A Dictionary of
Economics

John Black read Philosophy, Politics, and Economics at Oxford. He was Fellow and Tutor in Economics at Merton College, Oxford, from 1957 to 1966, and Professor of Economic Theory at the University of Exeter from 1967 to 1996. He has been Assistant, Associate or Production Editor of the *Review of Economic Studies* between 1958 and 1971, of the *Economic Journal* from 1971 to 1980, and of *Economic Policy* from 1985 to 1995. He has written *The Economics of Modern Britain, Essential Mathematics for Economists* (with J. F. Bradley), and *Housing Policy and Finance* (with D. C. Stafford), and has helped to edit books for the International Economics Study Group and the Centre for Economic Policy Research. He took early retirement in 1984 to concentrate on editorial work, and is now an Emeritus Professor of the University of Exeter, and Honorary Departmental Fellow at the University of Wales, Aberystwyth.

Oxford Paperback Reference

The most authoritative and up-to-date reference books for both students and the general reader.

*forthcoming

A Dictionary of
Economics

SECOND EDITION

Reissued with new covers
and corrections

JOHN BLACK

Oxford   New York

OXFORD UNIVERSITY PRESS

OXFORD

UNIVERSITY PRESS

Great Clarendon Street, Oxford OX2 6DP

Oxford University Press is a department of the University of Oxford.
It furthers the University's objective of excellence in research, scholarship,
and education by publishing worldwide in

Oxford New York
Auckland Cape Town Dar es Salaam Hong Kong Karachi Kuala Lumpur
Madrid Melbourne Mexico City Nairobi New Delhi Shanghai
Taipei Toronto

With offices in
Argentina Austria Brazil Chile Czech Republic France Greece
Guatemala Hungary Italy Japan South Korea Poland Portugal
Singapore Switzerland Thailand Turkey Ukraine Vietnam

Published in the United States
by Oxford University Press Inc., New York

British Library Cataloguing in Publication Data
Data available

Library of Congress Cataloging in Publication Data
Data available

ISBN–13: 978–0–19–860767–0

9

Typeset by Kolam Information Services Pvt. Ltd, Pondicherry, India

Printed in Great Britain by
Clays Ltd, St Ives plc

Contents

Preface

This dictionary aims to provide for the needs of students of economics at A-level and in the 'mainstream' part of first degree courses, and of lay readers of journals such as *The Economist*. To this end it includes several concepts in mathematics and statistics which are widely used in standard economics texts, and various terms connected with personal finances, including insurance, pensions, and investment on the stock exchange. It is not intended to cater for the full needs of economics researchers or postgraduate students, or the wide range of specialist subjects within economics. It almost entirely excludes 'great names' in economics, except insofar as they have 'laws' or theorems named after them. An asterisk immediately before a word indicates that it has a separate entry (disregarding the distinction between singular and plural).

The author is indebted for general background ideas and concepts to innumerable teachers, colleagues, pupils, and authors whose work he has edited. He is indebted for comments, suggestions and encouragement to Jane Black, Max Corden, Jonathan Levin, Paul Mizen, Malcolm Sawyer, Molly Scott Cato, Peter Sinclair, and his commissioning editor Angus Phillips. He is indebted for office facilities and secretarial help to the Departments of Economics at the University of Exeter and the University of Wales, Aberystwyth. None of these individuals or institutions is responsible for any errors or omissions.

A

AAA rating *See* triple A rating.

ability to pay The principle that any *tax should fall on those who can afford to pay. Paying for *public goods or *income redistribution requires taxes: taking account of ability to pay means that these should increase with the income or assets of taxpayers, and as some minimum consumption is needed for subsistence, taxes should be progressive rather than proportional. Ability to pay is oppposed to the *benefit principle, which suggests that only those who benefit from any given public expenditure should be taxed to pay for it. The main objections to the ability to pay criterion are that it is hard to measure ability to pay reliably, and that taxing income reduces the incentive to work. However, collection of taxes from those who cannot afford to pay is unpopular, expensive, and sometimes impossible. Given the scale of taxes necessary to run a modern society, use of the ability to pay criterion for taxation seems inevitable.

absolute advantage The use of less resources per unit of output than other producers. With only one type of resource, such as hours of work, a producer with lower inputs has an absolute advantage. In a world with many factors of production absolute advantage is often hard to measure. In any case, absolute advantage gives no advice on what to do with resources, which are best employed where their *comparative advantage is greatest.

absolute value *See* modulus.

absorption The total of expenditure on real goods and services, for consumption, investment, and by the government. Absorption is the use of output: it excludes exports and includes imports. This is contrasted with *production, which includes exports and excludes imports. The absorption approach to *devaluation looks at its effects on various forms of expenditure, and points out that devaluation can only improve the balance of payments on current account if production increases relative to absorption.

abstinence Refraining from or at least postponing consumption which could have been afforded. Where the funds not being spent arise from current income, abstinence is thus the same as *saving; but the term also covers refraining from running down past savings or spending windfall gains.

ACAS *See* Advisory, Conciliation and Arbitration Service.

accelerated depreciation The right to *write off capital goods for tax purposes faster than the rate at which they would normally be depreciated. This is intended to encourage *investment, as it enables a company to defer its taxes when it invests. Under accelerated depreciation a firm's profits net of *depreciation, and thus its tax liabilities, are lower than they would have been under normal depreciation. Once the capital goods are written off, profits net of depreciation become higher than they would have been under normal depreciation, and tax bills rise again.

accelerator A model relating *investment to changes in *output. The accelerator model asserts that firms invest more when output is rising and less when it is falling. This seems reasonable: a rise in *demand leads some firms to produce more, and leads them and other firms to expect that demand will rise further. The rise in output raises the ratio of output to *capacity, and the expectation of further rises in demand makes firms believe it would be profitable to have more capital equipment. Accelerator-type models do help empirically to explain variations in both *fixed investment and *investment in stocks and work in progress.

accelerator–multiplier model *See* multiplier–accelerator model.

acceptance Adding one's signature to a *bill of exchange, thereby accepting *liability to pay the bill at *maturity if the original signatory fails to do so. Acceptance of a bill of exchange by an institution of high financial standing, such as a *merchant bank, makes the bill safer to hold and thus easier to sell. The acceptor is taking a *risk, and makes a charge for this.

acceptance schedule, job *See* job acceptance schedule.

accepting house A financial firm that is willing to accept *bills of exchange, that is, to guarantee that they will be paid on the due date. An accepting house uses its financial reputation to earn a fee for acceptance, and its specialized knowledge of financial markets to avoid taking too many risks of accepting bills where it is actually going to have to honour its *guarantee. The principal London accepting houses form the Accepting Houses Committee.

accession countries Countries applying to join the European Union (EU). This includes the 'Visegrad countries', the Czech Republic, Hungary, and Poland; the Baltic countries, Estonia, Latvia, and Lithuania; and others including Slovenia, Slovakia, Romania, Turkey, and Cyprus. Many of these had *'Europe Agreements' with the EU, by which they received trade concessions and undertook to bring their laws and institutions into forms compatible with full EU membership. Ten countries: Poland, the Czech Republic, Hungary, Estonia, Latvia, Lithuania, Slovakia, Slovenia, Malta, and Cyprus joined the EU in 2004, and Bulgaria and Romania expect to in 2006, but Turkey is still waiting.

access, market *See* market access.

accommodatory monetary policy A policy of allowing the supply of money to expand in line with the demand for it. If the *demand for money rises because of sustainable real growth in the economy, accommodatory monetary policy is desirable, and failure to expand the *money supply obstructs real growth. If, however, the cause of rising demand for money is a temporary, unsustainable surge in real activity, *inflation in prices and wages, or both, accommodatory monetary policy allows these excesses to continue too long. When obvious *excess demand or high inflation eventually forces a shift to a more restrictive monetary policy, this will have to be severe and may cause a serious *slump. Real world authorities find it very hard to assess exactly how accommodatory their monetary policies should be.

account(s) A statement about activities over some period. Accountability is the obligation to produce such a statement: the directors of companies are accountable to their shareholders, and in the UK ministers are accountable to

Parliament for the activities of their departments. Accounts take various forms:

1. A statement of the relations between two parties: a *bank account records the deposits, borrowing, and withdrawals of a customer. Firms keep accounts of the goods and services provided to customers: goods provided on account are supplied on credit, and an account rendered is a demand for payment for goods and services supplied.

2. A systematic summary in money terms of the activities of a business over some period, usually a year. The two main statements in such accounts are the *profit-and-loss account and the *balance-sheet. A profit-and-loss account shows receipts and payments, and the profit or loss made during an accounting period. A balance-sheet lists the *assets and *liabilities of a firm on specified dates, at the start and end of an accounting period. Accountants are producers and *auditors of accounts: they are often required to be professionally qualified, where the accounts have to be credible to creditors, law courts, and the tax authorities. Firms' accounts have to be certified as accurate by professional auditors, but even so have sometimes been discovered to be highly misleading.

3. National income and expenditure accounts are surveys of the economic activities of a nation. They include analysis of the production of goods and services, the distribution of incomes, and the expenditures of investors, consumers, and the government. In the parts of national income accounts relating to transactions with the rest of the world, the *current account records sales and purchases of goods and services, property incomes and transfers, and the *capital account records sales and purchases of assets, including both real *foreign direct investment, inwards and outwards, and financial transactions, sales and purchases of securities abroad, and the making and repayment of international loans. *See also* appropriation account, bank account, capital account, checking account, current account, current (bank) account, deposit account, merchandise account, profit-and-loss account, and unit of account.

accounting *See* cost accounting, creative accounting, inflation accounting, and management accounting.

accounting period The period of time, normally a year, to which a set of company accounts refers.

accounts, consolidated *See* consolidated accounts.

accounts payable The part of a firm's *liabilities, as shown in its *balance-sheet, consisting of bills received from suppliers on which payment is due but has not yet actually been made.

accounts receivable The part of a firm's *assets, as shown in its *balance-sheet, consisting of bills sent to customers on which payment is due but has not yet actually been received.

accumulation, capital *See* capital accumulation.

acid rain Rainfall of abnormally high acidity. This results from atmospheric pollution by emissions of sulphur dioxide (SO_2) and nitrogen oxides (NO_x), mainly as the result of combustion of fossil fuels in power stations and internal combusion engines in cars and lorries. Wet deposition occurs at considerable distances downwind of the sources of pollution, so that the problem is international. Acid rain causes problems for human health, damage to buildings through corrosion, and environmental damage, including for example killing fish in Scandinavian lakes and causing die-back in German forests. In all cases the actual scale of damage is uncertain. The sources of acid rain can be reduced by methods including flue gas desulphurization for power-plants, and switching to low sulphur coal.

acquisition (company) *Company expansion through the purchase of other businesses. If these are unincorporated, terms are agreed with the owners. If the other business is a company, its *shares are bought. Where some, but not all, of the shares of another company are bought, special rules govern the treatment of existing shareholders who do not wish to sell their holdings.

ACT See Advance Corporation Tax.

action See anti-dumping action, and industrial action.

actuarially fair odds See fair odds.

actuary An expert who uses statistical records to predict the future. An actuary uses records of the occurrence of uncertain events, such as death at given ages, or fire, theft, and accidents to cars, to predict how frequently similar events are likely to occur in the future. These predictions take account of observed trends in health or crime, as well as past facts. Actuarial expertise enables *insurance companies to write policies with an expectation of making profits, but not with complete reliability.

adaptive expectations The model of *expectations formation in which expectations adjust gradually towards observed values of the variable concerned. At any given time people hold expectations about the future values of economic variables, such as the rate of *inflation. Under adaptive expectations, if the level observed in the current period equals what was expected, the expectation does not alter. If actual and expected values differ, the expectation for next period is formed using a *weighted average of this period's expectation and this period's actual, for example $2/3$ of the old expectation and $1/3$ of the actual. Under a constant actual, adaptive expectations rapidly come to be almost correct. If the actual oscillates around a stable *mean, under adaptive expectations the expectation will be randomly too high or too low. In either of these cases, while adaptive expectations will not be exactly right, they tend to be so little out that people may well feel satisfied with them. Under an actual with a *trend, however, adaptive expectations lag behind, and are seriously wrong in the same direction in successive periods. This leads people to look for some better way of forming expectations.

adequacy, capital See capital adequacy.

adjustable peg A system where countries stabilize their *exchange rates around *par values they retain the right to change. Under this system a country undertakes to intervene in the foreign exchange market to keep its currency within some margin, for example 1 per cent, of some given exchange rate parity, the 'peg'. The country retains the right to adjust the parity, however, that is to move the peg. This was more or less the case under the *Bretton Woods system in the 1950s and 1960s. This system provides opportunities for *speculators at times when it appears that the peg is going to have to move, but it has not yet done so.

adjustment *See* cyclical adjustment, partial adjustment, and seasonal adjustment.

adjustment costs The costs of making changes in the economic *variables one controls. Any economic agent, whether an individual, a firm, or a government, has a *utility function which determines what the optimal levels of the variables they control would be, if they were free to make a fresh start in setting them. When actual levels differ from these optimal levels, adjustment costs must be considered. If adjustment costs are lump-sum, or increase proportionally or less than in proportion to the changes made in any one period, it will pay to make at once any change that is worth making at all. If adjustment costs increase more than proportionally to the size of the change, however, it pays to adjust only gradually. There are in fact cases where adjustment costs more if done rapidly than if done gradually. In adjusting its labour force, for example, a firm may find that small increases present no recruitment problem, and small decreases can be accommodated by not replacing *natural wastage due to retirements and other voluntary departures, whereas rapid recruitment poses serious selection and training problems, and rapid decline involves *redundancies, which are expensive and damaging to morale.

adjustment, price and quantity The relative timing of price and quantity adjustments. In any market, if supply or demand conditions change, both price and quantity may need to adjust eventually. The timing of price and quantity changes, however, can vary. In some markets, a *market-maker sets the price: for example, in normal retail shops the seller sets a price, and in the short run any change in demand results in changes in the quantity sold. If this leads to an accumulation of *stocks in excess of their normal level, this may in time to lead to price cuts. If the market-maker's stocks become inconveniently low, the price may be raised. In other markets, in the short run the quantity is fixed: this happens, for example, in fish markets, where price adjusts to clear the market. If the resulting price is low, this discourages supply as producers make losses; if the market-clearing price is high, the prospect of profits draws in additional supplies.

adjustment programme A package of policy measures designed to cure *balance-of-payments problems. Adoption of a satisfactory adjustment programme is frequently made a condition of assistance from the *International Monetary Fund (IMF). Curing balance-of-payments problems requires decreasing *absorption relative to production. This can be approached via reducing absorption, by cutting government spending and/or increasing taxes. It can also be approached via increasing production by using resources more efficiently; this often involves increased use of the market mechanism and *devaluation of overvalued currencies.

adjustment to factor cost *See* factor cost.

administered price A price set by some form of administrative process, rather than adjusting to clear a market. The levels of and changes in administered prices often require the consent of the government or of some official regulatory body. Administered prices may be maxima, as in the case of *rent controls, or minima, as with *minimum wage laws and some agricultural policies.

administration The situation of a *company in financial difficulties whose affairs are put into the hands of an administrator by court order. The object of administration is to enable the company to survive as a going concern, or if that proves impossible, to get a better price for its assets than immediate *liquidation would produce.

ad valorem tax A tax proportional to the price of the object being taxed. This is contrasted with a *specific tax, at a rate per unit of quantity, independent of the price. Ad valorem taxes are often preferred to specific taxes because specific taxes are considered unfair as they fall proportionally more heavily on poorer consumers who choose cheaper and lower quality goods. Ad valorem taxes are also preferred because their real value is not eroded by *inflation.

Advance Corporation Tax (ACT) The system by which UK companies deduct income tax at source when distributing *dividends to their shareholders. With a tax rate of $100t$ per cent, companies must pay the Inland Revenue $£t/(1 - t)$ for every £1 distributed to shareholders. These payments are treated as a payment on account of the company's own *corporation tax.

advances Bank loans to their customers. These may be *unsecured loans, but are often secured by the bank holding stocks and shares or *life insurance policies owned by the borrower.

advantage *See* absolute advantage, and comparative advantage.

adverse selection The tendency for any *contract offered to all comers to be most attractive to those most likely to benefit from it. For example, if an insurer offers *health insurance without any medical examination, the expectation is that people with poor health prospects are likely to accept it, while people with better health prospects, who can get better terms from a more selective insurer, will reject the unconditional contract. In trying to be non-selective, adverse selection causes the worst risks to select themselves.

adverse supply shock A sudden reduction in the supply of an input necessary for an economy. This could result from natural disasters such as floods or earthquakes; from human, animal, or plant diseases; or from major political upheavals such as war or revolution. To oil importers, the sudden price increases imposed by the *Organization of Petroleum Exporting Countries (OPEC) in the 1970s appeared as adverse supply shocks. Such a shock reduces the *real income an economy can produce even at full employment of its available resources.

advertising Activity designed to sell products. It seeks to attract the attention of potential customers, inform them of the existence and attributes of a product, and persuade them to start or continue to buy it. It works via the media, that is, newspapers or television; by shop displays, posters, or mailshots; or through the actual design of products themselves and their packaging. While there is a logical distinction between informative and persuasive advertising, psychologically these are extremely difficult to distinguish. Political, charitable and religious bodies, and the government advertise, as well as commercial organizations.

Advisory, Conciliation and Arbitration Service (ACAS) A UK quango providing facilities for conciliation, arbitration and mediation in *industrial disputes.

AFDC See Aid to Families with Dependent Children.

AFL–CIO See American Federation of Labor and Congress of Industrial Organizations.

after-sales service The provision after goods have been sold of services which make them more useful to customers. This can include advice on and training in the use of the product; routine maintenance, servicing and repairs in the event of breakdown; provision of materials and spare parts; replacement under *warranty in the event of failure of the goods supplied; and updating if the product is developed further. Customers' expectations of cheap and efficient after-sales service are of great importance in making products competitive, and lack of customer confidence in the quality and price of after-sales services may make products unsaleable. See also competitiveness.

after-tax income The income remaining to an individual or a company after *direct taxes have been paid. It takes no account of liability to *indirect taxes when the income is spent.

age–earnings profile A graph showing the mean earnings of workers at various ages. Such profiles can be drawn up for all workers, or for specified groups of workers, for example manual, female, or professional workers.

agency See bond-rating agency, credit-rating agency, debt-collection agency, export-credit agency, and regulatory agency.

agent See principal–agent problem.

agglomeration economies The *external economies available to individuals or firms in large concentrations of population and economic activity. These arise because larger markets allow wider choice and a greater range of specialist services. Agglomeration economies are believed to explain the tendency of conurbations to contain an increasing share of the population of many countries. Beyond some point further agglomeration gives rise to diseconomies due to congestion and pollution.

aggregate demand The total of intended or *ex ante attempts to spend on final goods and services produced in a country. In a *closed economy aggregate demand is the sum of consumption, investment and government spending on goods and services. In an *open economy it is this plus export demand and minus imports. A rise in aggregate demand is a necessary condition for an increase in real output. It is not a sufficient condition, however, unless an economy has spare *capacity to produce the goods and services demanded. If the goods demanded are available only as imports, these rise; if the extra goods are not available at all, inflationary pressure is created.

aggregate demand schedule A diagram showing for each level of *national income the total level of aggregate demand in an economy that would result from it. *Internal balance in the economy requires that aggregate demand is equal to national output.

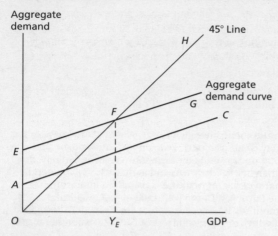

FIGURE 1: *Aggregate Demand Schedule*

The horizontal axis shows real GDP; the vertical axis shows aggregate real domestic expenditure. *AC* shows consumption for each level of GDP. *EFG* shows total domestic spending for each level of GDP. In a closed economy this is Consumption + Gross Investment + Government Spending on real goods and services; in an open economy it is these plus Exports minus Imports. *OFH* is a 'forty-five degree line', showing where real GDP produces domestic spending equal to itself. The line is so-called because its slope is 45°, provided the same scale is used on both axes. Equilibrium GDP is at Y_E, where *EFG* cuts the 45° line.

aggregate supply The total amount of real goods and services that the enterprises in an economy are willing to provide at any given ratio of prices to wages. This can be increased by rising *productivity due to increases in the volume of productive equipment or improvements in technical knowledge or the quality of the labour force. Whether actual output equals aggregate supply depends on two conditions. First, there must be sufficient aggregate demand to match the supply: if there is not, output is demand-constrained. Second, there must be a sufficient supply of labour to satisfy firms' demand for it: if *real wages are low, aggregate supply by firms may require more employment than the labour supply forthcoming at these wages, in which case output is constrained by labour shortages. In an economy where firms are not perfectly competitive, the concept of aggregate supply is dubiously applicable. *See also* demand-determined output.

aggregation The relation between the behaviour of totals and that of their components. Suppose, for example, that for each of N individuals $i = 1, 2, \ldots,$ N, i's consumption, C_i, is given by $C_i = a_i + b_i Y_{di}$, where Y_{di} is i's *disposable income. Can these *consumption functions be aggregated to give a function of the form $C = a + bY_d$, where C and Y_d are national aggregates? If all the b_i were equal, it would not matter if the a_i differed, as they could simply be added. If the b_i vary, however, a precise aggregate relation can only be derived from the individual consumption functions if we know how marginal changes in income will be distributed among the N individuals. If this is not known, any aggregate consumption function will only hold approximately. Similar problems arise with most economic aggregates.

AGM *See* annual general meeting.

agreement *See* commodity agreement, free-trade agreement, and no-strike agreement.

agricultural protection The use of *tariffs and trade controls on agricultural products to raise their prices in a country and thus to increase its farmers' incomes. This may be desired to slow down the tendency for the share of agriculture in total income and employment to decrease. It may also aim at increasing self-sufficiency in foodstuffs and agricultural raw materials in the interests of national security. Agriculture is protected in most industrial countries, particularly the European Union (EU) and Japan. Agricultural protection in advanced countries hinders economic growth in *less developed countries (LDCs), most of which are net exporters of agricultural products.

aid Economic assistance from one country to another, the recipient typically being a *less developed country (LDC). Aid is usually intended either to provide humanitarian relief in emergencies, to promote economic development, or to finance military expenditure. Aid may take the form of outright gifts of money, which may be tied to purchases from the donor, or untied and available for expenditure anywhere. It may take the form of *soft loans, on terms easier than those available to the borrower in world capital markets. Aid may also be given in kind, including food, plant and equipment, military supplies or technical assistance. Bilateral aid is given directly by a donor to a recipient country; multilateral aid is channeled through an international organization, without direct contact between donors and particular recipients. How much actual good is done by aid varies widely from case to case, and is often the subject of considerable controversy. *See also* grant in aid, tied aid, and untied aid.

Aid to Families with dependent Children (AFDC) A US federal welfare programme, originally set up in 1936, enabling states to use federal grants to provide financial support for poor children. AFDC now accounts for a major part of the overall cost of the US social security programme.

allocation, resource *See* efficient resource allocation.

allocative efficiency *See* efficiency.

allowance *See* family allowance, and tax allowance.

allowances, capital *See* capital allowances.

All-Share Index, Financial Times *See* Financial Times Actuaries All-Share Index.

alpha stocks The most actively traded securities in the *Stock Exchange Automated Quotations System (SEAQ). About 100 securities came into this category when it was in official use by the London Stock Exchange. These were shares of companies with high turnover and high *market capitalization. Alpha stocks had numerous *market-makers, and immediate publication of transactions in them was required. They were contrasted with beta, gamma and delta stocks which were those of smaller companies, and less intensively traded.

amalgamation *See* merger.

American Federation of Labor and Congress of Industrial Organizations (AFL–CIO) The main US labour federation. The cumbersome name results from the amalgamation in 1955 of two associations, the AFL representing mainly craft unions, and the CIO representing mainly industrial unions. The AFL–CIO operates mainly at the political level: wage and other industrial bargaining is carried on by its member unions. It is the US equivalent of the UK's *Trades Union Congress (TUC).

amortization The building up over a period of a fund to replace a productive asset at the end of its useful life, or to repay a loan. In the case of a loan, the amount required for amortization depends on the interest rate which can be earned on the accumulated fund. In the case of replacement of physical assets, the amount needed depends not only on the interest rate, but also on the expected lifetime of the asset and on the rate of inflation, which affects the expected cost of replacement.

amplitude of oscillation The difference between the maximum and minimum points of a regular oscillation. If $f(t)$ fluctuates over time with a maximum of a and a minimum of b, its amplitude is $(a - b)$.

analysis of variance A statistical technique based on decomposing the overall *variance of some characteristic of a population into parts correlated with other characteristics, and *residual variation. In particular, analysis of variance is used to test whether sections of a population appear to differ significantly in some property. For example, if y_i is the personal income of individual i, analysis of variance can be used to test whether there are significant regional differences in mean income. The overall variance of the population is analysed into the part due to differences within regions, and the part due to differences between regional means. The larger the proportion of total variance due to differences between group means, the higher the probability that the groups are really different; whereas the higher the proportion of overall variance due to within-group variance, the more likely it is that apparent differences between group means arise from sampling error.

anchor, nominal *See* nominal anchor.

animal spirits The term used by John Maynard *Keynes to convey the idea that major investment projects are usually undertaken not on the basis of careful calculation of the profits they are expected to make, but on the strength of 'hunches' of *entrepreneurs that, beneath the uncertainties that would make a rational and cautious person delay a decision, there is an opportunity to be grasped by whoever has the courage to try.

announcement effect The effect of an announcement of a change in policy, even before it is actually put into effect. For example, a promise by the government to reduce taxes next year may lead to an immediate increase in consumer spending, or an immediate rise in interest rates. Policy announcements can produce such effects only if the policy-maker has some credibility.

annual general meeting (AGM) A meeting of the voting *shareholders of a company, or the members of an association, at which the officers report on the last year's activities, and accounts are submitted for approval. AGMs normally elect the chief officers and directors of companies, and the chief officers and commitee members of associations. In the UK, company AGMs appoint the company's *auditors. Companies are required by law to hold AGMs, and associations are usually required to do so by their constitutions.

annualised percentage rate of interest (APR) The rate of interest on any loan calculated as interest paid per unit of the principal still outstanding, expressed as an annual rate. Thus, if the interest on a loan where no repayments are made is 2 per cent per month, the APR is 26.8 per cent rather than 24 per cent. Where a loan is repaid in instalments and the nominal interest rate is expressed as a percentage of the original capital, the APR may be considerably higher than the nominal interest rate. In the UK lenders are legally obliged to inform borrowers of the APR on mortgage, credit card, or other loans.

annual report and accounts An annual report on a company's or other organization's activities during the last *financial year, and *accounts covering this period. The annual report is normally presented by the chairman at the annual general meeting of shareholders or members, and the accounts are presented by the treasurer. These form a major source of information on companies and other organizations. Copies of the annual report and accounts are usually sent to shareholders and members, either in full or in summary form.

annuity A contract by which a financial institution such as an *insurance company agrees to provide a regular income for life. The name annuity arises from annual payments, but the payments can in fact be of any agreed frequency. The recipient will be a named person; it is also possible to contract for full or reduced payments for life to surviving spouses or other dependents. The payments may be fixed in money terms, or *index-linked. Annuities enable the recipients to spend their capital as well as their income without the danger of running out of funds before they die.

ante, ex *See* ex ante.

anti-dumping action The procedure by which complaints of *dumping are investigated and the case for the imposition of anti-dumping duties is assessed. Anti-dumping actions are processed by importing countries. A tariff commission or similar body investigates whether dumping has occurred, and whether it is causing injury to the domestic industry. Given the lack of any agreed definition of dumping, and the probable lack of impartiality in national tribunals judging cases between domestic complainants and foreign suppliers, the threat of anti-dumping actions has an all-round protectionist effect. There is a strong case for establishing an agreed international body to adjudicate all applications for anti-dumping actions.

anti-dumping duty A tariff imposed to protect domestic producers of a good against competition from *dumping of imports. Such duties are imposed only after investigation of complaints by domestic producers. As it is difficult to define dumping, and there is no internationally agreed procedure for deciding when it has occurred, the threat of anti-dumping duties is a general obstacle to the expansion of international trade.

anti-monopoly policy *See* monopoly policy.

anti-pollution measures Policies to reduce or eliminate *pollution. These include taxes, quantitative restriction or prohibition of activities causing pollution; *zoning regulations to locate polluting activities where they will do the least harm; and support for research into the effects of pollution and the discovery of methods of production with fewer harmful *by-products. Education of industrial firms and the general public can both increase voluntary avoidance of pollution, and generate political support for compulsory methods of reducing it, either by taxation or controls. *Incentives to avoid pollution can also be given by imposing legal liabilities on polluters either to compensate particular victims, or to pay for the general costs of cleaning-up operations.

antitrust The US term for policies designed to restrict monopoly and promote competition. The Antitrust Division of the US Department of Justice and the *Federal Trade Commission are the main agencies for antitrust policy. The name comes from the US use of trusts to describe large firms formed by amalgamation. US antitrust measures frequently work by making practices such as *price discrimination illegal. The very name embodies an anti-monopoly position. This can be contrasted with UK terminology, where the *Monopolies and Mergers Commission (MMC), now replaced by the Competition Commission (CC), was given discretion to judge whether any particular monopoly or merger was harmful.

APEC *See* Asian Pacific Economic Cooperation.

appreciation *See* capital appreciation, and stock appreciation.

appreciation, currency A rise in the price of a country's currency in terms of foreign currency. This makes foreign goods cheaper relative to home-produced goods, which tends to increase imports, and it makes home-produced goods dearer abroad, which tends to decrease exports. Currency appreciation is thus generally bad for a country's *balance of trade. Lower import prices, however, tend to reduce *inflation.

appreciation, stock *See* stock appreciation.

apprenticeship A system by which firms take on workers, typically young ones, for an initial period of employment during which they are supposed to spend part of their time training. *Training for apprentices may be provided by formal instructional courses, either within the firm or at outside institutions, by learning on the job working under the supervision of experienced workers, or in both ways. At the end of their training, apprentices receive some form of formal vocational qualification. Apprentices are frequently paid less than fully qualified workers, and are not guaranteed a job at the end of their training.

appropriation account An account showing what has been done with the total funds available to a company or other organization. This shows the division of total funds between tax payments, real investment, making external loans or purchasing securities, retention of cash balances, and distribution to shareholders.

appropriation bill A US federal legislative bill authorizing expenditure. This has to be approved by both houses of Congress.

APR *See* annualized percentage rate of interest.

a priori From first principles. The assumptions of an a priori argument are axioms, that have to be assumed, and cannot be derived from empirical evidence. While it is generally unwise in economics to base policy prescriptions on purely a priori arguments, all economic arguments necessarily contain some a priori elements.

arbitrage Buying a good or asset in one market where price is low, and simultaneously selling in another market where price is higher. This does not involve taking any *risks. Arbitrage tends to prevent the price of the same good or asset in different markets from moving further apart than a margin equal to transactions costs. Interest arbitrage is borrowing in a market with lower interest rates and simultaneously lending in a market with higher ones. *See also* no arbitrage.

arbitrageur A person or company who undertakes a set of transactions involving buying in one market and selling in another, where the prices are known simultaneously. Thus, although a profit can be made if the prices are different, an arbitrageur takes very little *risk. The term arbitrageur is also used to describe those who buy and sell companies or parts of companies at pre-arranged prices, again taking very little risk. An arbitrageur is contrasted with a *speculator, who buys and sells in markets where the prices are not known simultaneously, so that beween purchase and sale the speculator is massively at risk.

arbitration A system for settling disputes by submitting them to the judgement of a mediator acceptable to both parties. An arbitrator may be an independent individual, or a committee, often containing nominees of both parties with an independent person in the chair. Arbitration is often used in commercial and labour disputes, as it is usually quicker and cheaper than legal or *industrial action. It may be binding, where both parties are obliged by law or by contract to accept the results. Even when it is not binding, the parties may well accept the result rather than face the delays, costs and risk involved in resort to legal or industrial action. *See also* pendulum arbitration.

arc elasticity The ratio of the proportional change in one variable to the proportional change in another, as actually measured between two points over a discrete range. Arc elasticity is distinguished from *point elasticity, which is the limit taken by arc elasticity as the two points move closer together. Point elasticity cannot be directly observed, but must be found by statistical inference from actual observations, whereas arc elasticity is measured directly.

area, free-trade *See* free-trade area.

argument An independent variable determining the value of a *function. The argument of a function of one variable, for example $y = f(x)$, is the variable x; the value of x determines the value or values of y. In a function of more than one variable, for example $y = f(x_1, x_2)$, x_1 and x_2 are the arguments of $f(\ )$. If for example $y = x^2 + z^2$, the values of both x and z are needed to determine the value of y.

arithmetic mean The sum of a set of N numbers, $x_1, x_2, \ldots, x_N$, divided by N, denoted by $(\Sigma_i x_i)/N$. This can be calculated for any set of finite numbers, whether positive, zero, or negative.The arithmetic mean, or *unweighted average, is what is normally meant by the use of 'average' without further comment.

arithmetic progression A *series of numbers, where the rule for getting from each one to the next is to add a constant. Thus if $x_1 = a$, $x_2 = a + b$, $x_3 = a + 2b, \ldots, x_N = a + (N-1)b$.

Arrangement, Multi-Fibre *See* Multi-Fibre Arrangement.

A-share An *ordinary share in a company which, while it receives the same dividends as other ordinary shares, does not give its holder any voting rights. A shares are issued to enable the group controlling a company to raise capital from outside without parting with *control. Because A-shareholders are excluded from control, these shares generally trade at a lower price than voting ordinary shares in the same company.

Asian Pacific Economic Cooperation (APEC) An association of nations around the Pacific rim aiming at the creation of a Pacific free trade area. APEC was set up in 1990; its members include Australia, Canada, Chile, China, Indonesia, Japan, Malaysia, Mexico, New Zealand, Singapore, and the US. It aims at creating a free trade area for its industrialized members by 2010, and its less-developed members by 2020. When complete this will cover a large percentage of world trade.

assembly line A device moving a good being produced, for example a car, past a sequence of workers or machines. As it passes each work-station, a particular task is performed. Tasks may include adding components, working on components already in place, or checking the work of earlier stages. Assembly-line production allows *economies of scale, by keeping down the time needed to move workers or machines from one task to another. Under this system no task can be done until the one before is finished, so that breakdowns of machines, non-arrival of inputs, or the absence of any worker may hold up the entire process. Responsibility for the quality of the end-product is very widely spread, which may make it difficult to locate the cause of defects or to motivate workers to prevent them.

assessment, tax *See* tax assessment.

asset motive The incentive to hold money as a *store of value. If prices are expected to be stable, money is a poor store of value as it earns little or no interest. When *inflation is expected, money does even worse as a store of value. If prices fall, however, money is an attractive asset, and if there is thought to be any chance of falling prices, this can prompt a desire to hold money as an asset.

asset prices The prices of assets, including land and buildings, productive equipment and *securities. As assets can be sold again, their present prices are strongly influenced by *expectations about their future prices, and by the interest rate at which future values are discounted. As stocks of assets are very large compared to any one period's new asset creation, asset prices are anchored much less firmly than goods prices to costs of production. It is common for asset prices to vary widely over quite short time periods; see for example the large differences between the maximum and minimum prices of individual shares reported within any one year.

assets Possessions of value, both real and financial. Real assets include land, buildings or machinery owned. Financial assets include cash and securities, and credit extended to customers. The assets side of a company's *balance-sheet includes both real and financial assets. Asset management is managing for others, for a fee, their portfolios of real or financial assets. *Asset-stripping is selling off the assets of companies. Assets is also used in a metaphorical and usually favourable sense to describe things that cannot actually be owned, as in the phrase 'a company's best assets are the skill and loyalty of its employees'. *See also* current assets, intangible assets, liquid assets, portfolio of assets, and tangible assets.

asset-stripping A pejorative description of the process of dividing up the assets of a company in cases where the total value of the parts when separated is greater than their value when combined. Examples could include selling off unused or under-utilized land or buildings, or selling off activities where heavy investment carries tax allowances which the company cannot use to other companies whose large present profits make the tax allowances valuable to them. A more favourable description of asset-stripping activities is corporate restructuring. Advocates of corporate restructuring argue that so-called asset-stripping is only profitable because the assets were being inefficiently used, or simply neglected, in the first place.

asset, wasting *See* wasting asset.

Assisted Area A UK region made eligible for special government assistance to encourage investment because of persistently above-average *unemployment. Development Areas are eligible for more help than Intermediate Areas. Grants for these areas are also available from the European Union (EU) through the European Regional Development Fund (ERDF). Although special help for Assisted Areas has been available under various schemes since the 1930s, regional differences in unemployment have been very persistent.

association *See* housing association, and trade association.

assurance *See* equity-linked assurance, and insurance.

asymmetric information A situation where economic agents do not all have the same *information. This is of course the actual situation in any real economy. No economic agent has access to full information; each has some information that others do not. Information is available to some agents and not to others for various reasons. Some information is private, concerning the state of the agent's own mind; for example, the maximum amount I would be willing to bid in an auction. Other information is objectively measurable, for example the level of a firm's stocks, but only the firm and not its rivals can measure it. Even if private information is passed to others, if they cannot check it independently they may not believe it. Equally, for any agent there will be many things which others know but they do not. Every agent thus has to decide what *strategies to follow, knowing that others know things that they do not, and that they cannot be sure how far their own information is shared by other people.

asymptote A value which a given function approaches arbitrarily closely as its *argument changes, but does not actually reach while the argument is finite. For example, if the total cost of an output x is given by $TC = a + bx$, where a and b are constants, *average cost is given by $AC = TC/x = (a/x) + b$. AC can thus be bought within any given distance above b, however small, by taking a sufficiently large x, but AC exceeds b (denoted $AC > b$) for any finite x. Average cost asymptotes to b.

atomistic competition A situation where the participants on both sides of a market are so numerous that the assumptions of *perfect competition are actually realistic. This can only occur when *economies of scale are non-existent, or all available economies of scale are achieved at a level of output negligibly small relative to the size of the market.

auction A sale where the price is fixed by an auctioneer who invites bids, and awards the article being auctioned to the highest bidder. In an English auction the highest bid is publicly announced at each stage, and other parties are given a chance to make higher bids. In a sealed-bid auction the bids are not publicly announced: each bid is submitted sealed, and a time limit is set at which the auctioneer opens the bids and awards the article to the highest bidder, without further bids being invited. In a Dutch auction the auctioneer announces a decreasing series of prices, and the article is awarded to the first bidder. In any of these types of auction there may or may not be a reserve price, which is the lowest bid the seller will accept; this may or may not be published. The auctioneer normally charges the seller and possibly also the buyer a fee calculated as a percentage of the realised price.

audit The process of checking *accounts. Auditors check whether the accounts of a company, private trader, or association are complete and consistent, whether they agree with other records of purchases, sales and inventories, and whether they comply with legal requirements and professional standards. *Companies are legally required to have their accounts externally audited, and many other bodies are required to do so by their own constitutions. Many companies and other organizations employ internal auditors, to check the accuracy and completeness of their internal bookkeeping. The audit provides a safeguard against both fraud and incompetence in accounting. *See also* efficiency audit.

auditor A person or accountancy firm employed to check the *accounts of a company, private trader or association. Auditors check whether accounts are complete and consistent, and whether they are in agreement with other records of purchases, sales and inventories. They may certify that accounts present a 'true and fair view' of a company's finances, or they can 'qualify' them, that is, add adverse comments. The auditors of UK companies are elected by the *annual general meetings of the companies' shareholders, and are required to be professionally qualified accountants. Other bodies such as charities are required to have their accounts audited, but their auditors need not be professionally qualified, and are often unpaid. Many companies and other organizations also employ internal auditors, to check on the accuracy and completeness of the firms' internal bookkeeping, as a safeguard against both fraud and confusion in accounting.

autarky An economy with no external trade. The term is also applied to the policy aim of reducing a country's dependence on foreign trade, for example by *tariffs and *quotas, even if foreign trade cannot be entirely eliminated.

authorized capital The nominal value of the *shares a company is empowered to issue. Companies often extend their authorized capital in advance of actual issue of new shares. This allows the timing of capital issues to be fixed in the light of the firm's need for new capital and the state of the capital market and allows *share options to be exercised.

autocorrelation A measure of the relation between the value of any item in a *time series and those coming before or after it. First-order autocorrelation refers to the relation of each item to those immediately before or after. Suppose that the data are x_t, x_{t+1}, x_{t+2}, etc, where t represents time. If the series is stationary, replace each x_t by its deviation from the average value of the series; if the series is trended, replace each x_t by the deviation from its trend value. Denote these deviations z_t, z_{t+1}, z_{t+2} etc. The value of $z_t z_{t+1}$ is found for each t. If the *expected value of this product is zero, there is no first-order autocorrelation; the successive observations are independent. If the expected value of $z_t z_{t+1}$ is not zero, the series has positive or negative first-order autocorrelation. The existence of second-order or higher-order autocorrelation is measured by taking the expected values of $z_t z_{t+2}$, $z_t z_{t+3}$, etc. Positive autocorrelation means that deviations from *equilibrium tend to persist from period to period; negative autocorrelation means that deviations from equilibrium tend to be reversed. Many economic time series, such as *unemployment or the inflation rate, show positive autocorrelation.

automatic stabilizers *See* built-in stabilizers.

automation Production by machinery, usually computer-controlled, without the need for immediate human intervention. This is particularly useful where extreme accuracy is required, or in processing dangerous materials, where it may be difficult and expensive to protect human operatives. While the operation of automated plants uses very little labour, designing, producing and setting up the equipment usually requires very large amounts of *skilled work. Human operatives may also be used as an additional safeguard to monitor the working of automated equipment. For any given level of output automation usually means fewer but better jobs.

autonomous consumption That part of *consumption which does not depend on current income. If aggregate consumption, C, is given by $C = a + bY_d$, where Y_d is *disposable income, a can be regarded as autonomous consumption. $a > 0$ because even those with no income need to consume to live, and can finance expenditure by running down assets or borrowing. The level of a is influenced by total assets held, expectations of future income or acquisitions of assets through legacies, and social conventions about minimum acceptable standards of living.

autonomous investment That part of *investment which is not explained by changes in the level of output. This includes investment in public services, which are determined by government policy, investment to exploit new technical knowledge or geographical discoveries, and considerable amounts of replacement of existing capital as it wears out. In fact most investment is autonomous in this sense.

average A statistical summary measure of size. The average of a set of numbers may be weighted or unweighted. The unweighted average or arithmetic mean of a set of N numbers $x_1, x_2, \ldots x_N$ is their sum divided by N, written $(\sum_i x_i)/N$. In an unweighted average an equal weight is given to each number; this is often appropriate if the data concern individuals. A weighted average gives a 'weight' to each observation, denoted w_i; it is then the sum of the products of observations and their weights, $(x_i w_i)$, divided by the sum of the weights, written $(\sum_i x_i w_i)/(\sum_i w_i)$. A weighted average is appropriate in considering, for example, the average income of people in Latin America. Brazil has far more inhabitants than Uruguay, and if the x_i were average income for each country, natural weights w_i would be the populations of the various countries. *See also* moving average, unweighted average, and weighted average.

average cost Total cost of production divided by quantity produced. Average fixed cost necessarily decreases with output. Average variable cost may decrease with output up to the point where limits to *capacity become a constraint, after which it tends to rise. If average variable cost rises faster than average fixed cost falls, this produces a *U-shaped average cost curve. Where a firm has multiple products, as most actual firms do, the whole concept of average cost depends on the ability to attribute particular costs to particular products, which is often a matter of judgement.

average cost curve, U-shaped *See* U-shaped average cost curve.

average cost pricing The policy of setting prices so as just to cover average costs, allowing the producer to *break even. This is clearly not a sensible policy for a profit-maximizing firm, but it may be so for a government-controlled firm, or for a private but non-profit-making body. Average cost pricing is contrasted with *marginal cost pricing, which is sometimes argued to be the first-best pricing policy for a producer operating in the public interest. This is correct, however, only if it can be assumed that any losses can be financed without the taxes needed to finance these losses imposing transactions and deadweight costs. Where such costs are assumed to be heavy, average cost pricing, where goods are sold at the lowest price consistent with covering average costs, so that there are no losses to be financed, can be urged as a *second-best optimum.

average propensity to consume *See* propensity to consume.

average propensity to import *See* import propensity.

average propensity to save *See* propensity to save.

average revenue *See* revenue.

avoidable cost That part of the cost of any output that could be saved by not producing it. Some costs are clearly not avoidable, for example capital costs. Other costs might prima facie appear to be avoidable, but may actually not be. For example, ceasing production would save on fuel, materials and labour; but fuel and materials may be bought on long-term contracts, and employees laid off may be entitled to pay in lieu of notice. Thus these costs too may not be avoidable in the short run.

avoidance, tax *See* tax avoidance.

axiom A 'self-evident' proposition; that is, one which is believed to be true, but has to be assumed and cannot be proved.

axis A line in a graph along which one variable is held constant, often at zero, while only the other varies. Axes are normally drawn at right angles. Each axis of a graph should be clearly labelled to show what is being measured along it, and the scale and units of measurement in use.

B

back door The system by which the *Bank of England acts to change the UK money supply by dealing in *Treasury bills on its own initiative at the market rate. This is distinguished from the front door, when it lends to *discount houses at their initiative, as *lender of last resort.

backward-bending supply curve A *supply curve for a good showing that less would be supplied at a higher price. Supply from a competitive industry normally rises with price, so the supply curve slopes upwards. Higher prices induce existing firms in the industry to supply more, and attract new entrants to the industry. A backward-bending supply curve can only occur if these assumptions break down. Existing suppliers may react to higher prices by producing less because of the *income effects of higher prices: peasant farmers, for example, could choose to work less when prices rose. Higher prices are unlikely to cause exit from an industry, but if the supply of possible entrants is *inelastic, too few new entrants might come in to offset the effects of reduced effort by existing suppliers, and a backward-bending supply curve could result.

backward integration The expansion of a firm's activities to include the production of inputs formerly bought in from outside. Examples include a firm manufacturing its own components, mining its own mineral requirements, generating its own power supplies, or even growing food for its own works canteen. Backward integration may be pursued to improve the quality or reliability of inputs, or to increase a firm's *monopoly power by denying access to inputs to actual or potential rivals.

BACS *See* Bank Automated Credit System.

bad debt *Debt whose repayment is known to be impossible or unlikely. Failure of the borrower to make payments of principal or interest on the due dates is prima facie evidence that a debt should be suspect, but a debt can become bad even before the payments are actually due if the debtor is known or believed to be insolvent. If payments are delayed, creditors who think that ultimate payment is likely may be willing to formally *reschedule debts, or merely to wait for payment without any formal agreement. At what stage bad debts should be 'written off', that is, the creditors should cease to record them as assets in their accounts, is a matter of judgement. Institutions with numerous debts owing to them may make provision for losses without specifying which particular debts they regard as being uncollectable.

bad debt provision A statement in the accounts of a creditor of the extent to which it expects to have to write off bad debts, that is, to cease to record them as assets in its accounts. A firm with bad debts must at some stage decide to write them off. If it has numerous debtors, each of doubtful solvency, it is possible to make a 'bad debt provision', naming an amount by which it expects to have to write off bad debts, without the need to specify on which particular debts hope has been abandoned.

balance *See* external balance, internal balance, and invisible balance.

balanced budget Equality between total government receipts and expenditure. There is thus no need to borrow and thereby increase the *government debt. In a fluctuating economy it is neither possible nor desirable to have the budget exactly balanced each year. Some economists believe, however, that the budget should be balanced on average over a *trade cycle. Others maintain that there is no point in balancing the budget, and argue that there is in any case so much scope for dispute over the definition of the *budget deficit that the argument is pointless. For example, should the budget to be balanced be *cyclically adjusted? Should it include payments of nominal or of real interest by the government on its existing debt? Should interest on the debts of state-owned industries, or income on the assets of the national insurance fund, be included or excluded? The *Maastricht Treaty proposes an upper limit on budget deficits of 3 per cent of GNP, rather than balanced budgets, as an agreed constraint on the budgets of EU members.

balanced budget amendment A proposal to compel the US government to balance its budget by a consitutional amendment forbidding further government borrowing. Such an amendment is unlikely actually to be adopted. Even economists and politicians who believe that deficits are in general undesirable wish to retain discretion to allow them, in emergencies, to deal with a *slump in activity or a political crisis requiring increased military spending. They point out that short-run fluctuations in the budget position cannot be avoided because of the dependence of revenue on fluctuations in the level of activity. There is also too much scope for *creative accounting or the creation of off-budget but government-controlled special funds for a balanced budget to be legally enforceable.

balanced budget multiplier The argument found in *Keynesian economic models, that a rise in government spending on real goods and services combined with an equal rise in taxation, leaving the budget deficit or surplus unaltered, must increase the national product by exactly the amount spent. The effect of an extra £100 of real spending is to shift income from those who pay the £100 of extra taxes to the producers of the extra real output the government buys, so other incomes are unchanged, and the extra £100 of goods bought by the government are an addition to national output. This argument is as correct as its assumptions, which are that the savings propensities of taxpayers and government suppliers are equal, and that there are no repercussions elsewhere in the economy, either through the monetary system, or through the effects of extra taxes and spending on business confidence.

balanced growth *Growth of all sectors and regions of an economy at the same proportional rate. This is unlikely ever to be observed in any actual economy, and it is hard to understand why it should ever have been thought to be desirable. It is true that if growth is so unbalanced that some sectors or regions of an economy actually decline, this may give rise to problems of adjustment. A very wide variety of patterns of growth is still possible, however, even if sharp declines are avoided. Most economies will find that at any given time, for various reasons of geography, technical change and market prospects, optimal growth involves some degree of imbalance between sectors and regions.

balance of payments 1. An overall statement of a country's economic transactions with the rest of the world over some period, often a year. A table of the balance of payments shows amounts received from the rest of the world and amounts spent abroad. The *current account includes exports and imports, that is visible trade, and receipts from and spending abroad on services such as tourism. It also includes receipts of property incomes from abroad and remittances of property incomes abroad, and receipts and payments of international transfers, that is gifts. The *capital account of the balance of payments includes inward and outward *foreign direct investment, and sales and purchases of foreign securities by residents and of domestic securities by non-residents. The third element in the balance of payments is changes in official *foreign exchange reserves.

2. The difference between total receipts and expenditure in any category of payments. Overall payments, including changes in foreign exchange reserves, must balance by definition, but this is not true for any one category of payments. The balance of payments on current account is the difference between total receipts and expenditures on current account: if receipts exceed spending, there is a current account surplus, and if spending exceeds receipts there is a current account deficit. The balance of payments on capital account is the difference between receipts and expenditures on capital transactions with the rest of the world. Receipts come from the sale of securities or real capital assets to non-residents; expenditures are on loans to non-residents or purchase of real assets abroad. Changes in foreign exchange reserves are equal to the sum of the current and capital account surpluses. A balance-of-payments problem or crisis means that the balance-of-payments situation is not sustainable. This may be because foreign exchange reserves are being run down, or because they are being maintained, but only by borrowing abroad at a rate that cannot continue for long before foreign lenders get too worried about the safety of their loans to provide any more. A balance-of-payments crisis differs from a problem only in the speed at which exhaustion of exchange reserves or borrowing capacity is approaching: a problem calls for action sometime, a crisis for immediate action.

balance-of-payments crisis An unsustainable *balance of payments. This means that *foreign exchange reserves are falling rapidly, or are being maintained only by a level of foreign borrowing leading to difficulties in obtaining further loans. A balance-of-payments crisis may be ended by improving the balance of payments on current account, via a recession in domestic activity, or by *devaluation. It may alternatively be ended by changing policies so as to prevent *capital flight and induce inward capital movements. It may also help if a foreign loan can be obtained to allow time for the current account balance to improve.

balance of trade The excess of visible exports over visible imports. This is a major, but far from the only, component of the balance of payments on *current account.

balance-sheet A statement of the money values of the *assets and *liabilities of a firm or any other organization at some moment, particularly the end of a financial year. Assets can include money, securities, land, buildings and other capital equipment, stocks and work in progress, and amounts due from debtors. Liabilities include secured and unsecured debts. The excess of assets over liabilities is the *net worth of the firm; for a solvent firm this is positive, and is treated as a liability of the firm to its shareholders, so that the balance-sheet by definition balances. Any firm whose liabilities exceed its assets is insolvent. It should be noted that not all items on a balance-sheet are equally reliable. The value of cash held is certain, and the value of easily traded securities and commodities is reliably known, though liable to change rapidly; but the value of real assets such as land, buildings and equipment, of securities which are not readily traded, and of amounts due from debtors, are matters of estimation. A balance-sheet, which shows the state of affairs at a moment in time, is contrasted with a *profit-and-loss account, which shows flows over some period such as a firm's financial year.

balances with the Bank of England Balances held at the *Bank of England by UK commercial banks. Most payments by cheque involve the customers of different banks: the bank whose customer makes a payment has to transfer money to the bank whose customer receives it. This is done through the bank *clearing. Most of these payments are mutually offsetting, but the small residue of payments due to or from each bank at the close of the daily clearing is settled by the transfer of bankers' balances with the Bank of England.

balancing item An entry in a set of *accounts to cover the discrepancy between two different figures for the same item. This is used when two methods of measurement produce different results for figures which should by definition be the same if both methods were completely accurate. Statisticians include a balancing item, or statistical adjustment, rather than changing one figure to agree with the other, when they do not know which, if either, is correct.

ballot, strike See strike ballot.

bands, exchange rate See exchange rate bands.

bank A financial institution whose main activities are borrowing and lending money. Banks borrow by accepting *deposits from the general public or other financial institutions. Bank loans are an important source of finance for firms, consumers and government. *Commercial banks may be all-purpose, or may specialize. Investment banks specialize on loans to firms; merchant banks on financing capital market transactions and international trade; and savings banks on collecting and lending the savings of numerous, mostly small-scale, savers.

   *Bank accounts are held by individuals and firms to conduct their transactions, either by providing cash when it is needed or by transferring balances to other people as ordered by cheques, direct debits or electronic transfers. If banks become unable to provide their customers with their money when it is needed, this causes great loss and inconvenience. A bank run occurs if the customers of a bank lose confidence in it and all try to withdraw their money. To avoid this danger, most countries have public bodies which supervise banks, to prevent their getting into difficulties, and *central banks to rescue them if they do. In the US the central bank is the

Federal Reserve; in France the Banque de France; and in the UK the Bank of England. Bank rate, now abolished, was the special discount rate applied by the Bank of England to high-class borrowers.

There are also international banks. The World Bank, or *International Bank for Reconstruction and Development (IBRD) is an investment bank at the international level. The nearest international equivalent to a central bank is the *International Monetary Fund (IMF). The European Central Bank is part of the *European Monetary System (EMS). The *European Bank for Reconstruction and Development (EBRD) is a European investment bank, like the World Bank at a European level. *See also* central bank, clearing bank, commercial bank, investment bank, joint stock bank, member bank, merchant bank, and overseas bank.

bank account An account with a bank, held by an individual, firm or government. Money in an account may be instantly available, as in a current account (UK) or a checking account (US); or notice of withdrawal may be required, as in a deposit account (UK) or a time account (US). An account may be in credit, when the bank owes the customer money, or overdrawn, in which case the customer owes the bank money. Current accounts normally earn little or no interest, and may be liable to charges; interest is paid at somewhat higher rates on deposit accounts, and interest at considerably higher rates is charged on *overdrafts, which may also incur extra charges.

bank advances *See* advances.

Bank Automated Credit System (BACS) The system by which depositors instruct their banks to make payments to named accounts, without the need to use a cheque. BACS is widely used for payments of dividends and wages.

bank clearing *See* clearing, bank.

bank deposit *See* deposit.

banker's draft A cheque issued by a bank and sold to a customer. This may be acceptable to a third party who would not accept the customer's cheque for the amount, which may be too large to be covered by any bank card. The bank's credit is better than that of the customer, and a banker's draft is unstoppable.

Bank, Federal Reserve *See* Federal Reserve System.

Bank for International Settlements (BIS) An international bank based in Basle, founded in 1930 to co-ordinate payments of reparations after the First World War. Its possible role as the principal international bank was taken over after 1945 by the *International Monetary Fund (IMF). The BIS has acted as trustee for the *Organization for Economic Cooperation and Development (OECD) and the European Monetary Agreement, and as a clearing-house for *European Currency Units (Ecus). It sets capital adequacy ratios for European banks, and compiles statistics on international debt. Most European central banks are members of the BIS, as are those of Canada, Japan, and the United States.

banking The provision of payments facilities, credit and capital to individuals, firms and the government. Retail banking is the provision of payments, savings and credit facilities in relatively small quantities to large numbers of individual or small business customers. Investment banking is the provision of credit and capital in larger quantities to relatively large businesses. Universal banking combines these functions in the same banks, as for example in European countries including Germany. In the US and the UK the functions are largely separate: in the US through the *Glass–Steagal Act of 1933, and in the UK through voluntary choice by the banks. The argument against universal banking is that mistaken investments may impair the solvency of banks responsible for the payments system. Modern banking is increasingly adding further functions, including stockbroking and *portfolio management, mortgage finance, and insurance to these traditional activities. *See also* branch banking, fractional reserve banking, relationship banking, retail banking, and wholesale banking.

banking system The network of institutions responsible for providing banking services. This consists of two parts. First, there are the actual banks providing services to the general public; these may be universal banks, or specialist institutions dealing with particular types of banking business. These range from 'high street' banks, with numerous branches dealing with many small clients, to merchant banks specializing in financing capital market transactions or foreign trade. Second, there are higher-level institutions, which are not involved in direct contact with the general public. These are *central banks, which act as bankers for other banks and the government, and are responsible for monetary policy and macroeconomic management of the monetary system; and bank regulatory bodies, which supervise other banks and check their probity, *liquidity, and solvency. These higher-tier functions can be combined in the same institution, as with the *Bank of England for the UK, or separated, as in Germany.

bank loan A loan from a bank to an individual or firm. Bank advances for large amounts or for business purposes are normally made against *security, for example the title deeds of buildings or life insurance policies. Bank overdrafts or personal loans for small amounts are often unsecured, if the customer is regarded as a good risk.

bank note Paper money, issued by a bank. The issue of notes in most countries is either entirely confined to or subject to strict control by the *central bank. A bank note was originally a promise to pay coin on demand; this tradition is preserved by the form of words used on Bank of England notes in the UK.

Bank of Credit and Commerce International (BCCI) A large international bank operating in many countries, whose collapse in 1991 with a multi-billion pound shortage of funds provoked widespread suspicion of false bookkeeping and money-laundering, and widespread concern about the adequacy of supervision arrangements for international banks.

Bank of England The UK central bank. Originally founded in 1694 as a private bank to lend to the government and manage the *national debt, by the nineteenth century it had developed into a *central bank. In 1844 the Bank Charter Act formalized its status. Its main functions were controlling the *money supply, through the Issue Department, and acting as a banker for the government and other banks, through the Banking Department. The Bank came under formal government ownership when it was nationalized in 1946; the Governor and Directors are appointed by the government. It manages the national debt, and advised the government on *monetary policy until 1997, when it was made independent. It holds the national *foreign exchange reserves, in the Exchange Equalization Account, and administered *exchange controls until these were abolished in 1979. It is also responsible for supervision of the banking system, and acts as *lender of last resort in financial crises.

bank overdraft *See* overdraft.

bank rate The rate at which the Bank of England used at one time to *rediscount first-class bills for its customers. It has long been abolished. At one time many other interest rates were specified in terms of their margin above bank rate. It directly affected other interest rates only when the market needed to borrow from the Bank of England, but changes in bank rate were announced as a means of informing the City of the Bank of England's views on what commercial interest rates should be.

bank regulation The application to banks of public controls stricter than those on businesses in general. This is justified by concerns that bank failures may disrupt the rest of the economy in a way that other business failures do not. Banks provide most of the *money used in a modern economy, and lend on a large scale. If a bank is run irresponsibly, taking excessive risks and holding too small reserves, this is liable to cause a bank run by its customers if they suspect it of being illiquid or insolvent. If one bank defaults on its obligations, this is liable to undermine other banks or financial institutions. Most countries therefore empower either their *central bank or some other public institution to supervise banks, laying down rules for their lending and reserve holding, and monitoring the banks' accounts to check that the rules are being obeyed. In many countries the central bank acts as *lender of last resort, to prevent banks that are illiquid from defaulting. It is more important to safeguard banks' solvency than their liquidity; a solvent bank should be able to borrow liquid assets when it needs them, but no amount of liquidity can save a bank once it is known to be insolvent. Bank regulators have in the past also been concerned to restrain banks' use of monopoly power.

bankruptcy A legal arrangement to deal with the affairs of individuals unable to pay their debts. Bankruptcy proceedings may be started by the individual, or by unpaid creditors. The assets of a person adjudged bankrupt by a court are taken over by an official receiver and sold, the funds being used to repay creditors so far as possible. Those who have become bankrupt cannot accept credit without warning the lender that they are an undischarged bankrupt, and also face various restrictions on their future activities: in the UK, for example, they cannot be directors of companies or Members of Parliament. *See also* Chapter 11 bankruptcy.

Bank, World *See* International Bank for Reconstruction and Development.

ban, overtime *See* overtime ban.

bargaining, collective *See* collective bargaining.

bargaining power The ability to get a large share of the possible joint benefits to be derived from any agreement. This depends on the losses failure to agree is likely to cause to the various parties to a negotiation. In the absence of agreement, each party has a fall-back position: the less uncomfortable this is, and the longer any party can afford to stay in it, the stronger is their bargaining power. A party with a very uncomfortable fall-back position and an urgent need for an agreement has very little bargaining power. Bargaining power is increased by unity, financial reserves, and a reputation for toughness, and is decreased by division, shaky finances, and a reputation for being willing to compromise.

barriers *See* non-tariff barriers, and trade barriers.

barriers to entry Laws, institutions, or practices which make it difficult or impossible for new firms to enter some *markets, or new workers to compete for certain forms of employment. Barriers to entry may take various forms. The law may confer *monopoly rights on existing firms, or impose qualifications for licences for new operators which are so obstructively administered as to make new entry difficult. Existing firms may have monopoly control over essential inputs, sites, or technical know-how, protected by *patents or commercial secrecy. If the capital required for new plants is very large, this restricts the number of possible entrants. The fear of *price wars by existing firms may deter some new firms from trying to enter an industry. In some markets sheer gangsterism is used to discourage entry. Barriers to entry are often higher against foreign firms or individuals than against nationals: the *European Union tries to prevent this so far as EU residents are concerned, with varying success.

barter The exchange of one type of good or service for another, without the use of money. This developed to allow society to take advantage of the *division of labour and the gains from *specialization. Barter, however, is not at all convenient: a person who has goods of one type and wants goods of another has to find somebody who wishes to make the opposite exchange, either for their own use or as a professional intermediary. The use of precious metals as a medium of exchange, and the subsequent development of *money, avoided this inconvenience. Barter is nowadays only used when the monetary system has broken down, in countries subject to civil disorder or *hyperinflation, or internationally by countries with inadequate supplies of foreign exchange.

baseline A projection of how the economy will develop if existing *trends and policies continue unchanged. *Models of the economy may be based on theory, *econometrics, or some combination of these. Before it is possible to calculate the effects of changing any aspect of nature, technology, or economic policies, it is necessary to construct a baseline projection. This tracks the future of the economy if present levels or trends in natural phenomena, technology, and economic policy continue unchanged. Any calculation of the predicted effects of changes in nature, such as oil discoveries, changes in technology, or changes in official policies such as tax rates, tariffs, or interest rates, is then conducted in terms of the predicted departure of the economy from the baseline projection.

base (logarithms) The number whose powers are used as *logarithms. The most commonly used bases are 10, where if $y = \log(x)$, $x = 10^y$; and e, the base of *natural logarithms, often written ln, so that if $y = \ln(x)$, $x = e^y$. Logarithms to base 10 were originally popular: before the advent of electronic calculators they had to be looked up in numerical tables. Natural logarithms are nowadays more popular, since if $y = \ln(x)$, the rate of change of y over time equals the proportional growth rate of x, thus $dy/dt = (dx/dt)/x$. Most calculators now have keys for both logs to base 10 and natural logarithms (ln) to base e.

base *See* monetary base, and tax base.

base period The period whose data are identified with 100 (sometimes 1) in constructing an *index number. In the UK, for example, in 2001 official data on national income aggregates were using 1995 = 100 as their base. *Base-weighted or Laspeyres index numbers derive their weights from base-period data, but *current-weighted or Paasche index numbers do not.

base rate **1.** The rate of interest used by *commercial banks as a basis for charging for loans. Most borrowers pay a premium over base rate, whose size depends on how risky loans to them are considered to be, and what *collateral they can provide.
2. An informal term for the rate at which the Bank of England lends to *discount houses; this corresponds to the *minimum lending rate, abolished in 1981. This rate governs interest rates elsewhere in the banking system.

base-weighted index A weighted average of prices or quantities, where the weights used are the quantities or the prices of the base period. Where p_{ij} and q_{ij} are the prices and quantities of N goods, $i = 1, 2, \ldots N$, in period j, and t labels the latest period and 0 the base period, the base-weighted or Laspeyres price index is given by

$$P_B = (\Sigma_i p_{it} q_{i0})/(\Sigma_i p_{i0} q_{i0})$$

and the base-weighted or Laspeyres quantity index is given by

$$Q_B = (\Sigma_i p_{i0} q_{it})/(\Sigma_i p_{i0} q_{i0}).$$

base year *See* base period.

basic rate The normal rate of UK income tax. This was previously called standard rate. In 2000–01 it was 22 per cent. This rate applies to all taxable non-saving incomes above a lower limit, below which a lower rate is payable, and below an upper limit, above which a higher rate is payable; the basic rate in fact applies to most UK taxable income.

basis point A commonly used unit of measurement of changes or differences in interest rates. It is defined as 1 per cent of 1 per cent, so that a 50 basis points rise in the *rate of interest means a rise by 0.5 per cent.

batch production A method of production where output emerges in discrete units. It is often used when there is a requirement that a certain quantity of a product, for example wallpaper, should be of a uniform pattern and quality, but the required characteristics differ between different orders. If there is anything wrong with the product, batch production makes it relatively easy to identify the workers, machines, and materials responsible for any particular part of output. This helps to motivate those concerned to avoid defects in products, and makes it easier to avoid repeating mistakes.

Bayesian statistics A statistical model of how beliefs are updated in the light of experience. It is assumed that beliefs about parameters are regularly revised, using a weighted average of the previous belief, or 'prior', and the most recent observations. The relative weight given to recent observations depends on the variance of observations over time.

BBB The Standard and Poor rating of securities which are regarded as being of medium riskiness.

BCCI *See* Bank of Credit and Commerce International.

BEA *See* Bureau of Economic Analysis.

bear A trader who expects prices to fall. A trader on a stock or commodity market who believes that prices are more likely to fall than to rise will sell now any shares they own, in the hope of being able to buy them back cheaper when their price has fallen. In extreme cases bears speculate by selling forward shares or commodities that they do not actually hold, hoping to be able to buy them cheap before delivery is due. Because bears sell stock, their beliefs tend to be self-fulfilling. A bear market is a market where there are a lot of bears, and for some time prices tend to fall persistently. *See also* speculation.

bearer bond A *security where the person or organization holding the certificate of title is entitled to receive any interest and redemption payments. Such securities have no central register of holders; the owners are thus at considerable risk of loss by theft or accident. Bearer bonds are attractive to anybody seeking to remain anonymous in order to avoid taxation, controls on capital movements, or legal checks on the laundering of money derived from criminal activities. They are therefore illegal in some countries, including the UK.

bearer security *See* bearer bond.

bear market A stock market in which prices are expected to fall. A widespread belief that prices are more likely to fall than to rise, at least in the immediate future, leads investors to sell shares or defer purchases, and thus tends to be self-fulfilling.

before-tax income The income of an individual or company before deduction of *direct taxes.

beggar-my-neighbour policy A policy that seeks benefits for one country at the expense of others. Such a policy tries to cure an economic problem in one country by means which tend to worsen the problems of other countries. (Some authors use the term 'beggar-thy-neighbour': the meaning is identical). The term was originally devised to characterize policies of trying to cure domestic depression and unemployment by shifting effective demand away from imports onto domestically produced goods, either by the use of tariffs and quotas on imports, or by *competitive devaluation. More recently, beggar-my-neighbour policy has taken the form of reducing domestic inflation through currency *appreciation. This improves the terms of trade and thus reduces cost-inflationary pressure in the appreciating country, but tends to increase *cost inflation in the country's trading partners.

behavioural theories of the firm Theories of firm behaviour based on considering the objectives of individuals and groups within firms. In contrast to orthodox models of the firm based on the assumption of *profit maximization, with some allowance for risk-aversion, behavioural models consider the motives of managers and other groups within the firm. In small firms a preference for an easy life, or desire to remain one's own master, may limit ambition. In larger firms, pursuit of managerial perquisites, or empire-building based on love of power or prestige, may lead to maximization of turnover rather than profits. It is also argued that lack of information leads firms into choices based on *satisficing, rather than maximizing anything. *See also* risk-averse.

bell curve *See* normal distribution.

below-the-line Items following but not part of the *profit-and-loss accounts of firms or the income sections of *national income accounts. For firms below-the-line items indicate how profits are used, or how losses are financed. In national income accounts they are capital account transactions. In both cases below-the-line items refer to changes in the form in which assets are held, and not to transactions giving rise to *income.

benefit(s) *See* defined benefit, fringe benefits, housing benefit, marginal benefit, means-tested benefits, sickness benefit, social security benefits, supplementary benefit, unemployment benefit, and universal benefit.

benefit-cost analysis *See* cost-benefit analysis.

benefit principle The principle that the cost of public expenditures should be met by those who benefit from them. This is contrasted with the *ability to pay principle. The benefit principle is extremely difficult to apply. Public support for the disabled or unemployed cannot be paid for by these groups, who need support precisely because they have no incomes. If the group of beneficiaries is widened to include everybody who has been or could ever become disabled or unemployed, this includes everybody. Those without children may resent paying for education, but were presumably once educated themselves, and are going to need an educated labour force to look after them when they are old. The vast cost of maintaining a modern level of public services makes the use of the ability to pay principle for taxation inevitable.

benefits in kind Government provision of goods and services to those in need of them. This is contrasted with providing citizens with incomes sufficient to meet their needs via the market. Governments wishing to provide for the basic needs of their citizens, including subsistence, housing, education, and medical services, have to choose between these two methods. Providing income is supported by the *welfare economics argument that people vary in their individual tastes and needs, so that any available resources will be more efficiently used in providing goods and services that they choose for themselves. There are, however, various arguments in favour of benefits in kind. In the case of medical and educational services, the tasks of assessing and meeting needs are closely connected. Housing, medical services, and education are often regarded as *'merit goods': improved housing, health and education are supposed to benefit society at large as well as the individual recipient. There is a danger that if those in need of services for themselves, and more particularly for their children, were simply given enough money to pay for them, they might in fact prefer to spend some or all of it in more congenial ways, for example on drink. To try to combine the merits of market provision of services with the advantages of benefits in kind, it has been proposed that education should be supplied by the state issuing parents with *vouchers, which could be spent only at educational institutions, and would not otherwise be tradable.

benefits system The system of provision in cash and in kind of sufficient income and services to maintain minimum standards of welfare among a country's residents. This system has to support those unable to provide for themselves because they are too old or young to work, are disabled, ill, or simply unable or unwilling to obtain work. Such a system is necessarily expensive: choices which have to be made about it are between payments in cash and provision of *benefits in kind; between universal and *means-tested benefits; between unconditional benefits and benefits conditional on work or training; and between benefits as of right and benefits at the discretion of officials.

Benelux A customs union of Belgium, the Netherlands and Luxembourg, set up in 1948. It was a precursor of the *European Economic Community (EEC), which all three members joined when it was founded in 1958.

Bertrand competition *Competition between two or more firms in an industry where each assumes that the others will maintain their prices unchanged. This encourages the use of price-cutting as a form of competition, particularly if the products are good *substitutes. As price gets driven down towards *marginal cost, as should occur if the products are perfect substitutes, it is hard to see how firms under Bertrand competition could cover their *fixed costs.

Bertrand duopoly A market situation with two sellers, each of whom assumes that the other will hold their price unchanged. This leads to severe price competition.

BES See Business Expansion Scheme.

best See first-best, and second-best.

beta coefficient A measure of how variations in the return on a particular share correlate with variations in the return on a market index. The return on a share is the change in price plus any distribution of dividends. If S_t is the proportional return on a share from time $t - 1$ to time t, and M_t is the proportional return on the market index, β is calculated by finding the best fit to $S_t = \alpha + \beta M_t + \varepsilon_t$. $\beta < 0$ means that S_t moves against the market; a zero or low value of β means that the share has mainly idiosyncratic risk, independent of overall market movements; a positive value of β means that S_t moves with the market, and $\beta > 1$ means that the share more than reflects movements in the market.

beta stocks Shares in the second rank for frequency of trading on a *stock exchange. On the London Stock Exchange before the system was replaced in 1991 by Normal Market Size there were about 500 beta stocks, compared with about 100 *alpha stocks, the most frequently traded category, and over 3,000 gamma and delta, or less traded stocks.

Beveridge Report A report on social security, prepared by Sir William Beveridge during the Second World War, and published in 1944 as *Full*

Employment in a Free Society. This was widely regarded as the basis for the creation of the post-war *welfare state in the UK.

bias A tendency for estimates of variables to be systematically too high or too low. This may be due to the method of *sample selection, the way in which questions are put, or the calculations based on the data collected. Researchers can try to select samples by random methods which do not bias the results, and to put questions in a form which does not appear to invite any particular answer. If the extent of any remaining bias is known, methods of calculation can be changed to allow for it.

bid *See* hostile bid, and takeover bid.

big bang 1. A shorthand expression for the view that reforms should be carried out as rapidly as possible. This is contrasted with the view that major changes should be made gradually. These views clash in countries undertaking *liberalization or *structural transformation. The argument for rapid change is that it creates a sufficiently large group who have gained from change to make it politically irreversible, whereas gradual change encourages opposition, because the losers often suffer before the gainers benefit.
2. The change in 1986 when fixed commissions were abolished in the City. This usage is in connection with the UK financial sector.

big four The four largest UK high street banks, namely Barclays, Lloyds, HSCB (formerly the Midland), and National Westminster.

big push The argument that development can only succeed if the various sectors of an economy expand together, since each provides markets for the others. This argument for balanced growth takes little account of the possible use of external trade to complement a country's own production.

bilateral monopoly A market situation with a single buyer, or monopsonist, facing a single seller, or monopolist. This could arise where a single supplier firm faces a single government purchaser, for example the Ministry of Defence, or where a single trade union faces a single employer, for example a nationalized industry. Under bilateral monopoly, price and quantity are decided by bargaining between the two parties, each of whom can of course identify the other. *See also* monopsony.

bilateral trade A situation where trade between any two countries has to balance, or any imbalance has to be financed by credits arranged directly between the two countries. This is contrasted with *multilateral trade, which requires only that trade with all other countries combined should either balance, or be financed by overall credit from other countries. Bilateral trade has the disadvantages of *barter at the national level. It is more efficient to be able to run surpluses with some trade partners and deficits with others, and to be able to finance any overall surplus or deficit with loans to or from any other country. For a country with a *convertible currency, bilateral surpluses or deficits on either current or capital account are of no importance; only overall or multilateral balances matter. Bilateral trade can be defended only as a *second-best arrangement that is better than no trade at all in situations where the institutions that make multilateral trade possible have broken down.

bill A short-dated security, usually maturing in under a year. *Treasury bills are issued by the UK government; trade bills are issued by firms to obtain short-term finance cheaper than borrowing from the banks; *bills of exchange are issued by private firms to finance foreign trade. A bill specifies its *maturity date, for example 91 days from the date of issue, and the currency in which it is to be repaid. Bills carry no explicit interest; the interest on bills is provided by issuing them at a *discount to their redemption value. Bills can be traded before maturity; while their market price is subject to change with changes in the rate of interest, because of their early maturity dates large interest changes are needed to move bill prices very far. For example, a bill maturing in 6 weeks will be reduced in price by only 0.58 per cent by a rise in short-term interest rates from 5 to 10 per cent a year. Bills are thus regarded as *liquid assets. *See also* Treasury bill.

bill, appropriation *See* appropriation bill.

billion One thousand million (abbreviation bn. or b.). This usage is followed by all modern authors; a billion was once used to refer to a million million, but this meaning can safely be ignored unless dealing with long-dead authors, when the convention used needs to be checked.

bill of exchange A short-dated security issued to finance foreign trade. The customer pays an exporter not in cash but with a bill payable in usually 3 or 6 months. This can be sold in the discount market to provide immediate cash for the supplier. If the customer is not well known, a bill can be made more marketable by *acceptance by a merchant banker, who adds a signature to the bill guaranteeing payment if the issuer should default.

bill, trade *See* bill of exchange.

bimodal distribution A distribution with two distinct peaks, with a dip between. For example, human death rates per 1,000 are higher in infancy and in old age than in the years between.

binomial distribution The distribution giving the expected number of occurrences of a random event as the result of making a number of independent drawings, with a known and constant probability of the event occurring each time. If the probability of the event (for example 'heads' throwing a coin, or '6' throwing a dice) each time is p, and the probability of non-occurrence is $(1 - p)$, the binomial distribution gives the probability of exactly r occurrences out of n tries, where $0 \le r \le n$. This probability is given by $p^r(1 - p)^{n-r}{}_nC_r$, where ${}_nC_r$ denotes the number of ways of choosing r objects out of n. ${}_nC_r = n!/[r!(n - r)!]$, where $r!$ denotes 'r factorial', defined as $r! = r(r - 1)(r - 2) \ldots (2)(1)$.

BIS *See* Bank for International Settlements.

black economy Economic activities not reported to the tax, social security, and other public authorities. The term is intentionally somewhat pejorative, as participation in the black economy usually involves evasion of taxes and social security contributions, and sometimes enables workers to draw *social security benefits while working. It is also liable to involve breach of laws concerning health and safety, employers' liability, job security, controls on the employment of aliens, and so forth. Lack of records of activities in the black economy reduces the accuracy of official statistics on incomes and employment.

black market Trading which violates *rationing or *price control laws, usually both. Black markets can by definition exist only when governments attempt to control prices or ration quantities.

Black Monday 19 October 1987, the day on which world stock markets collapsed. In New York the *Dow Jones index fell by 23 per cent, and major falls occurred in London and other major stock markets worldwide. The collapse started widespread fears of a major world slump, which did not in fact occur.

Blair House Agreement An agreement on the liberalization of international trade in farm products concluded in November 1992 between the *European Community (EC) and the US. It included cuts in the volume of subsidized food exports.

blue book 1. A UK government publication, so called from the colour of its cover.
2. The annual *United Kingdom National Accounts*, published by the UK Office for National Statistics (formerly the Central Statistical Office (CSO)), providing data on UK national income and expenditure, both in the aggregate and by sectors. Before 1983 it was entitled *National Income and Expenditure*.

blue chip The equity shares of large and reputable companies. Such companies normally have high *market capitalization, and a liquid market in their shares.

Board, Federal Reserve *See* Federal Reserve System.

board of directors The governing body of a company, which appoints the company's officers. Most *company directors are elected by shareholders at general meetings of the company, but a board may be given powers of co-option. Boards include executive directors, employed by the company full-time or for a major portion of their time, and may include non-executive directors. These usually either have suitable commercial experience, or are selected because they have titles or hold offices which make the company look respectable. Directors are normally paid fees for their services to a company.

board, two-tier *See* two-tier board.

bond A security with a *redemption date over a year later than its date of issue. Bonds may be issued by firms, financial institutions, or governments. They may have a fixed redemption date, an option for the borrower to repay at any date over a period, or even be perpetuities. They may carry fixed interest, or interest variable with notice or linked to some financial index. Their interest and redemption payments may be specified in money terms, or *index-linked to a suitable price index. Finally, they may vary in the degree of risk attaching to them. Government bonds are called *'gilt-edged', and are generally regarded as very safe. Well-established firms issue 'investment-grade bonds', which are also regarded as safe, while financially adventurous firms issue *'junk bonds', where there is recognized to be a non-negligible danger that the borrower may default.

When bonds have a long time to go to *maturity, their market price is sensitive to changes in current and expected interest rates, which control the *present discounted value of future redemption and interest payments. A rise in interest rates lowers present discounted value; thus even bonds which are extremely safe, in the sense of absence of risk if held to maturity, suffer from large variations in their market value as interest rates change. Bonds are therefore not *liquid assets. This liability to price fluctuations diminishes as redeemable bonds approach maturity. *See also* bearer bond, granny bond, junk bonds, and premium bond.

bond-rating agency An agency specializing in assessing the creditworthiness of governments, municipalities and corporations issuing bonds. Standard and Poor and Moody's are leading US bond-rating agencies.

bonus A payment to a firm's employees additional to their normal pay. Bonuses may be linked to performance, either of the whole firm, a specified section of it, or the individual recipient. Bonuses provide *incentives to employees, both to exert themselves and to stay with the firm rather than looking for a better job elsewhere. Bonuses differ from normal pay in that there is no obligation to repeat them, and they are not pensionable. They are normally taxable.

bonus issue An issue of additional *shares in a company to existing shareholders, in proportion to their holdings. This is distinguished from a *rights issue, where existing shareholders are offered first option on new shares, at a preferential price, but only get them if they pay for them. Bonus issues bring in no cash to the company, and are made as a gesture of confidence, and a signal of a probable rise in *dividends.

bookkeeping, double-entry *See* double-entry bookkeeping.

book value The value which is put on assets in a firm's *accounts. This may be the original purchase price, or a revised figure based on a periodic revaluation. It is contrasted with trying to value assets at their current market prices. Book value is often used when the assets are non-marketed, so that regular revaluation would be expensive and unreliable, or where the assets are marketed but their price is volatile, so that 'marking to market' would produce very variable valuations. *Balance-sheets using book values may conceal either large hidden reserves or undeclared losses in a firm.

boom A period of optimism, high economic activity, and relatively low unemployment. In booms prices rise faster than usual, and primary commodity prices increase relative to those of industrial products.

Borrow, General Agreement to *See* General Agreement to Borrow.

borrowing Incurring debts to finance spending. This is done by individuals, firms, and governments. Borrowing can appear desirable when the benefits from using borrowed money are greater than the interest costs. This may be because of urgent need for individual spending or sudden falls in income, or favourable investment opportunities for firms. Incautious use of credit is liable to cause borrowers severe difficulties when repayments fall due. Similarly, governments borrow when their desire to spend outruns their ability to tax; too much of this causes *debt service to become burdensome. Countries borrow when they want to invest more than they save. This may be sensible if investment is very productive, but too much borrowing leads to balance-of-payments problems. *See also* foreign currency-denominated borrowing.

borrowing, consumer *See* consumer debt.

Borrowing Requirement, Public Sector *See* Public Sector Borrowing Requirement.

bottleneck The effective *constraint on the maximum speed or level of an activity. Its use in economics is a physical analogy to the maximum rate at which a liquid can be poured through the neck of a bottle. In production, transport, or administration, the effective constraint is often a shortage of some specific form of labour or some particular piece of equipment. In production this could be a machine; in transport, a narrow bridge or roadworks; in distribution, a queue for a checkout assistant; in administration, a queue to see the boss. A major role of efficient *management is to observe and remedy bottlenecks as they arise, or still better to foresee them and take action in time to prevent them from emerging.

bottom line The profit or loss on an activity. The expression derives from the custom in drawing up *accounts of showing the profit or loss at the foot of the statement.

bound A value which a given function cannot pass, and may or may not actually reach. A bound may be upper or lower. $f(x)$ is bounded from above, by an upper bound b, if $f(x) \leq b$ for all x. $f(x)$ is bounded from below, by a lower bound a, if $f(x) \geq a$ for all x. A given function may be bounded in both directions; for example Sin (x) has an upper bound of $+1$ and a lower bound of -1; in this case each is actually reached at particular values of x.

boundary, production possibility *See* production possibility frontier.

bounded rationality The argument that there is a finite limit to the amount of information the human brain can hold, and the amount of calculations it can understand. Teamwork and computers can vastly increase the amount of information that can be collected, and the calculations that can be performed, but using the information and understanding the implications of the calculations are still subject to severe limits. This casts doubt on the model of rational economic choice as considering all possible alternatives and choosing the best, or *optimization. In practice individuals and organizations consider only a relatively small number of alternatives, and frequently stop searching once they find a tolerable course of action, rather than seeking the best possible. This is known as *satisficing.

Bowley box *See* box diagram.

box diagram An expository device widely used in *welfare economics to explain *efficient resource allocation. This is often known as an Edgeworth-Bowley box, from its inventors. If an individual, firm, industry, or economy has two types of resources, and uses them for two different purposes, the box shows the amounts of resources available on its axes. Each point in the box represents a possible allocation of resources, measuring the amounts used for one purpose from one corner as the origin, and the amounts used for the other purpose from the opposite corner. *Indifference curves for the consumption of two goods, or *isoquants for the use of two inputs, using the opposite corners as origins, can then be inscribed in the box. Points where the indifference curves or isoquants are tangential represent Pareto-optimal allocations of resources. Points where the indifference curves or isoquants cross are not Pareto-optimal. A line joining all points of tangency, called the *contract curve, can be drawn across the box from one origin to the other. Moving along the contract curve more of one object of resource use is achieved, and less of the other. *See also* Pareto-optimality.

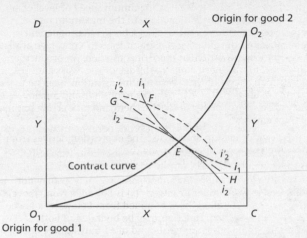

FIGURE 2: *Box Diagram*

The horizontal axis shows available supplies of factor X; the vertical axis shows available supplies of factor Y. Point O_1 at the SW corner of the box is the origin for good 1; point O_2 at the NE corner is the origin for good 2. Any point in the box shows an allocation of factors between the two industries: factors West and South of the point are used in good 1, factors East and North are used in good 2. i_1 and i_2 are isoquants for goods 1 and 2. Any point such as E where isoquants for the two goods are tangential to each other is a Pareto-optimal allocation. GEH is the common tangent to both isoquants; its slope shows relative factor prices. Any point such as F, where isoquants are not tangential, is not Pareto-optimal; the isoquant i'_2 is flatter than i_1, and output of one or both goods could be increased by moving towards E. O_1EO_2 is the contract curve. A similar argument applies to allocating fixed quantities of two goods between two consumers.

boycott A refusal to trade with the person, company, or country boycotted. The name comes from a nineteenth-century Irish land agent unpopular with his master's tenants. A boycott may involve refusal to buy goods and services from somebody, or to sell to them. A secondary boycott extends this to anybody who does not join in the original boycott. While it is hard to make a boycott completely effective, as trade can usually be conducted secretly or indirectly, this involves delay, expense, and inconvenience. A boycott is thus an effective form of pressure on individuals, firms, or countries whose conduct or opinions are widely disapproved of.

BP curve A curve drawn on the same diagram as the *IS* and *LM* curves, showing combinations of *Y*, GDP, and *r*, interest rates, at which the overall balance of payments is in equilibrium. This means that the current and capital account balances of payments sum to zero. As higher *Y* tends to produce a current account deficit, and higher *r* tends to produce a capital account surplus, the *BP* curve is upward sloping. If international capital mobility is high, the *BP* curve is flatter than the *LM* curve. *See also* the figure for *IS-LM* model.

Brady Plan An agreement in 1989 by which Mexico's external debt was restructured. The Plan was suggested by and named after the US Secretary of the Treasury. It involved a mixture of debt reduction and new money.

brain drain A pejorative description of the tendency for talented people from poor countries to seek employment in richer ones. Sometimes this migration occurs because, while similar skills are needed in both poor and rich countries, the rich pay more for them. In other cases brain drain occurs because the technical and economic backwardness of poorer countries means that job opportunities there are limited or non-existent. It is also possible that brain drain is encouraged because of tendencies in poorer countries to fill such good jobs as there are on a basis of family connections, political influence, and corruption, while on average richer countries, though subject to some of the same problems, tend to fill posts on a slightly more meritocratic basis.

branch banking The banking system under which *banks are allowed to have branches. This seems to most economists an obvious solution to the problem of providing bank services economically to geographically dispersed customers. Branch banking in some countries, including the United States, has sometimes been restricted to reduce the monopoly power of banks.

brand A name used to identify the maker or distributor of a good. A brand was originally a mark burned on the hide of an animal to identify its owner, or on the person of a convicted criminal to warn the public of their character. In some cases a brand name is that of the original maker, which has been retained by a new owner after the originator ceased to be an independent firm. Brand names benefit producers and distributors, as they facilitate *advertising and building up a reputation for a product or range of products. Branding may benefit consumers where it is difficult or impossible to discover the quality of a good by inspection before actual purchase. If the maker is easily identified, then a good which fails to give satisfaction in use will not be bought again. Producers and distributors know this, and have a strong incentive to maintain quality, and to make amends if they have failed; this incentive is weaker with unbranded goods where responsibility is hard to trace.

brand loyalty The tendency for consumers to prefer familiar names. Consumers frequently buy brands they have used before, or seen widely advertised, in preference to unbranded products or unfamiliar names. Brand loyalty is a form of *satisficing behaviour: actions which have produced satisfactory results in the past are repeated unless something goes wrong. This makes it difficult for new suppliers to enter a market, even if their product is in fact just as good or better, and as cheap or cheaper than established branded products. Brand loyalty may be rational for consumers, however, unless the cost of unsuccessful experiments with new brands or unbranded products is low. It may even be rational to prefer more widely advertised brands, on the argument that the seller would be wasting money advertising a product unless it was good enough for people to be likely to make repeat purchases.

Brandt Report The report of an Independent Commission on International Development Issues, chaired by Willy Brandt, former German Chancellor. The report, on steps to promote North–South co-operation, was published in 1980 as *North-South: A Program for Survival*. It included pleas for a reduction in Northern protectionism.

break-even The ratio of output to *capacity just sufficient to allow a business to cover its costs. Demand is usually subject to random fluctuations, and equipment sometimes fails, so capacity must exceed the average level of demand to avoid having to turn away too many customers at times of peak demand. Failure to satisfy demand not only loses immediate revenue, but decreases future demand, as customers who feel they cannot rely on the good or service being available seek alternatives. Firms thus have a strong incentive to hold adequate capacity, but this has to be paid for. Break-even is the ratio of output to capacity at which a firm can just cover its costs, so output below break-even level means losses; only if output is on average above break-even level will a firm make profits.

break-up value The sum a business could realize by ceasing operation entirely and selling off its *assets. For most firms break-up value is below value as a going concern, so they stay in business. If a firm's break-up value exceeds its value as a going concern, it is economically rational to close it down and sell off the assets. Many types of asset do not have liquid markets, so the process of closing down takes time, during which asset values may change. It may thus be very difficult to estimate a firm's break-up value, which makes closing it down a risky venture.

Bretton Woods 1. The venue of a conference held in 1944 to discuss the new international monetary arrangements to be set up after the Second World War. This led to the creation of the *International Monetary Fund (IMF) and the *International Bank for Reconstruction and Development (IBRD or World Bank).
   2. Shorthand for the *international monetary system resulting from the conference. This involved pegged exchange rates, to be altered only in the event of fundamental disequilibrium. The Bretton Woods system lasted until 1971, when it gave way to a system of *floating exchange rates.

broad money A relatively broad definition of money. This applies to definitions such as M2, which includes building society deposits, or M3, which includes interest-bearing bank deposits. It does not apply to M0 or M1. Broad money measures of the *money supply tend to be less stable relative to GDP than more narrow measures.

broker A person or company who does not trade as a principal, but puts buyers and sellers in touch with one another. Stockbrokers do this for stocks and shares; commodity brokers for commodities, insurance brokers for insurance policies, and shipping brokers for tramp and charter shipping.

Brokers are able to charge *commission for this service because of their specialized knowledge of the markets.

brokerage The fee, normally a small percentage of the price, charged by a broker for the service of putting buyer and seller in touch with one another.

bubble A cumulative movement in the price of an asset whose price is high mainly because *speculators believe it will rise still further. Such speculative behaviour can force prices to rise for some period on a path that is eventually realized to be unsustainable; at some point a bubble will burst, but it is hard to predict when this will happen.

budget A statement of a government's planned receipts and expenditures for some future period, normally a year. This is usually accompanied by a statement of actual receipts and expenditures for the previous period. The annual budget statement in the UK is a statement of the government's financial plans made in Parliament by the Chancellor of the Exchequer. The word budget originally meant the contents of a package; the budget is so called because it brings all the government's tax and spending plans together. A budget surplus means that total government receipts exceed total spending; a budget deficit means that spending exceeds receipts; and a balanced budget means that income and spending are equal. The *balanced budget multiplier is a calculation of the expected effects on national income if the government's receipts and expenditure rise by equal amounts. All calculations concerning budget surpluses and deficits depend on the exact definition of the government that is used. Items which could on some definitions be regarded as part of the budget but are in fact excluded, for example government-guaranteed borrowing by other bodies, are termed off-budget items. A related use of the term budget is the *budget constraint, which says that the spending of any body, whether government, firm, or individual, is limited by what they can finance, whether from present assets, from income, or by borrowing. A *budget line shows the combinations of goods which can be bought with a given sum of money. *See also* balanced budget, full employment budget, and unified budget.

budget constraint The limit to expenditure. For any economic agent, whether an individual, a firm or a government, expenditure must stay within limits set by the ability to finance it. The finance may come from income, from assets already held, or from borrowing; loans will be obtainable only if lenders believe that they are sufficiently likely to be repaid. The budget constraint thus says that the *present discounted value of total present and future expenditure cannot exceed the present discounted value of present wealth plus future income. Spending can only exceed income plus present wealth to the extent that it is possible to borrow. *See also* hard budget constraint, intertemporal budget constraint, and soft budget constraint.

budget deficit The excess of a government's total expenditure over its income. This has to be met by borrowing, which increases government debt. Budget deficits can be calculated for any level of government: central, local, state in federal countries such as Germany or the United States, or for general government, which is all these levels combined. It is important to distinguish whether the deficit is calculated including as expenditure the nominal or the real interest on government debt: conventional measures of the budget deficit use nominal interest, but an inflation-adjusted budget deficit would include real interest only. The cyclically adjusted budget deficit is what the budget deficit would be if the existing tax and spending rules were maintained but national income rose or fell to its normal level; this can only be estimated. *See also* cyclically adjusted budget deficit, and inflation-adjusted budget deficit.

budgeting, zero-base *See* zero-base budgeting.

budget line A graph showing what combinations of quantities of two goods can be afforded by a consumer with a fixed total amount to spend. If each good is available in any quantity at a fixed price per unit, the budget line is a straight line with a slope proportional to the relative price of the two goods.

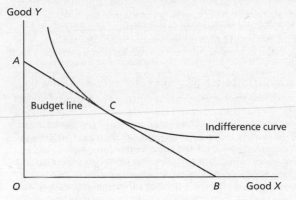

FIGURE 3: *Budget Line*

ACB is the budget line, showing combinations of goods *X* and *Y* that can be bought for given total spending. *C* is a consumer equilibrium, on the highest indifference curve consistent with the budget constraint.

budget surplus The excess of a government's total income over its expenditure. This can be used to repay government debt. Budget surpluses can be calculated for any level of government: central, local, state in federal countries such as Germany or the United States, or for general government, which is all these levels combined. It is important to distinguish whether the surplus is calculated including as expenditure the nominal or the real interest on government debt; conventional measures of the surplus use nominal interest, but an inflation-adjusted budget surplus would include real interest only. The cyclically adjusted budget surplus is what the surplus would be if the existing tax and spending rules were maintained, but national income rose or fell to its normal level; this can only be estimated.

budget year The fiscal year used by the US federal government. This runs from 1 October to 30 September in the following year. It corresponds to the UK fiscal year, which however runs from 6 April to 5 April in the following year.

buffer stock A stock of a commodity held for the purpose of stabilizing its price. If price is liable to fluctuate, because of variations in supply, demand, or both, a buffer stock operator can limit price rises by selling stocks and can limit price falls by buying stocks. This can be done either at the discretion of the manager, or in accordance with a pre-announced maximum selling price and minimum buying price. The price can only be kept within these limits if the prices set are consistent with long-run market conditions. If the minimum price is too high, stocks will tend to accumulate indefinitely, until the buffer stock runs out of funds; if the maximum price is set too low, stocks will run out during periods of high price. Successful stabilization requires that a buffer stock is provided with sufficient funds to be able to hold enough stocks to deal with periods of high demand, and not run out of funds during low price periods. With a selling price above the buying price, a buffer stock is bound to make a trading profit, but it has to meet storage, interest, and administrative costs. Whether it can break even after meeting these costs depends on having a sufficient margin between its buying and selling prices, and on judging correctly which market price changes represent short-run fluctuations, to be stabilized, and which reflect changes in long-run market conditions, to which it must in time adapt.

building and loan association A US co-operative institution providing mortage finance for home owners. This is the US equivalent of a UK building society.

building society A UK financial institution, whose main activity is accepting deposits from the general public to finance *mortgage lending on private housing. Building societies are the largest single source of mortgage finance. They also engage in some lending on commercial properties, and in other financial activities. Some provide current account facilities, including cheques and electronic transfers, for their depositors. Building Societies have recently been permitted to transform themselves into companies, and several have done so, while others have chosen to remain mutuals. *See also* demutualization.

built-in stabilizers Any features of the economy that tend to limit economic fluctuations through routine behaviour, without the need for specific decisions. The government's *budget provides obvious examples. If national income falls, the application of given direct and indirect tax rates cuts revenue automatically; if unemployment rises, the application of given benefit rules ensures that income maintenance payments rise. This raises the budget deficit, and limits the fall in incomes. Similarly, when national income rises the budget deficit falls. The advantage of built-in stabilizers over deliberate policy measures is that they operate automatically and immediately. When deliberate policy changes are needed, there is delay while the figures are collected, and further delay results from technical or political disagreement about the policy measures to be adopted. The disadvantage of built-in stabilizers is that they can only diminish fluctuations and cannot eliminate them completely. Any further *stabilization requires deliberate changes in policies, based on forecasts of the economy which are known to be unreliable. Some economists believe that partial stabilization through built-in stabilizers is probably about the most that can actually be achieved.

bull A trader who expects prices to rise. A trader on a stock or commodity market who believes that prices are more likely to rise than to fall will buy shares, in the hope of selling them at a profit when the price has risen. In extreme cases bulls speculate by contracting to buy forward shares or commodities for which they cannot afford to pay, hoping that when prices rise they will be able to borrow the cash needed for settlement. Because bulls buy stock, their beliefs tend to be self-fulfilling. A bull market is a market where there are a lot of bulls, and for some time prices tend to rise persistently. *See also* speculation.

bullion *Gold held in bulk, usually in the form of gold bars. Bullion is largely held by central banks, as part of their countries' *foreign exchange reserves.

bull market A stock market in which prices are expected to rise. A widespread belief that prices are more likely to rise than to fall, at least in the immediate future, leads investors to buy shares or defer sales, and thus tends to be self-fulfilling.

Bundesbank The German central bank. The Deutsche Bundesbank, with headquarters in Frankfurt-am-Main, had until 2002 a constitutional duty to protect the value of the German Mark, and acquired a formidable reputation for financial caution and monetary stability.

bundle of goods A collection of specified quantities and qualities of various types of goods and services. A *price index is constructed by measuring changes in the total cost of buying a given bundle of goods, whose composition depends on the purpose of the index.

burden *See* debt burden, and tax burden.

Bureau of Economic Analysis (BEA) The branch of the US Department of Commerce which assembles and publishes the US national income accounts.

business **1.** All forms of industrial and commercial profit-seeking activity. The business cycle refers to fluctuations in the aggregate level of economic activity, and the Business Expansion Scheme in the UK uses business in this sense.
2. The firms conducting these activities: businessmen or women are the directors and managers of firms.
3. The ownership/management side of firms, as opposed to their ordinary employees; this group is often referred to as the business community.

business cycle *See* political business cycle, real business cycle, and trade cycle.

business ethics The study of what standards businesses should observe in their dealings over and above compliance with the letter of the law. This covers questions such as fair dealing with their labour force, customers, suppliers, and competitors, and the impact of their activities on public health, the environment, and animal welfare. If a good reputation helps to gain and retain business, ethical conduct need not necessarily conflict with profit, but there are bound to be cases where it does. Particularly difficult questions of business ethics arise in multinational firms, where practices such as gifts to officials, which are essential to doing business at all in some countries, are regarded as criminal in others.

Business Expansion Scheme (BES) A UK fiscal device intended to encourage investment of *venture capital in new businesses. This operated from 1981 to 1994, when it was replaced by the Enterprise Investment Scheme (EIS). Investment under the BES was encouraged by tax concessions; it is not clear how far businesses coming into the scheme were really new, and how far it benefited businesses which would have been started in any case even without the scheme, or encouraged *creative accounting to enable businesses which were already in existence to participate.

business rate A UK tax on business premises, levied to finance local authorities. The rate per pound of valuation at which business rates are levied used to be decided by the local authorities themselves, but it is now set at a common national level, the uniform business rate. The valuation of premises for rating purposes is decided by a District Valuer.

buyer A person who buys things, usually for money. In their role as a consumer everybody is a buyer, but firms employ specialist buyers. In the case of goods which vary in quality, design or specification, or where suppliers are difficult to track down, a buyer is a highly skilled expert whose services are vital to the firm.

buyer's market A market in which conditions are better for buyers than for sellers. If sellers are numerous and under pressure to raise money quickly, while buyers are scarce and can afford to wait, it is likely that prices will be unusually low and that conditions of sale will be unusually favourable for buyers.

buy-out Change in *control of a company through its previous shareholders being bought out by new owners. These may already be connected with the firm: in a *management buy-out the firm is bought by its existing managers. A buy-out may alternatively be by outsiders. Finance may come from the purchasers' own resources, or from loans; in a *leveraged buy-out part of the price is raised by fixed-interest loans. *See also* leveraged buy-out, and management buy-out.

bygones Past events which play no part in rational present decision-making. For a firm, bygones include *sunk costs, and past operating profits and losses, except to the extent that these play a part in forming present expectations.

by-product A good produced incidentally to the production of some other good. Sale of a by-product makes production more profitable than if it had to be thrown away, or were costly to dispose of. The term by-product is used where one good would be produced for its own sake even if the other were useless. This is distinguished from *joint production, which is profitable only if both goods can be sold.

C

cabotage Transport of goods within a country by foreign carriers. Restrictions on cabotage are a common form of *protectionism. This is good for national carriers, but it may not be beneficial overall, as it deprives a country's producers of the cheapest or most convenient form of transport.

Cairns Group A group of countries formed in 1986 to exert pressure to ensure that the liberalization of agricultural trade remained a high priority in the *Uruguay Round of trade talks. The members of the Cairns Group are Argentina, Australia, Brazil, Canada, Chile, Colombia, Fiji, Hungary, Indonesia, Malaysia, the Philippines, New Zealand, Thailand and Uruguay. Farm exports of the Cairns Group exceed those of the European Union (EU) and the United States combined.

calibration Assigning numerical values to the parameters of models of the economy so that the quantities predicted for variables such as GDP are realistic. This procedure is used when the available statistics are inadequate to allow econometric fitting of a model.

call money Money lent in the London money market, repayable at very short notice. This is a highly *liquid asset for UK banks and other financial institutions. Because of transactions costs it is only practicable to lend money on these terms in large amounts.

call option A contract giving the holder the right but no obligation to buy a good or security on some future date at a pre-arranged price. A call option will be exercised only if the *spot price at the contract date exceeds the option price.

Cambridge equation The formulation of the *quantity theory of money as

$$M = kPY.$$

Here M is the demand for money balances, P is the price level, Y is the level of real national income and k is a parameter reflecting economic structure and monetary habits, namely the ratio of total transactions to income and the ratio of desired money balances to total transactions. The Cambridge equation is a modified form of the Fisher equation,

$$MV = PT,$$

with $k = T/(VY)$, where V is the *velocity of circulation and T is the real volume of transactions.

CAP *See* Common Agricultural Policy.

capacity The maximum output an industrial plant is considered capable of producing. This assumes normal working: if single-shift working is normal, output can sometimes be further increased by *shift work, using two or even three shifts. The capacity of a firm, an industry, or the economy as a whole can only be estimated subject to considerable problems of *aggregation. Firms or industries have equipment of varying types: some of this can only produce goods for which there is no demand; other equipment can produce goods that are wanted, but only at such high operating costs that its use is normally uneconomic. Because of the need for flexibility in both the timing and the composition of output, firms normally aim on average to operate at well under 100 per cent of capacity. In emergencies, however, the use of overtime, extra shifts, and deferring maintenance work can allow output to exceed capacity for limited periods. *See also* excess capacity, and spare capacity.

capacity utilization Actual output as a percentage of capacity. Capacity is the maximum output firms could produce with their existing equipment. Because demand fluctuates and equipment is liable to break down, firms normally aim to have more capacity than the average level of demand, and less than 100 per cent capacity utilization. Actual capacity utilization is expected to fluctuate: if it remains persistently above its normal level, this suggests that investment in new equipment would be profitable. If capacity utilization remains persistently below its normal level, this suggests that some equipment, normally the oldest and least productive, is not worth the cost of maintaining it and should be scrapped.

capital 1. Man-made means of production. Capital goods are goods designed to be used in production, for example machinery. *Capital consumption is an estimate of the investment needed to keep the capital stock constant. The *capital stock adjustment model explains investment as an attempt to bring the actual level of capital into line with what firms want, which depends on their output. *Human capital refers to skills and experience which enhance a worker's productivity. Human capital differs from material capital in that it cannot be bought or sold (except in the case of slavery), and thus cannot be used as collateral for loans.

2. A stock of financial assets, which can be used to provide an income. The capital of a company is the initial stock of money with which it started trading, plus subsequent retained profits. This capital may be spent on buying capital goods, or it may be circulating capital, held as money balances or used to give credit to customers. The *capital market is the system through which firms are provided with capital in this sense. Firms sell shares to investors; *capital gains are made if these shares, or other assets, rise in value and are resold at a profit. *Capital gains tax (CGT) is a tax on realized capital gains. The *capital asset pricing model (CAPM) is used to explain the prices of capital assets. The *capital account is the part of the balance-of-payments accounts concerned with transactions, such as international lending and foreign direct investment, which do not constitute income for the recipient. Capital account transactions change the form in which a given total of assets is held.

3. The social class of those who derive most of their income from owning property. *Capitalists are individual members of this class. *Capitalism is the economic system in which an important role in decision-making is taken by the owners of capital, including both its real and financial forms. *See also* authorized capital, cost of capital, human capital, issued capital, marginal efficiency of capital, marginal productivity of capital, paid-up capital, physical capital, risk capital, sources of capital, venture capital, and working capital.

capital account Transactions which do not involve income or expenditure, but change the form in which assets are held. Receipt of a loan, for example, is not income, but an exchange of cash now for a promise to repay, usually with interest, in the future. In a country's balance of payments, the capital account is a record of international exchanges of assets and liabilities.

capital accumulation The process of increasing the stock of man-made means of production. This is one of the main sources of economic growth in the short and medium run. Whether capital accumulation can raise long-run growth is a matter of controversy. *Solow-style growth models hold that in the long run the growth rate is set by population growth and the rate of *technical progress: capital accumulation raises output levels but is subject to decreasing returns, a tendency which is accentuated by the fact that much of the extra output is required for replacement of the capital stock as it wears out. *Endogenous growth models hold that the long-run growth rate can be increased through higher savings rates which permit more rapid capital accumulation.

capital adequacy Possession by a firm of sufficient capital for the business it is doing. This matters to the firm itself: if it is under-capitalized, a small adverse shift in cirumstances can impair its solvency. Capital adequacy therefore matters to a firm's creditors. In the case of banks and other financial institutions, it also matters to the regulatory authorities, who fear that the failure of particular firms might cause a general financial panic. How much capital is adequate depends on the risks a firm is taking.

capital allowances Deductions from a firm's taxable *profits in respect of investment expenditure. This encourages investment, since for any given level of gross profits, the more investment a firm does, the less tax it has to pay.

capital appreciation An increase in the prices of the assets owned by an enterprise. When increases in the value of land, buildings, equipment, or stocks are merely proportional to general *inflation in the economy, it is argued that they do not increase the real value of a business. They should therefore not be included in its profits for tax purposes, or in the national income accounts.

capital asset pricing model (CAPM) The theory that in a well-diversified portfolio of assets the valuation of a security depends not only on its own returns, but on how it contributes to overall risk. The value of a security will be higher, the lower its *beta coefficient; this measures the relation between returns on a particular security and returns on the overall market portfolio.

capital consumption Loss of value of capital equipment due to use, ageing, or *obsolescence. Part of the value of the capital stock owned by an enterprise is lost in any period through wear and tear in use. The passage of time also reduces its expected remaining useful life; and it may become obsolete through advances in technology or changes in factor prices. Capital consumption does not consist of any observable set of market transactions, but has to be estimated. It has to be deducted from the *gross profits of a business to obtain net profits, and from the *gross domestic product (GDP) of a country to obtain net domestic product.

capital deepening Investment to allow an unchanged volume of output to be produced at lower cost. This may be by saving on labour, fuel, or material inputs. Capital deepening is contrasted with *capital widening, where investment allows increased production by unchanged methods, using additional labour, fuel, and materials.

capital expenditure Expenditure by a company which cannot be treated as a *cost in calculating its profits. It thus has to be paid for either out of post-tax income, or by raising external finance. Capital expenditure may be on actually creating new capital goods, but is more usually on buying them from outside suppliers. It also includes the purchase of existing businesses, and of patents and trade-marks.

capital flight Large-scale and sudden movements of capital from a country, by residents or foreigners. The causes of capital flight include fear of public disorder or persecution leading to personal danger to its owners, fear of confiscation or drastically increased taxation, and fear of rapid inflation leading to a loss of its value by the country's currency. Control of capital flight is very difficult when its owners are really frightened that if they keep their wealth in the country they are liable to lose all or most of it; in these circumstances they are willing to take large risks and incur heavy transactions costs to get their money to safety abroad.

capital formation The process of adding to the stock of real productive equipment of an enterprise, either by actually constructing it, or more usually by buying it from outside suppliers.

capital gain An increase in the value of assets. This is the difference between their present value and the price at which they were purchased. If the general *price level is stable, real and nominal capital gains are equal. If there is general inflation of prices, capital assets show real gains only if their prices increase proportionally faster than the general price level, and assets with constant money values suffer real capital losses.

capital gains tax (CGT) A tax on increases in the value of assets. CGT is usually only collected on the realization of gains by sale or bequest; to tax unrealized capital gains would require regular valuations of all assets. In the UK capital gains tax has been levied since 1965. Only gains over some minimum sum each year are liable to tax, and until recently it was only levied on proportional gains greater than the rise in the *retail price index (RPI) since an asset was acquired. Certain forms of assets, including the main residence of any taxpayer, are exempt from UK capital gains tax.

capital gearing *See* gearing.

capital goods Goods intended for use in production, rather than by consumers. Some goods, such as power-stations and oil-drilling equipment, can clearly only be capital goods. Many goods are in fact capable of being used either for production or consumption: cars, for example, may be used for business purposes or privately, and furniture may be used in private homes or for business purposes in hotels and restaurants.

capital inflow *See* capital movements.

capital-intensity The ratio of capital employed to output in a process, a firm or an industry. Of all feasible techniques, firms normally choose the cheapest. Thus the capital-intensity of the preferred technique depends on the relative cost of using capital and other factors of production. A rise in the relative cost of using capital may lead to the choice of a less capital-intensive technique, if one is available.

capitalism The economic system based on private property and private enterprise. Under this system at least a major proportion of economic activity is carried on by private profit-seeking individuals or organizations, and land and other material means of production are largely privately owned. Capitalism does not imply complete *laissez-faire; it is compatible with having parts of the economy in public ownership, and with varying degrees of regulation of the private sector on grounds including public health and safety, enforcement of competition, and protection of the environment. Such regulation is, however, typically negative: the rules lay down what individuals or firms may not do, but initiative about what is done within these rules is decentralized. Capitalism is contrasted with *socialism, under which in principle all major economic decisions are taken collectively.

capital issues The main way in which new *shares come into existence. Money to fund newly floated companies, or to finance the expansion of existing ones, can be obtained by selling newly issued shares to the public. New issues are regulated by the stock exchange; in particular, firms are required to provide potential investors with a *prospectus giving information about the business's past results and forecasts of its future prospects.

capitalist A person whose income comes from the ownership of capital. In a capitalist economy with a well-developed *occupational pension system and where the majority of homes are *owner-occupied, it could be argued that most workers are to some extent also capitalists. The term is, however, normally applied only to people who derive a significant proportion of their income from property. In the nineteenth century a capitalist would typically have been a rentier, a landlord, or self-employed, but nowadays most capitalists also derive a significant fraction of their incomes from salaried employment.

capitalization, market *See* market capitalization.

capital–labour ratio The ratio of capital to labour employed in a process, a firm or an industry. This ratio depends on what techniques of production are feasible. Of all feasible techniques, firms normally prefer to use the cheapest. This means that the capital–labour ratio tends to be higher, the higher are wage rates relative to the cost of employing capital. As in most industries it is easier to vary labour input than capital stock in the short run, observed capital–labour ratios tend to fluctuate over the *trade cycle, being higher in slumps than in booms.

capital levy *See* capital tax.

capital loss A fall in the price of an asset. A capital loss is incurred when the price of an asset falls below what was paid for it, and is realized when an asset is sold for less than it cost. Sale at a lower price means a nominal capital loss; a real capital loss is incurred if an asset rises in price less than in proportion to general inflation since it was acquired, and is realized if it is sold for less than its purchase price adjusted for inflation. Capital losses are sometimes allowed as deductions in calculating liability to tax; usually capital losses on some assets can only be offset against capital gains on others.

capital market The *stock exchanges and other institutions where *securities are bought and sold. The securities concerned include both shares in companies and various forms of private and public debt. The capital market allows firms, governments, and countries to finance spending in excess of their current incomes. It also enables individuals, firms, and countries to lend to others savings they cannot employ as profitably themselves. Some transactions in capital markets involve the sale of newly issued shares and debt instruments, but the vast majority occur in *secondary markets, where existing shares and debt instruments change ownership. Many less developed countries (LDCs) and former planned economies find the lack of an efficiently organized capital market a serious obstacle to the efficient use of their savings, and thus to their overall economic development.

capital mobility The extent to which capital can be shifted between different uses, and in particular between different countries. This is restricted in various ways. Capital in use may be entirely sunk, or it may be possible to withdraw it from its present use only gradually, as existing equipment wears out. Capital mobility is hindered by *asymmetric information: investors do not have sufficient information, or sufficient confidence that such information as they have is reliable, about opportunities in different industries or foreign countries. International capital mobility is frequently limited by government controls, in both capital-importing and capital-exporting countries. Economic groupings such as the European Union (EU) have tried to increase capital mobility between their members, but not with complete success. *See also* perfect capital mobility.

capital movements Movement of capital between countries. Outward capital movements are movement of domestically-owned capital abroad; inward capital movements are movement of foreign-owned capital into a country. Capital movements may take the form of *foreign direct investment, that is, investment in real capital assets, the purchase of shares, or long or short-term loans. All such movements form part of the capital account of the balance of payments. *See also* short-run capital movements.

capital outflow *See* capital movements.

capital–output ratio The ratio of the capital used in a process, firm or industry to output over some period, usually a year. This ratio for any process depends on the relative cost of different inputs. Where *technology makes alternative techniques feasible, firms normally choose the cheapest, so capital–output ratios tend to be high when capital is cheap relative to other inputs. For a firm or industry, the capital–output ratio will depend on the mix of different outputs produced and different processes used. The capital–output ratio can be measured as an average ratio, comparing total capital stock with total output, or as a marginal ratio, comparing increases in capital used with increases in output. Both average and marginal capital–output ratios are taken to refer to normal levels of working: when output is abnormally low during a *recession, the average capital–output ratio is unusually high, but the marginal capital–output ratio is unusually low.

capital reserves Part of the net assets of a company in excess of the share capital originally contributed by shareholders. Capital reserves may arise from the sale of new shares at a price above their par value, from retention of profits, from the revaluation of assets, or from capital gains made by a company. Capital reserves are not normally distributable as dividends; this is in contrast to revenue reserves, which are available to maintain dividends in years of low current profits.

capital stock The total value of the physical capital of an enterprise, including *inventories as well as fixed equipment. This can be measured in various ways: historical cost is what the equipment originally cost to buy; written-down value is historical cost of equipment minus deductions for ageing and wear and tear in use; replacement cost is what it would cost to replace existing equipment with equivalent new items. Any of these may or may not be adjusted for inflation since the equipment was first acquired. Whether the capital stock of an enterprise should include the value of *intellectual property such as patents, or commercial goodwill such as trade-marks and brand names, is a matter of controversy. The capital stock of an industry, region, or country is the sum of the capital stocks of enterprises in it.

capital stock adjustment A model using the *capital-output ratio to explain investment. The model assumes that firms have a target capital-output ratio. If at any time actual capital stock is less than is implied by this ratio, the firm invests so as to close part of the gap during the next period. Partial adjustment is assumed, taking account of both uncertainty and costs of adjustment. Thus if Y is output and the desired capital-output ratio is a, the target capital stock is $K^* = aY$, and if the actual capital stock K is not equal to K^* then investment is

$$I = b(K^* - K) = b(aY - K), \text{ where } 0 \leq b \leq 1.$$

As with the *accelerator model, a rise in Y increases K^* and thus leads to investment.

capital tax A tax on individuals or companies based on the value of their capital. An alternative name for this is a capital levy. Such a tax requires capital to be valued, and would be difficult to collect if it could not be paid out of income received from the capital over some short period. Most countries have thus chosen to tax either income from capital, realized capital gains, or capital transfers, rather than capital itself.

capital transfers Transfers of assets between individuals, by gift or bequest, where the recipient regards the receipt as an addition to their capital rather than part of their income. There is no objective test of which transfers are of this nature; the UK capital transfer tax (CTT) effectively uses the size of the gift as a test, by allowing small amounts to be exempt from tax.

capital transfer tax (CTT) A tax on capital transfers from one person to another by gift or bequest. Governments have two motives for using a capital transfer tax rather than a *wealth tax if they want to tax capital. First, it is argued that a CTT is less discouraging to saving than a wealth tax. A CTT is less likely than a wealth tax to be resented, and thus avoided or evaded by taxpayers. Second, a wealth tax involves the regular identification and valuation of assets. When capital is transferred, particularly by inheritance, the legal procedures involved make it easier to identify assets, which have to be valued in any case for probate purposes.

capital widening Investment to increase capacity using unchanged techniques. This allows increased production, using more labour, fuel, and materials. Capital widening is contrasted with *capital deepening, where investment makes possible an unchanged level of output at lower cost, through savings of other inputs.

CAPM *See* capital asset pricing model.

capture, regulatory *See* regulatory capture.

carbon tax A proposed tax on the use of fossil fuels, designed to reduce world output of carbon dioxide (CO_2). The proposal has been prompted by fears that excess accumulation of CO_2 in the atmosphere will have serious effects on world climate.

card, credit *See* credit card.

cardinal utility The concept of personal *welfare as being measurable. Statements about both the level of welfare and the size of a change in welfare are thus meaningful. Cardinal utility is contrasted with *ordinal utility, in which the level of welfare is not measurable, so that only statements about the direction of changes in welfare are meaningful. Economists find that this distinction raises severe problems. No objective measure of utility has been discovered, but in the analysis of choice under conditions of *uncertainty models involving the assumption of cardinal utility have proved very useful.

carrier, flag *See* flag carrier.

carry forward losses The right to deduct past losses from present profits in calculating liability to tax. Most tax systems collect taxes from companies and unincorporated businesses which make profits, but do not make payments to firms making losses, presumably because it is believed that the fraudulent production of apparent losses would be too easy. This asymmetry in the treatment of profits and losses tends to discourage investment. To minimize this discouragement firms are allowed to carry forward losses. This means that if a firm has made a loss in one period, if and when it returns to profit it will be allowed to deduct the loss carried forward in calculating its *taxable income. It may thus pay a profitable business to acquire another business whose main asset is previous losses which can be carried forward for tax purposes.

cartel A formal or informal agreement between a number of firms in an industry to restrict *competition. Cartel agreements may provide for setting minimum prices, setting limits on output or capacity, restrictions on non-price competition, division of markets between firms either geographically or in terms of type of product, or agreed measures to restrict entry to the industry. Cartels suffer from problems of enforcement, which make them liable to break down. So long as the other members of a cartel stick to the terms of a cartel agreement, it usually pays any one member to cheat, for example by giving secret price discounts or covertly exceeding quota limits on output. Enforcement of cartel agreements is made more difficult if governments regard cartels as undesirable, and make the existence of the cartels or the policies they follow either illegal, or lawful but not legally enforceable. The *Organization of Petroleum Exporting Countries (OPEC) is the most famous cartel of recent times.

cash Literally, notes and coin; but cash is mostly used in economics as a synonym for money in general. The *cash flow of a firm is the pattern over time of its receipts and payments in money, as distinct from the pattern of sales and purchases, which may well be on credit. Cash down means payment in money and not credit. A cash discount means that the net price charged for goods is lower if payment is made immediately, or within some short time limit. A cash register is a machine for recording receipts of money; a cashcard is a card enabling the holder to withdraw cash from a machine or branch of their bank or other financial intermediary; and a cashpoint is a machine for dispensing cash to card-holders. *Cash limits are limits on the spending of government departments, expressed in money terms. The cash nexus is an expression describing the role of money payments in motivating and co-ordinating activities in a market economy.

cash discount A discount for prompt payment. Where goods are commonly sold on credit, it is often possible to obtain a reduction in price for prompt payment, in notes and coin, by direct debit, by cheque backed by a bank guarantee card, or by electronic transfer. Sellers are willing to offer cash discounts because immediate payment saves them both delay in receiving their money, and possible administrative costs or loss through default involved in credit sales or deferred payment.

cash flow The pattern over time of a firm's actual receipts and payments in money, as opposed to *credit. A major responsibility of the finance director of any business is to forecast its cash flow, on both current and capital account, and to ensure that the timing of receipts and payments is such that money is always available to meet any payments that have to be made. Business which appears profitable on the basis of *present discounted value may prove disastrous if the receipts come in too late relative to the payments due, so that the firm is forced out of business before the receipts arrive. A profitable business can normally borrow to deal with cash flow problems, but only if potential creditors can be convinced that their loans will be reasonably safe. Neglecting cash flow by taking on business before the necessary finance has been arranged is extremely risky. *See also* discounted cash flow.

cash limits Limits to spending set in cash terms. When any government or business organization forms its spending plans, it provides its managers who are responsible for spending with budgets. These budgets may be specified in real or in nominal terms: for example, the army can be told it can buy x tanks, or that it can spend £y on tanks. The objection to budgeting in *real terms is that it leaves managers with no incentive to shop around for the best value for money in their purchases, or to resist price increases when they bargain with contractors and wage increases when they negotiate with trade unions. With cash limits, if the managers make bad bargains or are weak in wage negotiations, they will get fewer real goods and services for their departments. The disadvantage of cash limits is that if prices or wages change for reasons which are really beyond the managers' control, the level of real spending will be higher or lower than the budgetary authorities intended.

cashpoint A machine from which the customers of banks or building societies can obtain cash. Such machines are operated by use of a combination of cards and computer code numbers. They are also used to provide customers with information, for example on the state of their balances, and to enable them to pass information to the banks, for example ordering new cheque-books.

cash ratio A minimum ratio of cash holdings to total liabilities of banks or other financial institutions. Cash ratios are supposed to guard against the collapse of such institutions due to lack of public confidence in their ability to repay deposits. It is hard to see how they provide much protection to depositors if an institution's other assets are inadequate, so that it is insolvent.

catch-up Learning by copying. A country's real economic growth may gain from the possibility of copying techniques from other countries with higher levels of productivity. Catch-up is believed to be most effective for countries which are not too far behind the current leaders, and are relatively open to trade and capital movements.

caveat emptor Latin for 'let the buyer beware'. Considered as a legal principle, this is inconsistent with much modern legislation and many regulations designed to promote public health and safety by protecting buyers, who cannot reasonably be expected to be experts on all the products they purchase, from the consequences of their own ignorance and the greed or incompetence of sellers. As a piece of advice, however, caveat emptor is still very sensible. While the law prohibits the sale of poisonous pasties, for example, and provides remedies for their victims, the vendor may not be traceable, or may turn out to be insolvent when sued for damages. Legal remedies invariably involve delay, expense, and inconvenience, and in any case financial compensation may not be much consolation if one has been maimed by a defective product. It is therefore prudent for purchasers to use as much caution and common sense as possible.

CBI *See* Confederation of British Industry.

CCC *See* Commodity Credit Corporation.

Cecchini Report A report on the gains expected as a result of the '1992' programme for unifying the European Community's internal market. The report was published in 1988 as *The European Challenge, 1992*.

ceiling (in the trade cycle) The maximum level of aggregate real output the economy can attain. The effective constraint may be scarcity of labour or capital, or limits on the money supply. Due to growing population, investment, and technical progress, the ceiling rises over time, but only at a limited rate. If the economy grows faster than this, and output reaches the ceiling, the rate of growth of actual output must fall. If investment is influenced by the *accelerator this slowdown in real growth can cause a downturn in activity. *See also* the figure for trade cycle.

ceiling price The highest permitted price of a good or service. If a government or other regulatory body sets out to prevent the price of a good from exceeding a ceiling price, this can be done in various ways. One is legal regulation, if this can be enforced. Another is market intervention, where the stabilization authority holds a *buffer stock of the good and stands prepared to sell it in unlimited quantities at the ceiling price. This requires that the good is storable, and that a sufficient initial stock is held. It is also possible to intervene to attract suppliers and discourage demand for a good when its price rises towards the ceiling.

census An official enquiry concerning the number and characteristics of the population of a given area. Censuses are normally carried out by official bodies, by means of questionnaires, reply to which is compulsory. In the UK censuses are normally held every ten years; the most recent was in 2001. Information is collected on personal characteristics such as age, sex, family status, and occupation; censuses may also collect information on other topics such as housing conditions, mobility, language, ethnic grouping, or religion.

census of production A systematic survey of productive enterprises, normally carried out by an official body with powers to compel firms to reply to questionnaires. Information is typically collected from enterprises on topics such as the nature of their products, the quantity and types of inputs used, the number and types of employees, and value added. The results of censuses of production can be used to draw up *input–output tables for the economy.

central bank A bank which controls a country's money supply and monetary policy. It acts as a banker to other banks, and a *lender of last resort. In some countries, including the UK, the central bank is also the main regulator of other banks. Any central bank is ultimately controlled by a country's political system; whether central bankers should be controlled by the current government, or should be independent is controversial.

central banker, conservative *See* conservative central banker.

central bank independence Independence of the central bank from immediate short-run control of its aims and operations by the government. This can be promoted by removing the government's right to sack the central bank's directors or to dictate its policies. An independent central bank is desired by those who believe stable money is good for the economy. This may sometimes conflict with government aims, whether these are increased employment or the protection of various vested interests in the economy. Governments are believed to be too easily tempted on short-run grounds into inflationary policies, through attempts to boost employment, or inability to resist groups lobbying for higher state spending and lower taxes. Thus, a central bank under the immediate control of politicians is liable to adopt monetary policies which lead to *inflation, or to fail to use monetary policy sufficiently vigorously to resist inflation. An independent central bank is expected to be better for monetary stability for two reasons. First, it can be legally committed to promoting monetary stability; and second, bankers are expected to favour price stability, since so many bank assets are denominated in money terms. In the long run central banks cannot be completely independent of politics: the banking system is part of a country's overall political structure. If central bank independence is enshrined in law, this can be changed; even if it is written into the constitution, constitutions can be and often have been amended.

central government The highest level of government in any country. It is contrasted with local government, and with state governments in federal countries such as Germany or the United States.

central planning The operation of a command economy through centralized decision-taking. In a centrally planned economy, decisions are taken at the centre and orders issued to enterprises concerning their production and investment plans. The advantages claimed for this system of a command economy are that all resources in an economy can be used in the public interest, and wasteful duplication of effort can be avoided. Critics say that the amount of *information required to achieve efficiency in a centrally planned economy is too great, and the *incentives to supply the centre with reliable information are too poor, for such a system to be able to perform as well as a decentralized system based on *competition between independent decision-takers. Central planning was tried on a large scale in the former Soviet Union and Eastern Europe. Experience there up to the 1980s was so unsatisfactory that the countries concerned are now shifting towards a less centralized economic system.

Central Statistical Office The UK government department responsible up to 1996 for publishing many major UK statistical sources. These include the *National Income Accounts, Economic Trends*, and the *Balance of Payments Accounts*. In 1996 it was merged with the Office of Population Censuses and Surveys to form the Office for National Statistics (ONS).

certainty equivalent The certain outcome which would confer the same *utility as an actual distribution of expected outcomes. For an investor with a linear utility function, the certainty equivalent of a distribution of uncertain outcomes equals the mean expected value of the uncertain outcomes; such an investor is *risk-neutral. For an investor with decreasing marginal utility, the certainty equivalent is less than the mean expected outcome of a distribution of uncertain outcomes; such an investor is *risk-averse. For example, if $U = \sqrt{x}$, where U is utility and x is the outcome, a project with equal chances of an outcome of 1 and 2 has an expected outcome of 1.5, but its expected utility is only $(1 + \sqrt{2})/2 = 1.207$ approximately, and the certain outcome giving this utility is approximately $1.457 < 1.5$. The excess of the mean expected outcome over its certainty equivalent measures the *risk premium required to induce a risk-averse investor to undertake a project with an uncertain outcome.

certificate of origin A document certifying that a good was produced in a given country. Such certificates are necessary in *free-trade areas, where the members do not have uniform external tariffs. They are needed to confine duty-free entry to goods produced in member countries, to avoid goods from non-members being imported to the free-trade area via members with low external tariffs and re-exported to members with higher external tariffs.

CES *See* constant elasticity of substitution.

CET *See* common external tariff.

ceteris paribus Latin for 'other things being equal'. This means that other things which could change are for the moment being assumed not to. All statements in economics include such a clause, either explicitly or implicitly: it is impossible to list all the things which could alter. Any explicit ceteris paribus clause in an economic statement is included to draw special attention to the points mentioned, and cannot be taken as exhaustive.

CFCs *See* chlorofluorocarbons.

CGEM *See* computable general equilibrium model.

CGT *See* capital gains tax.

chairman The member of a commitee or *board of directors elected or appointed to preside at its meetings. The chairman frequently has a casting vote. The holder of this office can of course be female, in which case some authors prefer to refer to her as a chairperson or even as 'the chair'.

Chancellor of the Exchequer The UK's chief finance minister. The Chancellor is a member of the cabinet, and is in charge of HM (Her Majesty's) Treasury, the UK ministry of finance. The Chancellor is responsible for overall supervision of monetary and fiscal policy, is the government's principal economic spokesman, and presents *budgets to parliament.

change, percentage *See* percentage change.

changing, expenditure *See* expenditure changing.

Chapter 11 bankruptcy A provision of US bankruptcy law by which a firm can apply to the courts for protection against all creditors while it is reorganized so as to enable it to pay its debts. The argument for such a provision is that it gives better results for creditors as a whole than allowing firms to be forced into *liquidation by any one creditor. The argument against is that if the market thinks a firm is capable of being made viable somebody solvent will buy it up; Chapter 11 merely gives incompetent or criminal managements more time to deplete the assets.

Charge, Community *See* Community Charge.

charge, front-end *See* front-end charge.

chartist A person who believes there are recurring patterns in the behaviour of market variables over time, so that study of past variations assists in predicting the future. The name comes from the use of charts or graphs to show the past behaviour of variables such as share prices. If a particular way of interpreting charts becomes fashionable, chartist predictions of price movements may influence expectations, so that for a time the predictions are self-fulfilling.

cheap money The maintenance of low interest rates during a period of depression to encourage investment. This policy was followed in the UK during the 1930s and 1940s. It was not very successful in stimulating investment in the 1930s, except in housing. While cheap money may have been a necessary condition for recovery, it was not a sufficient one: it was described at the time as 'trying to push on a string'. In the post-war period of widespread excess demand, cheap money merely worsened the problems which had to be tackled by rationing and price controls.

checking account An account with a US commercial bank which can be drawn on without notice, in cash or by writing a check. Until recently such accounts paid no interest. The UK equivalent is a current account.

cheque A written order by a customer to a bank to pay cash, or to transfer money on deposit to another account. It is convenient but not legally compulsory to use a form provided by the bank for this purpose. Cheques are convenient and very widely accepted; they are not *legal tender, and there is no compulsion to accept them. Most businesses require cheques to be supported by a bank card, unless the customer is well known to them. Cheques not supported by a bank card can be 'stopped', that is, the bank can be instructed not to honour them; cheques supported by a bank card cannot be stopped. Cheques will not normally be honoured by the bank unless the customer has a sufficient credit balance or an agreed *overdraft facility.

Chicago School A group of economists teaching at the University of Chicago, including Milton *Friedman, who believe in the explanation of all economic actions by self-interest, the merits of free markets, the futility of and possible harm from government attempts to control the economy, and the importance of the money supply in determining inflation.

chief executive The officer of a company or other organization responsible for seeing that decisions on principles by the *board of directors are actually implemented in day-to-day operations. The chief executive is frequently also Chairman or President of a company; opinion is divided as to whether these offices are better separated or combined. The US term for this is chief executive officer (CEO).

child benefit A state payment towards the cost of maintaining children. In the UK this is paid to the parent or guardian with custody of a child, or to the mother in two-parent households; it covers only part of the estimated costs of child-care.

Chinese walls The requirement that financial firms prevent transfers of information between staff who are dealing with different clients, which could lead to conflicts of interest or to *insider dealing. For example, if department A is advising clients with funds under management to buy or sell shares in company B, it should not know what advice department C is giving to B on a takeover bid that will affect its share price.

chlorofluorocarbons (CFCs) Chemicals widely used in refrigeration, air conditioning, and heat pumps. CFCs were originally adopted because they are non-toxic and were believed to be safe. It has since been discovered that their effect in the stratosphere is to deplete the *ozone layer, posing a worldwide threat to health through admitting increased solar radiation. An international agreement to reduce their use was reached in the *Montreal Protocol in 1987, and it was agreed to phase out their use in developed countries by the year 2000.

choice of techniques The choice of method of production where more than one method is possible. A technique is a set of inputs capable of producing a given output or set of outputs. If more than one set of inputs can produce the outputs, a choice of techniques must be made. A profit-maximizing firm prefers the technique for which the total cost of inputs is lowest. If some costs are sunk, for example buying long-lasting machines, choice of technique has to take account of expected input prices over the whole useful life of the machines. If the desired level of output is fixed, it pays to minimize costs for that output. If the desired level of output is uncertain, as is likely over a prolonged period, the chosen technique may have costs higher than the minimum possible for the expected most likely output, but more flexibility, so that costs are kept down when output is well above or below the average expected level.

choice, public *See* public choice.

cif *See* cost, insurance, and freight.

circular flow of incomes A simple model of a static economy, based on the assumption of a one-period lag between income and expenditure. If there were neither injections of new purchasing power into this flow nor leakages out of it, total income in each period would be equal to the spending arising from incomes in the previous period, and total income would remain constant over time. Injections of new purchasing power not derived from last period's income can be made by investment, government spending, or exports. Leakages from the circular flow, by which this period's income does not lead to incomes next period, are caused by saving, tax payments, or imports. If injections and leakages are equal, incomes will be constant; if injections exceed leakages incomes rise over time; and if leakages exceed injections incomes fall.

circulation, velocity of *See* velocity of circulation.

CITES *See* Convention on International Trade in Endangered Species.

City The City of London financial district or 'square mile'. This area includes the *Bank of England, the London Stock Exchange, *Lloyd's, and the headquarters of many UK banks, insurance companies, and other financial institutions. It also contains branches of many foreign and international banks and financial institutions. 'The City' is also used to stand for the people working there in the financial sector.

City Code The City Code on *Takeovers and *Mergers. This was originated in 1968 by a Takeover Panel under the auspices of the *Bank of England. It lays down a code of conduct for takeovers and mergers; the objective is to ensure that all investors are given equal access to full information and fair advice. The Code is not actually law, but bears a similar relation to correct City practice as the Highway Code does to safe driving.

claimant A person applying for any benefit from the state. Benefits, for example unemployment, sickness, or disability benefit, need to be claimed for two possible reasons. In some cases the person has a clear legal right to the benefit, but the civil servants administering the *benefits system need to be informed of the facts. In other cases payment of the benefit is discretionary: in this case the claimant has both to establish the facts and convince the administrator that he or she has a good case for receiving the benefit. Claimants' associations exist to help claimants to understand what benefits they are entitled to, or eligible to apply for, and to advise them on the procedures for claiming these benefits. It is believed that many people do not claim benefits to which they are entitled, or where they would have a good case for discretionary benefits, through either ignorance or embarrassment over the claims procedure.

classical dichotomy The view that real variables in the economy are determined purely by real and not by monetary factors, and nominal variables are determined purely by monetary factors and not by real ones. Keynesian economics is strongly opposed to this view, at least in any time-scale but the very long run. Given the widespread use of fixed money prices in contracts, debts, and tax systems it is hard to see how anybody can believe that the classical dichotomy holds in the short run.

classical model A model of the economy in which it is assumed that prices, wages and interest rates are flexible, so that all markets clear. In such an economy factors are fully employed, and the growth of output depends on the growth of available factor supplies. The *Solow growth model is an example of a classical model. Classical models are contrasted with models in which either nominal or real price rigidities prevent markets from clearing, and unemployment can occur in equilibrium. It is clear that classical models are not 100 per cent realistic; it is a matter of controversy how much light they shed on long-term trends in real world economies.

classical unemployment Unemployment caused by wages being too high relative to productivity, so that the firms in an economy cannot profitably employ all the labour on offer at these real wages. This type of unemployment can be reduced by a fall in wage costs relative to producer prices. This could be achieved in several ways: lower wages; a lower *tax wedge between what the employer pays and what the employee gets after tax; or improved *productivity through better equipment, better education and training, the reform of restrictive working practices, or improved management.

classification, industrial *See* Standard Industrial Classification.

Clayton Act A US Act of 1914 extending federal antitrust law. It forbade price discrimination, tying arrangements and exclusive dealing, and the acquisition of another corporation's stock where this led to monopoly or decreased competition. The Act allowed triple damages to those injured by breaches of antitrust law. Labour unions and agricultural associations were exempted from antitrust actions.

Clean Air Act Legislation setting standards for atmospheric pollution. In the US this requires the Environmental Protection Agency (EPA) to set air quality standards for pollutants, and to issue guidelines for control of emissions.

clean floating *See* pure floating exchange rate.

clearing bank A bank which is a member of the *clearing-house. Most large banks in the UK are clearing-house members; small banks which are not members have to use a clearing bank as their agent to get their cheques cleared.

clearing, bank The system for settling payments due from one bank to another. There are numerous *commercial banks, and in most transactions settled by a transfer of bank balances from buyer to seller, the two parties hold accounts with different banks. The bank clearing is an arrangement to reduce the amount of funds which needs to be transferred to settle all these payments. All the cheques are sent to a clearing-house, where the amounts payable to and from the customers of each bank are added up. Each bank then only needs to make a payment to other banks if total payments by its customers exceed total payments to them, and the bank need only receive a payment if the total receipts of its customers exceed their total payments. The actual settlement is normally done daily, by the transfer of balances held by the various banks with a central bank.

clearing-house An institution where claims by various banks against each other are offset. This greatly reduces the need for transfers of funds between banks, as each bank need only remit the net excess of its gross payments out over gross payments in, or receive the net excess of payments in over payments out.

clearing, market *See* market clearing.

cliometrics The application of quantitative methods in economic history. The main problem with applying econometrics to any but very recent economic history is the poor quality of the available data.

close company A company with very few members. In the UK a close company is one with five or fewer participants or directors, or one where five or fewer participants or directors would be entitled to more than 50 per cent of the assets in the event of *winding up.

closed economy An economy without contacts with the rest of the world. No economy is entirely closed, but the various possible forms of contact with the outside are restricted in several ways. Trade in goods and services may be limited by poor transport facilities, or by human agency. Some of this, such as *tariffs and *quotas on trade, is deliberate; other restrictions are by-products of conditions making a country unattractive to foreign firms, including poor infrastructure, disorder, lack of a satisfactory legal system, and corruption. International movements of capital may similarly be hindered both deliberately and as the result of uncongenial conditions for foreign investment. International movement of labour is widely restricted, by lack of transport facilities, differences of language and culture between countries, and by deliberate legal restrictions. Finally, the international diffusion of ideas, information, and techniques is inhibited partly by the effects of illiteracy and poor communications, and partly by deliberate censorship and persecution making countries unattractive to intellectuals. No economy, even the most advanced, is entirely open in all ways to all comers.

closed shop The requirement that all workers of certain grades in a given business or establishment belong to a recognized *trade union. This is desired by unions to increase their income and bargaining power.

closing prices Prices in a stock or commodity exchange at the end of a day's trading.

clustering The theory that firms in certain industries flourish best in areas where there are other firms of a similar type. This enables them to use the services of related industries providing inputs of goods and services, and possibly to gain from the training provided by other firms in a cluster by poaching their skilled labour force. This is held to explain the tendency of industries to concentrate in particular areas, for example Silicon Valley in California, with a high density of electronics and computer-based industries, and the M4 corridor in England. Economic development agencies often aim at the creation of new clusters; this is difficult to achieve, as it involves simultaneous investment in various industries and forms of technical education.

CMEA *See* Council for Mutual Economic Assistance.

coalition A group of individuals or firms who have separate objectives, but combine to adopt strategies or advocate policies. A coalition government is one relying on the support of two or more political parties. Coalitions are naturally unstable: the emergence of new situations or policy issues makes it difficult for them to agree. Members of any coalition are always interested in exploring the possibility that an alternative alliance might enable them to achieve more of their own objectives.

Coase theorem The argument that *externalities can be corrected by the market. Provided that *property rights are defined and there are no transaction costs, the creators and victims of externalities can internalize them by private *contracts. This will result in an efficient use of resources: the distribution of property rights between the parties affects only income distribution and not the overall income level. In such cases there is no need for state regulation or taxation to improve efficiency. This argument only applies, however, where transactions costs are absent. It does not apply in cases, such as traffic *congestion, where polluters and victims are numerous and hard to identify. In such cases transactions costs may be too high for a market solution to give any relief to the problems caused by externalities.

Cobb–Douglas function A model of the aggregate *production function. In this function, named after its American originators, aggregate output, Y, is a function of the inputs used in producing it, for example capital, K, and labour, L, of the form

$$Y = AK^\alpha L^\beta,$$

where A, α and β are positive constants. If $\alpha + \beta = 1$ this function has constant returns to scale; if K and L are each multiplied by any positive constant λ then Y will also be multiplied by λ. The Cobb–Douglas production function has also been applied at the level of the individual firm. With this production function, a cost-minimizing firm will spend a proportion α of its total costs on capital and a proportion β on labour. The term Cobb–Douglas function is also often applied to *utility functions as well as production functions, and to functions or more than two variables. If N is land, the production function could be given by $Y = AK^\alpha L^\beta N^\gamma$, where γ is a positive constant and $\alpha + \beta + \gamma = 1$. In a utility function of the Cobb–Douglas form, K and L are replaced by consumption levels of two forms of goods, and it is assumed that $\alpha + \beta < 1$.

cobweb A simple model used to illustrate the danger that time lags may introduce fluctuations into the economy. Suppose that the demand for a good is a decreasing function of its current price but, because of the time taken to plant and harvest crops, its supply is an increasing function of last year's price. The equilibrium price is where the supply and demand curves cross, but if price is not at this level in year 1, it will be above equilibrium level in year 2 if it was below in year 1, and vice versa. The price will thus oscillate, with increasing oscillations if the absolute slope of the demand curve is greater than that of the supply curve. This is not a realistic model: if the oscillations were as regular as it suggests, farmers would be able to predict what was going to happen and behave in a more sophisticated way. However, if there is also a random element to supply and/or demand, it may be difficult to detect the 'hog cycle' mechanism at work, and lags may help to magnify fluctuations in an industry.

The horizontal axis shows quantity supplied and demanded; the vertical axis shows price. It is assumed that supply depends only on last year's price and demand depends only on this year's price. E is the equilibrium point where supply and demand are equal.

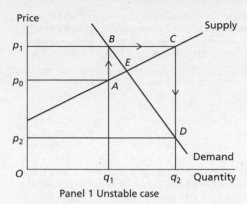

Panel 1 Unstable case

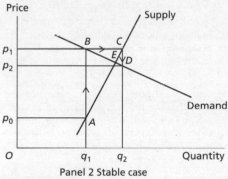

Panel 2 Stable case

FIGURE 4: *Cobwebs*

Panel 1 shows the case where supply is more elastic than demand. that is. the absolute slope of the supply curve is less than that of the demand curve. A price of p_0 in year 0 causes a supply of Oq_1 in year 1, leading to a price of p_1 at point B. This gives a supply of Oq_2 in year 2, leading to a price of p_2 at point D. This in turn leads to an output in year 3 further below E than p_0. Price and output tend to move further from the equilibrium E, until the system runs into some form of constraint, such as the fact that neither p nor q can fall below zero. The case in Panel 1 is explosively unstable.

Panel 2 shows the case where demand is more elastic than supply, that is, the absolute slope of the supply curve is greater than that of the demand curve. With corresponding labelling of points, price and quantity both approach the stable equilibrium E.

Code, City *See* City Code.

coefficient The numbers or algebraic expressions giving the structure of an expression or equation. For example, in $y = ax^2 + bx + c$, a is the coefficient of x^2, b is the coefficient of x and c is the constant term. *See also* correlation, and Gini coefficient.

coefficient of variation A measure of the importance of variability relative to average size. Size is measured by the mean, and variability is measured by the standard deviation, which is the square root of the mean square of deviations from the mean. Thus if there are N observations, x_i for $i = 1, 2, \ldots, N$, the mean is

$$\mu = [\textstyle\sum_1^N x_i]/N,$$

the standard deviation is

$$\sigma = \sqrt{\{[\textstyle\sum_1^N (x_i - \mu)^2]/ N\}},$$

and the coefficient of variation is

$$c = \sigma/\mu.$$

While the coefficient of variation is a convenient measure for variables such as consumption or gross investment, which are always positive, it is not convenient in dealing with variables such as net investment in stocks and work in progress, which can change sign and may thus have μ small or negative.

coin Money consisting of solid tokens, normally of metal. Coins were originally made of precious metals, normally *gold or silver, and were imprinted with patterns such as the sovereign's portrait to certify that their weight and fineness had been tested and approved. Sovereigns discovered that they could make profits by debasing the coinage, so that the material was of less value than the face value of the coin. This led to the rise of *token money, which does not claim to have intrinsic value. Since the rise of paper money, coinage has been largely used as small change. In a modern economy coins form only a small part of the total money supply. While the material costs are low, the processing costs of minting low-denomination coins mean that they may cost more to produce than their face value.

coincidence of wants The condition for a *barter transaction to be agreed upon. In the absence of money, if I want to trade a sheep for a goat, I have to find somebody willing to trade a goat for a sheep. The inconvenience of this led to the rise of professional traders, acquiring goods they did not want for themselves but could exchange again, and to the use of money as a *medium of exchange.

co-insurance Insurance covering only a proportion of total losses. This is often desirable since cover for the entire loss would create too much *moral hazard: the insured would take too few precautions to avoid the risk, for example of fire or motor accidents.

cointegration The property of a set of time-series, that a linear combination of them exists which is of a lower *order of integration than the highest-order series in the set. For example, two series which are I(1), that is of order of integration 1, are cointegrated if one can be expressed as a linear function of the other(s) plus a *stationary disturbance term. If a set of variables are cointegrated, the effects of a shock to one variable spread to the others, possibly with time lags, so as to preserve a long-run relation between the variables.

collateral A valuable article or property pledged as the security for a loan. In *mortgages, land or buildings are used as collateral; share certificates or life insurance policies with a surrender value are used as collateral for *bank loans; in pawnbroking the collateral pledged can be any portable valuable. If payments of interest and repayments of the principal are not made on time, in the last resort the lender can sell the collateral asset. This makes loans with collateral much safer for lenders than loans without adequate collateral. Individuals or firms who cannot offer collateral find it difficult and expensive to obtain loans.

collective bargaining The system by which wage rates, hours and conditions of employment in a firm or an industry are decided by negotiation between *trade unions representing the employees and employers or employers' associations.

Collector of Taxes A UK official responsible for the collection of *direct taxes on individuals and businesses. The Collector does not fix the amount payable, however; this is decided by an *Inspector of Taxes.

collusion Action in concert without any formal agreement. For example, firms may refrain from undercutting each others' prices, or from selling in each other's market areas. Collusion is common when anti-monopoly legislation makes explicit agreements illegal or unenforceable. Its existence is extremely difficult to prove.

column A list of variables arranged vertically. This may be part of a table, or a vector. A column vector is enclosed in brackets. The elements in either case may be numbers or algebraic expressions. A column is contrasted with a row, which is a list of variables arranged horizontally.

COMECON *See* Council for Mutual Economic Assistance.

command economy *See* central planning.

commercial bank A bank dealing with the general public, accepting deposits from and making loans to large numbers of households and small firms. Such banks are known in the UK as retail or high street banks. They also provide various services for depositors, including provision of cash and credit cards, storage facilities for valuables and documents, foreign exchange, stockbroking, mortgage finance, and executor services. Commercial banks are contrasted with *central banks, and with investment, merchant, and other specialist banks which deal little with the general public.

commercial bill *See* bill.

commercial policy The policies followed by governments affecting foreign trade. This covers the use of *tariffs, trade subsidies, *quotas, *voluntary export restraint agreements (VERs), and other *non-tariff barriers to trade, restrictions on rights of establishment for foreign businesses, and the regulation of international trade in services such as insurance. It is a matter of recurrent controversy whether commercial policy should be protectionist, or aim at an *open economy, and whether it should be entirely at each government's discretion, or should be governed by international rules negotiated through the *World Trade Organization (WTO) or regional groups such as the *European Union (EU) or the *North American Free Trade Agreement (NAFTA). *See also* protectionism.

commission A payment for the services of an agent or intermediary in a transaction. This payment is usually an increasing function of the value of the transaction. Commission may be payable by the buyer, the seller, or both; examples of agents working on a commission basis include sales staff, estate agents, stockbrokers and auctioneers.

commitment A promise by governments or central bankers about future policies. Commitment, sometimes pre-commitment, promises that monetary or fiscal policies will not be changed, or that if policy changes are needed they will take specified forms. This is hard to make fully credible, because governments cannot bind themselves by contract to keep promises, and may not want to exclude the possibility of reneging on them if circumstances change drastically. *See also* credibility.

commodity A standardized good, which is traded in bulk and whose units are interchangeable. Commodities are mostly the output of the *primary sector, that is agriculture and mining, or semi-processed products. Because these goods are standardized, commodity markets can trade spot goods by sample, and can trade in *futures and *forward contracts in commodities. *See also* spot market, and standardized commodity.

commodity agreement An international agreement intended to raise or stabilize the price of a primary product. This has been thought desirable since fluctuations in primary product prices lead to very unstable incomes for their producers, and corresponding fluctuations in the balance of payments of countries which export mainly primary products. Stabilization may be attempted by creating a *buffer stock, to be increased at times of low prices, thereby limiting their fall, and run down at times of high prices, thereby limiting their rise. Where variations in supply rather than demand are the cause of price fluctuations, a buffer stock may not greatly restrict variations in producer incomes. Increases in primary product prices may be brought about by restrictions on output, or in the case of agricultural products, restrictions on acreage planted or the number of livestock kept. Commodity agreements for various commodities including coffee, wheat, and tin have had a very chequered history, and there are currently no survivors. It has proved very difficult to get agreement on the financing of buffer stocks, or the allocation of quotas between different countries. The *Organization of Petroleum Exporting Countries (OPEC) is not exactly a commodity agreement, as it represents only producers; it does however, illustrate the difficulties facing such schemes.

Commodity Credit Corporation (CCC) A US federal agency set up in 1933 to provide price support for US farmers. Federal Treasury money is used to lend to farmers on the security of their crops; the loans and accumulated interest can be settled by delivery of the crops at support prices. The CCC sells the resulting stocks later if and when prices rise.

commodity exchange *See* commodity market.

commodity market A place or institution through which commodities are traded. *Markets were originally places or buildings, where traders could come together, which facilitated comparisons of price and quality. Non-standardized commodities such as fish and fresh vegetables, which need to be physically inspected, are often still traded in such markets; in other cases names such as the 'Corn Exchange' commemorate former physical centres which have been replaced by systems of traders linked by telephones and computers. Commodity markets include both *'spot' markets, where goods are traded for immediate delivery, and *forward and *futures markets, where prices are agreed in advance for trading at various dates in the future. Such trading is facilitated by market conventions on the specification and quality of the goods traded, and systems for adjudicating disputes. These are clearly essential for spot trades where the buyers do not physically inspect what they are getting, and even more so for forward and futures trading, where it is impossible to inspect crops which have not yet been grown or minerals which have not yet been mined.

commodity price index A price index of the prices of commodities, mainly agricultural and mineral products traded in bulk. Commodity price indices are used as leading indicators of economic fluctuations.

Common Agricultural Policy (CAP) The *European Union (EU) policy towards agriculture. This includes a *price support scheme which has led to excess production. As the supported prices are generally above world market levels, there is also an external tariff, and export subsidies are used to enable surplus products to be exported. Various grants to farmers are also available. The CAP absorbs up to two-thirds of total EU expenditure, raises the cost of living for EU consumers, damages non-EU farmers, and created great difficulties in reaching agreement in the *Uruguay Round of world trade talks.

common external tariff The tariff charged on trade with non-members by all countries in a *customs union or *common market. When used with capitals, Common External Tariff (CET) normally refers to the external tariff of the *European Union (EU).

common market A fully integrated market area. This covers not only complete freedom of internal trade, as in a *customs union, but also free *mobility of labour and capital. Full mobility of labour involves the right to reside and accept employment in all member countries, and mutual recognition of professional and technical qualifications, subject to satisfying local language requirements. Full *capital mobility requires lack of exchange controls, and full rights of establishment for firms in all countries. It is a matter of controversy whether a full common market can be established without a *single currency, and a common system of prudential regulation of banks and other financial institutions.

commons *Resources which are not owned, either privately or by the state, but are left open for free use by all comers. Examples include the air, fishery resources at sea, and public highways. As there is no price on using them, every user has an incentive to use them until the private marginal return falls to zero. If the resources are in unlimited supply, this is efficient; but if each user in fact reduces the supply available for others, it is not efficient, but leads to over-utilization, and in extreme cases such as over-fishing to the destruction of the resource. 'The tragedy of the commons' refers to the dangers of over-exploitation of resources due to lack of property rights over them. Beyond a certain intensity of use, some form of *rationing of the use of 'commons' becomes necessary for efficiency. This may be done by quantitative allocation, or by levying a charge for their use.

common stock The equity capital of a US corporation. Holders of common stock are entitled to attend and vote at general meetings, to receive declared dividends, and to receive their share of the residual assets, if any, if the corporation is wound up. Common stock corresponds to ordinary shares in UK companies.

Community Charge A UK system of local taxation introduced in 1990 for England and Wales (1989 for Scotland). It consisted of a flat rate charge per adult inhabitant of each local authority, with some exemptions, for example the disabled, and lower rates for low income earners. This tax, nicknamed the Poll Tax by its opponents, proved to be unpopular and difficult to collect, and was replaced in 1993 by the *Council Tax, based largely on property values.

community indifference curve A type of curve used in international trade theory, similar in shape to an individual's *indifference curve, but purporting to describe the tastes of a country. The community indifference curve through any collection of goods shows the amounts of goods needed to bring every member of the community up to their utility level in the original situation. Unless the community consists of a number of individuals with similar tastes and equal incomes, use of such a curve is a logical fudge: any change in foreign trade is liable to produce changes in *income distribution, which in the absence of compensation for the losers makes the use of community indifference curves illegitimate. However, the device is widely used by writers on international trade.

Companies, Registrar of *See* Registrar of Companies.

company A form of organizing a business, with a legal personality distinct from the individuals taking part in it. This has been found essential in organizing large and complex businesses. The formation of companies is controlled by the state. At various times in the UK, companies have been formed by royal charter, Act of Parliament, or registration with an official Registrar of Companies. A company is empowered to own assets, incur debts, and enter into *contracts, and may be sued and taxed. It may or may not have *limited liability for its shareholders: without limited liability shareholders are in the last resort responsible for meeting the company's debts; with it, they are liable only to the extent of any unpaid part of the book value of their shares. Under the UK Companies Acts there are three classes of company: private companies with unlimited liability, private companies with limited liability, and *public limited companies (PLCs). Private companies can place restrictions on the transfer of their shares, and cannot offer them to the general public. All UK companies are required to provide financial information to their shareholders, the Registrar of Companies, and the Inland Revenue, the obligations of PLCs being the most stringent. Further obligations on disclosure are required to qualify for listing of company shares so that they can be traded on stock exchanges. A company is governed by a *board of directors, elected at an *annual general meeting (AGM) of its ordinary shareholders. *See also* close company, holding company, joint-stock company, limited company, multinational, private company, public limited company, quoted company, shell company, and state-owned company.

company director A member of a company's *board of directors. Directors may be executive, that is, full- or part-time employees of the company, or non-executive. Non-executive directors are chosen either for their specialized knowledge and experience, or because their title or reputation is thought to confer respectability. The duties of directors are laid down by law, and their qualifications in the UK are laid down in the Company Directors Disqualification Act.

company law The law relating to the formation and operation of *companies. Laws are necessary for the existence of companies, which are artificial persons whose rights and obligations exist only in a legal framework provided by the state. Company law lays down the rights and duties of directors and shareholders, and determines the extent of *limited liability for a company's debts, and the amount of information a company is obliged to provide for its shareholders, the Registrar of Companies, and the tax authorities.

company taxation The system for taxing company *profits. Two systems are possible: in the 'classical' system the company is taxed as such. Any *dividends have to be paid out of post-tax company income, and are taxed again as the income of shareholders. In the *'imputation' system, company profits are taxed as though they were the income of shareholders, and dividends are not then taxed again. The argument against the classical system is that it impedes capital mobility between companies, as income left in the company where it is earned is taxed much less than income distributed as dividends and then reinvested in another company. The UK system of *corporation tax is a mixture of these systems: company income distributed as dividends is taxed on an imputation basis via *Advance Corporation Tax (ACT), while retained profits are taxed on a classical basis via Mainstream Corporation Tax.

comparative advantage Lower *opportunity costs than other countries. A country has a comparative advantage in producing a good, relative to another country or the rest of the world, if the relative cost of producing the good, that is, its opportunity cost in terms of other goods foregone, is lower than it is abroad. The law or theory of comparative advantage can be interpreted in either a positive or a normative sense. In its positive sense the law says that countries tend to export goods in which they have a comparative advantage and to import goods in which they have a comparative disadvantage. As real world trade is affected by *tariffs, subsidies, and monopoly this is an empirical generalization, not a logical necessity. In its normative sense the theory of comparative advantage says that it is beneficial both for a country and for the world as a whole if trade follows the lines it suggests.

comparative costs Comparative advantage expressed in terms of costs. The comparative costs of a good are low in a country which has a comparative advantage in producing it, and high in a country with a comparative disadvantage.

comparative statics The analysis of how the *equilibrium position in an economic model would change if the assumptions of the model were altered. Such changes can affect exogenously given quantities, for example a country's population, or parameters decribing behaviour, for example the propensity to save. 'Comparative' indicates that two or more equilibrium states of the economy are being compared. 'Statics' indicates that each state is simply considered as an equilibrium. Comparative statics is contrasted with *dynamics, which analyses how the economy would react to a change in the assumptions, and considers whether and how fast a new equilibrium would be approached. Many economists argue that comparative statics models are only of interest if some dynamic process exists by which the economy could get from an old equilibrium to a new one.

comparisons, interpersonal *See* interpersonal comparisons.

compensated demand curve The demand curve for a good as it would be if consumers were compensated for the effect of changes in its price. As this removes the *income effects of price changes, which are negative except for *inferior goods, the compensated demand curve for a normal good is less elastic than the market demand curve, which includes income effects.

compensating variation The amount of additional money needed to restore an individual's original level of utility if the price of any good consumed rises, or it ceases to be available. This assumes that the prices and availability of all other goods are unchanged. The compensating variation is contrasted with the equivalent variation, which is the amount of additional money needed to give the level of utility that an individual could have reached if the price of a commodity fell, or a new commodity became available.

compensating wage differential A differential in wages intended to compensate workers for special non-pecuniary aspects of a job. Examples would be extra pay for work which is abnormally dirty or involves unsocial hours.

compensation for externalities The principle that those causing adverse *externalities should compensate the victims. There are two different points involved here. The economic benefit of 'making the polluter pay' is that it creates an incentive to avoid creating pollution, unless avoiding it is too expensive to be worth while. This internalizes the externality concerned, and makes for economic efficiency, whether or not the charge the polluter pays goes to the victims of pollution. Where these are widely diffused it may be impossible or too expensive to identify and compensate them. Compensating the victims may be appealing on grounds of *equity, but is irrelevant to efficiency. It may indeed create inefficiency: if the victims could have avoided being damaged at low cost by changing their own conduct, getting compensation for actual damage may lead to too little evasive action being taken. On efficiency grounds, if the victims of externalities are compensated at all, it should only be for unavoidable damage.

compensation principle The welfare criterion that a change in the economy is beneficial if the gainers could afford to compensate the losers. This is known as the Hicks–Kaldor principle, from its originators. It is subject to the criticism that if the gainers could afford to compensate the losers, but do not in fact do so, and the new distribution of real incomes and structure of relative prices are different from the old, the same criterion could sometimes be passed by a change back to the old situation.

competition The situation when anybody who wants to buy or sell has a choice of possible suppliers or customers. With perfect competition there are so many suppliers and customers, with such good contact between them, that all traders ignore the effects of their own supplies or purchases on the market, and act as price-takers, able to buy or sell any quantity at a price which they cannot influence. Such intense competition is rather unusual in real life. The more usual condition is monopolistic or *imperfect competition, with a limited number of buyers or sellers. In this case buyers or, more usually, sellers realize that the amount they can trade is affected by the price they offer. With *monopoly there is only one seller, but this too is unusual. Monopolistic competitors have some monopoly power, but this is limited in the long run by potential competition from possible entrants to a market as well as actual competition from current rivals. In the case of one-off goods or services, competition takes the form of *'competitive tendering', where possible suppliers submit bids and the customer chooses one. This will be the cheapest, other things being equal, but buyers must take account of their confidence that bidders have the technical competence and financial resources to be able to deliver the goods and services they promise. Competition for markets is affected not only by price, but by various forms of non-price competition. These include quality, delivery dates, guarantees, reliability, availability of credit, and after-sales service. *Competitiveness is the ability to compete. Where firms in different countries are competing for markets, devaluation can help a country's firms. If their own currency falls, they have the choice of offering lower foreign currency prices, or of maintaining their price in foreign currency, and using the larger margin over costs to improve quality. *Competitive devaluation occurs when different countries in turn try to help their firms compete by devaluing.

While most economists welcome competition as a stimulus to cost reduction and quality improvement, many businessmen and trade unionists protest that competition is liable to lead to shoddy goods as prices are cut, and to depressed incomes for producers which may impair their ability to finance innovations. The term *'cut-throat competition' expresses the view that there are dangers in too intense competition. 'Unfair competition' is complained of when rivals compete by methods the complainant is unable or unwilling to match. If foreign firms receive subsidies from their governments which your own refuses to provide, or are allowed to break environmental rules while your own government enforces them, or rival firms break health and safety rules which you have to obey, competition is apt to feel unfair. *See also* atomistic competition, Bertrand competition, Cournot competition, cut-throat competition, imperfect competition, monopolistic competition, non-price competition, perfect competition, potential competition, and unfair competition.

Competition Commission (CC) A UK body set up in 1998 in replacement of the Monopolies and Mergers Commission (MMC) and the Restrictive Practices Court (RPC), with the same aims, controlling monopoly and encouraging competition. The CC is empowered to investigate situations of market domination, where an existing firm or group of firms acting in concert has 40 per cent or more of a market, and mergers where a proposed merged firm would have more than 25 per cent of a market. It can also investigate restrictive practices or illegal collusion referred to it by the Office of Fair Trading (OFT). The CCs decisions are only recommendations; where breaches of current laws are concerned, enforcement is dealt with by the OFT; new legislation, or prohibition of rejected merger proposals, is up to the government.

competition policy Government policy concerning competition. This may be concerned with the structure of industries, or with the behaviour of firms within them. As regards the structure of industries, governments have sometimes favoured monopolies, as with the UK postal service, or regulated entry, as with telephones, television and public transport, and have sometimes restricted them via monopoly legislation and the setting up of the UK *Monopolies and Mergers Commission (MMC), now the Competition Commission (CC). As regards the conduct of firms, governments have legislated against various practices which were thought to inhibit competition, including retail price maintenance (RPM), exclusive dealing, and refusal to supply. In the UK the *Office of Fair Trading (OFT) is responsible for enforcing these rules. On the other hand, governments have supported self-regulatory bodies, which are sometimes held to operate against competition between firms in their industries and against entrants to them. *See also* antitrust.

competitive devaluation Attempts by two or more countries to improve their competitive position relative to the others by devaluing their currencies. For each country, devaluation gives at least a temporary cost advantage, which improves the competitiveness of domestic firms. They can either maintain their prices in domestic currency and cut their foreign currency prices, or raise their prices in domestic currency and use the revenue gained to improve the quality of their products. Each country only retains the advantage thus gained until the next competitor devalues.

competitive equilibrium Equilibrium when all markets are competitive. This is possible only in an economy in which increasing returns are absent. If *externalities are also absent, it can be shown that a competitive equilibrium is Pareto-optimal.

competitiveness The ability to compete in markets for goods or services. This is based on a combination of price and quality. With equal quality and an established reputation, suppliers are competitive only if their prices are as low as those of rivals. A new supplier without an established reputation may need a lower price than rivals to compete. With lower quality than rivals, a firm may not be competitive even with a low price; with a reputation for superior quality, a supplier may be competitive even with a higher price than rivals. Similar propositions apply to a country's exports.

competitive tendering The system of purchasing goods or services by inviting bids or 'tenders' and choosing the supplier from among the bids received. Other things being equal, the cheapest tender will be chosen, but purchasers will also be guided by their views on the technical and financial capacity of the bidders to deliver the goods and services reliably. Competitive tendering is also used in selecting applicants to run *franchises or *contracted-out public services.

complementarity A relation between two goods or services in which a rise in the price of one decreases demand for the other. Complements are contrasted with *substitutes, when a rise in the relative price of either good increases demand for the other. Examples of pairs of goods which are complements would be ham and eggs, or car tyres and petrol. Any pair of goods can be either substitutes or complements; every good must have

substitutes, but a good may have no complements. No good can be
complementary to all other goods in the aggregate.

complex conjugates A pair of complex numbers, whose real parts are
equal but whose imaginary parts are equal and opposite. Thus where a and b
are any real numbers, $(a + ib)$ and $(a - ib)$ are complex conjugates. The sum and
product of any pair of complex conjugates are always real, since

$(a + ib) + (a - ib) = (a + a) + i(b - b) = 2a$ and

$(a + ib)(a - ib) = (a^2 + b^2) + i(ba - ab) = (a^2 + b^2).$

complex number A number with both a real and an imaginary part, for
example $(a + ib)$, where a and b are real numbers and i is defined as the square
root of -1. The sum, difference, product, and ratio of any pair of complex
numbers are themselves complex numbers. For any two complex numbers
$(a + ib)$ and $(c + id)$,

$(a + ib) + (c + id) = (a + c) + i(b + d),$

$(a + ib) - (c + id) = (a - c) + i(b - d),$

$(a + ib)(c + id)\quad = (ac - bd) + i(bc + ad),$ and

$(a + ib)/(c + id)\quad = [(a + ib)(c - id)]/[(c + id)(c - id)]$

$\quad = [(ac + bd)/(c^2 + d^2)] + i[(bc - ad)/(c^2 + d^2)].$

In each case it is possible that for the particular values of a, b, c and d chosen
the real or the imaginary part of the resulting complex number may be zero.

compliance costs The costs to a firm of complying with laws and
regulations affecting the markets it trades in. This may include extra record-
keeping, using extra staff to maintain * 'Chinese walls' between departments,
and employing compliance officers to monitor the behaviour of other
members of staff.

compounding, continuous *See* continuous compounding.

compound interest A loan where the interest due each period is added to
the amount outstanding. The interest of earlier periods thus itself earns
interest in later periods. At an interest rate of $100r$ per cent per period, after 1
period an original loan of A amounts to $A(1 + r)$; after two periods to $A(1 + r)^2$;
and after N periods to $A(1 + r)^N$. These successive values form a *geometric
progression with common ratio $(1 + r)$.

computable general equilibrium model A model of the economy so
specified that all equations in it can be solved numerically, by use of a
computer. How complex such a model can be depends on the computing
power available: this is continually increasing. Computable general
equilibrium models can be used to analyse the economy-wide effects of
changes in particular parameters or equations: the effects of changes in the
budget deficit, or of changes in international trade policies, for example, can
be modelled in this way.

computerized trading Use of a computer programme to track various
pieces of market information, such as share or commodity prices, and to
execute specified trades if certain conditions are observed. For example, the
computer could be programmed to track the share prices of companies A and

B, and to sell A and buy B if the excess of B's price over A's falls below 20 per cent. Some stock exchanges do not allow fully computerized trading, but the computer can be programmed to ring a bell to prompt a human dealer to trade if the conditions are satisfied.

concavity A property of a function whereby if it is evaluated at three points, where $a < b < c$, its value at b is never less than, and may exceed, the appropriate weighted average of its values at a and c. If $y = f(x)$, y is concave if

$$f(b) \geq [(b - a) f(a) + (c - b) f(c)]/(c - a),$$

and it is strictly concave if

$$f(b) > [(b - a) f(a) + (c - b) f(c)]/(c - a).$$

A decreasing marginal utility function is thus concave, and a person with such a utility function is *risk-averse.

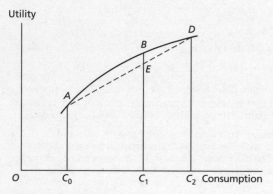

FIGURE 5: *Concavity*

The horizontal axis shows consumption; the vertical axis shows total utility.

$$U(C_1) > [(C_1 - C_0)/(C_2 - C_0)] \, U(C_0) + [(C_2 - C_1)/(C_2 - C_0)] \, U(C_2).$$

ABD shows the utility function. AED shows the straight line connecting A and D. If the utility function is strictly concave, B lies above E. If the utility function is weakly concave, B lies at or above E.

concentration The extent to which a market is taken up by a limited number of firms. The commonest ways of measuring concentration are the n-firm concentration ratio—for example, the five-firm concentration ratio is the proportion of the market in the hands of the five largest firms; and the *Herfindahl index, which sums the squares of market shares expressed as decimals. Size may be measured by turnover, employment, or capital employed. *See also* export concentration.

concentration ratio, n-firm The proportion of a market taken up by the n largest firms. This is normally expressed as a percentage of the market as a whole. Size may be measured in various ways, including output, employment, and market capitalization of the various firms. The n-firm concentration ratio takes no account of the distribution of firm sizes either between the largest n firms, or within the tail of smaller firms. A three-firm concentration ratio of 90 per cent, for example, is consistent with the three largest firms having 35, 30, and 25 per cent of the market respectively, or 85, 3, and 2 per cent: these competitive structures are very different.

concert party A group of investors acting in collusion in stock exchange transactions, for example buying shares to secure a *takeover. This may be done to avoid attracting attention and to evade disclosure requirements.

conciliation Resolving disputes by producing an agreement acceptable to all parties. This function may be perfomed by the parties themselves, or by a neutral intermediary, such as the UK's *Advisory, Conciliation and Arbitration Service (ACAS). Conciliation may work by persuading some parties that their demands are impossible, or that the fears of other parties are reasonable. It often works by subdividing the points in dispute, so that compromise can be reached by each side giving way on issues which do not matter much to them in return for gains on points they consider vital. Conciliation may also work by producing verbal formulae that each party accepts on a different interpretation: this does not resolve the real disputes, and stores up trouble for later.

conditional distribution The distribution of some characteristic for fixed values of some other characteristic(s). For example, if c stands for number of dependent children and a for the age of the head of family $f(c \,|\, a_i)$ is the frequency distribution of the numer of dependent children in families with heads aged a_i.

conditionality The practice by which the *International Monetary Fund (IMF) makes its loans conditional on the borrowing country adopting an approved *adjustment programme or policy package. Critics claim that the actual conditions are sometimes based more on economic dogmas than on understanding of the borrowing countries' real problems, and in particular that they tend to be too deflationary. Conditionality is justified on the argument that the IMF has limited total resources, and that there is no point in using them in cases when a country's trade or macroeconomic policies make it unlikely that their balance-of-payments problems can be solved even with an IMF loan.

conditions *See* initial conditions, necessary and sufficient conditions, and working conditions.

Confederation of British Industry (CBI) A federation of UK companies, mainly from the manufacturing sector. The CBI was founded in 1965; it collects information from members, and lobbies government on their behalf on matters such as economic policy, tax rules, employment legislation, competition policy, and industrial standards.

confidence, consumer *See* consumer confidence.

confidence interval The interval which contains the true value of a parameter of the population sampled with a given probability, for example 95 per cent, as inferred from a *sample. The width of the confidence interval is an increasing function of the probability required, an increasing function of the sample standard deviation, and a decreasing function of sample size.

congestion A situation when too many people or vehicles are trying to use the same facilities for them to work with maximum efficiency. This may result in a fall in the quality or quantity of services provided. Congestion is a source of *external diseconomies: while drivers on crowded roads, for example, are themselves inconvenienced, a cost they bear themselves, they also cause delay, higher fuel costs, and a greater chance of accidents to other road users.

conglomerate A business conducting activities in different industries with very little in common. A conglomerate merger is a merger between firms operating in completely different industries.

conglomerate merger A merger between firms which operate in different sectors of the economy. Such a merger offers no economies of scale except possibly in raising finance, but tends to reduce riskiness in so far as the component businesses are exposed to independent sources of fluctuation in profits.

conjectural variation A proposed approach to the problem of how equilibrium is reached under *oligopoly. Instead of Cournot competition, where each firm takes the others' outputs as given, or Bertrand competition, where each firm takes the others' prices as given, under conjectural variation each competitor assumes that others will follow any change in their price or output to the extent of some proportion λ, which need not equal either 0 or 1.

conjugates, complex *See* complex conjugates.

conservative central banker A central banker with a higher valuation of price stability relative to activity levels than the average for a country's population. It is argued that because a conservative central banker can acquire a reputation for anti-inflationary policies, appointing such a central banker may allow a country a more favourable trade-off between employment levels and price stability than could be achieved with a central banker whose preferences coincided with those of the average citizen.

conservative social welfare function A method of evaluating economic changes which puts more weight on reductions in welfare than on increases. The extreme form of this is the Pareto criterion by which nobody must lose, but less extreme forms are common. Policy-makers are well aware that resentment for injuries is more intense and more persistent than gratitude for favours. Many protectionist policies can best be justified on the grounds that they prevent losses by particular groups, regardless of the cost to other people. Where a utilitarian would favour any change which gave a larger gain to a poorer group than it caused losses to a richer one, a policy-maker with a conservative social welfare function might resist it. *See also* protection.

consistent preferences The assumption that a rational individual will choose consistently. If set A of goods is preferred to set B, and set B is preferred to set C, then for consistency A must be preferred to C. The assumption of such consistency is the basis of revealed preference. A problem arises over the time scale on which consistency is to be expected: over any short period individuals desire variety. Consistent preferences do not imply that if I choose ice cream rather than rice pudding today I must make the same choice tomorrow. Over any long period, however, individuals' needs and tastes may change. When considering the collective preferences of groups of people, as shown by voting, there is no reason to assume consistent preferences: a committee may well vote to choose A rather than B, B rather than C, and C rather than A.

consolidated accounts The combined *accounts of all the members of a group of companies. Such accounts show the profits and losses, assets and liabilities of the group as a whole, netting out any transfers of income and any debts between them. The parent companies of groups are required to produce and file consolidated accounts.

Consols UK government undated securities. The name is short for Consolidated Fund Annuities; the Consolidated Fund is the government's account at the Bank of England into which tax revenues are paid. Consols are redeemable at par at the government's discretion, but the holders have no right to demand redemption. The nominal yields of 2½ or 3 per cent are below current interest rates, so the possibility of redemption is remote. As perpetuities, the price of Consols is proportional to $1/r$, the reciprocal of the long-term interest rate.

consortium A group of companies or banks combining to run a project. This method is used for projects too large or risky to appeal to any one firm on its own. The Channel Tunnel, for example, was constructed by a consortium.

conspicuous consumption The theory that some consumption expenditures are undertaken not to maximize independent individual utility functions, but to impress other people. Consumers who spend in order to display their wealth will not necessarily prefer cheaper goods to dearer ones, provided a high price is well publicized. The existence of conspicuous consumption casts doubt on *welfare economics based on rational choice by consumers with independent tastes.

constant A number which does not change.

constant elasticity of substitution (CES) The property of production or utility functions such that the ratio between proportional changes in relative prices and proportional changes in relative quantities is always the same. A CES function may be written

$$z = k[\delta x^\rho + (1 - \delta)\, y^\rho]^{1/\rho},$$

where z is output or utility, x and y are inputs and k is a constant. The ratio of proportional changes in relative quantities to proportional change in relative prices is the elasticity of substitution,

$$\sigma = 1/(1 - \rho);$$

if

$$1 > \rho > 0, \sigma > 1$$

and the goods are good substitutes; if

$$\rho < 0, \sigma < 1$$

and the goods are poor substitutes. The Cobb–Douglas function is the case corresponding to $\rho = 0$; in this case $\sigma = 1$. *See also* the figure for elasticity of substitution.

constant of integration An arbitrary number which can be added to any *indefinite integral. Consider a function $f(x)$. Its first derivative is $df(x)/dx = g(x)$. $f(x)$ is thus the indefinite integral of $g(x)$. But the first derivative of any function $h(x) = f(x) + k$, where k is any constant, is also $g(x)$, since $dk/dx = 0$. Thus $h(x)$ is also an indefinite integral of $g(x)$. In calculating the definite integral of $g(x)$, that is the integral of $g(x)$ over the range from $x = a$ to $x = b$, the constant of integration disappears, since it is added when evaluating $h(x)$ at one limit and subtracted again evaluating $h(x)$ at the other.

constant prices A common set of prices used to value the output of a firm or economy in successive periods. Changes in the real activity of an enterprise or an economy are measured by valuing its real inputs and outputs each year at the same, constant, set of prices. The prices used may be those of some particular date, or average prices over a period. It is difficult to find such a set of constant prices, as the type and quality of goods continually changes. It is impossible to observe the 1990 price of a good not marketed until 2000, or the 2000 price of a good not marketed since 1990. The longer the period covered, the larger is the proportion of total production subject to such difficulties, and the less reliable are comparisons of income or production at constant prices.

constant returns A constant ratio between inputs and outputs. With constant returns to scale a uniform percentage increase in all inputs in a productive process results in an equal percentage increase in output. Such a production function is linear homogeneous.

constrained maximum The maximum possible value for a function, consistent with satisfying one or more inequalities. For example, a consumer seeks to maximize utility subject to a *budget constraint, that is, a limit on the amount he or she can spend. In this case, if wants are assumed insatiable, the budget constraint is always effective, but in other problems constraints may not be effective. There may be any number of constraints, each of which may or may not be effective. For example, consider the problem of maximizing $U = f(x, y)$ subject to $g(x, y) \leq 0$. If it is known that the constraint is not effective, it can be disregarded. If it is known that it is effective, that is that $g(x, y) = 0$, then it may be possible to use the constraint to express x in terms of y, turning U into a function of y only, which is then maximized in the normal way. In cases where it is not known whether the constraint is effective, a *Lagrange multiplier is frequently used. The original problem is replaced by that of finding a stationary value of

$$L = f(x, y) + \lambda g(x, y).$$

The three equations

$$\partial L/\partial x = 0, \ \partial L/\partial y = 0 \text{ and } g(x, y) = 0$$

are used to determine x, y and λ. This gives the x and y which maximize U subject to the constraint; if $\lambda > 0$ the constraint is effective.

constrained minimum The minimum possible value for a function, consistent with satisfying one or more inequalities. For example, a firm seeks to minimize the costs of producing a given output. In this case the constraint is always effective, but in other problems constraints may not be effective. There may be any number of constraints, each of which may or may not be effective. For example, consider the problem of minimizing $C = f(x, y)$ subject to $g(x, y) \geq 0$, where x and y are inputs.

If it is known that the constraint is not effective, it can be disregarded. If it is known that it is effective, that is that $g(x, y) = 0$, then it may be possible to use the constraint to express x in terms of y, turning C into a function of y only, which is then minimized in the normal way. In cases where it is not known whether the constraint is effective, a *Lagrange multiplier is frequently used. The original problem is replaced by that of finding a stationary value of

$$L = f(x, y) + \lambda g(x, y).$$

The three equations

$$\partial L/\partial x = 0, \ \partial L/\partial y = 0, \text{ and } g(x, y) = 0$$

are used to determine x, y and λ. This gives the x and y which minimize C subject to the constraint; if $\lambda > 0$ the constraint is effective.

constraint A condition which has to be satisfied for any economic activity to be feasible. Constraints may arise from facts of nature; for example, a country has only a certain amount of land available. They may arise from human actions in the past: a country's capital stock is pre-determined by its past investment, and its working population by its past immigration policies. Such constraints can be changed by human action, but only gradually. Constraints may arise from the limits on available technology; this again can be improved on by research and development, but only gradually and subject to uncertainty. Finally, constraints are imposed on human agents by the need to motivate others: people will not work without pay or lend without interest. Constraints are usually expressed in terms of inequalities, since while the economy cannot use more of a resource than there is, some can be left unemployed. Economic problems typically take the form of maximizing or minimizing some objective function subject to satisfying a number of constraints, each of which may or may not be effective. *See also* budget constraint, integer constraint, and liquidity constraint.

consultant An outside specialist hired by an enterprise to advise on particular technical, commercial, or legal aspects of its activities. A person or firm employed as a consultant normally has a reputation for technical expertise and experience. Consultants have no executive authority within the organizations which hire them: their function is to give advice to the management, which will not necessarily act on it. Consultants are often employed in the course of resolving internal disputes in an organization about its best course of action.

consumer A purchaser of goods and services for the personal satisfaction of themselves or other members of their households, as distinct from use to generate further income. Consumer credit is credit given for the purchase of consumption goods. *Consumer protection is legal measures to protect the health and safety or the financial interests of consumers. A consumer association is a body created to promote the interests of consumers of goods and services, by spreading information and lobbying for laws to protect consumers against producers, who are usually much better organized.

consumer behaviour The way in which consumers choose how to spend their incomes. One theory of consumer behaviour views consumers as having *utility functions showing the levels of satisfaction they will derive from every possible set of goods and services. They choose their expenditures to maximize their utility subject to the constraints imposed by their incomes and the prices facing them. This view assumes that tastes are given, independent, and fully known, and that information is free, complete, and reliable. Critics of this position point out that the set of available goods and services is continually changing, that knowledge about what is available is partial, expensive, and unreliable, and that consumers' own tastes evolve as they age and their marital status changes. It should also be pointed out that a large proportion of consumers are members of multi-person households, and are attempting in their spending to please more than one person. Consumers thus work partly on a basis of *satisficing, that is, repeating satisfactory purchases until something goes wrong, and partly on a basis of trial and error, to explore their own reactions to products they have not previously tried. This position leaves more scope for *advertising to influence purchases than the view that consumers maximize a fixed utility function subject to known constraints.

consumer borrowing *See* consumer debt.

consumer choice *See* consumer behaviour.

consumer confidence The willingness of consumers to spend their incomes. This is likely to be higher if their expectations concerning future incomes are optimistic, and lower if they are worried about job security. Long-term and short-term income expectations affect consumer confidence through people's ideas of their 'permanant income'; short-term income expectations also affect their spending through tightening or relaxing *liquidity constraints for those subject to them. Consumer confidence can be measured through surveys, asking questions such as 'Do you expect your income next year to be higher/the same as/lower than your income this year?'

consumer credit Credit granted to consumers by suppliers of goods and services. This may be granted by the suppliers themselves accepting payment by instalments or on deferred terms, or by the use of credit cards and other systems by which the supplier is paid at once by a credit institution, which then collects in instalments from the customer.

consumer debt The amount owed by consumers at any time as the result of past acceptance of consumer credit. The amount of consumer debt rises each month through new purchases on credit, and the addition of interest payable on existing debt; it falls each month through repayments, and the writing-off by creditors of *bad debts which they have given up hope of collecting, where debtors are dead, bankrupt, or untraceable.

consumer durables Long-lived goods bought for final consumption. Their services are expected to be enjoyed over a period longer than that (normally a year) used in national income accounting. They include private cars, boats, and caravans, and domestic items such as furniture, televisions, video recorders, washing machines, refrigerators, home freezers, and vacuum cleaners. Footwear and clothing are not normally treated as consumer durables, although they are frequently made to last for several years. House purchase is normally treated as investment and not as spending on consumer durables.

consumer expenditure Spending on private consumption. This can be divided into spending on non-durable goods such as food, drink, or tobacco; spending on consumer durables, such as cars and furniture; spending on services, such as travel and entertainment; and spending on housing, either as rent or as the imputed rent enjoyed by owner-occupiers.

consumer goods Goods designed for use by final consumers. These are mostly bought by consumers, but some, such as business cars, are bought by enterprises, and many are exported. Many consumer goods are held in inventories by shops and wholesalers.

consumerism The view that economic life should be organized for the benefit of consumers, rather than producers. Because consumers are individuals while producers are mostly organized in firms, and consumers spread their purchases over a much wider variety of goods and services than most firms produce, consumers are mostly less well informed and less organized than producers. Consumerism takes the view that where the interests of consumers and producers clash, the law should take the side of *consumer protection against firms' profits or their workers' job security.

consumer non-durables Non-durable goods, such as food, drink or tobacco, designed for use by final consumers. Some of these are in fact used by businesses, for example food for works canteens, and many are exported. Some non-durables such as wine actually have quite long shelf lives: they are non-durable in the sense that they can only be used once when they are finally consumed.

consumer price index A price index covering the prices of consumer goods. This is contrasted with a more general price index, such as the *GDP deflator, which also includes investment goods and goods purchased by the government.

consumer protection Laws to protect consumers. These concern minimum health and safety standards, information and labelling requirements, the provision of advice to consumers, and regulation of consumer credit. The principal official US agencies concerned are the Food and Drug Administration and the Consumer Product Safety Council. UK acts protecting consumers include the Sale of Goods Act, the Trade Descriptions Act, and the Consumer Credit Act. UK public corporations also have consumer councils to handle complaints.

consumer rationality The assumption that consumers, at least sane and sober adults, are the best judges of their own interests. This is the basis for leaving consumption patterns to be decided by the market; consumers face fixed prices of goods and services, which reflect the costs of production, and are left to maximize their own utilities by choosing whatever combinations of goods and services suit them best. Consumers cannot in fact have complete and reliable information on the quality of all the goods and services on offer. Governments clearly do not rely completely on consumer rationality: there are numerous laws about the health and safety standards goods must satisfy, and some goods such as narcotics or pornography are banned, while others such as alcohol and tobacco products are taxed heavily.

consumer sovereignty The proposition that it is the tastes of consumers rather than the preferences of producers which determine what goods are provided. This is contrasted with the theory of producer dominance: industry decides what to produce and *advertising brainwashes consumers into buying it. Neither view is completely justified: in a market economy consumers cannot be compelled to buy any particular goods, and many new products and new brands of existing products fail to secure a market share. On the other hand consumers can only choose between the goods which are made available to them. In most countries both producers and consumers are constrained by numerous laws concering health and safety and consumer protection.

consumer surplus The excess of the benefit a consumer gains from purchases of goods over the amount paid for them. An individual demand curve shows the valuation put by a consumer on successive units of a good. Goods whose value to the consumer is higher than their price are bought; purchasing stops when their marginal utility is equal to their price times the marginal utility of money. If the marginal utility of money is treated as constant, consumer surplus can be measured by the area below the demand curve but above the price. The marginal utility of money is not in fact believed to be exactly constant, but if the good absorbs only a small proportion of income the error involved is small. A more serious problem is that the elasticity of the demand curve depends on the breadth of the category of goods considered: demand for food as a whole is much less elastic than demand for a particular foodstuff such as eggs, holding all other food prices constant. The system of measurement thus produces an estimated consumer surplus on a group of goods larger than the sum of surpluses on the members of the group. Adding the consumer surpluses for the market as a whole involves assuming that the marginal utility of money is equal for all consumers; if there are wide differences in income this is not plausible.

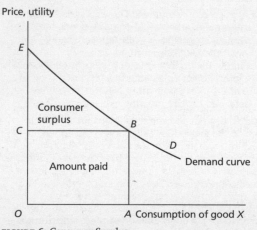

FIGURE 6: *Consumer Surplus*

The horizontal axis shows the quantity of good X consumed; the vertical axis shows its marginal valuation and its price. EBD is the consumer's marginal valuation of X. For a price-taker this is also the demand curve. OC is price per unit. OA is the amount consumed. $OCBA$ is the amount spent (= price × quantity). $OEBA$ is total value to the consumer. $CEB = OEBA - OCBA$ is consumer surplus. For convenience the demand curve is drawn meeting the price axis at a finite price. If the demand curve is asymptotic to the price axis, consumer surplus can still be found provided the demand curve between O and A has a finite integral.

consumption Spending for survival or enjoyment, as opposed to providing for future production. National income accounting distinguishes private consumption and consumption by government bodies. Private consumption is divided between spending on non-durables, which are goods and services for immediate enjoyment, and spending on durables, such as cars, which are expected to provide services over a number of years. All these distinctions are rather arbitrary at the edges: for example, spending on travel to work counts as consumption, though few people enjoy it. Cars bought by individuals are reckoned as consumption, while cars bought by their employers count as investment. Identical pills count as private consumption in the UK if bought privately, but as government consumption if provided free by the National Health Service (NHS). Spending on building dwellings by convention counts as investment rather than consumption; consumption includes the imputed income from the services of owner-occupied dwellings. *See also* autonomous consumption, capital consumption, and conspicuous consumption.

consumption externality An external cost or benefit arising from a consumption activity. These are very common: external costs include noise from television or power mowers affecting neighbours; external benefits include the sight of well-kept gardens and antique motor cars. Some consumption externalities, such as garden bonfires, mainly affect close neighbours and can to some extent be limited by mutual agreement. Others, such as the effects on other traffic of towing caravans on crowded roads, affect complete strangers, so that informal social control is very difficult.

consumption function A function showing how the consumption of an individual or a country as a whole is determined. Individual consumption is an increasing function of income, for individuals whose income is exogenously determined. For individuals who can choose how much to work, consumption and income are jointly determined, but still tend to rise or fall together. Consumption is also affected by many other factors, including size of dependent family, total assets, and factors affecting 'permanent income', such as job security and pension prospects. Aggregate consumption is an increasing function of the national total of disposable incomes; it is also affected by factors such as total assets, the age distribution of the population, and the distribution of incomes, if the poor tend to save a lower proportion of their incomes than the rich.

consumption goods *See* consumer goods.

consumption possibility line *See* budget line.

contagion The tendency of investors to doubt the solvency of some firms or countries when others are in trouble. Default by one bank, for example, may trigger a run on other banks, or default on its debts by one LDC government may make it harder for others to borrow, even when there is no objective evidence to justify this. Fears of contagion may force central banks to support institutions in financial difficulties which they would otherwise leave to their fate, or induce the IMF to assist countries whose policies they do not regard as completely satisfactory, to avoid the greater evil of widespread financial collapse.

content, local *See* local content.

contestable market A market which can be entered without *sunk costs and left without loss. In such a market potential as well as actual competition is a constraint on what the actual producers can charge. It is difficult to produce examples of fully contestable markets: most activities involve some sunk costs for entrants, and most producers aim to stay in business for some extended time, largely because of the losses involved in exit.

contingent fee A fee payable only if an activity is successful. For example, a UK estate agent only receives commission if a sale is achieved, and some training establishments offer 'no pass, no fee' terms. UK lawyers, however, are not allowed to work on a contingent fees basis, where they only get paid if they win their client's case, whereas US lawyers can work on this basis. The argument for contingent fees is that without them poor litigants cannot afford to sue; the argument against them is that they are believed to encourage excessive litigation.

contingent liability A liability which will only arise in certain specific circumstances. For example, a guarantee of somebody else's debts will only have to be honoured if they fail to pay up. Insurance companies incur contingent liabilities when they issue fire or accident insurance policies: they will only have to pay out if policy-holders have fires or accidents. Contingent liabilities create problems for accountants in valuing businesses, particularly with contingencies whose likelihood is difficult to assess.

contingent market A market in which contracts will only be carried out in certain states of the world, which may not occur. Some contingent markets do exist: for example, *options markets, where the holder of a put option will only choose to exercise it if the market price is below the option price, and the holder of a call option will only choose to exercise it if the market price is above the option price. Many contingent markets do not exist: in some cases this is because too few people would be interested on trading in them to make a market economic to run. In other cases a contingent market cannot be organized because the contingencies themselves, such as the invention of currently unimagined new products, cannot be specified in advance.

contingent protection Instruments of import restriction which are not actually used unless they are thought to be needed, but are available should a domestic industry be threatened by a surge of imports. This includes measures such as *anti-dumping duties. Contingent protection is a disincentive to *less developed country (LDC) suppliers investing in building up markets in industrial countries.

continuity The absence of sudden jumps in a function. A function $y = f(x)$ is continuous if as x changes by arbitrarily small amounts there are no sudden changes in y. Some functions are continuous for all values of x, for example $y = x^2$. Other functions are continuous except at particular values of x. The function $y = 1/x$, for example, is continuous except at $x = 0$: as x approaches 0 from above, y becomes indefinitely large; as x approaches 0 from below, y becomes indefinitely large and negative; and for $x = 0$, y is not defined. In commonsense terms, y is a continuous function of x if its graph, with x and y on the axes, can be drawn without removing one's pen from the paper.

continuous compounding The charging of interest or discounting of future receipts on a continuous basis. At a rate of $100r$ per cent, added annually, after N years a loan will have grown to $(1 + r)^N$ times its original value. If interest is added v times a year, it will grow to $(1 + r/v)^{Nv}$, which is greater the larger is v. As v tends to infinity, $(1 + r/v)^{Nv}$ tends to a limit e^{rN}, where e is the exponential constant. Similarly, if a future receipt due in N years is discounted to find its present value at a continuous rate r, its present value with continuous discounting is e^{-rN} times what is due at the end of the N years.

continuous distribution A frequency distribution in which the variable concerned can take any value, and not only discrete values such as integers.

continuous time The treatment of time in dynamic economic models as a continuous variable. Processes in continuous time are described by differential equations. This is contrasted with the treatment of time as a discrete variable, where processes are described by difference equations.

continuous variable A variable which can take any value, and is not confined to particular values, such as integers. The techniques of calculus apply only to continuous variables. Many economic variables, including prices and incomes, are measured in money terms: as money comes in discrete units, it is not a continuous variable. Economic models frequently treat monetary variables as continuous: this is very convenient, and as the units are so small it is thought to introduce negligible errors.

contract A legal agreement between two or more parties, specifying the actions to be taken and payments to be made by each party. A contract may also specify how any dispute over its interpretation will be resolved, by arbitration or legal action. A contract of employment is a contract between an employer and a worker specifying the work to be performed by the employee and the payments and working conditions to be provided by the employer. Contracts may be contingent, that is, may stipulate that actions shall be taken only in specific circumstances, as for example in insurance policies. The terms permitted in legally enforceable contracts are governed by legislation. In many cases possible variations in circumstances are so complex, or are so difficult to verify objectively, that a completely specified contract is impossible or too inconveniently complicated. In such cases an *implicit contract is an unwritten or only partially written understanding between two parties as to how each will behave as circumstances vary. *See also* forward contract, futures contract, implicit contract, and service contract.

contract curve The line in a *box diagram running between the two origins, showing where indifference curves or isoquants for the two outputs are tangential. Only points on this curve represent Pareto-optimal allocations of resources; points off it are not Pareto-optimal. If the *indifference curves or *isoquants through any point in the box are not tangential, then a shift in resource allocation to some point on the contract curve can allow more of either output to be obtained without giving up any of the other. *See also* box diagram.

contracted-out (services) Services paid for by one body, for example a UK local authority, but provided under contract by an outside supplier. This is contrasted with services provided by *direct labour, employed by the authority. Examples include refuse collection, office cleaning, and the provision of school meals. The argument for contracting-out of services is that it introduces competition in their provision, which should make them cheaper. Critics of contracted-out services argue that this may be at the expense of quality. Supporters of the system argue that quality criteria can be built into the contracts, and that it may in fact be easier to ensure compliance with quality standards by outside suppliers with a legally enforceable contract than by a well-unionized direct labour force.

contract of employment A contract between an employer and an employee, stating the job description, pay, and conditions. These can include normal hours of work, arrangements for overtime, holiday entitlement, disciplinary and grievance procedures, period of notice on either side, and any arrangements for redundancy pay beyond the statutory entitlement.

contract, service *See* service contract.

contractual savings Savings made on a regular basis in conformity with a contract. This could be via life insurance policies, or a repayment mortgage. Individuals may adopt these forms of savings as a method of self-discipline. They have the disadvantage that escape from the contract generally involves financial penalities; this may give trouble if income falls, for example through unemployment, or if special needs arise. Continuing with contractual savings does not necessarily mean that an individual is a net saver, as they may be financed by running down other assets, or getting into debt via personal loans or use of credit cards.

contradiction, proof by *See* proof by contradiction.

contribution, defined *See* defined contribution.

contributions, National Insurance *See* National Insurance contributions.

contributory pension scheme A pension scheme in which scheme members are required to contribute to the scheme's funds, usually by deduction of a percentage of their pay. This is contrasted with a non-contributory pension scheme, where the entire cost is borne by the employer. In a contributory pension scheme the employer normally also bears part of the cost.

control *See* credit control, dividend control, exchange control, export control, import control, pay control, pollution control, price control, quality control, and rent control.

control (of a company) The ability to win votes at company general meetings. Any person or group holding over 50 per cent of the voting ordinary shares can exercise control; in practice control is usually possible with considerably under 50 per cent of the voting shares, provided that the other shareholders do not combine.

convenience, flag of *See* flag of convenience.

Convention on International Trade in Endangered Species (CITES)
An international treaty drawn up in 1972 to regulate international trade in species currently threatened with extinction, or which it is considered might

become threatened. The point of such trade restrictions is to decrease the demand for specimens from endangered species. A trade ban, however, does nothing to encourage nations to promote the survival of species, which are frequently endangered because of human encroachment on their habitat. Critics of CITES argue that it would be more effective to allow trade conditional on the exporting country adopting an effective conservation programme.

convergence A tendency for two or more economies to become more similar. This may be, for example, in respect of per capita incomes, real growth rates, inflation rates, interest rates, methods of economic organization, or social policies.

convergence criteria A set of criteria which it is stipulated that a set of countries must satisfy for it to be practicable or desirable for them to adopt a common currency. Such criteria were laid down for *European Monetary Union (EMU) by the *Maastricht Treaty of 1993. The criteria set limits to divergencies in inflation rates, and changes in exchange rates during the period leading up to union, and set maxima of 3 per cent for budget deficits and 60 per cent for the ratio of government debt to GNP. It is a matter of controversy whether satisfying these criteria is either necessary or sufficient for monetary union to work satisfactorily, and how many European countries are likely to satisfy them.

convergent series A series for which the sum of the first N terms tends to a finite limit as N tends to infinity. For example, in the geometric progression

$$1, \ r, \ r^2, \ldots, r^N, \text{ where } -1 < r < 1,$$

the sum of the first N terms tends to a finite limit as N increases. This can be shown as follows; denote the sum of the first N terms by S_N. Thus

$$S_N = 1 + r + r^2 + r^3 + \ldots + r^{N-1}.$$

Multiplying each term by r,

$$rS_N = r + r^2 + \ldots + r^{N-1} + r^N.$$

Subtracting the second series from the first,

$$S_N - rS_N = 1 - r^N.$$

As N increases without limit, r^N tends to zero, so $(1-r) S_N$ tends to 1 and S_N tends to $1/(1-r)$. One might at first sight expect a series to be convergent if its individual terms tend to zero as N increases, but this is not correct. Consider for example the series $1, \frac{1}{2}, \frac{1}{3}, \ldots \frac{1}{N}$; the first term is 1, the second $\frac{1}{2}$. The next two terms sum to over $2 (\frac{1}{4}) = \frac{1}{2}$; the next four sum to over $4 (\frac{1}{8}) = \frac{1}{2}$; and by taking successive groups of terms it is clearly possible to add amounts larger than $\frac{1}{2}$ indefinitely, so the series is not convergent.

convertibility The right to change money into foreign currency. A currency is convertible if holders can change it into foreign currency without permission from the authorities. A fully convertible currency is convertible by any holder, for any purpose. A currency may be convertible for non-resident but not for resident holders. Under current account convertibility holders have the right to convert their currency for any current account purpose, such as trade or foreign travel, but not for capital account purposes such as making loans or buying assets abroad. Current account convertibility requires that the authorities can monitor the use of funds; under full convertibility this is not necessary.

convertible currency A currency which the holder has the right to change into any other currency. A fully convertible currency can be exchanged into any other currency by any holder and for any purpose. More limited forms of convertibility are possible: currencies may be convertible only by non-residents, or only for current account but not for capital account purposes. If a currency is convertible only by non-residents, it is necessary to control payments from residents' into non-residents' bank accounts. Similarly current account convertibility requires official scrutiny of all foreign payments to check their purpose. With full convertibility no controls are necessary.

convertible debenture A company share which is a debenture, in the sense that it pays a regular dividend but carries no vote, but which the holder has the right at some future date to exchange for *ordinary shares on pre-arranged terms. This gives the holders relative security during the early years of a venture, while enabling them to participate in the long-run benefits if things turn out well.

convexity A property of sets whereby if any two points are members of a set, any convex linear combination of them is also a member. If points with coordinates shown by $(a_1, a_2, a_3, \ldots, a_N)$ and $(b_1, b_2, b_3, \ldots, b_N)$ are members of a convex set, any linear combination $(c_1, c_2, c_3, \ldots, c_N)$, where $c_i = \lambda a_i + (1 - \lambda)b_i$ for all i, $0 < \lambda < 1$, is also a member of the set. For example, if a and b are sets of goods which can be produced in an economy with constant returns to scale technology in all industries, then c can also be produced, using λ of all resources in the proportions used to produce a, and $(1 - \lambda)$ of all resources in the proportions used to produce b. The country's production possibility frontier thus encloses a convex set.

The horizontal axis represents good X, the vertical axis good Y. $ABCD$ in Panel 1 is a convex set: every linear combination of any two members of the set is also a member of it. $EFGH$ in Panel 2 is not a convex set: points in the triangle FGH can be expressed as linear combinations of members of the set, but are not themselves members of it.

co-operation Agreement by two or more individuals, firms, or governments to work together. Co-operation as a method of co-ordinating economic activity is contrasted with *competition, where individuals, firms or governments operate independently and sometimes in opposition to each other. All economic systems use some mixture of both mechanisms; the optimal division of functions between them is a matter of controversy. In many cases firms or countries co-operate in some activities, such as research or the setting of industrial standards, while competing in other activities, especially current sales.

co-operative society A business owned by its employees or customers. The Co-operative Wholesale Society in the UK is a co-operative of co-operatives.

coordinates The method of specifying position on a diagram. The most common form in economics is 'Cartesian' coordinates, that is a grid with the axes at right angles.

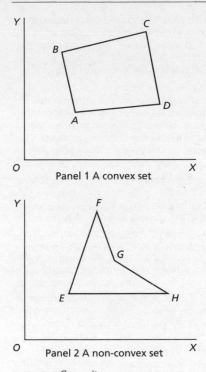

Panel 1 A convex set

Panel 2 A non-convex set

FIGURE 7: *Convexity*

co-ordination failure A situation where activities which could have benefited two or more parties does not take place because they fail to concert their plans. In a less developed country (LDC), for example, one might find mineral resources which are not mined because there is no transport to export them, and a railway which is not built because there is no freight for it to carry. If both projects went forward, both would be profitable, but neither is started, because the firms concerned do not know about, or do not trust, each other. The same problem can affect governments: a number of countries may be afraid to liberalize their trade because of worries about the effects on their balance of payments, whereas if they could all agree to liberalize at once, all could benefit.

co-ordination, policy *See* policy co-ordination.

copyright The exclusive right to reproduce artistic, dramatic, literary, or musical work, or to authorize its reproduction by others. Copyright persists for a finite period after the author's death; it can be sold or inherited. It also extends to films and television, and is one of the main forms of intellectual property.

core A central region in an economy, with good communications and high population density, which conduce to its prosperity. The core is contrasted with the *periphery, outlying regions with poor communications and sparse population. Some regional economists argue that the differences between core and periphery tend to increase as migrants and investment are attracted to the core. Large populations give core regions considerable voting power, which means that government policies tend to be more responsive to core than to peripheral needs.

core inflation A measure of inflation of consumer prices excluding the prices of certain items. This may apply to food, whose prices are subject to seasonal fluctuations, fuel, whose prices are subject to large variations, for example because of actions by OPEC, and other seasonal or erratic items. The use of a measure of core inflation may assist in the production of better inflation forecasts. Core inflation is unlikely to be politically acceptable as a basis for indexation of pensions or other benefits, as consumers do in fact have to pay for food and fuel.

corner (a market) To create a situation in a speculative market where other people have between them contracted to deliver more of a good or security than is available. However high a price has to be agreed to obtain such contracts, the holder can make a large profit by forcing the counter-parties who cannot deliver to pay to be released from their contracts. A corner can only be made in a speculative market, since it relies on other people promising to sell goods or securities they do not actually possess. Attempts to create a corner usually fail, because a high price brings in supplies from unexpected sources.

corner solution A solution to a system of equations where some variables are zero. For example, firms typically do not produce many goods, and individuals typically do not consume all available goods. This is contrasted with an interior solution, in which all variables are non-zero. Statements of optimality conditions in terms of equality of marginal costs and marginal benefits are correct only for interior solutions. With corner solutions, as a price or output variable which is already zero cannot be reduced, the optimality condition applicable is an inequality, showing that it is not desirable to increase it.

corporate equity The net assets of a company after paying all creditors, including debenture and preference shareholders. This is the net amount available for ordinary shareholders.

corporate income tax A tax on the profits of firms, as distinct from taxation of the incomes of their owners. There are strong arguments for having separate income tax schemes for firms and individuals: the system of allowances and progressive tax rates appropriate for a tax on individual incomes is quite different from a sensible scheme for taxing firms.

corporate sector That part of the economy which is conducted by companies working for private profit. This is contrasted with the parts of the economy run by the government, nationalized industries, individuals, or voluntary bodies such as charities, which in the UK are counted as part of the personal sector.

corporation A collective body carrying on economic activities, able to sue and liable to be sued, and to pay taxes, as an entity distinct from the individuals running or employed by it. A public corporation is a state-owned body; a private corporation is a synonym for a company. Corporation tax (UK) and Corporation Income Tax (US) are taxes on the profits of companies. *See also* multinational, and public corporation.

Corporation Tax The UK system of company taxation. This is levied on the trading profits of all companies, with slightly lower rates for smaller companies. It is paid in two parts: Advance Corporation Tax (ACT) is effectively income tax deducted at source from dividends paid to shareholders, and Mainstream Corporation Tax is any remaining tax due after ACT has been paid.

corporatism The system of reaching economic decisions through negotiation between centralized corporate bodies representing economic groupings, notably employers and workers. This is contrasted with a reliance on decentralized bargaining between individuals or limited groups. The supporters of corporatism have hoped that it could improve the trade-off between inflation and unemployment, by inducing all parties to adopt a consensus view on prices and incomes. Empirical testing of such claims is extremely difficult, due to the difficulty of measuring the real effectiveness of apparently centralized procedures.

correlation The extent to which two variables vary together. Linear correlation between two variables x and y depends on the sign and size of

$$\Sigma_i(x_i - \mu_x)(y_i - \mu_y),$$

where μ_x and μ_y are the means of x and y. The two variables are positively correlated if this sum of products is positive, and negatively correlated if the sum of products is negative. The strength of correlation is measured by the correlation coefficient

$$r = [\Sigma_i(x_i - \mu_x)(y_i - \mu_y)]/[n\sigma_x\sigma_y],$$

where there are n pairs x_i, y_i, and σ_x and σ_y are the standard deviations of x and y. r varies between +1 and –1, being +1 if x and y are perfectly positively correlated and –1 if x and y are perfectly negatively correlated; if $r = 0$, x and y are independent. r does not depend on the units in which x and y are measured. *See also* rank correlation, and serial correlation.

correlation of returns The extent to which the returns on one project are good or bad at the same time as the returns on another. Suppose that x and y are the returns on two risky projects, with expected means μ_x and μ_y. The returns are positively correlated if the expected value $E[(x - \mu_x)(y - \mu_y)]$ is positive, they are negatively correlated if this expected cross-product is negative, and they are independent if the expected cross-product is zero. The more strongly the returns on different projects are correlated, the less reduction in overall risk can be obtained by combining them in one firm or one portfolio. The nearer they are to independence, the more overall risk can be reduced by combining projects; overall risk can be reduced still further if projects can be found with returns which are negatively correlated.

corruption The use of bribery to influence politicians, civil servants and other officials. Bribes may be in cash or in kind; almost any official action or inaction can be influenced by corruption. Officials may have to be bribed to do things they are legally supposed to do anyway, or to do them promptly.

They may be bribed to neglect their duties, to the advantage, for example, of speculative builders putting up flats without planning permission and in disregard of building regulations. Officials or politicians with discretion over decisions, such as the location of public works, can be bribed to exercise it in particular ways. Corruption can be used to influence elections, or to get laws changed. (In the nineteenth century, one US state was described as having 'the best legislature money can buy'.) Corruption is extremely bad for social efficiency: it undermines public confidence that decisions will be sensible, or that laws will be either fair or consistently enforced. Many countries make corruption inevitable by paying their civil servants and police so poorly that they cannot live without taking bribes.

'corset, the' A colloquial name for the Supplementary Special Deposits Scheme. This was a UK monetary device used from 1973 to 1980, controlling the growth of bank deposits and interest-bearing eligible liabilities. The scheme was abandoned because the effect of imposing quota limits to the expansion of particular institutions was thought to be anti-competitive.

cosine The ratio in a right-angled triangle between the side adjacent to an angle and the hypotenuse. The cosine of angle x is written cos x. If a circle of unit radius is drawn, measuring angles anti-clockwise from due East, cos x is the horizontal coordinate of the point on the circle at angle x. The cosine is thus an oscillatory function. If x is measured in radians, cos x fluctuates between a minimum of -1, reached when $x = \pi$ or $x = \pi \pm n(2\pi)$, where n is any integer, and a maximum of $+1$, reached when $x = 0$ or $x = \pm n(2\pi)$. If x is measured in degrees, cos x has a minimum of -1 when $x = 180°$ or $x = 180° \pm n(360°)$, and a maximum of $+1$ when $x = 0°$ or $x = \pm n(360°)$. *See also* the figure for trigonometric functions.

cost(s) The value of the inputs needed to produce any good or service. This has to be measured in some units or numeraire, usually money. Opportunity cost is cost measured in terms of alternative output forgone in order to produce a good. Total cost includes fixed or overhead costs, and variable costs. Fixed costs must be incurred if any output is produced: for example, paying for buildings and a manager. Sunk costs are fixed costs which cannot be recovered even if an enterprise is closed down completely: for example, the cost of sinking a mine shaft or digging a canal. Variable costs depend on the level of output: these include the costs of labour, fuel, and materials. Where it is possible to allocate costs to particular products, average cost is total cost divided by the amount produced. Marginal cost is the addition to variable costs needed to produce a unit increase in output. Average and marginal cost curves show these costs for various levels of output. Costs can be considered in the short and long run. In the long run more inputs can be changed than in the short run, so more costs are variable and fewer are fixed.

Social cost is cost including the external costs of an enterprise, such as the value of smoke damage, noise, and river pollution, as well as the direct costs to its proprietors. *Cost–benefit analysis compares total social costs with total social benefits, again including external costs and benefits as well as those accruing to the producer.

Cost accounting is the techniques used by accountants to allocate and analyse costs. *Cost-plus pricing is a system of setting prices in contracts by measuring costs and adding an agreed percentage mark-up. Normal cost pricing is this system applied not to actual costs but to what costs would have been at a normal level of output. The cost-of-living index measures the cost of buying a fixed bundle of consumer goods, selected to resemble the purchases of a typical household. Factor cost is the prices of products facing producers, subtracting from market prices any indirect taxes and adding any subsidies: the resulting price is the amount available to producers to pay for inputs and their own profits. *Cost, insurance, and freight (cif) is the price of imports at their port of entry. *See also* adjustment costs, average cost, avoidable cost, comparative costs, compliance costs, factor cost, fixed cost, joint costs, historical cost, opportunity cost, overhead cost, private cost, real costs, replacement cost, selling costs, social cost, sunk costs, transport costs, and variable cost.

cost accounting The branch of accounting concerned with the costs of economic activities. This includes measuring the costs of activities already carried out, so that their profitability can be assessed, and estimating the likely costs of future activities, to assist management in planning and in tendering for contracts. It is concerned generally only with private costs.

cost–benefit analysis The attempt to compare the total social costs and benefits of an activity, usually expressed in money terms. The costs and benefits concerned include not only direct pecuniary costs and benefits, but also *externalities, meaning external effects not traded in markets. These include external costs, for example pollution, noise, and disturbance to wildlife, and external benefits such as reductions in travelling time or traffic accidents. If total social benefits of an activity exceed total social costs this can justify public works such as motorway building, or subsidizing projects which are not privately profitable. If total social costs exceed total social benefits this can justify preventing projects such as building in green belts, even when these would be privately profitable. Because non-marketed costs and benefits are difficult to measure and evaluate, the results of cost–benefit analysis can be highly controversial.

cost centre A section of a firm whose costs and revenues are distinguished from those of other sections. If most costs and revenues can be reliably attributed to a particular cost centre, so that the profitability of each cost centre can be measured, this can be a valuable tool of management accounting. If costs and revenues cannot be reliably attributed and have to be distributed arbitrarily between cost centres, the whole process is liable to be a waste of time, or positively misleading.

cost curve A curve relating costs to the quantity of a good produced. The total cost curve or schedule shows total costs at each level of output; the average cost curve shows total costs divided by quantity produced; and the marginal cost curve shows the addition to total costs caused by any increase in output. The marginal cost curve thus shows the slope of the total cost curve at any level of output. Any of these curves may be drawn for fixed costs, variable costs, or both combined. Cost curves can be constructed for the short run, in which few inputs can be adjusted, or for the long run, in which all inputs can be adjusted. A U-shaped average cost curve means that at low levels of output average cost falls as output increases, but after some point average cost tends to rise. Short-run average cost curves seem likely to be

Cost

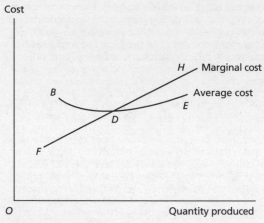

FIGURE 8: *Cost Curves*

U-shaped because at low levels of output fixed costs must be spread over few units, while at output levels which are high relative to plant capacity marginal costs tend to be high. Long-run average cost curves may well not be U-shaped.

BDE is the average cost curve, *AC*. *FDH* is the marginal cost curve, *MC*. *D* is the minimum point of the average cost curve. Left of *D*, $MC < AC$ so *AC* falls; right of *D*, $MC > AC$ so *AC* rises. At *D*, $MC = AC$ and $d(AC)/dQ = 0$.

cost-effectiveness The achievement of results in the most economical way. This approach assesses efficiency by checking whether resources are being used to produce any given results at the lowest possible cost. Cost-effectiveness is most relevant as a concept of efficiency in cases such as the provision of defence, education, health care, policing, or environmental protection, where a monetary evaluation of the results achieved is often difficult and controversial. In such cases it is interesting to consider whether the results could be achieved at lower cost independently of the question of whether or not they are worth achieving at all.

cost function *See* cost curve.

cost inflation Inflation due to increases in particular prices or wage rates being passed round the economy. Increases in costs cause producers to raise prices; increases in prices cause workers to demand higher wages; and increases in wages in one occupation lead to demands for increases in others to restore differentials. The cumulative effect of all these processes leads to a cost-inflationary spiral, which it is extremely difficult to stop. Cost inflation is contrasted with *demand inflation, where high levels of demand lead to shortages of goods and labour and thus to price and wage increases. It is probably better to regard cost and demand inflation not as two kinds of inflation, but as two ways of looking at the inflationary process as a whole: excess demand can start inflation, and cost inflation keeps it going.

cost, insurance, and freight (cif) The value of imports when they enter a country. Cif value is the value of goods when they reach the port of entry to their country of destination: it includes their purchase price in the country of origin, and the freight and insurance costs of shipping them to a foreign port. Cif does not include import duty or costs of transport within the country of destination.

cost minimization The assumption that any enterprise will try to produce its output at the lowest possible cost. This is clearly desirable for a profit-maximizing firm. It is likely to appeal to public bodies also, as a saving of cost in any one project will either allow lower taxes, or free resources for other desirable uses. Cost minimization does however have to be taken with some provisos. First, it refers to the cost of providing goods or services of a specified quality; it does not mean achieving lower costs by cutting standards. Second, it does not imply operating at the lowest point of a U-shaped cost curve, unless the market will accept the level of output which this entails. If there are large *economies of scale, the desired output may well be less than the minimum point on the cost curve: what is socially desirable is producing what is wanted at minimum cost, not achieving low average cost via producing things nobody wants. Third, actual firms have to anticipate that demand will fluctuate over some range: cost minimization means achieving low average costs over a range of outputs. This may involve choosing flexible equipment and working methods, involving higher average costs than could be achieved if a constant level of output was required.

cost of capital The rate of return an enterprise has to offer to induce investors to provide it with capital. The cost of loan capital is the rate of interest that has to be paid. The cost of equity capital is the expected yield needed to induce investors to buy shares. When a firm uses both methods of raising capital, its cost of capital is the average of the costs of capital raised by the two methods, weighted by the proportion of funds raised in each way. The cost of capital depends on the apparent riskiness of the purpose for which it is to be used, the collateral offered for any loans, and the overall financial soundness and reputation of the borrower.

cost of living index An index of the cost of maintaining a given standard of living. This is found by measuring the total cost of some given basket of goods and services. The composition of the basket has to be changed periodically, both to take account of changes in the proportions of income spent on different goods as relative prices change, and of changes in the types of goods and services purchased because of changes in tastes or technology. The main UK cost of living index is the *Retail Price Index (RPI).

cost of protection The total cost to an economy of adopting protectionist trade policies. In the short run, this is the cost to consumers of having to buy more expensive domestic products rather than cheaper or better quality imports. This normally exceeds the private gains to domestic producers. Defenders of *protection argue that if the labour employed in protected production would otherwise have been unemployed, there may be a net gain to the country. In the longer run, protection has other costs: among these are the discouragement to technical improvements given by not having to compete with imports, and the diversion of business effort from improving production into *rent-seeking. It is argued that in the long run protection cannot cut a country's natural rate of unemployment: it merely diverts labour from potential export industries into import-competing ones.

cost-plus pricing A contract providing that price will equal measured costs plus an agreed percentage mark-up for profit. This procedure is criticized because it gives the producer no incentive to keep down costs; rather, the incentive is to increase costs needlessly, thereby increasing the profit margin also. Cost-plus pricing is often used, however, in projects, for example in military spending, where the customer wants the product urgently and there is great uncertainty about costs. Under these circumstances a cost-plus contract may give a lower expected price than a fixed-price contract, because any fixed price agreed would include a substantial risk-premium for the producer.

cost-push inflation *See* cost inflation.

cost schedule *See* cost curve.

Council for Mutual Economic Assistance (CMEA or COMECON) An international organization of the former planned economies of the USSR and its allies. The CMEA was founded in 1949, and included the USSR, Bulgaria, Czechoslovakia, East Germany, Hungary, Poland, and Romania in Central and Eastern Europe, plus Cuba, Mongolia and Vietnam. CMEA members tended to trade relatively intensively with each other. The organization broke up in 1991, as part of the collapse of both the USSR and faith in central planning.

council *See* Wages Council, and works council.

council housing State-financed housing for rent, provided in the UK through local authorities. This has for many years been the second largest category of housing in the UK, below owner-occupation but above private rented housing. Council housing is allocated on the basis of need, with priority for factors including number of children, and the quality and degree of overcrowding of present accommodation, with top priority for the homeless. Rents are generally held below a market-clearing level; a large proportion of council tenants in fact receive concessional rents and/or housing benefit to assist with payment. There are usually waiting lists to obtain council tenancies.

Council of Economic Advisers A US body of three academics appointed to advise the President on the state of the economy. They assist in the preparation of the President's annual Economic Report to the Congress, and in the formulation of US government economic policy.

Council Tax The main UK tax levied by local authorities. Council Tax is payable by the occupants of dwellings at rates depending on their valuation, as assessed in seven bands by the District Valuer. A reduced rate of Council Tax is payable by sole occupants of houses, and some low-income households are exempt. The rate at which Council Tax is levied is decided by individual local authorities, subject to upper limits fixed by the central government.

counter party The other party in any transaction. For an exporter, the counter party is the foreign customer; for a lender, the counter party is the borrower. In any transaction, counter-party risk is the risk that the other parties may fail to fulfill their side of any contract or informal bargain. In many markets, market-makers can reduce counter-party risks for both sides by substituting themselves as the counter party for both outside buyers and sellers. Outsiders are left dealing with 'the market', and do not have to worry about the solvency or honesty of a particular trading partner.

counter-party credit risk The risk when selling goods on credit that the purchaser may fail to make payments when they become due. Credit for short periods can be given against a trade bill, which can be discounted, so that the seller gets cash immediately and passes the credit risk to whoever buys the bill. For longer-term credits it may be possible to insure the risk, possibly via an official agency such as the UK *Export Credits Guarantee Department (ECGD) or the US *Export–Import Bank.

counter-trade International trade conducted by barter. In general, barter is inefficient compared with the use of money, and bilateral trade is inefficient compared with multilateral trade. Counter-trade is thus clearly a second-best policy. It has nevertheless been used by many countries, including formerly planned economies. Its defenders argue that while counter-trade is not ideal, for an economy which has allowed its monetary system to break down, in the short run it is better than no trade at all.

countervailing duty A *tariff imposed to offset the effects of some foreign policy such as an export subsidy, which domestic producers claim gives an unfair advantage to foreign competitors.

countervailing power The use of organizations to protect their members against monopolistic exploitation by others. Examples include the formation of co-operatives to protect consumers from suppliers and the formation of *trade unions to protect workers against monopsonistic employers. The alternative is control of the monopolists by public regulatory authorities. Critics of the use of new monopolies to fight old ones point to the danger that the old and new monoplies may collude to exploit the rest of the community. A monopolist and the trade union representing its employees, for example, may unite to exploit both their customers and 'outsiders' excluded from jobs in the industry.

counting, double *See* double counting.

coupon 1. The dividends due on a security. With a bearer security, the holder claims payments due by using a physical coupon attached to the documents of title.
   2. Tokens, usually paper, used as evidence of entitlement under rationing schemes.

Cournot competition Competition between two or more firms, where each assumes that the others will hold the quantity they produce unchanged. If there are only two firms, that is duopoly, Cournot competition produces an equilibrium with price lower and total output higher than with monopoly. A Cournot equilibrium becomes more similar to a perfectly competitive equilibrium the more firms there are, and the better substitutes their products are for one another. The Cournot assumption is not very realistic: over time one would expect the firms to realize that the others do vary their quantities, and adopt a more sophisticated forecasting technique.

Cournot duopoly A market situation with only two sellers, each of whom fixes their own output on the assumption that the other will hold quantity sold unchanged. This is the two-firm case of Cournot competition.

covariance A measure of the degree of association between the values of two random variables. If x and y are two variables, with mean values μ_x and μ_y, where i runs from 1 to N, the covariance of x and y is defined as

$$\text{cov}(x, y) = [\Sigma_i(x_i - \mu_x)(y_i - \mu_y)]/[\Sigma_i (x_i - \mu_x)^2 \Sigma_i(y_i - \mu_y)^2]^{\frac{1}{2}}.$$

This is the sum of the products of deviations of each variable from its mean, divided by the product of their standard deviations. The highest value cov (x, y) can take is +1, where x and y are perfectly correlated; the lowest value it can take is –1, when x and y are perfectly negatively correlated. If cov $(x, y) = 0$, x and y are independent.

cover 1. The protection against risk which an insurance policy provides for the policy-holder. This may be limited as to the type of risk covered: for example, a motor policy may cover third-party risk only, or extend to protection against fire, theft, and accidental damage. Cover may also be limited in extent, covering losses only above some minimum or below some maximum amount.

2. The ratio of the total profits of a business to its dividend payments. High dividend cover means that dividends are unlikely to be cut if profits decrease, whereas low dividend cover leaves investors exposed to cuts in dividends if a company encounters bad times.

covered, times *See* times covered.

CPI *See* consumer price index.

crash, stock market *See* stock market crash.

crawling peg exchange rates The proposal that official intervention in foreign exchange markets should take the form of limiting the rate of change of exchange rates, as opposed to setting any particular level. A 'crawling peg' could take several forms, among them the following. The authorities could pre-announce a trend rate of movement in par exchange rates by small regular changes in the same direction, for example ½ per cent a month. They could retain discretion to change par rates in either direction by up to a low limit, for example 1 per cent a month. Alternatively, they could announce that the par rate would be continually adjusted to be equal to the average of market rates over some period of the past, for example a year. In all cases it is assumed that market rates would be held within fixed limits around the par rates by intervention in the market. The merit of crawling peg systems is that if they succeed in avoiding the need for large sudden jumps in exchange rates, they reduce the profits to be made from speculation. Their disadvantage is that if exchange rates start a long way from equilibrium, the limited rate of adjustment may be too slow to bring market rates near to equilibrium levels before *foreign exchange reserves run out.

creation, trade *See* trade creation.

creative accounting Devising new financial methods, or new ways of presenting old ones, in order to evade controls on one's activities. Examples include the creation of special accounts to which transactions can be relegated so as to appear as off-balance-sheet items, or selling assets and leasing them back, thus exchanging present receipts from the sale for future liabilities in the rentals payable. Creative accounting is very useful in shifting receipts between apparent income and apparent capital gains, if these are subject to different tax rates or rules.

creative destruction The effect of technical progress in one part of the economy in lowering the value of existing capital in other parts. If a new good displaces demand for an old one, the capital used in making the old good may become worthless; if a new method of production has lower costs even including any necessary capital costs than the variable costs of producing on old equipment, the price of the product is likely to fall so far that operating the old machines becomes uneconomic. This destroys the livelihood of the owners of old equipment. If they had anticipated this they might never have invested in the industry. In general, the fear of losses though creative destruction forces firms to write off capital goods faster than they are expected to wear out, and discourages investment in equipment which is not expected to pay for itself fairly quickly. Technical progress creates similar problems for human capital: new products and techniques may make old skills worthless and cause *technological unemployment.

credibility The extent to which policy announcements are believed. Policy announcements by monetary or fiscal authorities are credible if it is rational for people to believe that the authorities will in fact stick to their announced policies. Credibility is thus relatively easy to achieve if the announced policies are compatible with what people would predict on the basis of the authorities' past conduct; it is increasingly difficult to achieve the more announced policies depart from what the authorities' past record would lead people to expect. A promise to desist from past bad habits, for example budget deficits or inflationary increases in the money supply, will gain credibility only gradually even if the authorities manage to live up to it.

credible threat A threat that the maker is exected to carry out. A's threat to B is that if B acts in certain ways, A will harm B. This threat is credible only if it is rational for B to believe that A will carry it out; if the threatened action also harms A, the threat will not seem credible to B. This holds unless B believes that A will feel that loss of credibility from failure to carry out the threat is even worse than the direct effects of the action itself. A reputation for ruthlessness or even irrationality thus makes threats more credible.

credit 1. The system by which goods or services are provided in return for deferred rather than immediate payment. Credit may be provided by the seller, or by a bank or finance company. Trade credit is when the buyer is a business; consumer credit when the buyer is an individual. A credit card is a plastic document issued by a bank or other financial intermediary, allowing the holder to obtain credit.
   2. The reputation for financial soundness which allows individuals or companies to obtain goods and services without cash payment.
   3. A positive item, that is, a receipt or asset in accounts. *See also* export credit, export credit agency, subsidized credit, and trade credit.

credit card A card, normally made of plastic, which allows the holder to obtain goods and services up to some limit without immediate payment. The supplier gets paid at once by the bank or other financial institution issuing the card; the card-holder then pays off the debt in arrears, often by instalments. Use of a credit card usually involves a commission, paid by the seller, and the purchaser is often charged interest.

credit control 1. The policy of controlling aggregate demand by means of restriction of access to credit. This may simply mean using monetary policy instruments, that is, the quantity of money and the interest rates. It may also involve regulation of particular types of lending, for example hire purchase restrictions, exhortations to banks against lending for speculative purposes, or quantitative limits on lending by particular institutions.

2. The system of monetary control adopted in the UK during the 1970s, when banks and other deposit-taking finance houses were required to maintain minimum reserve asset ratios.

3. The systems by which commercial organizations seek to ensure that they get paid in reasonable time for goods and services supplied on credit.

credit creation A name for the process by which the banks collectively can make loans in excess of extra *base money they receive. If base money increases, through a balance-of-payments surplus or open market operations by the central bank, this will mostly be paid into somebody's account with a commercial bank. The bank concerned can then lend most of the extra money out, which in turn raises deposits at other banks. Collectively, if banks hold $100n$ per cent of their total assets in base money, they can increase loans, and thus total deposits, by up to $£1/n$ for every £1 of extra base money. How close to $1/n$ the credit multiplier actually is depends on the proportion of the total money supply which the banks' customers choose to hold as cash rather than bank balances.

credit crunch *See* credit squeeze.

credit cycle The theory that *trade cycles are caused by fluctuations in credit. Booms occur because banks and other lenders become over-optimistic in granting credit. At some stage their mistakes lead to defaults and a loss of confidence, leading to a slump. During this lenders are over-cautious, and bad debts are gradually written off. After a while bankers recover from the shock and start lending again, which leads to a recovery, in the course of which they once again become over-optimistic, leading to the next cycle.

creditor nation A country with positive net foreign assets. Foreign assets include outward foreign direct investment and loans to foreigners. Against this must be offset any external liabilities: inward foreign direct investment, and foreign deposits in domestic banks and ownership of domestic securities. A country is a creditor nation if its external assets exceed its external liabilities.

creditors The balance-sheet item showing debts owing to others. This is divided between payments due in under a year, and other debts.

credit rating An assessment of the probability that an individual, firm, or country will be able and willing to pay its debts. Such an assessment is based on all available information about the subject's total assets and liabilities, exposure to risk, and past record in making prompt payment of interest and principal when due. An individual, firm, or government with a good credit rating can borrow or obtain goods on credit more easily and cheaply than one whose credit rating is poor. A credit-rating agency is a firm specializing on collecting and analysing information relevant to providing credit ratings for others.

credit-rating agency A firm which collects information affecting the credit-worthiness of individuals or companies, and sells the resulting credit rating for a fee to interested parties. These include firms considering lending to the individual or company, or providing them with goods or services on credit.

credit rationing Non-price restriction of loans. This takes place when lenders will not make loans to all applicants willing to pay the interest rate demanded, even though they satisfy all collateral requirements and other tests of credit-worthiness. The absence of credit rationing does not mean that lenders simply announce an interest rate and grant loans at it to all comers. There is an unlimited supply of fools and rogues, who would accept on any terms loans which they would be unable or unwilling to repay. Loans of this sort are reduced to acceptable proportions by collateral requirements and other tests of credit-worthiness. These tests are not infallible, however, so lenders may prefer to ration credit rather than raise interest rates to clear the market for loans. They will do this if they believe that a higher interest rate would lead to a worse incidence of bad debts than a lower interest rate which produces excess demand for loans.

credit restriction *See* credit control.

credit risk, counter-party *See* counter-party credit risk.

credit squeeze A policy package intended to restrain the level of demand by restricting credit. This may include restricting the money supply, raising interest rates, restricting the level of lending by particular banks or other credit intermediaries, or restricting the type of transactions for which credit is available. For example, limits could be placed on the maximum percentage of the price of goods which could be covered by hire purchase, or the maximum percentage of house prices which could be covered by a mortgage.

credit standing *See* credit rating.

creditworthiness The opinion of potential lenders about the safety of loans to any particular borrower. This is a matter of judgement; apart from some governments, the only people to whom it would be perfectly safe to lend do not need to borrow. The profits of firms are liable to variation through bad luck, bad management, or fraud; the incomes of individuals are liable to variation through unemployment, poor health, or folly. Credit-rating institutions exist to assess the creditworthiness of firms, banks, and foreign governments; their assessments affect the willingness of banks and other credit institutions to make loans. These assessments, however much expertise goes into forming them, are still only opinions and may prove to be wrong.

creeping inflation Inflation at moderate rates but persisting over long periods. This is the normal state of affairs in many countries. If inflation is rapid, it inflicts serious losses and builds up strong political support for measures to control it. Once inflation falls to low levels, other problems such as maintaining full employment claim the attention of the authorities, and measures to reduce inflation further command little political support. It can also be argued that the danger of the *liquidity trap during recessions makes low rather than zero inflation the best target for monetary management.

crisis *See* balance-of-payments crisis, debt crisis, and oil crisis.

criteria, convergence *See* convergence criteria.

criterion, welfare *See* welfare criterion.

critical path analysis The system of planning complex processes whose components take time and have to be carried out in a given sequence, by starting at the end and working out when each activity needs to begin. If this is not done correctly, projects cannot be completed on time because necessary inputs are not available, and costs overrun because workers and machines are kept waiting.

cross-elasticity of demand The ratio between the proportional change in demand for a good and the proportional change in the price of a different good. This is calculated assuming that the price of the good itself is constant. Thus if q_x is the quantity of good x, and p_y is the price of good y, the cross-elasticity of demand is given by

$$\varepsilon_{xy} = (dq_x/q_x)/(dp_y/p_y) = (p_y/q_x)(\partial q_x/\partial p_y).$$

If $\varepsilon_{xy} > 0$, x and y are substitutes; if $\varepsilon_{xy} < 0$, x and y are complements.

cross-holding (of shares) The position when two companies each hold shares in the other. If such holdings were of significant size this would make it difficult for either company's shareholders to displace the existing management; if both were majority holdings it would be impossible to vote out either set of directors so long as they agreed.

cross-partial derivative The effect of changing one argument of a function of two or more variables on the derivative of the function with respect to another argument. If $y = f(x, z)$, the derivative, or first derivative, of y with respect to x is written $\partial y/\partial x = f_x$. If z changes, holding x constant, this may change f_x. The second-order cross-partial is written $f_{xz} = \partial f_x/\partial z = \partial^2 y/\partial x \partial z$. For example, if

$$y = (x + z)^2 = x^2 + 2xz + z^2, \quad f_x = 2x + 2z, \text{ and } f_{xz} = 2.$$

f_{zx} is found in the same way, and is always equal to f_{xz} (at least, for any function likely to appear in economics). By analogy, think of y as the height of land where x and z give position on a grid running North–South and East–West. The cross-partial gives the change in the North–South gradient as one moves in an East–West direction.

cross-price elasticity *See* cross-elasticity of demand.

cross-section data Data for a number of individuals, firms, industries, or countries relating to the same time period. This is contrasted with *time-series data, where figures for the same individual, firm, industry, or country are given in successive time periods. Cross-section data on personal savings, for example, allow a relation between income and savings to be calculated.

The propensity to save derived from a cross-section study can be compared with that derived from time-series data.

cross-subsidization The provision of a good or service at a loss, which is met by the supplier from profits made on other goods and services. Where the goods and services concerned have joint costs, or are complementary in demand, the extent of any cross-subsidy is very difficult to determine. Some economists argue that lack of transparency makes cross-subsidization likely to lead to inefficient decisions as to which goods and services should be subsidized. It is also argued that even where subsidies are justified, cross-subsidization may be an inequitable method of paying for them.

crowding out The possibility that an increase in one form of spending may cause another form to fall. This could happen in various ways: Suppose for example that government spending on *public works rises. This might use scarce resources, such as skilled engineers, diverting them from alternative investment projects which are thus delayed. Alternatively, if increased demand causes inflation, this might lead to tighter monetary policy, thus cutting other forms of spending. Finally, if private investors are made nervous by increased government debt, a rise in public works might scare off private investment. Total crowding out occurs if other spending falls by 100 per cent of the rise in public works. Partial crowding out occurs if other spending falls, but by less than public spending rises. It is possible that crowding in may occur, that is, other spending is actually increased, if conditions are such that the Keynesian multiplier works, or through favourable effects of an overall rise in spending on the confidence of private investors.

CSO *See* Central Statistical Office.

CTT *See* capital transfer tax.

culture, dependency *See* dependency culture.

cum dividend Sale of shares including the right for the purchaser to receive a dividend already declared but not yet paid. This is contrasted with ex dividend, which is sale of shares where the vendor retains the right to a dividend already declared but not yet paid.

cumulative frequency distribution The proportion of a frequency distribution below any given value. If $f(x)$ is the frequency distribution, where x is continuously distributed between a minimum value a and a maximum value b, the cumulative frequency distribution is written

$$F(c) = \int_a^c f(x)dx.$$

$F(a) = 0$; for $a < c < b$, $0 < F(c) < 1$; and $F(b) = 1$.

cumulative preference share A share where dividends to the holder must be paid, including any arrears due from previous years, before any dividends can be paid to ordinary shareholders.

currency Another name for money. A country's own currency is that used for internal transactions. Foreign currency is the money of other countries. The Currency School in the nineteenth century urged that the banks should supply money according to some fixed rule, arguing that the alternative, Banking School, view that money should be supplied 'in accordance with the needs of trade', would put no monetary check on inflation. *See also* convertible currency, hard currency, over-valued currency, soft currency, trading currency, and under-valued currency.

currency appreciation *See* appreciation, currency.

currency area, optimum *See* optimum currency area.

currency depreciation *See* depreciation, currency.

currency reform Replacement of a currency by a new one. This has frequently been done simply for convenience, because inflation has made the value of units of the old currency inconveniently small. It may sometimes have been hoped that a new name for the currency would assist in making a promise of less inflationary monetary policy more credible. Currency reform has also been used to take money out of circulation because the holders wish to avoid bringing the size of their assets to the notice of the tax authorities or the police, or by imposing a limit on the amount of new money any individual can obtain.

currency risk The risk that changes in exchange rates will affect the profitability of any activity between the time when one is committed to it and the time when it is carried out. This affects foreign trade, foreign lending, and foreign direct investment. Commitment may arise from a contract, as in export sales or foreign currency loans, or from incurring sunk costs, as in foreign direct investment or setting up foreign distribution systems for exports. It is possible to reduce currency risk by use of forward currency markets, at a cost, but only for relatively short time periods.

currency snake *See* snake in the tunnel.

currency, vehicle *See* trading currency.

current account Transactions where the payments are income for the recipient. A country's balance of payments on current account includes trade in goods, or visibles; trade in services, or invisibles; payments of factor incomes, including dividends, interest and migrants' remittances from earnings abroad; and international transfers, that is gifts. Current account is contrasted with *capital account, where transactions do not give rise to incomes, but represent changes in the form in which assets are held.

current account deficit An excess of expenditure over receipts on current account in a country's balance of payments.

current account surplus An excess of receipts over expenditure on current account in a country's balance of payments.

current assets Assets turned over frequently in the course of business. These include cash, debtors (other than bad debts), and stocks. Current assets are contrasted with fixed assets, which last some years and are depreciated.

current (bank) account A UK bank account bearing no interest and requiring no notice for withdrawals. This is contrasted with a deposit account, where interest is paid and notice of withdrawal is required. The distinction has become blurred with the introduction of bank accounts under various proprietory names which are withdrawable on demand but yield some interest, generally at a very low rate. The US name for a current account is a checking account.

current liabilities Debts due to creditors which are due for payment within the next 12 months. These have to be shown separately in balance-sheets from longer-term liabilities.

Current Population Survey (CPS) A survey of US households by the US Census Bureau. This provides many economic data, including employment, unemployment, wages and hours worked, and other social and economic data including school enrolments, living arrangements, annual incomes, and poverty.

current prices Measurement of economic magnitudes using the prices actually prevailing at any given time, for example, 2002 GDP at 2002 prices. This may mean the prices in force at some particular date, for example 1 April, or the average of prices observed over the year; in years of high inflation these could differ significantly. Measurement of economic variables in current prices is contrasted with measurement at constant prices. Comparisons in current prices record nominal and not real differences, whereas comparisons in constant prices record real changes.

current-weighted index A weighted average of prices or quantities, where the weights used are proportional to the quantities or prices of the most recent period. This type of index is also known as a Paasche index. Where p_{ij} and q_{ij} are the prices and quantities of goods $i = 1, 2, \ldots, N$ in period j, and 0 labels the base period and t the latest period, the current-weighted or Paasche price index is given by

$$P_C = [\Sigma_i p_{it} q_{it}]/[\Sigma_i P_{i0} q_{it}]$$

and the current-weighted or Paasche quantity index is given by

$$Q_C = [\Sigma_i p_{it} q_{it}]/[\Sigma_i p_{it} q_{i0}].$$

curse, winner's *See* winner's curse.

curve *See* cost curve, demand curve, Laffer curve, Phillips curve, reaction curve, supply curve, and yield curve.

Customs and Excise The UK tax authority responsible for collecting indirect taxes, including customs duties, revenue duties on alcoholic drinks and tobacco, and value-added tax (VAT).

customs drawback A refund of customs duty collected on imports, paid when they are re-exported.

customs duty A tax on imports, or tariff.

customs union A group of countries with free trade between members and a *common external tariff on trade with non-members. These trading rules will govern a large proportion of trade, but may exclude particular sectors of the economy, such as agricultural products. A customs union is distinguished from a *free-trade area, which has free trade between members but where members are allowed different tariffs on trade with non-members.

cuts in expenditure Reductions in government spending. These may refer to changes in actual government spending which have already taken place, or, more usually, to announcements of planned reductions. Cuts in actual spending may be due to the application of unchanged spending rules in changing circumstances: for example, a reduction in unemployment benefits when employment rises during a boom. They may alternatively be due to a change in policy about spending, for example increasing the stringency of tests for eligibility for benefits. Similarly, announced plans to cut spending may be in anticipation of a reduction in the need for it, or an indication of changes in policy. In an inflationary economy, government spending has to rise in money terms if it is to stay constant in real terms; 'cuts' often take the form of money increases smaller than anticipated increases in costs.

cut-throat competition Competition between suppliers of goods or services, by price cutting or otherwise, which is so intense as to endanger the survival of some or all of the competitors.

cycle *See* credit cycle, Kondratieff cycle, life cycle, stop-go cycle, and trade cycle.

cyclical adjustment The adjustment of figures such as GDP, government spending, or the budget deficit to show what they would be if total activity was at its trend or normal level. This can only be done by the use of a model showing how these aggregates are related to the level of activity, and a model of the long-run trend in activity. In the absence of generally agreed models for these, cyclically adjusted figures must be treated with a great deal of caution.

cyclically adjusted budget deficit A calculation of what the government's budget deficit would be if the economy was at a normal level of activity. This is normally done by assuming that the rules and rates concerning spending and taxes are unchanged. As taxes are an increasing and government spending is a decreasing function of national income, during a slump in activity the cyclically adjusted budget deficit will be smaller than the actual, and an actual deficit may correspond to a cyclically adjusted budget surplus. Such adjustments usually do not take account of the probable effect of changing national income on the interest costs of government debt, nor do they take account of the fact that if the budget deficit is itself a target for government policy, a change in activity rates may be accompanied by discretionary changes in government tax and spending policies.

cyclically adjusted PSBR A calculation of what the Public Sector Borrowing Requirement would be if the economy was at a normal level of activity. This is normally made by assuming unchanged rules and rates for taxes and government spending.

cyclical unemployment Unemployment during the recession phase of business cycles, which can be expected to disappear during the next boom. Because of continual changes in techniques and tastes, it is difficult to tell during any recession how much of the increase in unemployment is cyclical, and curable on Keynesian lines by a recovery in total effective demand, and how much is structural, due to a decline in the industries where people were formerly employed, and curable only by the rise of new forms of activity. Because of lags in hiring and firing, cycles in employment are normally lagged on cycles in production.

D

data mining The production of spurious relationships in econometrics by running too many regressions. Standard tests of significance answer the question, given the variance of the data, what chance is there that an apparent relation could have arisen by chance? A coefficient is significant at the 5 per cent level, for example, if a result this far removed from zero would only have arisen by chance in 5 per cent of cases. When such tests were devised, regression calculations involved so much hard labour that probably only a few had been performed. The number-crunching power of modern computers is such that there may well have been thousands of regressions performed for each published result, so that apparent good fits may well owe a lot to chance.

date, redemption *See* redemption date.

dawn raid A move without notice by one firm to buy a substantial part of the shares of another. There is normally a limit to the amount of shares that can be bought without giving notice of a takeover bid; a dawn raid is often the prelude to a formal bid.

DCE *See* domestic credit expansion.

DDD A Standard and Poor's credit rating indicating that servicing of a security is in default or in arrears.

deadweight burden of taxes The excess of the total harm done by a tax over the actual revenue raised. An indirect tax raises the price of the taxed good to the consumer. The quantity sold falls, as consumers only buy units of the good for which their benefits exceed the tax-inclusive price. There are thus some units where the benefit to the consumer would be higher than the cost of production, but lower than the tax-inclusive price. The *consumer surplus which could have been made on these units is lost; this is the 'triangle of loss'. Similarly, direct taxes are liable to reduce effort, since workers will only exert effort whose cost to them is less than net-of-tax pay. They will not work where the cost to them is less than the pre-tax wage but more than the post-tax wage; the *producer's surplus which could have been made on these units is lost. Most taxes produce some deadweight burden: a well-designed tax system seeks to minimize the deadweight burden involved in raising any given total tax revenue.

deadweight debt Debt incurred without leading to the creation of any specific asset from which the cost of debt service can be met. This applies to personal debts incurred to finance consumption, business debts incurred to finance operating losses, and government debt incurred to finance wars or unemployment benefit. This is contrasted with personal debt incurred to finance training which increases earning power, debt incurred by firms to finance profitable investment projects, and government debt incurred to finance education or improvements to infrastructure, which may give no direct return but do increase the economy's tax base.

dealing *See* exclusive dealing, and insider dealing.

dear money High interest rates, which make it expensive to borrow. How high rates need be to constitute dear money depends on the rate of inflation: only interest rates greater than the rate of inflation make borrowing expensive in *real terms. If the central bank is using monetary policy to reduce aggregate demand, dear money and tight money, or difficulty in gaining credit, tend to go together. During a financial panic, however, a central bank may seek to make money dear but not tight: the aim is to induce lenders not to increase precautionary balances or call in debts, as holding cash is expensive, while they remain confident that they will be able to obtain credit if they really need it.

death duties Taxes levied on a person's estate after their death. These may be levied to discourage inherited wealth, or simply as a convenient source of government revenue. In the UK death duties have taken various forms: estate duty was replaced by capital transfer tax, which in turn was replaced by inheritance tax. All these have been extended to include taxes on transfers made before death, as without this death duties would be too easy to avoid.

debenture A secured loan raised by a company, usually with fixed interest and sometimes with a fixed redemption date. Debenture holders have no control over the company so long as their interest is paid and any conditions of the loan are complied with, but if the interest is not paid or the conditions are broken they can take control of the company, and they rank before other shareholders in the event of liquidation. Convertible debentures are debentures carrying a right to convert to equity shares at some future date.

debenture, convertible *See* convertible debenture.

debt Money owed by one person or organization to another. A debt contract states the terms of borrowing; what interest and redemption payments the borrower must make, and what collateral must be provided. Debt contracts stipulate the currency in which payment is due; foreign currency debt is debt where the interest and redemption payments due are in some currency other than the debtor's own. Debt may have interest or redemption payments linked to a price index. Debt service is the money required to make the interest and redemption payments due. A debt collector or debt-collection agency is a person or firm specializing on collecting debts on behalf of other people. Secured debt is debt where the borrower provides collateral, which the lender is entitled to take over if the promised payments are not made. *Mortgage debt is debt secured on houses, other buildings, or land. With unsecured debt the lender has no special claim on any particular part of the borrower's assets. International debt is debt owed by individuals, firms, or the government of one country to residents of another, or to international agencies. LDC debt is the debt of less developed countries. If debtors cannot pay, they may default, or the lender may agree to 'roll over' or reschedule debt. This means that the lender agrees to defer the receipt of interest or redemption payments, or to make fresh loans to cover the payments due on the old debt. A *debt crisis occurs when there is widespread inability to pay debts, or widespread fear of default. If private parties do not pay their debts, there is usually some legal process available to compel them to pay, or to make them bankrupt if they cannot pay. Sovereign debt is the debt of governments, which cannot be compelled to pay unless they submit voluntarily to legal processes. *See also* bad debt, deadweight debt, government debt, national debt, non-marketable debt, non-performing debt, and sovereign debt.

debt burden The cost of servicing debt. To an individual or business, this is what they have to pay in interest and redemption payments. In the case of government debt, it would appear that as what is paid from one set of citizens is received by another, the aggregate debt burden should be zero. This is subject to two objections: first, where the debt is held externally, payments to non-residents are a real burden on residents. This is increased for the country as a whole if the need for external debt service worsens the country's *terms of trade. Even where debt is held by residents, it is usually impossible for the government to finance debt service except by the use of taxes which distort incentives, so that taxation reduces the real wealth of taxpayers by more than the amount the government receives. This *deadweight burden arises from the existence of government debt, even if this is held by residents.

debt-collection agency A firm specializing in the collection of debts on behalf of other firms. Such firms need skills in tracing the addresses of debtors, discovering whether they have concealed assets, and bringing pressure to bear to make debtors who can pay do so. This may involve legal proceedings, or publicity to make it more difficult for defaulters to obtain credit from other lenders.

debt crisis Inability or unwillingness of major debtors to service their debts, or serious fears of this. A debt crisis occurs if major debtors are unable or unwilling to pay the interest and redemption payments due on their debts, or if creditors are not confident that these payments will be made. This is most likely to happen when debts are large, and interest rates rise or the economy slumps. The international debt crisis of the 1980s occurred when several major less developed countries (LDCs) had difficulty meeting their debt obligations.

debt deflation A situation when spending is depressed because individuals and firms have too much debt. This causes them to be cautious about both spending and further borrowing, preferring to reduce their debts. As one person's debts are another person's assets, debt can only reduce aggregate spending if debtors have higher spending propensities than their creditors, or if debtors tend to be liquidity-constrained whereas their creditors typically are not; both these possibilities seem plausible.

debt for equity A system by which firms or countries with excessive debt exchange part of their debt obligations for equity, held initially by the former creditors. This may be beneficial for both debtors and creditors. The debtors gain from a reduction in *gearing: when the profits of firms or export receipts of countries are low, less of them has to be spent on debt service. The creditors may also expect to gain, if the debtor's recovery prospects are uncertain. Holders of debt will lose if things go very badly for the debtors and they default, while if things go well the creditors do not share in the benefits. Holders of equity get little if things go badly, when the debtors might default anyway, but they do at least share in the benefits if things go well.

debt management The management of the debt of a company or government to keep down its expected cost and ensure that funds are always available when needed. This includes forecasting when net borrowing will be needed, choosing the type of securities to be issued or redeemed, and timing the maturity dates of outstanding debt to prevent excessive concentration of redemption payments at particular dates, which might give rise to difficulties in funding them.

debtors The part of the assets shown in a balance sheet consisting of debts due to a firm. Debts due to be paid in the next accounting period have to be distinguished from those due to be paid later.

debt relief An agreement by the creditors of an indebted firm or country to accept reduced or postponed interest and redemption payments from the debtors. This may be in the interest of creditors if they believe they can expect more from debtors making real efforts to pay tolerable bills than from hopelessly insolvent debtors who would be liable simply to default.

debt rescheduling *See* rescheduling of debt.

debt service The payments due under debt contracts. This includes payment of interest as it becomes due, and redemption payments. Where debt is long-dated, a large proportion of debt service consists of interest payments. Where debt is short-dated, most debt service consists of redemption payments. If an individual, firm or country has difficulty in servicing debt, the shorter-dated their debts are, the worse their problems. Debt service problems can thus be eased if creditors can be persuaded to convert short-dated into longer-term debt.

debt service ratio The ratio of a country's debt service payments to its total export earnings. This is normally expressed as a percentage. The higher a country's debt service ratio, the more likely it is to have difficulty in servicing its debts, either from export earnings or by raising new loans. A high and rising debt service ratio is a sign of a coming debt crisis.

decentralization The dispersal of the power and duty to take decisions away from the centre and towards other bodies. Within the public sector this means leaving decisions to local or regional rather than central government. In the private sector it means devolving decisions to divisions or subsidiaries of firms instead of taking them at headquarters. Decentralization may also be pursued by transferring decisions from the state to private bodies such as housing associations, or by breaking up monopolistic companies.

decile The boundary of a tenth part of a distribution. If all incomes, for example, are arranged in descending order, the first decile is the income such that 10 per cent of incomes lie above it, and 90 per cent lie below.

decreasing balance depreciation The system of accounting for the depreciation of assets by assuming that they lose a fixed percentage of their remaining value each year until they are finally scrapped, when their remaining value is written off. This results in a steadily decreasing stream of depreciation allowances.

decreasing function A function whose value falls as its argument rises. If $y = f(x)$, y is a decreasing function of x if and only if $dy/dx \leq 0$ for all x. If $dy/dx < 0$ for all x then y is a strictly decreasing function of x.

decreasing returns to scale A ratio of output to inputs that falls as inputs rise. A uniform proportional increase in all inputs results in a less than proportional inrease in output.

deductibility The tax concession available in many countries including the US by which certain contributions to charities can be deducted from gross income to arrive at taxable income. The argument for these concessions is that through them the state can encourage donations to worthy causes, by lowering the net cost to individual donors, while decentralizing the decision as to what causes should be supported.

deductibles The part of any insured loss which has to be borne by the insured party. The UK term for this is an excess. The point of making the insured bear the first part of any loss is partly to reduce moral hazard by making them more careful, and partly to avoid the administrative cost of processing numerous small claims.

deepening, capital *See* capital deepening.

default Failure to make payments such as the interest or redemption payments on debt on the due date. Default may be partial or total, ranging from a slight delay in payment accompanied by apologies and promises that payment will soon be forthcoming to total and defiant repudiation. Default is frequently avoided by creditors agreeing to reschedule debt, which they may prefer as it avoids showing bad debts in their own accounts. The main deterrent to default for individuals and firms is that bankruptcy or insolvency make it difficult to carry on trading. For countries, which as sovereign debtors cannot be made bankrupt, the deterrent to default is that it makes future loans very difficult to obtain.

defence spending Military spending by governments. It is not in fact possible to determine whether military expenditure is for national defence, for offensive operations or threats, or for internal repression. The classification of military and civil spending is often arbitrary: building strategic roads or railways may be listed as civil expenditure, whereas in some countries full-time Olympic athletes are paid for by the army.

deferred share A company share on which dividend payments may be deferred. If this is done, the deferred payments take priority over dividends on any lower-ranking share until they have been paid.

deficiency payment A subsidy paid to farmers when the prices at which certain products can be sold is below a target set by government policy.

deficit *See* budget deficit, current account deficit, and trade deficit.

deficit, US The United States government deficit. This grew vastly during the 1980s and continued in the 1990s in spite of repeated political pledges to reduce it and an attempt via the Gramm-Rudman-Hollings Act to do this by legislation. The deficit disappeared in the late 1990s due to growth in the US economy. 'The deficit' is not the same as the deficit in the US balance of payments on current account, though the budget deficit has been a major cause of the external deficit.

defined benefit A provision of a pension scheme by which the benefits to be received by the pensioner do not depend on the financial performance of the pension fund. Under a defined benefit scheme the risk of poor financial returns on the pension fund is borne by the employer or insurance company running the scheme, and does not affect the pensioner so long as the company remains solvent. A defined benefit scheme is contrasted with a *defined contribution scheme, where the rules fix what the member pays, and the benefits depend on the financial returns on the fund built up under the scheme.

defined contribution A provision of a pension scheme by which the rules fix the contributions to the scheme by employers and employees. The benefits paid to pensioners are determined by what can be afforded from the pension fund built up by these contributions. A defined contribution scheme is contrasted with a *defined benefit scheme, in which the benefits to the pensioner are independent of the financial performance of the pension fund, the risk of poor performance falling on the employer.

definite integral An integral evaluated between some upper and lower limits. If the first derivative of the function $F(x)$ is $f(x)$, then the indefinite integral of $f(x)$ is $F(x) + k$; the definite integral of $f(x)$ between a lower limit of a and an upper limit of b is written $\int_a^b f(x)dx = F(b) - F(a)$. If $f(x)$ is plotted as a curve, the definite integral gives the area above the x axis and below the curve lying between $x = a$ and $x = b$.

deflation 1. A progressive reduction in the price level. This would make real interest rates exceed nominal interest rates, which might make it impossible to lower nominal interest rates during a slump sufficiently to make real investment appear profitable. This is known as the *liquidity trap.
2. A reduction in activity due to lack of effective demand. This could be brought about deliberately by the monetary authorities in order to reduce inflationary pressure, or could occur through a collapse in confidence which the authorities were unable to avert. *See also* debt deflation.

deflationary gap An estimate of the difference between the level of effective demand required for a normal level of economic activity at any time, and the actual level during a recession. The deflationary gap thus provides an estimate of the amount by which effective demand needs to rise to restore a normal level of activity.

deflator *See* expenditure-based deflator, and GDP deflator.

degrees of freedom The number of variables in a set which can vary independently. For example, if N variables x_i, $i = 1, 2, \ldots, N$, are to have a mean μ, then there are only $N - 1$ degrees of freedom in choosing them, since once any $N - 1$ are chosen the remaining one is determined, as the mean is defined as

$\mu = (\sum_1^N x_i)/N.$

The number of degrees of freedom is thus the number of variables minus the number of restrictions holding between them.

deindustrialization The tendency for the industrial sector to account for a decreasing proportion of GDP and employment. In advanced countries large improvements in industrial productivity in the twentieth century increased real incomes. Consumers and government have largely chosen to spend these on services, including education, medical care, banking and insurance, entertainment and tourism. An increasing proportion of economic activity thus consists of services.

Delors Report A report proposing a single currency and common monetary policy for the *European Community (EC). The *Report on Economic and Monetary Union in the European Community* was published in 1989. It was produced by a committee chaired by Jacques Delors, the President of the EC, and proposed a progression through monetary convergence to the setting up of a European System of Central Banks (ESCB) and a common European currency.

demand The quantity of a good or service that people want to buy. The demand function relates demand to the factors determining it: these include customers' incomes, the good's own price and the prices of competing goods and of other goods in general; factors affecting the demand of individuals, for example their family circumstances; and factors affecting demand at particular times, for example weather conditions. The demand curve relates the demand for a good to its own price, holding all other factors constant. Price elasticity of demand is the proportional increase in quantity demanded divided by the proportional reduction in price. Income elasticity of demand is the proportional increase in quantity demanded at a given price divided by the proportional rise in income. Aggregate demand is the total demand for goods and services in the economy. Effective demand is what is actually demanded, as contrasted with notional demand, which is what people would demand if all markets were in equilibrium. Effective demand thus excludes consumer goods people cannot afford to buy because they cannot get jobs, and investment spending for which firms cannot obtain finance. Demand management is the use of monetary and and fiscal policies to control the level of effective demand in the economy. Excess demand is the excess of the demand for a good or service over its supply, at its present price. Demand inflation occurs when price and wage increases are stimulated by perceptions of excess demand in the economy. Derived demand is the demand for a factor of production or an intermediate good, which depends on output of the final product. *See also* aggregate demand, cross-elasticity of demand, derived demand, effective demand, excess demand, income elasticity of demand, and inelastic demand.

demand curve A graph relating demand for a good or service to its price. The price of the good is usually shown on the vertical axis and the quantity demanded at each level of its own price on the horizontal axis. Other factors affecting demand are assumed constant, including incomes, the prices of other goods, and other factors such as fashion and the weather. A demand curve may represent the demand of an individual consumer, or of the market as a whole. The demand curve for a good is normally downward-sloping, that is, more is demanded at a lower price. The demand curve may shift if incomes or the prices of other goods alter, or if there are changes in other factors, for example competition from new products. *See also* compensated demand curve, downward-sloping demand curve, kinked demand curve, and market equilibrium.

demand-deficiency unemployment *See* Keynesian unemployment.

demand-determined output The situation when effective demand is the only constraint on output. This is likely to be the case only during a deep slump. At most times there are shortages of particular skills or types of equipment which restrict output in some parts of the economy, even when output in other parts is demand-determined. The ability to fill shortages by the use of imports and inward migration of particular types of labour means that an open economy is closer to having its output demand-determined than a closed economy would be.

demand for money The amount of money people wish to hold, or the function determining this. Some economists have referred to the demand for transactions, speculative, and precautionary balances, but money held for one purpose can always be used for another, so it seems more sensible to think in terms of different motives affecting the amount of money holdings people want. The transactions motive means that, because money is used in most transactions, individual money holdings are an increasing function of incomes, and business holdings are an increasing function of turnover. At any given level of real activity, money holdings at any given interest rate and expected rate of inflation are proportional to the price level. Because money is one way of holding assets, the amount demanded is also an increasing function of total net assets. The demand for money, or liquidity preference, is widely held to be a decreasing function of both interest rates and the expected rate of inflation. The size of this effect is not agreed, and because interest rates and inflation are correlated, it is difficult to separate their effects on the demand for money. The speculative motive refers to *Keynesian models of money demand, in which liquidity preference is an increasing function of any expected rise in interest rates: such an increase would lower security prices, which makes money seem relatively attractive as an asset. The precautionary motive for holding money exists because *liquidity is an insurance against uncertain prospects, so that the demand for money is a decreasing function of confidence in the stability of people's incomes, and is higher when the future seems more uncertain. *See also* interest-elasticity of the demand for money.

demand function A function showing how the demand for any good or service is determined. Both at the individual and aggregate level, demand depends on income, and on the price of the good concerned. The demand curve plots demand against the good's own price, holding other factors constant. Demand also depends on other factors, including the prices of other goods, particularly those of close substitutes and complements; and on factors such as the weather or changes in fashion. Demand for consumer durables is influenced by consumers' existing stocks of them: the more people have such goods already, the fewer will wish to buy them.

demand inflation Inflation due to excess demand. As resources are not perfectly mobile between different regions and sectors of the economy, demand inflation can occur even if the level of effective demand in the economy as a whole is below the level needed for normal levels of employment. The higher the aggregate level of activity, the larger the proportion of areas and industries which experience excess demand for goods and labour of various sorts, and the more powerful is demand-inflationary pressure. Demand inflation is contrasted with *cost inflation, in which price and wage increases are transmitted from one sector to another. It is sensible to regard these as different aspects of an overall inflationary process: demand inflation explains how inflation starts; cost inflation explains why inflation once begun is so difficult to stop.

demand management The use of monetary and fiscal policy to influence the level of aggregate real effective demand in the economy. Policy-makers may aim at various targets: a high and stable level of activity and employment; a somewhat lower level, designed to cure inflation; or the balance of payments. Whatever the aim, the monetary and fiscal authorities can only influence the level of effective demand, and cannot decide it: this is done by a large number of decentralized consumers, investors and export customers. Demand management may be content with trying to avoid large deviations of effective demand from target, or may attempt 'fine-tuning', attempting to control effective demand more closely and on a shorter time-scale. Critics argue that because of lags in both information and the effects of policies, attempts at fine-tuning may actually tend to destabilize rather than stabilize the economy.

demand-pull inflation *See* demand inflation.

demand schedule *See* demand curve.

demarcation The reservation of particular tasks to workers with specialized skills. Some degree of demarcation is essential to health and safety, for example insisting that gas installations are fitted by qualified engineers. Members of professions or craft-based unions face the temptation to insist on high levels of demarcation to exploit their monopoly power. A demarcation dispute is a protest by one union against other workers performing jobs which are regarded as the preserve of its own members. Excessive demarcation leads to inflexibility and inefficiency; too little leads to electrical fires and collapsing buildings.

democracy, industrial *See* industrial democracy.

demographic transition The process by which countries pass from a situation of high birth and death rates to one of low rates. *Less developed countries (LDCs) typically have high birth and death rates: as development starts, death rates tend to fall earlier than birth rates, resulting in rapid population increase of up to 3 per cent per annum. More education and higher living standards reduce the birth rate, and advanced countries tend to have low birth and death rates and a low or even negative rate of natural increase. A similar process is observed in many immigrant groups; on movement to more developed countries, their death rate falls fast and their birth rate falls towards the host country level more gradually.

demographic unemployment Unemployment whose immediate cause is changes in the labour force. Demographic unemployment can arise if the number of new workers entering the labour force through natural increase or inward migration exceeds the number leaving the workforce through retirement or emigration.

demutualization The conversion of financial or other institutions owned by their members into companies owned by shareholders. This has happened in recent years to many, but not all, UK building societies and insurance companies, and the AA. Critics of demutualization argue that demutualized institutions will be run for the benefit of their shareholders rather than their customers. Supporters of demutualization argue that in practice the members of mutual institutions have almost no influence on the conduct of the directors, and that while many members continue to be shareholders after demutualization, efficiency is improved by allowing other firms to become shareholders, thus exposing the institutions to the market pressures that affect companies.

dependency culture A situation where welfare provision leads many people to depend permanently on state handouts and drop out of the labour market. Some economists believe this could be avoided by placing time limits on welfare handouts, or making receipt of benefits conditional on accepting training or *workfare.

dependent variable The variable on the left hand side of a regression equation, whose variations are correlated with those of the explanatory or right-hand variables. In the linear regression equation

$$y_i = \alpha + \beta x_i + \gamma z_i + \varepsilon_i,$$

for example, where there are N observations, $i = 1, 2, \ldots, N$, and ε_i is the error term, y is the dependent variable and x and z are explanatory variables. A lagged dependent variable is a right-hand or explanatory variable which was a dependent variable in an earlier period.

depletable resources Resources which can be used only once. Examples include deposits of coal, oil or minerals. This is in contrast to renewable resources, which can be used without being used up, for example solar energy or tidal power. In many cases whether resources are depletable or renewable depends on how they are used. Over-cropping of land or deforestation may diminish future productivity, whereas moderate levels of use with regular replanting would allow the same resources to be used on a sustainable basis. It is not always known until too late just how intensively resources can be used before they become depletable.

deposit An account with a bank or other financial institution, such as a building society in the UK. Deposits may be on current account (UK), or checking account or sight deposits (US), which bear no interest and can be withdrawn on demand, or deposit accounts (UK) or savings accounts or time deposits (US), which bear interest but require notice of withdrawal. In recent years new types of account have blurred this distinction somewhat. Deposits may originate from the account holder placing money obtained from elsewhere in the bank, or from advances by the bank itself. *See also* import deposit, special deposits, and time deposit.

deposit account A deposit with a bank which requires notice for withdrawal, and where interest is paid. This is UK terminology; the corresponding US term is time account. This is contrasted with a current account (UK; in US, checking account) which is repayable on demand and does not bear interest. The distinction has been blurred in recent years by the creation of numerous accounts combining withdrawal on demand and payment of a low rate of interest.

deposit insurance Insurance of the depositors with banks or other financial intermediaries against default by the bank. This is normally either paid for through premiums charged to all banks, or funded by a central bank or government. The advantage of deposit insurance is that it safeguards individuals and small businesses against ruin through losing their money. The disadvantage of deposit insurance is that it makes large businesses disregard the risks being taken by the banks or other credit institutions. Deposit insurance forces the taxpayer or prudent institutions to subsidize more reckless ones. This problem can be mitigated somewhat by limiting the compensation payable in respect of any one account, or better, to any one depositor.

Depository Institutions Deregulation and Monetary Control Act (DIDMCA) A US act of 1980 which imposed uniform reserve requirements on US commercial banks, savings banks, mutual savings banks and savings and loan associations, empowered the Federal Reserve to ask for supplemental reserves, and removed some interest rate ceilings. The Act was intended to increase competition in US banking.

depreciation Loss of value of capital goods due to wear and tear, ageing, or *obsolescence. The value of a capital good is assumed for accounting purposes to decrease each year. The amount by which to 'write down' an asset in a balance-sheet can be estimated in alternative ways. Straight line depreciation assumes that the asset loses an equal amount of its value each year over its expected lifetime, the number of years allowed for write-down depending on the type of asset. Decreasing balance depreciation assumes that the asset loses a constant percentage of the value remaining each year after deducting previous write-downs until it is finally scrapped, when the remaining value is written off. *See also* accelerated depreciation, decreasing balance depreciation, and straight-line depreciation.

depreciation, currency A fall in the price of a currency in terms of other currencies. This makes a country's imports dearer relative to home-produced goods, which tends to decrease imports, and it makes exports cheaper abroad, which tends to increase exports. Currency depreciation is thus usually good for a country's balance of trade. Higher import prices tend to increase inflation, however, so the benefit to the balance of trade may not be permanent.

depressed area A region with persistently higher unemployment and lower per capita incomes than the rest of the economy. National governments and the European Union (EU) have tried to improve the position of depressed areas by making them eligible for various forms of assistance to increase investment in them and improve their job prospects.

depression *See* slump.

Depression, Great *See* Great Depression.

deregulation The removal or relaxation of government regulation of economic activities. Advocates of deregulation argue that excessive regulation increases costs and restricts entry to markets in industry, finance and transport, and that consumers are better protected by competition. The financial and transport sectors have been extensively deregulated in recent decades in the US, UK and other countries. Critics of deregulation argue that it can result in lower standards of service and greater financial risks to customers, and that more competition may prevent some socially valuable services being paid for by cross-subsidization from the monopoly profits on other services. Increasing scientific information and political concern about environmental problems is in any case still leading to more regulation rather than less. *See also* financial deregulation.

derivative The rate at which the value of a function increases as its argument increases at any point, if this is defined. In a graph, the first derivative of a function is its slope. If $y = f(x)$, its first derivative at a point x_0 is the limit to which

$$[f(x_0 + a) - f(x_0)]/a$$

tends as a becomes indefinitely small. The first derivative can be written as

$$f'(x), f_x, dy/dx \text{ or } y'(x).$$

The second derivative is defined as the first derivative of the first derivative, and so on. If a function has several arguments, its partial derivatives are its derivatives with respect to one argument, holding the other argument constant; thus if $y = f(x, z)$, $\partial y/\partial x$ is the derivative of y as x increases, holding z constant, and $\partial y/\partial z$ is the derivative of y with respect to z, holding x constant. *See also* cross-partial derivative, first derivative, partial derivative, and second derivative.

derivative (financial) A tradable security whose value is derived from the actual or expected price of some underlying asset, which may be a commodity, a security or a currency. Derivatives include futures contracts, futures on stock market indices, *options and swaps. Derivatives can be used as a hedge, to reduce risk, or for speculation. A derivatives market is a market such as the *London International Financial Futures and Options Exchange (LIFFE) on which derivatives are traded.

derived demand The demand for an input to a productive process. This depends on the output of the good or service being produced. Derived demand also depends on the price of the input and the prices of other inputs which are substitutes for or complements to it. If other inputs are good substitutes, the elasticity of derived demand may be high; but if other inputs are poor substitutes, the elasticity of derived demand may be very low, especially if the input accounts for only a small proportion of total costs.

deseasonalized data *See* seasonal adjustment.

destruction, creative *See* creative destruction.

determinant A number derived from the values of the elements of a square matrix. For example, if a_{ij} are the elements in the ith row and jth column of a 2×2 matrix, its determinant is given by $\Delta = a_{11}a_{22} - a_{12}a_{21}$; the derivation of determinants for larger matrices is similar in principle. A major function of determinants is to check whether the rows or columns of a matrix are independent; if they are not independent then the determinant is zero. It can be seen that if

$$a_{11}/a_{12} = a_{21}/a_{22}, \Delta = 0.$$

deterrents to entry *See* barriers to entry.

Deutschmark (DM) The currency of West Germany, and since German Monetary Union in 1990 of the whole of Germany. The DM has been replaced by the Euro in 2002.

devaluation A fall in the price of a currency in terms of other currencies. Less foreign currency can be bought with a unit of the currency that has been devalued. If the price of the pound in dollars falls from $2.00 to $1.60, the pound is devalued by 20 per cent. The dollar thus appreciates relative to the pound: the price of a dollar in pounds rises by 25 per cent, from £0.50 to £0.625. Devaluation and depreciation are similar: devaluation is generally used for a discrete change in the exchange rate brought about as a matter of policy, whereas depreciation occurs gradually through the working of the foreign exchange markets. Devaluation makes exports cheaper abroad in terms of foreign currency, and imports dearer at home in terms of home currency, and thus tends to improve the balance of trade. The rise in import prices contributes to inflation, however, so that any improvement in the balance of trade produced by devaluation may only be temporary. *See also* competitive devaluation.

developing country *See* less developed country.

development aid *See* aid.

development area An area of the UK eligible for government grants to expand investment and improve employment. Areas of persistent high unemployment are designated as assisted areas; these are either development areas or intermediate areas. Development areas are those with the most serious problems. They are also eligible for grants from the European Union (EU).

development economics Economics applied to the problems of *less developed countries (LDCs). Its main special feature is the need to devote attention to aspects of the economy including the institutional framework, provision of *infrastructure such as power and transport facilities, and problems of population and agriculture, which in advanced economies can often be taken for granted.

development, greenfield *See* greenfield development.

dichotomy, classical *See* classical dichotomy.

DIDMCA *See* Depository Institutions Deregulation and Monetary Control Act.

difference The change in value of any variable from one time period to the next. If x_t is the value of x at time t, the first difference is defined as $\Delta x_t = x_t - x_{t-1}$. The second difference is the first difference Δx_t minus the previous period's first difference Δx_{t-1}, thus

$$\Delta^2 x_t = \Delta x_t - \Delta x_{t-1} = x_t - 2x_{t-1} + x_{t-2}.$$

The same principle applies in calculating further differences. If it is desired to measure differences forward from time t, use is made of the notation

$$\nabla x_t = x_{t+1} - x_t.$$

difference equation An equation involving the values of a variable at different times, assuming a discrete measure of time. Such an equation can be written in terms of the current value of the variable and its differences. For example,

$$x_t + ax_{t-1} = b$$

can be written as

$$(1 + a)x_t - a(x_t - x_{t-1}) = (1 + a)x_t - a\Delta x_t = b.$$

The same principle applies to equations in any N successive periods; they can be written in terms of x_t and its $N - 1$ differences.

differential The rate of change of a variable over time, where time is treated as a continuous variable. The rate of change of y, dy/dt, is frequently denoted by a dot over the y, or $\dot{y}$; d^2y/dt^2 is represented by two dots over the y, or $\ddot{y}$, and so on.

differential equation An equation relating the value of a variable to its own derivatives with respect to time, treating time as a continuous variable. This is contrasted with difference equations, in which time is treated as a discrete variable. A first-order linear differential equation, for example, can be written as

$y(t) = a + b(dy/dt)$ or $y = a + b\dot{y}$.

The solution of differential equations makes use of the same procedures as integration; many differential equations have analytical solutions, while others have to be solved numerically on a computer.

differentiation, product *See* product differentiation.

diffusion of innovations The spreading of innovations round the economy, and between countries. This may proceed by simple copying of an innovation, possibly under licence, or by modifying and adapting an innovative idea to apply it to related problems elsewhere in the economy.

dilemma, prisoners' *See* prisoners' dilemma.

diminishing marginal product The tendency for successive extra units of any input to a productive process to yield smaller increases in output. If one input to a productive process rises, while other inputs are held constant, total output may increase; if it does, the input has a positive marginal product. As successive extra units of an input are applied, however, after a certain point output is likely to rise at a diminishing rate. Whether marginal products diminish is a matter of fact: at low levels the marginal product of an input may increase. Beyond some point, however, marginal product usually diminishes. In farming, for example, it is usually possible to get more output from an acre by applying more labour, fertilizer, or irrigation water. If marginal product did not diminish as more of these inputs were used, the world could be fed on the output of one acre of land, which is clearly impossible.

diminishing marginal rate of substitution *See* marginal rate of substitution.

diminishing marginal utility *See* marginal utility.

diminishing marginal utility of money *See* marginal utility of money.

diminishing marginal utility of wealth *See* marginal utility of wealth.

diminishing returns, law of *See* diminishing marginal product.

direct investment abroad *See* foreign direct investment.

direct investment, foreign *See* foreign direct investment.

direct labour The use by a UK local authority of its own employees for work such as refuse collection or maintenance of its housing stock. This is contrasted with the system of having such work contracted-out to independent firms. Supporters of the direct labour system argue that it gives the authorities full control over the quality of work done. The system's critics argue that because of lack of competition, work done by direct labour tends to be relatively expensive, and that if a council's workforce is strongly unionized it may be easier to enforce compliance with standards by an outside contractor.

director *See* board of directors, company director, and non-executive director.

directorates, interlocking *See* interlocking directorates.

direct tax A tax on income or capital, for example income tax. Direct taxes are so called because it is normally assumed that the real burden of payment falls directly on the person or firm immediately responsible for paying them, and cannot be passed on to anybody else.

dirigisme Willingness of the state to intervene in the economy, either systematically or ad hoc. This is contrasted with laissez faire, in which there is a preference by the state for non-intervention.

dirty floating *See* managed floating exchange rate.

discomfort index *See* misery index.

discount A difference in prices. A cash discount or a discount for prompt payment is a reduction in price allowed to customers who pay cash, or pay promptly. A security stands at a discount if its present market price is below the price at which it is due to be redeemed. The *present discounted value of payments due to be received at a future date is found by reducing them by a percentage per period, for each period by which the receipt is delayed. Discounting bills of exchange means buying at a reduced price the right to receive payment when it becomes due. Discount houses are financial institutions which specialize in discounting bills. *See also* cash discount and quantity discount.

discounted cash flow The method of calculating the net present value of a project by adding the *present discounted values of all expected net cash flows at various future dates. If the expected net receipts at time N are R_N, and the rate of interest is $100r$ per cent, the present discounted value of net receipts at time N is $R_N/(1 + r)^N$, and the discounted cash flow is the sum of these into the future, denoted by

$$F = \sum_1^\infty R_N/(1 + r)^N.$$

A project may have an indefinite life, or it may be expected that for $N > N^*$, $R_N = 0$. Some of the R_N may be negative; this will be the case if construction takes time and there is a running-in period before a new project is expected to make profits. There may also be closing-down costs at the end of a project.

discounted present value *See* present discounted value.

discount house A city institution specializing in discounting bills of exchange.

discounting the future Placing a lower value on future receipts than on the present receipt of an equal sum. This may be because of the risk that a payment may not in fact be made, or that the person entitled to receive such a payment may not be alive to enjoy it. It may also be due to an expectation that the wealth of the recipient will have increased by the time the payment is due, thus lowering the marginal utility derived from any given sum. Finally, it may be merely because the payment occurs in the future: this is referred to as pure time preference. There is no obvious way in which the effects of these three reasons for discounting the future can be distinguished.

discount rate The interest rate at which future receipts or payments are discounted to find their present value. If the discount rate is $100r$ per cent per annum, the *present discounted value of a payment of A due in N years time is $V = A/(1 + r)^N$. *See also* test discount rate.

discount window Lending by district Federal Reserve Banks to US depository institutions.

discouraged worker A person who drops out of the labour market after a period of unemployment. This follows a period when they have been unable to get work of a type they regard as suitable for their qualifications, or in some cases to get any work at all. Discouragement may result from recognition that disuse is causing their skills to deteriorate, from fear that employers regard prolonged unemployment as being in itself a bad signal, or through sheer depression arising from idleness and poverty.

discrete distribution The distribution of a variable that can take only discrete values, such as integers. If $f(x_i)$ is the frequency of occurrences of x_i, where $i = 1, 2, \ldots, N$, in a discrete distribution, $f(x_i) \geq 0$ for each i, and $\sum_1^N f(x_i) = 1$. A discrete distribution is contrasted with a *continuous distribution, where i can take any value over some interval.

discrete time The treatment of time in dynamic economic models as a discrete variable. Processes in discrete time are described by difference equations. This is contrasted with the treatment of time as a continuous variable, where processes are described by differential equations.

discrete variable A variable which can only take certain particular values, for example integers. This is contrasted with a *continuous variable, which can take any value over some interval. Calculus is only applicable to continuous variables. Many economic variables are defined in money terms: money is strictly a discrete variable, but it is convenient for many purposes to treat money and monetary variables such as prices and incomes as though they were continuous.

discretionary policy Policy where the choice of policy measures, their extent and their timing, is entrusted to the judgement of policy-makers. This is contrasted with *rules-based policy, where policy-makers either follow pre-announced rules, or always follow well-defined precedents. The argument for preferring rules to discretion is that if the authorities act at their discretion it is difficult for other parties to predict what they will do. Actions of the monetary and fiscal authorities which cannot be forecast constitute a further source of disturbances in the economy, and are thus liable to destabilize rather than stabilize it. The main argument for discretionary policies rather than exclusive reliance on rules is that rules can only cope with types of disturbance which were thought of in advance, at least as possibilities. If anything really new occurs, such rules will be impossible to apply. Even in reacting to disturbances of types whose possibility has been anticipated, rules for policy can only be as good as the model of the economy on which they are based. Many economists doubt whether the working of the economy is sufficiently well understood for it to be desirable to adopt binding policy rules: considerable discretion needs to be left to the policy-makers.

discretionary spending Spending which a government body is empowered but not legally required to undertake. This can include both spending on real goods and services, such as public works, and grants to individuals or organizations. Discretionary spending is contrasted with *mandatory spending programmes, where certain forms of spending are required by law or by the rules governing schemes like pensions or disability benefits. Supporters of discretionary spending argue that it enables local government to respond to variations in public opinion about what forms of public spending are desirable. Critics say that it makes the availability of some public services depend on where people live.

discriminating monopoly A situation where a single firm sells in more than one market, and need not charge the same price in each. For maximum profits a monopolist sets prices so that at the amounts sold, marginal revenue in each market equals marginal cost. If the elasticity of demand is not the same, the profit-maximizing price will be higher in markets with less elastic demand, and lower in markets with more elastic demand. Discriminating monopoly is only possible when the monopolist can identify which market each customer belongs to, and where resale between markets is costly or impossible.

discrimination *See* price discrimination, racial discrimination, and sex discrimination.

discrimination (trade) Treatment of imports on a different basis according to their country of origin. In a free-trade area, customs union, or common market, imports from non-members are subject to tariffs while imports from members are admitted tax-free. Even treating free-trade areas and common markets as single trading units, it is possible to discriminate between different non-members: there may be preferences in tariffs for goods from particular countries, or special quota arrangements applying to particular sources of imports. Discrimination is contrasted with the principle of *most favoured nation (MFN) treatment, by which goods from all countries are admitted on the most favourable terms granted to any supplier. While the *General Agreement on Tariffs and Trade (GATT) and now the *World Trade Organization (WTO) commit countries in principle to non-discrimination, most world trade is in fact subject to various forms of discrimination.

disease, Dutch *See* Dutch disease.

diseconomies of scale A tendency for making an operation larger to decrease its average efficiency. At the level of the plant, this may arise from congestion, as more people or machines in the same locality get in each others' way. It may also be possible to dispose of small amounts of waste products without noticeable environmental damage, whereas large amounts require special and expensive disposal arrangements. At the level of the firm, which can have multiple plants, it is harder to see how diseconomies of scale can arise. Very large organizations may require many layers of management, increasing the mental and social distance between managers at the top and workers at the bottom, with adverse effects on mutual understanding and motivation. Larger organizations may also be less flexible in the face of changes in techniques or markets.

diseconomy, external *See* external diseconomy.

disembodied technical progress Improvements in technical knowledge that allow more output to be obtained from given inputs without the need to invest in new equipment. Disembodied technical progress is contrasted with embodied technical progress, where improved techniques can be exploited only by investing in new equipment embodying the new knowledge. Most real world innovations require for their utilization that some but not all the capital equipment used be replaced; whether a given innovation is embodied or disembodied is thus a matter of degree.

disequilibrium A situation in which plans cannot be carried out. Ex ante plans for spending and selling, or for producing and consuming, cannot be carried out if they are inconsistent with each other, or with objective facts. Disequilibrium can arise in particular markets, in the level of activity as a whole, or in the external relations between countries: it is the normal state of the real world economy. It produces discrepancies between ex ante plans and ex post facts, which lead to a dynamic process of change. Economic *dynamics studies whether the reactions to disequilibrium tend to reduce its extent or to exacerbate it. *See also* fundamental disequilibrium.

disguised unemployment Unused labour which does not appear as open unemployment. Firms hoard labour for which they have no use, because sacking workers is illegal or too politically risky, or because they are subsidized to do so. Family firms and peasant agriculture keep unproductive relations on the payroll. During recessions many of the self-employed are also largely idle (self-unemployed?). It can be argued that many of those on training schemes of various sorts are really also disguised unemployed.

disincentives Economic arrangements which weaken the inducements to work or save, or make it actually pay not to. High marginal tax rates provide disincentives to effort, and means-tested benefits give rise to the 'poverty trap', which means that it may not benefit individuals to accept low-paid work.

disintermediation Replacement of the use of financial intermediaries by direct contact between the providers and users of capital. For example, instead of savers depositing their money in banks and the banks lending to industry, disintermediation means that industrial firms borrow direct from the general public.

disinvestment The process of reducing the capital stock. So far as fixed capital is concerned, this may be by scrapping, or by non-replacement of capital goods as they wear out. Stocks and work in progress can also be reduced. Individuals and firms can disinvest by selling capital goods to each other, but this does not reduce the overall total in the economy unless disused capital goods are exported.

dismissal for cause Termination of employment by the employer sacking the worker for unsatisfactory conduct. Grounds for dismissal for cause could include incompetence, failure to obey instructions, absenteeism, dishonesty, drunkenness at work, or breach of health and safety regulations. Dismissal for cause is distinguished from *redundancy, where there is no complaint about the employee, but the employer's need for labour has changed or ceased. A UK employee who disputes the existence or seriousness of the cause cited for dismissal can sometimes take a case of wrongful dismissal to an industrial tribunal.

dismissal, unfair *See* unfair dismissal.

dispersion The extent to which any variable is spread out rather than concentrated at some particular value. Dispersion can be measured in various ways. The range is simply the difference between the highest and lowest values. This is usually not regarded as a satisfactory measure, as it disregards the distribution of all other values, while the extreme values themselves may be outliers due to freaks or errors of measurement. A commonly used measure of dispersion is the standard deviation, which is defined as the square root of the mean of squared deviations of the variable from its own mean. Thus if x takes N different values, x_i for $i = 1, 2, \ldots, N$, with mean μ, the standard deviation is given by

$$\sigma = \sqrt{[\Sigma_1^N (x_i - \mu)^2 / N]}.$$

To allow for the fact that different variables have different means, comparisons of dispersion frequently use the coefficient of variation, which is the ratio of the standard deviation to the mean, or $v = \sigma / \mu$. This is not satisfactory when x can take negative values, so that its mean may be small or negative.

disposable income Personal income actually available for spending. This is total or gross income minus direct tax and social security contributions.

dispute, industrial *See* industrial dispute.

dissaving Decreasing net assets by spending beyond one's income. This may be done either by spending money taken from bank balances or the proceeds of selling assets, or by incurring debts. People with positive net assets can dissave relatively easily: even if their assets are not very liquid, they can usually be used as collateral for loans. Individuals with negative net assets find dissaving difficult; lending to them appears increasingly more risky as their net asset position worsens.

distorted prices Prices of goods and services which do not reflect the true social cost of providing them. Prices may be distorted by monopoly on the part of the sellers, by legal regulation, or by failure to take account of external costs and benefits created by the production of the good concerned.

distortions Economic situations in which the incentives facing firms and individuals fail to reflect true social opportunity costs. Distortions can be created by externalities, taxes, or monopoly. The effects of some externalities could be corrected by appropriate taxes, for example congestion taxes on urban traffic. Some distorting taxes could be removed; for example tariffs have been greatly reduced over the past 50 years. Given the need for vast government revenue to pay for services that everybody agrees that the state needs to provide, eliminating all taxes is clearly impossible. Monopoly can to some extent be controlled by legislation, but given the prevalence of economies of scale the economy cannot be based on atomistic competition between small firms. The theory of second best attempts to tackle the problem of what to do when some distortions can be reduced, but others cannot be removed. *See also* domestic distortion.

distribution 1. The shares of income received by different sections of the community. The functional distribution of incomes refers to the shares of income derived from the services of labour, land, and capital; personal income distribution refers to the relative number of personal incomes of various sizes.
  2. The process of moving goods and services from producers to final consumers, via a network of wholesalers and retail shops. 'The distributive trades' refers to workers in this sector.
  3. A function showing the probability of various possible outcomes of a stochastic process. *See also* frequency distribution, conditional distribution, continuous distribution, discrete distribution, frequency distribution, log-normal distribution, normal distribution, symmetrical distribution, and uniform distribution.

disutility The psychological cost of work or other unpleasant experiences. There is no separate disutility function: an individual's utility is assumed to be a function of both consumption and work performed, with utility an increasing function of consumption and a decreasing function of work. It is possible that some people derive positive marginal utility from doing some work, but it is generally assumed that in equilibrium the marginal utility of work is negative. Disutility, or a reduction in utility, may also be produced by adverse *externalities, such as noise, air, or visual pollution.

divergence indicator A measure of how far the exchange rates of currencies of members of the *Exchange Rate Mechanism (ERM) of the European Monetary System (EMS) diverged from their agreed central parities with the *European Currency Unit (Ecu).

divergent series A series where the sum of the first N terms does not tend to any finite limit as N increases. A geometric progression, for example a, ar, ar^2, . . . , ar^N, is divergent unless $-1 \leq r < 1$.

diversification A spread of the activities of a firm or a country between different types of products or different markets. Practically all firms are diversified to some extent: the truly single-product firm is highly exceptional, and even it may supply various markets. Even very small shops usually sell a range of products. The advantage of diversified markets is that a firm or country will be less risky, as its markets are unlikely all to slump at the same time. A disadvantage of diversification is that every product and every market demands slightly different expertise; too wide a range may overstrain the capacity of management, leading to expensive mistakes when managers operate outside their area of competence.

diversion, trade *See* trade diversion.

divestment The disposal of part of its activities by a firm. This sometimes reflects the commercial judgement that the activity concerned would be more profitable operating independently or run by another firm. In other cases, divestment is required by anti-monopoly regulators to reduce a firm's monopoly power.

dividend A payment of income by a company to its shareholders. Dividends are so called because a company is legally required to divide any sum available for distribution between its shareholders in proportion to the number of shares held. Co-operative society dividends are payments to customers who are members, the total sum available being divided between customers in proportion to the value of their purchases. *See also* cum dividend, ex dividend, and stock dividend.

dividend control Restrictions on the distribution of dividends by firms. These may be imposed as part of a prices and incomes policy; they usually take the form of preventing or limiting increases in dividends. If wages are controlled, political considerations may require a balancing restriction on profits. Profits themselves are impossible to control, as they are never known till too late. Dividend controls are not fully parallel to wage controls, as undistributed profits are retained by firms and are available for distribution after the controls are relaxed, but they may be the best the authorities can offer as a sop to labour.

dividend cover The ratio of total earnings for equity in a company to dividends paid out. This is normally more than 1, as some profits are retained, but it is possible for a company which has built up reserves from past profits to pay dividends for periods when the cover from current profits is less than 1, or even negative.

division of labour The system by which different members of any society do different types of work. This has two advantages: it allows individuals to specialize on types of work at which they have a *comparative advantage, and it allows them to acquire specialized skills, both through training and by learning from experience on the job how to work efficiently and avoid mistakes. The division of labour in modern industrial societies is so extreme that no individual could create unaided more than a minute fraction of the goods and services he or she uses. Critics of extreme division of labour argue that over-specialization is bad for intellectual and emotional development, leading to narrow-mindedness and feelings of alienation. Some variety of tasks is therefore likely to improve overall efficiency, by increasing awareness of problems and motivation to solve them. A broader experience of different tasks also makes for more flexibility: workers can replace one another during absences due to holidays, illness, or emergencies, and find it easier to get new jobs if they lose their present ones.

divorce of ownership and control of companies *See* control (of a company).

DIY *See* do it yourself.

DM *See* Deutschmark.

do it yourself (DIY) Tasks carried on within a household which are also frequently performed by a paid specialist. The term covers mainly decorating, home improvements and motor repairs. DIY stores sell materials for use in such activities. Do-it-yourself activities are encouraged by the tax system, which requires employed labour to be paid for out of taxed income, whereas family labour is tax-free. Much DIY activity is carried out for physical exercise and mental relaxation, as well as to save money.

dollar ($) A unit of currency adopted by several countries, notably the United States. Other countries using dollars include Australia, Canada, Fiji, Hong Kong, Jamaica, Singapore and New Zealand. Any mention of 'a dollar' without qualification normally refers to the US dollar, unless it occurs in a context which implies that it means the local currency.

dollar standard A system of exchange rate management in which other countries peg the exchange rates of their currencies with the US dollar, and hold their *foreign exchange reserves mainly in the form of US dollars. It was argued that the *Bretton Woods exchange rate system operating in the 1950s and 1960s was effectively a dollar standard. More recently the decline of the US's dominant position in the world economy has made the adoption of a dollar standard less likely.

Domar *See* Harrod-Domar growth model.

domestic credit expansion The part of any increase in the money supply which is not due to a balance-of-payments surplus. The money supply can increase through a balance-of-payments surplus, on either current or capital account. This leads to a rise in foreign exchange reserves, and a corresponding increase in base money if this is not sterilized by the monetary authorities. Alternatively, the money supply can rise through lending by the banking system to either the state or the private sector. This extra internal bank lending is domestic credit expansion.

domestic distortions Factors causing departures of a country's internal economy from Pareto-optimality. Such factors include the existence of *externalities, *monopoly, and discriminatory taxes. These are contrasted with international distortions, such as those arising from *tariffs and trade *quotas. Trade theorists have argued that it is not efficient to attempt to correct for domestic distortions by imposing distortions in international trade, and that it is preferable to attack domestic distortions directly.

domestic product The value of the total product of enterprises operating in a country, regardless of their ownership. This is contrasted with national product, which is the product of enterprises owned by residents, regardless of where they operate. To get from domestic to national product it is necessary to add the profits of enterprises owned by residents but operating abroad, and to subtract the profits of enterprises operating in the country but owned by non-residents.

domestic rates A UK system of local taxation of householders. This operated up to 1990 in England (1989 in Scotland), when it was replaced by the Community Charge. Domestic rates were levied on the occupants of houses in proportion to their ratable value, which was assessed by a District Valuer. The rate charged per pound of ratable value was decided by local authorities, subject to 'capping', or maximum limits set by the central government.

dominant firm A firm with a position of strong leadership in its markets. Such a position may be due to large economies of scale, possession of essential patents, or legal restrictions on entry. It is possible for a firm to lose its dominant position, through anti-monopoly action or technical innovation by smaller rivals.

dominant strategy A strategy for one party in a game which gives results at least as good for them as any other, whatever strategy the opponent adopts. If strategy A dominates strategy B there is no point in using B. Descriptions of games can be simplified by omitting dominated strategies.

domino effect The tendency of one country's accession to an organization, or adoption of a policy, to induce other countries to follow suit. In the case of joining trade blocs, this could be because the bloc benefits members at the expense of outsiders. In the case of policies, if one country gives tax concessions or subsidies to attract foreign investment, this may divert it from other countries, which induces them to offer similar concessions.

dotcom company A name for companies devoted to providing internet access and various activities including sales over the Net. These recently became very fashionable; a bubble in dotcom shares developed, and burst in 2001. It remains to be seen what their long-term future will be.

double counting The attempt to find the total product of an economy by adding up the gross sales of each enterprise, without subtracting purchases of inputs from other enterprises. As firms buy large amounts of fuel, materials, and services from one another, simply adding gross outputs results in double, or multiple, counting of output. Double counting is avoided by subtracting purchased inputs from gross output to get *value-added for each enterprise. The national product is total value-added.

double entry bookkeeping The system of keeping accounts in which, as a check on accuracy and consistency, every payment appears twice, in different accounts, once as a credit and once as a debit. Thus a sale appears as a credit for the department making it, and a debit for the customer, while a purchase appears as a debit for the department making it and a credit for the supplier. Double entry books can if desired be represented in a single table, using rows for credits and columns for debits. As a check on double entry accounts, every debit item must have a corresponding credit, and the totals of all credit and debit entries must be equal.

double taxation The collection of taxes on the same income by two countries. This is liable to occur when an economic asset earns income in one country but is owned in another. If countries tax both the profits of firms operating in their territories, and the incomes of their residents, double taxation will occur unless there is an agreement between the two countries to prevent it. Double taxation is thought to be undesirable as it hinders international factor mobility.

double taxation agreement An agreement between two countries to avoid double taxation of the same income. Any income earned in one country by assets whose owner is a resident of the other is taxed only once, at the rate of whichever country has higher tax rates. The absence of such agreements would discourage international investment. As most advanced economies have both inward and outward capital movement, double taxation agreements between them are relatively easy to arrive at.

Douglas *See* Cobb–Douglas function.

Dow Jones Industrial Average A leading index of US stock market prices. This is an index of the thirty most widely traded US industrial shares. Dow Jones also publish indexes of transportation and utilities stocks, and a composite index which is an average of all three.

down payment The part of the price of goods sold on hire purchase or instalment credit that has to be paid immediately. When hire purchase controls formed part of UK monetary policy, varying the required minimum down payment was used to influence demand for the goods concerned. In the absence of hire purchase controls, sellers may require no down payment.

downside risk The risk that the outcome of a project will be below the expected mean return. From the point of view of a lender financing a project, the downside risk is that a project may not yield enough to enable the borrower to repay a loan.

downstream *See* forward integration.

downward-sloping demand curve A demand curve showing that the quantity demanded decreases as price increases. Demand curves are normally assumed to slope downwards, which is consistent with the outcome of empirical demand studies. This is not a logical necessity: it is theoretically possible for Giffen goods to exist. For such goods, the substitution effect of a price rise in decreasing demand is small, and the income effect, which is positive if the good concerned is inferior, is large enough to outweigh the substitution effect and produce an upward-sloping demand curve. Empirically, this seems not to occur: this is not surprising, since narrowly specified goods may be inferior but are likely to have good substitutes, while widely specified goods may have poor substitutes but are unlikely to be inferior.

draft, banker's *See* banker's draft.

drag, fiscal *See* fiscal drag.

drawback, customs *See* customs drawback.

drawing rights The right of members of the *International Monetary Fund (IMF) to acquire foreign currency from the Fund in exchange for their own, to an extent proportional to the size of their quota. Drawing rights were extended after 1970 by the creation of *Special Drawing Rights (SDRs), which enabled members to obtain further amounts of foreign currency.

dual economy An economy in which modern industries, mines or plantation agriculture exist side-by-side with backward sectors, with little interaction between them. This situation may occur in less developed countries (LDCs) with foreign investment in extractive industries using expatriates for their more skilled work. If the rest of the economy consists of subsistence farming and traditional handicrafts, technology transfer from the advanced sector may be minimal.

duality The fact that economic problems stated in terms of one set of variables can also be considered in terms of an alternative set. For example, in *linear programming, the problem may be to maximize the value of output subject to resource constraints. The dual problem corresponding to this involves choosing shadow prices to minimize the value put on resources, consistent with firms breaking even producing outputs subject to constraints imposed by the available techniques of production. It can be shown that these approaches lead to the same results. Which problem is simpler to handle computationally varies from case to case.

dummy variable A variable included in a regression to denote the presence or absence of some characteristic. Such a dummy can only take the values 1 or 0. Dummies can be used, for example, to show particular seasons in quarterly data, to show whether workers are married or single in unemployment data, or to show membership of the European Union (EU) in foreign trade data.

dumping Selling goods in a foreign country at a price which local producers regard as unfairly low. This may mean selling at less than the long-run average costs of production plus transport costs; charging a lower price in export markets than is charged for comparable goods in home markets; or simply selling at a price with which producers in the importing country cannot compete. *Anti-dumping duties are tariffs imposed in response to alleged dumping.

duopoly A market situation with only two sellers, each of whom must take account of the other's expected reactions. A Cournot duopolist assumes that the rival will hold constant their quantity produced; a Bertrand duopolist believes that the rival will hold constant the price charged. Duopolists may make more complex assumptions, for example that the rival will react to their actions according to some conjectural reaction function. *See also* Bertrand duopoly, Cournot duopoly, and Stackelberg duopoly.

duopsony A market situation with only two buyers. This is the parallel on the demand side to duopoly, which is a market situation with only two sellers.

durable consumer goods *See* consumer durables.

durables, consumer *See* consumer durables.

Durbin–Watson statistic (DW) A statistic used to test for autocorrelated disturbances. If z_t are the residuals of a series, that is, the differences between the actual series and the values predicted by a regression on the explanatory variables, the DW statistic is given by the ratio of the sum of squares of first differences in residuals to the sum of squares of residuals. Thus

$$DW = \sum_t (z_t - z_{t-1})^2 / \sum_t (z_t)^2.$$

A value of DW near to 2 indicates absence of autocorrelation in the disturbances. It should be noted that DW is not a satisfactory test when the explanatory variables include lagged values of the series itself.

Dutch disease The effect of an increase in one form of net exports in driving up a country's exchange rate, which handicaps the sale of other exports and impairs the ability of domestic products to compete with imports.

The name comes from the supposed effects of natural gas discoveries on the Netherlands economy.

duty/ies *See* anti-dumping duty, countervailing duty, customs duty, death duties, estate duty, excise duty, and stamp duty.

DW *See* Durbin–Watson statistic.

dynamics The study of how economies change over time. Change may occur as a result of exogenously determined factors, and endogenously as individuals, firms, and governments react to observed disequilibria. Dynamics is contrasted with *comparative statics, which is concerned with how changes in exogenous factors or behavioural assumptions will alter equilibria. Dynamics is concerned with the questions whether, in what manner, and how rapidly an economy will approach any new equilibrium.

early retirement Retirement before the normal age. This is common in many countries. In some cases it is chosen by workers who prefer either leisure or part-time work to continuing in their career occupations, particularly if their health is making full-time work a strain. In other cases it is imposed by employers as an alternative to redundancy.

earmarking A linkage between a particular tax and a particular type of state expenditure. Such linkages are unpopular with Treasuries because of their inflexibility. In the UK, for example, television licence revenue goes to support the British Broadcasting Corporation (BBC), but Road Fund Licence revenue is not assigned to building and maintaining roads.

earned income Income received in return for work. This is distinguished from unearned income, which is income from property, such as rent, dividends or interest. At one time the UK income tax system charged lower rates on earned income.

earnings The pay of the employed labour force. Earnings include payment for overtime and bonuses, as well as basic pay. They are distinguished from wage rates, which refer to normal time working only and exclude bonuses. Earnings normally rise faster than wage rates when activity increases, and fall relative to wage rates when activity declines. *See also* transfer earnings.

earnings–age profile *See* age–earnings profile.

earnings, company The part of the profits of a company available for equity shareholders, after deducting debenture interest. Companies may distribute these earnings in dividends, pay tax, or retain them to expand the business. Share prices are believed to depend strongly on company earnings. *See also* retained earnings.

earnings per share The amount of company earnings available per ordinary share issued. These earnings may be distributed in dividends, used to pay tax, or retained and used to expand the business. Earnings per share are a major determinant of share prices.

earnings–price ratio *See* price–earnings ratio.

East Asian tigers Four East Asian economies, namely Hong Kong, Singapore, South Korea and Taiwan, whose incomes and trade have grown extremely rapidly in the period since the 1950s.

easy fiscal policy A policy of cutting taxes, increasing government spending, and not worrying about the resulting budget deficits and increases in government debt. Such a policy is likely to be advocated when the economy is depressed. While this policy is tempting when investment and employment are below normal, it has dangers for the future. Taxes can be raised again when the economy recovers, but once people have got used to increased state spending, cuts are politically very unpopular, and servicing a large government debt has deadweight costs. Any government that adopts an easy fiscal policy is thus storing up trouble for its successors.

easy monetary policy A policy of having low interest rates and easy access to credit, to stimulate real economic activity. Such a policy is likely to be adopted in times of depression, when investment and employment are both below normal. A danger of easy monetary policy is that entrepreneurs may be tempted by easy credit to start up businesses which are viable only with very low interest rates, but are not sufficiently profitable to pay the normal interest rates which are likely to be restored when the economy recovers.

EBRD *See* European Bank for Reconstruction and Development.

EC *See* European Community.

ECB *See* European Central Bank.

ECGD *See* Export Credits Guarantee Department.

e-commerce The practice of advertising and selling goods and services over the Internet. This is a growing substitute for the traditional use of mail-order catalogues by people who prefer or are obliged to shop from home. Business to business (B2B) use of the Net is also growing. For the firms which are selling, a website is cheaper and more flexible than printing and mailing catalogues.

econometrics The application of statistical methods to economics. In econometrics a model of some aspect of the economy is set up, stated in mathematical terms. This model is compared with the available statistical facts about the economy; the model and the facts will invariably fail to match precisely. Econometrics uses statistical tests to tackle various questions, including: How well or badly does the model fit the observed facts? Does any other available model fit them any better? In any model, how large is the estimate of the effects of one variable on any other, and how reliable is the estimate? How far into the future, and with what degree of reliability, can the model predict any variable of interest? Econometrics is hampered by the fact that the relevant statistics may be unavailable, or wrongly recorded, and that variables of interest in many models, for example expectations, are not directly observable.

Economic and Social Research Council (ESRC) A UK *quasi-autonomous non-government organization (quango) set up to fund research and postgraduate training in Economics and other disciplines in the social sciences. ESRC was previously called the Social Science Research Council (SSRC).

economic growth *See* growth.

economic growth, stages of *See* stages of economic growth.

economic imperialism Domination of the economies of colonies by their rulers, or of politically independent countries by foreign or multinational companies. It can be argued that true independence is impossible for small, weak, and backward countries faced with domination of their trade, and possibly their extractive industries, by large, sophisticated and monopolistic firms based in the advanced countries. The dependency of peripheral countries is accentuated when the rules governing international trade and investment are written by the most advanced countries.

economic integration *See* integration, economic.

economic integration, European *See* European economic integration.

economic man A person who is entirely selfish and entirely rational. While such a person in pure form is a caricature met only in economic models, there is a sufficient element of this in enough people to make economic models relevant to real life. Real people are in various ways both better and worse than economic man. Economic man may only obey laws because of the penalties for being caught, and only keep bargains from concern for his reputation, but he is free from malice and dogmatic resistance to change.

economic rent A payment for the services of an economic resource which is not necessary as an incentive for its production. Unimproved land, which is valuable purely on account of its location, commands a rent based on its value to the user. Nobody had to be paid to make it, so rent paid to a landlord is economic rent. In the case of land which has been improved, however, for example by drainage, part of the rent is a necessary incentive for the improvements. If landlords knew that no rent could be charged, the land would not be improved. People with special abilities may receive some element of economic rent, but it is hard to distinguish this from a return on the time and effort that leading baritones or barristers put into their specialized training.

economics The study of how scarce resources are or should be allocated. *Microeconomics examines how production and consumption are organized, what is produced, and who benefits. *Macroeconomics considers how aggregates such as output, employment, and the general price level are determined. *Positive economics is concerned with what actually happens, or what would happen under various conditions. *Normative economics considers what would be the best methods of economic organization, from the point of view of both equity and efficiency. The analysis of economic policy requires both normative and positive economics: normative economics to choose the objectives of policy, and positive economics to check whether the proposed objectives are feasible, and what methods of organization would be the most effective means of achieving them. *See also* development economics, industrial economics, institutional economics, international economics, labour economics, Marxian economics, neoclassical economics, new classical economics, normative economics, positive economics, supply-side economics, transaction cost economics, urban economics, and welfare economics.

economic sanctions *See* trade sanctions.

conomic welfare, net *See* net economic welfare.

economies, agglomeration *See* agglomeration economies.

economies of scale The factors which make it possible for larger organizations or countries to produce goods or services more cheaply than smaller ones. Economies of scale which are internal to firms are due to *indivisibilities and the *division of labour. Specialized equipment usually comes in units of some minimum size, so that a larger total output makes it economic to use more specialized equipment. The division of labour means that it is possible with a larger workforce to restrict the range of tasks performed by each individual worker. Also, in a larger firm the breakdown of any particular piece of equipment, or the absence of any individual worker, causes less disruption to production. Against these sources of economies of scale have to be set the increasing difficulty of co-ordinating and motivating people in larger organizations. How large a firm can become before the problems of scale outweigh the economies varies widely between different industries. Economies of scale which are external to firms, but operate at the national level, arise from similar causes; there is scope for more specialist services in a large economy than in a small one.

economies of scope The benefits arising from carrying on related activities. These are similar to economies of scale, but whereas with economies of scale cost savings arise from carrying on more of the same activity, with economies of scope cost savings arise from carrying on related activities. Specialized labour, equipment, and ideas used in one activity are often also useful in related activities. Given the prevalence of multi-product firms, a great deal of what is normally referred to as economies of scale is in fact economies of scope.

economy *See* black economy, closed economy, dual economy, external economy, free-market economy, market economy, mixed economy, open economy, and unofficial economy.

economy, command *See* central planning.

economy, planned *See* central planning.

ECSC *See* European Coal and Steel Community.

Ecu *See* European Currency Unit.

Ecu, hard *See* hard Ecu.

Edgeworth *See* box diagram.

EEC *See* European Economic Community.

EEOC *See* Equal Employment Opportunity Commission.

effect *See* announcement effect, income effect, Pigou effect, and substitution effect.

effective demand *Ex ante spending, that is plans to purchase, by people with the means to pay. Effective demand is contrasted with notional demand, the demand that would exist if all markets were in equilibrium. Effective demand thus excludes the extra goods that unemployed workers would buy if they could get jobs, or that frustrated would-be entrepreneurs would buy if they could obtain finance.

effective exchange rate A country's exchange rate, taking a weighted average of its bilateral nominal exchange rates against other currencies. The weights are normally based on the value of trade with other countries. The effective exchange rate is a nominal and not a real exchange rate, but it helps to explain the contribution of exchange rates to changes in a country's competitiveness better than simply looking at its rate against one currency, for example the US dollar, which may be distorted by variations peculiar to the particular foreign currency chosen.

effective protection The effects of a *tariff system on an industry's value added, taking account of tariffs on imported inputs as well as on output. Defining units of output and imported inputs so that their prices would be 1 under free trade, if the tariff on output is $100t$ per cent and the tariffs on imported inputs are $100s$ per cent, and a units of imported inputs are used per unit of output, with zero tariffs value added per unit of output is $(1-a)$. With tariffs value added per unit is $[(1+t) - a(1+s)]$. The rate of effective protection e is then defined by

$$(1+e) = [(1+t) - a(1+s)]/(1-a),$$

so that

$$e = (t - as)/(1-a).$$

Effective protection is increased by higher tariffs on output, and decreased by higher tariffs on imported inputs.

efficiency Getting any given results with the smallest possible inputs, or getting the maximum possible output from given resources. Efficiency in consumption means allocating goods between consumers so that it would not be possible by any reallocation to make some people better off without making anybody else worse off. Efficiency in production means allocating the available resources between industries so that it would not be possible to produce more of some goods without producing less of any others. Efficiency in the choice of the set of goods to produce means choosing this set so that it would not be possible to change it so as to make some consumers better off without others becoming worse off. Efficiency is also referred to as Pareto-optimality. *See also* technical efficiency, and X-efficiency.

efficiency audit A process of checking whether an organization is working as efficiently as possible. This may be done internally, as management tries to improve profitability, or externally by regulatory bodies, for example those in the UK responsible for supervising privatized utilities. The two standard methods of efficiency audit are the engineer's approach, of comparing practice with what theory suggests is possible, and the statistician's approach, of comparing performance with that of similar enterprises elsewhere in the economy, or in other countries.

efficiency–equity trade-off A clash between making decisions on grounds of efficiency, and considerations of equity or fairness. When a good is exceptionally scarce, for example, efficiency suggests that its price should rise, both to direct available supplies to the uses in which the highest valuation is put on them, and to induce additional supplies. Rationing by price is liable to hurt poorer consumers most, however, and is thus often held to be unfair or inequitable. Similarly, efficiency suggests that it is not rational to tax other consumer goods but exempt food, while equity suggests exempting food from tax as the poor spend relatively more of their incomes on it.

efficiency frontier *See* production possibility frontier.

efficiency wages Wages which employers prefer to pay even if some workers would be willing to accept less. This concept arises from a model of the labour market in which workers' living standards affect the quantity and quality of work they perform. An employer paying the efficiency wage buys effective units of labour as cheaply as possible; employing workers who would accept less is not worthwhile since they will give less good value for the wages paid. Where ability to work is concerned, the efficiency wage concept only applies when employment is long-term, since casual employees' ability to work depends on their past rather than their future consumption. Wages affect motivation as well as ability, however, and employers may well find that paying wages workers regard as fair is actually more cost-effective than paying lower wages which are regarded as exploitative. Higher wages can also be expected to reduce quits, saving on recruitment and training costs, and reduce shirking and abenteeism. If employers believe that present wages are in fact efficiency wages, this helps to account for the frequent failure of wage rates to fall in spite of large-scale unemployment.

efficient asset markets *See* efficient markets hypothesis.

efficient markets hypothesis The theory that where assets are traded in organized markets, prices take account of all available information, so that it is impossible to predict whether some assets will give better risk-adjusted returns than others. This cannot be predicted because it depends on news, that is information which is not yet available, and cannot be deduced from information which is available. The efficient markets hypothesis is very attractive to economists, who are notoriously bad at predicting anything, and welcome a scientific explanation that this is inevitable. Evidence does not fully confirm the hypothesis, which is clearly not believed by market analysts and their employers, who spend billions annually on trying to predict which shares will give the best returns. The market analysts argue that their work contributes to the flow of new information which market prices then take into account.

efficient resource allocation A situation in which it is not possible to reallocate available resources so as to achieve more of one objective without accepting less of another. This applies whether the resources are those available to an individual, a firm, or a government. If an individual could gain by shifting expenditure from one good or service to another, the existing allocation is not efficient. If a firm could shift resources so as to achieve more of one objective, profits for example, without accepting less of another, say growth, the existing allocation is inefficient.

EFTA *See* European Free Trade Association.

EIS *See* Enterprise Investment Scheme.

elastic More than unit proportional response of one variable to a proportional change in another. Elasticity of demand is defined as $\varepsilon = -(p/q)(dq/dp)$, where p is price and q is quantity. If demand is elastic, $\varepsilon > 1$; the proportional rise in quantity is more than a proportional cut in price, so total spent rises as price falls. This is contrasted with inelastic demand, where $\varepsilon < 1$, so total spent falls as price falls. If supply is elastic, an increase in price increases supply more than in proportion. This is contrasted with inelastic supply, where an increase in price increases supply less than in proportion.

elasticity The ratio between proportional change in one variable and proportional change in another. Economists find this concept useful because comparisons of proportional changes are pure ratios, independent of the units in which the variables, such as price or quantity, are measured. Price elasticity, sometimes own-price elasticity, compares proportional change in quantity of a good supplied or demanded with proportional change in price. Elasticity of supply is the ratio of proportional increase in quantity supplied to proportional increase in own price. Elasticity of demand is the ratio of proportional rise in quantity demanded to proportional fall in price. This is usually defined as $-(p/q)(dq/dp)$, where p is price and q is quantity; the negative sign makes the elasticity of demand positive. This convention on signs is common but not universal; the usage adopted by any given author needs to be checked. Cross-price elasticity is the ratio of proportional increase in quantity demanded to proportional rise in the price of a related good. Income elasticity of demand is the ratio of proportional increase in quantity of a good demanded at an unchanged price to proportional increase in income. Elasticity of substitution is the ratio of proportional change in relative quantities of two goods demanded to proportional change in their relative prices. Where p_x and p_y are the prices of goods x and y and q_x and q_y are the quantities, the elasticity of substitution is defined as

$$-[d(q_x/q_y)/d(p_x/p_y)][(p_x/p_y)/(q_x/q_y)]$$

to make its sign positive. As

$$(x/y)(dy/dx) = d(\log y)/d(\log x),$$

elasticity equals the ratio of changes in the logarithms of the two variables (with appropriate sign). The elasticities approach to *devaluation considers the effects of devaluation on a country's balance of trade mainly by looking at a country's elasticity of supply of exports and elasticity of demand for imports, and the supply and demand elasticities of the rest of the world. *See also* arc elasticity, point elasticity, and price elasticity,

elasticity of demand The ratio between proportional change in quantity demanded and proportional change in price. This is on the assumption that income and other prices remain unchanged. It is common to insert a minus sign in the definition, so where q is quantity and p is price, elasticity of demand is given by

$$\varepsilon = -(p/q)(dq/dp).$$

This is to get the elasticity positive, to avoid confusion when discussing larger or smaller elasticities. Some authors do not use the minus sign, however; it is necessary to check the notation in use. *See also* cross-elasticity of demand, and income elasticity of demand.

elasticity of expectations The ratio of the proportional change in the expected value of a variable to a proportional change in its current value. Let us assume that the current value is altered by a shock. If the elasticity of expectations is less than 1, people expect short-run changes to be at least partly reversed, so the market is likely to be stable. If the elasticity of expectations is actually 1, expectations are myopic, and each new situation is expected to continue. If the elasticity of expectations exceeds 1, short-run changes lead to the expectation of further changes in the same direction. This can lead to *bubbles, and tends to make markets unstable.

elasticity of substitution The ratio of proportional change in relative quantities of two goods demanded to proportional change in their relative prices. Where p_x and p_y are the prices of goods X and Y and q_x and q_y are the quantities, the elasticity of substitution, *ES*, is defined as

$$-[d(q_x/q_y)/d(p_x/p_y)]\ [(p_x/p_y)/(q_x/q_y)],$$

to make its sign positive. The better substitutes any two goods are, the higher the *ES* between them. For perfect substitutes *ES* is infinite. Where *ES* > 1, as a good gets relatively cheaper it takes a larger share of total expenditure. If *ES* < 1, as a good gets relatively cheaper it takes a smaller share of total expenditure. If *ES* = 1, the two goods take constant shares of expenditure whatever their relative prices.

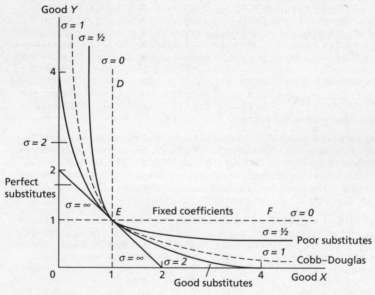

FIGURE 9: *Elasticity of Substitution*

The horizontal axis shows consumption of good X; the vertical axis shows consumption of good Y. (Alternatively, use of factor X and use of factor Y.) The utility function is given by

$$z = [x^\rho + y^\rho]^{1/\rho}.$$

The elasticity of substitution is

$$\sigma = 1/(1 - \rho).$$

Point *E* is where

$$x = y = 1, \text{ and } dy/dx = -1.$$

With perfect substitution, $\sigma \to \infty$, and the indifference curve is the straight line connecting $x = 0$, $y = 2$, and $x = 2$, $y = 0$.

If the goods are good substitutes, $\sigma > 1$. For example, if $\rho = \frac{1}{2}$, $\sigma = 2$. The indifference curve through E then meets the Y axis at $y = 4$ and the X axis at $x = 4$.

The case where $\rho = 1$ corresponds to the Cobb–Douglas case where $z = \sqrt{(xy)}$ $= 1$; in this case the indifference curve through E asymptotes to the Y axis as $x \to \infty$ and to the X axis as $y \to \infty$.

If the goods are poor substitutes, $\sigma < 1$. For example, if $\rho = -1$, $\sigma = \frac{1}{2}$; the indifference curve through E approaches the asymptote $y = \frac{1}{2}$ as $x \to \infty$ and the asymptote $x = \frac{1}{2}$ as $y \to \infty$.

If there is no substitutability between X and Y, $\sigma \to 0$ and the indifference curve is the L-shaped curve DEF.

elasticity of supply The ratio of the proportional rise in the quantity of a good supplied to a proportional rise in its price. The concept is only appropriate to an industry in which the firms are price-takers: that is, the market sets the price and firms adapt their outputs to it. For any one firm, elasticity of supply will be larger in the long run than in the short run. In the long run more equipment can be installed, and more workers can be taken on and trained, whereas in the short run output can be increased only by taking on more workers who may not be well trained. For the industry, long-run elasticity of supply will depend not only on the elasticity of supply of existing firms, but on entry and exit. Long-run elasticity of supply will be larger, the easier it is for firms to enter the industry as the result of higher prices or to leave as the result of lower prices.

elasticity of technical substitution The ratio of proportional change in the relative quantities of two inputs used by a firm to proportional change in their relative prices, holding total output constant. This elasticity has the same role for the firm as the *elasticity of substitution has for the consumer. If it is high, a small change in the relative cost of two factors leads to a large change in relative quantities used by a cost-minimizing firm. If it is small, a large change in relative factor prices causes a cost-minimizing firm to make only a small change in factor proportions.

electronic trading Trading stocks and shares or commodities through the use of a computer network. The network transmits information on offers to trade by *market-makers and others, and data of trades done. It can also be made to conduct the actual trades, though this part is often still done by telephone. Electronic trading is contrasted with the traditional market organization of having individual dealers meet and proceed by 'open outcry', that is, trade conducted verbally with all offers and trades done out loud so that competitors on both sides of the market can follow what is happening.

eligible liabilities The class of liabilities against which banks are required to hold specified percentages of reserve assets.

eligible paper Securities considered suitable for rediscounting by a central bank. In the UK the Bank of England will rediscount Treasury bills, short-dated gilts, and any first-class security accepted by a British bank or discount house. In the US eligible paper is securities which can be rediscounted with the Federal Reserve. Eligible paper is suitable for bank portfolios as it can quickly be turned into cash.

embargo 1. A prohibition on trading with a country, generally or in some particular goods. A general embargo is intended as an expression of disapproval, for example of practices such as Apartheid in South Africa; an embargo on particular products is generally based on defence considerations, to prevent the spread of advanced weaponry, for example during the Iraq–Iran war in the 1980s.
   2. A prohibition on releasing or quoting published material until some deadline. This is generally intended to avoid diplomatic embarrassment or opportunities for insider trading by synchronizing the release of information through various channels.

embodied technical progress Improvements in technical knowledge which can be exploited only by *investment in new equipment; technical improvements are embodied in the equipment. Embodied technical progress is contrasted with *disembodied technical progress, where new knowledge can be exploited with unchanged equipment. In practice many innovations require partial but not total replacement of equipment for their utilization, so the embodiment of technical progress is a matter of degree.

emerging markets Stock exchanges in countries where investors are unused to trading. These are mainly newly industrialized countries (NICs), such as Taiwan or Brazil, or newly liberalized economies, such as Hungary or Poland. Because of thin markets and lack of experience of both investors and market regulators, emerging markets are often even riskier than stock exchanges in countries where they have been long established.

EMI *See* European Monetary Institute.

emissions Substances given off by people or productive processes. These may be solid particles or liquids deposited in rivers or the sea, or solid particles and gases put into the atmosphere. Emissions are an inescapable fact of life: people emit carbon dioxide when they breathe. Economists are interested in emissions which have adverse external effects on people, animals, or plants. *Pollution can be checked in the short run by taxing or restricting activities involving a lot of harmful emissions, and in the longer run by research on alternative productive techniques involving fewer or less harmful emissions.

emission taxes Taxes designed to reduce damage to the environment by cutting emissions of products such as NO_x or CO_2. Emission taxes can be used as an alternative to, or a supplement for, quantitative controls on emissions. The arguments for using taxes are that they induce reductions in emissions where this can be achieved at least cost, and that they give an incentive to reduce emissions further even when they already comply with quantitative standards.

employee A person working for somebody else, for wages or salary, rather than working on their own account and selling their product or services. In the official economy the distinction is clear-cut: an employee has a contract of employment, and employers are liable for damage caused either by or to employees in the course of their duties. In the UK employers are required to collect income tax and National Insurance contributions from employees liable to them. Self-employed workers are responsible for their own insurance and for their tax and National Insurance payments. In the *unofficial economy the distinction between employees and self-employed contractors is extremely unclear.

employee stock ownership plan (ESOP) An arrangement for a US company to provide shares for its employees through a trust fund. Company contributions to ESOPs are tax-deductible. Employee share ownership is believed to make employees better motivated, better informed about their employer's business, and more loyal to the company.

employer An individual, company or government body that pays somebody wages to work for them. This is distinguished from hiring a self-employed person to do the work. In the UK employers have legal liabilities for the health and safety of employees: they are required to be insured for employer's liability, are responsible for deducting income tax from their employees' pay, and have to pay National Insurance contributions. The self-employed deal with tax and insurance for themselves. In fact large numbers of people employ part-time workers on an unofficial basis for jobs like cleaning and gardening without either employers or workers having any contact with the tax or National Insurance authorities.

employers' association A body representing employers in some sector of the economy. Such bodies may conduct collective bargaining with trade unions on behalf of their members, on wages, hours, and working conditions. They often also lobby the government about changes in laws affecting their members, for example concerning security of employment or health and safety measures.

employer's liability The liability of employers to compensate their employees for accidents and illnesses due to their work. Employers in the UK are compelled to insure themselves for this. It would be possible to run an economy on the basis that wages reflected the risks to health of various jobs, and employees were responsible for insuring themselves. There are two main arguments for imposing the liability on employers. One is economies of scale: there are far fewer employers than workers in the economy, so insurance by employers is less costly both to carry out and to enforce. The other argument is economy of information: on average employers have a broader experience of occupational risks in their industry, and they are responsible for working practices. They can use their experience to organize work in ways which keep down the risks run, and thus the cost of insurance.

employment 1. The state of being paid to work for somebody else.
2. The number of people employed, in this sense. This includes both full-time and part-time workers.
3. The state of being gainfully occupied: this includes self-employment as well as working for somebody else. Full employment is a state in which everybody wishing to be so is gainfully employed, in this sense. *See also* contract of employment, full employment, and over-full employment.

employment protection Regulations concerning the dismissal of workers by their employers. These concern matters such as the procedures to be followed, the reasons for which employees can be dismissed, and the compensation to which they are entitled in the case of redundancy or wrongful dismissal. Strong regulation of dismissal clearly benefits those who already have a job. There is a danger, however, that strong employment protection measures may make it harder for the unemployed and new entrants to the labour force to find jobs, as employers will be reluctant to take on new employees if it is liable to be difficult or expensive to get rid of them should they prove to be unsatisfactory, or if market changes mean that they are no longer needed.

EMS *See* European Monetary System.

EMU *See* European Monetary Union.

endangered species A species which is in danger of extinction. This occurs when total numbers fall so low that successful breeding becomes impossible, either because the survivors cannot locate one another, or because of a fall in the total genetic variety available to below a viable level. Many species have become endangered or extinct through human activities, through hunting them, changing their environment, or introducing exotic species which kill them or compete with them for resources.

endogenous Arising from the working of a system. This is contrasted with exogenous, which means imposed on a system from outside. *Monopoly in an industry, for example, could be endogenous, where economies of scale allow larger firms to drive out smaller ones, or it could be exogenous, where it is imposed by the state giving one firm a legal monopoly. What is endogenous depends on the scope of any analysis: parameters or institutions which are exogenous in a partial equilibrium model could be endogenous in a general equilibrium model.

endogenous growth Economic growth where the long-run growth rate is determined by the working of the system. This is contrasted with exogenous growth, where the long-run growth rate is determined from outside the system, by population increase and an exogenously given rate of *technical progress. Under both systems short-run growth can be speeded up by saving and investing more of the national income. In exogenous growth this speeding up is only transitory: growth gradually falls towards an exogenously determined long-run rate. In endogenous growth higher savings and investment, or the devotion of more resources to research and development, can increase the rate of growth for an indefinite period. Because it takes a long time for the differences between these models to show up, it is hard to tell which type of growth model gives a better approximation to real world economic growth.

endogenous variable, predetermined *See* predetermined endogenous variable.

endowment, factor *See* factor endowment.

energy, renewable *See* renewable energy.

energy tax A tax on the consumption of energy, which is urged by some economists. Such a tax would help to slow down exhaustion of the limited world stock of fossil fuels, and it is claimed that it would reduce global warming.

Engel curve A curve showing the relation between income level and spending on the consumption of some good, at a given price. The Engel curve for a good with unit income elasticity is a ray through the origin; with income on the horizontal axis and consumption on the vertical, the Engel curve for a necessity with less than unit income elasticity is flatter than a ray through the origin; and that for a luxury with more than unit income elasticity is steeper.

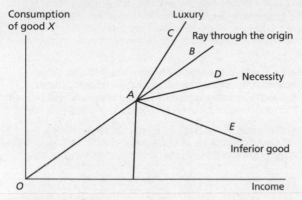

FIGURE 10: *Engel Curves*

The horizontal axis shows a consumer's total income; the vertical axis shows quantity of good X consumed at a given price. A shows initial consumption. OAB is a ray through the origin.

AC shows the quantity consumed as income rises for a luxury: AC is steeper than OAB. Consumption of X rises faster than total spending.

AD shows a necessity: AD is flatter than OAB. Consumption of X rises with total spending, but not as fast.

AE shows an inferior good: consumption of X falls as total spending rises.

enterprise 1. A business venture, private or public.
2. The combination of initiative, foresight, and willingness to take risks required to make a success of running a business. *See also* private enterprise, and state enterprise.

enterprise culture A climate of social opinion favourable to enterprise. This includes a willingness to take risks, a willingness to adopt new ways of doing business, respect for those successful in business, and willingness to allow others the freedom to compete and to retain a large proportion of their profits.

Enterprise Investment Scheme (EIS) A UK scheme to encourage the formation of new small companies, by giving income tax relief to individuals investing up to £100,000 in the equity of new companies. The EIS replaced the Business Expansion Scheme (BES) in 1994.

enterprise zone An area in which the government seeks to encourage investment and employment. This may be by making government grants available, by a relaxation of planning regulations, or by a reduction in taxation. This device has been adopted in both the UK and US to try to stimulate recovery in decayed urban areas. A danger of this policy is that such zones may simply divert investment and employment from neighbouring areas.

entitlement program A US term for a government spending programme where the rules give recipients a legal right to the payments concerned. There is thus no government discretion over who should be paid; the cost is open-ended and cannot be capped by policy decisions without getting Congress to change the rules. The existence of large entitlement programs, such as social security and Medicare, makes the problem of limiting total budgetary spending very difficult, as all reductions have to be made in non-entitlement parts of the budget.

entitlements Benefits to which the recipients have a legal right. Such benefits form part of mandatory expenditure for the government. They are contrasted with discretionary benefits, which the donor is empowered but not compelled to pay.

entrepôt A place where goods are imported and re-exported without processing. Entrepôt trade exists because of economies of scale in transport, and because the countries concerned have specialized commodity market institutions.

entrepreneur A person with overall responsibility for decision-taking in a business, who receives any profits and bears any losses. Entrepreneurs need not necessarily contribute either labour, which can be hired, or capital, which can be borrowed; but they must contribute either one of these or a credible guarantee, if their responsibility for possible losses is to be genuine. In a business run by a sole trader or partnership it is clear who is the entrepreneur; in incorporated businessses the role is dispersed among directors and shareholders.

entry Access to a market by a new supplier. An entrant may be a new firm, or a firm which has previously been active in other markets. It is possible to enter a new market from scratch, but many firms seeking to broaden their activities by entry to new markets do this by buying up a firm which already has market contacts. *Barriers to entry are factors making entry difficult. Entry is likely to be both most attractive and least subject to restrictions when a market is profitable and growing rapidly. *See also* barriers to entry, free entry, hit and run entry, innocent entry barriers, and strategic entry deterrence.

envelope curve A curve showing the maximum possible outputs obtainable by using a combination of two or more independent processes to pursue any objective. If all processes have constant or increasing returns to scale it is always possible to produce any amount efficiently using only one process. It pays to combine processes only when each has decreasing returns. This can apply to the use of different plants by a firm, or the use of internal production and external trade for a country. The envelope curve is found by taking a graph for one process, and superimposing on it the graph for a second process, using each point on the first process in turn as an origin. The envelope curve is the outer limit of all points attainable by using any combination of the two processes. The envelope theorem states that where both processes are represented by smooth curves, the slope of the envelope curve must be the same as that of the curve for each process at the point where it is used. That is, the marginal product of each process used must be equal, and is equal to the marginal product of the combination of processes. If these slopes were not equal, it would be possible to obtain better results by using more of one process and less of the other.

Another example of an envelope curve is long-run and short-run average cost (AC) curves. With cost curves, the object is to minimize cost. The long-run AC curve is the envelope curve drawn beneath all possible short-run AC curves. Each point on the long-run AC curve is also on a short-run AC curve, which is tangent to the long-run curve at that point.

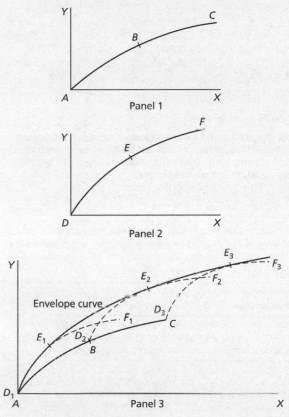

FIGURE 11: *Envelope Curve*

In each panel the horizontal axis represents an input, X, and the vertical axis represents an output, Y. In Panel 1, ABC represents process 1, and in Panel 2, DEF represents process 2. In Panel 3, ABC represents process 1; $D_1E_1F_1$ represents process 2 with A as origin; $D_2E_2F_2$ represents process 2 with B as origin; and $D_3E_3F_3$ represents process 2 with C as origin. $D_1E_1E_2E_3$ is the envelope curve. The slope of process 2 and the envelope curve at E_2 are equal to the slope of process 1 at B.

environment The conditions under which people, creatures, and plants have to live. The natural environment concerns matters such as the purity of air to breathe, water to drink and soil to cultivate, and several further aspects ranging from biodiversity to noise. The built environment concerns the effects on quality of life of human constructs such as buildings, roads, dams, or powerlines. The environment may be affected by pollution of the atmosphere, rivers, and seas, by the climatic effects of building and deforestation, by increasing human use of land for commercial agriculture and forestry, and by noisy and visually intrusive activities. Environmental economics is concerned with the effects of economic activity on the environment, and the costs and benefits of measures to control them.

Environmental Protection Agency (EPA) A US federal agency for research into pollution and the environment. The EPA is concerned with air and water pollution by solid wastes, pesticides, toxic substances, and radiation; it collaborates with other federal agencies and co-ordinates the anti-pollution policies of state and local governments.

EPA *See* Environmental Protection Agency.

Equal Employment Opportunity Commission (EEOC) A US federal commission set up by the Civil Rights Act of 1964. The EEOC deals with discrimination in wages, hiring, firing, training, and promotion, on the basis of age, colour, race, sex, religion, or national origin.

equality The property of having the same value. This is symbolised by =, and applies to numbers or algebraic expressions. If x and y are real numbers, $x = y$ means that x and y are the same. If x and y are complex numbers, $x = a + ib$ and $y = c + id$, where a, b, c and d are real, $x = y$ if and only if $a = c$ and $b = d$. If $\mathbf{x}$ and $\mathbf{y}$ are vectors, $\mathbf{x} = (x_1, x_2, \ldots, x_N)$ and $\mathbf{y} = (y_1, y_2, \ldots, y_N)$, $\mathbf{x} = \mathbf{y}$ if and only if $x_1 = y_1, x_2 = y_2, \ldots$, and $x_N = y_N$.

equalization, factor price *See* factor price equalization.

equalization grant A grant made by UK central government to poorer local authorities, to compensate for their lack of local taxable capacity.

equalizing wage differential A wage differential necessary to compensate workers for non-pecuniary disadvantages of a job. Such disadvantages could include danger, dirt, discomfort, an inaccessible workplace, low social regard, or unsocial hours.

equal pay The principle that the pay for any job should be independent of the sex, race, religion, or other personal characteristics of the person holding it. Equal pay for men and women is legally required in some countries, including the UK; it is, however, very difficult to enforce except in cases where employees have identical contracts of employment. It has been urged that to prevent evasion by minor variations in job description, the concept should be extended to 'equal pay for work of equal value', but it is enormously difficult to assess the 'value' of work. After many years of equal pay legislation and propaganda, the fact remains that in many countries including the UK women earn on average far less than men.

equation A requirement that a mathematical expression take some particular value. A quadratic equation, for example, takes the form

$ax^2 + bx + c = 0$. A solution is any value of x for which this is true. An equation may have more than one argument: for example, $ax^2 + bxy + cy^2 = 0$. A solution to this is any set (x, y) for which this equality is satisfied. With simultaneous equations, two or more equations must be satisfied by the same set of their arguments. There is no guarantee that any given equation or set of equations has any real solution, or if it does have one, that this is unique. In a few very special and simple cases it is easy to see whether there are any real solutions and locate them analytically. For many more complex equations and systems of simultaneous equations, it is not easy to tell whether they have solutions, or how many; locating solutions requires number-crunching procedures normally conducted on a computer. *See also* difference equation, differential equation, and simultaneous equations.

equilibrium A situation in which nobody has any immediate reason to change their actions, so that the status quo can continue, at least temporarily. This concept is applied in economics in a number of related ways. These concern microeconomics, macroeconomics, and game theory.

1. In *microeconomics, the simplest form of equilibrium analysis looks at a single market. Because repercussions in the rest of the economy are ignored, this is called *partial equilibrium analysis. Equilibrium price is that at which quantity supplied and quantity demanded are equal, and equilibrium quantity is that at which the marginal valuation put on the good by purchasers equals the marginal supply price, which for competitive producers is their marginal cost. Under normal assumptions the demand curve in a competitive market slopes downwards, and the supply curve slopes upwards. Equilibrium exists where the supply and demand curves cross: it is unique if they cross only once. The equilibrium price is the price that clears the market. Such an equilibrium will be stable because it will not pay either party to try to trade at any but the equilibrium price. In a more complex approach several markets are considered simultaneously: this is termed general equilibrium analysis. Repercussions of what happens in one market on the other markets are considered; *general equilibrium requires that all markets clear at once. The conditions for the existence and uniqueness of general equilibrium are often very complex, even in competitive equilibrium, that is a situation in which all markets are competitive.

2. In macroeconomics, equilibrium refers to situations when activity and price levels are such that the plans of various groups such as savers and investors are consistent, so that they can all be implemented. There is no reason, for example, why the *ex ante savings and investment of any individual or firm should be equal. In the aggregate, however, these plans can only be carried out if the level of national income is such that aggregate savings and investment plans in a closed economy are equal. As each individual's plans depend on expectations about what others will do, macroeconomic equilibrium may not exist, and may not be unique. If macroeconomic equilibrium does exist and is achieved, nobody has any immediate need to change their plans. If equilibrium is not in fact achieved, then at least some people's ex ante intentions must be thwarted, which may induce them to alter their plans. Macroeconomic equilibria may or may not be stable. A stable equilibrium is one where the result of failure to achieve plans is to change them in a way that brings the economy closer to equilibrium. An economy in which disequilibrium induces changes in spending plans which move the economy towards equilibrium is self-equilibrating or self-stabilizing. There is no guarantee, however, that disequilibrium will produce such a result. If it does, convergence may be towards a stationary equilibrium or steady state, or towards a steady growth path. It is also possible that the reactions to disequilibrium may lead to perpetual oscillations.

3. A third application of equilibrium is in game theory. A strategy is a rule adopted by an individual agent whose own actions are made conditional on those they observe in others. An equilibrium in strategies exists if, given the strategies that all other agents are using, no individual agent finds any change of strategy to be desirable. Such an equilibrium may involve all parties taking the others' strategies as given: this is called a Nash equilibrium. Alternatively, one agent may anticipate the reactions of others and act as a 'Stackelberg leader' in strategy choice, while other agents act as followers. This gives rise to a Stackelberg equilibrium (named, like the Nash equilibrium, after its inventor). *See also* competitive equilibrium, general equilibrium, market equilibrium, multiple equilibrium, Nash equilibrium, partial equilibrium, perfect equilibrium, and tangency equilibrium.

equilibrium price A price at which the quantity of a good supplied is equal to the quantity demanded. If the supply curve is upward-sloping and the demand curve is downward-sloping, this price is unique. *See also* the figure for market equilibrium.

equilibrium quantity The quantity of a good supplied and demanded when the price is such that these quantities are equal, so that the market is in equilibrium. With normally sloped supply and demand curves, if the price is above the equilibrium price, the quantity supplied is above the equilibrium quantity, which in turn is above the quantity demanded. *See also* the figure for market equilibrium.

equilibrium, tangency *See* tangency equilibrium.

equities The ordinary shares (UK) or common stock (US) of companies. The owners of these shares are entitled to the residual profits of companies after all claims of creditors, debenture holders, and preference shareholders have been satisfied. Equities thus have a higher variance of expected yield than other shares; this effect increases with a company's gearing. *See also* corporate equity and debt for equity.

equity–efficiency trade-off *See* efficiency–equity trade-off.

equity (fairness) The concept of distributive justice used in *welfare economics. Equity as fairness has several possible meanings, not always consistent. Sometimes it means equality; sometimes that differences in deserts should be followed by differences in rewards; and sometimes that expectations should not be disappointed. These interpretations of equity can conflict: applying the concept of equity to pensions, for example, equity as equality implies at least approximate equality of pensions; equity as matching rewards to deserts implies that a career of hard and responsible work should earn a higher pension than one of slacking or routine casual work; and equity as conforming to expectations means that people should not be disappointed of the pensions they have been led to expect. *See also* horizontal equity, and vertical equity.

equity-linked assurance A system of life insurance where the benefits to be received are linked to the level of an index of equity share prices. The benefits may have some guaranteed minimum, but above this they reflect the behaviour of equity prices up to the time when the policy matures.

equity, negative *See* negative equity.

equity withdrawal Raising a new or increased *mortgage for some purpose other than buying or improving the mortgaged property. This is sometimes criticized as leading to excessive consumption; it may, however, be used as a means of raising capital to start or expand a business, which could benefit the economy. In other cases it is a means of raising a cheaper, secured, loan to pay off unsecured debts already incurred and paying a higher interest rate.

equivalence, Ricardian *See* Ricardian equivalence.

equivalent, certainty *See* certainty equivalent.

equivalent variation The amount of additional money needed to give the level of utility which an individual could have reached if the price of a commodity fell, or a new commodity became available. This is contrasted with the compensating variation, which is the amount of additional money needed to restore an individual's original level of utility if the price of any good consumed rises, or it ceases to be available.

ERM *See* Exchange Rate Mechanism.

erosion *See* soil erosion.

error *See* rounding error, and standard error.

errors, types 1 and 2 *See* type 1 and 2 errors.

error term *See* residual error.

escalator clause A clause in a contract linking the price or wage to be paid to some other price, or to the cost of living. This linkage may apply to all increases in costs, or only to those beyond some threshold level. If escalator clauses are widely used in contracts or wage bargains, they contribute to *cost inflation and make inflation difficult to stop. On the other hand contracts without escalator clauses may have to set prices or wages higher initially because of anticipations of possible increases in costs: this substitutes present inflation for the danger of future inflation implied by escalator clauses.

ESOP *See* employee stock ownership plan.

espionage, industrial *See* industrial espionage.

ESRC *See* Economic and Social Research Council.

estate duty A UK tax formerly levied on the estate of a dead person. It was based on the total value of the estate, with exemption for small estates. Estate duty has been replaced, first by capital transfer tax (CTT), and then in 1986 by inheritance tax.

Estimates Proposals on expenditure in the coming financial year included in the UK government's annual budget. These have to be approved by the House of Commons. The Select Committee on Estimates is an all-party parliamentary committee appointed to examine selected items in detail.

Estimates, Select Committee on *See* Select Committee on Estimates.

estimator, unbiased *See* unbiased estimator.

ethics, business *See* business ethics.

EU *See* European Union.

Euler's theorem A mathematical theorem relating marginal to average products. The theorem states that where a function is homogeneous of order n in its arguments, so that, for example, if $y = f(x, z)$, then $f(\lambda x, \lambda z) = \lambda^n f(x, z)$, the sum of the marginal product of each argument times its quantity equals ny. This implies that if $f(\ )$ is a production function with y as output and x and z the inputs, the amount of factors used times their marginal products equals total output if and only if $n = 1$. Thus if factors are paid their marginal products, only with constant returns to scale does the sum of factor earnings exhaust the total product. With decreasing returns to scale the entrepreneur is left with a profit, and with increasing returns to scale the firm cannot afford to pay its inputs their marginal products. Constant returns to scale are thus needed for a perfectly competitive equilibrium.

Euro (€) The unit of the single European currency, adopted in 1999 as part of *European Monetary Union (EMU) by 11 members of the European Union; Austria, Belgium, Finland, France, Germany, Italy, Ireland, Luxembourg, the Netherlands, Portugal, and Spain. It has a fixed value in terms of each country's domestic currency; for example, approximately 1.6 Deutschmarks, or 200 Portuguese escudos. Initially the Euro was only a common unit of account, and not a medium of exchange; in 2002 it replaced the domestic currencies of the 11, plus Greece, which has now joined the Euro zone, and Euro notes and coin circulate in all 12 countries. In 2004 the UK has not yet decided whether or when it will join.

Euro area The countries which from 2002 have abolished their national currencies and adopted the Euro. In 2003 there are twelve; Austria, Belgium, Finland, France, Germany, Greece, Italy, Ireland, Luxembourg, the Netherlands, Portugal, and Spain. The Euro area will expand if Denmark, Sweden, or the UK, the existing EU members who have not joined, or any new EU members decide to join.

Eurobond A bond issued in a Eurocurrency, that is, a European currency held outside its country of origin. Eurobonds are issued in bearer form, and the interest payments are free of withholding taxes. They are thus attractive to investors wishing to remain anonymous, for tax avoidance or other reasons. They may be of various maturities, and at fixed interest rates, or floating rates linked to the London Inter Bank Offered Rate (LIBOR).

Eurocurrency A currency held in a European country other than its country of origin. Such currencies need not themselves be European: there are large Eurodollar and Euroyen deposits. This market is useful for short- and medium-term international borrowing, mainly by banks and large companies, and for financing international trade and investment. Eurocurrency balances are attractive to those wishing to avoid national taxes or regulations.

Eurodollars *See* Eurocurrency.

Euromarket A market dealing in Eurobonds and Eurocurrencies, that is securities and currencies held in European countries other than their country of origin. There are large Euromarkets in several centres, including Brussels, Frankfurt, London and Paris.

Europe agreements Agreements between the European Union (EU) and countries applying to become members. These agreements concerned changes in the institutional and legal arrangements required before countries would accede, and provision for trade with them in the meantime. Europe agreements were made with several countries of Central and Eastern Europe, including Bulgaria, the Czech Republic, Hungary, Poland, Romania, and Slovenia.

European Bank for Reconstruction and Development (EBRD) An international bank founded in 1990 to assist in the transformation of the countries of Central and Eastern Europe and the former Soviet Union to market economies. The EBRD is empowered to make loans to both private and public sector borrowers. Most Western and Eastern European countries are members.

European Central Bank (ECB) The central institution of the *European Monetary Union (EMU). The ECB was set up in 1998, with power to control interest rates from 1999 and to issue Euro coins and notes from 2002. The ECB's offices are in Frankfurt; it has an Executive of six members drawn from member countries of the European Monetary Union (EMU), and a supervisory board of these plus the central bankers of the 12 EMU members.

European Coal and Steel Community (ECSC) A European body established in 1952 with France, West Germany, Italy, and the three Benelux countries, Belgium, Luxembourg, and the Netherlands, as members. It established a *common market in coal and steel, abolishing tariffs and quantitative restrictions on trade in these goods between its members. It also provided for the regulation of mergers and restrictive practices, setting up a Parliament to set the rules and a Court to enforce them. The ECSC became merged in 1958 in the *European Economic Community (EEC), which extended the same principles to all manufactured goods.

European Commission The main executive body of the *European Union (EU). The commissoners are appointed by member country governments, two each by larger and one each by smaller members. The Commission is responsible for initiating action in the EU: it accepts joint responsibility and takes decisions by majority vote.

European Community (EC) The main institution of European unity, formed in 1967 from the European Atomic Energy Community, the European Coal and Steel Community (ECSC), and the European Economic Community (EEC). In 1993 its title changed to the European Union (EU). Its six founder members were Belgium, France, (West) Germany, Italy, Luxembourg, and the Netherlands. Denmark, Ireland, and the UK joined in 1973, Greece in 1979, and Portugal and Spain in 1986.

European Currency Unit (Ecu) A unit of account introduced by the
*European Economic Community (EEC) when forming the *European
Monetary System (EMS) in 1979. The Ecu was a form of international money
used by various offical European bodies in their accounting, but very little by
other financial markets. Its value was equal to a weighted average of the
currencies of several member countries. The Ecu was superseded by the Euro,
when this was adopted in 1999.

European Economic Community (EEC) The European common market set
up in 1958 by the original six members of the European Coal and Steel
Community (ECSC). These were Belgium, France, (West) Germany, Italy,
Luxembourg, and the Netherlands. The EEC was combined with the European
Atomic Energy Community in 1967 to form the *European Community (EC). The
aims of the EEC included the abolition of tariffs and quota restrictions on trade
between members, the adoption of a common tariff on trade with non-members,
full mobility of workers and capital between members, harmonization of social
and economic legislation, and a *Common Agricultural Policy (CAP).

European economic integration The process by which the various
countries of Europe are becoming more closely linked, particularly in trade
and finance. This is partly the result of natural economic developments: trade
through the rise of intraindustry trade, which is increasingly important in
industrialized countries situated close together, and financial links via the
general move to financial deregulation and the abolition of exchange
controls. Integration has also been promoted by deliberate policy, through the
formation of numerous European institutions, including the European
Community (EC), now the *European Union (EU), the *European Free Trade
Association (EFTA), and the European Monetary Union (EMU), with the Euro as
a common European currency. Several Eastern European and Mediterranean
countries joined the EU in 2004, and further integration will follow if and
when Bulgaria, Romania, and Turkey join.

European Free Trade Association (EFTA) An association of European
countries with free trade between them, established in 1959. The original
members were Austria, Denmark, Norway, Portugal, Sweden, Switzerland,
and the UK. Finland and Iceland joined later; Denmark and the UK left when
they joined the European Economic Community (EEC) in 1973, as did Portugal
in 1986 and Austria, Finland, and Sweden in 1995. EFTA is a *free-trade area
and not a *customs union, and the free-trade provisions are restricted to
goods originating in member countries. EFTA has an industrial free-trade
agreement with the European Union.

European Monetary Institute An European organization set up to study
the problems of organizing a *European Central Bank (ECB).

European Monetary System (EMS) A European organization set up in
1979 to co-ordinate monetary policy and exchange rates in Europe. Its main
practical activity has been running the *Exchange Rate Mechanism (ERM); its
other activity has been discussing the possibility of movement towards a
*European Monetary Union (EMU), which would involve the closer
co-ordination of monetary policy under a European System of Central Banks
(ESCB), and ultimately a common European currency, and the setting up of a
*European Central Bank (ECB) to control it.

European Monetary Union (EMU) The common monetary system for
Europe. This includes co-ordination of monetary policies, the creation of the
*European Central Bank (ECB), and the adoption of the single European
currency.

European Single Market The target of complete integration of the
economies of members of the European Community (EC), now *European
Union (EU). According to the Single European Act of 1986 this process should
have been completed by 1992. This was supposed to allow free movement of
goods, workers, and capital between member countries, and to remove
discrimination in the award of public contracts, transport, and insurance. It
was believed that this would lead to considerable gains in efficiency.

European Union (EU) The name since 1993 of the former European
Community (EC). The EU was formed with twelve members; Belgium, Denmark,
France, Germany, Greece, Ireland, Italy, Luxembourg, the Netherlands,
Portugal, Spain and the United Kingdom. Austria, Finland and Sweden joined
in 1995; ten Central and Eastern European and Mediterranean countries joined
in 2004, and applications from Bulgaria, Romania, and Turkey are pending.

Europe, fortress *See* fortress Europe.

evasion, tax *See* tax evasion.

evolutionary theory of the firm The view that the survival of firms is
an evolutionary process. Because of limited information and bounded
rationality, firms cannot deliberately choose strategies which guarantee
survival. Actual survival is due to a combination of a corporate philosophy
which leads to the choice of strategies appropriate to a firm's economic
environment, and sheer chance.

ex ante As viewed in advance. The ex ante value of a variable is what the
person or organization responsible expects it to be. An individual's ex ante
savings, for example, is the amount they intend to save. Ex ante is
contrasted with *ex post, meaning as viewed after the event. Ex ante plans
may not get carried out: individuals may save more than they intended if
the goods they meant to buy are not available, or may save less if their
incomes fall unexpectedly. Ex ante investment is what a firm intends to
invest. Actual or ex post investment may be less than ex ante if building
operations are delayed, or ex post investment may be more than ex ante if
goods produced cannot be sold, so that stocks accumulate unexpectedly. It is
necessary for equilibrium that when aggregated over the whole economy ex
ante plans should be consistent. Ex ante variables usually cannnot be
directly observed: individuals or firms often do not announce their
intentions, and even if they do one may not necessarily believe the
announcements. This is in contrast to ex post variables which are all in
principle observable and consistent.

excess capacity Equipment in excess of the amount firms find it economic
to maintain, given their expectations of demand for their products. Firms
normally aim to have equipment capable of producing more than the average
expected demand for their products: this is to allow for random fluctuations
or expected growth in demand, and for occasional breakdowns of equipment.

All capacity costs money to maintain; excess capacity is that which is not worth the maintenance costs, and so is likely to be scrapped.

excess demand A situation when the quantity of a good demanded exceeds the quantity supplied. In markets where a *market-maker maintains the price by buying all supplies offered and supplying the demands of other market participants, excess demand can be directly measured. In all other markets it cannot be directly observed, but has to be inferred from various market signals. These include abnormally long queues or unusually late delivery dates; unusually low or zero stocks; abnormal efforts by customers to find alternative suppliers; and in the labour market, a widening of normal fields of recruitment. Excess demand makes it likely that prices or wages will rise.

excess profits Profits which are larger than the writer regards as normal. There is no objective definition of excess profits: opinions that profits are excessive are normally based on comparisons, either with the rate of return on capital obtainable in other industries with a comparable degree of risk, or with the past profits of the same company.

excess supply A situation where at the existing price the quantity of a good or service supplied is greater than that demanded. In markets where a *market-maker stabilizes the price by meeting all other people's offers to supply and their demands, excess supply can be measured directly. In all other markets excess supply cannot be measured directly, but has to be inferred from various market signals. These include the absence of queues or abnormally early delivery dates; exceptional selling efforts by producers; abnormally high or rising levels of stocks; and in labour markets, unusually high figures for unemployment. Excess supply makes price cuts likely, and wage cuts possible though unlikely.

exchange 1. Trading one good or asset for another. This usage appears in the phrase 'fair exchange is no robbery', and in exchange of contracts between the buyer and seller of land or buildings. *See also* voluntary exchange.
  2. A place where trading is carried on: thus shares were traded at the stock exchange, corn was traded at a corn exchange, and workers were hired at a labour exchange. In many cases most of the trade is nowadays done electronically; the stock exchange is an institution rather than a physical place. *See also* commodity market, and stock exchange.
  3. Money, from its use in trade; money is a *medium of exchange. Foreign exchange is the money of other countries. An exchange rate is the price at which one currency can be traded for another, and different currencies are traded in the foreign exchange market. *See also* foreign exchange, and medium of exchange.

exchange control A system under which holders of a national currency require official permission or approval to convert it into other currencies. Exchange control may apply to all holders of a currency, or some holders, normally non-residents, may be exempt. Where non-residents are allowed convertibility, exchange control has to be applied to transfers from resident to non-resident domestic currency bank accounts. Exchange controls can be applied with varying degrees of strictness; frequently they are much more stringent on obtaining foreign currency for capital account than for current account purposes.

Exchange Equalization Account A UK government account at the *Bank of England, in which the country's gold and foreign exchange reserves are held. This account is used to intervene in the foreign exchange market.

exchange rate The price of one currency in terms of another. This can be quoted either way round: if one pound is worth two dollars, one dollar is worth 50p, or half a pound; it is necessary to check which system is being used. A par exchange rate is that agreed between governments, or registered with a central authority such as the *International Monetary Fund (IMF) or *European Monetary System (EMS). A market exchange rate is the actual price on foreign exchange markets. Market prices of foreign exchange are liable to fluctuate, between narrow margins in a fixed exchange rate system, and much more widely under a floating or flexible rate system. In countries with exchange controls, there may be *multiple exchange rates: the price of foreign currency varies according to the use the central bank believes a purchaser intends to make of it. In countries with *convertible currencies there is at any one time only a single exchange rate with any given foreign currency. Because of transactions costs and some element of monopoly in dealing with small buyers and sellers of currencies, banks generally charge more to sell foreign exchange than they offer to buy it, particularly in the case of small amounts and low-denomination notes. In the markets used by banks and large commercial organizations the range of prices is much smaller. There are three exchange rates between any three currencies: where all are quoted on foreign exchange markets, arbitrage ensures that they will be consistent. Major currencies have quoted rates with all other currencies; where trade contacts between small and remote countries are small or non-existent, there is no foreign exchange market, and anybody wishing to shift between two such currencies has to trade via a major currency, such as the US dollar.

All this refers to nominal exchange rates: these are contrasted with real exchange rates, which compare the relative prices of different countries' products. A country's real exchange rate may change either through a change in its nominal exchange rate, or through a domestic inflation rate faster or slower than its trading partners. *See also* crawling peg exchange rates, effective exchange rate, fixed exchange rate, floating exchange rate, misaligned exchange rate, multiple exchange rates, and realignment of exchange rates.

exchange rate bands Limits to variations in exchange rates. A country commits itself to hold the exchange rate between its own currency and some foreign currency or currencies within a limited band. Exchange rate bands may be broad or narrow: under the *Exchange Rate Mechanism (ERM), for example, at one time most members of the *European Monetary System (EMS) agreed to keep their currencies within 2¼ per cent of parity with the *European Currency Unit (Ecu), an average of European currencies, while the UK and Italy only committed themselves to broader bands, of 6 per cent each side of parity.

Exchange Rate Mechanism (ERM) A feature of the *European Monetary System (EMS), by which EMS members agreed to maintain the relative prices of their currencies within narrow limits. This was done by keeping each country's value in *European Currency Units (Ecus) within 2¼ per cent of an agreed parity grid of par values. Some currencies, including sterling, were allowed a wider range of 6 per cent. These values could be realigned only by mutual agreement. The ERM was founded in 1979, and over the first few years parities were realigned several times. The UK joined the ERM in 1990, but was forced to leave it in 1992 by speculation against the pound. The ERM was replaced when the Euro was adopted in 1999. *See also* narrow-band ERM.

exchange rate regime The system by which exchange rates between different currencies are determined. There are a number of possible systems, ranging from the *gold standard, under which all countries are permanently committed to maintaining fixed exchange rates, to a freely floating system in which no effort is made to stabilize exchange rates, which are left to be determined entirely by market forces. Under the gold standard each country makes its currency convertible into gold at a fixed price, or the central bank operates buying and selling prices which differ only by a small percentage, and trade in gold is not controlled. The exchange rate between two currencies on the gold standard cannot move far from par, since this would make it profitable for *arbitrageurs to buy gold from one central bank and sell it to the other. Under the *Bretton Woods system, which operated from after the Second World War until 1971, countries registered par values for their currencies with the *International Monetary Fund (IMF), and undertook to keep market exchange rates within a small margin of variation from these rates. The difference from the gold standard was that countries retained the right to change their par rates in the event of 'fundamental disequilibrium', which was never defined. This 'adjustable peg' system meant that government commitment to existing par rates lacked credibility, so that speculators frequently forced countries with weak currencies to devalue. Since 1973 the world has been on a flexible exchange rate system. As governments are worried that speculation might lead to violent instability in exchange rates, floating is generally not 'pure' or 'clean', but 'managed' or 'dirty', with considerable intervention by central banks to try to limit fluctuations in exchange rates, not always successfully.

Under a generally adopted fixed exchange rate system, each country has a choice as to whether to join it or opt for flexible rates. Under a floating rate system, no country has this choice: if other currencies are all floating against each other, a single country can choose to peg its exchange rate with some other, usually a larger country with which it does a lot of its trade. Some smaller countries peg their currencies to the US dollar or French franc, but their exchange rates with all other currencies still float. Alternatively, they can peg their currencies to a basket of other currencies: the rates with any single currency will still float. It is possible for a group of countries to decide to link their currencies, as in the *Exchange Rate Mechanism (ERM) of the *European Monetary System (EMS). This still leaves them floating relative to the currencies of non-member countries, such as the US dollar. Where a country decides to manage its exchange rate, this can be done either by discretionary action by the central bank, or by setting down rules about the procedure to be followed, for example a *'crawling peg' system, which attempts simply to slow down changes rather than aiming at any fixed target.

exchange restrictions *See* exchange control.

excise duty A tax levied on the consumption of particular goods. These may be levied to raise government revenue, and are often levied at higher rates on goods whose consumption is believed to have adverse effects on public health, public order, or the environment. Excise duties on alcoholic drinks, tobacco, and petrol are widely used for both purposes.

exclusion The legal right and practical ability to prevent others from using a good. If a good is to be a private good it must be possible to exclude others from using it at reasonable cost. If it is impossible or unduly expensive to exclude others from using a good, it cannot be sold, and thus can only be provided by a public body or a voluntary organization.

exclusive dealing An agreement between the producer and a distributor of certain goods that one will trade only with the other. This may apply generally, or within a particular country or district. In some cases this means that a retailer agrees to stock only one manufacturer's brands; in other cases a manufacturer agrees to sell through only one outlet in a given area. It is possible for both forms of restriction to apply. Such practices are criticized as being in restraint of trade. Economies of scale may sometimes make the actual trade flows stipulated in such agreements efficient, but it is argued that in such cases the same result would be produced by market forces, so that no agreement is necessary. Defenders of exclusive dealing arrangements argue that they promote efficient trading patterns by protecting both parties against opportunistic conduct by the other. Once one party has sunk capital in equipment designed for handling trade with the other, their partner can improve the terms they trade on by threatening to switch to rival partners; exclusive dealing arrangements help to prevent this. Suppliers may also fear loss of reputation if their goods are handled by unqualified distributors, or if customers fail to appreciate that unsatisfactory goods sold through an outlet linked with their brand name are not actually theirs.

ex dividend Sale of shares where the vendor retains the right to a dividend already declared but not yet paid. This is contrasted with cum dividend, where the sale includes the right of the purchaser to receive a dividend already declared but not yet paid.

executive, chief See chief executive.

exercise price The price at which an *option gives the right to buy or sell shares, commodities, or currencies. The option will only be exercised if this price is more favourable to the party holding it than the market price. A put option will only be used to sell assets if the exercise price is higher than the market price, and a call option will only be used to buy assets if the exercise price is lower than the market price.

exhaustible resources Resources of which only a finite quantity exists, so that any constant rate of extraction must eventually cause them to run out. As the earth is of finite size, this must in principle apply to every mineral resource. In the case of some resources, such as oil, known reserves which it is economic to exploit by known techniques would run out relatively soon. The continuation of modern civilization for more than a few decades therefore depends on some combination of discoveries of new reserves, improvements in technology so that currently inaccessible reserves can be exploited, or technical progress to devise alternative fuels. In the case of some other materials such as rare metals, improvements in recycling techniques can also be hoped for. Iron ore reserves are luckily so vast that we can assume that civilization will have come to a bad end for some other reason long before they approach exhaustion.

Eximbank *See* Export Import Bank.

exit 1. Departure of a firm from an industry. This will normally occur if a firm is making losses and sees no prospect that the market will recover. Exit is easier, the greater the second-hand value of the firm's assets. Employment protection legislation or other public regulations may hinder a firm wishing to discontinue part of its business while continuing to trade. If a firm is insolvent there is nothing the law can do to prevent it from exiting entirely from the economy, unless the government is willing to carry on the business at the taxpayer's expense. Where an enterprise is actually profitable but the firm owning it is not, due to excessive debt charges, the firm will normally exit but the enterprise will continue under new ownership.

2. The expression of preferences by leaving unsatisfactory situations: this can apply to selling shares, changing jobs, or migration between areas or countries. It is contrasted with 'voice', which is attempting to change the situation one is in by voting, lobbying, or use of complaints procedures or litigation.

exit, freedom of *See* free exit.

exit price The price below which firms will leave an industry. This is likely to be somewhat below the break-even price, as *sunk costs cannot be avoided by exit.

exogenous expectations Expectations which are not explained, but are taken as fixed by some exogenous forces. This is a convenient assumption in small economic models, where explaining expectations formation would involve extending the analysis too widely. It is also a sensible view of other people's expectations, which are historically determined in the short run, and cannot be influenced by the actions of any economic agents save the very largest, notably governments. In a more complete economic model, expectations need to be explained, and cannot sensibly be treated as exogenous.

expectations What people expect to happen. Some models simply take expectations as exogenous, that is, no analysis is attempted of how they are formed. Static or myopic expectations models assume that people expect the present situation, whatever it is, to continue. Adaptive expectations models assume that what people expect reacts gradually to what they observe. If actual observations are constant or vary randomly around a constant level, adaptive expectations gradually come to be approximately correct; but if the actual has a trend, adaptive expectations lag behind, and are systematically incorrect. Extrapolative expectations assume that observed trends over the past will continue in the future. Model-consistent, or rational expectations assume that people use all available information to avoid making predictable errors in their forecasts. The *expectations-augmented Phillips curve relates wage increases to unemployment, taking into account expectations about price inflation. Some expectations tend to be self-fulfilling: for example, if people expect the price of an asset to rise, they will buy or delay selling in anticipation of this, which itself tends to raise the price. In other cases expectations tend to be self-frustrating: for example, if farmers who anticipate higher prices grow more of a crop, this tends to limit any rise in price. Expectations cannot be directly observed, but have to be inferred from people's actions. Even if organizations announce their plans, such announcements are usually intended to influence other people's decisions, so cannot be taken at face value. *See also* adaptive expectations, elasticity of expectations, exogenous expectations, extrapolative expectations, rational expectations, and self-fulfilling expectations.

expectations-augmented Phillips curve A version of the Phillips curve, relating wage increases to demand pressure, taking account of expected inflation. If the expected rate of price increases is given, the Phillips curve shows wage increases as a decreasing function of the unemployment rate, or an increasing function of demand pressure. Wage increases lead to price increases, so actual inflation is an increasing function of demand pressure. If the expected inflation rate did not respond, and the Phillips curve stayed the same from period to period, it would be possible by the use of monetary or fiscal measures to expand demand to get permanently higher employment at the price of accepting a higher rate of inflation. The expectations-augmented Phillips curve assumes that if actual inflation rises, expected inflation will also increase, and the Phillips curve will move upwards so as to give the same expected real wage increase at each employment level. Under this model there is no long-run trade-off between unemployment and inflation. To achieve an unemployment rate below the *non-accelerating inflation rate of unemployment (NAIRU) would involve an ever-increasing rate of inflation. This is thought to be undesirable, since while moderate rates of inflation may do relatively little harm, *hyperinflation seriously interferes with the efficient running of the real economy by impairing the economic functions of money.

expectations, model-consistent *See* rational expectations.

expected inflation The rate of inflation that people expect. In fact, people are likely to have a frequency distribution of possible rates of inflation over any given future period; this may be different for different time horizons. Expected inflation cannot be directly observed, except by surveys in which people are asked to state their expectations, which normally produce only point estimates, of low reliability. The rate of inflation that people expect can be inferred from the difference between the prices of index-linked and unindexed government securities with the same maturity dates. The greater the expected rate of inflation, the greater the excess of the price of indexed securities over those of comparable unindexed ones.

expected utility The mean level of utility expected from future consumption or asset holdings, when only the distribution of possible values of these is known. If x is consumption, $f(x)$ its frequency distribution, and $U(x)$ the utility level given x, then expected utility is $E[U(x)]$. If utility is a linear function of x, then

$$E[U(x)] = U[E(x)],$$

that is, expected utility is the utility of the expected value of consumption. If utility is a concave function of consumption, that is,

$$d^2U/dx^2 < 0,$$

when the value of x is uncertain expected utility is less than the utility of expected consumption;

$$E[U(x)] < U[E(x)],$$

the difference requiring a risk premium.

expected value The mean of the distribution of the values an economic variable is expected to take. If p_t is the price of a good at time t, $E[p_t]$ is its expected value. To specify the time when an expectation is held, the expectation held at time $t - 1$ can be written $_{t-1}E[p_t]$ and the expectation held at time $t - n$ can be written $_{t-n}E[p_t]$. In the absence of any indication as to when an expectation was held, it is normally assumed that it refers to the previous period in a discrete-time model, and to the moment before the actual level of p_t becomes known in a continuous-time model.

expenditure Spending, by consumers, investors, or the government. Consumer expenditure is restricted to purchasing real goods and services; acquiring assets or making transfers to others by individuals does not count as expenditure. Government expenditure is treated differently: some government expenditure is on real goods and services, but government interest payments and transfer payments to individuals, such as pensions, are counted as government expenditure, and government spending is not clearly divided between current and capital account items, possible because these are hard to distinguish. An *expenditure tax would be a tax on individual consumer spending. National expenditure is what a country spends, as contrasted with national product, which is what it produces. *See also* capital expenditure, consumer expenditure, cuts in expenditure, government expenditure, and tax expenditure.

expenditure-based deflator A price index whose weights reflect the shares of different goods and services in expenditure, rather than shares in production. This includes import prices and excludes export prices.

expenditure changing An economic policy intended to change total expenditure. This may be through fiscal policy, for example a tax cut, or through monetary policy, via a reduction in interest rates. It is contrasted with an *expenditure switching policy, intended to divert expenditure from one outlet to another, for example the use of tariffs or import quotas to switch spending from imported onto home-produced goods. *See also* the figure for internal and external balance.

expenditure method The method of calculating domestic product using information on expenditure by various sectors of the economy, including consumers, investors, and the government. This naturally produces a figure at *market prices. The expenditure method is contrasted with the other two methods, the output method, which proceeds by adding the net outputs of various sectors of the economy, and the income method, which proceeds by adding up the incomes of various sectors.

expenditure, public *See* government expenditure.

expenditure switching A policy intended to divert an existing level of expenditure from one outlet to another. For example, tariffs or import quotas could be used to divert existing spending from imports onto home-produced goods. This is contrasted with *expenditure changing policies, intended to increase or decrease total spending. The distinction applies to the impact effect of the policy concerned: if an expenditure switching policy is successful it will produce multiplier effects which also change total spending. *See also* the figure for internal and external balance.

expenditure tax A suggested alternative to income tax, taxing expenditure in place of income. This is defended on the grounds that it would tax people on what they take out of the economy rather than what they put in. A system of allowances in respect of special occasions of major expenditure, such as marriage, family formation, and major illness would probably be necessary. On the other hand an expenditure tax would be better than a progressive income tax for people with very irregular incomes. Direct measurement of individuals' total expenditure would probably be impossible, given the extent of the *unofficial economy. Levying an expediture tax would therefore involve measuring savings as well as income. A major difficulty with a change to an expenditure tax is posed by the transition: in their life cycles people accumulate assets during their working lives and run them down after retirement. Those who retire near to the change-over date would have paid tax on their incomes while they were accumulating their assets, but would be taxed on their expenditure while they reduced them. This would be widely regarded as unfair.

exploitation 1. Making use of something. An oil-rich country, for example, exploits its mineral resources. This is an entirely value-free usage; it is contrasted with the pejorative usage.

2. Taking unfair advantage of somebody. Sweatshop employers are said to exploit ill-informed immigrant workers, and multinational firms are accused of exploiting less developed countries (LDCs) from which they buy primary commodities on monopolistic terms.

exponent Another name for a power; if $y = x^n$, n is the exponent. An exponent need not be an integer; if z is the natural logarithm of x, so that $x = e^z$, we have $y = x^n = (e^z)^n = e^{zn}$, which can be calculated using the series for powers of e.

exponential A mathematical function with the property that it is equal to its own first derivative. Define $e^x = \exp(x) = 1 + x + (x^2/2!) + (x^3/3!) + \ldots + (x^N/N!) + \ldots$, where $N!$ denotes N factorial $= N(N-1)(N-2)\ldots(2)(1)$. If this series is differentiated term by term, the same series is obtained; every term equals the derivative of the term following, and the derivative of 1 is 0. The same series with $x = 1$ gives $e = \exp(1)$, the exponential constant, which is the base for natural logarithms: the natural logarithm (ln) of e^x is x. If $x = gt$, the exponential e^{gt} grows over time at the proportional rate g.

exportables Goods and services of types which could be exported, whether they are in fact exported or not. Many countries consume at home some of the goods they export: for example, Argentines eat beef and Venezuelans burn oil. Where exports and goods for domestic use are identical or similar, their prices tend to move together.

export concentration Concentration of exports on a narrow range of categories of goods and services, or a narrow range of countries. The higher its degree of export concentration, the more liable are a country's balance of trade and national income to disruption by fluctuations in the sectors of the world economy in which it is concentrated. More widely dispersed markets give a lower degree of risk. Export concentration is generally highest in some of the oil-exporting countries, and some of the world's smaller primary commodity exporters. It is generally low in industrial counties.

export control Restriction of exports by governments. This is less common than export promotion, but can occur in a number of special cases. These include defence considerations, where governments prevent the export of advanced weapons and equipment used in making them to countries which they regard as unfriendly. Some countries restrict the export of raw materials to encourage the growth of domestic processing industries. Some countries have restricted the export of machinery to try to prevent the rise of foreign industries to compete with their own. Export controls are little used, partly because they have an immediate adverse effect on the balance of trade.

export credit The system of selling exports on credit rather than for cash payment. Exports of commodities and consumer goods are frequently financed by trade bills, or short-term credit. These are normally payable in 3 or 6 months, giving the buyer time to ship goods and distribute them for resale, thus providing the money to pay the bills. If the seller needs immediate cash, bills can be discounted, that is sold to discount houses. Producer goods normally need longer-term credit. This may be given by the sellers, or by intermediary financial institutions. The length of credit available is an important factor affecting the marketability of capital goods exports. Many countries promote their exports by providing either subsidized export credit, or guarantees on more favourable terms than can be obtained commercially. Export credits are governed by international agreement between the OECD countries.

export credit agency A body set up to provide credit to export customers or guarantees of credit granted by exporters. Where the interest charged for credits or the premiums charged for guarantees are below what is available in the market, state subsidies for export credit agencies are a form of export subsidy.

Export Credits Guarantee Department (ECGD) A UK government department responsible for encouraging UK exports by insuring exporters against risks. These include both the risk of default on the part of export customers, and the risk of loss through the imposition of import licensing or exchange controls by the importers' governments. Export credits may be for any period up to 10 years; the premiums charged may constitute an implicit subsidy if they fail to reflect the full cost of risks.

Export Import Bank (Eximbank) An agency of the US federal government set up to promote US trade. The Eximbank assists US exports by providing finance, or guaranteeing or insuring private loans to finance them.

export incentives Devices used by countries to encourage exports. These can include tax incentives for exporters, allowing them exemptions from the normal provisions of anti-monopoly legislation, preferential access to capital markets, priority allocations of materials in countries where these are controlled, allowing exporters to retain export earnings rather than having to exchange them at the official exchange rate in countries with over-valued currencies, and official honours for successful exporters.

export-led growth Growth in which exports increase faster than other components of national expenditure. This can occur either because foreign incomes are growing faster than at home, or because domestic products are becoming more competitive in world markets, through lower prices, increased variety, or quality improvements. The disadvantage of growth led by domestic consumption or investment is that it is liable to lead to balance-of-payments problems, as imports tend to rise faster than exports. Export-led growth will also tend to increase imports, but it is less likely to involve a country in balance-of-payments problems than growth led by an expansion of domestic spending.

export multiplier *See* foreign trade multiplier.

export promotion 1. Government activities to help sell exports by providing export incentives at home, and various forms of practical assistance for exporters abroad. These include advice on local trading laws and practices, the provision of export credits or guarantees on favourable terms, and diplomatic pressure, including tying aid to export sales.
    2. A strategy for promoting economic development in less developed countries (LDCs). This involves running an open economy, relying on foreign markets to allow export-led growth. This strategy has been successfully used by many countries, including the *newly industrialized countries (NICs) of East Asia. It is contrasted with the strategy of import replacement, where countries started to industrialize by protecting local industries against imports.

export restraint, voluntary *See* voluntary export restraint.

exports Goods and services produced in a country and sold to non-residents. Visible exports are goods sent abroad; invisible exports are services sold to non-residents. Some invisibles, for example air and sea transport, are services performed abroad. In the case of other invisibles, non-residents come to a country to use the services of hotels, hospitals, universities or casinos. In the case of services such as insurance the location of the service is not defined. Export of capital means making loans to non-residents or buying real assets located abroad. This should not be confused with exporting capital goods. Some countries do both, but it is perfectly possible, like some oil-exporting countries, to export capital without producing capital goods, and many industrial countries are capital goods exporters while borrowing abroad. *See also* net exports.

export subsidy A subsidy to exporters, so that the price per unit received by the producers of exports is higher than the price charged to foreign customers. Direct export subsidies are prohibited by international agreement, but other government measures with similar effects are not uncommon. Exporters may be allowed refunds on tariffs on their inputs, subsidized credit, preferential access to ordinary credit in an economy, or assistance with their capital costs or training costs. In economies with either currency or direct controls on imports, exporters can be allowed priority in the allocation of scarce materials or foreign currency. Firms competing with imports which they claim have received export subsidies may be able to obtain countervailing import duties to offset the effects of these subsidies.

export surplus An excess of exports over imports.

ex post The value of a variable as it appears after the event, that is, what actually occurred. Ex post is contrasted with *ex ante, which means looking at things before the event; that is, ex ante concerns people's plans. If what actually happens is correctly recorded, ex post figures for the economy must be consistent, whereas ex ante plans need not be consistent. If the economy were in equilibrium, the ex ante and ex post values of all variables would be equal.

exposure to risk The extent to which lending institutions would lose if particular borrowers or classes of borrower were to default on their obligations. Exposure to risk can be kept down both by choosing relatively safe forms of investment, such as the government debt of countries considered unlikely to default, and by avoiding having too large a percentage of assets invested in the debt of any one borrower or class of borrower.

external balance A sustainable pattern of transactions with the rest of the world. With no capital movements, in a static economy external balance requires a zero balance of payments on current account, since otherwise foreign exchange reserves would become exhausted if there was a current account deficit, and would expand without limit if there was a current account surplus. Without capital movements a growing economy which needs to add to its foreign exchange reserves requires a current account surplus just sufficient for this purpose. With capital movements, external balance means that these are at a sustainable level, at least in the medium run. In an economy with good domestic investment opportunities and low savings, capital inflows and a current account deficit could represent external balance. Conversely, in an economy with high savings and poor domestic investment opportunities, capital outflow and a current account surplus could represent external balance. Common signs of external imbalance are falling foreign exchange reserves and rapidly rising external debt. *See also* the figure for internal balance.

external diseconomy A cost arising from an economic activity which does not fall on the person or firm controlling the activity. For example, factories pollute the atmosphere or rivers, and traffic using crowded roads inflicts delay on other vehicles and health damage on pedestrians. While conscience may restrain some polluters, in general activities which cause external diseconomies are carried on in excess of the levels that would be socially optimal. External diseconomies can be restricted by prohibiting some polluting activities and taxing others, but a complete cure on these lines is difficult because in many areas, including power generation and transport, a modern economy relies on polluting activities on a massive scale, and no 'green' alternatives are available.

external economy A benefit arising from an economic activity which does not accrue to the person or firm controlling the activity. For example, lambs on farms and externally attractive buildings give pleasure to the general public who cannot normally be charged for the privilege of looking at them. The full benefits of innovations rarely accrue to the innovators: other people can use an innovation as inspiration for further development, and can learn from the first innovator's mistakes. While considerations of altruism and prestige influence some people to expand activities confering external economies beyond what would privately be most profitable, in general such activities tend to be conducted on a smaller scale than would be socially optimal.

externality A cost or benefit arising from any activity which does not accrue to the person or organization carrying on the activity. External costs or diseconomies are damage to other people or the environment, for example by radiation, river or air pollution, or noise, which does not have to be paid for by those carrying on the activity. External benefits or economies are effects of an activity which are pleasant or profitable for other people who cannot be charged for them, for example fertilization of fruit trees by bees, or the public's enjoyment of views of private buildings or gardens. Externalities may be technological or pecuniary. Technological externalities affect other people in non-market ways, for example by polluting their water supply; they create a prima facie case for intervention in the interests of efficiency. Pecuniary externalities mean that other people are affected through the market: for example, a new industry may raise labour costs for other employers, or reduce the value of their capital by capturing their customers. Pecuniary externalities do not create any prima facie case for intervention, except possibly on grounds of income distribution. *See also* compensation for externalities, consumption externality, internalizing externalities, network externality, and production externality.

external labour market The system by which recruitment for senior appointments in an organization is mainly by open competition. It is contrasted with an internal labour market, in which senior posts are filled mainly by promoting existing employees in lower-grade jobs. The main merits of an external labour market are that open competition provides a wider choice for senior appointments, and that outsiders may bring new ideas to an organization. The main merits of internal labour markets are that a firm is likely to know more about the strengths and weaknesses of existing employees than outsiders, and that a reputation for internal promotion as its preferred strategy may assist in recruitment and retention of staff.

extrapolate Extend an apparent pattern beyond the actual observations on which it is based. Extrapolation can be applied both to cross-section and time-series data. The elasticity of demand for any good can only be calculated for price levels which have actually occurred. An economist asked to forecast what would happen if price rose a little above its previous maximum, or fell below its previous minimum, can only rely on extrapolation. If demand is inelastic over the whole observed range, it would seem sensible to assume that it would still be inelastic over these extensions to its range. A growth rate for the economy can be calculated from past data on GDP. If asked what growth is likely in the future, it seems likely that if growth in the recent past has been slow, it will continue so. Extrapolation is not proof, but it is used to provide hypotheses whose falsity would be surpising.

extrapolative expectations Expectations based on the assumption that recent trends will continue, for some time at least. In an economy which was growing steadily, such expectations would produce correct forecasts. In an economy subject to both stochastic and cyclical fluctuations, forecasts produced by extrapolation will not be completely reliable, but it may be difficult to do any better. To extrapolate it is necessary to decide what span of the past to consider in calculating past trends, and how far into the future to project any forecasts. Extrapolative forecasts will of course miss changes in trends due to major shocks. Most actual forecasting methods contain some element of extrapolation. The resulting expectations may not be right, but major departures come as surprises.

F

factor cost The value of goods and services at the prices received by sellers. This is the market prices paid by purchasers, minus any indirect taxes, plus any subsidies provided by the government. Factor cost is so called because the value of output at factor cost is the amount available to pay for bought-in inputs and for the services of the factors of production used. Factor cost thus involves treating any profits of the firms concerned as payment for factor inputs.

factor endowment A country's stock of factors of production. The term endowment is rather misleading. So far as land is concerned, its area and location, and the minerals under it are given by nature; but the quality of the land can be improved by drainage or irrigation, and damaged by deforestation and erosion, and known mineral resources reflect effort put into investigating them. The labour force at any time is given by history, but in the long run can be affected by health and social measures which affect birth and death rates, and by policies towards immigration and emigration. The capital stock, again, is pre-determined at any moment by past investment, but its growth is affected by savings and by policy on international capital movements. Human capital can be affected by education and training.

factor incomes Incomes derived from selling the services of factors of production. In the case of labour, this means wages, plus the part of the incomes of the self-employed which is a reward for their own labour. Income from land is rents, including part of the incomes of the self-employed, and part of the imputed incomes of owner-occupiers of houses. Incomes from capital and entrepreneurship are received as dividends, interest, the retained profits of companies and the part of the incomes of the self-employed which is a return on their own capital and entrepreneurship.

factor incomes from abroad Incomes received by residents of a country from activities carried on abroad. This includes remittances by migrants working abroad, profits earned by companies operating abroad, and interest received on loans made abroad. Gross factor incomes from abroad are the total amounts so received; net factor incomes from abroad are these receipts minus any expenditure on similar items earned within the country by non-residents. Net factor incomes from abroad can thus be negative.

factoring Buying goods for resale without further processing. Debt factoring is buying debts due from another business's customers and collecting them.

factor-intensity The relative proportions of various factors of production used in producing goods and services. The factor-intensity of the techniques of production used by a cost-minimizing firm depends on the relative prices of different factors of production. For any given set of relative factor prices, some goods are produced using a lot of labour and little capital: such goods are labour-intensive. Others are produced using a lot of capital and very little labour: such goods are capital-intensive. Agricultural goods may be produced using a lot of land and relatively few other inputs: such products are land-intensive.

factor market The bargaining system in which the prices of the various factors of production are determined. In most economies there is no one institution in which factor prices are determined. Wage rates in Europe are typically decided by a series of negotiations between employers or groups of employers and *trade unions. These negotiations are linked in the sense that what happens in one wage bargain has effects on others, but there is no formal organization of this interaction. Collective bargaining over wages is less common in the US. Even in Europe many occupations, for example domestic cleaners, have no collective bargaining at all. Negotiations over rents of land and the terms on which capital is made available to firms are similarly very decentralized. The argument for referring to this non-system as a market is that it involves a fair degree of competition, and generates a set of factor prices.

factor(s) of production Any resource used in the production of goods or services. Factors of production can be broadly classified into three main groups: labour, or human services; capital, or man-made means of production; and land, or natural resources. Each of these broad groups of factors of production can be subdivided in various ways, for example labour with various amounts of human capital, or land with various mineral contents. *See also* fixed factors, and immobile factors.

factor price equalization A tendency for international trade to reduce international differences in relative factor prices. In the *Heckscher–Ohlin model explaining *inter-industry trade, countries specialize in the production and export of goods whose production requires relatively large inputs of their more plentiful factors of production, and import part or all of their requirements of goods requiring large inputs of their scarcer factors. Imports of goods intensive in scarce factors lower the demand for them, and therefore their factor prices. Exports raise the demand for, and thus the price of, abundant factors. Trade thus tends to reduce international differences in relative factor prices. If there were no transport costs and no restrictions on international trade, complete factor price equalization could result. In the presence of transport costs and *trade barriers, trade tends merely to reduce international factor price differences. The fact that actual divergences in factor prices are large and persistent has complex causes. These include the fact that factors with the same name but in different countries may not have much else in common, and the influence of increasing returns, which cause half of real world trade to be *intra-industry rather than inter-industry.

factor prices The prices of the services of factors of production. For labour of various types the factor price is the appropriate wage rate; for land, the rent paid; and for capital, the interest rate. The purchase prices of land and capital goods are not factor prices in this sense. In competitive equilibrium, factor prices would be equal to the marginal product of each factor. In fact not all goods or factor markets are competitive, and the prices of some factors are fixed for some time in advance by contracts. This makes the relation between factor prices and marginal products less clear-cut. Any residual profits after factors have been paid can be argued to be the reward of either entrepreneurship or monopoly; these are hard to distinguish.

factor productivity The value, at constant prices, of the output of a plant, a firm, or an industry per unit of factor input. The factor concerned may be a particular factor only, such as labour or land. *Productivity is often used to mean labour productivity, that is output per unit of labour employed, which may rise or fall for a variety of reasons. These include changes in effort, in the quality of labour employed, in managerial efficiency, in technical knowledge, in the amount of other factors, such as capital, which are employed with each unit of labour, or in the level of output when returns to scale are not constant. Total factor productivity relates the value of output to total factor inputs, aggregated at some set of relative prices. This can change through changes in effort, managerial efficiency, or available techniques, or through scale effects when the ouput level varies.

factor proportions, variable *See* variable factor proportions.

facts, stylized *See* stylized facts.

failure *See* co-ordination failure, and market failure.

fair gamble *See* fair odds.

fair odds The odds which would leave anybody betting on a random event with zero expected gain or loss. For example, if there is 1 chance in 100 that my house will burn down during the next year, actuarially fair odds are 99 to 1 against this happening. If I bet £1, which I lose if my house does not burn down, but get £99 if it does, my expected gain is $(1/100)(£99) - (99/100)(£1) = 0$; the odds are thus actuarially fair.

fair trade Arguments for the use of *protection to help domestic producers compete with imports whose suppliers have some cost advantage claimed to be unfair. There is no straightforward method by which aspects of comparative advantage, such as cheaper labour or cheaper power in one country than another, can be distinguished from 'unfair' cost advantages, such as export subsidies. International differences in labour protection laws or in the regulation of environmental externalities are sometimes cited as unfair advantages, which call for market intervention on 'fair trade' lines. 'Fair trade' is basically an emotive term for protection.

Fair Trading, Office of *See* Office of Fair Trading.

family allowance A UK welfare benefit paid to the parents or guardians of dependent children. The arguments for family allowances are a desire to avoid child poverty, and considerations of horizontal equity, as people with families have more demands on their incomes than childless people with the same income. Family allowances are contrasted with the use of children's allowances as part of the direct tax system: family allowances are more egalitarian, as the poorest parents may lack sufficient income for tax allowances to benefit them. Family allowances are a universal benefit; this contrasts with the US position, where *Aid to Families with Dependent Children (AFDC) is a means-tested benefit targeted towards needier families.

Family Expenditure Survey (FES) A regular survey of the spending of a sample of households in the UK. The FES is a source of data on the earnings as well as the expendure of UK households.

Family Income Supplement (FIS) A UK system of state benefit payments to increase the incomes of some lower-paid workers with family responsibilities.

fan chart A diagram in which the past history of a variable is plotted against time, but its future is shown as a range of forecast values rather than a point. After the present is passed on the time axis, the graph fans out, hence the name. The fan chart is a useful way of reminding policy-makers and the public that forecasts of any economic variable are not perfectly reliable, but are subject to a degree of uncertainty increasing with time.

FAO *See* Food and Agriculture Organization.

Farm Credit System (FCS) A US federation of banks and lending associations of farmers to provide credit to farmers and ranchers. FCS bonds are guaranteed by the US federal government.

farm subsidies Subsidies to farmers. These may take the form of price support payments, to increase farm incomes per unit of output, or direct payments to farmers, for example as compensation for taking land out of cultivation. Such subsidies are designed to increase farm incomes, and slow down the tendency in modern economies for farmers to leave the land. Whether such subsidies are called food or farm subsidies, the benefits are divided between consumers, farmers and landlords.

FCS *See* Farm Credit System.

FCO *See* Federal Cartel Office.

FDIC *See* Federal Deposit Insurance Corporation.

feasible set The set of resource allocations which satisfies all constraints in an economic model. For a consumer, for example, the feasible set is all spending plans which satisfy his or her budget constraint.

Fed *See* Federal Reserve System.

Federal Cartel Office (FCO) The US agency responsible for monitoring mergers, as part of antitrust policy.

Federal Deposit Insurance Corporation (FDIC) A US regulatory body responsible for chartering banks, and insuring depositors against bank failure. While the guarantee covers only a limited sum per depositor, the system leaves only very large depositors with any interest in the safety of banks' lending policies. The FDIC is largely financed by charges on the banks.

federal fiscal system The fiscal system in a federation, with state as well as federal governments. In such a system taxes may be levied, and expenditure incurred, at both levels. It is possible for the central government to tax more than it spends, and make transfers to the states, or for the states to tax more than they spend and make contributions to central funds. In either case, in adding up the total taxes and spending of the government, transfers between the various levels should be netted out.

Federal Reserve System (Fed) The US system of central banking. This consists of a Board of Governors in charge of twelve District Reserve Banks (a district here means a group of states). The Governors are appointed by the

President, with Senate approval. They fix reserve and margin requirements and discount rates, through the Federal Open Market Committee, provide discounting facilities, and appoint the directors of the twelve District Reserve Banks. The District Banks supervise member banks in their regions: member banks are subject to stricter reserve requirements than other banks, but in return can obtain cheaper services from the Fed. The Fed acts as agent in collecting taxes and administering federal government debt, and Federal Reserve Notes form the US currency.

Federal Savings and Loan Insurance Corporation (FSLIC) A US institution to insure the shareholders of federal savings and loan associations, or *thrifts. It is financed by premiums paid by the insured institutions and loans from the federal government.

Federal Trade Commission (FTC) A US federal agency charged with formulating competition policy and maintaining competitive enterprise. The FTC seeks to prevent restraints on trade and price discrimination, and to ensure disclosure of credit costs. It is empowered to investigate and declare illegal unfair and predatory competitive practices. It acts through voluntary compliance wherever possible, or litigation if this fails.

fee, contingent *See* contingent fee.

fiat money Money which circulates only because the state says it shall. Originally money was accepted by users because it consisted of materials which were themselves valuable, such as gold or silver. Rulers originally stamped it into coins merely to certify their contents. Later the contents were decreased in value, and the state required coins to be accepted as worth more than their intrinsic value. Later still banknotes originally gave the holder the right to receive coin to the same face value on demand. Present-day money consists of paper notes with negligible intrinsic value, which is legal tender because the state says it shall be, or of book or computer entries, where the same comments apply. Modern money is fiat money. As its cost of production is negligible there is a great temptation to over-issue it, which many governments are unable to resist. Their subjects often prefer to use as a *store of value objects such as gold or diamonds, which the government cannot debase because they cost real resources to produce.

fiduciary issue The amount of *high-powered money issued by a central bank in excess of its holdings of gold reserves. In the UK in the nineteenth century the fiduciary issue was restricted to control the power of the Bank of England to issue money; during banking crises the Bank of England had to be specially authorized, by suspension of the Bank Act, to exceed this limit. In the twentiethth century nearly all high-powered money has come to consist of a fiduciary issue.

FIFO *See* first-in, first-out.

FIMBRA *See* Financial Intermediaries, Managers and Brokers Regulatory Association.

final goods Goods for use by final users, including consumers, investors, the government, and exporters, as distinct from intermediate products. It is not at all easy to distinguish final goods in practice: fuel, for example, may be bought by consumers or businesses.

Finance Act The UK legislation by which Parliament approves or amends the Chancellor of the Exchequer's budget proposals.

finance, public *See* public finance.

financial assets Money and claims, as distinct from physical assets such as land, buildings or equipment. Financial assets include money, securities giving a claim to receive money, such as bills or bonds, and shares giving indirect ownership of the physical and financial assets of companies. The claims held as financial assets include the obligations of individuals, companies and governments, domestic and foreign. Financial assets include shares in financial institutions, and derivatives such as *options.

financial deregulation The removal or relaxation of regulations affecting the type of business financial firms may undertake, the type of firms permitted to deal in particular markets, or the terms on which dealing is allowed. Financial deregulation has been fashionable in recent years in many countries. Regulations which have been relaxed include controls on the interest rates at which banks can lend or borrow, controls on operations by banks outside their country of registration, and restrictions on the types of business particular financial institutions can transact. Deregulation has been favoured as leading to more competition and efficiency gains, but is open to criticism where it exposes people to risks which through lack of experience they may fail to understand.

financial derivative *See* derivative (financial).

financial futures Futures contracts in currencies or interest rates. Futures contracts, like forward contracts, commit both sides to a transaction on a future date at a pre-arranged price, but futures contracts can be traded in futures markets. These contracts can be used either for *hedging, to reduce the risks traders are exposed to, or for *speculation, taking on extra risk for the sake of expected profits. Financial futures are traded in the UK on the *London International Financial Futures and Options Exchange (LIFFE).

financial innovation Changes in financial institutions, financial instruments, or business practices in the financial sector. Today's familiar practices, including the use of cheques, cash and credit cards, electronic fund transfers, *futures and *options markets and *derivatives were all innovations when they started. Other innovations have included abolition of fixed commissions and the introduction of screen-based stock exchange dealing, the blurring of the distinctions in the UK between banks and building societies, and the introduction of index-linked government debt. Financial innovation may introduce new dangers to financial stability until experience of new ways is accumulated; it also makes naïve use of statistical series a possible source of error by policy-makers if statistical procedures lag behind the way the real world system is run.

Financial Intermediaries, Managers and Brokers Regulatory Association (FIMBRA) A UK self-regulating organization (SRO) set up under the Financial Services Act to regulate organizations marketing and managing securities, unit trusts, and unit-linked life assurance policies, and independent financial advisers. FIMBRA became part of the system of protection for the private investor under the Personal Investment Authority (PIA) in 1994.

financial intermediary A firm whose main function is to borrow money from one set of people and lend it to another. Financial intermediaries are able to operate profitably because of the economies of scale in collecting savings from many sources and making them available for large loans, and in handling information about large numbers of small debtors or the risks of lending to single large ones. Firms wishing to borrow large amounts do not want the trouble of negotiating with numerous small lenders, and lenders can use financial intermediaries to get a spread of risks in their lending without the high transactions costs of making numerous single small loans to the ultimate users of their money. The use of financial intermediaries reduces risk and transactions costs for both lenders and borrowers.

financial markets The markets in which financial assets are traded. These include *stock exchanges for trading company shares and government debt, the money market for trading short-term loans, the foreign exchange market for trading currencies, and a number of specialized markets trading financial derivatives. Most financial markets now operate minute-by-minute via computer and telephone linkages rather than traders meeting in person, but many participants still prefer to be near to other major market participants, which is why financial markets tend to be concentrated in large business centres such as Frankfurt, London, New York, or Paris.

financial ratios Ratios between various items in a company's accounts and the market value of its shares. These include the *price-earnings (P/E) ratio, that is the ratio of the market price to earnings per share, and the price-dividend (P/D) ratio, that is the ratio of the market price to the latest dividend paid per share. These ratios are used in comparing the merits of investing in different companies. The market price is of course affected by information more recent than the latest published earnings and dividend figures.

financial repression The imposition of liquidity constraints through allocation of loans by administrative means rather than use of the market. Financial repression may be adopted through a desire to influence the distribution of investment in the economy, or to facilitate extortion by those responsible for allocating funds.

financial sector The part of the economy concerned mainly with lending and borrowing, long or short term. This includes banks, non-bank financial intermediaries such as building societies (UK) or savings and loan associations (US), as well as merchant banks, insurance companies, pension funds, and a range of financial managers and advisers.

financial security *See* security.

Financial Services Act The UK legislation governing the regulation of investment business by means of the *Securities and Investment Board (SIB) supervising a system of self-regulating organizations (SROs).

Financial Times Actuaries All-Share Index An index of the prices of shares traded on the London Stock Exchange, including ordinary shares and fixed-interest stocks and covering the financial sector as well as industry. This index covers most trade in the London market.

Financial Times Actuaries Share Indexes Share indexes for various sectors of the London Stock Exchange: the widest coverage is that of the FTA

World Share Index, based on 2,400 share prices from twenty-four countries. The widest UK index is the FTA All-Share Index, based on 800 shares and fixed-interst stocks.

Financial Times Industrial Ordinary Share Index (FT 30) An index of the share prices on the London Stock Exchange of thirty leading UK industrial and commercial companies. This index excludes banking and insurance shares and government stocks. This index started from a base of 100 in 1935.

Financial Times Share Indexes A group of share indexes published by the *Financial Times* of London. They include the Financial Times Industrial Ordinary Share Index, the Financial Times–Stock Exchange 100 Share Index (Footsie), and a number of other widely used share indexes.

Financial Times–Stock Exchange 100 Share Index (FT–SE 100 or Footsie) An index of 100 equities traded on the London Stock Exchange. This index, with a base of 1000 in 1984, covers a list of companies with over £1bn of market capitalization, and is used as the basis for UK futures contracts.

financial year The year used as an accounting period by any organization. This can coincide with the calendar year, but frequently does not. In view of the need to prepare and audit accounts at the end of each financial year, it would be very inconvenient for the accountancy profession if all companies' financial years were to coincide.

financing, official *See* official financing.

fine tuning The effort to make precise adjustments in the level of activity via fiscal and monetary policies. Many economists do believe in the use of fiscal and monetary policies to try to get the level of effective demand into a satisfactory range, but do not believe that efforts at fine tuning are likely to be successful. This is because of lags and minor inaccuracies in the data on which policies are based and our incomplete understanding of the precise mechanisms by which policies affect the economy. Incessant attempts at minor adjustments based on inaccurate data and dominated by short-term objectives may simply act as one more source of random shocks to the economy.

firm The basic unit of decision-taking in a decentralized economy. The theory of the firm models how a firm would behave given assumptions about its objectives, which may include profit maximization, avoidance of risk, and long-run growth. Many firms are run by sole traders, and others are partnerships; larger firms are usually organized as companies. A single firm may have numerous establishments or branches, such as factories or shops. *See also* dominant firm, evolutionary theory of the firm, incumbent firm, managerial theories of the firm, marginal firm, multinational, multi-plant firm, multi-product firm, representative firm, and worker-controlled firm.

firm-specific human capital Specialized skills, experience, or qualifications which are of value only to one specific employer. Skills may be firm-specific because the equipment the firm operates is unique, or because, while the skills are in principle industry-specific, the firm is a monopolist in the industry. Because the holder of firm-specific skills is faced with a monopsonist employer, acquisition of such skills is not particularly attractive to workers; the employer will probably have to pay for any necessary training.

first-best A state of the economy in which all the necessary and sufficient conditions for efficiency are satisfied simultaneously. If all but one such condition were satisfied, it would always be beneficial to satisfy the remaining one. First-best is contrasted with second-best, which states that if two or more of the conditions for efficiency are not satisfied, changes which cause some more, but not all, of the efficiency conditions to be satisfied may not be beneficial.

first-degree price discrimination Price discrimination where consumer are charged the maximum amount they are willing to pay for each unit of a good. This means that the producer obtains all the gains from the good being available, and there is no consumer surplus. Producers generally do not have sufficient information about their customers to be able to practice first-degree price discrimination. In contrast, second-degree price discrimination, where customers are offered a choice of possible contracts, and third-degree price discrimination, where different prices are charged to different classes of customer, are relatively common.

first derivative The rate at which the value of a function increases as its argument increases at any point, if this is defined. In a graph, the first derivative of a function is its slope. If $y = f(x)$, its first derivative at a point x_0 is the limit to which $[f(x_0 + a) - f(x_0)]/a$ tends as a becomes indefinitely small. The first derivative is written dy/dx or $y'(x)$. A function $y(x)$ has a stationary value at x_0 if dy/dx evaluated at x_0 equals zero. A zero first derivative is a necessary but not a sufficient condition for a function to take a maximum or a minimum.

first-in, first-out (FIFO) An accounting convention which assumes that when a firm uses materials it uses first those which it has held in stock longest, so that the first stocks to enter its stores are the first to leave. FIFO is contrasted with last-in, first-out (LIFO), which is the convention that the first stocks to be used are those most recently acquired.

first-mover advantage The benefit from being first in the market with a new product. This leads to a temporary monopoly, which may be profitable, and may last for some time if it can be protected by patents. It can be argued, however, that it is not necessarily a long-term benefit to move first. Later entrants may be able to use the first mover's invention without paying for the research costs, and can learn from the first mover's mistakes. It has been suggested, for example, that the UK suffered during the 20th century as a result of being first with the industrial revolution in the 18th and 19th centuries.

first-order conditions The conditions for a function to take a stationary value. If $y = f(x)$, the first-order condition for a stationary value is $dy/dx = f_x = 0$. For a function of several variables, $y = f(x_1, x_2, \ldots, x_N)$ the first-order conditions for a stationary value are $\partial y/\partial x_i = f_i = 0$ for each i. First-order conditions give necessary but not sufficient conditions for a maximum or minimum. It is necessary to go on to consider second- or higher-order conditions to check whether a stationary value of a function of one variable is a maximum, a minimum, or a point of inflection, and whether a stationary value of a function of several variables is a maximum, a minimum, or a saddle point.

FIS *See* Family Income Supplement.

fiscal drag The tendency under progressive tax systems for the proportion of incomes collected in taxes to rise under inflation. This results from the fact that the threshold at which income tax becomes payable, and the thresholds for the application of higher tax rates, are fixed in money terms. Inflation thus tends to increase the proportion of incomes collected in direct taxes. The existence of some *specific taxes tends to reduce the proportion of incomes collected in indirect taxes when prices rise, however, and the fact that many taxes are collected in arrears also tends to reduce fiscal drag, which is not necessarily positive overall, considering all taxes.

fiscal neutrality The aim of devising a fiscal system which does not cause distortions in the economy. For example, if the tax system allows firms to write off some types of equipment faster than others with a similar actual life, this tends to divert investment into the types of equipment benefiting from more generous allowances. Fiscal neutrality aims to avoid this type of perverse incentive. When it comes to the incentives to work and to save, it is difficult to see how fiscal neutrality can be achieved: taxes inevitably distort the incentive for individuals to enjoy leisure or engage in do-it-yourself activities rather than spend time on paid work, and for businesses to spend effort on *tax avoidance and evasion rather than more efficient production.

fiscal policy The use of taxation and government spending to influence the economy. This may work via changing tax rates or the rules about liability to tax, or via changes in government spending on real goods and services or transfer payments. Fiscal policy can be used both to influence the level of aggregate demand in the economy, and to change the incentives facing firms and individuals so as to encourage or discourage particular forms of activity. *See also* easy fiscal policy, and tight fiscal policy.

fiscal stance The tendency of the tax and spending policies embodied in a government's budget to expand or contract the economy. This involves comparisons with a normal budgetary position. It is argued that a government's fiscal stance cannot be inferred purely from its actual spending and tax revenues, as these are affected by fluctuations in activity. The fiscal stance should therefore be found by comparing the full employment budget surplus or deficit with some normal level. This type of measurement of fiscal stance can only be carried out with the use of a model of how national income changes are reflected in government spending and tax revenues.

fiscal system, federal *See* federal fiscal system.

fiscal year The year used for accounting purposes by a government. In the UK, for example, the fiscal year runs from 6 April to 5 April. The US budget year runs from 1 October to 30 September.

fixed cost The part of total costs which does not depend on the level of current production. This includes items such as management costs and the costs of plant security. Fixed costs do not affect the profit-maximizing level of output in the short run, though in the longer run a firm which cannot cover its fixed costs will become insolvent and exit.

fixed exchange rate A system in which a country's exchange rate remains constant. Normally this means that the exchange rate between the country's currency and some other currency or basket of currencies stays within some small margin of fluctuation around a constant par value. A fixed exchange rate cannot be established by mere policy statements by the government or central bank issuing the currency. Effective policies to maintain a fixed rate and a credible commitment to stick to them are both needed. Maintenance of a fixed exchange rate requires that a country hold sufficient *foreign exchange reserves, which are used for intervention in the foreign exchange market to absorb small variations in willingness to hold its currency, and that monetary and fiscal policies are used sufficiently vigorously to keep these variations small.

fixed factors Factors of production which cannot be withdrawn from a firm even if its output falls. Factors may be fixed because their use is essential if a firm is to stay in business at all. Some are sunk costs, which cannot be recovered even if the firm goes out of business completely.

fixed-interest security A security whose return is fixed, up to some redemption date or indefinitely. The fixed amounts may be stated in money terms, or indexed to some measure of the price level. A fixed-interest security is liable to vary in price with the rate of interest, its price rising as the rate of interest used to find the present discounted value of the fixed receipts falls. This sensitivity to changes in the interest rate increases with the time to maturity of any security.

fixed investment Investment in durable capital equipment, which is expected to last for a long period, and is written off over several years. This is contrasted with investment in stocks and work in progress, which is goods expected to be used up quickly, and not depreciated at all. Fixed investment is not necessarily geographically immobile: it includes goods vehicles and mobile equipment like cranes and earth-movers.

fixprice An economic model in which prices are fixed in the short run, and quantities adjust faster than prices. This is contrasted with a flexprice model, in which quantities are fixed in the short run, and prices adjust faster than quantities. The real world is a mixture of markets where relative prices adjust faster than quantities, for example the foreign exchange market and stock markets, and markets where quantities adjust faster than relative prices, for example the labour market and markets for industrial products.

flag carrier A business which is regarded as contributing to national security and/or national prestige. It is often believed by governments that flag carriers, such as national airlines, should be supported whether or not they are economically viable.

flag of convenience A national registration for a ship which does not correspond to its actual ownership or control. Owners may choose this for tax reasons, to avoid stringent controls on safety and manning prevailing in their own countries, or to allow the use of foreign crew at lower wages than those payable to their own nationals. The practice is bitterly criticised both by national seamen's unions and by owners who do not avail themselves of the opportunities for cost savings offered by the use of flags of convenience.

flexible exchange rate *See* floating exchange rate.

flexible prices Prices which are able to adjust in either direction, as necessary to clear markets. The prices of primary products, that is, fuels, minerals and crops are generally flexible except when there is government intervention in the market. The prices of industrial products are normally less flexible. It is held that with flexible prices there could be no unemployment. This is true by definition for perfectly flexible prices, but if industrial goods prices and wage rates are sticky, making them a bit more flexible would not necessarily help to restore full employment. If prices are expected to fall, but not immediately, this gives an incentive to postpone purchases until prices have actually fallen, which could make recessions worse.

flexible wages Wages which are free to move up and down as necessary to preserve equilibrium in labour markets. Wages are notoriously not normally flexible, particularly not flexible downwards. This is due to a number of reasons. Trade unions are usually strongly opposed to wage cuts, but so are non-unionized workers. This may be because wages are a sign of social status as well as a purely economic reward. Individuals and groups of workers are keenly aware of their differentials compared with others whose skills they regard as inferior: accepting a wage cuts means losing status compared to other groups. It is sometimes argued that flexible wages would prevent unemployment. While perfectly flexible wages would by definition prevent involuntary unemployment, it is not clear that if wages are sticky, making them slightly less so would help. An expectation that wages are due to fall gives an incentive to postpone employing people until after this has actually occurred, so a small increase in wage flexibility might not be beneficial for employment.

flexprice An economic model in which quantities are fixed in the short run, and prices adjust faster than quantities. This is contrasted with a fixprice model, in which prices are fixed in the short run, and quantities adjust faster than prices. The real world is a mixture of markets where relative prices adjust faster than quantities, for example the foreign exchange market and stock markets, and markets where quantities adjust faster than relative prices, for example the labour market and markets for industrial products.

flight, capital *See* capital flight.

flight from money The tendency when inflation is very high for people to abandon the use of money, or at least that of their own country. Under *hyperinflation people refuse to accept money, and try to spend any they receive as quickly as possible. They may substitute other goods, such as cigarettes, as a *medium of exchange, revert to barter, or shift to foreign currency if sufficient is available. Whatever may be the relation between low levels of inflation and economic efficiency, there is no doubt that inflation at levels high enough to cause a flight from money is extremely bad for the efficient working of an economy.

floating, clean *See* pure floating exchange rate.

floating, dirty *See* managed floating exchange rate.

floating exchange rate An exchange rate with no government or central bank action to keep it stable. This is also known as a flexible exchange rate. In a pure or 'clean' float there is no government or central bank intervention at all in the foreign exchange market, and determination of the exchange rate is left to market forces. In a managed or 'dirty' float the monetary authorities of one or both of the countries do intervene in the foreign exchange market, but at their own discretion and not with any systematic effort at complete stabilization of the exchange rate.

floor price The lowest price that a commodity stabilization scheme is intended to allow. The simplest way to ensure that price does not fall below this floor is to stand ready to buy the commodity at the floor price: this can succeed only if the stabilizing body has sufficient funds to be able to buy all the supplies on offer. A second method is to take measures to restrict supply when the market price approaches the floor level.

floor (to trade cycle) The lowest level of real national product during the slump phase of a trade cycle. In a closed economy this will be the lowest level of *injections to the circular flow of incomes plus their multiplier effects. Investment is likely to be at the minimum of non-postponable replacements needed to keep businesses going, plus any non-postponable autonomous investment. Government spending will also have minimum levels, including items such as defence expenditure, long-term public works, pensions and income maintenance payments to the unemployed. *See also* the figure for trade cycle.

flotation The process of making the shares in a public company available for sale to the investing public. Flotation may raise money to finance new company activities, or may enable the owners of existing private companies to realize their assets. It also applies in the *privatization of state-owned businesses. Different methods are used in flotations according to whether likely purchasers of shares are believed to be individual investors or institutions.

flow, cash See cash flow.

flows Economic processes happening over time. These are contrasted with stocks, which are amounts existing at a moment of time. Income, expenditure, and exports are flow variables; capital, the labour force, and debt are stocks. For flow variables an indication of the unit of time over which they are measured is essential: for example, output per hour worked, or pay per week.

fluctuations The tendency of all economic variables to continual variation over time. This combines very short-run variations which appear to be random, or 'white noise', and cyclical oscillations of varying lengths, including 'inventory cycles' of under 2 years, 'trade cycles' of 5 to 10 years, 'building cycles' of around 20 years, and long or 'Kondratieff cycles' of 60 years or more. Such fluctuations appear over all time periods for which we have any data. As they are all happening simultaneously, detecting any one requires sophisticated statistical techniques, and regular oscillations are in the nature of 'stylized facts'.

flying picket A UK term for a picket by strikers at premises other than their normal place of work. A flying picket may seek to persuade workers at the premises picketed to join in industrial action, or to dissuade delivery drivers from making deliveries to or collections from the premises. Use of flying pickets is particularly attractive for strikers whose support at their own place of work is sufficiently solid for little picketing there to be necessary. This practice is now illegal.

fob *See* free on board.

Food and Agriculture Organization (FAO) An agency of the United Nations (UN), responsible for problems of agricultural production and nutrition. It conducts research, provides advice, and promotes education and training in productive techniques in agriculture, forestry, and fishing, in the distribution of their products, and in nutritional standards.

food stamps Documents issued to poor families in the US to entitle them to obtain free or cut-price foodstuffs. This is a working example of the use of *vouchers, a method of ensuring the use of public assistance for an approved purpose, in this case the provision of basic foodstuffs, rather than providing assistance in cash which can be used for any purpose.

food subsidies Subsidies to the sale of foodstuffs, which allow the price paid by the consumer to be below the amount received by the vendor. Food subsidies have been adopted in various countries. They increase the incomes of farmers, and decrease the cost of living for the poorest members of society, who spend the largest share of their incomes on food. As a method of helping the poorest, food subsidies are highly inefficient, as most of the benefit goes to those who do not need it.

footloose industry An industry where there are few advantages in any particular location, so that small differences in cost can lead to large shifts in location. This is contrasted with extractive industries tied to particular inputs, service industries which need to be close to their markets, and industries with large sunk costs, where major shifts in location are difficult.

Footsie *See* Financial Times–Stock Exchange 100 Share Index.

forecasting The production of estimates of future economic events. This includes events which have already occurred, when the official version of the facts has not yet been published. Economic forecasters rely on two standard techniques. One is the use of econometric models based on published statistics of past events. The other is the use of survey data, on the replies of businessmen or others to questions about what they expect to happen. It is possible to combine these in one forecasting method. Economic forecasting is undertaken by various government, academic, and private bodies.

foreclosure Taking over by a lender of a mortgaged property, because of failure by the borrower to comply with the conditions of the *mortgage. This failure usually consists of failure to make interest and amortization payments by the due dates. Foreclosure is usually only resorted to by lenders when considerable arrears have arisen, and normally requires authorization by a court.

foreign aid *See* aid.

foreign currency-denominated borrowing Borrowing denominated in a currency other than that of the debtor's country. If government debt is denominated in foreign currency, this removes the temptation for the government to cause or permit domestic inflation to ease its debt burden. If a country has a record of past inflation, and lenders expect this to continue, foreign currency-denominated borrowing may be cheaper than borrowing in domestic currency, where high interest rates are required to compensate lenders for the risk of further inflation.

foreign direct investment The acquisition by residents of a country of real assets abroad. This may be done by remitting money abroad to be spent on acquiring land, constructing buildings, mines, or machinery, or buying existing foreign businesses. Inward foreign direct investment similarly is acquisition by non-residents of real assets within a country. Once a country has real assets abroad, if these make profits which are ploughed back into expanding enterprises, this should ideally be shown in the balance of payments as receipts on current account balanced by an outflow on capital account. In fact balance-of-payments accounts often show only net remittances of profits as a current account item, ignoring profits earned abroad and ploughed back in both current and capital accounts.

foreign exchange Other countries' money. The foreign exchange rate is the rate at which one country's money can be turned into another's. Foreign exchange reserves are stocks of gold or convertible foreign currency held by central banks or governments to enable them to intervene in foreign exchange markets to influence the exchange rate.

foreign exchange control See exchange control.

foreign exchange markets The markets where foreign exchange is traded. This includes both spot markets, for immediate delivery, and futures markets for delivery on future dates at pre-arranged prices. There is no one place for this market, which operates via computer and telephone connections. The total turnover of world foreign exchange markets is enormous; it is many times total international trade in goods and services. See also intervention in foreign exchange markets.

foreign exchange rate See exchange rate.

foreign exchange reserves Liquid assets held by a country's government or central bank for the purpose of intervening in the foreign exchange market. These include gold or convertible foreign currencies, for example US dollars for countries other than the United States, or DM for countries other than Germany, and government securities denominated in these currencies. Foreign exchange reserves can also include balances with international institutions, notably the *International Monetary Fund (IMF). They do not include working balances of foreign currencies or short-dated foreign securities held by a country's banks or other firms, but in an emergency some of these could probably be added to a country's foreign exchange reserves.

foreign investment The acquisition by residents of a country of assets abroad. These assets may be real, in the case of foreign direct investment, or financial, in the case of acquisition of foreign securities or bank deposits. Foreign investment may be carried out by the state or the private sector, and foreign securities required may represent private or government debt. It is also possible for foreign residents to invest in real or financial assets in a country: this is inward foreign investment. Net foreign investment is the excess of outward over inward foreign investment.

foreign trade *See* trade.

foreign trade multiplier The ratio of the resulting increase in domestic product to an addition to exports. This is a class of formula rather than any one specific formula. In the simplest possible economy with only one form of leakage, say a savings propensity s, the foreign trade multipier (FTM) is $1/(1 - s)$. In a more realistic economy, with leakages of t tax payments out of each 1 of income, s savings out of each 1 of disposable income, and m imports out of each 1 of spending, 1 of exports generates $(1 - t)$ of disposable income, $(1 - s)(1 - t)$ of spending, and $(1 - m)(1 - s)(1 - t)$ of extra domestic incomes. The FTM is thus $1/[1 - (1 - m)(1 - s)(1 - t)]$. A truly realistic model which distinguished between direct and indirect taxes and between imports of intermediate inputs to production and final goods would produce a more complex FTM formula.

fortress Europe An expression of worries about European isolationism. The fear is that closer integration will lead not only to fewer obstacles to trade and mobility of capital and labour within Europe, but also to intensified restrictions on trade and factor mobility with the rest of the world.

forty-five degree line A line on an economic diagram showing points at which the amounts on the two axes are equal: in particular, the line showing positions where total expenditure equals total income. This assumes that both axes use the same scale. The position where a curve showing expenditure as a function of income crosses the 45 degree line represents an equilibrium level of income. *See also* the figure for aggregate demand schedule.

forward contract A contract in which a price is agreed for commodities, securities or currencies to be delivered at a future date. A forward contract is made with an identified counter-party, and the individual or firm entering into a forward contract remains exposed to the risk that the counter-party may fail to carry out their side of the bargain. Foward contracts may be used for hedging, to decrease risk, or as a speculation, taking on risk for the sake of an expected profit.

forward integration The inclusion in the same firm of 'downstream' activities which use or distribute the products of an 'upstream' activity. An example of this is the ownership of filling stations by oil companies. Forward integration may be adopted to improve efficiency by better co-ordination of the different levels of production, or to exploit monopolistic advantages at one level to reduce competition at another.

forward-looking behaviour Behaviour based on anticipation of the results which present decisions will bring in the future. There is a prima facie case that all economic decisions should be forward-looking. This is extremely difficult to achieve in practice, however, because of the absence of reliable information about the future. It can be argued that the tendency for some economic agents to use rule-of-thumb decision methods, as in satisficing models, makes their behaviour more predictable and thus assists other agents in making forward-looking decisions.

forward market A market in which forward contracts are entered into, that is contracts for the delivery at some future date of commodities, securities or currencies.

forward price The price at which commodities, securities, or currencies are to be delivered in a forward contract. The forward price and the spot price, that is the price for immediate delivery, may differ, and the same commodity may have different forward prices for delivery at different dates. Divergencies between these prices are limited by the costs of storage and possibilities of intertemporal substitution.

fractional reserve banking A banking system in which banks hold minimum reserves of cash or highly liquid assets equal to a fixed percentage of their deposit liabilities. The minimum percentage of reserves may be adopted voluntarily as a matter of commercial prudence, or required by law or convention. In either case the intention of minimum reserve requirements is to safeguard the ability of banks to meet their obligations.

franc fort The policy of using the foreign exchange rate as an inflation anchor. This policy seeks to control inflation by tying the currency to that of a country with an established reputation for low inflation. The franc fort (strong franc) policy was followed in the 1980s and early 1990s by both France and Belgium, who attempted to restrain inflationary expectations by linking their currencies to the German DM.

franchise The system by which independent firms are authorised to use a common business system. This may include the use of a brand name, designs, patents and operating systems, and provision of equipment, training, capital, or credit by the franchiser. This system combines the advantages of incentive for the operating firms and economies of scale in research, development, and advertising for the franchiser. The holders of franchises are subject to supervision of their operations in order to maintain the reputation of the franchised product.

fraud The use of misrepresentation for economic gain. The misrepresentation may be through positive statements, or conduct liable to mislead. Fraud includes obtaining goods on credit or loans which one knows cannot be repaid, continuing to trade when unable to pay one's debts, or making payments to creditors knowing that others with equal or prior claims cannot be paid. Fraud is difficult to prove, as its effects are hard to distinguish from those of bad luck or incompetence. Where fraud is proved, the courts have powers to undo transactions, and to take over the personal assets of officers responsible for fraud by companies.

freedom, degrees of *See* degrees of freedom.

freedom of entry *See* free entry.

freedom of exit *See* free exit.

free enterprise An economy in which the initiative for production and consumption decisions lies with individuals and companies. This is contrasted with a planned economy, in which initiative lies with the government. In any economy firms and individuals have to conform to rules set by the government; companies indeed owe their very existence to laws. Business in a 'free market economy' is subject to innumerable rules concerning health and safety, consumer protection, competition, control of land use, etc. It also has to pay taxes to finance the public sector. The rules, however, act only as constraints, and individuals and firms are free to make any choices consistent with the rules.

free entry The absence of any obstacle to new entrants to a market. Barriers to entry may be legal or economic. Legal barriers include monopoly rights for an incumbent, exclusive possession of necessary *patent rights by an incumbent, or licensing of entrants. While legal barriers to entry are common, it is possible in some cases that they may be absent. Economic barriers to entry include the need for large amounts of capital to enter, and the difficulty of competing with the established experience, market contacts, and reputation of incumbents. These are more difficult to remove than legal barriers.

free exchange rate *See* floating exchange rate.

free exit The absence of obstacles to leaving a market. Difficulties over exit may be economic or legal. The main economic barrier to exit is sunk costs, which cannot be recovered by leaving a market. These mean that firms stay in lines of business which they would not enter if they were not already engaged in them, given what they now know. Similarly, employment protection laws and redundancy costs keep workers in existing jobs who the employers would not now take on. It is difficult to see how the law can prevent a firm from leaving a business completely, especially if it is insolvent. It is possible, however, to have legal obstacles to leaving parts of a type of business while retaining other parts. Railways, for example, have common carrier obligations to provide services on their tracks, and can only withdraw part of their services with approval from industry regulators. Similar restrictions apply to public utilities.

free good A good which is not scarce, so that its availability is not an effective constraint on economic activity. A good is not a free good merely because its market price is zero: it may in fact be scarce, but be underpriced by the market because of a lack of enforceable property rights over it. A really free good has a shadow price of zero. A good may be free under some but not all circumstances; 'free as air' is a proverbial expression, but in mines and other confined spaces air has to be provided at great expense.

freehold Land or property in the UK held for use by the owner without obligation to any landlord. Freehold is contrasted with leasehold, where a ground landlord is entitled to ground rents and reversion of the property at the end of the lease, and may be entitled to impose restrictions on the use of the property. Freehold property is subject to public controls on its use through planning laws, and to other restrictions such as public rights of way.

free lunch A policy or combination of policies which produces advantages without any offsetting disadvantages. The term arises from the saying that 'there is no such thing as a free lunch'. Any policy normally has some adverse side-effects: for example tariffs benefit some domestic firms but damage consumers. It may be possible to find a combination of policies, including compensation for losers, which is beneficial all round. Adoption of a free lunch policy package is Pareto-optimal: such a package must be difficult to devise, since any obvious free lunch policy package would have been adopted already.

freely floating exchange rate *See* floating exchange rate.

free market A market in which people buy and sell voluntarily, without legal compulsion. Neither the quantities traded nor the price at which trade takes place are subject to control by third parties. This is not to say that such markets operate without legal regulation: the participants have to conform to laws concerning health and safety, weights and measures, labelling requirements, and so on. The essential point about these rules, however, is that they lay down what traders must not do: for example, misrepresenting the weight of their product. The actual initiative to trade still lies with the market participants, on both sides. Free markets are contrasted with a planned economy, where one party may be ordered to buy, or the other to sell. Where there are price controls but not quantity controls, a market is partly but not wholly free.

free-market economy An economy in which a substantial majority of economic activity is organized through free markets, in which the parties choose the quantities and prices traded without central direction. This is contrasted with a centrally planned economy, in which a substantial majority of economic activity is carried on through central directions to people and firms as to what they must buy and sell, and at what prices. Very few if any economies are either totally free-market-based or centrally planned; most have substantial elements of each. The most laissez-faire economies have large public sectors, and the most planned economies, such as the former Soviet Union, usually have a free market in fresh fruit and vegetables grown on small plots. Most real world economies fall somewhere between the extremes, with substantial elements of both types of economic organization.

free on board (fob) The value of exports when they are placed on a ship, lorry or aeroplane to leave a country. Fob thus includes costs of production and of transport to the port of embarkation, but does not include the costs of freight and insurance in getting them to their foreign destination. Free on board is contrasted with *cost, insurance and freight (cif), the value of goods on arrival at a foreign port, which includes freight and insurance.

free port A seaport or airport where national *tariffs are not levied. This is intended to encourage entrepôt trade, as goods can be shipped in and out without having funds tied up in tariff payments and free from the administrative expenses involved in claiming tariff drawbacks when goods are re-exported. Tariffs are payable when goods are shipped from a free port into the rest of the national territory.

free rider A person or organization who benefits from a *public good, but neither provides it nor contributes to the cost of collective provision. They thus free ride on the efforts of others. The free-rider problem means that many public goods are under-provided, or have to be provided by governments which can collect taxes to pay for them. The same problem occurs internationally, when governments prefer to leave others to bear the costs of international institutions to maintain world security, and the expensive measures needed to restrain global warming or destruction of the ozone layer.

free trade A policy of unrestricted foreign trade, with no *tariffs or subsidies on imports or exports, and no *quotas or other trade restrictions. Free trade implies that this regime applies to most goods, though there may be exceptions, for example agricultural goods or military equipment. It has usually been interpreted as applying only to trade in goods and not in services, but a similar policy can be applied to trade in services. A free-trade policy can be adopted unilaterally, or on a multilateral basis by joining a free-trade area. This is a group of countries which have no tariffs or other restrictions on trade between them, but remain free to control their trade with non-members of the area. Again this may apply to most but not all types of goods.

free-trade agreement A treaty between a group of countries setting up a free-trade area. Such a treaty normally contains exceptions for particular products, and transitional arrangement for the early years of the agreement.

free-trade area A group of countries with free trade between them, but retaining independent *tariff systems on trade with non-members. There are several free trade areas, including the *European Free Trade Area (EFTA) and the *North American Free Trade Agreement (NAFTA). The free trade arrangements must apply to a substantial proportion of trade, but some sectors, such as agricultural products or defence equipment, may be exempted from the free-trade provisions. To avoid the country with the lowest external tariff on any good being used as a route for imports to other members, tariff-free trade is confined to goods certified as being produced in member countries. A free-trade area is contrasted with a *customs union, which has both free trade between members and a *common external tariff.

free-trade zone An area of a country where national tariffs are not applied. This is intended to encourage industries which rely largely on producing goods for export using large amounts of imported inputs. Having the inputs duty-free saves on the interest costs of having money tied up by tariffs, and avoids the administrative expense of claiming tariff drawbacks on the exports. National tariffs have to be paid on goods shipped from a free-trade zone to the rest of the national economy.

freeze, pay *See* pay freeze.

frequency distribution A function describing the distribution of random drawings of a variable. If the variable, x, can take values over a continuous range from a minimum of a to a maximum of b, the frequency distribution will be $f(x)$. The integral of $f(x)$ from a to b, $\int_a^b f(x)dx$, must be 1. The cumulative frequency distribution, $F(c)$, shows the proportion of drawings equal to or less than c; $F(c) = \int_a^c f(x)dx \leq 1$. Where the variable can only take one of a range of discrete values from a minimum of v_1 to a maximum of v_N, the frequency distribution takes the form $f(v_i) = f_i$, where $\sum_i f(v_i) = 1$. *See also* cumulative frequency distribution.

frictional unemployment The unemployment that would exist because, as people change jobs because some sectors of the economy grow and others contract, it is not practicable to dovetail precisely leaving old jobs and starting new ones. At times of fairly full employment, frictional unemployment may form an appreciable fraction of total unemployment. Under conditions of high unemployment its contribution is probably negligible, except in sectors with localized labour shortages.

Friedman, Milton US monetarist economist, born in 1912 and awarded the Nobel Prize for Economics in 1976. Friedman is a strong believer in the merits of competition and free enterprise, and in the importance of money. He introduced the concept of *permanent income as an explanation of both consumption behaviour and liquidity preference. His analysis of the importance of money included both a stress on the monetary causes of inflation during periods when the quantity of money was increasing, and the contribution of money to the Great Depression of the early 1930s, when the Federal Reserve allowed the US money supply to fall by a third. He is sceptical about the possibility of stabilization by discretionary action by the monetary authorities, and has advocated a slow but steady increase in the quantity of money as the best contribution the government can make to stable growth of the real economy.

friendly society A UK institution for small savings and life insurance. Friendly societies are non-profit-making institutions owned by their members. They are regulated under Friendly Society Acts, and have limited power to offer tax-free investments and life insurance.

fringe benefits Benefits, other than pay, bonuses, and pensions, provided for employees by their employers. Such benefits may include company cars, sports facilities, free or subsidized catering facilities, health services or insurance, childcare facilities, free or subsidized accommodation or cheap mortgages. Employers provide fringe benefits for various reasons: to improve the health, morale and thus the performance at work of their employees, to stimulate loyalty to the firm, and to reduce their own and their employees' joint tax liabilities. Some fringe benefits are taxable, others partly taxable: this is an area of perpetual battle between the revenue authorities and tax accountants.

front-end charge An initial fee by the management of an investment or unit trust, or life insurance policy. This is calculated as a percentage of the initial sum invested, and is distinct from and additional to any annual management fee based on the value of the assets managed.

frontier, production possibility *See* production possibility frontier.

FSLIC *See* Federal Savings and Loan Insurance Corporation.

FTC *See* Federal Trade Commission.

FT index *See* Financial Times Share Indexes.

fuel Materials used to obtain energy through combustion. This is the main source of energy, without which very few economic activities are possible. The main fuels used in the modern world are coal, oil, and natural gas, and nuclear material for use in reactors; wood remains important in many less developed countries. Many activities use energy in the form of electricity, which is mostly fuel-based, though hydro-electricity provides part of the supply. Other possible non-fuel energy sources are solar energy, wind energy, and tidal power: these provide only a tiny part of present and prospective world energy requirements. Fuel thus seems indispensable for the foreseeable future.

full cost pricing The practice of setting prices so as to cover what average cost would be at a normal rate of production, plus a conventional mark-up. At times when output is low, actual average costs exceed those when output is normal, as fixed costs have to be spread over a lower output level. One argument for full cost pricing is that firms frequently have to quote a price for much of their output before they know what total output is going to be, and before they know some of their costs. Under these conditions their cost calculations are bound to be partly notional.

full employment A situation when every worker available for employment has a job. It is very unlikely that this can ever be achieved, even when there is general excess demand in labour markets. Some forms of unemployment probably cannot be reduced to zero. These include frictional unemployment, where people leaving jobs in declining sectors of the economy have not yet obtained a job in the expanding sectors. They also include search unemployment, where workers are unemployed while looking for jobs whose type, pay, and working conditions match their expectations. If these expectations are unrealistic it may take some time for them to learn from experience that they are aiming too high. There will also be people whose past or present conduct makes it hard for them to obtain or keep jobs. When economists talk of full employment, they normally mean fairly full employment, in which unemployment has been reduced to the categories mentioned here. Many doubt whether even this unemployment level can be sustained if it is below the *non-accelerating inflation rate of unemployment (NAIRU).

full employment budget The government's budget as it would be if the rates and rules for taxes and expenditure stayed the same, while national income was at full employment level. If the actual level of national income is lower than this, tax receipts are lower and government spending on unemployment and other means-tested benefits are higher than with full employment. The full employment budget deficit would thus be smaller than the actual budget deficit. It should not be assumed that if the level of unemployment fell substantially the budget deficit would fall, or the budget surplus would rise, as much as this type of calculation suggests. A rise in real national income might well stimulate government spending through discretionary improvements in real services or more generous income maintenance payments, or discretionary tax cuts.

full employment national income The level of real GDP which would be consistent with full employment. Whether this means an unemployment rate low enough to be socially acceptable, or the *non-accelerating inflation rate of unemployment (NAIRU) is ambiguous, unless one is sufficiently optimistic to believe that these unemployment rates are the same. It is difficult to say what the full employment national income would be. If unemployment is largely Keynesian in nature, due to lack of effective demand, or classical, due to excessive real wages, it may be fairly straightforward to work out what the labour force could produce if the unemployed went back to jobs similar to those they held before. Where unemployment is structural, due to mismatch between the skills and location of the unemployed and the economy's labour requirements, the unemployed require retraining before they can be employed. In this case working out how much they could eventually produce is much less simple.

full line forcing The practice of supplying distributors with goods only on the condition that they carry the full range of a firm's products. This may be used as a monopoly device: for example, if some car spares are highly specific to a make, while others are generic products available cheaper from rival suppliers, full line forcing protects the manufacturers from being undercut on the spares other people can make as well. Manufacturers defend full line forcing on the grounds that they need to protect their reputations with customers who may not appreciate that spares they are being sold are inferior substitutes.

function A relation between two or more variables. If y is a function of x, written $y = f(x)$, when the value of the argument x is known, the function tells us how to find the value of y. If y is a single-valued function of x, for each value of x there is only one value of y. In the linear function $y = ax + b$, for example, or the quadratic function $y = ax^2 + bx + c$, y is a single-valued function of x. For some functions, however, there may be more than one value of y for any given x, or there may be no real values of y. For example, if $y = \sqrt{x}$, when $x > 0$ there are two values of y, since for any y such that $y^2 = x$, it is always also true that $(-y)^2 = x$. When $x < 0$, however, there are no real values of y, but two 'imaginary' numbers, iz and $-iz$, where $z^2 = -x$. It is also common to have a function of several variables, for example $y = f(x_1, x_2, \ldots, x_N)$. In this case every x_i from x_1 to x_N needs to be specified to determine y. *See also* decreasing function, homogeneous function, implicit function, increasing function, inverse function, linear function, log-linear function, monotonic function, non-linear function, oscillatory function, piecewise linear function, step function, and trigonometric function.

functional income distribution The distribution of income between the owners of the various factors of production. Wages accrue to labour, rent to landlords, and interest, dividends, and retained profits of companies to capital. The incomes of the self-employed pose a problem for functional income distribution, as they often contain elements of the rewards of labour, land, capital, and entrepreneurship; disentangling these is a matter of convention. Functional is contrasted with *personal income distribution, the division of total income between individuals. The relation between functional and personal income distribution depends on the distribution of the ownership of property. Most individuals in a modern economy have both earned and property incomes for part of their lives. There is a positive correlation between these, as high earned incomes enable people to save, and property incomes help families to invest in professional training for their children, which leads to high earned incomes.

fund(s) *See* loanable funds, mutual fund, and offshore fund.

fundamental disequilibrium The condition of the balance of payments under which the original rules of the *International Monetary Fund (IMF) allowed countries to devalue their currencies. No formal definition of fundamental disequilibrium was ever produced, but it was widely assumed that it meant severe balance-of-payments problems which could not be cured without devaluation. In the event the rules proved unenforceable and member countries devalued as and when they chose anyway.

fundamentals The determinants of asset prices or exchange rates which are not dependent on the initial expectations of market participants or on the methods of short-run forecasting they employ. Fundamentals are thus the forces of supply and demand which determine the levels to which asset or currency prices will converge after sufficient time for the effects of initial expectations to fade away, assuming that any fluctuations set up by speculative forces are stable.

funding The conversion of government debt from short-term forms, or bills, to long-term forms, or bonds. This is regarded as a form of monetary policy, since bills are more liquid than bonds, and form part of the banks' liquid reserves, whereas bonds do not. Funding tends to raise long-term interest rates, as bonds have to be sold, and lower short-term interest rates, as bills become scarcer.

Fund, Know-How *See* Know-How Fund.

future good A good to be delivered at a future date. A futures contract is an agreement to buy or sell on a future date at a price fixed when the agreement is made.

futures contract A contract to buy or sell a good, share or currency on a future date, at a price decided when the contract is entered into. A futures contract entails for both parties both the right and the obligation to trade; it is contrasted with an *option, which confers only the right to trade on one party and only the obligation on the other. Futures contracts can be used to reduce risk by traders who have to hold a good and want protection against a low price, or who know they are going to have to buy and want protection against a high price. The contract can also be used to speculate by a trader who has a different opinion about expected price movements from that prevailing in the futures market. With some futures contracts, each party actually contracts with a market authority, which balances its buying and selling contracts, and collects margin payments from each side to ensure that they will be able to honour their contracts.

futures *See* financial futures, and interest-rate futures.

futures market A market organization through which futures contracts are traded. These contracts commit both parties to buy and sell commodities, shares, or currencies on a future date at a price fixed when the contract is made. To ensure that both parties will be able to carry out their side of the bargain, the actual contracts are made between each side and the market organization, which requires both parties to make margin deposits with it of a given percentage of the market price of a contract. In most futures markets no actual delivery is made: the difference between the contract price and the spot price when the contract matures is paid by one party to the market organization, and by the market organization to the other. If the spot price is above the contract price the futures buyer gains and the futures seller loses; the opposite holds if the spot price is below the futures price.

G

G7 *See* Group of Seven.

G10 *See* Group of Ten.

gain, capital *See* capital gain.

gains from trade The improvement in welfare possible as the result of countries being able to trade with one another, as compared with having autarkic economies. Gains from trade arise from two principal sources. One is differences in *factor endowments: countries have different natural resources, and different proportions between labour of various types and stocks of capital. Countries can thus gain from inter-industry trade, exporting goods which their resources are relatively well adapted to produce, and importing goods where they have no or poor production possibilities. The other source of gains from trade is *economies of scale: *intra-industry trade in differentiated products allows countries to produce on a substantial scale while their consumers enjoy the benefit of having a wide variety of product types available. While the gains from inter-industry trade accrue mainly to a country's plentiful factors of production, and its scarce factors may lose through trade, the gains from intra-industry trade are available to all. Thus where both forms of trade are substantial, it is likely that all factors in an economy gain from trade.

gambling Taking on bets at less than actuarially fair odds. On the assumption that the gambler understands the odds, there are three possible reasons for being willing to gamble. One is that the gambler may have a non-concave *utility function, with marginal utility increasing over some range of incomes. This means that even if the expected value of losses exceeds that of gains, the benefit from the gains exceeds the damage through the losses. A second reason, which may affect businesses, is that to a gambler already insolvent or near to *insolvency, gambling may appear worthwhile because gains can be kept while creditors bear any losses. A third reason for gambling is that people actually enjoy excitement, and gamble for pleasure. This applies particularly to cases such as lotteries where punters incur a large chance of a small loss to obtain a small chance of a large gain.

game *See* repeated game, strategic game, and zero-sum game.

game theory The modelling of economic decisions by games whose outcome depends on the decisions taken by two or more agents, each having to make decisions without information on what choices the others are making. Game theory distinguishes between one-off games and repeated games, where reputation established through earlier games affects the conduct of subsequent ones. It also distinguishes between zero-sum games, where the game affects only the distribution of a given total of resources, positive-sum games, where some players can gain more than others lose, and negative-sum games, such as fighting over resources, where the game itself can decrease the amount available to be shared. Game theory is widely used in analysing both industrial organization and economic policy.

gamma stocks Shares of relatively small companies, in which trade on the London Stock Exchange was infrequent. This was part of a system of classification of shares which has now been replaced.

GAO *See* General Accounting Office.

gap *See* deflationary gap, inflationary gap, technology gap, and yield gap.

GATS *See* General Agreement on Trade in Services.

GATT *See* General Agreement on Tariffs and Trade.

gazumping Reneging by the seller of a property on an agreement to sell. This is usually because of a higher offer by an alternative buyer. It is possible because of the existence of delays between an agreement to trade and the signing of a legally binding *contract, and usually occurs when property prices are rising.

GDP *See* gross domestic product.

GDP deflator A price index used to assess whether there has been a real rise or fall in *gross domestic product (GDP) from one year to another. GDP at current prices is divided by the GDP deflator to obtain an index of GDP at base-year prices. A GDP deflator is based on a broader class of goods than the *Retail Price Index (RPI), since it needs to take account of the prices of investment goods and goods bought by the public sector as well as consumer goods prices.

gearing The ratio of a company's debt to its equity. Gearing (UK) or leverage (US) is the ratio of a company's debt to the part of its capital owned by shareholders. High gearing or leverage means high reliance on debt financing. This is risky for the shareholders, as debt service absorbs a large proportion of profits in a normal year, and in a bad year the cost of debt service may exceed total profits. This could lead to dividends being reduced or passed, and possibly to loss of control of the company to creditors or debenture holders.

GEMU *See* German Economic and Monetary Union.

General Accounting Office (GAO) A US agency responsible to Congress for ensuring that funds voted by Congress are spent as prescribed by law.

General Agreement on Tariffs and Trade (GATT) An agency of the United Nations (UN), based in Geneva, founded in 1948 to promote international trade. By 1995 it had over 100 members, including most leading trading countries. GATT successfully concluded several rounds of multilateral negotiations to reduce world tariffs, but was unable to prevent the spread of *non-tariff barriers to trade such as voluntary export restraints (VERs). The latest round of GATT negotiations, the *Uruguay Round, finished in 1994. This included measures affecting trade in agricultural products and services, and intellectual property rights, all of which had been omitted from earlier rounds. It also led to the replacement of GATT by the *World Trade Organization (WTO).

General Agreement on Trade in Services (GATS) An international agreement on trade in services, arrived at in 1994 as part of the *Uruguay

Round of negotiations under the *General Agreement on Tariffs and Trade (GATT). The GATS is very limited in scope: it is a long way from providing for world-wide market access and 'national', that is, non-discriminatory treatment for foreign providers of services. Its provisions apply only to services included by members in a positive list: this is around half of all services in high-income countries and a very small proportion elsewhere. Even within these positive lists there are numerous exceptions. As with the GATT, a prolonged series of further negotiations seems likely to be needed before anything approaching free trade in services is achieved.

General Agreement to Borrow An agreement made in 1962 by the Group of Ten (G10) countries to extend international credit. The agreement is a misnomer, as the countries actually agreed to lend via the *International Monetary Fund (IMF) to enable each other to borrow extra reserves if this was necessary to defend their currencies. The agreement was later extended to other members of the IMF.

general equilibrium The approach in economics of considering all markets in an economy simultaneously. For general equilibrium all markets must be in equilibrium, and no change of actions in any market must pay any agent. General equilibrium is contrasted with the *partial equilibrium approach, in which some part of the economy is considered, neglecting what is happening in other markets. General equilibrium models are conceptually and mathematically more complex than partial equilibrium models.

general government The whole of the government sector, including central government, local government, and government at intermediate levels, like the states in federal countries such as Germany or the USA.

general government final consumption The spending of general government, that is, government at all levels, on real goods and services, excluding investment. General government final consumption includes items such as defence spending, the provision of administration, law and order, schools, and hospitals. It excludes government spending on pensions, unemployment benefit, other income maintenance payments, and debt interest. It also excludes government investment spending, for example on road construction or publicly-owned housing.

General Household Survey A UK sample survey used to obtain information on the labour force and on household expenditure.

general human capital Skills and qualifications of value in a wide range of occupations. This clearly applies to general skills such as literacy and numeracy. General human capital is contrasted with forms of human capital, such as medical, legal or technical skills or qualifications, which are of value only in particular occupations. As general human capital improves the outside earnings opportunities of those who acquire it, employers have little incentive to provide the training necessary, which must be paid for by individuals, their families, charities or the state.

Generalized System of Preferences (GSP) Agreements by members of GATT (now the World Trade Organization, WTO) to grant market access to the exports of less developed countries subject to preferentially lower tariffs than the normal level. GSP agreements were made by various European countries and Japan in 1971–2, by Canada in 1974 and by the US in 1976. The GSPs were subject to various exceptions concerning sensitive sectors, such as textiles, and never affected very much international trade. Their value has been eroded by the tariff reductions negotiated over recent decades.

generations, overlapping *See* overlapping generations.

geometric mean The Nth root of the product of a set of N numbers, x_1, x_2, . . . , x_N. This is written as $(\Pi_i x_i)^{1/N}$. This is defined only when all the x_i are positive. The logarithm of the geometric mean equals the arithmetic mean of the logarithms of the x_i.

geometric progression A sequence of numbers such that each is a constant multiple of the one before. For example, a, ar, ar^2, ar^3, . . . , ar^N is a geometric progression (GP). A loan of principal a, with compound interest added annually at $100i$ per cent, will amount after 1 year to $a(1 + i)$, after 2 years to $a(1 + i)^2$, and after N years to $a(1 + i)^N$. Here $r = (1 + i)$. A geometric progression is convergent, that is, the sum of its first N terms tends to a finite limit $a/(1 - r)$, as N tends to infinity, if $-1 < r < 1$.

German Economic and Monetary Union (GEMU) The reunification in 1990 of East and West Germany. This included the replacement of the East German currency, the Ostmark, by the Deutschmark, at a one-for-one exchange rate, and the setting up of the *Treuhandanstalt* to rationalize and privatize East Germany's state-owned firms. The immediate result of GEMU was a massive slump in East German GDP and a large budget deficit for the united Germany. East German industry consisted largely of firms producing low quality products by methods involving excessive use of fuel and reckless pollution of the environment, and East German wages were increased towards Western levels. This left Germany with a choice between large-scale unemployment and massive subsidies to keep East German firms in business to prevent it; either choice required vast transfers to the East.

gestation, period of *See* period of gestation.

Giffen good A good for which quantity demanded falls when its price falls. This can in theory occur: a Giffen good must be inferior and also have poor substitutes. A fall in the price of a good increases real purchasing power: if the good is inferior the *income effect of this rise in real income is negative. The *substitution effect of a price fall cannot be negative, but if the good has poor substitutes the positive substitution effect is small. If the substitution effect is smaller than the negative income effect, the overall effect of a fall in price is a fall in consumption. Giffen goods are in practice unlikely to be found, since narrowly defined classes of goods may be inferior but are unlikely to have poor substitutes, while widely defined classes of goods may have poor substitutes but are unlikely to be inferior.

gift tax A tax on gifts between the living (or *inter vivos*). This is contrasted with a tax on transfers of wealth by inheritance. A gift tax is designed to counter the loss of revenue from inheritance taxes through people transferring their wealth to their relations or friends while still alive. A gift tax normally contains some exemptions, for example a certain sum per annum. It may be made progressive, either on the sum given by any one donor to a particular beneficiary, on the total sum transferred, or on the total received in gifts and bequests by a single beneficiary.

gilt-edged security A fixed-interest security issued by the UK government. Gilts may be irredeemable Consols; long-dated, with 15 years or more to maturity; medium-dated, with 5 to 15 years to maturity; or short-dated, with under 5 years to maturity. Gilt-edged securities are considered extremely safe from risk of default, but are liable to fluctuate in price inversely with current interest rates, long-dated securities being most at risk. Index-linked gilts are also available, reducing the risk from inflation.

Gini coefficient A statistical measure of inequality. If y_i is the income of individual i, for example, the Gini coefficient is half the expected absolute difference in the incomes of any two individuals i and j chosen at random, as a proportion of the mean income. In a Lorenz curve, the Gini coefficient is the ratio of the area between the diagonal and the Lorenz curve to the total area under the diagonal.

Ginny Mae *See* Government National Mortgage Association.

giro A system of money transfer available even to those without bank accounts. The UK Girobank system works via post office branches, and Bank Giro enables bank customers to make giro payments. The Department of Social Security (DSS) also makes use of giro cheques for benefit payments.

Glass–Steagal Act A US law passed in 1933 prohibiting banks from acting both as lenders and as investors in companies. This Act forbids universal banking in the US, whereas such banking is common in other countries including Germany. The Act was passed due to a belief that universal banking made banks excessively risky, and had contributed to the collapse of the US banking system during the Great Depression.

globalization The process by which the whole world becomes a single market. This means that goods and services, capital, and labour are traded on a worldwide basis, and information and the results of research flow readily between countries. The rise of cheap sea transport and the telegram contributed to this process in the 19th century. Cheap air travel, the telephone, and the computer, together with the rising importance of multinational companies and general relaxation of controls on trade and international investment, continued the process in the 20th century. It is possible that the rise of the internet and the start which has been made on liberalizing international trade in services will continue this movement in the 21st century. The world has still a very long way to go, however, before its economy is fully globalized. In particular, international mobility of labour is tightly restricted, and poor transport and communications in most less developed countries (LDCs) mean that only the economies of the richer and more advanced countries are at all seriously globalized.

global maximum A value of a function as high as or higher than that for any other values of its arguments. The sufficient condition for a maximum of a function of a single argument, in terms of a zero first and negative second derivative, shows only that the function takes a local maximum. In some special cases it can be shown that a function has only one stationary value: for example, a quadratic, whose second derivative is constant. In this case any local maximum must also be global. In other cases it is necessary to check whether or not a given maximum is global. The function $y = ax^3 - bx$, for example, where a and b are both positive, has stationary values at $x = \pm \sqrt{(b/3a)}$; $x = -\sqrt{(b/3a)}$ gives a local maximum, but this is clearly not a global maximum since y can be made indefinitely large by taking large values of x. The same point applies with functions of more than one argument. *See also* the figure for maximum.

global minimum A value of a function as low as or lower than that for any other values of its arguments. The sufficient condition for a minimum of a function of a single argument, in terms of a zero first and positive second derivative, shows only that the function takes a local minimum. In some special cases it can be shown that a function has only one stationary value: for example, a quadratic, whose second derivative is constant. In this case any local minimum must also be global. In other cases it is necessary to check whether or not a given minimum is global. The function $y = ax^3 - bx$, for example, where both a and b are positive, has stationary values at $x = \pm \sqrt{(b/3a)}$; $x = \sqrt{(b/3a)}$ gives a local minimum, but this is clearly not a global minimum since y can be made indefinitely large and negative by taking large negative values of x. The same point applies with functions of more than one argument. *See also* the figure for maximum.

global warming The effect of burning fossil fuels increasing the quantity of carbon dioxide in the atmosphere so that the earth warms up. This is a danger rather than a scientific certainty. There are fears that it could cause large-scale climatic changes, and raise the sea level through melting the polar icecaps, with catastrophic results. While the scale of these possible effects is uncertain, worry about them has given rise to a desire to restrict the use of fossil fuels and to the *Kyoto Protocol of 1997.

glut A situation of unusually large supply of a good. This is likely to drive its price down considerably, particularly if it cannot be stored, or if storage facilities are full.

GNMA *See* Government National Mortgage Association.

GNP *See* gross national product.

gold A precious metal, widely used both as a form of money and for jewellery and other ornamental purposes. Gold was already used in these other ways before its use as money and the invention of coinage. Gold coinage was at one time in general circulation, but the monetary use of gold is now confined to holdings of gold bullion by central banks as part of their *foreign exchange reserves. Gold is still widely used as a store of value by individuals who mistrust government-created money because it is so vulnerable to inflation. Gold costs real resources to mine, so that its value is not liable to be destroyed by inflation, unlike fiat money. The *gold standard was a system of fixing foreign exchange rates by making the currency of each country convertible into gold at a fixed price.

gold and foreign exchange reserves *See* foreign exchange reserves.

gold backing, hundred-per-cent *See* hundred-per-cent gold backing.

golden handshake A provision of an executive's contract giving entitlement to a large bonus on leaving a firm's employment.

golden rule The rule that an economy can maximize its consumption if the rate of growth is equal to the marginal product of capital. Suppose that in steady-state growth the capital–output ratio is z; with a growth rate of g, a proportion gz of output must be invested. The marginal product of capital is m, assumed to be a decreasing function of z. Extra capital produces extra output of mdz, while a higher capital–output ratio requires extra investment of gdz; thus raising z above the level at which $m = g$ decreases the output left for consumption. If the rate of profit equals the marginal product of capital, the golden rule implies that it is socially beneficial for investment to equal profits and consumption to equal wages.

gold exchange standard *See* gold standard.

gold parity The official par value in terms of gold of the currency of a country on the gold standard.

gold points The values of exchange rates under the gold standard at which it became profitable to ship gold from one country to another. For example, if the dollar rose relative to the pound sterling, a firm holding sterling with a dollar payment to make could buy gold from the Bank of England, ship it to New York, and sell it to the Federal Reserve Bank for dollars. The gold points were the lowest price of dollars which made this profitable, and the highest price of dollars which made it profitable to ship gold from New York to London. In peacetime conditions modern transport makes shipping gold so cheap that the gold points would be very close together: the possible fluctuations in market exchange rates under a gold standard would thus be very small.

gold standard A system for fixing *exchange rates by the central bank or government of each country making its currency freely convertible into gold at a fixed price. Under this system the par value of exchange rates is set by the amount of each currency that can be obtained for a given quantity of gold. Exchange rates thus cannot shift further from parity than the limits set by the transactions costs of shipping gold between different countries, which is usually a very small percentage of its value. The same applies if gold actually circulates within each country, provided it can be imported and exported freely.

good(s) **1.** Things people prefer more of rather than less: thus income, leisure and security are goods, while pollution and risk are bads.
   2. Economic assets taking a tangible physical form, such as houses or clothes. These are contrasted with services, such as transport, which cannot be stored, or insurance, which has no physical embodiment. Some economic goods in sense **1**, such as restaurant meals, are combinations of services and goods in sense **2**. *See also* capital goods, consumer goods, final goods, free good, future good, Giffen good, homogeneous good, inferior good, intermediate good, merit goods, normal good, producer good, and public goods.

Goodhart's law The observation by Professor Charles Goodhart that when an empirical regularity starts to be exploited as a basis for economic policy, it is liable to break down. This is one application of the *Lucas critique, that the observed behaviour of economic systems is affected by the economic policies in force. If the policy regime changes, the behaviour of the economy is liable to change, so that econometric models fitted during earlier policy regimes become unreliable as a basis for predicting the effects of new policies.

goodwill An intangible asset, representing the fact that a business as a going concern is worth more than its tangible assets. This is usually due to the accumulated know-how and trade contacts of its staff. Goodwill is not normally included as an asset in balance-sheets, but is listed if a company has taken over another business for more than the value of its tangible assets. It is then required to be written off over a period.

Gosplan The central planning agency of the former Soviet Union. It was responsible for drawing up successive five-year plans and annual operational plans, and for auditing enterprises to check whether the plans had been fulfilled.

government Sometimes central government only; on other occasions general government. This the total of all levels of government, including central and local government, and state governments in federal countries such as Germany or the United States. It is always necessary to check what level of government is being referred to in any particular context. Similarly government deficits, and government debt, are used with various definitions of the government sector. *See also* central government, general government, and local government.

government debt Debt owed by the government at any level. It is necessary to net out any debt owed by one level of government to another, such as central government debt held as financial reserves by local authorities. Government debt may be measured gross or net, when some firms or individuals are indebted to the government, for example through local authority mortgages. The status of debt carrying a government guarantee but issued by other bodies, such as nationalized industries, is ambiguous; such debts may or may not be included in estimates of government debt. Where government securities fluctuate in market value, government debt is normally calculated using their par values.

government expenditure Spending by government at any level. It is necessary to net out payments by one level of government to another, for example central government grants to local authorities. Government expenditure consists of spending on real goods and services purchased from outside suppliers; spending on employment in state services such as administration, defence and education; spending on transfer payments to pensioners, the unemployed and the disabled; spending on subsidies and grants to industry; and payment of debt interest.

Government National Mortgage Association (GNMA) A US institution which guarantees securities issued by the Federal Housing Administration and the Veterans Administration. The GNMA is familiarly known as 'Ginny Mae.'

government production The part of the income of government which derives from the services of factors owned by the state or local authorities. This includes rent received from state-owned land and buildings, for example local authority housing. It is also possible for the state to operate productive services such as public utilities, either directly or through public corporations:

any profits these make form part of the government's share of the national product. Where the government sector provides services to the public such as administration, defence, law and order, education, and health services, these form part of government production, and are by convention valued at what they cost.

government regulation *See* regulation.

government spending on real goods and services Government spending on buying goods, for example military equipment, or employing people, for example policemen. This is contrasted with government spending on transfers or interest payments: spending on real goods and services is part of the gross domestic product, whereas spending on transfers or interest payments is not.

government transfer payments Payments of income by the government which are not made in return for current services rendered. This includes payment of state pensions and unemployment and other social security benefits, by the government itself or the National Insurance Fund. While the state provides most transfer payments, some are also made by charities and individuals.

gradualist monetarism The policy of stabilizing *inflation by gradually decreasing the growth rate of the money supply until it approaches the real growth rate of the economy. This is contrasted with the *'rational expectations' view that with a pre-announced and credible commitment to lower the growth rate of money rapidly, stable prices could be achieved via a 'short sharp shock', with little delay and at no greater cost in unemployment than is entailed by a gradual monetary squeeze. One argument for the gradualist approach is that if inflation has reduced the level of *real money balances that people want to hold, once inflation is cut this will recover. Thus it is not necessary to cut the money supply as much as the short sharp shock technique suggests. The monetary authorities do not actually know what level of real balances the economy will settle down to, and a gradual reduction in monetary growth allows them to find this out by trial and error.

Gramm–Rudman–Hollings The sponsors of the US Balanced Budget and Emergency Deficit Control Act of 1985, which attempted to reduce the US fiscal deficit, eventually to zero, by setting legal targets.

granny bond A security with state guarantees on both the interest to be paid and the price at which it can be redeemed at any time. These are thought of as suitable assets for savers with small total wealth and limited financial sophistication, of whom 'grannies' were assumed to be typical examples. Provision of such guarantees cannot be afforded except by the state. Securities of this type have typically been made available only to limited classes of holders, in relatively small amounts. This restriction is partly because the guarantees might be expensive to honour, and partly because if such securities were freely available, it would be difficult for many businesses to borrow at all.

grant, equalization *See* equalization grant.

grant in aid A US federal grant to state or local government. These grants are used to ensure that public services can be maintained in poorer states or in times of depression.

gravity model The theory that the contact between different locations is ruled by an inverse square law, similar to that governing gravitation. A consumer's custom, for example, is divided between possible shopping centres in proportion to $1/x_i^2$, where x_i is the distance to centre i. This model has also been applied to international trade between countries.

Great Depression The worst depression in living memory. At present this position is still conceded to the world depression in the early 1930s. As this is believed to have contributed to the rise of Hitler to power in Germany and thus to the Second World War, it is to be hoped that this depression will retain the title indefinitely.

greenfield development A factory erected on a previously undeveloped site, as contrasted with extending or converting an existing plant. Greenfield development allows firms to avoid the congestion and pollution problems of the areas around many old sites. It also allows an old plant to continue in use while its successor is being built. A disadvantage of greenfield development is that it may be necessary to invest in providing new sites with power, transport and other facilities already in place in an old site. Greenfield developments are also liable to costly delays through planning objections from prospective neighbours and environmentalists who prefer greenfield sites to remain green fields.

greenhouse gases Carbon emissions tending to increase the proportion of carbon dioxide (CO_2) in the earth's atmosphere. This is believed to have a greenhouse effect, decreasing radiation of heat from the earth and causing temperatures to rise. This could cause climatic changes, and raise the sea-level by melting part of the polar icecaps. It has been suggested that this could be prevented by introducing carbon taxes to decrease emissions of carbon dioxide, and by halting deforestation in tropical areas and promoting reforestation of temperate areas of the world, since trees act as a sink for CO_2.

green issues Policy issues arising from concerns about the *environment. Various environmental problems arise from economic activity and in particular from economic growth. These include climatic change due to excessive usage of fossil fuels, deforestation, erosion, extinction of plant and animal species and loss of biodiversity, and health problems due to air and water pollution, radiation, and excessive use of fertilizers and pesticides. There are serious doubts as to whether economic growth at present and prospective rates is sustainable, or whether it is leading the world towards massive catastrophe.

green paper A UK government publication, intended to stimulate public discussion on an issue, without necessarily committing the government to legislation, or as to the lines this might take. This is contrasted with a white paper, which is a UK government publication generally intended as a prelude to legislation, and giving some indication of its likely form.

green pound A notional unit of currency, used as part of the European Community's *Common Agricultural Policy (CAP). The green pound was devised when the shift to flexible exchange rates in the early 1970s led to the prices of farm products fixed under the CAP becoming unstable when translated into UK pounds sterling at market exchange rates.

green revolution Large improvements in recent decades in agricultural productivity in less developed countries (LDCs), due to improved plant varieties and widespread use of fertilizer and pesticides. This has raised living standards in many countries, and staved off a Malthusian crisis which might otherwise have resulted from persistent high population growth rates.

gross An indication that something which could have been subtracted has not been. The word appears in economics in a variety of contexts. The gross weight of a product includes packaging; net weight is gross weight minus the weight of any packaging. Gross investment is total investment spending, before making any deduction for *capital consumption, which is subtracted to get net investment. Similarly, gross domestic product (GDP) is the total of production for consumption, investment and government use, before making any deduction for capital consumption; net domestic product is GDP minus capital consumption. Gross assets are total assets held, disregarding any liabilities; net assets are gross assets minus liabilities.

gross domestic capital formation A measure of total investment. 'Gross' indicates that it is measured without subtracting any allowance for *capital consumption; 'domestic' that it refers to investment in the country regardless of ownership. It thus includes investment in the country by companies owned by non-residents, and excludes investment abroad by resident firms.

gross domestic fixed capital formation The part of domestic gross investment that consists of durable goods rather than stocks and work in progress. 'Fixed' is contrasted with 'circulating' capital, and does not refer to geographical immobility; thus vehicles, ships and aircraft are all included in this aggregate.

gross domestic product (GDP) One of the main measures of economic activity. 'Gross' indicates that it is calculated without subtracting any allowance for *capital consumption; 'domestic' that it measures activities located in the country regardless of their ownership. It thus includes activities carried on in the country by foreign-owned companies, and excludes activities of firms owned by residents but carried on abroad. 'Product' indicates that it measures real output produced rather than output absorbed by residents. GDP is reported at both current and constant prices.

gross fixed investment The total spent on fixed investment, before making any deduction for depreciation of the existing capital stock. This is contrasted with net fixed investment, which is gross fixed investment minus an estimate of *capital consumption. The figures for gross fixed investment are relatively reliable, as it is mainly carried out via observable market transactions, whereas capital consumption and thus net fixed investment are estimates, not based on observing market transactions.

grossing up Finding the gross amount of any receipt of income which is actually paid net of income tax. This allows a taxpayer's total gross income to be calculated; for example, if a UK taxpayer receives £78 net of tax and the tax rate is 22 per cent, their grossed up income is £100. Any allowances due are then subtracted to find taxable income, and tax payable. The total tax payable is compared with tax already deducted at source: if too little tax has been deducted the taxpayer then gets a demand for the remainder, and if too much tax has been deducted the taxpayer gets a refund.

gross investment Spending on creating new capital goods, before making any allowance for *capital consumption. Gross investment consists of gross fixed investment, plus net investment in stocks and work in progress. Gross investment is distinguished from net investment, which measures the change in the capital stock after allowing for capital consumption. Gross investment is in principle based on observable market transactions; by contrast, capital consumption is based on calculations about the rate at which capital goods wear out or become obsolete. These calculations are not based on market transactions: thus they, and estimates of net investment based on them, are less reliable than measures of gross investment.

gross national product (GNP) One of the main measures of national economic activity. 'Gross' indicates that it is measured without subtracting any allowance for *capital consumption; 'national' that it includes residents' incomes from economic activities carried on abroad as well as at home, and excludes incomes produced at home but belonging to non-residents. 'Product' indicates that it measures real output produced rather than real output absorbed by residents. GNP is reported at both current and constant prices.

gross profit The profits of companies before deducting depreciation allowances or taxation but after deducting debt interest.

gross trading profit The profits of companies before deducting depreciation allowances, taxation, or debt interest. This is the profit derived from a company's trading activities. Debt interest has to be deducted from it to get gross profit. A company with high *gearing and a large interest bill may make a loss overall, even if its gross trading profits are positive.

Group of Seven (G7) An informal group of leading industrial countries, whose leaders meet periodically to discuss economic problems and policies. The G7 nations are Canada, France, Germany, Italy, Japan, the United Kingdom, and the United States.

Group of Ten (G10) An informal group of leading industrial countries, whose leaders meet periodically to discuss economic problems and policies. The G10 is also known as the Paris Club. The G10 nations are Belgium, Canada, France, Germany, Italy, Japan, the Netherlands, Sweden, the United Kingdom, and the United States.

growth An increase in an economic variable, normally persisting over successive periods. The variable concerned may be real or nominal, and may be measured in absolute or in per capita terms. Growth in real economic variables such as GDP for short periods or at low rates may occur by simply having similar activities conducted on a larger scale. Rapid or persistent growth is likely to involve changes in the nature of economic activity, with new products or processes, and new types of labour skills, capital goods and economic institutions. Every innovation gives rise to problems in devising satisfactory measures of economic aggregates: the more rapid and persistent a growth process, the more difficulty there is in measuring it reliably. Growth models seek to simulate the growth processes of economic aggregates.

Unlimited growth poses problems over limited natural resources, pollution and congestion. Only experience will reveal how long it is sustainable. *See also* balanced growth, endogenous growth, export-led growth, immiserizing growth, non-inflationary growth, steady-state growth, and zero growth.

growth model *See* Harrod–Domar growth model, and Solow growth model.

growth rate The proportional or percentage rate of increase of any economic variable over a unit period, normally a year. If a variable measured over discrete time intervals grows from 1 to $1 + x$, this is a proportional growth rate of x, or a percentage growth rate of $100x$. If working in continuous time, a continuous growth rate g means that a variable grows from 1 at time 0 to e^{gt} at time t. If $y_t = y_0 e^{gt}$, $dy_t/dt = gy_0 e^{gt}$, and $(dy_t/dt)/y_t = g$. As $\ln(y_t) = gt$, $d[\ln(y_t)]/dt = g$; the rate of change of the natural logarithm of any variable equals its growth rate. *See also* natural growth rate, warranted growth rate.

guarantee A promise that if a good is unsatisfactory it will be repaired or replaced, or that if a loan is not repaid the guarantor will repay it. Some guarantees are legally enforceable, which protects the holder of the guarantee provided that the guarantor is solvent. Even if a guarantee is not legally binding, the guarantor risks loss of reputation if the guarantee is not honoured.

hard budget constraint A limit to spending by some private or public body, where the results of breaching it are expected to be catastrophic. For example, managers whose firms fail to break even, or to achieve the required rate of profit, may expect the result to be loss of their jobs or closure of their firms. This is contrasted with a soft budget constraint, where the consequences of breaching set limits are not expected to be serious: managers expect that if they make losses the state will meet them. The vogue for *privatization is based partly on the belief that this is the only way to get people to treat budget constraints as hard.

hard currency A currency which is convertible into other currencies, and whose price in terms of other currencies is expected to remain stable or rise. This is contrasted with a soft currency, which is not convertible into other currencies, or whose price in terms of other currencies is expected to fall. Hard currencies are attractive to hold as private stores of wealth or national foreign exchange reserves.

hard Ecu A proposal for a European Currency Unit (Ecu) that would initially be equal in value to a bundle of European currencies, but could not subsequently be devalued relative to any member currency. The hard Ecu would thus be at least as hard as the hardest member currency, and harder than the remainder. This should make the hard Ecu and debt denominated in it attractive as assets both to private investors and to national authorities as a form of foreign exchange reserves. The concept has been superseded by the adoption of the Euro.

hard landing The difficulty of ending a period of excess demand and inflation without provoking a *recession. It is difficult to judge exactly how much fiscal and monetary restraint is needed to stabilize effective demand at a high level and inflation at a low one. Checks applied too little or too late fail to cure excess demand; checks that are too severe are liable to damage business confidence and start a recession. This is known as a hard landing, as contrasted with the ideal of a *soft landing, where the timely use of moderate restraints succeeds in producing a smooth transition to price stability with high employment.

hard loan A loan on normal market terms as regards interest, including a risk premium appropriate to the borrower's credit rating, the maturity date, the currency in which interest is paid, and when repayments are due. This is contrasted with a *soft loan, which may be at a concessional interest rate, with an expectation that interest payments and capital repayments can be easily rescheduled or paid in soft currency.

harmonization The idea that the taxes and regulatory rules in countries belonging to economic blocs should not diverge too widely. If capital and labour were perfectly mobile between countries, it could be argued that the members of common markets would have to adopt identical tax and regulatory regimes. With no mobility, any set of different taxes and rules would be viable. With imperfect mobility, harmonization is needed: large divergences of tax or regulatory regimes would distort the location of economic activities, but minor discrepancies have little effect.

Harrod–Domar growth model A growth model, named after its originators, which considers the consequences of fixed capital–labour ratios and savings propensities. In this model, the labour force, measured in efficiency units to allow for technical progress, grows at an exogenously fixed natural growth rate, n. There is a fixed capital–output ratio, v, and a fixed propensity to save, s. If national income is Y, savings are sY. With income Y, desired capital stock is vY, and if this grows at a constant proportional rate g, desired investment is gvY. Ex ante savings and investment are equal only if $sY = gvY$, or $g = s/v$. The only growth rate which makes this possible is $w = s/v$, the warranted growth rate. If $w = n$, growth is possible with a constant percentage of the labour force employed. If $w < n$, that is, the warranted growth rate is less than the natural rate, equilibrium growth of national income involves steadily increasing unemployment. If $w > n$, equilibrium growth becomes impossible once full employment is reached, and the resulting slow-down in growth produces a slump. The Harrod–Domar growth model can be contrasted with the *Solow growth model, in which v adjusts to accommodate any combination of s and n. The Harrod–Domar model points to the problems which can arise if v and s are rigid; the Solow model looks at what the world would be like if these problems were solved.

Harrod-neutral technical progress Technical progress which increases the efficiency of labour, so that the labour force in efficiency units increases faster than the number of workers available. Technical progress of this form is thus labour-saving. It is contrasted with Hicks-neutral technical progress, where the efficiency of all factors increases in the same proportion.

haven, tax *See* tax haven.

hazard, moral *See* moral hazard.

hazardous waste Waste which is dangerous to health and safety. This can be, for example, because it contains toxic chemicals or infectious biological materials, or is explosive or radioactive. Most countries attempt to control the disposal of hazardous waste by regulating its storage, transport and processing. Severe problems arise when, because of past scientific ignorance of its effects, or failure to enforce rules about waste disposal, hazardous waste products have become widely dispersed in unrecorded sites.

Health and Safety at Work Act The UK Act of Parliament laying down standards of health and safety at work, and providing for their enforcement through a Health and Safety Commisson. The Act is designed to protect both workers and the public from hazards to health and safety arising from a variety of causes, including unfenced machinery, toxic and explosive substances, excess noise, atmospheric pollution, and inadequate heating and lighting of premises. It imposes on employers the duty of providing safety training, and providing safety equipment and ensuring that employees use it.

health insurance Insurance against medical expenses and loss of earnings due to accident or illness. This may cover individuals only, or extend to their dependents. Health insurance schemes may be compulsory or voluntary, and their cost may fall on individuals or on their employers. Compulsory schemes can cover any form of health risk. Voluntary schemes typically charge premiums related to members' apparent risk, depending on factors such as age, sex and occupation. A voluntary scheme which did not charge premiums related to apparent risk for members would be subject to *adverse selection: it would attract people with high risks, and would therefore need to charge high premiums. These would make it unattractive to people who appeared to be better risks, who would find that they could get cheaper cover from more selective schemes. Voluntary schemes usually also often exclude the cost of treatment for conditions that members are known to have when they first join. Health insurance may also exclude risks believed to be under a member's own control, for example pregnancy.

health service *See* National Health Service.

Heckscher–Ohlin model The standard model of the theory of *inter-industry trade, named after its Swedish originators. In this model countries have the same constant-returns-to-scale production functions for each good, but different amounts of capital relative to their labour supply. In the absence of trade, goods which require large amounts of labour relative to capital would be relatively cheaper in the more labour-abundant countries, and relatively dearer in the more capital-rich countries. If trade becomes possible, countries export goods intensive in the use of their more plentiful factor, and import goods intensive in the use of their scarce factor. This tends to equate relative prices in different countries, and relative factor prices. If there were free trade and no transport costs, complete relative price and *factor price equalization could result. This model does not attempt to explain *intra-industry trade.

hedge fund An investment fund specializing in taking speculative positions in markets, for shares or currencies. This may involve selling short, that is, selling forward shares or currency which the fund does not actually possess, in the expectation that the price will fall. Hedge funds are thus extremely risky; they are in principle the only form of investment fund which can profit from bear markets, though in practice most do not.

hedging Activities designed to reduce the risks imposed by other activities. If a business has to hold stocks of a commodity, it runs a risk of making losses if the price falls. This loss can be avoided by hedging, which involves selling the good forward, that is for delivery at an agreed price on a future date, or by selling in the *futures market. If the good is homogeneous, it may be possible to remove the risk completely by hedging. If the good is not homogeneous, the price of the particular goods held may not move in precisely the same manner as the standard commodity traded in forward or futures markets, but provided that there is some correlation between the two prices, hedging reduces the risk. An alternative method of hedging the risk of stock-holding is to buy a *put option, which allows but does not compel the holder to sell at the contract price. Similarly, a firm which knows it will have to obtain supplies of a good at a future date may wish to protect itself against the risk that when the time comes the cost of the goods will be very high. It can hedge this risk by buying forward or buying a futures contract, or by buying a call option, which gives it the right but not the obligation to buy at the contract price.

Herfindahl index An index of concentration in an industry. The index calculates the sum over all firms of the squares of their market shares, expressed as proportions. Thus $H = \sum_i s_i^2$, where s_i is the market share of the ith firm. If there are N firms, the lowest value H can take is when all N firms have equal shares, so that $s_i = 1/N$ for all i, and $H = N(1/N^2) = 1/N$. The highest value H can take is 1, which is approached as the market share of the largest firm tends to 1 and the market shares of the rest tend to zero. H thus rises as concentration increases.

heteroscedasticity Having different variances. Data are heteroscedastic if their variations are not consistent with being random drawings from the same population. This is contrasted with *homoscedasticity, where the data appear consistent with being random drawings from the same distribution. Many statistical procedures are not strictly valid for heteroscedastic data. Data on time-series drawn from a world with changing structures, or cross-sections of different industries or countries, can easily turn out to be heteroscedastic.

heterotheticity The property of a family of curves, that they differ in shape as well as scale. The isoquants for an industry where larger firms find it economic to use more capital-intensive techniques than smaller firms must be heterothetic. Heterotheticity is contrasted with *homotheticity, the property of a family of curves that they all have the same shape, and differ only in size.

Hicks-neutral technical progress Technical progress where with any given factor proportions the average and marginal products of all factors increase in the same proportion. Thus if $y = f(x, z)$, where y is output, x is labour and z is capital, and the function $f(.)$ has constant returns to scale, output after Hicks-neutral technical progress where the productivity of each factor rises to $\lambda > 1$ times its former level is given by $y^*(x, z) = f(\lambda x, \lambda z) = \lambda y$. This is contrasted with other definitions of neutrality, for example Harrod-neutral or pure labour-augmenting technical progress, where labour productivity rises but that of capital does not, so that output after technical progress is given by $y^*(x, z) = y(\lambda x, z)$.

high-powered money Money of forms that qualify it to be used as commercial bank reserve assets. Such money is 'high-powered' because if the commercial banking system maintains a reserve ratio of a, an additional £1m of high-powered money allows total deposits to expand by £$(1/a)$m. Some monetarists have argued that if the central bank controls 'base' or high-powered money, the rest of the money supply will adapt automatically.

high-tech Modern jargon for processes involving the use of advanced technology. High-tech is mainly associated with a narrow range of industries, including aeronautics, atomic energy, chemicals and pharmaceuticals, computers, military equipment and telecommunications. High-tech is of greatest importance in the OECD countries, Russia, and the newly industrialized countries (NICs). High-tech is of particular interest to the great powers because of its military implications. The actual definition of high-tech itself changes rapidly: last decade's high-tech is often this decade's standard industrial technology.

hire purchase (HP) The system by which goods are made available to the buyer for immediate use, but payment is made by instalments. HP may or may not require a down-payment; instalments are spread over an agreed period, and until the final instalment is paid the goods remain the property of the seller, who can reclaim them if payments are not made on time. Goods being bought on HP cannot legally be sold or given away. The cost of goods bought on HP normally exceeds the price for cash payment. HP is widely used in buying durable goods such as cars, furniture, and household appliances. HP controls were at one time used in the UK as part of government policies to control aggregate demand.

hiring Taking on new employees. This is an important function of the management of a firm. Hiring is less subject to regulation than firing, so far as the number of new workers taken on is concerned. There are however various legal restrictions on how new workers are chosen; for example discrimination by race or sex may be illegal, while on the other hand discrimination by nationality may be compulsory.

histogram A diagram representing the distribution of a variable, where information is about discrete ranges of values. Areas in the diagram are proportional to the number of observations in each interval, for example personal incomes between £10,001 and £11,000 per annum. If the figures are in proportions, the total area must sum to 1; if they are percentages, the area sums to 100. If actual numbers are represented the total can be anything. When class intervals differ in width, as in the example below, the height of each column is chosen to make the area proportional to the number of observations in the interval shown. Where intervals are open-ended, for example 'incomes above £1m', some arbitrary assumption has to be made about the upper end of the top interval.

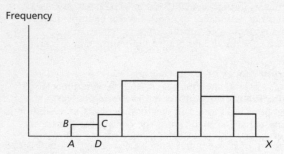

FIGURE 12: *Histograms*

The horizontal axis represents values of variable *x*; the vertical axis represents frequency. *ABCD* shows the proportion of the population with values of *x* between *A* and *D*.

historical cost The system of accounting in which assets are valued and depreciation allowances are calculated for firms using the prices paid for assets when they were first bought or built. The great merit of this system is that it uses prices based on actual market transactions; any other method of accounting for assets involves using valuations not based on market transactions. During a period of stable prices historical cost accounting is quite sensible, but in a period of sustained inflation it systematically undervalues assets, and calculates depreciation allowances well below the replacement costs of capital goods, so that profits are systematically overestimated.

hit-and-run entry Entry to a market in the expectation of making an immediate profit, possibly followed by withdrawal. This can only occur if the entrant does not incur *sunk costs. If there are sunk costs entry will only be profitable if the entrant expects to stay in the market long enough to recoup them. Absence of sunk costs is probable only through *economies of scope: firms with skills or facilities which can be put to a variety of uses can afford hit-and-run entry to a particular market.

hoarding, labour *See* labour hoarding.

hog cycle *See* cobweb

holding company A company whose sole function is holding shares in other companies.

holding, nominee *See* nominee holding.

holiday, tax *See* tax holiday.

home bias The tendency for consumers to spend relatively more on their own country's products than the world average, and relatively less on the products of other countries. This is due partly to international differences in tastes, partly to government policies concerning tariffs and non-tariff barriers to trade, and partly to the cost and difficulty of obtaining full and reliable information on what foreign products are available. A similar effect is shown in international differences in portfolio holdings. Investors tend to hold relatively more of their own country's bonds and shares than the world average, and relatively less foreign bonds and shares.

homogeneous function A function where multiplying all the arguments by any constant λ multiplies the value of the function by λ^α is homogeneous of order α. Thus, for example,

$$y = (\beta x + \gamma z)/(\delta x + \varepsilon z)$$

is homogeneous of order 0, since multiplying both x and z by λ leaves y unchanged;

$$y = (\beta x + \gamma z)$$

is homogeneous of order 1, or linear homogeneous, as multiplying both x and z by λ multiples y by λ;

$$y = (\beta x + \gamma z)^2$$

is homogeneous of order 2, since multiplying both x and z by λ multiplies y by λ^2; but

$$y = (\beta x + \gamma z^2)$$

is not homogeneous of any order.

homogeneous good A good which has uniform properties, any unit being interchangeable with any other. Goods which differ in specifications or quality, or bearing different *brand names which affect the confidence of customers are not homogeneous. Units of money, or securities of the same type, are completely homogeneous. Some primary products and basic materials are almost homogeneous, apart from their physical location, but other primary products and most manufactured products are not homogeneous. Economic aggregates invariably involve treating as if they were homogeneous goods which in fact are not.

homoscedasticity Having the same variance. Data are homoscedastic if their variations are consistent with being random drawings from the same population. This is contrasted with *heteroscedasticity, that is, having different variances. Many statistical procedures are only strictly valid for homoscedastic data. Data on time-series drawn from a world with changing structures, or cross-sections of different industries or countries, can easily turn out to be heteroscedastic.

homotheticity The property of a family of curves that their shapes are all the same. If a family of indifference curves or isoquants $f(x, y)$ is homothetic, the gradient dy/dx at any point depends only on the ratio of y to x and not on their absolute size. Many widely-used functions including the *Cobb–Douglas and *constant elasticity of substitution (CES) functions have this property. It is contrasted with *heterotheticity, the property of families of curves where size and shape are not independent.

horizontal equity The view that people in similar circumstances should be treated equally and that differences in needs should be reflected by differences in treatment. Applying this concept to the tax system, for example, it would appear unjust to tax two similar workers at different rates. Some might argue on similar grounds that it is unjust to impose the same taxes on people with burdensome obligations such as mortgage payments as on other taxpayers with equal incomes but no similar obligations. Horizontal equity is distinguished from *vertical equity, which is concerned with questions such as how far large differences in income should be moderated by redistributive taxation.

horizontal integration Combining two or more enterprises at the same stage of production. This may allow cost savings, if there are *economies of scale in any of the processes involved, or if it is possible to eliminate duplication of effort, for example in raising finance or in *research and development (R&D). Horizontal integration is contrasted with vertical integration, where enterprises at successive stages of production are combined.

horizontal merger A merger between firms at the same stage of production. This may be desired because of cost savings from combined operation, or because a larger firm will be able to use monopoly power against its customers or monopsony power against its suppliers and workers. A horizontal merger is contrasted with a vertical merger, where a firm merges with a supplier or a customer.

horizon, time *See* time horizon.

hostile bid A *take-over bid whose acceptance is opposed by the directors of a company. A bid may be opposed because the directors feel that the company is better off independent, through concern for their own job security, or because they hope to get a higher offer either from the present or a rival bidder.

hot money Money in bank balances or liquid securities which is liable to rapid removal to other countries if the holders suspect that the currency will depreciate. An inflow of hot money may make a country's balance of payments situation look satisfactory, but also makes it subject to sudden deterioration. There is no objective test showing in advance how hot actual money holdings are.

hours of work The number of hours per day or per week that a worker is contracted to perform. This may be decided by negotiation, individually or through trade unions, or limited by law. Work in excess of these hours is overtime; work for less is short-time, if temporary, or part-time work, if regular.

household A group of people living together in shared accommodation and with common domestic expenses. A household usually but not always contains people who are related or cohabiting. Whereas the individual is the recipient of incomes, the household is the unit through which a lot of consumption expenditure is decided. The General Household Survey is a source of information on the composition of household expenditure in the UK.

household production Production of goods and services within the household, rather than through formal or informal market organizations. In pre-industrial societies, and in some *less developed countries (LDCs), a substantial proportion of economic activity takes this form. In modern economies it is less important, though this is partly a matter of accounting conventions. A considerable part of people's time even in advanced economies is taken up with tasks like cookery, cleaning, child-minding, gardening, driving and car maintenance, and do-it-yourself building and decorating. All these can in principle be provided commercially, and are in fact performed by employees for a minority of richer households. These services are generally ignored in national income accounting.

housing *See* council housing, owner-occupied housing, and rented housing.

housing association A non-profit-making body providing low-cost housing for people who cannot afford to become owner-occupiers, or cannot manage their own housing. Dwellings may be for rent, or for purchase on concessional terms. Housing associations in the UK are financed by a mixture of charitable donations, public funding and commercial borrowing.

housing benefit Payments under the UK social security system to assist low-income households with housing costs. It is necessary to have a separate benefit for housing because of the wide variations in housing costs between areas and different types of housing tenure.

HP *See* hire purchase.

human capital The present discounted value of the additional productivity, over and above the product of unskilled labour, of people with skills and qualifications. Human capital may be acquired through explicit training, or on-the-job experience. Like physical capital, it is liable to obsolescence through changes in technology or tastes. Unlike physical capital, it cannot be sold in a society without slavery: this means that it cannot be used as collateral for loans. The training needed to create human capital has to be paid for. Training for firm-specific human capital, which does not improve workers' earning ability outside the firm, can be provided by employers. General or vocational human capital, which can be used by other employers, will increase workers' outside earning power, so employers are in general reluctant to provide this type of training. The cost of creating human capital thus mostly falls on individuals or their families, charitable institutions, or the state. *See also* firm-specific human capital, and general human capital.

hundred-per-cent gold backing A reserve rule requiring the bank issuing a currency to hold gold of equal value. The only difference between this and a solid gold currency would be the saving in transactions costs from not having to handle the gold. This type of rule is generally regarded as unacceptable for the same reasons as the use of gold coinage itself.

hyperbola A function which can be expressed as the ratio of two linear functions. A rectangular hyperbola takes the form

$$y = (\alpha + \beta x)/(\gamma + \delta x).$$

This function is continuous except at $x = -\gamma/\delta$, which forms an asymptote, where y tends to plus infinity as x approaches it from one side and to minus infinity as x approaches it from the other side. The inverse function takes a similar form:

$$x = -(\alpha - \gamma y)/(\beta - \delta y),$$

so that x is continuous except at the asymptote $y = \beta/\delta$.

hyperinflation Very rapid inflation; it is sometimes reckoned to set in when price increases exceed 50 per cent per month. Such rapid inflation not merely makes money useless as a store of value, but seriously affects its use as a medium of exchange, and greatly disrupts productive economic activity.

hypothesis, null *See* null hypothesis.

hypothesis testing Testing whether there are statistical grounds for disbelieving any statement. Economic data are based on records, which may be inaccurate, and on samples, which may not be truly representative. Statistical testing can never prove any statement based on these data to be true, only that there is no reason to believe that it is not. Hypothesis testing involves avoiding two types of error: accepting statements when there is good reason to doubt them, and rejecting them when there is in fact no good reason to do so. The modus operandi of hypothesis testing is to ask, given the apparent variance of the data, what is the probability of having obtained any given result purely through sampling error? The more unlikely any result is to have arisen from sampling error, the less reason there is to disbelieve it. Making any test more or less stringent increases the probability of one form of error and decreases the chances of the other. What test is best depends on the seriousness of the consequences of being wrong. Lenders, for example, risk a small loss of possible profit if they reject an honest and competent borrower, and total loss of their money if they accept a dishonest or incompetent one.

hysteresis Dependence of the *equilibrium position of a system on what happens during the process of dynamic adjustment. This undermines the traditional distinction between comparative statics and dynamics. *Comparative statics considers the new equilibrium of the economy after a change in some exogenous variable: this does not depend on the starting point. *Dynamics analyses what happens when the economy is not in equilibrium: this affects whether equilibrium is approached, and how fast, but the equilibrium position itself is taken to be independent of the process of getting there. Under hysteresis this dichotomy breaks down: events during the dynamic process of adjustment affect where the economy finishes up. The productive potential of an economy, for example, depends not only on its current stocks of capital and labour but also on recent economic history. The economy may be less productive after a slump than it would have been with the same stocks of capital and labour but a past history of full employment. Unemployment leads to atrophy of specialized skills and general enthusiasm for work; and depression involves close-downs of business organizations and losses of business contacts. A slump may thus have a permanent effect in lowering the economy's full-employment output. The practical importance of hysteresis is a matter of controversy.

I

IBRD *See* International Bank for Reconstruction and Development.

ICC *See* Interstate Commerce Commission.

IDA *See* International Development Association.

identification problem The problem of estimating the parameters of structural equations when all that can be observed is equilibrium positions. For example, in the market for a particular good, if demand conditions vary and supply conditions do not, comparing prices and quantities at different times allows us to determine the supply equation; if supply conditions vary and demand conditions do not, we can estimate the demand equation; but if both supply and demand conditions vary, regressing quantity on price tells us nothing. The identification problem can be resolved only if either theory or the results of other studies inform us that some explanatory variables affect one side of the market but not the other.

identity (symbol ≡) An equation which must hold by definition of the variables involved. Thus $z \equiv x + y$ means that z is defined as the sum of x and y. Many economists do not use this notation consistently, but write = even when the relation concerned is really an identity.

idiosyncratic risk Risk of a type which affects each individual case largely independent of others. This could apply to the risk of an individual dying, of a house catching fire, or a car having an accident, during any period. Idiosyncratic risk allows insurance companies, by pooling risks, to insure customers, while keeping their own overall risk exposure relatively small. This is contrasted with market risk, where events such as a slump, a flu epidemic, or a hurricane, affect large numbers of individuals in a similar manner.

if and only if (iff) Equivalence between two statements. 'If A then B' means A is a sufficient condition for B and B is a necessary condition for A. 'If B then A' means B is a sufficient condition for A and A is a necessary condition for B. If both these statements are true, 'A if and only if B', written 'A iff B', means that each of A and B is a *necessary and sufficient condition for the other; either both are true or both are false. The two statements are thus equivalent.

IFC *See* International Finance Corporation.

iff *See* if and only if.

illiquidity 1. The property of not being easily turned into money. Some assets are illiquid because there are no markets on which they can easily be traded: for example, unsecured loans to bank customers. Other assets are illiquid because while they can be traded, the price that can be obtained may be hard to predict, especially if a quick sale is required. This applies to shares in companies, or to houses. This is contrasted with *liquidity, the property of being turned into money rapidly and at a fairly predictable

price. Apart from money itself, short-dated securities or bills are the main
asset of this form.

2. The property of having illiquid assets. A business may have problems
over meeting its obligations because, although it believes itself to be solvent,
its assets are not liquid. If its own view of its solvency were shared by credit
institutions it would be able to obtain liquidity on credit, but the information
which leads it to feel solvent may be private, for example confidence in new
products, and not convincing to creditors. It is possible that businesses forced
into liquidation through illiquidity eventually pay their creditors in full, that
is, experience shows that they really were solvent. A business which is
insolvent, on the other hand, is liable to fail, however liquid its assets may be.

illusion, money *See* money illusion.

imaginary number A number (symbol i) whose square equals a real
negative number. Imaginary numbers were invented to allow equations to be
solved when they have no real roots. For example, 1 has two real square roots,
+1 and −1. The equation $x^2 = 1$ thus has two real roots, $x = 1$ and $x = -1$. The
number −1 has no real square roots, so the equation $x^2 = -1$ has no real roots.
However, the 'imaginary' number, denoted by i, allows the equation $x^2 = -1$ to
have two imaginary roots, $x = i$ and $x = -i$. By convention i always precedes any
coefficient other than 1 or −1.

IMF *See* International Monetary Fund.

immigration Movement of foreign nationals to reside in a country. This
does not include people on short visits, for business or as tourists. Immigrants
may come with the intention of permanent settlement, with the intention of
returning home after a prolonged stay, or be uncertain at the time of arrival
how long they will wish to stay. Immigration is motivated by 'push' and 'pull'
factors. Push factors could be poverty or persecution in the country migrants
are leaving; pull factors could be economic opportunity or freedom in the
country they go to. In many cases both factors may be at work; people want to
leave country A to avoid persecution, but prefer to go to B rather than C
because economic opportunities are better in B; or they want to leave A to
escape from poverty but prefer B to C as a destination because they are better
treated in B. Most countries welcome immigrants with great wealth or scarce
skills, but seek to limit immigrants with neither.

immiserizing growth Growth of national or regional production which
actually decreases welfare. This could occur if the effect of growth of part of
the world economy was to worsen its *terms of trade so much that its welfare
actually fell. This is unlikely for a single country, as even if growth worsens its
terms of trade, much of the resulting loss falls on other countries exporting
similar products. It could conceivably apply to a group of countries
specializing on exporting a product in *inelastic demand, for example oil
exporters. It has been suggested that it could apply to LDCs as a group: this
seems unlikely given the wide variety of goods they export, many of them
manufactures with elastic world demand. It must be remembered that worse
terms of trade do not necessarily imply immiserizing growth: if trade
accounts for 20 per cent of national income, the terms of trade have to
worsen by over 5 per cent for each 1 per cent growth of output for growth to
be immiserizing.

immobile factors Factors which do not move readily between sectors, regions, or countries when relative rewards or job opportunities change. Immobility of labour between occupations may be due to lack of qualifications, or to inadequate information on job opportunities. Labour mobility between regions or countries is restricted by social ties, and by housing markets which are often organized so as to favour those who stay put over those who move. Mobility between countries is also hindered by differences of language and social customs, and frequently by legal restrictions. Mobility of capital, while often greater than that of labour, is also limited by lack of information, by differences between countries in law and commercial practices, and in many cases by legal restrictions.

impact effect The part of the effect of any economic event that acts immediately, or during a short time period. In the *multiplier model, for example, the impact effect of an injection of investment, government spending, or exports is 1 unit of further income for each unit spent. After leakages into tax payments, savings and imports, a second round of k units is created; then a further round of k^2, and so on. The eventual multiplier effect adds up to $1/(1-k)$, which is larger than the impact effect of 1. Some economic events have impact effects larger than their overall effects: for example, a temporary cut in VAT on cars would be expected to lead to planned car purchases being brought forward to take advantage of the tax saving, so its impact effect on the number of cars bought could exceed the eventual cumulative total effect.

impatience *See* discounting the future.

imperfect competition A market situation with a limited number of sellers. This is also known as *monopolistic competition: each firm realizes that the price it can charge is a decreasing function of the quantity it sells, so that it faces a downward-sloping demand curve. Imperfect competition assumes that sellers do not attempt to forecast the reactions of individual competitors; this is contrasted with *oligopoly, which assumes that firms take account of the expected reactions of individual rivals.

imperialism, economic *See* economic imperialism.

implicit contract A situation when people or firms expect to have continuing dealings with one another, and so need to agree the terms on which these will take place, but a formal or explicit contract between them is impossible or impracticable. The difficulties which make implicit contracts preferable to formal legal contracts arise mainly from uncertainty about the future and problems in getting information that can actually be proved to be reliable. A formal legal contract has to specify what is to happen under any given circumstances. If the number of possible sets of circumstances is very large then a legal contract might be excessively complicated to negotiate, and actual compliance with it might be impossible to monitor. In many cases, such as possible future innovations, circumstances may change in ways which cannot even be imagined in advance, let alone described in legally binding terms. An implicit contract implies that, while if circumstances develop in some ways the parties can behave as though there were a legal contract between them, if circumstances develop in other ways they simply have to trust one another to behave reasonably.

implicit function A relation between two variables treating them symmetrically. For example, the linear function $y = \alpha x + \beta$ can be inverted to give x as an explicit function of y, $x = -\beta/\alpha + y/\alpha$, or it can be written as an implicit function, $\alpha x - y = -\beta$. It is always possible to express an explicit function in implicit form, but it is often difficult and sometimes impossible to express an implicit function in explicit form: for example, if $x^2 + x^3 + y = 0$, try expressing x as an explicit function of y.

importables Goods of types which could be imported, whether or not they actually are. The UK, for example, both produces and imports butter.

import control Administrative restriction and allocation of imports. This may be imposed for balance-of-payments reasons, to reduce spending on imports, or for industrial policy reasons, to protect domestic producers of import substitutes. Administrative import controls reduce competition in the economy, and provide opportunities for corruption; programmes of economic liberalization generally include the abolition of import controls, or their replacement by tariffs.

import deposit A requirement to place a blocked deposit in advance with the central bank as the condition for obtaining foreign currency to pay for imports. Such a deposit has the effect both of imposing a tax on imports, and of reducing the money supply in circulation.

Import Duties Act, 1932 The UK Act of Parliament marking the end of the era during which *free trade was the accepted normal national trading policy. The Import Duties Act imposed a 10 per cent tariff on most items from non-Commonwealth countries, except food and raw materials, thus marking the end of free trade and the start of the policy of Imperial Preference.

import duty *See* tariff.

imported inflation Inflation due to increases in the prices of imports. Increases in the prices of imported final products directly affect any expenditure-based measure of inflation. Increases in the prices of imported fuels, materials, and components increase domestic costs of production, and lead to increases in the prices of domestically produced goods. Imported inflation may be set off by foreign price increases, or by depreciation of a country's exchange rate.

import levy *See* tariff.

import licence A permit from the government to import particular goods. The requirement for import licences may be intended to protect domestic producers from competition, to improve the balance of trade by restricting imports, or to facilitate government control over dangerous materials such as explosives. Even if a licence can be obtained, the requirement imposes extra transactions costs and delay on buying imports, and in some countries necessitates bribing the officials who issue licences.

import penetration The proportion of the market for a particular type of good that is supplied by imports. A rise in import penetration may result from an increase in demand which cannot be met from domestic sources, from worsening of the *competitiveness of domestic suppliers, or from relaxation or removal of restrictions on imports.

import propensity The proportion of the national income that is spent on imports. This can be measured both on average and at the margin. The short-run marginal propensity to import may be higher than the average, particularly at periods of high demand, because of supply constraints in the domestic economy.

import quota A quantitative limit to imports of some type of good. This may be set in terms of value or physical units. A quota in physical units is liable to lead to a rise in the average price of products imported, as higher-priced products generally carry a higher profit margin.

import restriction *See* import control.

imports Goods and services bought by residents of a country but provided by non-residents. Visible imports are goods physically brought into the country. Imports of services, or invisible imports, may involve the supplier entering the country, for example to put out oil-well fires, or residents going abroad to enjoy the services of airlines, hotels, or entertainments. For some invisible items, such as payment of royalties on patents, the location of the service is not defined. Capital import means accepting foreign loans or selling real domestic assets to non-residents. This should not be confused with the import of capital goods. Many countries in fact do both, but it is perfectly possible to import machinery without borrowing abroad, or to borrow abroad, for example to finance government spending on armaments, without importing capital goods.

import substitution A strategy for the industrialization of less developed countries (LDCs), of concentrating initially on replacing imports by domestically produced substitutes. This has the advantage that it is already known what markets exist for the products, but the disadvantage that as the imports most easily displaced fall, further progress becomes ever more difficult. If a country is small, its whole domestic market for a product may make it impossible for domestic producers to take full advantage of *economies of scale. The strategy of import substitution is contrasted with that of *export promotion, where LDCs' industrial effort concentrates on products that can be sold in world markets.

import surcharge A temporary additional tax on imports, imposed in addition to normal tariffs, in response to balance-of-payments problems. Such a temporary tax may be very effective in reducing imports, as it creates an incentive to postpone them until it has been removed.

import tariff *See* tariff.

imputation system The system of *corporation tax used in the UK since 1972. Dividends distributed to shareholders are subject to tax, but taxes on company profits collected in *Advance Corporation Tax (ACT) are treated as tax credits at basic rate for investors receiving dividends. Shareholders have the grossed-up value of their dividends treated as taxable income: if the basic rate of tax is t, the grossed up value of dividends is the amount received times $1/(1 - t)$. With basic rate tax already paid, shareholders are only liable for the excess of their own marginal tax rate over basic rate, and can claim refunds if their marginal rate of tax is lower than basic rate or if they are not subject to income tax.

imputed charge for consumption of non-trading capital An estimate of *capital consumption in respect of government assets such as offices, schools, or hospitals which are not run as profit-making businesses. The charge is in principle the amount which would need to be spent on new building to keep the real stock of assets constant.

imputed income Income attributed to the owner of an asset which could have been rented out to somebody else to produce a cash income, where the owner in fact uses the asset themselves. An example of an imputed income is the rental value of *owner-occupied housing: this is included in both the national income and consumption in the UK national income accounts. The argument for this is that without it national income would appear to fall whenever a rented house was purchased by its tenant. In some countries, though not the UK, the imputed income from owner-occupied housing is subject to income tax.

IMRO *See* Investment Management Regulatory Organization.

incentive-compatibility The requirement in economic models that people and firms are not assumed to act in ways contrary to their own interest. If a suggested equilibrium involves people choosing A when B is available to them, and they would prefer B to A, then the suggested equilibrium is not incentive-compatible. Policies have to be designed so that self-interest induces people to behave in the way that the authorities want.

incentives Rewards or penalties designed to induce one set of people to act in such as way as to produce results that another set of people want. As rewards for good results, incentives can include higher pay, better working conditions, better job security, better promotion prospects, or simply prestige. As penalties for poor results, incentives may take the form of lower pay, worse working conditions, poorer promotion prospects, demotion or sacking, or simply loss of reputation. Incentives may be applied in response to actual results, such as output or profits, or to management's perceptions of inputs, such as attendance and disciplinary record. Incentives cannot be based on inputs or outputs which cannot be observed by management: to motivate these it is necessary to rely on self-respect or team spirit. *See also* export incentives, and investment incentives.

incidence of taxation The distribution of the real burden of taxation. The distinction between direct and indirect taxes is based on the assumption that the real burden of *direct taxes falls on the person or firm responsible for paying them, whereas the real burden of *indirect taxes can be passed on to somebody else, usually a firm's customers. Neither assumption need be correct. If an income is a pure rent, the burden of a direct tax cannot be passed on; but taxes on earned incomes affect the incentives to work, taxes on property incomes affect the incentives to save, and taxes on profits affect the incentives to take risks. It is therefore possible that some of the real burden of direct taxes can be passed on, to employers, borrowers, or customers. Also, unless the goods concerned are in perfectly elastic supply, some of the burden of indirect taxes will fall on the suppliers of the goods taxed rather than the customers. Discovering who actually bears the real burden of paying taxes is extremely difficult.

income **1.** The amount an individual can spend in a period while leaving his or her capital unchanged. For an individual with neither assets nor debts, personal income can be defined as receipts from wages, or earned income, plus receipts from transfers, such as pensions. Taxable income is this minus any tax allowances. Net or disposable income is income after payment of direct taxes. Real income is money income deflated by a consumer price index, to find its purchasing power at constant prices. For an individual with assets or debts, income from rent, dividends and interest, or unearned income, has to be added to earned and transfer income. Interest paid out should logically be deducted, though actual tax systems tend to restrict such deductions. For individuals with real or financial assets, the distinction between receipts which are treated as income and those which are treated as *capital gains is a highly technical and often arbitrary matter. For individuals with financial assets consisting of money or securities whose value is denominated in money terms, interest received should logically have losses in real purchasing power due to inflation deducted in measuring their real income. Tax systems, however, generally ignore this point and treat cash receipts as income.

2. The amount that can be spent consistently with being able to maintain the same level of spending in the future. This is defined as permanent income: it is exceedingly difficult to measure objectively, as it is a forward-looking concept. Permanent income is affected by expected levels of earned income, unearned income, and transfers from the state or other individuals due to be received over a whole lifetime of unknown length. This can only be estimated, and not measured.

3. The receipts of firms or public corporations from sales or payments of interest and dividends by other firms. These appear as the income side in income and expenditure accounts. Only any net profits in these accounts can be considered to be income in a sense comparable with individual incomes.

4. A macroeconomic aggregate, equal to the sum of individual earned and unearned incomes, the undistributed profits of companies, and property income accruing to the government. National income does not include *transfer payments, which merely transfer part of the national income from one set of individuals to another. If transfers are large, personal incomes before taxation can exceed national income. National income is derived from *gross domestic product (GDP) at factor cost by two main adjustments. First, *capital consumption has to be subtracted; this is an estimate of the amount that would have to be spent on replacement investment to keep the nation's capital stock unchanged. Second, net property income from abroad has to be added, as national income refers to the income of residents, regardless of whether this arises from activities carried on domestically or abroad. The income approach is one of three methods used in national income accounting to measure aggregate economic activity: this approach works by adding the incomes of all sectors of the economy. The other approaches are the *output method, looking at the outputs of various sectors, and the *expenditure method, which adds the expenditures of various sectors of the economy.

5. The income effect of a change in price is the change in demand for a good whose price has altered which would have resulted if prices had stayed the same, but incomes had risen or fallen sufficiently to bring consumers to the same level of welfare as after the price change.

6. Income support is government payments to keep people's incomes up to some prescribed minimum level, in the event of illness, old age, disability or unemployment making them unable to earn it for themselves. Negative income tax is a system in which this is done through a combined tax and social security system, which collects tax if income is above a certain level and pays out if income is below it.

7. Income distribution is concerned with the shares of total income going to different groups. Functional income distribution looks at the shares of different types of income, for example wages and profits; personal income distribution looks at the shares of income going to people whose total incomes are of various sizes. *See also* circular flow of incomes, disposable income, earned income, factor incomes, imputed income, permanent income, taxable income, and unearned income.

income approach to GDP *See* income method.

income change, compensating *See* compensating variation.

income distribution The division of total income between different recipients. Functional income distribution is the division of income between the owners of the different factors of production. Personal income distribution is the distribution of incomes classified by size. Income distribution can be measured before and after the deduction of direct taxes and the addition of transfers.

income effect The part of the response in the demand for a good to a change in its price which is due to the rise in the real income of consumers resulting from a price decrease. This effect is normally positive, except for inferior goods, for which the income effect is negative.

The horizontal axis shows quantity of good X; the vertical axis shows quantity of all other goods at constant relative prices, measured by Y. ABC is

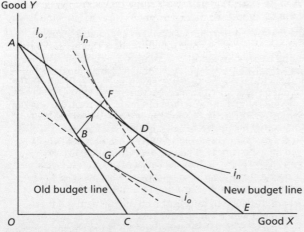

FIGURE 13: *Income and Substitution Effects*

the old budget line, at original prices. B is the old equilibrium, where the consumer reached indifference curve i_o. ADE is the new budget line, after the price of X is reduced. D is the new equilibrium, where the consumer reaches indifference curve i_n. The shift from B to D can be decomposed in two alternative ways.

1. Point F on i_n shows the equilibrium with the old prices but the new welfare level; the slope of i_n at F is equal to the slope of ABC. The shift from B to F is the income effect, as real income rises while relative prices are unchanged; the shift from F to D is the substitution effect, as relative prices change holding real income constant.

2. Alternatively, point G represents the situation with the old welfare level but the new relative prices; the slope of i_o at G is equal to the slope of ADE. The shift from B to G is the substitution effect, as relative prices change holding real income constant; the shift from G to D is the income effect, as real income rises holding relative prices constant. For very small changes, BF and GD are equal and parallel, as are BG and FD. For discrete changes in price these equalities are only approximate.

income elasticity of demand The ratio of proportional increase in quantity demanded to proportional increase in income, with all prices held constant. A luxury is a good with an income elasticity of demand in excess of unity: a higher proportion of income is spent on luxuries as income rises. A necessity has an income elasticity of demand which is positive but less than unity: as income rises, spending on a necessity rises, but the proportion of income spent on it falls. An inferior good has a negative income elasticity of demand: as income rises, spending on inferior goods falls. *See also* the figure for Engel curve.

income expansion path A graph showing how income is divided between different uses, for example importables and exportables, as its total level rises. With unit income elasticity of demand for each, the income expansion path is a ray through the origin; if consumption is biased towards importables as income rises, the income expansion path has a slope between a ray through the origin and the importables axis.

income from employment Income from wages and salaries earned working for another person, firm, or government body. It can be measured including or excluding benefits in kind, such as housing, company cars, or free health insurance received from employers. It can also be measured net or gross of deductions by employers, including superannuation contributions, income tax, and national insurance contributions.

income from self-employment Income of individuals derived from carrying on unincorporated businesses, as sole traders or partners. This is a combination of wages for their own or their family's work, and a return on the capital employed in the business. It can be measured inclusive or exclusive of any imputed income, such as the services of an owner-occupied farmhouse or a flat over a shop. It can also be measured gross or net of depreciation allowances on the capital equipment employed.

income inequality *See* inequality of incomes.

income method The procedure of measuring domestic product by adding the factor incomes received by various members of the economy. This approach is largely based on information derived from the tax system. Its results are compared with the figures produced by the expenditure method, which uses information on expenditures by various sectors of the economy including consumers, investors, and the government, and the output method, which uses information on the net outputs of various sectors of the economy.

income per capita *See* per capita income.

income redistribution The use of taxation, government spending, and controls to change the distribution of real incomes. Taxation may be more or less progressive. Government spending programmes may be generally available, or may be targeted or means-tested to try to concentrate benefits on the relatively needy. Controls may be used to alter income distribution: for example, rent controls were originally designed to prevent housing shortages from shifting income from tenants to landlords, and minimum wage legislation aims to benefit low-paid workers at the expense of their employers. The extent of income redistribution through the tax system can be measured by comparing the inequality of income distributions before and after tax. The ability of the state to redistribute incomes is limited by the need to avoid too much damage to the incentives to create income by work, savings, and enterprise.

incomes and prices policy *See* prices and incomes policy.

incomes policy *See* prices and incomes policy, and tax-based incomes policy.

income support Payments by the state to bring people's incomes up to a socially acceptable level. Such payments are made to various groups, including the old, the disabled, the sick, and the unemployed. Making such payments is justified on equity grounds, and on the argument that allowing incomes to fall below some minimum level carries dangers to public health, and to public order if poverty encourages crime. The availability of income support gives rise to *moral hazard: support for the sick or disabled could encourage malingering, support for the unemployed could impair the incentives to seek work, and state pensions undermine the incentives to private savings. Many modern economies find the cost of income support schemes a serious problem.

income tax A tax on income. Income tax is normally zero on some bands of small incomes, both on equity grounds and because of the expense of collecting tiny amounts of tax. It is then normally proportional up to some upper limit; income beyond this is taxed at higher rates. Thus income tax is usually progressive. An individuals's taxable income is calculated after deducting various allowances, in respect of assorted items which may include mortgage interest payable, charitable donations, responsibility for dependents, age allowances, medical insurance, and superannuation contributions. Income for tax purposes may include or exclude imputed items such as the value of the services of owner-occupied houses. *Capital gains may be included as income, excluded, or taxed separately from income. Income tax may be collected from individuals in arrears, or by deduction at source through *pay-as-you-earn (PAYE) in the UK, or a withholding tax on incomes from employment and payment of dividends net of tax by companies, in the US. *See also* corporate income tax, and negative income tax.

income velocity of circulation The ratio of national income to the stock of money, on some definition. This is considerably smaller than the actual velocity of circulation, as there is a high ratio of total transactions to income in a modern economy: firms buy factor inputs in one set of markets and sell outputs in another, and there is a lot of trade in intermediate products. In any case there is a far larger volume of transactions on capital account than on income account.

incomplete information Not having available all possible information; this is the normal situation when economic decisions have to be taken. There is in principle an unlimited amount of information we could have: most of us possess only a minute fraction of this, and only by knowing it all could we tell for certain which bits were relevant. 'Incomplete information' normally indicates that the person or firm taking a given decision lacks some particular pieces of information which other people do have available.

incomplete markets Situations where certain goods or services cannot be traded because there is no organized market on which to trade. Markets may be incomplete for various reasons. One is that the goods concerned have not yet been invented, so that no contract involving them can be specified. Another is that while the conditions of a contract could be specified, this would be so complex that the legal bills would outweigh the benefits. Another is that there are too few people interested in contracts of a given type to make an organized market in them worth the costs of operating it.

increase in the book value of stocks and work in progress The increase over some period in the value of stocks and work in progress as shown in firms' accounts. This can be decomposed into two parts: the value at current prices of the real increase in stocks and work in progress, and stock appreciation, that is changes in the value of the original level of stocks due to price increases. The real change in stocks forms part of gross domestic product (GDP); stock appreciation does not.

increasing function A function whose value increases as its argument increases. If $y = f(x)$, y is an increasing function of x if and only if $dy/dx \geq 0$ for all x. y is a strictly increasing function of x if and only if $dy/dx > 0$ for all x.

increasing returns to scale Average productivity increasing with output. In a productive process this means that increasing all inputs in the same proportion results in a more than proportional increase in output.

incremental capital–output ratio *See* capital–output ratio.

incumbent firm A firm which is already in position in a market. In a fully *contestable market, where the goods produced by different firms are homogeneous and there are no *sunk costs, there is complete symmetry between an incumbent firm and would-be entrants. If goods can vary in quality, so that reputation matters, and if there are any sunk costs, the incumbent is in a stronger competitive position than potential entrants: the incumbent has established market contacts, and has already incurred the sunk costs. An incumbent will have a further competitive advantage if cost savings come from *learning by doing: an existing firm has a start on any new entrant in the experience from which cost reductions are derived.

indefinite integral A function whose *first derivative is equal to a given function. If $g(x)$ is the derivative of $f(x)$, then $f(x) + k$, where k is any arbitrary constant, is the indefinite integral of $g(x)$. This is written $\int g(x)dx = f(x) + k$.

independence, central bank *See* central bank independence.

independent risks Risks on projects where there is no relation between the results of one and those of the other. If the outcomes are the random variables x and y, with means μ_x and μ_y, the risks are independent if the expected value $E[(x - \mu_x)(y - \mu_y)] = 0$.

independent taxation of spouses A system of personal taxation in which individuals are taxed on the basis of their own income only, independent of their marital status and the income of their spouse. The UK in 1990 introduced a system which is not quite independent taxation of spouses, since a married man's allowance was retained, and some taxable items and allowances are transferable between spouses. This system was introduced because the previous system of joint taxation of spouses was felt to involve both breaches of financial privacy for married women, and tax discrimination against marriage, since aggregated incomes made spouses liable to tax at higher marginal rates than under independent taxation.

index *See* base-weighted index, cost of living index, current-weighted index, discomfort index, price index, trade-weighted index number, value index, and volume index.

indexation A system by which wages, prices, or the interest and redemption payments on securities are not fixed in money terms, but are adjusted in proportion to a suitable index of prices, such as the *Retail Price Index (RPI). Similarly pensions can be linked either to prices or to wage rates. Indexation of prices and wages is intended to stabilize real incomes and income differentials; when applied subject to time lags, it does this only approximately.

indexation (funds) A system for making the performance of an investment or unit trust mimic that of a share index. This is done by holding, in proportions approximating to their weights in the index, all the shares concerned or a sufficiently large sample of them.

Index, Laspeyres *See* base-weighted index.

index-linked An economic variable whose value is linked to an index number. Index-linked government securities have their interest and redemption payments linked to a suitable price index, for example the *Retail Price Index (RPI). Wage rates and pensions may also be index-linked, again normally to the RPI. Index-linked securities or pensions may be linked either to the RPI or to some index of share prices. The advantage of index-linked securities or incomes is that they protect the holder against the effects or large unforeseen changes in the value of money. A wide spread of index-linking arrangements in an economy may help to make inflation more difficult to stop, as it eliminates the effects of price increases in reducing the real claims on the rest of the economy of holders of cash and of securities whose value is fixed in cash terms.

index number A number showing the size of some variable, relative to a given base. The base may be assigned any value, but is normally chosen to be either 1 or 100. For a time series, the base may be the value at a given date; for cross-section data, it may be some chosen instance, or the mean of the items covered. Where an index number describes a constructed variable, such as 'the price level', which is an average of prices, or gross domestic product (GDP), which is an aggregate of many different sectors, it is a weighted average of the index numbers for the various components. A *base-weighted or Laspeyres index uses as weights the relative sizes of the different items at the base period; a *current-weighted or Paasche index uses as weights the relative sizes of the component items during the current period.

Index of Industrial Production An index of the volume of production covering the productive sectors of the economy. This is a weighted average of the indexes for manufacturing, mining and quarrying, public utilities and construction. It is mainly based on measures of physical volume; it excludes private and public services.

index, Paasche *See* current-weighted index.

indicative planning An attempt to promote economic growth by influencing expectations. Indicative planning attempts to combine the advantages of decentralization and central planning. Growth in an economy may lag because of pessimistic expectations: firms do not expect other firms to invest, and do not feel that market prospects make it profitable for them to invest. Central planning would tell firms to invest, but this is thought to be too rigid. Under indicative planning the government sets out to produce a set of forecasts of activity in various sectors, which if believed would persuade each firm that its own investments would be profitable. In view of the difficulty of forecasting technical progress and taste changes, it is doubtful whether indicative planning can do any better than simply proclaiming overall targets for macroeconomic policy.

indicator A variable used in deciding on the use of *policy instruments. Policy indicators are distinguished from both targets and instruments. Economic policy targets include objectives such as high levels of employment and growth, low and stable levels of inflation, or maintenance of particular exchange rates. Policy instruments are variables the government or central bank can control, or at least influence, such as tax rates or the money supply. Policy indicators may themselves be targets, but frequently are not. They are preferred to targets for use in decision-taking because they are available sooner or can be measured more reliably than targets. Policy instruments cannot be indicators for the authority that decides them, but where decision-making is decentralized, one authority's instrument may be used as another's indicator. *See also* leading indicator.

indifference curve A diagram representing the preferences of an individual. If the amounts of two goods consumed are shown on the axes, an indifference curve connects combinations of the two goods giving equal welfare. Combinations above any indifference curve are preferred to those on it, and these are preferred to those below. The indifference curves for any individual cannot cross. The slope of an indifference curve at any point shows the marginal rate of substitution between the goods, and the *elasticity of substitution measures its curvature. Since the axes represent goods, indifference curves are downward-sloping by assumption. They are generally assumed to be convex to the origin, but this, if correct, is a psychological fact and not a logical necessity. Consumers who are price-takers cannot be in equilibrium, with maximized utility, at any point where their indifference curve is concave to the origin. Indifference curves can also be drawn up with a good, for example income, on one axis, and a bad, such as work done, on the other. *Community indifference curves are drawn for countries in international trade theory, but such curves are valid only for rather restrictive assumptions about income distribution within a country.

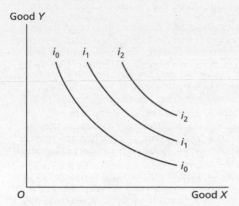

FIGURE 14: *Indifference Curves*

The horizontal axis shows consumption of good X; the vertical axis shows consumption of good Y. i_0 shows a lower level of utility than i_1, which in turn shows a lower level of utility than i_2. Indifference curves for the same individual cannot cross. The curves are drawn concave upwards: this is a plausible empirical assumption, not a logical necessity. They may or may not meet the two axes. *See also* the figure for elasticity of substitution.

indirect tax A tax on spending on goods or services, for example value-added tax or taxes on alcohol and tobacco. The term indirect tax is used because it is usually assumed that the real incidence of such a tax will not fall on the firm immediately responsible for paying it: the tax will rather be passed on to the customer, who thus bears the tax burden indirectly. Whether this assumption is correct depends on the elasticity of supply of factors to the industry concerned: only if this supply is perfectly elastic will an indirect tax be passed on completely.

indirect utility function A function giving utility as a function of income and prices. In an indirect utility function, utility is expressed as an increasing function of non-work income and the wage rate for work performed, and a decreasing function of the prices of goods and services consumed. This is contrasted with a normal or direct utility function, where utility is an increasing function of goods or services consumed and a decreasing function of work performed. The partial derivative of the indirect utility function with respect to any good's price equals–(quantity consumed) × (marginal utility of income); the partial derivative of the indirect utility function with respect to the wage rate equals (amount of work performed) × (marginal utility of income).

Individual Savings Account (ISA) A UK scheme designed to encourage savings, by allowing individuals to invest a limited sum annually in assets which are not subject to income tax or capital gains tax. This replaced the Personal Equity Plan scheme in 1999. The permitted limits can vary annually; in 2000–2001 they were either a 'mini ISA' of up to £3,000 in stocks and shares, a 'mini cash ISA' of up to £3,000 in securities such as building society deposits, and a 'mini insurance ISA' of up to £1,000 in life insurance, or up to £7,000 in a 'maxi ISA' in stocks and shares.

indivisibility The existence of a minimum scale at which any technique can operate. This applies to all productive techniques. In some cases the minimum scale is so small that it has no economic effects, but in other cases it is sufficiently large to make the technique unavailable to small firms. Indivisibilities in techniques are a major source of both *economies of scale and *economies of scope.

induced investment Investment in response to changes in output. This applies at a macro- rather than a microeconomic level. Investment by a firm cannot be a technical reponse to its own past output, which has already been produced with the capital in place. Investment may, however, be affected by ouput changes through their effects on profits. When output rises, because overhead costs can be spread more widely profits rise, and this both provides funds for investment directly and makes it easier to borrow. Investment is not determined by future changes in a firm's output: output and investment plans are formed simultaneously. Investment by each firm responds to expectations about market prospects, which are influenced by changes in the incomes of its customers. Induced investment is contrasted with autonomous investment, which is determined by long-run factors independent of short-run changes in income, such as technical innovations.

induction, proof by *See* proof by induction.

industrial action Action taken by trade unions or informal groups of workers to bring pressure to bear on employers when *industrial disputes have not been settled by negotiation or arbitration. Such action by workers can include go-slows, 'working to rule', overtime bans, or strikes. Industrial action by employers can include temporary lay-offs or lock-outs.

Industrial Classification, Standard *See* Standard Industrial Classification.

industrial concentration *See* concentration.

industrial countries Countries whose GDP and exports contain a large share of industrial production. The list of countries which could be described as industrial is continually changing. The International Monetary Fund (IMF) uses the name for the group of mainly advanced economies included in the

*Organization for Economic Cooperation and Development (OECD). This group includes the United States, Canada, Japan, Turkey, Australia, New Zealand, and eighteen European countries; Austria, Belgium, Denmark, Finland, France, Germany, Greece, Iceland, Ireland, Italy, Luxembourg, the Netherlands, Norway, Portugal, Spain, Sweden, Switzerland, and the United Kingdom. This definition omits the newly industrialized countries (NICs), including Brazil, Korea, and Singapore, and the countries of the former Soviet Union and Central and Eastern Europe, of which several, including Russia and the Czech Republic, are heavily industrialized.

industrial democracy The principle that all those employed in a firm should have a say in how it is run. This can take various forms. In cases where capital requirements are relatively small, it is possible that a firm can be owned by those who work in it. In this case the workers can elect the directors and managers, and control all decisions taken. In cases where too much capital is required for this to be possible, or where the workers do not want to accept the risks involved in being owners, they can have a share in decisions, electing some directors. Alternatively, the actual direction of a firm can be by managers appointed by its owners, but workers can be consulted about decisions, either through *works councils elected by the employees, or through their trade unions. The owners of firms may feel that some degree of industrial democracy is actually desirable from their point of view, as it improves workers' motivation and lessens the chance that management will blunder into unpopular decisions leading to industrial disputes which could have been avoided.

industrial dispute A disagreement between employees and employers concerning pay, hours of work, working conditions, mannning levels, or job security. Industrial disputes may be settled by conciliation, that is discussion; by arbitration by some third party agreed on by both sides or prescribed by law; or by industrial action, including overtime bans, go-slows, or in the last resort strikes or lock-outs. The employees are normally organized by trade unions; employers may negotiate separately or via employers' associations.

industrial economics The aspects of economics concerned with the organization of productive activities. This includes the factors determining which activities are co-ordinated within firms and which through markets; the problems connected with providing incentives within firms to overcome *principal–agent problems; the relation between the structure of industries and their performance; and the public regulation of monopolies, mergers, and competition. 'The new industrial economics' is a name given to the application of game theory to the formal modelling of these areas.

industrial espionage The illicit acquisition of information by one business about the activities of another. Such information may include formulae, designs, business plans, or information about personnel. The methods of industrial espionage include theft of documents, phone tapping, and computer hacking, with or without help from corrupt employees of the firm being spied on.

industrialization The process of moving resources into the industrial sector. This is common in the early stages of economic development, when resources move out of primary production. Industrialization was the norm in the now advanced countries earlier in their development, and was energetically pursued by many LDCs and by the former planned economies of the ex-USSR and Central and Eastern Europe. In recent years most of the advanced economies have seen *deindustrialization; this is not really the reverse of industrialization, as it mainly involves a shift of resources from producing goods into service sectors.

industrial licensing *See* licensing.

Industrial Ordinary Share Index, Financial Times *See* Financial Times Industrial Ordinary Share Index.

industrial policy Official policies concerning the direction of economic activity to particular parts of the economy. For many years governments were concerned with the division of economies between industry and primary production; the less industrialized countries tried to encourage the growth of local industry, while the more industrial countries protected their native agriculture and mines. In more recent years attention has centred on trying to encourage the rise of *high-tech sectors using advanced technology. Policies have included using tax rules and government money to encourage *research and development (R&D), intervention in financial markets to direct investment funds into favoured sectors, and intervention in the mergers market to try to obtain firms large enough to gain economies of scale. Critics of industrial policy argue that governments have shown little talent at *picking winners to back when making specific interventions, and would do better by promoting generally favourable conditions for technical advance, such as generous provision for scientific and technical eduation.

industrial production, index of *See* index of industrial production.

industrial relations The relations between the management and workforce of an enterprise, particularly bargaining through *trade unions. This mainly concerns pay, hours and conditions of work, fringe benefits, security of employment, redundancy and redundancy payments, and disciplinary and grievance procedures. Many of these matters are affected by legislation, but the law may leave scope for disagreement, and in various ways the treatment received by employees may be more generous than is legally compulsory. Disputes in industrial relations may be resolved by negotiation, arbitration, or industrial action by either side.

industrial sector The part of the economy concerned with producing goods without much direct input of natural resources. This secondary sector is distinguished from the primary producing sector, that is agriculture, fishing, forestry, and mining and quarrying, which produces goods with large direct inputs of natural resources, and the tertiary sector, including transport, distribution, finance, health, education, and administration, which produces services.

industry 1. A sector of the economy, in which firms use similar factor inputs to make a group of related products. The *Standard Industrial Classification (SIC) is a partition of goods into sectors and sub-sectors.
2. A group of sectors, mainly in manufacturing and construction, typically producing physical goods rather than services. The Confederation of British Industry (CBI) is a UK organization representing firms in these sectors, and

the Department of Trade and Industry (DTI) is the main UK government department responsible for dealing with them.

3. Hard and persistent work. *See also* footloose industry, infant industry, nationalized industry, and service industry.

industry demand for labour The demand for labour by an industry as a function of the wage rate. At any given wage rate, industry demand for labour depends on output. If wage rates fall, this can raise industry demand for labour in three ways. First, labour may be substituted for other inputs; second, a reduction in costs may lower price and increase demand for the industry's output; and third, in the longer run a rise in profits may induce new firms to enter the industry and take on additional workers. Industry demand for labour is more elastic the better the opportunities for substitution between labour and other inputs, the more elastic demand for the industry's output, and the more elastic the supply of potential entrants.

industry supply curve *See* supply curve.

inefficiency Not getting the best possible results from the use of resources. This is costly to the economy, as it means either getting lower outputs than would have been possible, or using more resources than necessary to get any given results. X-inefficiency, or organizational slack, means that enterprises are producing the right outputs, but are using an unnecessary level of inputs. Allocative inefficiency means that while cost-effective methods are in use within enterprises, resources are being used to produce the wrong combinations of goods and services: different goods and services do not contribute to welfare in proportion to their opportunity costs. Many actual organizations suffer from both X- and allocative inefficiency. Wherever there are *external economies and diseconomies there may be actions that appear privately efficient but are socially inefficient, and actions that appear privately inefficient but are socially efficient. *See also* X-inefficiency.

inelastic Lacking in responsiveness. Where one variable, x, can affect another, y, the relation is inelastic if a proportional change in x is associated with a smaller proportional change in y, of whichever sign is appropriate. Demand for a good is inelastic if a fall in price produces a smaller proportional increase in quantity demanded, so that total revenue falls when quantity increases, and marginal revenue is negative.

inelastic demand Weak response of quantity demanded to price, so that a proportional fall in price produces a smaller proportional increase in quantity demanded. Total revenue thus falls when quantity increases, and marginal revenue is negative. Such a price will not be chosen by a profit-maximizing firm, but can occur as the equilibrium in a competitive industry.

inelastic supply Low response of quantity supplied to price. The supply of a good or service is inelastic if a given percentage increase in the price at which it can be sold produces a smaller percentage increase in the quantity supplied. Supply is inelastic if a rise in price causes little increase in output by existing firms and little entry to an industry of new firms. If it is easy to expand production in existing firms, or to attract entry of new firms, supply is not inelastic.

inequality The state of not being equal. If two numbers x and y are known not to be equal, but the direction of inequality is not known, this is written $x \neq y$. Inequality of known direction may be strong or weak. Strong inequality means x is larger than y, written $x > y$, or x is smaller than y, written $x < y$. Weak inequality means x is larger than or equal to y, written $x \geq y$, or x is smaller than or equal to y, written $x \leq y$. Where **x** and **y** denote vectors rather than numbers, the notation for inequalities is more complicated: a mathematics textbook needs to be consulted.

inequality of incomes Differences in income between individuals or families, or between different groups, areas, or countries. Inequalities between individuals are accounted for by differences in earning ability, and in property. Individuals who are economically inactive, through age, ill health, or inability to find a job usually have low incomes even after taking account of social security benefits, and those who can work have very varied earning power. Property is also unevenly distributed: inequalities in earned and property incomes are highly correlated and there is also a tendency for high-income earners to intermarry. This means that families or households also show great inequality of incomes. Inequality can be measured either before of after taking account of direct taxes and social security payments: these tend to reduce but fall far short of eliminating income inequality. Statistical measures of inequality include the *Gini coefficient. Regional and national income differences are similarly caused by differences in earning ability and national capital stocks.

infant industry A new industry which during its early stages is unable to compete with established producers abroad. Governments are often urged to support the development of new industries either by direct subsidies, or by protective *tariffs or other trade controls. It is not clear that it is necessarily a good idea for governments to support infant industries at all. Problems because of small scale and lack of experience in production, and lack of market reputation in selling, are part of the *sunk costs of becoming established, and it can be argued that new industries should not be started unless long-run profits are expected to be sufficent to repay these costs and leave something over. State support for infant industries is justified if there are external benefits, for example if the industry creates new skills which can then be exploited by other industries, or if the capital market is imperfect and the government is more far-sighted than private investors. Even if a new industry should be supported, an infant industry tariff is probably not a good method. The tariff raises the price of the good to consumers, thus slowing the growth of the market. If supporting an infant industry is worth while, a subsidy would do it at lower cost.

inferior good A good of which less is demanded at any given price as income rises, over some range of incomes. An inferior good thus has a negative *income elasticity of demand, over this income range. A good is most likely to be inferior if it has a close substitute of higher quality. It should be noted that a good cannot be inferior at all levels of income. *See also* the figure for Engel curve.

infinitesimal Extremely small. However small a number other than zero may be, it is always possible to find another even closer to zero. The derivative of a continuous function considers the limit to which the ratio between changes in a function and changes in its argument tends as both changes become infinitesimally small.

infinity (symbol ∞) An extremely large amount. However large any finite number may be, it is always possible to find one even larger. Infinity means an amount larger than any chosen positive number. A variable is said to tend to infinity, written → ∞, as it increases without limit. Similarly minus infinity, written – ∞, is less than any finite negative number.

inflation A persistent tendency for prices and money wages to increase. Inflation is measured by the proportional changes over time in some appropriate price index, commonly a consumer price index or a *GDP deflator. Because of changes in the type and quality of goods available, measures of inflation are probably not reliable to closer than a margin of 1 or 2 per cent a year, but if prices rise faster than this there is no doubt that inflation exists. Economists have attempted to distinguish cost and demand inflation. Cost inflation is started by an increase in some element of costs, for example the oil price explosion of 1973–4. Demand inflation is due to too much aggregate demand. Once started, inflation tends to persist through an inflationary spiral, in which various prices and wage rates rise because others have risen. The inflation tax is the real cost to the holders of money due to its loss of real purchasing power during inflation. *Hyperinflation is extremely rapid inflation, in which prices increase so fast that money largely loses its convenience as a medium of exchange. *See also* core inflation, cost inflation, creeping inflation, demand inflation, expected inflation, imported inflation, menu costs of inflation, repressed inflation, shoe-leather costs of inflation, underlying rate of inflation, and unexpected inflation.

inflation accounting The attempt to produce meaningful company accounts under inflationary conditions. During inflation, *depreciation allowances on capital goods based on historical cost do not provide for their replacement, and thus overstate profits, and increases in the prices of inventories also produce paper profits in excess of real ones. On the other hand, if interest rates increase in response to inflation. counting nominal interest payments as costs but taking no credit for the decrease in the real value of a firm's debts understates true profits. There are also difficulties if the prices of a firm's capital goods, inventories, or output change at different rates from the general price level. Despite massive efforts by the accountancy profession, no fully satisfactory method of inflation accounting has yet emerged.

inflation-adjusted budget deficit The budget deficit which would result if government expenditure was reckoned as including the real rather than the nominal interest paid out. For example, consider a government whose budget deficit before adjustment for inflation equals 2 per cent of GNP. If net government debt equals half of GNP, and nominal interest rates are 10 per cent but inflation is 5 per cent, then nominal debt interest equals 5 per cent of GNP, while real debt interest equals only 2 ½ per cent of GNP. In this case a nominal budget deficit equal to 2 per cent of GNP corresponds to an inflation-adjusted budget surplus equal to ½ per cent of GNP.

inflationary gap The excess of the actual level of activity in the economy over the level corresponding to the *non-accelerating inflation level of unemployment (NAIRU). If the inflationary gap is positive, inflation tends to speed up, and the larger the inflationary gap, the faster inflation speeds up. An inflationary gap thus gives rise to *demand inflation.

inflationary spiral The tendency for prices and wages to react in turn to increases in other wages and prices during a cost inflation. During this process prices rise to pass on increases in costs because of rises in wages and fuel or materials prices; while wages rise because of increases in the cost of living. If cost rises are partially absorbed, the spiral will gradually converge; if nobody consents to absorb cost increases, an inflationary spiral can continue indefinitely once it has started.

inflation tax The effect of inflation on the real value of money and government debt denominated in money terms. For example, if the population of a country hold money equal in value to 10 per cent of GNP and government debt equal in value to 30 per cent of GNP, annual inflation of 10 per cent removes an amount equal to 1 per cent of GNP from the real purchasing power of their money balances, and an amount equal to 3 per cent of GNP from the real value of their security holdings. This is equivalent to a tax of 4 per cent of GNP. The government can incur a nominal budget deficit equal to the yield of the inflation tax without increasing the real value of its debts, including issue of fiat money.

inflection, point of See point of inflection.

inflow, capital See capital movements.

information The data available to individuals, firms, or governments at the time when economic decisions have to be taken. There is in principle an indefinitely large amount of this; in practice even the largest and most sophisticated bodies, such as central banks and multinationals, know only a small fraction of it. Information concerns states of nature, technology, the decisions of other economic agents, and one's own preferences and plans. None of this is known with complete certainty; even one's own tastes may only be discovered through trial and error. *Asymmetric information is the normal situation, where each participant in a market knows some things the others do not, and does not know some things that other people do. Even the facts that people think they know will in any case usually not be 100 per cent correct. See also asymmetric information, incomplete information, and price-sensitive information.

information agreement An agreement by a number of firms to provide one another with information on their prices, discounts, and conditions of sale. This information is usually provided through a *trade association, either before or after changes are made. While such an exchange of information is not itself a restrictive practice, it could clearly assist in collusion. In the UK such agreements are required to be registered with the *Office of Fair Trading (OFT), and may be referred to the *Restrictive Practices Court (RPC).

infrastructure The capital equipment used to produce publicly available services, including transport and telecommunications, and gas, electricity, and water supplies. These provide an essential background for other economic activities in modern economies; the fact that they are not available or reliable is characteristic of *less developed countries (LDCs), and handicaps their development. Infrastructure services are generally either provided or regulated by the state.

inheritance tax A tax on amounts inherited by particular heirs. The tax rate can vary according to the relation with the deceased, for example spouses may be exempt; or progressively with the amount received. It is possible, as in the UK, to combine an inheritance tax with a tax on gifts *inter vivos*, that is while the donor is still alive, via a *capital transfer tax (CTT).

initial conditions The position from which an economic system is assumed to start. If a system obeys a known difference or differential equation system on a deterministic basis, knowledge of the initial conditions is both necessary and sufficient to calculate its state at any later time. If a system is partly stochastic, its current state owes less and less to initial conditions as time goes on, and long-term prediction of its state is not possible.

injections to the circular flow of incomes Forms of spending which do not derive from current income. These are investment spending by firms, government spending, and export sales to foreigners. If injections exceed *leakages from the circular flow, the income level starts to rise.

Inland Revenue The part of the UK civil service responsible for the assessment and collection of income and capital gains taxes.

innocent entry barriers Barriers to entry to an industry which result from natural, technical, or social conditions, but are not deliberately designed to restrict entry. For example, an existing firm may have cost advantages due to accumulated experience of production, or the techniques of production may require large sunk costs before production can start. In foreign trade, exporters find it difficult to sell to people whose languages they cannot speak or write; but people did not adopt their national languages deliberately to make it hard for outsiders to sell to them.

innovation The economic application of a new idea. Product innovation involves a new or modified product; process innovation involves a new or modified way of making a product. Innovation sometimes consists of a new or modified method of business organization. Many cases, for example the introduction of the credit card, have involved all these types of innovation. *See also* financial innovation, and diffusion of innovations.

input–output Study of the flows of goods and services between different sectors of the economy. An input–output table lists all flows of goods and services between sectors of origin and factor services, normally denoted by rows, and sectors of destination, including both intermediate and various types of final use, normally represented by columns. Input–output analysis then assumes that each activity has *constant returns to scale, and that the ratio of inputs to production for each sector is constant. On these assumptions it is possible to work out what gross outputs of all sectors are required for any set of final products, and what total factor inputs must be. These totals can then be compared with the available labour force and industrial capacity to see if such a programme is feasible. Input–output has sometimes been advocated as a part of a centralized economic planning mechanism. The results of its calculations can only be as reliable as its assumptions: constant returns, constant input proportions, and an economy that can be divided into a manageable number of sectors within each of which perfect aggregation is possible.

input prices The prices at which the services of factors of production, or supplies of fuels, materials, and intermediate products can be obtained. For capital goods, the interest and amortization costs of using them, rather than the prices of the capital goods themselves, are treated as input prices.

inputs The services of factors of production and usage of fuels, materials, and intermediate products necessary for a process of production. The relation of output to the use of various inputs is shown by a *production function. Inputs may be required in fixed proportions, or may be substitutable for one another. Where inputs are substitutable, profit maximization requires using the cheapest set of inputs that will produce any given set of outputs.

inside money Money which is an asset to the person or firm holding it, but is also a liability for somebody else in the economy. Inside money is contrasted with outside money, where the asset of the holder is not balanced by a liability for some other party. Bank balances, for example, are clearly inside money, while gold coinage is outside money. A rise in the real value of inside money does not increase the aggregate wealth of the economy, but redistributes it between the issuers and the holders of money. It is a matter of definition whether money which is a liability of the government counts as inside or outside money.

insider dealing Stock exchange transactions by 'insiders'. These are people who through their positions in or contacts with companies are able to obtain *price-sensitive information, such as profits figures or news of takeover bids, in a more detailed and accurate form, and in particular earlier, than 'outsiders', who have to rely on published information. Insiders are able to profit by their superior information, buying before share prices rise and selling before share prices fall. Insider dealing is restricted both by stock exchange regulations and by law in many countries; it is in practice extremely difficult to detect.

insiders and outsiders Those currently employed (insiders) and those who are not (outsiders). This distinction is used to help explain the persistence of unemployment in many economies. Wages and working conditions are determined by bargaining, either informally, or via *collective bargaining between trade unions and employers. The workers' representatives are very keen on protecting the jobs of present employees, the insiders, but less keen on providing job opportunities for potential employees, the outsiders. The workers' side have a strong interest in not making wages so high or working conditions so expensive as to handicap employers in competing to retain their existing markets, as losing these would lead to job losses. They have less interest in agreeing to wage levels and working practices which would make profits high enough to induce employers to expand and provide jobs for new workers. The domination of collective bargaining by insiders is believed to help explain why unemployment is so persistent in many countries.

insider trading *See* insider dealing.

insolvency Inability of an individual or company to pay debts as they fall due. This may lead an individual to become bankrupt, or a company to go into liquidation. In either case a trustee in bankruptcy or liquidator is appointed by a court to realize the available assets and pay off the debts so far as possible. An individual or business may be unable to pay debts because of *illiquidity rather than inadequate assets: if the assets are in fact sufficient creditors may eventually be paid in full. If creditors can be persuaded of this, insolvency can be avoided by rolling over old loans, or taking out new loans to pay off the old ones. It is an offence to trade knowing oneself to be insolvent, but for businesses with non-marketable assets, or whose principal asset is the future earning power of the proprietor, knowledge of insolvency is difficult to prove.

Inspector of Taxes A UK Inland Revenue official who receives tax returns from individuals and companies, and assesses the tax they are due to pay. The actual payment is then made to a different official, a Collector of Taxes.

instalment Payment of a total sum in regular amounts at intervals over a period, instead of making a single payment. Instalment payments are used in *hire purchase (HP), and it is often possible to arrange to pay taxes such as the UK Council Tax, or bills for credit cards and for utilities such as gas, electricity, and water, in regular instalments.

institutional economics The view of economics which stresses the importance of institutions in determining how economies really work. For example, the rules of land ownership are important in economic development in less developed countries (LDCs), and the lack of clearly defined and enforced *property rights is proving a handicap in the transformation from planned to market economies in Eastern Europe. This should not exclude the analysis of economic influences on institutional rules themselves; but once chosen, institutional forms show great persistence, and trying to model economies without taking account of them may lead to serious errors.

institutional shareholder A shareholder which is itself a company rather than an individual. Because small amounts of capital can only be used to hold shares either by concentrating on a few securities, which involves high risk, or buying very small holdings, which involves high transactions costs, an increasing proportion of individual investors choose to hold shares via institutions. These may be *unit trusts, investment trusts, pension funds, or insurance companies selling with-profits life policies. Institutional shareholders may act as *relationship investors, seeking a voice in the management of the companies whose shares they own, but usually adopt a passive role and refrain from participation in management decisions.

instrument, policy *See* policy instrument.

insurance The use of contracts to reduce and redistribute *risk. In an insurance contract, the insurer accepts a fixed payment, or premium, from the insured, and in return undertakes to make payments if certain events occur. In life insurance the event insured against is the death of the insured, or his or her survival to some agreed age. In insurance for fire and theft the event insured against is damage by fire or theft to the insured's property. In motor insurance the event insured against is loss by fire, theft, or damage to 'third parties', that is, anybody except the insured and the insurer. In health insurance the event insured against is medical expenses and/or loss of earnings through ill health. In every insurance contract the insured exchanges one evil for another. Without insurance there is a small chance of a large loss; with insurance there is a certain small loss, that is the premium, and possibly some further loss if the damage done by the event insured against exceeds the sum insured. The insurer makes the reverse exchange, accepting a new risk for the sake of the premium. Insurers are willing to take on risk in this way for two reasons. One is that they may be *risk-neutral, or at least less *risk-averse than the people they are insuring. The other factor which induces insurers to take on risks is that if they take on a number of risks of the same general type which are largely independent, the proportional dispersion of their returns will be smaller than the average of the individual risks they take on. Insurance thus both reduces overall risk, and transfers risk to those with a comparative advantage in risk-bearing. *See also* deposit insurance, health insurance, life insurance, and third party insurance.

insurance company A company whose main activity is providing insurance. This may include life, fire, motor, health, or many other varieties of insurance. As the premiums for policies are paid before claims occur, and in the case of life policies the funds collected accumulate for decades, insurance companies hold large stocks of assets. This makes them major participants in the market for government bonds, equity shares, and commercial and household mortgages.

intangible assets Assets of an enterprise which cannot be seen or touched. This includes goodwill, *patents, trade-marks, and copyright. In the case of goodwill there is no documentary evidence of its existence. There is in all these cases evidence that intangible assets exist, as they are occasionally bought and sold, but there is no continuing market, and in their nature they are non-homogeneous, so that their valuation is very uncertain.

integer A whole number. A great many economic variables, such as the number of firms in an industry, must be whole numbers: this is known as the integer constraint. Economists often find it convenient to ignore the integer constraint, and treat economic variables as though they were continuous. Even the national income can in fact only vary in steps, equal to the smallest unit of currency, but this is so small that it is felt that the convenience of being able to use calculus and other properties of continuous numbers outweighs any possible inaccuracy due to treating income as a continuous variable.

integer constraint The requirement that a variable be a whole number. This is often a nuisance in economics, as it prevents the use of calculus, and hence is often ignored. Integer constraints are sometimes important: for example, in considering the number of firms in an industry, if there are actually 371, it does no noticeable harm to use calculus which suggests that there should be 371.23; but if there are 2 firms, it is nonsense to assume there are 2.47.

integral A function whose *first derivative is equal to another function. If $f(x)$ is the first derivative of $g(x)$, then $g(x)$ is an integral of $f(x)$, and so is $h(x) = g(x) + k$, where k is an arbitrary constant, known as the constant of integration. The indefinite integral of $f(x)$ is written $\int f(x)dx = g(x) + k$. The definite integral is the indefinite integral evaluated over some range of x, from $x = a$ to $x = b$, written $\int_a^b f(x)dx = g(b) - g(a)$. If $f(x)$ is represented as a curve, its definite integral from a to b equals the area under the curve between a and b. While many functions have integrals which are easily calculated, some functions, for example that of the normal distribution, do not have indefinite integrals; their definite integrals have to be approximated by numerical methods. *See also* definite integral, and indefinite integral.

integration 1. The combination of different economic activities under unified control. This may involve vertical integration that is, either backward integration, where a business is combined with one supplying its inputs, or forward integration, where a business is combined with one using its outputs. It may also involve horizontal integration, where a business is combined with another which may use the same suppliers or sell in the same markets. *See also* backward integration, forward integration, horizontal integration, and vertical integration.

2. The organization of economic activities so that national boundaries do not matter. Complete economic integration would imply *free trade in all goods and services, perfect capital mobility, complete freedom of migration, complete freedom of establishment for businesses, and an unhindered flow of information and ideas. It would also imply the elimination of national differences in taxation, in the financing of social services, in the rules governing competition and monopoly, and in environmental regulation; and arguably a single currency. Complete economic integration is clearly a very distant prospect for the world as a whole, although some part of the way towards it has been covered in economic blocs such as the *European Union (EU) and the *North American Free Trade Agreement (NAFTA). Some further movement towards integration is widely considered desirable for countries with similar cultures; whether it is desirable at all where there are wide differences in culture is a matter of dispute.

3. The process of finding an integral. For many mathematical functions there are convenient standard forms, or rules for doing this. For example, the integral of x^α is always $x^{\alpha+1}/(\alpha + 1)$, provided $\alpha \neq -1$, (if $\alpha = -1$, the integral is $\ln x$); and the integral of $e^{\beta x}$ is $e^{\beta x}/\beta$; in both cases plus a constant of integration. Many other functions also have convenient standard form integrals. Some commonly used functions unfortunately do not have analytical integrals, for example the formula for the *normal distribution; definite integrals for these have to be found as approximations using numerical methods. *See also* constant of integration.

4. A property of time series, concerning the number of times they need to be differenced to produce a stationary series. *See also* order of integration.

intellectual property Private property rights in ideas. This may take the form of copyright, where material such as books or music can be copied only with permission from the copyright owner, who can charge for this; or *patents, where processes or product designs can only be used with permission from the patentee, who can charge a licence fee. Such property rights originally rest with authors or inventors, or their employers, but can be bought, sold or inherited.

intensity, capital *See* capital-intensity.

intercept The point where a given curve crosses an axis on a graph. The linear function $y = \alpha + \beta x$, for example, has an intercept on the x axis at $x = -\alpha/\beta$, and an intercept on the y axis at $y = \alpha$.

interest Payment for a loan additional to repayment of the amount borrowed. The rate of interest is the extra payment per unit of the loan, normally calculated as an annual rate. An interest-bearing security yields interest to the holder; some interest-bearing loans are used as money. Interest payments are made by borrowers to lenders. Simple interest means that, where interest is not actually paid out but is added to the principal of a loan each period, the amount added is the same each period. Compound interest means that, again where interest is not paid out to the lender, the amount to be added to the loan each period is the same percentage of the debt already accumulated: compound interest thus includes interest on past interest. Interest rates can be found for loans of any duration, from those repayable on demand to perpetuities. Many authors term rates on loans of under five years short-term rates, rates on loans from 5 to 15 years maturity as medium-term, and rates on loans for over 15 years as long-term rates; but usage is not uniform, and the terminology used by any author needs to be checked. Interest rates are commonly quoted in nominal terms. The *real interest rate is the nominal interest rate for any period, corrected for the effects of inflation. Writing interest rates and inflation rates as decimals, so that 8 per cent interest or growth is written as 0.08, if i_n is the nominal and i_r the real interest rate, where p is the rate of inflation over the period of a loan, $(1 + i_r) = (1 + i_n)/(1 + p)$ and $(1 + i_n) = (1 + i_r)(1 + p)$. A real interest rate may be considered ex ante, that is by taking as p the expected rate of inflation when the loan is first made, or ex post, using the actual rate of inflation up to the end of the loan. The interest-elasticity of investment measures the responsiveness of investment, I, to interest rates, i; this is $-(i/I)(dI/di)$. Similarly, the interest-elasticity of the demand for money, M, is $-(i/M)(dM/di)$. *See also* compound interest, natural rate of interest, rate of interest, and simple interest.

interest-elasticity of the demand for money A measure of the responsiveness of the demand for money to changes in interest rates. This is given by

$$\varepsilon = -(dM/M)/(di/i) = -(i/M)(dM/di),$$

where M is the demand for money and i is the interest rate.

interest equalization tax A US tax on foreign portfolio borrowing in the United States. This was intended to reduce capital outflows from the US.

interest payments Payment of interest due on loans. These may be owed by individuals, firms, or the government. Individual interest payments are mostly not tax-deductible, with some exceptions for mortgage interest. Interest payments made by firms have to be subtracted from trading profits to obtain total profits, and interest received has to be added. Interest payments by governments are an important part of government spending, especially in countries with high ratios of government debt to GDP.

interest rate(s) *See* rate of interest, long-term interest rate, real interest rate, and term structure of interest rates.

interest-rate futures A form of financial futures by which lenders and borrowers can agree in advance the rates at which they will be able to lend or borrow fixed sums on future dates. These futures can be used either to hedge, that is to reduce risks, or to speculate, accepting extra risks for the sake of expected profits. Interest-rate futures are traded in the UK on the *London International Financial Futures and Options Exchange (LIFFE).

interest-rate swaps Transactions by which financial institutions change the form of their assets or debts. Swaps can be between fixed and floating-rate debt, or between debt denominated in different currencies.

interim dividend A dividend payment based on interim profit figures for part of a company's financial year. Payment of an interim dividend normally carries a suggestion, but no guarantee, that a final dividend payment will follow.

interim report Any company report other than an annual report. Interim reports are often issued half-yearly. Figures for turnover, profit, or loss included in interim reports are usually not audited.

inter-industry trade Trade between countries where exports and imports consist of different types of goods. Such trade is based on differences in *factor endowments. Countries tend to export goods where they have relatively large amounts of the factors intensively used in producing them, and to import goods which they cannot produce themselves, or which they can only produce at great cost, due to a scarcity of the factors intensively used in producing them. With trade of this type, it is unusual for a country to import and export goods in the same classification. Inter-industry trade is contrasted with *intra-industry trade, which is based on economies of scale, and often takes place between countries with very similar factor endowments.

interior solution A solution to a system of equations where all variables are non-zero. For example, outputs of all goods are positive, or all prices are positive. This is contrasted with a corner solution, in which some variables are zero. Statements of optimality conditions in terms of equality of marginal costs and marginal benefits are correct only for interior solutions.

interlocking directorates The situation where two or more companies are linked by having some members of their *boards of directors in common. This ensures that the firms can be well informed on each other's position without the need for any formal arrangements.

intermediary, financial *See* financial intermediary.

intermediate good A good which is not itself a final good, but is used as an input for production. Intermediate goods include fuels and lubricants, natural and man-made materials, and components. A large proportion of gross output in a modern industrial economy consists of intermediate goods.

internal balance A situation where the level of activity in an economy is consistent with a stable rate of inflation. At higher activity levels inflation tends to rise, and at lower levels unemployment is unnecessarily high. Maintaining internal balance is one objective of macroeconomic policy. Internal balance is contrasted with external balance, which is a situation where the economy has a balance of payments, on current and capital account combined, which is sustainable, at least in the medium run. Some combination of monetary and fiscal policies should allow both internal and external balance to be maintained. A policy dilemma confronts any body controlling only one policy instrument if internal balance suggests that interest rates, for example, should be lowered, while external balance requires that they be raised.

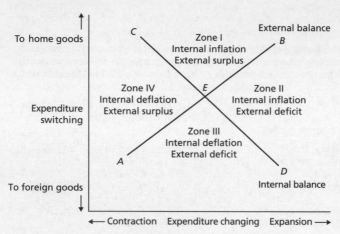

FIGURE 15: *Internal and External Balance*

The horizontal axis represents expenditure changing: movements to the right indicate expansion, and movements to the left contraction. The vertical axis represents expenditure switching: movements upwards represent a switch towards home-produced goods, and movements downwards a shift towards imports. *AEB* is the external balance line. With constant total expenditure, expenditure switching towards home goods, for example by devaluation, causes a shift towards external surplus, and switching towards foreign goods causes a shift towards external deficit. With no switching, expanding expenditure causes a shift towards external deficit, and contracting expenditure causes a shift towards external surplus. Thus *AEB* slopes upwards.

CED is the internal balance line. With constant total expenditure, switching towards home goods causes a shift towards internal inflation, and switching towards foreign goods causes a shift towards internal deflation. With no switching, expanding total expenditure causes a shift towards internal inflation, and contracting expenditure causes a shift towards internal deflation. Thus *CED* slopes downwards.

In Zone I there is internal inflation and an external surplus.
In Zone II there is internal inflation and an external deficit.
In Zone III there is internal deflation and an external deficit.
In Zone IV there is internal deflation and an external surplus.
In general a combination of expenditure changing and expenditure switching policies is needed to get to the equilibrium point *E*.

internalizing externalities Methods of getting those producing external costs or benefits to take account of them in their decision-taking. This is partly a question of information: once individuals or firms realize that their actions are causing external costs or benefits, conscience, business ethics, or a concern for their reputation may induce them to avoid or reduce activities causing external costs, and to increase activities conferring external benefits. Internalizing externalities also involves motivation, however. There is a disincentive to causing external damage if one is made to pay for it, by taxes on activities causing external damage, or an obligation to compensate the victims. Alternatively, prohibition or quantitative restriction of activities involving adverse externalities gives those causing them an incentive to avoid fines or jail for breaching such rules. Where damage is highly concentrated, a merger of firms may internalize the damage, since what were formerly external effects now become costs to the firm. This method may lead to problems over monopoly, and is not practicable where damage is widely diffused.

internal labour market The system by which recruitment for senior appointments in an organization is mainly from existing employees in lower-grade jobs. It is contrasted with an external labour market, in which recruitment is mainly by open competition. The main merits of internal labour markets are that a firm is likely to know more about the strengths and weaknesses of existing employees than outsiders, and that a reputation for internal promotion as its preferred strategy may assist in recruitment and retention of staff. The main merits of an external labour market are that open competition provides a wider choice for senior appointments, and that outsiders may bring new ideas to an organization.

Internal Market The unified market supposed to be introduced in the European Community (EC) in 1992. This was to involve free mobility of goods, funds, and labour throughout the EC.

internal market (health service) The system whereby one section of the UK National Health Service which uses facilities provided by other sections has to pay for them. This is intended to gain the cost-saving benefits of competition, and lead to more efficient utilization of the total resources used. It is independent of the question of whether patients should be required to contribute to the cost of treatment.

internal rate of return (IRR) The interest rate at which the net present value of a project is zero. If the net cash flow on a project starts off negative, and once it becomes positive it remains so, the IRR is unique; but if cash flow at the end becomes negative, as can happen if there are costs of making a plant safe after its useful life is over, the IRR may not be unique. A project is worth investing in if its IRR is greater than the rate of interest, including an appropriate risk premium.

Internal Revenue Service (IRS) The US federal government organization that assesses and collects personal and business federal taxes. This makes it parallel to the UK Inland Revenue.

International Bank for Reconstruction and Development (IBRD or World Bank) An international body set up in 1946 after the Bretton Woods conference to promote economic recovery and development. The IBRD was originally intended to assist in the reconstruction of countries in Europe and Asia damaged by the Second World War. It has since become a provider of both funds and technical and economic advice for *less developed countries (LDCs). The IBRD is funded by quota subscriptions of member countries, partly in gold and national currencies, but mainly in uncalled capital, which is, however, available in case of need to back IBRD guarantees of private loans to LDCs. The IBRD's own loans are only available for public sector or state-guaranteed projects, but it has an affiliate, the *International Finance Corporation (IFC), which can make and guarantee loans to private sector borrowers. It has another affiliate, the *International Development Association (IDA), specializing in loans on less stringent terms to the least developed countries.

international commodity agreement *See* commodity agreement.

international company *See* multinational.

international competitiveness *See* competitiveness.

international debt Debt owing by the government or residents of one country to the government or residents of another, or to an international institution. Such debt takes various forms: it may be long- or short-dated; fixed-interest or floating-rate debt; and denominated in the currency of the lender, the borrower, some third currency such as the US dollar, or an international currency unit such as the Euro. The borrower may be a private sector body, or a government: government or sovereign debt cannot be collected by any legal process unless the government chooses to submit to it. The lenders may be individuals or investment institutions holding bonds, banks making short-term loans, national governments or government-funded institutions, or international bodies such as the *International Bank for Reconstruction and Development (IBRD or World Bank). Because lenders prefer varied portfolios, many countries both lend and borrow internationally. Countries which are large net borrowers find that a high ratio of debt service to exports places a great strain on their balance of payments, which may lead to default.

international debt crisis *See* debt crisis.

International Development Association (IDA) A subsidiary of the *International Bank for Reconstruction and Development (IBRD or World Bank), established in 1960 to provide development aid and advice to the poorest less developed countries (LDCs). IDA is financed by the IBRD, and is willing to make loans on less stringent terms than IBRD itself.

International Economic Order, New *See* New International Economic Order.

international economics The parts of economics concerning the relations between different countries. This includes trade in goods and services, factor movements, including migration, capital movements and technology transfer, and international monetary arrangements, including exchange rates and exchange reserves. It also studies government policies affecting trade, factor movements, and monetary arrangements, international negotiations, regional institutions such as the European Union (EU) and North American Free Trade Agreement (NAFTA), and international institutions such as the World Trade Organization (WTO) and the International Monetary Fund (IMF).

International Finance Corporation (IFC) An international investment bank affiliated to the *International Bank for Reconstruction and Development (IBRD or World Bank), founded in 1956 to make loans to the private sector. IFC was set up to broaden the scope of IBRD, which lends directly only for projects in the public sector or with government guarantees, but lends to IFC to fund loans to the private sector.

International Monetary Fund (IMF) An agency of the United Nations, founded in 1946 to promote international monetary stability and co-operation. The IMF is financed by *quota subscriptions from member countries, partly in gold or convertible currencies and partly in their own currencies. It was intended to promote international trade through encouraging stable exchange rates and providing additional international liquidity to enable countries to avoid the need for trade restrictions and exchange controls. It administered a system of pegged exchange rates, the *'Bretton Woods' system, until this collapsed in 1971. It has also made loans to countries with balance-of-payments problems. Extra liquidity was provided by the introduction of *Special Drawing Rights (SDRs) after 1970, and various special facilities have been introduced since. Since the 1980s IMF loans have been mainly to less developed country (LDC) members. The IMF organizes regular meetings to discuss world monetary problems, and provides specialist advice on their balance-of-payments problems to members needing loans, sometimes making these conditional on at least part of this advice being accepted.

international monetary system The system of foreign exchange markets through which international trade and capital movements are financed, and *exchange rates are determined. If there were no national foreign exchange reserves and no world central bank, exchange rates would be entirely determined in the foreign exchange market. In fact most countries have central banks which hold foreign exchange reserves, which can be used to stabilize exchange rates, in the short run at least. In the longer run central banks and governments can use the instruments of monetary and fiscal policy to try to prevent balance-of-payments surpluses and deficits becoming so large that stable exchange rates cannot be maintained. There is no world central bank, but the *International Monetary Fund (IMF) was intended to act in place of one to provide extra liquidity for national central banks, and to co-ordinate macroeconomic policies so that exchange reserves would not be exhausted. The *General Agreement to Borrow, between the G10 central banks, also increased the effective size of national exchange reserves. In fact none of these arrangements has proved adequate to maintain stable exchange rates, and over the last thirty years even major currencies like the US dollar, DM, and yen have fluctuated considerably against each other, and there have been persistent disagreements over policy between the three countries concerned.

international money Money which can be used in settling international transactions. This may be a national currency, provided that it is acceptable to residents of other countries, which is nowadays likely only with a fully *convertible currency. At one time sterling was widely used as an international money, and the US dollar is still widely acceptable. Alternatively it could be a special type of money issued by some supra-national authority. No such money at present exists for use in private transactions: transactions between central banks can take place in *Special Drawing Rights (SDRs), which are the creation of the *International Monetary Fund (IMF). If the common European currency is successful, it will constitute international money so far as members of the *European Union (EU) are concerned, and may well come to be used as an international money by non-members as well. *Gold was at one time a form of international money, but has fallen out of use for domestic monetary purposes.

international payments Payments made between residents of different countries, or between residents and international bodies. These include payments for exports of goods and services, payment of property incomes, and international transfers or gifts; these are current account transactions. They also include sales and purchases of securities, and making and repayment of loans, which are capital account transactions; and transfers of foreign exchange reserves between central banks and governments. International payments may be made in a country's own currency if foreigners are willing to hold it; in a national currency acceptable to both parties, such as the euro or the US dollar; or in an international money, such as *Special Drawing Rights (SDRs) issued by the *International Monetary Fund (IMF).

international reserves *See* foreign exchange reserves.

International Settlements, Bank for *See* Bank for International Settlements.

international trade *See* trade.

International Trade Classification, Standard *See* Standard International Trade Classification.

international transactions *See* international payments.

interpersonal comparisons Comparing the welfare of one individual with that of another. This raises problems in economics analogous to the dispute over cardinal and ordinal *utility. For exact interpersonal comparisons to be possible, it would be necessary to measure people's utility levels, which is notoriously not possible. If no interpersonal comparisons are acceptable, however, then it becomes impossible to explain why society should tax the rich to help the starving or homeless, rather than taxing the poor to subsidize the rich. Economists are forced to argue as though large differences in income make interpersonal comparisons possible, while small income differences do not, with the margin between large and small differences left undefined.

interpolation Inserting missing data into a series. This is normally done by assuming that the data grew according to some known rule over the period when data are missing. Except in the case of series which are known to grow in a smooth manner, this procedure is extremely unreliable.

Interstate Commerce Commission (ICC) A US agency set up to regulate rail traffic across state boundaries. The ICC was intended to regulate both monopolistic pricing and the standard of service provided. Its jurisdiction has since been extended to include transport by inland waterways, roads, and pipelines.

intertemporal budget constraint The requirement that the total spending of an individual, firm, or government must be within the funds available to it over some long period. This period is a lifetime for individuals; for firms and governments, which are potentially immortal, the period is not well defined. Spending can exceed income plus net assets in any short period if credit is available, but lenders will only be willing to provide credit if they believe the borrower's intertemporal budget constraint is satisfied, so that repayment of debts is possible. Uncertainty about future income prospects and interest rates makes intertemporal budget constraints very difficult to apply in practice.

intertemporal substitution The extent to which similar goods or services at different times are substitutable. If fares at peak periods are higher than off-peak, for example, this can induce travellers for whom off-peak travel is a good substitute for peak-period travel, such as shoppers, to change to off-peak journeys, while travellers such as office workers, for whom journeys at different times are poor substitutes, tend to stick to the peak periods.

interval, confidence *See* confidence interval.

intervention in foreign exchange markets Action by central banks or other monetary authorities to influence an exchange rate. A currency will be sold to keep its price relative to other currencies down, or bought to keep its price up. Intervention in the foreign exchange market may be 'unsterilized', meaning that it is allowed to alter the domestic money supply, which rises when foreign exchange is bought and falls when foreign exchange is sold. This is distinguished from 'sterilized' intervention, where the central bank sells securities when it buys foreign currency, so as to keep the domestic money supply constant. *See also* sterilization.

intervention, intra-marginal *See* intra-marginal intervention (in foreign exchange markets).

intra-industry trade Trade where goods of the same classification are both imported and exported. In some cases this results from seasonal factors: for example, a country may export apples in the autumn and import them in the spring. In other cases the reason is transport costs: a large country may export goods over one border and import similar goods over another. In most cases, however, intra-industry trade results from *economies of scale. It allows consumers to have access to numerous varieties of a type of good, of which the country produces a few on a large scale, which it exports, and imports the others. Intra-industry trade is contrasted with *inter-industry trade, which arises from differences in resources between countries, so that any type of goods is normally exported or imported, but not both.

intra-marginal intervention (in foreign exchange markets) Intervention in the foreign exchange market by the central bank or other monetary authorities before an exchange rate has reached the limit to which it is desired to restrict fluctuations. This is contrasted with intervention when the rate reaches its limit, to prevent it from moving any further. Central banks may choose intra-marginal intervention because they are de facto pursuing a policy of keeping the exchange rate within a narrower band than that to which they are committed by agreement. They may also wish to intervene before the rate reaches its limits because of a fear that sudden movements in the market rate, even within the permitted band, will influence speculative opinion about further movements. In such a case a small intervention within the limits may help to prevent the start of a major swing in market opinion, which if unchecked would require intervention on a much larger scale when the limit was reached.

intrapreneur A manager whose status changes from company employee to proprietor of an independent firm. This change is encouraged and possibly financed by the former employer, in the expectation that increased autonomy and improved incentives for the intrapreneur will raise the parent firm's profits.

invention The idea of a new product, or a new method of producing an existing product. This is distinguished from an *innovation, which is the development of an invention to the stage where its use becomes economically viable.

inventories Stocks of goods held by businesses. These may be fuel, materials, or components awaiting use in production, goods in process, for example cars on assembly lines, or stocks of finished products awaiting sale to distributors or final users. Additions to inventories forms a small, but by far the most volatile component of national expenditure.

inverse function A function which reverses the effect of another function. If $y = f(x)$, then the inverse function can be written $x = f^{-1}(y)$. The inverse of the inverse function is the original function. While for some functions, for example the linear function, the inverse is of the same form as the original function, for many other functions this is not the case. Inverse functions need not be unique: for example if $y = x^2$, $x = \pm \sqrt{y}$. In matrix algebra, the inverse of a matrix A is a matrix which reverses the operations performed by A; if $y = Ax$, $x = A^{-1}y$. A^{-1} exists only if A has the same number of row and columns and these are independent; if A^{-1} does exist, it is unique and $A^{-1}A = AA^{-1} = I$, the identity matrix.

investment **1.** The process of adding to stocks of real productive assets. This may mean acquiring fixed assets, such as buildings, plant, or equipment, or adding to stocks and work in progress. This is the *Keynesian definition of investment: it is a flow concept. Investment goods are goods designed to be used for investment rather than consumption. Gross fixed investment is spending on new capital equipment; net investment is gross investment minus *'capital consumption', an estimate of the loss of value of capital goods through wear and tear, the passage of time, or technical obsolescence. Investment allowances are tax allowances which lower taxation on the profits of firms which invest. Foreign direct investment is investment spending carried out abroad. Some forms of spending designed to raise future productivity, such as *research and development (R&D) to produce new technical knowledge, and training to improve the skills of the workforce, are conventionally not counted as investment, although as they add to the stock of *human capital they logically could be.

2. The acquisition of financial assets, such as company shares. 'Investors' are the people who own such assets; 'investments' are what they hold. In the sense of a list of assets this is a stock concept. The *Investor's Chronicle* is a UK journal specializing in information for and advice to investors. Investment trusts and investment banks are financial institutions which typically hold securities as investments, in this sense, rather than themselves conducting physical investment in the Keynesian sense.

Investments in the financial sense are often used to fund investment in the Keynesian sense, for example when companies sell new shares to finance the building of new factories. The two senses of investment are not invariably linked, however: real investment can be paid for from retained profits, without the use of financial intermediaries; and firms can use the proceeds of share issues to pay off debt or to finance the acquisition of other firms, rather than spending the money on physical investment.

Investment is often considered in conjunction with *savings. At the world economy-wide level, investment and savings ex post, on some definition, must be equal. At the level of the individual, firm, government, or country, however, there is no reason why savings and investment should be equal either ex ante or ex post. *See also* autonomous investment, foreign investment, induced investment, inward investment, and planned investment.

investment bank A US bank similar to a merchant bank in the UK.

investment incentives Arrangements designed to encourage investment, by increasing its rewards or decreasing its costs. Many such incentives work via the tax system. Accelerated depreciation means that firms are allowed to write off investments faster than the true rate of capital consumption: this lowers measured profits and thus taxes paid in the early years after an investment is made. Initial allowances enable the whole cost of investment goods to be written off when they are purchased. Investment allowances enable part of the cost of investment to be written off when it is made, while still allowing full depreciation allowances to be claimed later; investment allowances are thus a form of investment subsidy. Non-tax incentives for investment include preferential treatment for firms which invest in matters such as allocations of materials, access to financial markets, or planning permission for development.

investment income Income received from the interest on government or commercial bonds, from equity share holdings, or from deposits in building societies and other financial intermediaries. Individuals receive investment income both directly from their own holdings of financial assets, and indirectly in the form of payments from pension funds and insurance companies, which in turn derive their income from holding similar assets.

investment income surcharge Additional income taxes on investment or 'unearned' incomes.

investment in stocks and work in progress The value of the real change in stocks, both of inputs and finished products, and of work in progress, during any period. This is a small, but by far the most unstable component of total GDP in modern economies; it can become negative during downswings in activity.

Investment Management Regulatory Organization (IMRO) A UK self-regulating organization (SRO), responsible for regulating any institution which offers investment management. The IMRO draws up and enforces a code of conduct for such institutions; it is recognized by and reports to the *Securities and Investment Board (SIB).

investment trust A company that invests its shareholders' funds in a portfolio of securities. These are normally quoted on a stock exchange;

trusts may select from a wide range, or concentrate on securities from particular sectors or countries. They may aim for varying combinations of income and capital growth. Using investment trusts gives investors the benefits of a varied portfolio without excessive transactions costs, and the services of professional management. Investment trusts are distinguished from unit trusts, where a trustee holds the portfolio for the benefit of the unit holders.

investor, relationship *See* relationship investor.

invisible balance The balance of trade in invisibles. This is the excess of receipts from sales of services such as transport, tourism, and consultancy over payments for imports of invisible items.

invisible hand An expression introduced by Adam Smith as an analogy for the way in which the working of *markets allows economic activity to be co-ordinated without any central organization. Self-interest working through markets induces people to produce goods and services to meet the needs of other people whom they may never meet and for whom they need feel no goodwill. Equally, the market system allows people to satisfy their own wants from the produce of others who are similarly only connected with them through markets. The invisible hand is not a panacea, lacking the ability to deal with the provision of public goods, *externalities, *monopoly and problems of income distribution.

invisibles International trade in services. Invisible exports are sales of services to non-residents; invisible imports are purchases of services from non-residents. Invisible items include the services of airlines and shipping, hotels and other tourist facilities, banking, insurance, medical services and education, and various forms of consultancy.

involuntary unemployment Unemployment which is not desired by the unemployed person. This is contrasted with voluntary unemployment, where the person prefers to be unemployed, although many economists feel that this is not a very helpful distinction. During search unemployment, workers are unemployed while searching for jobs for which they are qualified, and which pay at least their reservation wages. This unemployment is involuntary in the sense that once suitable jobs are found, they would rather take them than go on searching. Unemployment is voluntary in a sense, however, if they could have found jobs already if they had been willing to consider something demanding lower qualifications, or had been willing to accept lower wages. Are workers who are not considered by employers to have the ability to do the only types of work they will accept voluntarily or involuntarily unemployed?

inward investment Investment in a country by non-residents. This may be measured gross, or net of capital consumption on existing non-resident-owned assets in the country and disposal of assets by non-residents to residents.

IOU An unsecured promise to pay: literally, 'I owe you'.

irredeemable security A security with no *redemption date. Interest on an irredeemable security is payable for ever, but the original sum borrowed is never to be repaid. Securities may also be termed irredeemable if the borrower has the right, but no obligation, to redeem them, as is the case with UK 'consols'.

irreversibility The fact that changes, once made, cannot be reversed. Irreversibility is usual in economic activity. Humans, animals, and plants once dead cannot be brought back to life. Present goods can often be turned into future goods by storage, but no process can turn future goods into present goods. Physical productive processes are not fully reversible, because of friction and time lags. Financial transactions cannot be fully reversed because of transactions costs.

irrigation The use of water pumped from boreholes or diverted from rivers to assist agriculture. This makes it possible to use otherwise uncultivable land, and to produce larger and more reliable crops on land already in use.

IRS *See* Internal Revenue Service.

IS curve A curve showing where *ex ante savings and investment are equal. This is a condition of equilibrium in macroeconomic models. The IS curve shows those combinations of national income, Y, and interest rates, r, at which ex ante investment, I, will equal ex ante savings, S. It is usually assumed that when income rises, savings rise considerably and investment changes little. When interest rates rise, investment falls sharply while savings change little. Given these assumptions, to preserve equality between ex ante savings and ex ante investment, if Y rises r must fall; thus the IS curve, drawn with its origin at the lower left corner of a diagram, slopes downwards. *See also* the figure for IS–LM model.

IS–LM model A model often used as an extremely simple example of *general equilibrium in macroeconomics. The IS curve shows the combinations of national income, Y, and interest rate, r, at which ex ante savings and investment are equal. The LM curve shows the combinations of Y and r at which the supply of and the demand to hold money are equal. Where the IS and LM curves cross, both the market for goods and the market for money balances are simultaneously in equilibrium. IS–LM is a pure

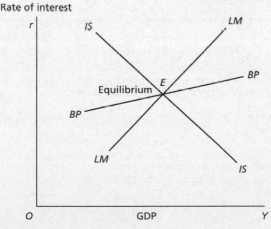

FIGURE 16: *IS-LM-BP Diagram*

*comparative statics model: it suppresses consideration of how the price level is determined and whether the labour market is in equilibrium. IS–LM is a teaching device and not a realistic model of any actual economy.

The horizontal axis shows real GDP, labelled Y; the vertical axis shows the rate of interest, labelled r. $ISEIS$ shows the IS curve. This is the locus of combinations of Y and r at which savings and investment are equal. Because higher Y increases savings and lower r increases investment, the IS curve is downward sloping. $LMELM$ shows the LM curve. This is the locus of combinations of Y and r at which the supply and demand for money are equal. Because higher Y increases the demand for money and higher r decreases it, the LM curve is upward sloping. E is the equilibrium point, at which the IS and LM curves cross. $BPEBP$ shows the BP curve. This is the locus of combinations of Y and r consistent with overall equilibrium in the balance of payments. Because increases in Y tend to worsen the current account, and increases in r tend to improve the capital account, the BP curve slopes upwards. With high international capital mobility, BP is very elastic, and is flatter than the LM curve, as drawn. Under earlier conditions of strict capital controls and low international capital mobility, BP may have been steeper than LM.

The IS–LM diagram is frequently drawn omitting the BP curve.

isocost curve A curve showing the combinations of factor inputs that can be bought for any given sum. If firms are acting as price-takers in factor markets, the isocost curve is a straight line, whose slope represents the relative prices of different factors' services. In equilibrium a firm will use the factors it buys to produce the largest possible output, corresponding to the *isoquant tangential to the iscost curve.

isoquant A curve showing the various combinations of different inputs which can be used to produce any given output. An isoquant shows only technically efficient combinations: the curve shows the minimum level of each input necessary for given levels of output and other inputs. What points on an isoquant are economically efficient depends on the prices of factor services,—shown by an *isocost line—and the economically efficent set of inputs is that at which an isoquant touches the lowest possible isocost line. Isoquants are generally drawn convex to the origin: this is a technical fact and not a logical necessity. Their curvature shows how readily factor inputs can be substituted: as more of one factor is used, it becomes increasingly difficult to substitute it for the other factors.

issue 1. The amount of shares or stock available, or the amount of banknotes in circulation.
2. The process by which new shares are distributed. In a bonus issue (UK) or scrip issue (US) extra shares are given to existing shareholders. In a rights issue new shares are sold on preferential terms to existing shareholders. New issues of shares may be sold in various ways: in a tender issue they go to the highest bidders; in a public issue, offer for sale, or placing, the company fixes the price and shares are bid for by investment institutions or the general public. An issuing house, usually a merchant bank, may buy the whole issue at an agreed price and then sell it on, or it may underwrite the issue, that is, guarantee that it will buy any shares nobody else takes up. *See also* bonus issue, and rights issue.

issued capital The part of the authorized capital of a firm which has actually been issued to shareholders. Any authorized but unissued capital remains available for issue when required, for example to allow executives to take up share options.

J

J-curve A model of the delayed effects of *devaluation on the *balance of trade. Devaluation allows the foreign price of exports to fall and the domestic price of imports to rise immediately. Time is needed, however, for orders to be obtained and contracts negotiated before the quantity of exports rises and the quantity of imports falls. There is thus likely to be an initial worsening of the trade balance—the downward part of the J—for, say, two or three quarters, before the trade balance starts to improve—the upward part of the J—following devaluation.

job 1. A task, as in 'Give us the tools and we will finish the job'. A jobbing builder or gardener carries out tasks for pay on a self-employed basis.

2. Paid employment. Jobs may be full- or part-time, permanent or temporary. The job market is the mainly informal system through which jobs are filled.

3. A racket or crime, as in 'a put-up job', or 'jobbery'.

job acceptance schedule The set of characteristics of jobs that workers engaged in job search are willing to accept. Acceptance depends on pay, prospects, working conditions and location. If workers are searching while unemployed, their job acceptance schedules are liable to change: normally they become willing to accept lower pay or worse working conditions, and more willing to accept a change in location or type of work, as unemployment lowers both their expectations and their liquidity.

jobber A dealer in shares or commodities who holds a stock of the asset and trades as a principal. Jobbers are contrasted with brokers, who operate in the same markets, but put people who want to buy and sell in touch with each other, and do not trade for themselves. A more modern name for a jobber is a *market-maker.

job characteristics, non-monetary *See* non-monetary job characteristics.

job quits *See* quits.

jobseeker's allowance The new name for the UK's unemployment benefit, introduced in 1996. The change in name was presumably intended to encourage the recipients to try to get jobs so that they would cease to need the allowance.

job vacancy *See* vacancy.

joint costs Costs which are shared by two or more products. It may be possible for a firm to measure the *marginal cost of each product separately, but joint costs make it impossible to measure the average cost of each product.

joint production Production where the processes giving outputs of different goods are connected. Producing the goods concerned separately would result in increased costs. Where one good would still be economic to produce even if the other had no market or required costly disposal, the other good is a *by-product. In many cases joint production is an obvious result of natural phenomena: for example, nature equips chickens with both wings and breasts. In other cases joint production is undertaken because it offers firms *economies of scope, allowing expensive equipment to be more fully used.

joint-stock bank A bank operated by a joint-stock company. This is contrasted with a private bank, owned by an individual, family or partnership. The large commercial or 'high street' banks in the UK are all joint-stock banks.

joint-stock company A legal arrangement by which investors pool their funds to carry on a business. Investors receive shares in proportion to the funds put in, and the shareholders elect directors to manage the business. Shareholders receive any distributed profits as dividends, proportional to the number of shares they own. Joint-stock companies generally also have *limited liability for their shareholders.

joint supply The supply conditions when outputs are produced jointly. If two or more goods are produced by the same process in completely inflexible proportions, there is no supply curve for each good separately, only for the fixed combination of goods. If the proportions can be varied, the supply curve for each good depends on the extra costs involved in changing the production process so as to obtain more of it. Pigs, for example, always have both fat and lean parts, but it is possible by varying their breed, diet, and age at slaughter to change the proportions considerably.

joint venture A business where the provision of risk capital is shared between two or more firms. This is a method of organization often adopted for projects which are too large or too risky for any one firm to attempt alone. The firms joining in such a venture may provide different forms of expertise: for example it is common for firms investing abroad to seek local partners. Foreign firms can provide technical expertise, but locals have advantages in familiarity with local conditions and business practices, in marketing and in dealing with national governments and the labour force.

judgement, value *See* value judgement.

junk bonds Bonds issued on very doubtful security. The finances of the firm issuing them are regarded as so insecure that there is serious doubt as to whether the interest and redemption payments promised will actually be made. Junk bonds are thus risky to hold, and lenders will only hold them if the promised returns are high enough to give an acceptable expected rate of return, after allowing for a non-negligible probability of default.

just-in-time A system of production using minimal inventories, and relying on prompt and frequent deliveries of materials and components from suppliers arriving just before they are needed. This system also relies on prompt and reliable reporting of stock holding, which is facilitated by the use of computers. It has the advantages of reducing the space needed to store inventories, and the interest costs of financing them. It also helps to improve reliability: with low stocks few unsatisfactory inputs are bought before their defects are discovered. The just-in-time system may merely transfer the burden of holding stocks to suppliers, and is easily disrupted if transport arrangements break down.

Kennedy Round The round of international *trade talks held under the *General Agreement on Tariffs and Trade (GATT) in 1964–7. The round was named after US President John F. Kennedy. The agreement arrived at cut tariffs on most world trade in manufactures by about a third, implemented over the following five years. No agreement was reached on agricultural protection, or on *non-tariff barriers to trade (NTBs).

Keynes, John Maynard (Lord) A British economist, largely responsible for the creation of modern *macroeconomics. He was born in 1883, was editor of the *Economic Journal* from 1911 to 1945, and wrote several books, of which the most important was *The General Theory of Employment, Interest and Money* (1936). This book first persuaded theoretical economists to take seriously the possibility of unemployment as an equilibrium state of the economy. It also helped to persuade politicians that government policy could contribute to higher and more stable levels of economic activity. He acted as an economic adviser to the UK government during both World Wars, and took part in the Bretton Woods negotiations leading to the creation of the *International Monetary Fund (IMF) and the *International Bank for Reconstruction and Development (IBRD or World Bank).

Keynesian A view of the economy modelled on that of John Maynard (Lord) Keynes, or an economist holding such views. The Keynesian view of a capitalist economy is that it has the capacity to remain for long periods in a short-term equilibrium involving substantially lower output than would be consistent with full employment. While the economy is in this state output is to a large extent demand-determined, and the level of output can be affected by monetary and fiscal policies. This view of the economy is contrasted with the view, sometimes called 'classical' or 'neoclassical', that the economy has a tendency towards a natural level of activity, so that the main role for economic policy is promoting growth from the supply side, for example by encouraging savings and enforcing competition in markets. Critics of the Keynesian position urge that, by trying to expand output by *demand management when what is needed is *supply-side policy, Keynesian policies, however laudable their motivation, in fact tend to promote inflation.

Keynesian unemployment Unemployment due to lack of *effective demand for goods and services which people could have been employed to produce. Keynesian unemployment can be reduced by the use of monetary or fiscal policy to increase effective demand. This demand-deficiency unemployment is contrasted with *classical unemployment, where wage rates are too high relative to productivity for employment to be profitable, and with *structural unemployment, where the unemployed lack the skills needed by prospective employers, or firms do not have the equipment needed to take on more workers. If unemployment is of these other types, more effective demand alone cannot cure it, but merely causes inflation.

Keynes Plan An alternative set of proposals for international monetary institutions proposed by J. M. (Lord) Keynes at the Bretton Woods negotiations on post-war monetary arrangements in 1944. The Keynes Plan would have involved the creation of an international monetary unit, 'bancor'. The plan was rejected and the *International Monetary Fund (IMF) was set up instead, on lines proposed by the United States.

kind, benefits in *See* benefits in kind.

kinked demand curve A demand curve as it would appear to a firm which expected that if it raised its price, rivals would not follow suit, whereas if it cut its price, rivals would respond by cutting theirs. The demand curve would thus appear more elastic for price rises than price falls. This would lead to a sharp vertical jump in marginal revenue at the existing output, making it likely that small changes in costs would not shift the marginal cost curve enough to make the firm want to change its price. This type of expectations would lead to a tendency for prices to be sticky at their existing levels.

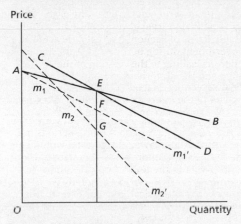

FIGURE 17: *Kinked Demand Curve*

The horizontal axis shows quantity produced; the vertical axis shows price charged. AEB is the demand curve for a firm's products if its rivals hold price constant. m_1Fm_1' is the marginal revenue curve corresponding to AEB. CED is the demand curve if rivals match all price changes. m_2Gm_2' is the marginal revenue curve corresponding to CED. If the firm expects that rivals will match all price cuts, but will hold their prices constant in the face of price increases, the kinked demand curve is shown by AED. The marginal revenue curve corresponding to AED is shown by m_1FGm_2'. The price charged to maximize profits will not change if any shift in the marginal cost curve is sufficiently small to allow it to pass between F and G after the shift.

knight, white *See* white knight.

know-how Practical economic knowledge, enabling firms to achieve results. Some of this is technical in nature, and can in principle be made into private property by the use of *patents, although these may be difficult to enforce. Much practical know-how, however, takes forms such as modes of organization, professional standards, or systems of incentives, which cannot be privatized by patents.

Know-How Fund A UK government agency set up to provide technical assistance to the countries of Eastern Europe and the Former Soviet Union in transforming themselves into market economies after the collapse of central planning.

Kondratieff cycle A supposed long cycle in economic activity, with a period of 60 years or more. Economic records in most countries do not go back far enough on a reliable basis to allow this theory to be properly tested. If it is correct, the remarkable spurt of growth in world incomes and trade from 1950 to 1980 may turn out to have been a boom phase in a long cycle.

kurtosis A measure of how 'humped' a frequency distribution is, compared to a *normal distribution with the same mean and variance. The kurtosis of a variable x with mean μ can be measured by $K = E(x - \mu)^4/[E(x - \mu)^2]^2$; for a normal distribution $K = 3$. A distribution with $K > 3$ is slim and long-tailed, with more weight in its centre and extremes and less at medium distances from the mean than a normal distribution. A distribution with $K < 3$ is fat and short-tailed, with less weight in its centre and extremes and more at medium distances from the mean than a normal distribution.

Kyoto Protocol An international agreement signed in 1997, designed to reduce emissions of greenhouse gases in the interests of controlling global warming. Critics have denounced the Protocol as quite inadequate for its declared purpose. It has been ratified by the EU, but not by the US, which considers the reductions proposed to be impracticable.

labour Human beings as factors of production. The labour supply consists of all those able and willing to work, including the self-employed and unemployed as well as employed workers. Labour is very varied in its levels of skills and qualifications. Labour economics is the aspects of economics concerned with the supply and demand for labour. Organized labour refers to the role of *trade unions in negotiating over wages, hours and working conditions, disciplinary procedures and redundancy, and in representing labour interests at the political level. *See also* direct labour, division of labour, organized labour, and sweated labour.

labour–capital ratio *See* capital–labour ratio.

labour economics The aspects of economics concerned with the supply and demand for labour. This includes factors affecting the participation rate, wage bargaining and organized labour, training, hours and conditions of work, practices concerning hiring, redundancy and labour turnover, migration and the age of retirement.

labour force The number of people available for work. This is affected by many factors. The population of working age is affected by the school-leaving age and the size of the further and higher education system, which keeps down the number of young workers, and the retirement age and pension system, which keeps down the number of older workers. Among the population of working age, the *participation rate is affected by the social security system, which determines how much income is available without working, and how easy it is to qualify for it. Health standards affect the proportion of the population which is disabled, and family structure affects how many people stay out of the labour market to care for children and the elderly. The availability of child-care facilities affects how many parents are available for part-time work, and the availability of part-time jobs affects how many people can work at all. Past *unemployment affects the number of *discouraged workers who have effectively withdrawn from the labour force. The labour force is also affected by a country's immigration policy and the degree of effort put into actually enforcing it.

labour hoarding Retention by a business of more workers than are required to produce the present level of output. This may be based on expectations that output will recover so that the surplus workers will soon be needed again. It may be more efficient to retain workers than to incur redundancy payments by sacking them and then have to meet recruitment and training costs replacing them a few months later. Labour hoarding may, however, simply be a form of organizational *slack. Managers know that redundancies are unpopular and bad for morale, so both natural sympathy for their employees and the desire for a quiet life make them willing to retain unnecessary labour so long as the shareholders

in a private firm, or the taxpayers in a state-owned one, are willing to
bear the cost.

labour-intensity The proportion of labour in the total inputs to a
productive process. Some processes involve large amounts of labour and
few other inputs: for example, the production of haircuts. Others involve
large amounts of other inputs and little labour: for example, the operation
of nuclear power stations. Labour-intensive processes are those where the
ratio of labour to other inputs is relatively large. Where alternative
techniques of production are possible, labour-intensity can be varied in
response to changes in the relation between real wages and the cost of using
other inputs.

labour market The processes by which workers and employers are brought
into contact, and wages and conditions of work are decided. Some of these
involve formal institutions: contacts between workers and employers may be
arranged by employment exchanges or agencies, either public or private.
Wages and conditions of work are frequently decided by negotiation between
*trade unions respresenting workers and associations representing
employers. The hours and conditions of work, and the rules about hiring and
firing, are frequently subject to legal regulation. Much of the labour market,
however, does not involve formal institutions or negotiations. Jobs are filled
by press or other advertisements, or informal contacts via other present or
past employees. Where trade unions are absent or weak, wages, hours and
conditions are settled by individual haggling. Work for private households
and small employers is largely part of the informal or *unofficial economy,
where official rules on hiring, firing, pay, working conditions, or anything
else are widely disregarded. *See also* external labour market, and internal
labour market.

labour mobility *See* mobility of labour.

labour productivity *See* productivity.

labour standards The proposal that access to markets for imports
should be restricted to those made by labour whose pay and working
conditions are up to some minimum standard. Supporters of this proposal
argue that it would improve labour conditions in LDCs. Opponents argue
that difficulties in policing it would mean that labour standards would
simply serve as an excuse for protectionism in richer countries, and that
losing employment opportunities would in any case harm workers in
LDCs.

labour supply The supply of work effort. This is determined by many
factors. The *participation rate is the proportion of the population of
working age who decide to seek work, rather than staying at home or
dropping out. This is affected by rates of pay, the availability of jobs, and
the rules of the social security system, which determine how much
income is available without working. The size of the national labour force
is also affected by immigration policy. The supply of workers with the
specific skills or qualifications needed for particular types of work is
affected by a country's education and training systems, and any past
restrictions on entry to particular occupations. Given the size of the

potential labour force the number of hours worked per week, or weeks worked per year, is affected by the *wages offered. Higher pay may induce those in a given occupation to work longer, and may induce entry by people from other occupations. If pay or the ease of getting work varies over time, labour supply at periods of high demand may be boosted by *intertemporal substitution: people work more when the going is good, with the intention of taking time off later. While some occupations have fixed working hours and strict control on absenteeism, many part-time workers have some flexibility over hours worked, and in many industries overtime is not compulsory and absenteeism is not strictly controlled, so that workers do have some choice over hours worked. The actual degree of effort while at work is difficult to measure, but is probably subject to similar influences.

labour theory of value The theory that the *value of goods or services is determined by the amount of direct and indirect labour inputs needed to produce them. This view ignores the role of scarce natural resources in production, and the fact that the cost of using capital goods depends not only on the labour used to produce them but also on the interest rate. It also takes no account of the fact that labour is nowhere near uniform in quality, as is shown by the vast variations in the wage rates paid for labour with different skills. While labour is probably the most important single factor of production, it is not the only one, and basing value upon one factor alone is an oversimplification.

labour turnover The inflow and outflow of labour employed by an enterprise. Some of this is because of fluctuations in total employment over time, either seasonally or cyclically. Some turnover results from geographical mobility of activitiy, notably in the construction sector. Some results from the aging of the labour force: older workers retire and young ones enter employment. There is also a large amount of turnover for personal reasons. Workers may leave jobs because they dislike their boss, because their families move, because they want a variety of experience to improve their qualifications, because they become mature students, because they get a better job, or simply because they are bored. Employers sack workers because they are dissatisfied with their work, or because changes in technology or organization eliminate the need for them. The result of all these factors is that, even ignoring temporary and seasonal work, an appreciable percentage of the labour force change their jobs each year, and the typical worker's career includes several different jobs.

Laffer curve A curve showing the relation between tax rates and revenue raised, named after its inventor. If any activity is taxed, revenue starts from zero with a zero tax rate, and rises as the rate is increased. The tax tends to discourage the activity, however, so that at some point the total revenue raised turns down. This tendency is accentuated by the effect of higher tax rates in promoting tax evasion. It is hard to discover the rate of any given tax which gives maximum revenue except by trial and error.

Lagrange multiplier A notional variable introduced to help in finding *constrained maxima and minima. Suppose that a function $y = f(x, z)$ has to be maximized subject to the constraint that $g(x, z) \leq k$. One approach to this problem is to locate a stationary value of the expression $L = f(x, z) - \lambda[g(x, z) - k]$. Where f_x denotes $\partial f(x, z)/\partial x$, etc, L takes a stationary value where $L_x = L_z = 0$; but $L_x = f_x - \lambda g_x$ and $L_z = f_z - \lambda g_z$. If the constraint is not binding, $\lambda = 0$ and y is maximized where $f_x = f_y = 0$. If the constraint is binding, $\lambda > 0$ and a stationary value of y exists at the values of x and z found by solving the three equations $L_x = 0$, $L_y = 0$ and $g(x, z) = k$. L is the Lagrangean expression, and λ is the Lagrange multiplier. λ can be regarded as a *shadow price, giving the effect on y of an increase in k. For example, y could be utility, which is maximized subject to the constraint that total spending on x and z is less than or equal to income, k.

lags *See* time lags.

laissez-faire A policy of complete non-intervention by governments in the economy, leaving all decisions to the market. If there were perfect markets everywhere, with no *externalities, and we were indifferent to income distribution, laissez-faire would be a first-best policy. In fact there are numerous market imperfections and many externalities, and there is considerable concern about income distribution. Laissez-faire cannot seriously be defended as *first best. There are however government failures as well as market failures, and one might attempt to defend laissez-faire as a *second-best policy. Most economists nowadays accept a major role for centralized policy in enforcing competition, regulating externalities, and trying to correct some of the income inequalities engendered by free markets.

land Natural resources as *factors of production. These are used in economic activity in a variety of ways: for growing crops and keeping animals; for extracting minerals; and to provide sites for buildings, transport and leisure facilities. Land as provided by nature can be changed by human activities: agricultural land can be improved by fertilizers and drainage, or ruined by erosion. *See also* marginal land.

landlord The owner of land or buildings, entitled to use them or to charge others *rent for their use. The rent received is partly a pure economic rent, and partly a return on capital used in improving land or constructing buildings. A landlord's relation with tenants is governed by contracts and legal controls affecting both rents and security of tenure. A ground landlord is one who has granted tenants a lease, which may fix ground rents in advance, and impose conditions on the tenant.

land use planning *See* planning (land use).

Laspeyres index *See* base-weighted index.

last-in, first-out (LIFO) The system of accounting for stocks which assumes that any goods withdrawn from inventories will be those most recently acquired. LIFO is contrasted with first-in, first-out, (FIFO), which assumes that any goods withdrawn from inventories will be those which have been in stock longest.

last resort, lender of *See* lender of last resort.

laundering, money *See* money laundering.

LAUTRO *See* Life Assurance and Unit Trusts Regulatory Organization.

law of large numbers The fact that where individual members of a population are subject to idiosyncratic differences, the average behaviour of a group is more predictable than that of any individual member of it. This tendency of groups to behave more systematically than individuals increases with the size of the group. This law underlies the ability of actuaries to predict death rates, and of statisticians to detect the effect of price changes on demand.

law of one price The proposition that where the same good or asset is traded in different *markets, the prices will not diverge. If prices do diverge, a profit can be made by *arbitrage, that is buying in the cheaper market and selling in the dearer. This assumes that information about both prices is available, and that goods or assets can be transferred freely between the markets. By extension, the law of one price can be taken to imply that where there are costs of transferring goods or assets, prices will not diverge by more than the transfer costs; they may of course diverge less than this. The application of this law to goods markets is inhibited by the fact that transfer of goods between markets takes time as well as money.

layoffs Sacking by firms of labour which is not required. This may be permanent, if the firm is ceasing the operations which gave rise to the jobs, or temporary, if demand is low but is thought likely to recover.

LBO *See* leveraged buy-out.

LDC *See* less developed country.

leader *See* loss leader, and price leader.

leading indicator An economic time-series which tends to rise or fall earlier than variables of interest, such as GDP. A series may be a leading indicator either because the activity measured actually changes earlier than the rest of the economy, or because statistics on it are collected more fequently or more promptly, and are processed and published sooner. Leading indicators are clearly useful in economic forecasting.

leads and lags The ability of traders to bring forward or defer the timing of transactions. If a country's currency is expected to be devalued, importers have a strong incentive to buy now before import prices rise, and exporters have a strong incentive to delay selling goods, or delay converting the foreign exchange they get for them, as it is expected soon to be worth more. This ability to make changes in timing means that a country's currency can come under strong speculative pressure, even with apparently stringent *exchange controls.

leakages from the circular flow of incomes Uses of income which do not give rise to a further round of incomes. These are saving by individuals or firms, payment of taxes to the government, and purchase of imports from foreigners. If leakages exceed *injections to the circular flow, incomes will start to decline.

learning by doing Improvements in *productivity due to experience of operating a process. It is open to argument whether the relevant experience is that of a particular producer, a national industry or the world as a whole. Except in the case where *spill-overs are worldwide, learning by doing gives a competitive advantage to existing producers, who necessarily have more experience than new entrants. Learning by doing is often characterized by making productivity an increasing function of cumulative total output of a product. This is probably misleading: if output has been spread over a long period of time, it is doubtful whether the earlier parts are relevant. In particular, skills are likely to be lost if they are not exercised.

lease A contract giving the right to use land or buildings for a set period, in return for payment of ground rent to the landlord. The rent payable may be fixed, or subject to periodic review. Leases may be for any period: 999 years is not unknown. A lease may impose conditions on the tenant, for example concerning the maintenance of premises or the use to be made of them.

leasehold The form of tenure of land or buildings by which the tenant has a lease.

leasing The practice of hiring items of equipment, rather than buying them outright. This enables firms to manage with less capital than they would need if all their equipment had to be bought. It also shifts to the owners the risk of *obsolescence; this will be reflected in the rentals demanded. Leasing may give tax benefits where a new firm has no profits against which it can set tax allowances on any equipment it buys. It may also enable local authorities to avoid cash limits on their expenditure.

least-developed countries The world's poorest countries. Least developed countries were defined in 1971 by the *United Nations Conference on Trade and Development (UNCTAD) as those with very low per capita incomes ($100 or less at 1968 prices), a share of manufacturing in GDP of under 10 per cent, and a literacy rate under 20 per cent. By 1990 there were over 40 such countries, with average per capita incomes of under 10 per cent of the world average.

least squares *See* ordinary least squares, and two-stage least squares.

least-squares regression *See* linear regression.

legal tender Forms of *money which a creditor is legally obliged to accept in settlement of a debt. It is necessary to have some rules on this so that it is clear when debts have been defaulted on. What the rules should be is a matter of convenience. Coin and banknotes are generally legal tender, with some exceptions: small denomination coins are not legal tender in large amounts, and nobody is legally obliged to give change, so that large notes are not legal tender for small amounts. Nobody is obliged to accept cheques. Actual payment is very often accepted in forms that are not legal tender, for example payments by cheque or electronic transfer, but this is at the discretion of the party accepting the payment.

leisure Time spent in enjoyment. This enters into people's *utility functions, in addition to their consumption of goods and services. Actually measuring leisure is difficult: it could be defined simply as time not spent working, but it is doubtful whether time spent travelling to work if employed, or looking for work if unemployed, should count as leisure. The provision of leisure facilities, including cultural activities, sport, and entertainments, is a major sector in modern economies.

lemon An unsatisfactory product, where quality cannot reliably be checked before purchase. Even if some goods of the same type are in fact perfectly satisfactory, their price is lowered by the risk that the purchaser may get a dud. If customers are *risk-averse, the price will also be lowered by a risk premium. The market for second-hand cars is a typical example of the market for lemons at work.

lender of last resort The function of providing *liquidity for the banking system at times of crisis. This is one of the duties of the *central bank. In the event of a run on the banks or other financial panic, the central bank should be willing to lend to soundly run banks or other financial institutions in order to avoid a general collapse of the financial system. It may be necessarily to suspend temporarily the normal limits on the money supply and restrictions on the forms of collateral acceptable. If the institution in difficulties is not believed to have been soundly run, the central bank is left with a difficult decision: lending too easily may encourage other banks to take undue risks in the belief that they are 'too big to fail' and the central bank will always bail them out, while if central bank assistance is withheld, the collapse of badly run institutions may also bring down good ones.

lending, property *See* property lending.

lending rate, minimum *See* minimum lending rate.

Leontief paradox The observation by Wassily Leontief that in spite of being the world's most capital rich country, the US appeared on average to have exports that were slightly more labour-intensive than its imports. This was thought to be paradoxical because the *Heckscher–Ohlin model of international trade led people to expect that US exports would be capital-intensive and its imports would be labour-intensive. Two possible explanations for the paradox are: first, that the simple Heckscher–Ohlin model ignored the role of natural resources in affecting trade; and second, that because of its large investments in *human capital which gave it a highly skilled labour force, the effective US labour supply was much larger than the mere numbers of workers would suggest.

Lerner *See* Marshall–Lerner conditions.

less developed country (LDC) A country with less advanced technology and/or lower income levels than the advanced industrial countries. Most LDCs have high dependence on *primary sectors in their production, and more so in their external trade. Most have low average incomes, though a few of the smaller oil exporters such as Kuwait have per capita incomes comparable to those in industrial countries. Being an LDC is a matter of degree. Many countries in Sub-Saharan Africa are LDCs on any possible criterion, but many of the *newly industrialized countries (NICs) such as China have a mixture of very poor primary producing sectors and more advanced industry. Members of the *Organization for Economic Cooperation and Development (OECD) are not classed as LDCs, though Turkey, which is a member, has lower per capita income than some NICs. The former planned economies of the ex-USSR and Eastern Europe present similar problems of classification: Tadjikistan is clearly an LDC, and the Czech Republic and Russia are clearly not, but many are hard to classify.

leverage The ratio of a company's debt to its equity, that is to the part of its total capital owned by its shareholders. High leverage (US) or gearing (UK) means high reliance on debt financing. The higher a company's leverage or gearing, the more of its total earnings are absorbed by paying debt interest, and the more variable are the net earnings available for equity shareholders.

leveraged buy-out A buy-out of the equity of a firm largely financed by borrowing. This is risky for the purchasers, as interest on the loan will absorb a large proportion of any operating profits. If the firm does badly, this may leave nothing for the equity holders.

levy, capital See capital tax.

levy, import See tariff.

liabilities The items on the debit side of a balance sheet. These include unpaid bills from suppliers, unpaid taxes, and secured and unsecured debt of various sorts. The net equity value of the firm is included as a liability to make the total equal to total assets. *Contingent liabilities are those which may arise, for example if the firm is called upon to honour guarantees. See also current liabilities, and eligible liabilities.

liability 1. The legal obligation to make some payment. This includes payment of compensation to employees injured at work, or to customers injured by defective products such as unsafe cars, or paying other people's debts if one has guaranteed them and they default. See also contingent liability, employer's liability, and product liability.
   2. The legal obligation to pay debts. *Unlimited liability means that the individual or company concerned must make the payment if their assets permit; if not, they can be made bankrupt or liquidated. Unlimited liability normally applies to individuals, and firms trading as sole traders or partnerships. *Limited liability, which applies only to companies, means that their shareholders are liable for the company's debts only to the extent of losing the money originally put into a business, plus any unpaid portion of the par value of shares purchased. See also limited liability, and unlimited liability.

liberalization A programme of changes in the direction of moving towards a free-market economy. This normally includes the reduction of direct controls on both internal and international transactions, and a shift towards relying on the *price mechanism to co-ordinate economic activities. In such a programme less use is made of licences, permits and price controls, and there is more reliance on prices to clear markets. It also involves a shift away from exchange controls and multiple exchange rates, towards a *convertible currency. The extent to which an economy is controlled can vary greatly;

liberalization is a matter of degree, and does not imply a shift to total laissez-faire. *See also* trade liberalization.

liberal trade policy A trade policy aimed at allowing a country's residents to take part in international trade with the minimum of interference. This involves the reduction of *tariffs, the relaxation or removal of quantitative trade controls, and replacement of discretionary controls by rules, and of quantitative controls by tariffs. It also involves the replacement of multiple exchange rates by a uniform system of exchange rates, and the replacement of exchange controls by sufficient devaluation to allow a satisfactory balance of payments without controls. Trade policy is capable of many degrees of dirigisme, and liberalization of trade policy does not necessarily involve a shift to complete laissez-faire.

LIBOR *See* London Inter Bank Offered Rate.

licence, import *See* import licence.

licensing Allowing another firm, for payment, to make use of a *patent or trademark. This is a method of profiting by a patent without investment on the scale necessary to exploit an innovatory idea for oneself. The other possibility would be to sell the patent to somebody who could afford to exploit it, but licensing allows the inventor to retain ownership.

life assurance *See* life insurance.

Life Assurance and Unit Trust Regulatory Organization (LAUTRO) A UK self-regulating organization (SRO) responsible for regulating organizations offering life assurance and unit trusts as principals. LAUTRO was merged in the Personal Investment Authority (PIA) in 1994.

life cycle The lifetime pattern of income and consumption. Assuming that children are supported by their parents, young adults start with low incomes, which rise with age until sometime in middle age, after which they fall, possibly quite sharply, on retirement. Little earned income is usually received after retirement. Consumption is generally highest in the early years of adult life when household goods have to be bought and children reared. This results in a pattern of savings, which are generally small in early adult life, large for a period after the children are grown, and negative during retirement. Household assets thus tend to rise before retirement and fall afterwards. Whether assets actually start and finish at zero depends on social habits as regards inheritance: most people leave positive assets at death, if only because they do not know when this will occur. The life-cycle model of savings suggests that the distribution of assets will be uneven between households even if their lifetime incomes and social attitudes are the same.

life insurance A contract providing funds on death or at a certain age. A life insurance (or assurance) policy is a contract whereby, in return for lump-sum or regular premiums, the company provides an agreed sum to the policy-holder's estate in the event of death before some agreed date, or to the policy-holder upon survival to this date. Life policies may be 'without profits', that is, for a fixed sum of money, or 'with profits', in which case the sum paid out reflects the profits the insurance company has been able to make by investing the premiums. Life insurance policies can also be arranged to provide the policy-holder with an annuity income after retirement, and make provision for surviving spouses or other dependents. *See also* with-profits life insurance.

LIFFE *See* London International Financial Futures and Options Exchange.

LIFO *See* last-in, first-out.

limit A value which is approached as some process continues indefinitely. For example, consider the process starting with some finite number $x \neq 0$, and dividing by 2; thus $x_t = x_{t-1}/2$. As this process continues, x approaches the limit zero, written $x \to 0$, but never actually reaches it in finite t.

limit, cash *See* cash limits.

limited company A company whose ordinary shareholders have limited liability.

limited liability The system by which shareholders in a company are not liable for its debts beyond the nominal value of their shares. Where shares are fully paid up, with limited liability the shareholders cannot be called on for any further funds. If shares are partly paid up, limited liability means that shareholders are liable only to the extent of the unpaid portion of the nominal value of their shares. Limited liability makes it possible to raise capital for purposes considered too risky for investors to be willing to provide funds on the basis of unlimited liability.

limit pricing A policy for an incumbent firm of discouraging entry to its markets by charging low enough prices for entry to appear unprofitable to other firms. This is contrasted with a policy of short-run profit maximization, where the price is high enough to attract entry, which will lead to a gradual loss of sales, as customers come to know of alternative suppliers. There is thus a trade-off between large but temporary and smaller but more sustained profits.

linear approximation A straight line used in economic models to give an approximation to a function which is in fact non-linear. Where the tangent to a curve at a given point is used as a linear approximation, the errors involved tend to be small near the point of tangency, and to increase rapidly with distance from it. Linear approximations are widely used for ease of computation.

linear equation An equation in which the arguments appear only as first and not as any higher powers. Thus, for example, $ax + by + c = 0$ is a linear equation; but $ax^2 + by + c = 0$ is not. The graph of a linear equation containing only two variables is a straight line, hence the name.

linear function A function of the form $y = a + bx$, where a and b are constants. A linear function is so called because its graph is always a straight line. The equation $y = 0$ can always be solved for a linear function with $b \neq 0$ by using the formula $x = -a/b$. A linear function may have N arguments, $x_1, x_2, \ldots, x_N$, taking the form

$$y = a + b_1 x_1 + b_2 x_2 + \ldots + b_N x_N.$$

For each i, only x_i and no power of x_i appears as an argument.

linear programming A mathematical procedure for finding the maximum or minimum value of a linear objective function subject to linear constraints. Where only small numbers of variables and constraints are involved, it is possible to proceed by assuming every possible set of the constraints to hold exactly and solving this as a system of simultaneous equations. Each solution is checked to see if the remaining constraints are satisfied: if they are it is feasible. The objective function can then be evaluated at every feasible solution and the feasible solution(s) giving the highest value for the objective function can be selected. If the number of variables concerned is large this procedure is impossible; linear programming works by selecting a set of constraints yielding one feasible solution, and adding constraints one by one, and excluding others, if making this change gives a feasible solution and increases the objective function; this procedure stops when no further change in the set of constraints can increase the objective function.

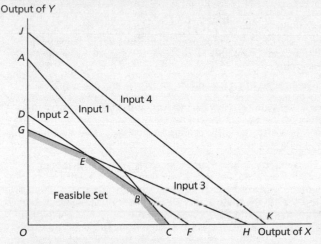

FIGURE 18: *Linear Programming*

The horizontal axis shows output of good X; the vertical axis shows output of good Y. The constraints are imposed by limits on the inputs available, where output of X and Y requires minimum quantities of each input per unit. ABC shows the constraint imposed by the available quantity of input 1; only outputs on or below ABC can be produced. $DEBF$ shows the constraint imposed by the available quantity of input 2. GEH shows the constraint imposed by the available quantity of input 3. JK shows the constraint imposed by the available quantity of input 4. Input 4 will never be an effective constraint, but each of the others may be. The feasible set of outputs is shown by $OGEBC$. If production is at E, input 1 is not an effective constraint; if production is at B, input 3 is not an effective constraint.

linear regression A statistical method of measuring the extent to which variations in one variable are associated with variations in others. It is assumed that the relation between one selected variable, the 'left-hand' or dependent variable, and the others, the 'right-hand' or independent variables, can be described by a linear function of the form

$$y_i = \alpha_0 + \alpha_1 x_{1i} + \alpha_2 x_{2i} + \ldots + \alpha_N x_{Ni} + \varepsilon_i,$$

where ε_i is a stochastic error term. The aim is to pick estimated values of α_0, α_1, etc, which minimize the sum

$$\Sigma_i \varepsilon_i^2 = \Sigma_i [y_i - (\alpha_0 + \alpha_1 x_{1i} + \alpha_2 x_{2i} + \ldots + \alpha_N x_{Ni})]^2,$$

that is 'unexplained' variance in y. While the various x's are referred to as independent variables, and y as the dependent variable, regression is only a measure of association, and does not imply either that there is any causal relation, or, if there is one, that y is caused by the x's.

liquid assets Assets which are themselves *money, or can be converted into money with minimum delay and risk of loss. Short-dated marketable securities such as Treasury bills are liquid assets. Longer-dated securities, which may change in value as interest rates vary, are not liquid, nor are shares or commodities whose price is liable to vary, even if they are readily marketable. Real assets such as unincorporated businesses or houses are doubly illiquid: they cannot reliably be sold quickly, and the price they will fetch is very uncertain.

liquidation The process of closing down a business and disposing of its assets. This may be done by selling it to a new owner as a going concern, or by selling off the various assets separately. The aim of liquidation is to produce as large as possible a sum of money, which can be used to pay off existing debts of the business, any remaining surplus being available for distribution to the owners or shareholders.

liquidity 1. The property of assets, of being easily turned into money rapidly and at a fairly predictable price. Apart from money itself, and deposits with non-bank financial firms such as building societies, short-dated securities such as Treasury bills are the main assets of this form. This is contrasted with illiquidity. Some assets are illiquid because there are no markets on which they can easily be traded: for example, unsecured loans to bank customers. Other assets are illiquid because while they can be traded, the price that can be obtained may be hard to predict, especially if a quick sale is required. This applies to shares in companies, or to houses. 2. The property of having liquid assets. Without these a business may have problems over meeting its obligations because, although it believes itself to be solvent, this view is not shared by credit institutions. The information which leads it to feel solvent, for example confidence in new products, may be private and not convincing to creditors.

liquidity constraint The fact that it is not always possible for inviduals or firms to borrow as much as they would like to. Individuals, given their expectations, may prefer to consume now and pay later, if they expect that in the future their incomes will be higher or their needs will be less than they are now. Firms may believe that it would be profitable to invest in projects they can only finance by borrowing. Where an individual or a firm has *collateral which will make a loan to them safe, or where their reputation inspires lenders to provide loans without collateral, their desired spending plans can be carried out. Individuals and firms without collateral or reputation cannot borrow as much as they would like, or possibly not at all: they are thus liquidity-constrained. Most borrowers are potentially liquidity-constrained: small expenditures can be financed by loans, but for large expenditures a liquidity constraint would apply.

liquidity preference The factors determining the amount of money people want to hold. In Keynesian monetary theory liquidity preference is affected by three main considerations: the volume of transactions which people and firms expect to need to conduct, or the *transactions motive; their expectations concerning movements in interest rates, or the *speculative motive; and their degree of uncertainty about the future, or the *precautionary motive. Liquidity preference, or the desire to hold money, is an increasing function of the expected level of money income, of fears that interest rates are likely to rise so that capital losses will be made on securities, and of fears of recession and unemployment. The L in the LM curve refers to liquidity in this sense.

liquidity ratio The proportion between a bank or other financial institution's holdings of liquid assets and its total liabilities. Minimum liquidity ratios may be imposed by law or convention, or adopted voluntarily as a matter of commercial prudence.

liquidity trap A situation in which *real interest rates cannot be reduced by any action of the monetary authorities. This is liable to arise if prices are expected to fall. If general price falls are expected, holding money will produce an expected real gain equal to minus the expected rate of inflation. The real interest rate cannot be reduced beyond the point at which the nominal interest rate falls to zero, however much the money supply is increased. The monetary authorities are thus unable to promote investment by cutting real interest rates, even if investment would be responsive to a real interest rate cut if one should occur.

listing Agreement by a stock exchange to allow a company's shares to be traded. This is conditional on the company complying with the exchange's requirements as regards the information provided to investors. A listed share is included in the exchange's physical and electronic displays of information on dealings.

living, standard of *See* standard of living.

Lloyd's A London institution whose members provide *insurance of all types on a world-wide basis. In Lloyd's individual investors, or 'names', provide limited cash funds and accept unlimited liability for insurance policies. The policies are arranged by managers on behalf of *syndicates, that is groups of names. Companies have recently been allowed to join Lloyd's. Lloyd's does not itself provide insurance, but does maintain a central fund to back syndicates which might otherwise default, which would damage the reputation of Lloyd's as a whole. Lloyd's had operated profitably for centuries before the 1980s, but in recent years some syndicates have made losses of billions of pounds. These losses have led to large cash calls on names, which have been followed by allegations of mismanagement and some complex litigation.

LM curve A curve used in macroeconomic models to represent the conditions for equilibrium in the money market. The *LM* curve shows those combinations of national income, *Y*, and the interest rate, *r*, at which the ex ante demand for money holdings, *L* (for liquidity preference), equals the ex ante supply of money balances, *M*. It is usually assumed that the demand for money balances rises when national income rises and falls when interest rates rise, while the supply of money is taken to be exogenous. Under these assumptions, when *Y* increases *r* must increase also, so that the *LM* curve slopes upwards, when drawn on a diagram with the origin in the lower left-hand corner. *See also* the figure for *IS-LM* model.

loan Money lent, which has to be returned, usually with interest. Loans may be secured, that is backed by *collateral, which the lender can sell to get their money back if the borrower fails to pay, or may be unsecured. If a debtor cannot pay all debts in full, unsecured creditors rank below secured ones in their claim on such assets as are available. Soft loans are ones where it is expected that if the borrower has problems in paying, the terms will be relaxed, allowing reductions or delay in payments; hard loans are ones where it is expected that the conditions will be strictly enforced. *See also* bank loan, personal loan, revolving loan, roll-over of loans, secured loan, soft loan, syndicated loan, term loan, tied loan, and unsecured loan.

loanable funds A theory of the determination of the *rate of interest by the need to equate the demand for funds for investment with the supply of available savings. This was popular in pre-Keynesian thinking, when the level of national income was taken as fixed by long-term supply-side factors. It is contrasted with the Keynesian liquidity preference theory, in which interest rates are determined by the need to equate the supply and demand for money balances. *See also* supply-side economics.

loan-loss reserve A reserve fund held by a financial institution which believes that some of the loans it has made are liable to turn into *bad debts, but does not know, or does not wish to specify, which of its debtors are likely to default.

loan portfolio The collection of loans held as assets by a financial institution. Such institutions hold loan portfolios for two reasons: first, their total assets are often too large for it to be practicable to lend to only one borrower; and second, a number of loans are safer than one large one, especially if the borrowers have a degree of spread, either geographically or by industry. This makes it safe to predict that even if some borrowers default, the profits on the ones who do not will make the portfolio profitable as a whole.

lobbying Activities devoted to informing politicians of the views of various interest groups, and persuading them to draft legislation or to vote in accordance with these views. Lobbying is conducted by numerous interest groups; the methods vary greatly. Some lobbying is purely informative; no reasonable objection can be made to this, as it is clearly desirable that legislators should know about people's problems, and how any proposed legislation will affect them. At the other extreme lobbyists can use clearly criminal methods such as bribery and blackmail. In between are methods involving financial support for political activities, which many countries believe cannot be prohibited but need to be regulated.

local authority housing *See* council housing.

local content The proportion of inputs to a product supplied from within a country. Minimum levels of local content may be required for a product to qualify for tariff-free movement between the countries of a *free trade area, or for an inward foreign direct investment to qualify for tax concessions.

local government A unit of government which does not claim sovereign powers. Thus the states of federal countries such as Germany or the USA are not local governments, whereas French *départements* and UK counties are. The powers of local governments are entirely delegated from above. Their finance may be provided from the central government, or they may be empowered to levy taxes themselves. They may have discretion over some policies, or be required to administer policies laid down centrally. There may be any number of layers of local government, possibly with overlapping functions.

local maximum A value of a function which is greater than at any nearby value of its argument, or set of values of its arguments. It is a necessary condition for a local maximum of $y = f(x)$ that $dy/dx = 0$; provided this is satisfied, it is a sufficient condition for a local maximum that $d^2y/dx^2 < 0$. A local maximum may also be a global maximum, if there is no value of x for which y is greater. This need not be the case, however: consider the function $y = x^3 - 3x$. $dy/dx = 0$ when $x^2 = 1$; and $d^2y/dx^2 = 6x$. y has a maximum at $x = -1$, but this is only a local and not a global maximum, since y can be made indefinitely large by taking a large enough positive value of x. *See also* the figure for maximum.

local minimum A value of a function which is lower than at any nearby value of its argument, or set of values of its arguments. It is a necessary condition for a local minimum of $y = f(x)$ that $dy/dx = 0$; provided this is satisfied, it is a sufficient condition for a local minimum that $d^2y/dx^2 > 0$. A local minimum may also be a global minimum, if there is no value of x for which y is lower. This need not be the case, however: consider the function $y = x^3 - 3x$. $dy/dx = 0$ when $x^2 = 1$; and $d^2y/dx^2 = 6x$. y has as a minimum at $x = 1$, but this is only a local and not a global minimum, since y can be made negative and indefinitely large by taking a large enough negative value of x. *See also* the figure for maximum.

location The position of a firm's premises. The aspects of position which matter vary with the business. For hotels, the proximity of natural features such as beaches or ski-slopes, or man-made attractions such as cathedrals or the Acropolis is important. For distribution and commerce, easy access to transport facilities, such as railway stations or motorway exits is important. For some financial firms the proximity of other firms is vital: witness the concentration of banks and other financial businesses in Wall Street or the

City of London. Many other businesses find it an advantage to be near transport facilities and large numbers of customers, but not one great enough to warrant paying the high rents which prevail in very popular centres, so that they prefer to locate somewhere cheaper. As moving is itself expensive, the location of production is strongly influenced by history.

lock-out A form of industrial action by employers, in which workers are excluded from their place of work and their pay, but not dismissed.

locomotive principle The idea that growth in an economy, or in the world economy, depends on growth in some leading sector or leading country. The leader, which may be an industry with favourable investment opportunities, or a country with a strong balance of payments, can by expanding serve as a locomotive to pull the less dynamic parts of the economy or of the world after it.

logarithm The power to which any base number over 1 needs to be raised to give any positive number. If x is the log to base y of z then $z = y^x$. Logarithms have the property that the logarithm of the product of any two numbers is the sum of the logs of the two numbers. Logarithms can be taken to any base over 1: the two forms most commonly used are logarithms to base 10, written $\log(x)$, and *'natural' logarithms to base e, written $\ln(x)$; these are provided by most calculating machines. $\ln(x)$ is the indefinite integral of $1/x$. *See also* natural logarithm.

logarithmic scale A scale on a diagram where distances represent the logarithm of a variable. Log scales are used particularly in diagrams with time on one, usually the horizontal, axis, and some real or nominal variable such as GDP or the price level on the vertical axis. The slope of a curve in such a diagram shows the proportional growth rate of the variable, and a constant proportional growth trend is represented by a straight line. If both axes use logarithmic scales, the slope of a curve is proportional to its elasticity. Neither zero nor negative numbers can be represented on a log scale.

In both panels of Figure 19 on the next page the horizontal axis shows time, and the vertical axis shows the real GDP of an imaginary economy. Panel 1 uses a natural scale; Panel 2 uses a logarithmic scale. It is assumed that the economy has alternating booms, each lasting five years, and slumps each lasting two years.

Panel 1 leads the government's apologists to argue that its growth policies are successful, as growth is greater in each successive cycle. It leads the government's critics to argue that cycles are becoming more severe, showing that the government's stabilization efforts are incompetent.

Panel 2 shows that both are wrong. Growth is actually slowing down, but fluctuations are also becoming less severe. (The figures were picked to make the economy grow by 100, 90, 80 per cent, etc. in successive booms, and shrink by 10, 9, 8 per cent, etc. in successive slumps.)

logistic curve A curve showing the behaviour over time of a variable x where

$a < x < b,$

and the growth of x is governed by the rule

$dx/dt = \alpha(x - a)(b - x).$

GDP Natural scale

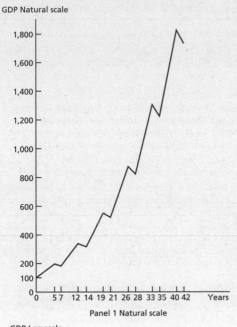

Panel 1 Natural scale

GDP Log scale

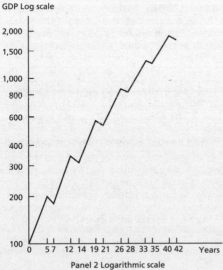

Panel 2 Logarithmic scale

FIGURE 19: *Logarithmic Scales*

This type of curve can be fitted as an approximation to economic phenomena such as the proportion of consumers using a new product, or firms using a new technique, where $a = 0$ and $b = 1$.

log-linear function A function in which the logarithm of the dependent variable is linear in the logarithm of its argument. Thus $\ln(y) = \alpha + \beta \ln(x)$ is log-linear.

log-normal distribution The distribution such that the logarithms of the variables are normally distributed. This distribution naturally results from the effects of a large number of independent but multiplicative sources of variation. It is contrasted with the *normal distribution, which results when there are numerous independent and additive sources of variation. The log-normal distribution is upward skewed, with a mean larger than its mode, whereas a normal distribution is symmetrical about its mean.

log-rolling Co-operation between representatives in national or local legislatures to support other members' bids for public money in return for support for measures to benefit their own constituents. Log-rolling is blamed for wasteful public expenditures: a coalition formed on this basis may push through a group of measures most of which each member would have opposed if not voting strategically.

Lomé Convention An international agreement reached in 1975 by the *European Economic Community (EEC) granting associate status to French overseas territories.

London Inter Bank Offered Rate (LIBOR) The rate of interest on short-term wholesale loans in the London money market: this is the rate at which banks lend to each other. LIBOR is used as a bench-mark for variable-rate loans within the UK and internationally. A less developed country (LDC), for example, might be offered a loan at LIBOR plus 3 per cent.

London International Financial Futures and Options Exchange (LIFFE) A financial futures market opened in London in 1982 to provide for trade in options and futures contracts. These include government bonds, stock indices, currencies and interest rates. The London Traded Options Market merged with LIFFE in 1992; LIFFE added Options to its title, but kept the acronym unchanged.

long-dated security A security with fifteen or more years to maturity when first issued. Such securities are particularly liable to fluctuations in their market price when current interest rates change.

long position A situation where dealers in commodity, currency or security markets are holding stocks they have no current arrangements to sell, because they are speculating on a rise in their prices.

long rate *See* long-term interest rate.

long run A period sufficiently long that everything can be changed, which can ever be changed at all. The long run is contrasted with the short run, in which very few things can be changed, and with the medium run, in which more things can be changed than in the short run, but not so many as in the long run. In the long run, for example, a firm can build new premises, carry out research and development programmes to devise new processes and products and apply them, and recruit and train managers and skilled workers. In the short run most of these things are impossible: the firm can only buy more fuel and materials, and recruit additional untrained workers. Long-run supply and demand curves are typically more *elastic than the corresponding short-run curves.

long-run average cost *See* average cost.

long-run marginal cost *See* marginal cost.

long-run Phillips curve A curve showing the long-run relation between inflation and unemployment. This is drawn adopting the assumption that the appropriate short-term Phillips curve is that augmented for inflation, and assuming that at each point on the long-run Phillips curve actual and expected inflation are equal. If models featuring a *non-accelerating inflation rate of unemployment (NAIRU) are correct, the long-run Phillips curve is a vertical line at the NAIRU. If such models are not correct, there could be a non-vertical long-run Phillips curve, which while it was steeper than the short-run curves, was still not actually vertical. This would leave some scope for a long-run trade-off between inflation and unemployment, which does not exist if the long-run Phillips curve is vertical.

long-term interest rate The rate of interest paid on government securities with a long period to maturity, say fifteeen years or above.

long-term unemployment Unemployment for relatively long periods, for example a year or more. This causes more severe problems than short spells of unemployment, from the point of view of both the financial position and the morale of the unemployed and their families. Similar problems arise where shorter periods of continuous unemployment are interrupted only by brief spells in work. It appears that the probability of getting a job decreases the longer a worker has been unemployed. It is not clear whether this is because unemployment makes workers less employable, or simply that those harder to employ tend to stay unemployed longer. Long-term unemployment suggests a need for help with retraining or relocation.

Lorenz curve A graphical representation of inequality. Personal incomes in a country, for example, are arranged in ascending order: the cumulative share of total income is then plotted against the cumulative share of the population. The slope of this curve is thus proportional to per capita income at each point of the population distribution. For complete equality of income the Lorenz curve would be a straight line; it becomes more curved as inequality rises. The *Gini coefficient is a measure of this inequality.

loss The result of a business operation where expenditures exceed receipts. Business losses may arise internally, through failure to produce enough of anything the market will buy to cover production expenses, or externally, through failure of others to pay bills due, or to repay debts. The effect of losses is to reduce a business's capital. If losses proceed so far that the total assets of a business become less than its liabilities, the business is insolvent, and should either be closed or rescued by a fresh injection of capital. *See* capital loss, and triangle of loss.

loss leader A good which is priced low, possibly even below cost, to attract customers who are expected to buy other goods which yield a profit. The use of loss leaders can be profitable only if consumers are more conscious of the relative prices of some goods than of others. This may be so, if goods differ in how easily their quality is checked, and how frequently they are bought. Selling cheap goods about which customers are well informed may be used to attract custom for other goods on which they are less well informed, and can therefore be exploited.

Louvre Accord An agreement reached in February 1987 between the G6 industrial countries concerning exchange rates of other currencies against the US dollar. At this meeting the countries agreed 'to cooperate closely to foster stability of exchange rates around current levels'.

loyalty, brand *See* brand loyalty.

Ltd *See* limited company.

Lucas critique The argument that it is dangerous to attempt to predict the effects of major policy changes by using econometric models of the economy based on data recorded when different policies were in place. Individuals and firms are assumed to choose their actions in the light of existing policies: for example, choice of hours of work takes account of current income tax policy. If there is a major policy change, this changes the incentives in the system, and will change people's conduct. It cannot be assumed that the effects of a major policy change can be predicted just by changing particular parameters in a few fitted equations. The general implication of this critique is that the effects of policy changes are hard to forecast: they can be learned by experience, but only when it is too late to alter them.

lumpiness *See* indivisibility.

lump of labour The view that there is a fixed total amount of employment available. If this were true, it would be correct to argue that that limiting hours worked would create more jobs, and making the elderly retire early would create jobs for the young. This view ignores the possibility that the demand for labour may depend on the relation between wage rates and the value of work to employers. Allowing for this, preventing employers from employing the most experienced workers, or from employing people for longer hours per week, might actually reduce total employment, by lowering the value of the work employers get for the wages they offer.

lump-sum tax A tax whose amount is not affected by the tax-payer's actions, or at least by some aspects of them. In the UK, for example, a television licence is only payable by those who have a TV set, but its amount does not depend on whether they have a new and large or an old and small TV. A completely lump-sum tax would be a poll tax payable by all residents. Because it is impossible to extract much from the poorest members of society, actual taxes usually contain escape clauses which do make paying the tax

something the taxpayer can influence by their own conduct. The UK
*Community Charge, for example, had lower rates for some groups and
exemption for others. The advantage claimed for lump-sum taxes is that they
do not distort incentives at the margin. This is paid for by the fact that
they are highly regressive in their distributive effects, collecting the largest
proportion of incomes from the poorest taxpayers.

luxury A good or service whose consumption at any given price rises more
than in proportion to an increase in income. The income elasticity of demand
for a luxury is thus more than unity. A luxury is therefore a good on which
richer people spend a higher proportion of their incomes than do poorer
people. This is contrasted with a *necessity, whose consumption at any given
price rises less than in proportion to income. *See also* the figure for Engel
curve.

M0 The narrowest definition of the UK money supply. This includes notes and coin in circulation, and banks' till money and balances with the Bank of England.

M1 A less narrow definition of the money supply. In the UK M1 includes notes and coin in circulation plus private sector current accounts plus deposit accounts transferable by cheque. In the US it includes currency outside the Treasury and Federal Reserve Banks, demand deposits of commercial banks, and other checkable deposits.

M2 A possible definition of broad money. In the UK, M2 includes notes and coin in circulation plus non-interest-bearing bank deposits plus building society deposits plus National Savings accounts. In the US it includes M1 plus money market deposit accounts, balances in money market mutual funds, and savings and time deposits of under $100,000.

M3, M4, and M5 A variety of alternative broader definitions of broad money as M1 plus assorted other deposits at banks and other financial intermediaries.

M3, sterling *See* sterling M3.

Maastricht convergence criteria *See* convergence criteria.

Maastricht, Treaty of A treaty concluded in 1993 between members of the *European Community (EC). This changed its name to European Union (EU), and set out a programme for progress towards a *European Monetary Union (EMU) and the creation of a *European Central Bank (ECB). The treaty included convergence criteria, including a 3 per cent limit to budget deficits and a 60 per cent limit to debt–GDP ratios for members to be eligible to join the EMU. The treaty also included a *Social Chapter, containing various employment protection provisions. The UK originally opted out of the Social Chapter, but has since accepted it.

macroeconomics The macro aspects of economics, concerning the determination of aggregate and average figures in the economy. This considers what determines total employment and production, consumption, investment in raising productive capacity, and how much a country imports and exports. It also asks what causes booms and slumps in the short run, and what determines the long-term growth rate of the economy, the general level of prices and the rate of inflation. Macroeconomics considers how these matters can and should be influenced by government through monetary and fiscal policies. It is contrasted with *microeconomics, which is concerned with micro questions, such as the incentives operating on individuals and firms in the economy, the organization of production, and the distribution of incomes.

maintenance Work on buildings and equipment which is necessary to keep them in good condition. This includes lubrication, checking for wear and damage, and the replacement of worn or defective parts. Maintenance is expensive in labour and materials, but cutting down on routine maintenance is generally false economy as it leads to breakdowns, accidents, and unsatisfactory quality of output.

majority shareholder A shareholder who owns a majority of the voting shares of a company. This gives control of the appointment of the company's directors, and gives them the final say on company policy.

maker, market- *See* market-maker.

Malthusian problem The fear of economists that per capita incomes would be driven down to subsistence level by a tendency for population to grow faster than output. This was named after the eigtheenth-century UK economist T. R. Malthus. For much of the world this problem has been kept at bay for the last two centuries by a combination of geographical discoveries, technical progress, and falling birthrates. The experience of Sub-Saharan Africa in recent decades, however, shows that the problem is not extinct.

managed currency *See* intervention in foreign exchange markets.

managed floating exchange rate The system under which a country's exchange rate is not pegged, but the monetary authorities try to manage it rather than simply leaving it to be set by the market. This can be done in two ways: small fluctuations in the exchange rate can be smoothed out by the authorities buying the country's currency when its price would otherwise fall and selling it when its price would otherwise rise. The authorities can also influence the exchange rate through their macroeconomic policies. Higher interest rates tend to bring inward capital flows and improve the trade balance through their effect in depressing domestic activity; lower interest rates have the opposite effects. This type of exchange rate management is sometimes referred to as a 'dirty float'. There is no obvious justification for the pejorative description, and this policy regime is in fact widespread.

managed trade International trade conducted in accordance with plans negotiated by government bodies. This is the natural mode of trade for planned economies, but is not convenient for *market economies. While governments in market economies have sufficient powers to prevent trade they do not approve of, they have no adequate means of inducing private firms to supply exports they have promised that their country will provide or to buy imports they have promised their country will accept. Also, managed trade must either be bilaterally balanced, or involve negotiation between several governments, which is liable to be very cumbersome and unlikely to produce agreement.

management 1. The decision-making role in organizations. If things are going smoothly, there is not much for management to do, but if things go wrong or new opportunities arise, somebody has to decide on hiring and firing workers, investing in new machines or scrapping old ones, marketing new products and dropping old ones, and how to raise the necessary finance. The role of management is to take these decisions.

2. The people who do the managing. This may involve a hierarchy, with junior, branch, or assistant managers exercising limited discretion, and the Managing Director as the overall boss of an organization, laying down general lines of policy, and hiring and firing assistant managerial staff to carry out the decisions.

3. Overall control of aggregate demand. *See* demand management.

management accounting The part of accounting devoted to providing information useful to the management of an organization. This is contrasted with the process of producing official accounts, which have to satisfy a company's *auditors and its Inspector of Taxes. Management accounting involves the collection and processing of information which will help in actually running a firm. This includes things like checking on the stocks, to ensure that enough are kept to avoid running out too often, but not so many that they incur excessive interest costs and deterioration from age before items are needed, and ensuring that the staff are not purloining them. Management accounting includes elements of operations research, checking whether the order of operations, or the processes used to deliver products, are efficient. It also includes cost accounting, to discover which operations are profitable and which cost more than they bring in.

management buy-out Acquisition of the equity capital of a firm by its managers. If the managers own or can borrow sufficient capital for a buy-out, this has the advantage of concentrating control in the hands of people with experience of the firm's problems.

managerial theories of the firm The theory that the conduct of firms must be explained in terms of the motivation of managers. Such theories are alternatives to *profit maximization as explanations of how firms are run. Profit maximization makes sense if there is full information and firms are run in the interests of their shareholders.This is open to two main objections, based on information and motivation. On the information side, *satisficing theories urge that firms do not have the information needed to maximize: they run by rules or habits so long as the results are tolerable, and if the current rules give poor results, they use trial and error to search for better ones. On the motivation side, decisions are taken by the directors, who are interested in maximizing their own welfare so long as the shareholders will allow it. This is a typical case of the *principal–agent problem. The interests of top management are best served by growth of the firm, managerial pay and perquisites, and an easy life; the shareholders' interests matter only as a constraint on these. The possible brakes on the directors' autonomy are concentrated ownership, which is unusual, and the threat of *takeovers by rival management groups who offer the shareholders a better deal. The effectiveness of this sanction is a matter of controversy.

mandatory spending programme The part of government spending which the government is legally obliged to carry out. This is contrasted with *discretionary spending, where the government is empowered to spend in certain ways but is left with discretion as to the detailed composition of spending and possibly its total. For example, spending on pensions or judges' salaries is usually mandatory, while placing contracts for defence equipment is usually discretionary, subject to a limit on the total spent.

margin A proportion of the value of a transaction which traders have to deposit to guarantee that they will complete it. Buying shares on margin means contracting to buy them without actually putting up the full cash price immediately. To safeguard the other party, a buyer is required to deposit a margin, that is a percentage of the price sufficient to protect the seller against loss if the buyer cannot complete.

marginal The effect per unit of a small change in any variable. Marginal cost is the addition to total cost from a small increase in output, per unit of the increase. Marginal revenue is the effect on total revenue of a small increase in sales, per unit of the increase, allowing for any effect of quantity sold on price. The marginal social cost of any activity is the effect of a small increase in the activity on total social costs, per unit of the increase, including any *externalities as well as direct costs to the producer. Similarly, marginal social benefit is the effect on total social benefit of a small increase in an activity, per unit of the increase, including externalities as well as direct benefits to the producer and purchaser. Marginal land, or land on the margin of cultivation, is land which would just become worth farming if output prices rose slightly, or would go out of cultivation if prices fell slightly. A marginal firm is one which would just be induced to enter an industry by a small rise in profitability, or would just be induced to leave the industry by a small worsening in market conditions. The *marginal rate of substitution between two goods shows the amount of one which would be needed to compensate a consumer for a small reduction in the availability of the other good, per unit of the reduction. The criteria for efficiency in economic activity are often stated in terms of equality between marginal rates of substitution for consumers and marginal rates of transformation for producers. Marginal equality is only the correct criterion when quantities can vary in both directions. If the quantity of one good is already zero, its output cannot be reduced, and the efficiency condition is transformed into an inequality. It should also be stressed that marginal equalities define only local optima; with increasing returns, local optima may not be global ones. Marginal conditions are appropriate only when dealing with continuous variables. Some economic variables, such as the number of firms in an industry, cannot vary continuously but are subject to *integer constraints.

marginal benefit The additional benefit from an increase in an activity. This is the addition to total benefit resulting from a unit increase if it varies discretely, or the addition to total benefit, per unit of the increase, if it varies continuously. Marginal private benefit is marginal benefit accruing to the person or firm deciding on the scale of the activity, excluding any external benefits; marginal social benefit includes external benefits as well as private benefit accruing to the decision-taker.

marginal cost The additional cost from an increase in an activity. This is the addition to total cost resulting from a unit increase if it varies discretely, or the addition to total cost, per unit of the increase, if it varies continuously. Marginal cost may be short-run, when only some inputs can be changed, or long-run, when all inputs can be adjusted. Marginal private cost is marginal cost falling on the person or firm deciding on the scale of the activity, excluding any external costs; marginal social cost includes external costs as well as private cost falling on the decision-taker.

marginal cost pricing The policy of setting the price of a good or service equal to the marginal cost of producing it. If demand at this price is equal to output, it can be argued that marginal cost pricing is optimal, since marginal

costs and benefits are equal. If the good or service is produced under
conditions of increasing returns to scale, however, marginal cost will be
below average cost and the firm will make a loss. Paying for this loss requires
a subsidy, either from the state or via cross-subsidization from some
profitable activity conducted by the firm. As taxes impose deadweight costs,
marginal cost pricing is not normally adopted in practice in industries with
decreasing average costs.

marginal efficiency of capital (MEC) The highest interest rate at
which a project could be expected to break even. This depends on the
immediate profits expected from operating the project, and the rate at
which these are expected to decline through reductions in the real price of
the output, or increases in real wages and fuel and materials costs. If all
possible projects in an economy are arranged in descending order of their
MEC, theory suggests that investors will proceed with those with MEC
higher than the interest rate plus an appropriate risk premium, and reject
those whose MEC is lower than this. The MEC is contrasted with the
marginal product of capital, which is concerned only with the immediate
effect of additional capital on possible output, and not with how long the
resulting profits can be expected to persist.

marginal firm A firm which would just be induced to enter an industry by
a small rise in profitability, or would just be induced to leave the industry by a
small worsening in market conditions.

marginal land Land on the margin of cultivation. Such land would become
just worth farming if output prices rose slightly, or would go out of
cultivation if prices fell slightly.

marginal physical product The addition to output, measured in physical
terms, as the result of a small increase in any factor input, per unit of the
increase. This disregards any effects of the change in output on the price at
which it can be sold, in contrast to *marginal revenue product, which also
takes this into account.

marginal private cost *See* private cost.

marginal product The addition to output from a small increase in any
input, per unit of the increase. Marginal physical product measures this in
physical terms, disregarding any effects of the change in output on the price
at which it can be sold. Marginal revenue product equals marginal physical
product times marginal revenue per unit of additional output sold. *See also*
diminishing marginal product.

marginal productivity of capital The extra value of potential output, at
current prices, resulting from a small increase in capital, per unit of the extra
capital. This is contrasted with the *marginal efficiency of capital (MEC),
which is the highest interest rate at which a project can be expected to break
even. The marginal productivity of capital considers only the marginal
revenue from the extra output which an increase in capital makes possible; if
this exceeds the interest on the cost of the capital, it results in a profit. This
profit margin is subject to erosion over time if the real price of the product is
expected to fall, or real wages or fuel and material costs are expected to rise.
The MEC is the interest rate at which prospective profits have to be

discounted to make their *present discounted value equal to the cost of the capital.

marginal propensity to consume *See* propensity to consume.

marginal propensity to import *See* import propensity.

marginal propensity to save *See* propensity to save.

marginal rate of substitution The additional amount of one product required to compensate a consumer for a small decrease in the quantity of another, per unit of the decrease. The marginal rate of substitution is proportional to the slope of an *indifference curve between the two products.

marginal rate of technical substitution The additional amount of one input required to keep output constant for a small decrease in the quantity of another input, per unit of the decrease. The marginal rate of technical substitution is proportional to the slope of an *isoquant between the two inputs.

marginal rate of transformation The amount by which one output can be increased if another is reduced by a small amount, per unit of the decrease, holding total inputs constant. The marginal rate of transformation can be calculated at the level of the firm, the industry, a country, or the world as a whole. It measures *opportunity costs, and is proportional to the slope of the *production possibility frontier.

marginal revenue The increase in total revenue when the quantity sold increases by a small amount, measured per unit of the increase in sales. If the seller is a price-taker, marginal revenue is equal to price. Where the seller faces a downward-sloping demand curve, where p is price and q is quantity sold, and the elasticity of demand is defined as

$$\varepsilon_d = -(p/q)(dq/dp),$$

marginal revenue is

$$m = d(pq)/dq = p + q(dp/dq) = p[1 - (1/\varepsilon_d)].$$

Positive marginal revenue thus requires that $\varepsilon_d > 1$.

marginal revenue product The addition to total revenue from a small increase in any factor input, per unit of the increase. This takes account both of the effect of the extra input in raising the quantity produced, and the effect of an increase in the quantity sold on the price that can be charged for it. Marginal revenue product equals *marginal physical product times marginal revenue per unit of additional output sold.

marginal social benefit *See* social benefit.

marginal social cost *See* social cost.

marginal tax rate The amount by which tax revenues increase per unit increase in value in a taxed activity. At the microeconomic level the marginal tax rate for an individual or firm can usually be found from published tax rules. At the macroeonomic level this is less straightforward, due to the complex interaction of various rules and rates. The marginal income tax rate at the national level, for example, depends on the distribution of additional taxable income between individuals with basic marginal tax rates, those with higher tax rates, and those on lower rates or exempt from tax.

marginal utility The addition to an individual's utility from a small increase in consumption of any good, per unit of the increase. It is usually assumed that, at least beyond a certain point, the marginal utility of any particular good decreases as more is consumed. This is a psychological generalization and not a logical requirement. The marginal utility of any good may also depend on the amounts of other goods consumed. Actually measuring marginal utility is impossible, just as it is impossible to measure the absolute level of utility.

marginal utility of money The amount by which an individual's utility would be increased by a small addition to their money holding, per unit of the increase. It is assumed that other assets held do not change, so that the extra money represents a net increase in total wealth. In considering particular goods, it is convenient to assume that the marginal utility of money is constant. The demand curve for any good can then be found, using the argument that the quantity consumed will be adjusted so that the marginal utility of good X equals its price times the marginal utility of money. In considering the overall utility of the invidivual, it seems sensible to assume that the marginal utility of money, taken here as being equal to the marginal utility of wealth, decreases. Having more money to spend may raise utility, but given that money cannot buy love or life there is probably some upper bound to the utility level that can be achieved even with unlimited wealth.

marginal utility of wealth The increase in an individual's utility consequent on a small increase in their total wealth, per unit of the increase. It seems sensible to assume that for most individuals the marginal utility of wealth is a decreasing function of the wealth already achieved. This is for two reasons. First, while more wealth is always pleasant, as it cannot buy love or life there is probably some upper bound to utility which cannot be exceeded even with unlimited wealth. Second, the fact that most individuals are *risk-averse suggests that the marginal utility of wealth is a decreasing function. If it were constant, individuals should logically be risk-neutral, and if it were increasing they should be risk-loving.

margin requirement The percentage of the value of a transaction which a buyer or seller is required to deposit as a margin. This is needed to protect one party to a contract against loss if the other side's commitments are not met.

market 1. A place or institution in which buyers and sellers of a good or asset meet. A market was originally a building, and still is for some goods, for example cattle or vegetable markets, and for some services, for example Lloyd's for insurance. Nowadays in many cases the market is a network of dealers linked physically by telephone and computer networks, and linked institutionally by trading rules and conventions. Markets facilitate trade in goods, as in commodity markets; in securities, for example the bond market, the capital market, or the stock exchange; in labour services, as in the labour market; or in foreign exchange, in the foreign exchange market. Spot markets handle trade in goods or services for immediate delivery. Markets also exist for goods, services or assets for future delivery, that is trade in forward or futures contracts, and for derivatives, for example options or market indices.

2. A market economy is one in which markets play a dominant role in co-ordinating decisions. The prices formed in markets convey information and provide motivation for decision-takers. Market forces are the supply and demand factors which determine prices and quantities in a market economy. An efficient market is one where prices reflect all available information about the good or asset concerned. *Market failure refers to a failure of market prices to reflect correctly social costs and benefits. This may be due to externalities, lack of information, or monopoly. It can also arise because markets are incomplete, meaning that it is impossible to trade some goods for others; or where markets are very thin, that is, there is little trading activity, so that there are few records of recent trades to provide information on the prices at which it may be possible to buy or sell in the future. *See also* black market, buyer's market, capital market, commodity market, common market, contestable market, contingent market, efficient markets hypothesis, emerging markets, Eurobond market, factor market, financial markets, forward market, free market, futures market, incomplete markets, internal market, labour market, missing markets, money market, order-driven market, over-the-counter market, perfect market, property market, quote-driven market, secondary market, segmented market, seller's market, spot market, and unlisted securities market.

marketable security A security which can be sold in a secondary market. This is contrasted with a non-marketable security, for example National Savings in the UK, which are not marketable, and can only be turned into cash by selling them back to the issuer. Assets such as mortgages which are individually non-marketable may be made marketable by *securitization, combining them into packages which can then be marketed.

market access The freedom to sell in a market. Market access may not be available for natural or institutionally imposed reasons. Natural obstacles include distance and inability to meet the requirements of customers; institutional obstacles include legal restrictions on entry, tariffs and quotas, and public procurement rules excluding possible suppliers. Inability to compete on price may result from nature or policy; in increasing returns industries, lack of access to some markets limits total output and may cause high costs. Similarly, in industries where technical progress is partly due to *learning by doing, past lack of market access contributes to present inability to compete. Improved market access for their producers is therefore an important aim of governments entering trade negotiations.

market capitalization The market value of a company's issued shares. This is the share price times the number of shares issued.

market clearing Setting the price of a good or security so that the ex ante quantities supplied and demanded are equal. If the price does not equate ex ante supply and demand, then either market participants' plans cannot be carried out, or there must be intervention by a *market-maker or a government body to provide extra goods or securities if demand exceeds supply, or to take goods or securities off the market if supply exceeds demand.

market economy An economy in which a substantial proportion of economic decisions are taken by the use of markets. This is contrasted with a planned economy, in which most major decisions are taken by a centralized decision-making process working in quantitative terms. The advantage of a market economy is that prices fixed by markets convey information about the relative demand for various goods and services and the relative costs of providing them. The prices also provided incentives to increase profitable and decrease unprofitable activities. The disadvantages of a pure market economy are that *externalities are disregarded, the market may be distorted by *monopolies, and the resulting income distribution may be socially unacceptable. In practice most economies are based on varying mixtures of markets and government planning.

market entry *See* entry.

market equilibrium The situation when supply and demand in a market are equal at the prevailing price. The equilibrium price is determined by supply and demand.

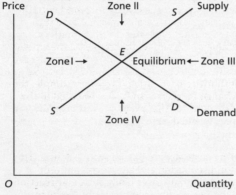

FIGURE 20: *Market Equilibrium*

DD is the market demand curve, which is downward sloping. *SS* is the market supply curve: this must be upward-sloping, or possibly horizontal, for a competitive market to exist. *E* is the equilibrium point, where the supply curve *SS* and the demand curve *DD* intersect. At any other point, there is some form of disequilibrium.

In Zone I, an excess of the price which customers are willing to pay over the price at which producers are willing to provide supplies leads to an increase in quantity.

In Zone II, an excess of supply over demand at a given price leads market-makers to cut prices.

In Zone III, an excess of the price at which producers are willing to provide supplies over the price which customers are willing to pay leads to a fall in quantity.

In Zone IV, an excess of demand over supply leads market-makers to increase prices.

market failure A brief label for the view that the market does not provide a panacea for all economic problems. There are various ways in which an unregulated market may fail to produce an ideal state of affairs. The main sources of market failure are *monopoly, *externalities, and income distribution. Profit maximization under monopoly implies under-provision and over-charging for goods. If the production or consumption of a good involves external economies, it is under-provided by an unregulated market, and if they involve external diseconomies, the good is over-provided. *Public goods are under-provided in a pure market economy. It is also possible that the market may give rise to a distribution of incomes which is regarded as socially unacceptable. The various sources of market failure provide a prima facie case for considering public regulation of some goods, public provision of others, and redistribution of incomes. All these measures, however, are also exposed to potential failings, which need to be considered in arriving at a *second-best design for a mixed economy.

market forces The forces of supply and demand, which determine equilibrium quantities and prices in markets. These are contrasted with the government and monetary authorities, which are able to some extent to modify the outcome of unrestricted market processes. In some matters government powers are considerable: for example, the market alone would leave to starve those without property and unable to work; governments are able to prevent this through income support for the unemployed, retired, and disabled. In other matters the authorities have little power: for example, the total turnover of the foreign exchange markets is so large compared to the foreign exchange reserves of most countries that exchange rates can diverge very little from what market forces would dictate.

market for lemons See lemon.

marketing The process of getting customers to buy a firm's products. This involves making arrangements for distribution and advertising current products. It also covers market research to discover likely customer reaction to potential new products, and whether possible modifications to existing products would improve their appeal. In the long run no amount of marketing skill can sell products customers do not like, but poor marketing can make a product fail even though consumers might have liked it.

market-maker A trader in a goods or securities market who holds a stock of the good or security and is willing to buy or sell at pre-announced prices. These prices only apply up to some limited quantity, but up to this limit they provide *liquidity for other people or firms who want to buy or sell. For larger deals the market-maker will negotiate over price. The market-maker's profits come from the difference between their ask, or selling price, and their bid, or buying price. These prices have to be adjusted over time to keep supply and demand approximately balanced. If demand persistently exceeds supply at the market-maker's offer price, this must rise, otherwise stocks will become exhausted; if supply persistently exceeds demand at the market-maker's bid price, this must fall, otherwise stocks will rise above the level the market-maker is willing and able to finance. The spread between a market-maker's bid and offer prices has to be large enough to cover operating costs and a premium to cover the risks they are taking, and small enough not to attract too much competition from rival market-makers.

market mechanism *See* market economy.

market power An indefinite concept concerned with the strength of the position of the dominant firm in a market. Market power can be regarded as high if the dominant firm has the ability to act as a price leader, if it can dictate the conditions of sale for its products, if it is able to deter entry, or if it can make persistently super-normal profits.

market prices The method of measuring national income at the prices customers actually pay. Gross domestic product (GDP) or any other national income accounting aggregate at market prices uses the prices customers pay, including any indirect taxes and subtracting any subsidies. This is contrasted with *factor cost, the prices of goods and services actually received by the sellers. To get from market prices to factor cost indirect taxes are subtracted and consumer subsidies added.

market risk The risk taken by any trader on a market who holds either a long or a short position, that the price will change. The holder of stocks of goods, securities, or currencies not hedged by futures sales runs the risk of losing if the price falls; the seller of futures for goods, securities or currencies they do not hold runs the risk of losing if the market price rises. Market risk in some markets can be reduced by hedging. Market risk exists even if the other party's side of any bargain fully and promptly; it is contrasted with *counter-party risk, which is the risk that the other party to a deal may fail to deliver punctually, or at all.

market share The share of a market held by a particular firm. The size of this depends largely on the definition of the market: a firm with a small share of a market broadly defined in geographical and industrial terms may have a much larger share of its local market, or the market for a more narrowly defined type of product. This point may be important if monopoly legislation makes decisions, for example on reference to the *Monopolies and Mergers Commission (MMC), now the Competition Commission (CC), in the UK, depend on market share.

market structure The pattern of market shares in an industry. This is concerned with how many firms there are, and how they vary in size. Two common measures used in describing market structure are the N-firm *concentration ratio and the *Herfindahl index. The five-firm concentration ratio, for example, shows the total market shares of the largest five firms as a proportion of the whole market. This has defects; there is a lot of difference between a market in which the largest firm has 82 per cent of all sales and the next four firms have 2 per cent each, and a market in which five equal firms have shares of 18 per cent; yet each produces a five-firm concentration ratio of 0.9. The Herfindahl index works by adding the squares of the proportional shares of all firms. If there are N firms, the largest possible Herfindahl index approaches a maximum of 1 as the biggest firm has nearly all the sales and the rest minute amounts, and a minimum of $1/N$ if all firms have equal market shares. Both measures are completely static; a more dynamic approach to market structure might enquire how far the leading places tend to be occupied by the same firms, and how fast the identity of the market leaders changes.

Market, Unlisted Securities *See* Unlisted Securities Market.

mark-up The excess of the selling price of a product over the cost of making or buying it. The mark-up on any product has to cover the overheads of the firm, as well as providing a profit margin.

Marshall–Lerner condition A condition for *devaluation to improve a country's *balance of trade. Suppose that trade between two countries is initially balanced, and that country 1 devalues by a small proportion k. If exports are in perfectly elastic supply in each country, domestic price and income levels do not change, and the price elasticity of demand for imports is α in country 1 and β in country 2, the balance of trade changes as follows. In terms of country 1's currency, 1's import prices rise by k, and the quantity imported falls by αk; spending on imports rises by $(1-\alpha)k$. Export prices stay the same in 1's currency, but in 2's they fall by k, so quantity sold rises by βk. The balance of trade thus improves by $(\alpha+\beta-1)k$ times the initial level of trade; this is positive if $\alpha + \beta > 1$. In terms of country 2's currency, A's import spending falls by αk, and export receipts rise by $(\beta-1)k$, so again the balance of trade improves by $(\alpha + \beta - 1)k$ times initial trade, as before. The Marshall–Lerner condition clearly needs several qualifications: it is only an approximation for large k; countries do not generally devalue when their trade is initially balanced; and it takes no account of imported inflation in the devaluing country, nor of the multiplier effects on income of an improved trade balance. However, the general point it makes is valid: devaluation is likely to be most effective in improving the trade balance if the demand elasticities are large in both countries, and will not be very helpful if $\alpha + \beta$ is close to 1.

Marshall Plan A large programme of US aid to assist recovery of the European economies from the effects of the Second World War. The Plan was proposed by the US Secretary of State, George C. Marshall. From 1948 to 1951 the US provided assistance in grants and loans to various European countries, including Austria, France, West Germany, Italy, the Netherlands and the UK. The main role of this aid in promoting recovery is thought to have been the provision of reserves to restore confidence in financial stability, and the provision of working capital to allow liberalization of production and prices.

Marxian economics An alternative form of economics based on the theories of Karl Marx. This includes the *labour theory of value, and a theory of exploitation by which surplus value is appropriated by capitalists; which has been extended to cover exploitation of less by more developed countries. The theory predicts the rise of monopolies, the immiserization of the proletariat, and an eventual breakdown in capitalist society due to under-consumption.

massaging statistics Adjusting figures so as to remove apparent discrepancies. These are numbers which are assumed to be due to miscounting or computational errors. Massaging may also be done to bring the figures into conformity with theories about how the economy works, or to manipulate results for the political convenience of some user, often the government.

mass production Production on a large scale, using mechanized methods to produce standardized goods. This is contrasted with handicraft production, which turns out non-standardized products. Mass production is responsible for the remarkable cheapness of manufactured products in modern industrial societies. The advent of computer-controlled assembly has allowed considerable variation in the final products, albeit using highly standardized components.

material resources *See* resources.

matrix An array of elements laid out in rows and columns. The elements may be numbers, algebraic expressions, or a mixture of these. An $m \times n$ matrix has m rows (running from left to right) and n columns (running from top to bottom). In a matrix A, a_{ij} represents the element in the ith row and the jth column. Matrices are a convenient compact way of expressing systems of linear relations, for example the coefficients of an *input–output system.

maturity The date when a security is due to be redeemed. The further any security is from maturity, the more its market value is liable to fluctuate if there are changes in the rate of interest; the nearer to maturity, the more stable its market price. For example, if the rate of interest is 5 per cent, a security paying £5 at the end of each year with a redemption value of £100 is worth £100 whatever its maturity. If the rate of interest rises to 6 per cent, a security with 1 year to maturity falls in price by 0.94 per cent; with 5 years to maturity, it falls by 4.21 per cent; with 15 years to maturity it falls by 9.71 per cent; and a perpetuity, with no redemption date, falls by 16.67 per cent.

maximin The highest value of a set of numbers, each found by taking the minimum of some further set. The maximin is a useful concept in game theory. Suppose that i possible strategies of firm A, which seeks to maximize the outcome, say the market share of A, are represented by the rows in a pay-off matrix, and j possible strategies of firm B, which seeks to minimize the outcome, are represented by the columns in the same matrix. Entries x_{ij} represent the outcome if A chooses strategy i and B chooses strategy j. If A has to choose its strategy first, B will choose the row minimum, that is the strategy with the minimum x_{ij}. A therefore chooses the strategy i for which this row minimum is greatest: this is the maximin. If the choices are simultaneous, and A does not know what strategy B will choose, the maximin value of x_{ij} is the worst outcome that can result for A.

maximization, utility *See* utility maximization.

maximizing profits *See* profit maximization.

maximum The highest value a function takes for any value of its arguments. A maximum may be local or global. For example, $y = 1 - x^2$ has a global maximum of $y = 1$ when $x = 0$; there is no value of x which gives a higher y. It is a necessary condition for a local maximum of a function $y = f(x)$ that $dy/dx = 0$; given that $dy/dx = 0$, it is a sufficient but not necessary condition for a local maximum that $d^2y/dx^2 < 0$. Consider, however, the function $z = x^3 - 3x$. This has a maximum $z = 2$ at $x = -1$, but this is only a local maximum, that is, z is higher for $x = -1$ than for nearby values of x. Sufficiently large positive values of x can make z larger without limit, so that z

does not have a global maximum. The maximum of a set of x_i, $i = 1, 2, \ldots, N$, written

$$\arg \max[x_1, x_2, \ldots, x_N]$$

is the largest value of any x_i.

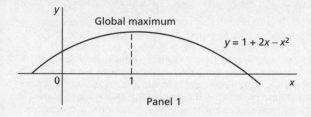

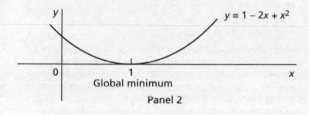

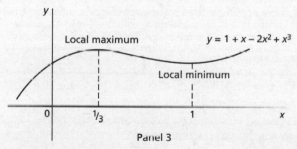

FIGURE 21: *Maxima and Minima*

The horizontal axis shows x; the vertical axis shows $y = f(x)$.

In Panel 1, $y = 1 + 2x - x^2$; $dy/dx = 2 - 2x$, so $dy/dx = 0$ for $x = 1$. $d^2y/dx^2 = -2$, so this is a global maximum.

In Panel 2, $y = 1 - 2x + x^2$; $dy/dx = -2 + 2x$, so $dy/dx = 0$ when $x = 1$. $d^2y/dx^2 = 2$, so this is a global mimimum.

In Panel 3, $y = 1 + x - 2x^2 + x^3$; $dy/dx = 1 - 4x + 3x^2$, so $dy/dx = 0$ for $x = 1$ and $x = 1/3$. $d^2y/dx^2 = -4 + 6x$, thus when $x = 1$, $d^2y/dx^2 = 2$, so there is a local minimum; but when $x = 1/3$, $d^2y/dx^2 = -2$, so there is a local maximum. *See also* constrained maximum, global maximum, and local maximum.

mean The unweighted average of a set of numbers. The arithmetic mean, μ_x, of the numbers x_i, $i = 1, 2, \ldots, N$, is given by their sum divided by N, so $\mu_x = (\sum_i x_i)/N$. The geometric mean is defined as the Nth root of the product of the numbers, that is $(\prod_i x_i)^{1/N}$. The logarithm of the geometric mean of the numbers x_i equals the arithmetic mean of their logarithms. The arithmetic mean can be calculated for any set of numbers, whether positive, zero, or negative; the geometric mean exists only when they are all non-negative. *See also* arithmetic mean, and geometric mean.

means test A test applied as a condition of receipt of some benefit, for example a pension. This may be applied to an individual, a family, or a household, and may take account of income, capital, or both. Benefits are usually payable only if an applicant's capital or income falls below some limit. Means tests are expensive to administer, and infringe the privacy of applicants: they are thus unpopular. The rules of eligibility for benefits are bound to lead to apparent anomalies at the margin, wherever this is drawn. Means testing is contrasted with making benefits universal, that is independent of the applicant's means. *Universal benefits are very expensive, so high taxes are needed to pay for them: this makes it likely that means testing will continue to be used despite its disadvantages.

means-tested benefits Benefits which are available only to claimants whose income or assets fall below some limit. These are contrasted with *universal benefits, which are available to everybody in particular categories, for example based on age, regardless of income or assets. The argument for means-tested benefits is that the cost of providing universal benefits is very high, so that they have to be kept small. With means-testing, expenditure can be targeted to those in most need, and the level of benefits can be much larger. The argument against means testing is that means tests are expensive to administer, and intrusive. There is some fear that means-testing concentrates benefits on the articulate and unscrupulous rather than those in most need, who may well be inarticulate and nervous, and fail to receive benefits to which they were really entitled. There is also resentment among those who have built up assets by hard work and savings when they are later treated less generously than those who have not worked or saved.

mechanism, price *See* price mechanism.

median A measure of the mid-point of a set of numbers. The median of a set of N numbers, $x_1, x_2, \ldots, x_N$ is found as follows: arrange the numbers in increasing, or decreasing, order of size. If N is odd, the median is the central number, the $(N + 1)/2$ th (whichever end one counts from). If N is even, the median is defined as the mean of the central pair, that is the $N/2$ th and the $(N/2) + 1$ th (again, whichever end one counts from). The median can always be calculated, whether the x_i are positive, zero, or negative. A merit of the median as a statistic describing, for example, household income, is that it is very insensitive to extreme figures caused by measurement errors or mistyping the data.

median voter The voter whose preference on any issue on which preferences can be described by a single number equals the median for all voters. If a decision is made by voting, where all electors take part and vote non-strategically, the median voter has the decisive vote: a side including the median voter always wins. While few decisions are in fact taken by direct voting, and many actual votes are cast strategically, the median voter argument draws attention to the need for parties which disagree to appeal to those whose views are relatively central if they are to get a majority.

Medicaid A US government scheme to pay for medical treatment for the poor.

Medicare A US government scheme to pay for medical treatment for the elderly.

medium-dated security A security with between five and fifteen years to maturity when first issued.

medium of exchange The use of money to simplify the process of exchanging one's products for those of the rest of society. Without a medium of exchange it is necessary to find a person willing to *barter the goods one is selling for the goods one wishes to buy. With a medium of exchange this is unnecessary: sales to one person finance purchases from another.

Medium-Term Financial Strategy (MTFS) The policy adopted by the UK government in 1980 of controlling inflation by embarking on a long-term programme of steady reductions in government borrowing and in the rate of growth of the money supply. This self-imposed constraint on policy-making involved a target range for the growth of Sterling M3 falling by 1 per cent each year.

member bank A bank that belongs to a clearing system. In the US a member bank is one that belongs to the Federal Reserve System.

menu costs of inflation The part of the real cost of inflation due to the need to notify customers of price increases. This is mainly printing costs; extra costs due to inflation can be significant only for goods not subject to much short-term price variation in the absence of inflation.

Mercado Comun del Sur (MERCOSUR) A Latin American common market agreed in 1991 by the Argentine, Brazil, Paraguay, and Uruguay. MERCOSUR contains the majority of the population of Latin America.

mercantilism A belief in the merits of balance-of-payments surpluses to increase the money supply and stimulate the economy, and advocacy of *protectionism to achieve this. Critics claim that in the long run mercantilist policy is self-defeating, as more money increases the price level until any trade surplus vanishes, leaving only real losses from restrictions on trade.

merchandise account The part of the *balance-of-payments accounts referring to visible trade, or merchandise imports and exports.

merchant bank A bank dealing mainly with other firms rather than the general public. Merchant banks engage in a variety of specialist activities, including: financing foreign trade by accepting bills of exchange; providing hire purchase and industrial finance; underwriting new issues; advising on and arranging finance for mergers and takeover bids; and investment management for institutions and wealthy individuals.

MERCOSUR *See* Mercado Comun del Sur.

merger A combination of two or more firms into a single new firm. This takes over all the assets and liabilities of the merging firms; shares in the new firm are divided between the shareholders of the original firms on an agreed basis. Merger procedures in the UK are subject to the *City Code on Takeovers and Mergers. A merger may allow economies of scale or scope between the firms, which should lead to gains in efficiency. It may however also reduce competition, so that mergers in the UK may be referred to the *Monopolies and Mergers Commission (MMC), now the Competition Commission (CC). *See also* conglomerate merger, horizontal merger, and vertical merger.

merit goods Goods or services whose consumption is believed to confer benefits on society as a whole greater than those reflected in consumers' own preferences for them. This implies that they have beneficial external effects, presumably by making the consumers better or more productive people. Merit goods are therefore sometimes subsidized by the government, and sometimes provided by charities. In some cases plausible mechanisms for beneficial *externalities can be suggested: well educated people are more likely to be employed, and well housed people may be less likely to become criminals. In other cases, however, it is hard to think of any plausible mechanism by which such externalities could arise: how, for example, does watching grand opera make people better citizens?

MFA *See* Multi-Fibre Arrangement.

MFN *See* most favoured nation.

microeconomics The micro aspects of economics, concerning choices. It considers questions such as: how is it decided, and how should it be decided, what enterprises should operate; what goods and services should be produced; what techniques of production should be used; at what prices should goods be sold, or on what terms should they be given away; and how should incomes be distributed amongst the members of society? Microeconomics is contrasted with *macroeconomics, which is concerned with the size of aggregates such as employment and income, rather than their composition.

mid-market price The mid-point between the lowest price at which any market-maker is willing to sell a security and the highest price at which any market-maker is willing to buy it.

migrants' remittances Money sent by migrant workers in foreign countries to their former homes. These remittances have three main purposes; to maintain family members still in their old homes; to assist family members to join them in their new homes; and to prepare the way for their own return to their native countries, to retire or set up in business. Migrants' remittances form part of the *invisibles section of the balance of payments on current account; in some countries an important part.

migration Movement of people between regions or countries. Immigration and emigration are usually reserved for migration into and out of countries. Migration may be temporary, with the intention of returning in the future, or permanent; or migrants may not have decided between these alternatives at the time of migration. Migration is affected by push and pull factors. Push factors include lack of employment opportunities, lack of other facilities, and fears of disorder or of persecution on grounds of race, religion or politics in the areas people leave. Pull factors include favourable employment opportunities, good health and educational facilities, public order and freedom, and a favourable climate, particularly for retirement, in the areas people move to.

military–industrial complex An expression used to describe the combination of a country's armed forces and the parts of its industry related to military supply. In both the armed services and industry there are bound to be people whose careers are based on developing expertise in the production and use of weapons and related support equipment. The military–industrial complex in major powers has sometimes been accused of being motivated by its vested interests to influence policy in ways which promote international tension and thus lead to arms races or even war.

Millenium Round The latest series of trade negotiations, under the World Trade Organization (WTO). This started in the Seattle conference of 1999, and is likely to last for some time, as in 2002 the final agenda had not yet been agreed.

Miller *See* Modigliani–Miller theorem.

minimax The lowest value of set of numbers, each found by taking the maximum of some further set. The minimax is a useful concept in game theory. Suppose that i possible strategies of firm A, which seeks to maximize the outcome, say the market share of A, are represented by the rows in a pay-off matrix, and j possible strategies of firm B, which seeks to minimize the outcome, are represented by the columns in the same matrix. Entries x_{ij} represent the outcome if A chooses strategy i and B chooses strategy j. If B has to choose its strategy first, A will choose the column maximum, that is the strategy with the maximum x_{ij}. B therefore chooses the strategy j for which this column maximum is lowest: this is the minimax. If the choices are simultaneous, and B does not know what strategy A will choose, the minimax value of x_{ij} is the worst outcome that can result for B.

minimum The lowest value a function takes for any value of its arguments. A minimum may be local or global. For example, $y = 1 + x^2$ has a global minimum of $y = 1$ when $x = 0$; there is no value of x which gives a lower y. It is a necessary condition for a local minimum of a function $y = f(x)$ that $dy/dx = 0$; given that $dy/dx = 0$, it is a sufficient but not a necessary condition for a local minimum that $d^2 y/dx^2 > 0$. Consider, however, the function $z = x^3 - 3x$. This has a minimum $z = -2$ at $x = 1$, but this is only a local minimum, that is, z is lower for $x = 1$ than for nearby values of x. Sufficiently large negative values of x can make z lower without limit, so that z does not have a global minimum. The minimum of a set of x_i, $i = 1, 2, \ldots, N$, or

$$\arg \min [x_1, x_2, \ldots, x_N]$$

is the smallest value of any x_i. *See also* the figure for maximum, constrained minimum, global minimum, and local minimum.

minimum efficient scale The minimum level of any activity at which all known economies of scale can be enjoyed. In some cases there is no finite level of output at which further cost savings cease: this is the case, for example, when marginal cost is constant and fixed costs can be spread over an ever larger output. In such cases it is convenient to define the minimum efficient scale as the level of output beyond which further increases in scale give cost savings below some minimum level. For example, this could be defined as a level of output where further doubling would reduce average cost by under 1 per cent.

minimum lending rate (MLR) The immediate successor of bank rate. From 1971 to 1981 MLR was the minimum rate at which the Bank of England would lend to UK discount houses; it was used as a bench-mark for other interest rates. MLR was replaced in 1981 by base rate.

minimum wage A minimum level of pay laid down by law, for workers in general or of some specified type. Its supporters argue that this prevents the exploitation of ignorant or vulnerable workers. Opponents of a minimum wage argue that it must either be so low as to be ineffective, or will destroy jobs, especially if exceptions are not allowed for handicapped or inexperienced workers with abnormally low productivity. Critics also argue that minimum wages cause inflation, both by raising the pay of some workers directly, and because workers with wages just above the minimum demand pay increases to restore their traditional differentials with groups whose pay has been raised.

minority shareholder A shareholder who owns only a minority of the voting shares of a company. The vast majority of shares are in fact held by minority shareholders. A minority shareholder can always be voted down by the majority if that majority is united, but usually there is no single majority shareholder. Most companies are in fact controlled by individuals or groups who are only minority shareholders, as the rest do not vote.

mint A factory producing coinage. When the coinage was the most important part of the money supply, mints were important and profitable. Now that coin is confined to use as small change, mints are unimportant and the production of low-denomination coins is frequently unprofitable.

MIRAS *See* mortgage interest relief at source.

misaligned exchange rate An exchange rate which is inconsistent with a satisfactory balance of payments. If a country's currency is priced too high, this makes imports excessively attractive and exports hard to sell, which is liable to result in an unsustainable current account deficit. Equally, if a currency is underpriced it tends to result in a current account surplus so large as to overstimulate the economy. Unfortunately, frequent changes in market conditions and in the relative inflation rates in different countries make it very difficult to judge when any given currency is misaligned.

misery index An index of overall economic performance, taking account of both unemployment and inflation. An alternative name for this is a discomfort index. A simple form of misery index is the sum of the inflation and unemployment rates, but equal weights are not necessarily the best. The relative weights placed on unemployment and inflation should reflect beliefs about the relative importance of the harm done by these two evils.

mis-match Differences between the skills and location of unemployed workers and available job vacancies. These help to explain why *unemployment exists at the same time as unsatisfied demand for labour. Mis-match may occur because the location and skill patterns of new entrants to the labour market, those finishing education and immigrants, do not match the pattern of those leaving the labour market through retirement or emigration. It is increased by rapid changes in the pattern of demand for labour through changes in tastes or technology. Methods by which mis-match can be reduced include retraining, migration, industrial relocation, and changes in the relative wages of different occupations.

missing markets The lack of markets in which to trade in various future and contingent goods. It is sometimes argued that the economy would be optimally organized if there were markets in which all present, future, and contingent goods could be traded. In fact, however, most of these markets are missing, for various reasons. Some future goods cannot be traded because the law forbids contracts for future labour, by which effectively people sell themselves into slavery. Many future goods cannot be traded because the people who would wish to trade in them have not yet been born. Many markets in contingent goods cannot exist because the actual occurrence of the contingencies is private information which cannot be objectively confirmed. Finally, many markets which could exist in fact do not, because not enough people would wish to trade in them to allow an efficient market to be organized.

mixed economy An economy with a mixture of state and private enterprises. Some economic activities are carried on by individuals or firms taking independent economic decisions, co-ordinated by markets; others are carried on by organizations under state ownership and control, with some degree of centralized decision-taking. Most actual economies are mixed, in the sense of having substantial elements of both forms of economic organization.

mixed strategy The use of a random mixture of strategies. The choice between two or more strategies on any particular occasion depends on using some randomizing device, such as tossing a dice. Agent using mixed strategies do not know what their own actions will be on any particular occasion until the randomizing device has been used. The benefit of adopting a mixed strategy is to make it impossible for any opponent to predict a player's actions with certainty, however well they understand the player's psychology.

mix of policies The use of *policy instruments in combination. If a government has only one objective, it will often be possible to achieve it using only one policy instrument. If more than one policy instrument is available, and use of each involves adverse side effects which increase more than proportionally as it is used more, it may pay to use a mix of policy instruments to reduce these side-effects. If the government has more than one objective, as it always has, at least n independent policy instruments are needed to allow n separate objectives to be obtained, other than by coincidence. This too dictates using a mix of policy instruments. If more than n instruments are available, the mix should again be chosen to reduce total adverse side-effects.

MLR *See* minimum lending rate.

MMC *See* Monopolies and Mergers Commission.

mobility, capital *See* capital mobility.

mobility of labour The ability of workers to change jobs. This may be between different firms, different occupations, different locations, or different countries. In all cases there are obstacles to mobility. Workers changing employers lose seniority, which may affect their pay, vacations, and redundancy rights, and may lose in terms of their pension rights. Workers changing occupations lose in terms of the weight given to their experience and possibly to their formal qualifications. Workers changing location face problems over housing. International mobility of labour is hindered by immigration controls, problems over recognition of their qualifications, and differences of language. Governments and supra-national organizations such as the *European Union (EU) attempt to improve labour mobility in the interests of economic efficiency, but perfect mobility of labour seems extremely unlikely.

mode The most frequent or most likely value of a variable. Where the variable is discrete, the mode is the value with the highest share of the distribution. The number of children in a family, for example, may be 0 or any whole number: if the mode is 2 this means there are more families with two children than of any other particular size. Where the variable is continuous, the mode is at the maximum of the frequency distribution. For example, if x lies between 0 and 1 and is distributed with frequency distribution $f(x) = 6x(1-x)$, the mode is at $x = 0.5$, where $6x(1 - x)$ is a maximum.

model A simplified system used to simulate some aspects of the real economy. Economics is bound to use simplified models: the real world economy is so large and complicated that it cannot be fully described in finite time or space. A good model concentrates on the point it is studying and leaves out anything not essential to this. Models vary between the very simple, for example the *IS-LM* model, and large econometric models with thousands of equations. The results of any change in the assumptions of an economic model can be worked out, either by theory or numerical calculation; whether the results generalize to the real world can only be found out by experience. If model-builders have picked the right aspects of reality to include in their models, there will be some approximate resemblance between the model's predictions and the real economy.

model-consistent expectations *See* rational expectations.

Modigliani–Miller theorem The theory that in a perfect capital market the cost of capital to a firm is independent of the method of financing used. Capital can be raised by borrowing, issuing equity shares, or retaining profits instead of paying dividends. The Modigliani–Miller theorem asserts that in a perfect capital market it does not matter to a firm whether it uses debt or equity, or what dividend policy it follows. The fact that firms do worry about their leverage and dividend policies reflects the effects of the tax system and imperfection in the capital market.

modulus The size of a number, in the sense of its distance from zero. The modulus or absolute value of a real number x (symbol $|x|$) is the difference between x and zero, regardless of sign. Thus if $x > 0$, $|x| = x$ and if $x < 0$, $|x| = -x$. The modulus of a complex number, $x = a + ib$, is defined as $|x| = \sqrt{(a^2 + b^2)}$.

monetarism The school of economics that maintains that the quantity of money is the main determinant of money incomes. This is often combined with the view that markets tend to clear, and that people form *rational expectations. On the positive side, this leads to the policy recommendation that the best contribution the government can make to stable economic growth is to keep the money supply growing steadily at a rate equal to the growth of aggregate supply plus any target rate of inflation, which may well be zero. On the negative side, it suggests that attempts at *demand management on 'Keynesian' lines can do no good, and are liable simply to add one more source of shocks to the economy. *See also* gradualist monetarism.

monetary accommodation *See* accommodatory monetary policy.

monetary base The part of the money supply which is eligible to count as reserves in the banking system. Some monetary theorists argue that if the monetary authorities can control the amount of base money the rest of the *money supply will adjust automatically. How far this is true depends on how stable bank reserve ratios are, and on how far base money is also held outside the banking system, for example as notes and coin in general circulation.

monetary control *See* monetary policy.

monetary overhang That part of the money supply that people are holding merely because they have not been able to spend it. In an economy with *repressed inflation, people hold more money than they really want, because shortages of real goods and services make it impossible to spend it as they would wish. If the controls which kept inflation repressed are removed, monetary overhang tends to produce a burst of open inflation.

monetary policy The use by the government or central bank of interest rates or controls on the money supply to influence the economy. The target of monetary policy may be the achievement of a desired level or rate of growth in real activity, the price level, the exchange rate, or the balance of payments. Methods of monetary policy include setting the interest rate charged by the central bank, sales or purchases of securities to control the money supply, and changes in the required reserve ratios of banks and other financial institutions. The central bank can affect other interest rates both through *open market operations to affect the probability that banks are going to need to borrow at its own lending rate, and by the *announcement effects of changes in the central bank's minimum lending rate, which are regarded by the markets as statements about the authorities' forecasts and objectives. Monetary policy works through the effects of the cost and availability of loans on real activity, and through this on inflation, and on international capital movements and thus on the exchange rate. Central bank and government pronouncements on monetary and other economic questions can be effective in reinforcing practical measures of monetary policy, but do not provide a substitute for them. *See also* accommodatory monetary policy, easy monetary policy, and tight monetary policy.

Monetary Policy Committee (MPC) A committee set up when the Bank of England was granted independence in 1997 to advise on monetary policy and changes in interest rates. The MPC consists of the Governor of the Bank and eight other members, drawn half from the Bank's own staff and half from outside. The MPC meets monthly, and its minutes are published, with a short time lag.

monetary system The system by which an economy is provided with money. It is possible for a small country simply to use some other country's money, but most countries choose to provide their own. This is partly for reasons of national prestige, partly because governments derive *seigniorage from providing money, and partly because of a belief that economic stability can be promoted by using *monetary policy to adapt to localized shocks, or to insulate the economy from the effects of foreign shocks. An independent monetary system must include a mint to provide coinage and a central bank to provide base money. It usually includes a system of commercial banks to provide deposit, loan, and payments facilities. It then needs a regulatory body to supervise the banks, to minimize the chance of bank failure, and a *lender of last resort, to prevent failure of any one bank turning into a system-wide crash. These supervisory and last-resort functions may be combined in a single *central bank, as in the UK, or dealt with by separate bodies, as in Germany and the US.

monetary union Two or more countries with a single currency. Countries which formerly had independent monetary systems unite to adopt a single currency, or keep separate currencies but enter into a permanant and credible agreement to maintain a constant exchange rate between their currencies. A monetary union requires either a single central bank or the adoption of effective policy co-ordination between the central banks of the member countries; the Euro zone in fact has both.

money 1. A medium of exchange and store of value. This may consist of physical objects, that is notes and coin; or of book or computer entries, that is bank deposits. Money was originally a physical substance such as *gold or silver, which was valued for its own sake before it came to be used as coinage. Coins and notes are now usually tokens, whose intrinsic value is below their face value; fiat money is money whose value derives from a decision, or fiat, of the state. In many monetary systems one can distinguish between 'base money', or 'high-powered money', issued by the central bank or the government, and ordinary money, issued by other banks, which are required to hold as reserves base money equal to some fraction of their total deposits. Real money balances are the *quantity of money divided by some suitable price index, such as the *GDP deflator, to find its real purchasing power. The demand for money is the amount people want to hold. The income elasticity of demand for money is the ratio of a proportional change in the demand for money to a proportional increase in incomes. The interest elasticity of demand for money is the ratio of a proportional change in the demand for money to a proportional change in interest rates. The demand for money is also affected by expectations of inflation, which affect its usefulness as a store of value, and by institutional changes, such as the rise of the credit card over recent decades. The *quantity theory of money is a formula relating the quantity of money, the price level, and real activity. The supply of money is the amount the banking system is willing to provide. There are several alternative definitions of the money supply, M0, M1, etc. (for details of these see their separate entries.) Monetarism is the belief that money is of primary importance in determining what happens to the economy.

2. A verbal shorthand for 'monetary policy'. Thus cheap money means that loans are cheap and easily available; tight money or dear money mean that loans are expensive and hard to obtain. The money market is the system of institutions through which short-term loans are obtained.

3. A synonym for wealth in general. Easy money is earnings which are quick though not necessarily legal; money-grubbing is attaching undue priority to getting rich; 'love of money is the root of all evil' stigmatizes covetousness rather than the currency. 'Value for money' is simply a claim to efficiency, and 'The Money Programme' on UK TV deals with economic affairs in general. *See also* broad money, call money, cheap money, dear money, fiat money, flight from money, high-powered money, inside money, interest-elasticity of the demand for money, international money, marginal utility of money, neutrality of money, outside money, quantity of money, quantity theory of money, and token money.

money at call and short notice The most liquid UK bank assets after cash. Money is lent to other banks and non-bank financial institutions such as discount houses, repayable on demand (call) or at up to 14 days notice (short notice). These are secured loans, bearing interest, usually at low rates.

money illusion Mistaking nominal for real changes. People may interpret rises in their own wages, or the prices of goods and services they sell, or assets that they own, as real gains rather than as part of a general process of price and wage inflation. Money illusion is likely in societies with a history of wage and price stability. The more inflation persists, the more likely people are to assume that when their wages or prices rise, their real position is not improved as everybody else's prices and wages are probably rising too.

money laundering The use of often complex series of transactions to conceal the ultimate source of money holdings. It is widely used to camouflage receipts from illegal activities, including drug trafficking, corruption, fraud, and tax evasion.

money market The market for very short-term loans. In lending money for very short periods, for example overnight, transactions costs are quite large relative to the interest that can be earned, so transactions in the money market are usually for large amounts, and the participants are mainly banks and other financial institutions such as discount houses, though large firms and a few exceptionally rich individuals also participate.

money multiplier A formula relating changes in money supply to changes in income. It relates an initial change in some form of money to the change in the money level of national income which will ultimately result. The money multiplier is a class of formulae rather than any particular formula. For example, if the banking system creates n units of ordinary money per unit of high-powered money which it holds, and the public hold v units of ordinary money per unit of income, then the money multiplier for high-powered money is (n/v); that is, (n/v) units of extra income will result from a rise of 1 unit of high-powered money.

money supply The amount of money in an economy. This may be the country's own money, supplied by its banking system, or foreign money, used in preference to domestic money. There is no single accepted definition of what constitutes money: while notes and coin are *legal tender and must be included in any definition, and bank deposits repayable on demand are unlikely to be excluded, there are various types of deposit in non-bank financial intemediaries such as building societies, and various forms of highly *liquid security, which can be included or excluded in various ways. Even unused postage stamps and uncashed postal orders could be used as money, though they are not included in any current definition. For various definitions applied in the UK see M0 to M5. Most economists believe there is some long-run connection between the money supply and inflation, but because the quantity of money varies differently according to which definition is used, checking this statistically presents problems. The monetary authorities can influence the money supply through monetary and fiscal policy, but have difficulty in controlling it precisely. The money supply on narrow definitions has the best correlation with inflation, but is hard to control since many forms of *broad money can easily be converted into narrow money on the initiative of the holders.

money supply, real *See* real balances.

money wages Wage rates measured in money terms. This is contrasted with *real wages, which is money wages deflated by a suitable price index, for example the UK Retail Price Index (RPI), to find their real purchasing power. Wage bargaining is normally in terms of money wages.

monitoring The process of checking whether individuals or firms are actually behaving as they should. This applies to seeing whether laws imposed by the government are being obeyed; whether instructions issued by regulatory agencies to firms are being complied with; whether orders by employers to their employees are actually being carried out; and whether the other party is complying with the terms of a *contract. Monitoring is necessary because it may not be in the private interest of firms to obey laws and regulations, or in the private interests of employees to obey their employers. Monitoring is expensive: in designing laws and issuing private orders it is thus sensible to bear in mind the trade-off between desirable aims and keeping down monitoring costs.

Monopolies and Mergers Commission (MMC) A UK body appointed to investigate monopolies, mergers, and anti-competitive practices referred to it by the Director General of Fair Trading or the Secretary of State for Trade and Industry. The MMC did not initiate its own enquiries, and its reports led to changes only through government action, legislation, or voluntary compliance to avoid these. The MMC has now been replaced by the Competition Commission. (CC)

monopolistic competition A market situation with a limited number of sellers, where each believes that the price that can be charged is a decreasing function of the quantity sold. Monopolistic competitors believes they face downward-sloping demand curves, but do not attempt to anticipate the reactions of individual competitors. Under monopolistic competition it is expected that free entry will eliminate abnormal profits. Monopolistic competition is contrasted with *oligopoly, where firms do attempt to forecast the reactions of individual competitors.

monopoly A market situation with only one seller. A natural monopoly exists when the monopolist's solo position is due either to the exclusive possession of some essential input, or to the existence of economies of scale so great that no entry by competitors is possible once an incumbent firm is established. A statutory monopoly exists when the entry of competitors is forbidden by law. Bilateral monopoly means that as well as there being only one seller, there is also only one buyer in a market. *Monopolistic competition is a situation with more than one seller, each able to fix a price, that is, each with some monopoly power. The *Monopolies and Mergers Commission (MMC) was a UK body set up to oversee monopolies and mergers.

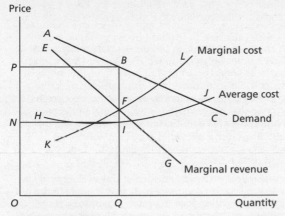

FIGURE 22: *Monopoly*

The horizontal axis shows the quantity sold by a monopolist; the vertical axis shows cost and price. *ABC* shows the demand curve, and *EFG* shows the corresponding marginal revenue curve, *MR*; *HIJ* shows the average cost curve, and *KFL* shows the corresponding marginal cost curve, *MC*. Profits are maximized when output is set at *OQ*, to make *MC* = *MR* at *F*. This is sold at price *OP*. *OPBQ* is total revenue and *ONIQ* is total cost. *NPBI* is monopoly profit; while this is drawn positive here, there is no guarantee that a monopolist will be able to make positive profits. *See also* bilateral monopoly, discriminating monopoly, natural monopoly, sheltered monopoly, and statutory monopoly.

monopoly policy Government policy towards monopolies. This is motivated partly by a belief that monopoly may lead to inefficient use of resources, and partly by a desire to promote a more equal income distribution than tends to result if some firms have monopoly power. The two main approaches to monopoly policy are attempts to control market structure, and attempts to control monopolists' behaviour. Market structure can be tackled by regulating *mergers, forcing monolithic firms to split up, or controlling anti-competitive practices tending to inhibit entry to monopolized markets by firms established in other markets. Monopolists' behaviour can be controlled through taking them into public ownership by nationalization, or by subjecting them to price controls and other forms of supervision by regulatory bodies such as the UK Office of Telecommunications (Oftel). In some cases public policy actually supports monopoly: giving the postal service monopoly powers is justified by the argument that this allows it to use the profits on services in densely populated areas to cross-subsidize postal services in remote rural areas.

monopoly power The degree of control monopolists have in their markets. This is an elusive concept to measure. If monopoly is interpreted broadly as lack of competition, monopoly power can be judged by concentration measures such as the *Herfindahl index. If monopoly is interpreted strictly as there being only a single seller, it has been suggested that monopoly power could be measured by the ratio of price to marginal cost.

monopoly profit An excess of profits over the normal rate which a firm is able to make by exploiting a monopoly position. If the market were open to competitive entry, such profits would be competed away, or the monopolist would be obliged to restrict them voluntarily by a *limit pricing policy to deter entry. A monopoly position allows a firm to retain any excess profits. It does not, however, guarantee that there will be any abnormal profits: one of the simplest ways of becoming a monopolist is to make a mistaken investment in *sunk costs which does not earn enough revenue to be profitable. Entry does not occur because other firms learn from the monopolist's mistakes and refrain from loss-making investment.

monopsony A market situation with only one buyer. Unless the supply is perfectly elastic, a monopsonist has an incentive to exploit the fact that a reduction in the quantity bought will reduce the price. Monopsony is the equivalent on the demand side to *monopoly on the supply side of a market.

monotonic function A function where, as the value of the argument rises, the value of the function always changes in the same direction. Thus if $y = f(x)$, either $dy/dx > 0$ for all x, in which case y is an increasing function of x, or $dy/dx < 0$ for all x, in which case y is a decreasing function of x. With a monotonic function there is no value of x for which $dy/dx = 0$, so that there is no maximum or minimum for y.

Monte Carlo methods A method of investigating the behaviour of economic models which are too complicated for analytical solutions to be possible. A system is started off at a large number of initial positions chosen at random, and followed through a numerical simulation to see what happens. Monte Carlo methods can be used to check whether a system has an *equilibrium, and whether this is stable for any starting point, or for some limited region of possible starting points.

Montreal Protocol An international agreement reached in 1987 to reduce the production and consumption of *chlorofluorocarbons (CFCs) and halon, substances which deplete the ozone layer in the upper atmosphere. This was amended in 1990 to target the phasing out of CFCs and halon by 2000. The agreement also provides for trade bans on CFCs and CFC-using products. CFCs and halon are inert and non-toxic substances, CFCs being widely used in refrigeration, foams, aerosols, and dry cleaning, and halon in fire extinguishers. It has become possible to replace these by less ozone-destructive products.

Moody's One of the main US credit rating agencies.

moral hazard The danger that if a contract promises people payments on certain conditions, they will change their conduct so as to make these conditions more likely to occur. For example, moral hazard suggests that if possessions are fully insured, their owners are likely to take less good care of them than if they were uninsured, or even to connive at their theft or destruction.

moratorium A suspension of the obligation to repay debts: this may apply to the principal, interest, or both, and may apply to all debts or only to particular types of debt. The payments are only deferred and not cancelled. The object is usually to give time to make arrangements to refinance the obligations of some particular debtors. It is justified by the fear that their collapse might start a general financial panic. The drawback with a moratorium is that it makes it very difficult for anybody to obtain any new credit, both by freezing the assets of possible lenders and by creating fears of similar measures to intervene in credit markets in the future.

mortgage A loan using a real asset, such as a house or other building, as *collateral. If the interest and redemption payments are not made, the lender or mortgagee can foreclose on the collateral, that is, can take it over and sell it to repay the loan. Mortgages can be for any period: 20 or 25 years is not unusual. With a repayment mortgage the principal is paid off gradually over the life of the mortgage. With an endowment mortgage the principal is paid off at the end of the mortgage from a capital sum built up by an endowment insurance policy. Mortgage interest relief is a UK income tax reduction allowed to a taxpayer in respect of part or all of their mortgage interest payments.

mortgage interest relief A UK tax allowance by which payers of mortgage interest are allowed to claim part of all of this as a deduction in calculating their taxable income. The argument for such relief is that those with mortgage payments are worse off than other taxpayers with equal incomes but no mortgage. The argument against is that such tax relief costs the government money which could be better spent on improving housing for those too poor to afford to buy their homes.

mortgage interest relief at source (MIRAS) The system by which mortgage interest relief to UK taxpayers was given through the lending institutions, so that the borrower paid interest net of tax relief to the lender. This system has now been abolished.

most favoured nation (MFN) A county with rights under a trade agreement. An MFN clause stipulates that imports from the partner country will be treated no less favourably than imports of similar goods from any other country. In the case of tariffs, this means no other foreign goods face a lower tariff than those from the partner country. With quota restrictions on trade the meaning of MFN is unclear.

movements, capital *See* capital movements.

moving average A time series obtained from the original series by averaging the figures for a number of consecutive periods. For example, suppose that x_t is the original series for years $t = 1, 2, \ldots, N$. A moving average y_t can be calculated by averaging x_t for a number of periods centred on t, say $t - 2, t - 1, t, t + 1$ and $t + 2$. When the original series fluctuates either cyclically or randomly, y_t fluctuates less, which makes it easier to follow what has happened. Moving averages do have some disadvantages, however. First, it is not possible to construct a moving average for the most recent periods: in the example above, for the two most recent periods for which x_t is available. Also, suppose that nothing much has happened to x_t except at time t^*; suppose $x_{t^*} = 1$ and all other x_t are approximately zero. y_t will be approximately zero except at times $t^* - 2$ to $t^* + 2$; for these y_t is approximately 0.2. Thus y_t rises by approximately 0.2 from $t^* - 3$ to $t^* - 2$, and falls by approximately 0.2 from $t^* + 2$ to $t^* + 3$, though nothing much actually changed at these times, while from $t^* - 1$ to t^* and from t^* to $t^* + 1$, y_t hardly moves when the only major change in x_t was taking place. In this case use of a moving average actually obscures what was happening.

MTFS *See* Medium-Term Financial Strategy.

multicollinearity The problem which arises in *multiple regression when the explanatory variables are not themselves independent. This makes it impossible to fit significant coefficients to explanatory variables which are related to one another.

Multi-Fibre Arrangement (MFA) An international agreement, started in 1973 and renewed several times, between countries exporting and importing textiles and clothing. MFA has restricted exports of these products from less developed countries (LDCs) to the industrialized countries. This was done to slow down declines in employment in the textile industries in importing countries, and it has substantially increased the cost of clothing in the advanced countries. The MFA is contrary to the guiding principles of the *General Agreement on Tariffs and Trade (GATT) and the *World Trade Organization (WTO). The textile industry has been made an exception through protectionist pressure mainly because the industry combines high labour-intensity and relatively simple technology, and has been one of main entry routes to industrialization in LDCs, which have a comparative advantage in this area. Under the Uruguay Round, the MFA is due to be phased out by 2004.

multilateralism The belief that international economic relations should be conducted on the basis of equal treatment for all non-nationals. This applies both to trade, where multilateralism implies multilateral trade rather than preferential arrangements within trade blocs, and to international capital movements. Multilateralism also implies that negotiations over international trade and investment should be conducted through multinational bodies and not on a bilateral basis.

multilateral trade Trade carried on between a group of countries where there is no need for the trade between any pair of countries to balance. This follows naturally if all countries in the group have *convertible currencies.

multinational A firm conducting business in more than one country, through branches or subsidiary companies. Many large firms are multinationals, and a considerable proportion of international trade is between multinationals and their own foreign branches or subsidiaries. While multinational operation presents some legal and organizational problems, many firms find it worth while. It brings them closer to suppliers and markets, they can take advantage of international differences in resources and costs, the benefits of research and development can be spread over wider markets, and it gives a wider spread of risks. Multinational operation also improves their bargaining position in negotiating with national suppliers, governments, and trade unions.

multi-plant firm A firm which operates two or more plants. These may be either branches or run by subsidiary companies; most large firms are in fact multi-plant.

multiple equilibrium The possibility that *equilibrium is not unique. The conditions for equilibrium are that no agent should want to act differently, given their expectations of the reactions of all other agents in the system. These conditions may be satisfied at more than one set of values of the relevant variables. In macroeconomics, for example, there could be two equilibrium levels of national income: a high-level state where everybody is optimistic and spends freely, causing a boom; and a low-level equilibrium where everybody is pessimistic and hoards their money, causing a slump. Where multiple equilibria are locally stable, after a small disturbance a system will return to the equilibrium it was at before, but large disturbances may cause the system to shift to a different equilibrium.

multiple exchange rates The system by which a country's currency has more than one exchange rate with any foreign currency. The rate which applies to any transaction may depend on the holder of the currency, or on the purpose for which it is being used. Multiple exchange rates may discriminate between resident and foreign holders of the currency, between export and import of different types of goods, or between current and capital account payments. Multiple exchange rates are criticized as distorting international trade. They require elaborate administration, and provide scope for political favouritism and corruption over deciding what rate should apply to any given transaction. Most of the world's leading economies do not use multiple exchange rates, but have unified foreign exchange markets.

multiple regression Linear regression with two or more explanatory variables. Variable y, for example, may be explained by variables x_i, $i - 1, 2, \ldots, N$. The regression equation is then

$$y_t = \alpha + \beta_1 x_{1t} + \beta_2 x_{2t} + \ldots + \beta_N x_{Nt} + \varepsilon_t.$$

multiplier 1. A formula relating an initial change in spending to the total change in activity which will result. The multiplier is applicable in an economy in which supply is elastic, so that activity is demand-determined. It is a type of calculation rather than any particular formula; the example which follows is only one of many possibilities. Consider an initial unit of extra spending on domestic goods, which may be investment, real government spending, exports or an autonomous rise in consumption. This spending creates incomes for suppliers, who in turn spend part of it, and so on, indefinitely. Each round of spending will be equal to the previous round minus leakages into payment of taxes, savings, or spending on imports. If a unit of income leads to t of tax payments then disposable income rises by $(1 - t)$. Of this $s(1 - t)$ is saved and $(1 - s)(1 - t)$ is spent; and of this spending $m(1 - s)(1 - t)$ is spent on imports and $(1 - m)(1 - s)(1 - t)$ is spent domestically. Thus each round of domestic spending is $r = (1 - m)(1 - s)(1 - t)$ times the size of the previous round, and the sum of these is $1 + r + r^2 + \ldots = 1/(1 - r)$. If spending at each round involves time lags, the multiplier process will take unlimited time to complete. If the leakages t, s and m are large, however, as they are in most modern economies, r is sufficiently small that most of the process is completed in the first few rounds. For example, if $t = 0.4$, $s = 0.2$, and $m = 0.3$, $r = (0.6)(0.8)(0.7) = 0.336$, so $1/(1 - r) = 1.506$ approx; but the first three rounds account for 1.449 of this, or over 96% of the full multiplier effect. *See also* balanced budget multiplier, foreign trade multiplier, and money multiplier.

2. A mathematical device used in dealing with constrained maximum and minimum problems. *See* Lagrange multiplier.

multiplier–accelerator model The model deriving economic fluctuations from the interaction of the multiplier and the accelerator. The multipier makes output rise following a rise in investment, and the accelerator makes investment increase when output increases. Once expansion starts, if the accelerator is strong the economy tends to explode; but if the accelerator is weak, as empirical studies suggest, expansion slows down, which lowers investment and causes incomes to decline. A slump follows, during which investment is low and capital wears out. Once capital has fallen sufficiently relative to output, investment starts again and the economy expands. This can produce persistent *trade cycles of alternating booms and slumps.

multi-product firm A firm which makes more than one type of product. In the literal sense most firms produce more than one type of good or service, even if the range is not very wide. Some quite small firms such as shops make or trade in a wide variety of products. The term multi-product firm is often reserved for firms which make products which differ significantly in description or construction, especially if they differ sufficiently to come under different categories of the *Standard Industrial Classification (SIC).

mutual fund A financial institution which holds shares on behalf of investors. In the UK these are called unit trusts. Investors buy shares, or 'units' in the fund, which uses their money to buy shares in companies. An investor selling back the units gets the proceeds of selling a fraction of the fund's portfolio. A mutual fund's management benefits from appreciation of the shares the fund holds only to the extent that its management charges are a percentage of the market value of its portfolio.

NAFTA *See* North American Free Trade Agreement.

NAIRU *See* non-accelerating inflation rate of unemployment.

name (at Lloyd's) A member of one or more syndicates at *Lloyd's providing insurance. A name contributes limited cash when joining a syndicate, and accepts unlimited liability for its obligations. Members share in the profits or losses of syndicates in proportion to the cash they have put in, but are liable for all losses if other members cannot pay. Traditionally, it was assumed that people would only become Lloyd's names if they could afford to lose large amounts. In recent years large losses by some syndicates have led to calls for cash from names. These calls have led to widespread hardship among names who have paid, and extensive litigation involving names who have refused to pay.

narrow-band ERM The relation between members of the *Exchange Rate Mechanism (ERM) of the European Monetary System (EMS) which agreed to limit fluctuations of their currencies relative to those of other members to 2 1/4 per cent. This was in contrast to the position of other members, namely the UK and Italy when they were members of ERM, which were allowed 6 per cent margins of fluctuation.

NASDAQ *See* National Association of Securities Dealers Automated Quotation System.

Nash equilibrium A situation in which two or more agents are taking decisions on their *strategies, where no agent can gain by any change in their strategy given the strategies currently being pursued by the others. Such a non-cooperative equilibrium is usually not *Pareto-optimal, and could be improved on by some form of co-operation.

national accounts *See* national income accounts.

National Association of Securities Dealers Automated Quotation System (NASDAQ) A US securities market, originally for over-the-counter securities not listed on regular stock exchanges. It is now a computer-based market, with a system of market-makers, and is a strong rival to the New York Stock Exchange (NYSE).

National Bureau of Economic Research (NBER) A private non-profit US organization founded in 1920 to promote objective quantitative analysis of the American economy. The NBER is a major provider of high quality analysis of micro, macro and international aspects of the US economy.

national debt The debt of a country's government. This may be owed to residents or foreign lenders. In some countries net national debt is smaller than the apparent total, as some government securities are held by other public bodies such as civil service pension funds. In other cases the true national debt is higher than the apparent figures, due to government guarantees of the debts of other bodies such as local governments and state-owned industries. If national debt is held by foreigners, the whole of the interest and redemption payments are claims on national resources. Where the debt is held domestically, the real burden of debt is only the deadweight losses due to the taxes needed to service it.

National Economic Development Council (NEDC) A UK forum for the discussion of economic affairs between representatives of industry, the trade unions and the government. The NEDC, byname 'Neddy', was set up in 1962 and abolished in 1992. It was served by a secretariat, the National Economic Development Office (NEDO). Several 'little Neddies' were set up related to particular industries.

National Health Service (NHS) The UK system of state-financed medical treatment, covering GP services, pharmaceuticals, hospitals, and dentistry. NHS treatment is available to all; some forms of treatment are charged for, with exemptions for children, pensioners, and those on very low incomes. The NHS makes some use of an internal market based on fund-holding GP practices and hospital trusts. Because of advances in medical technology and an ageing population, the NHS has to ration many forms of non-emergency treatment by queueing. Private and privately insured medical services are available as an alternative, but the NHS provides the great majority of UK medical treatment.

national income 1. The total income of residents of a country, measured at factor cost after deducting capital consumption. This equals gross national product at factor cost minus capital consumption. This sense is used in technical discussions of national income accounting concepts. *See also* full employment national income.

2. Any one of the many possible measures, that is, national product or domestic product, gross or net, and stated in either market prices or factor cost. One or other of these is meant when the term is used in general discussions of economic policy; it is often difficult to check which concept any given author or speaker has in mind, and indeed they are frequently uncertain or inconsistent themselves.

national income accounts Accounts showing the main aggregates relating to national income and its components; these include gross domestic product (GDP), gross national product (GNP), national income after deducting capital consumption, and components including consumption, net and gross investment, government expenditure, exports and imports. National income accounts frequently also include data on stocks as well as flows: that is, the domestic stock of productive capital, and external assets and liabilities. National income accounts normally include information on changes in price levels, and show the various aggregates at both current and constant prices, that is, in both nominal and real terms. Data normally refer to whole years; where they are provided for shorter periods, they may or may not be seasonally corrected.

National Institute of Economic and Social Research (NIESR) An independent UK body carrying out research into both macro- and microeconomic aspects of the economy.

National Insurance contributions (NICs) Charges levied in the UK on employees, employers and the self-employed to help to pay for social security.

These contributions are levied as fixed percentages of wages, with exemptions for very low incomes, and a maximum rate of employee's contributions. NICs form part of the *tax wedge between the cost of labour to employers and the cash benefit of working to their employees.

nationalization Bringing under government ownership and control resources and activities formerly operated by private businesses or local organizations.

nationalized industry An industry whose ownership has been taken over by the state. Motives for nationalization varied: in some cases industries were nationalized because they were *natural monopolies, such as public utilities, so that public ownership was expected to give consumers a better deal. Some industries were nationalized because large subsidies were neeeded to avoid run-downs in output and employment. In other cases the aim was to reduce the power of private capitalists, and take public control of 'the commanding heights of the economy'. Critics of nationalization claimed that the absence of a *hard budget constraint led to over-manning and inefficiency, that monopoly power led to lack of response to consumer needs and complaints, and that government interference with management decisions concerning pricing and investment obscured responsibility for their performance. In many countries formerly nationalized industries have in recent years been privatized, that is, sold off to private owners. *See also* privatization.

national product The total value of income produced by factors of production owned by residents of a country. This includes income from factors owned by residents but operating abroad, and excludes the value of factors operating domestically but owned by non-residents. This is contrasted with *domestic product, which is the value of incomes produced domestically, regardless of ownership. Gross national product (GNP) is calculated before deducting an estimate of capital consumption; net national product is GNP minus capital consumption.

National Savings Bonds carrying a UK government guarantee of both their principal and interest. They may be for fixed sums of money, or index linked to the retail price index. The National Savings Bank is a UK institution providing safe securities for individuals to hold. These are widely held: they provide a return which is completely safe, but on average somewhat lower than that on other investments. The amount of National Savings bonds any individual can hold is limited.

national treatment The requirement often included in trade agreements that governments treat the products of foreign firms on an equal basis with those of domestic firms. This implies that once goods have been subjected to border measures such as tariffs and quotas, they should be treated in the same way as domestic goods in matters such as taxes and excise duties.

natural growth rate The growth rate of national income which would just maintain a constant unemployment rate. If there is no technical progress and the labour force grows at rate g, this will be the natural growth rate. If there is also technical progress at rate p, the natural growth rate is given by $n = g + p$. In a *Solow growth model the actual growth rate converges on the natural rate, whatever the ratio of saving to income. In a *Harrod–Domar growth model, if the warranted growth rate is above the natural rate, the economy will expand until it reaches full employment. At this point growth of actual output must fall below the warranted rate, and there will be a recession. If the warranted growth rate falls below the natural rate, there will be a tendency to ever-increasing unemployment. In *endogenous growth models, no natural growth rate exists.

natural logarithm A logarithm to base e. This is written $\ln(x)$; if $y = e^x$, $x = \ln(y)$. $\ln(x)$ is the integral of $1/z$ from $z = 1$ to $z = x$. A natural logarithm can be found as the sum of an infinite series; provided $|x| < 1$,

$$\ln(1 + x) = x - (x^2/2) + (x^3/3) - (x^4/4) \text{ etc.}$$

Differentiating term by term,

$$d[\ln(1 + x)]/dx = 1 - x + x^2 - x^3 + \text{etc.} = 1/(1 + x).$$

natural monopoly A monopoly based on an overwhelming cost advantage for the incumbent firm. This may be because it possesses some unique natural resource, for example a mine tapping the only known deposits of a particular mineral; or because of past capital installations which would have to be duplicated by a competitor, for example domestic electricity supply. This is contrasted with a *statutory monopoly, where the incumbent's position is based on laws to exclude possible rivals. Where the incumbent's advantage derives from sole access to the necessary technology, this is a natural monopoly if it is based on inability of others to match the know-how, but not if it is based merely on exclusive possession of *patents.

natural rate of interest The rate of interest which would be compatible with a stable level of economic activity in an economy with a constant price level. Attempts to set a market rate of interest below the natural rate lead in the short run to an expansion of real activity above the level consistent with stable prices, and in the longer run to inflationary rises in prices and money wages.

natural rate of unemployment The unemployment rate which would prevail in an economy with a constant rate of inflation. This is a function of various man-made institutional factors, including the extent of industrial monopoly, the social security system, minimum wage legislation, restrictions on mobility between occupations and trade-union organization. All of these can be influenced by policy. At any time the natural rate of unemployment will also be affected by the past history of actual unemployment, if the effect of unemployment is to make people less employable. 'Natural' is used here to indicate that this unemployment rate cannot be permanently reduced simply by *demand management: any attempt to do this will result in ever-rising inflation. It does not mean that this level of unemployment is either desirable or inevitable.

natural resources Factors of production provided by nature. This includes land suitable for agriculture, mineral deposits, and water resources useful for power generation, transport and irrigation. It also includes sea resources, including fish and offshore mineral deposits. The effective availability of natural resources is strongly influenced by human activities: most agricultural land has been drained and fertilized, mineral resources have been surveyed, and the accessibility of resources depends on the provision of transport links. Some apparently natural resources are in fact man-made: a large part of the

Netherlands, for example, has been reclaimed from the sea over many centuries. Natural resources can also be depleted by over-exploitation, leading to deforestation and erosion.

natural wastage The proportion of the labour force who quit their jobs each year for reasons other than being sacked by their employer. This includes workers who retire, and those who leave for personal reasons. These vary greatly, including the need to look after children or sick or elderly relatives, the fact that a spouse is moving jobs, taking up a full-time educational course, desire to broaden their experience to improve their curriculum vitae, having found a better job, dislike of the boss, or sheer boredom. For these various reasons an appreciable percentage of a firm's labour force will leave in any year: this often makes possible gradual reduction in the labour force without the need for *redundancies.

NBER *See* National Bureau of Economic Research.

near money Securities which are very close substitutes for money. Short-dated securities with a government guarantee which are either marketable, or redeemable by the government at short notice, are such substitutes. They are not themselves money, but are so near to being money that their existence reduces the demand to hold money proper.

necessary and sufficient conditions Logical relations between two statements. Consider propositions B and C. 'B is a sufficient condition for C' means that if B is true, C is always true. 'B is a necessary condition for C' means that C cannot be true unless B is true. 'B is a sufficient condition for C' thus implies 'C is a necessary condition for B'. A condition can be sufficient but not necessary; if B is a sufficient condition for C, C cannot be false when B is true, but C could well be true when B is false. Equally, a condition can be necessary but not sufficient; if B is a necessary condition for C, C cannot be true if B is false, but C could well be false when B is true. It is however possible for the same condition to be both necessary and sufficient; this means that B is true if and only if (written iff) C is true. Thus if B is a necessary and sufficient condition for C, C must likewise be a necessary and sufficient condition for B; the two statements are thus equivalent.

necessity A good or service whose consumption by an individual, at a given price, rises less than in proportion to increases in their income. The *income elasticity of demand for a necessity is less than one. Necessities are thus goods on which poorer people spend a larger proportion of their incomes than richer people. A necessity is contrasted with a luxury, which is a good or service whose consumption rises more than in proportion to income. *See also* the figure for Engel Curve.

NEDC *See* National Economic Development Council.

negative A number less than zero, written $x < 0$ or $x \leq 0$. $x < 0$ indicates that x is strictly negative, that is, always less than zero; $x \leq 0$ indicates that x is negative in a weaker sense, including zero as a borderline case.

negative equity The position of the owner of an asset whose value is less than the amount of debt secured by a *mortgage on it. For example, a house owner with a mortgage of £100,000 on a house whose market value is only £90,000 has negative equity of £10,000. The providers of mortgage finance do not lend more than they believe the security is worth, but negative equity can occur if house prices fall after a mortgage is taken out, as occurred in the UK in the early 1990s, or if borrowers get into arrears on their repayments.

negative income tax A proposal to combine income tax and social security in a single system. Under this system, all citizens would report their pre-tax incomes; they would then pay tax if their incomes after deducting any allowances to which they were entitled came above some cut-off level, and would receive payments if their income was below the cut-off. The advantage of such a system is that it would remove any stigma attaching to claiming benefits, as every citizen would be subject to the same system. The disadvantage is that either the minimum post-tax-and-benefits income would have to be very low, or tax rates would have to be very high, given the present distribution of pre-tax incomes. There are also problems arising from the fact that, in the UK at least, the unit for taxation is the individual whereas the unit for benefits is the household.

neoclassical economics The approach in economics of analysing how individuals and firms should behave to maximize their own objective functions, assuming that activities are coordinated by the *price mechanism, and that markets clear so that the economy is in equilibrium at all times. In this type of model, macroeconomics is largely a study of the growth of factor supplies, which determine real output, and of the effects on the price level of growth in the quantity of money.

net An indication that something has been subtracted. The word appears in economics in a variety of contexts. Net price is price after subtracting any discounts, for prompt payment or otherwise. Net weight is the weight of a product excluding packaging. Net investment is total or gross investment minus an estimate of *capital consumption. The net national product is similarly equal to gross national product, the total of all value added in the economy, minus capital consumption. Net exports are total exports minus total imports. The net assets of a firm are its total, or gross, assets minus its liabilities. The *Net Book Agreement in the UK fixed the minimum prices at which books might be sold, forbidding reductions by booksellers.

Net Book Agreement A UK agreement allowing publishers to fix the retail prices of their books. This was allowed as an exception to the general prohibition of *resale price maintenance. It was argued that the agreement helped to keep small and specialized booksellers in business, and was thus good for the reading public. The NBA was abandoned in 1995.

net capital formation *See* net investment.

net domestic product The value of incomes produced by factors of production operating in a country, regardless of their ownership, and after subtracting an estimate of capital consumption.

net economic welfare The concept of a broader measure of economic welfare than income per head. This could include in addition to ordinary measures of income items such as the following: the cost of effort; the value of household production, including services such as child-care and looking after the sick and elderly; any depletion of the stock of natural resources; and the value of changes in the natural environment. While such a measure of overall welfare would be of great interest if one could trust it, the actual observation and valuation of these things is so difficult that any proposed measure would be highly subjective.

net exports Exports less imports, either in total, or of any category of goods and services. It is thus negative when imports exceed exports.

net foreign assets The total of assets owned by residents of a country, but situated abroad, minus assets located within the country but owned by non-residents. A country's overseas assets include both foreign direct investment and holdings of foreign securities, and foreign holdings of domestic assets include both inward foreign direct investment and foreign holdings of domestic securities. Net foreign assets can thus be either positive or negative.

net investment The net increase in the amount of capital. This equals gross investment minus an estimate of *capital consumption. Net investment is harder to measure than gross, since while gross investment is mainly based on actual market transactions in acquiring capital goods, capital consumption is not based on observing market transactions, but is an estimate of the loss of value of the existing capital stock due to wear and tear, the passage of time, and obsolescence.

net national product The value of the incomes produced by factors of production owned by residents of a country, whether operating domestically or abroad, measured after deducting an estimate of *capital consumption. Net national product thus includes the earnings of factors owned by residents and operating abroad, and excludes the earnings of factors operating domestically but owned by non-residents.

net present value The present value of a security or an investment project, found by discounting all present and future receipts and outgoings at an appropriate rate of interest. If the net present value thus calculated is positive, it is worth while investing in a project, provided it can be financed. If the receipts or outgoings are subject to uncertainty, picking the appropriate rate of discount is difficult.

net profit The profits of an organization after all expenses have been taken into account. This can be measured either before or after deduction of taxes payable.

net property income from abroad The excess of property incomes received from abroad over property incomes paid to non-residents. Property incomes include rent, dividends and interest remitted from abroad plus the retained profits of companies operating direct investment abroad. In practice company profits earned abroad and reinvested, which should be counted both as receipts of property income and as capital outflows, tend to get omitted from balance-of-payments statistics, so net property income from abroad is not reliably reported.

net tangible assets The tangible assets of an organization less its current liabilities. This is different from total assets minus total liabilities. On the assets side it excludes intangibles such as goodwill, and on the liabilities side it excludes debts not due for payment within the next financial year. A positive figure for net tangible assets thus gives no guarantee of an organization's long-run solvency, but it is sometimes regarded as a good indicator of its ability to survive in the immediate future.

net transfer income from abroad The excess of transfers from abroad received by the residents of a country over the payments of transfers abroad. Transfers include government grants to overseas bodies, and private charitable donations.

net wealth The wealth of an individual after subtracting any debts owed from his or her total gross assets.

network externality An external economy deriving from being connected to other people, for example through the telephone system or the internet. The larger the proportion of the population connected to such a network, the greater the benefits to each of them.

net worth The net value of an organization's assets, after deducting any liabilities. Net worth can only be measured reliably if assets are correctly valued: this cannot usually be done simply by using balance-sheet figures. Where assets are not readily marketed and goodwill is important, any figure for net worth may be very unreliable.

net yield The interest or dividends on securities, net of tax, that is after deduction of the normal rate of income tax, as a percentage of their price. For taxpayers with a personal marginal income tax rate lower than the normal rate, net yield is higher than that reported; similarly, for taxpayers with a personal marginal income tax rate higher than the normal rate, net yield is lower than that reported.

neutrality of money The view that the level and growth rate of the money supply does not affect the real working of the economy. Unless there is complete price flexibility, this cannot be true in the short run. Even in the long run, fluctuations in the money supply affect real activity even if the trend does not. Given the growth rate of the money supply, in the long run its level can be expected to affect only the price level and not real activity. In the long run the rate of inflation depends on the growth rate of the money supply. There is widespread agreement that extreme inflation, or hyperinflation, is bad for real activity, and so is a falling price level; how moderate inflation affects real activity is a matter of controversy. Money can be neutral only in a limited long-run sense.

neutral taxes Taxes which do not cause inefficiency by distorting the structure of incentives. Poll taxes and lump-sum taxes on economic rents may be neutral, but it is hard to find any others. Direct taxes can avoid discrimination between occupations, but cannot avoid giving incentives to leisure and do-it-yourself activity rather than paid employment, and to a shift to the *unofficial economy. Value-added tax (VAT) could avoid discrimination between different goods and services, but because of income distribution considerations and various vested interests it is usually not imposed at a uniform rate on everything; and again it cannot avoid shifting activity to the informal sector. The tax treatment of various types of investment spending by companies provides particularly spectacular examples of non-neutrality.

new classical economics A school of economics based on the assumption that all economic agents hold *rational expectations and that all markets clear. The consequence of this is a belief that unemployment is essentially voluntary, produced by the provision of perverse incentives by the state, and that discretionary government policies are destabilizing. This leads to the advocacy of *laissez-faire policies, and to a belief that inflation can be controlled by strict monetary policy at zero real cost. Few economists believe this entirely, but many are affected to some extent by this type of analysis.

New Deal The package of policies adopted in the US in the 1930s under President Franklin D. Roosevelt to promote economic recovery from the great depression. This included price stabilization through the National Recovery Adminstration, extension of collective bargaining through the Wagner Act, promotion of financial stability through the creation of the *Securities and Exchange Commission (SEC) and the *Federal Deposit Insurance Corporation (FDIC), social security including the creation of *Aid to Families with Dependent Children (AFDC), and a programme of public works including setting up the Tennessee Valley Authority (TVA).

New International Economic Order (NIEO) A set of proposals to improve the position of *less developed countries (LDCs) by changing their terms of trade with and their arrangements for borrowing from more advanced economies. These were originated at the United Nations (UN) in 1974, and urged through the *United Nations Conference on Trade and Development (UNCTAD). These proposals included measures to improve the terms of trade for exporters of primary products, measures to improve the access of LDC producers to markets for industrial exports in the more developed countries, and a reduction in international debt burdens, particularly for the poorer indebted LDCs. These proposals have led to very little action by the advanced economies.

new issues The value of sales of newly issued shares in public companies. This is one of the main sources of finance for companies.

newly industrialized country (NIC) A country which has recently increased the proportion of industrial production in its national income and of industrial exports in its trade. The NICs have been the most rapidly growing part of the world economy in the last quarter of the twentieth century. There is no standard list of NICs: they include the 'East Asian tigers', Hong Kong, Korea, Singapore and Taiwan, and various other countries including Brazil, China, India, Malaysia, Mexico, South Africa and Thailand, and their number is growing.

new orders The value of orders for goods obtained by firms in those sectors where goods are made to order rather than made first and then sold off the shelf. This is principally the construction industry and those parts of manufacturing industry selling producer goods. Changes in new orders are a leading indicator of changes in economic activity.

new protectionism The revival of protectionism, with the support of some additional arguments. These are based partly on the introduction of strategic considerations, and partly on considering the effects of assuming widespread increasing returns to scale in industry. The strategic argument for protection is that one country may by protecting its own industry deter others from entering into competition with it. The effect of increasing returns, with resulting imperfect competition, is that protecting a country's home market increases the output of its own industry, thus decreasing its average costs and improving its ability to compete internationally. Protection also cuts rivals' output, thus increasing their average costs and impairing their ability to compete. None of these arguments affects the objection that all forms of protection are *beggar-my-neighbour policies, so that all countries could gain by agreeing to abstain from them.

New York Stock Exchange (NYSE) The oldest and largest US stock exchange.

NHS *See* National Health Service.

NIC *See* National Insurance Contribution: *see also* newly industrialized country.

NIEO *See* New International Economic Order.

NIESR *See* National Institute of Economic and Social Research.

Nikkei index The principal index of Japanese share prices.

1992 The European Community's programme aimed at unifying the EC's *internal market by 1992. The target was the elimination of all barriers to the movement of goods, people and capital within the EC. This involved the removal of border controls, the liberalization of financial markets, the harmonization of VAT rates, the standardization of industrial regulations, and the opening up of government procurement to all EC members.

no arbitrage The assumption that the resale of goods or services is impossible, or sufficiently costly to be unusual. This allows sellers to practice third-degree price discrimination, where different prices are charged to different types of customer. If arbitrage were cheap the extent of possible price discrimination would be limited, and if arbitrage were costless price discrimination would be impossible.

noise, white *See* white noise.

nominal anchor A mechanism for determining the general price level in an economy. The need for equilibrium in markets for goods and factor services determines the structure of relative prices, but this could be achieved with any absolute price level. The monetary authorities may simply proclaim an intention to keep some price index stable, but this promise may lack credibility. A nominal anchor is a way of making such promises credible. Possible methods include using a commodity such as gold or silver as money, or adopting a fixed exchange rate with some other currency such as the DM which already had a reputation for price stability.

nominal protection The proportional price increase in imported goods caused by a tariff. With a proportional tariff rate t, the price of imports inside the country is $(1 + t)$ times their external price. The tariff rate thus measures nominal protection. This is contrasted with *effective protection, the proportional increase in value-added in the industry producing a good, taking account of tariffs on any imported inputs used in producing it. The more heavily imported inputs are taxed, the less effective protection is given by any rate of nominal protection.

nominal variable An economic variable measured in money terms. Examples include national income data, and price and wage levels. Nominal variables are contrasted with real variables, which are measured in physical units, such as employment or steel production, and variables which are pure numbers, such as elasticities and percentage shares.

nominee holding A share holding registered in a name other than that of the real owner. This is sometimes done for sheer convenience, for example when *unit trusts hold shares which are ultimately the property of their own unit-holders. In other cases it is done to avoid revealing the identity of the owner, for example when shares are being acquired prior to a takeover bid.

non-accelerating inflation rate of unemployment (NAIRU) The unemployment rate at which *inflation remains constant. This features in models where the rate of inflation depends on demand pressure. In such models, if demand is high, firms aim on average to raise their own prices faster than they expect other prices to increase, which causes inflation to speed up. If demand is low, firms aim on average to raise their own prices more slowly than they expect other prices to increase, which causes inflation to slow down. The NAIRU is the unemployment rate corresponding to a level of demand pressure which causes firms on average to aim to keep their own price increases in line with the price increases they expect elsewhere. This stabilizes the rate of inflation at whatever level it has already reached.

non-contributory pension scheme A pension scheme in which members are not required to contribute to the cost of their pensions, which is entirely met by their employer. This is contrasted with a contributory pension scheme, in which the members are required to contribute to meet at least part of the cost.

non-discrimination Equal treatment for comparable cases. This is contrasted with discrimination, which is differences of treatment on what are considered irrelevant grounds. In employment, for example, non-discrimination implies not choosing employees on grounds of sex, race, or religion, for positions where these grounds are not directly relevant to the duties to be performed. In international trade, non-discrimination means treating all transactions with non-nationals equally. The question of what differences are in fact irrelevant gives rise to problems: the principle of non-discrimination may conflict with actuarial evidence. In pensions, for example, it is an actuarial fact that women on average live longer than men; whether they should therefore receive lower pensions for equal contributions is the subject of controversy.

non-durables, consumer *See* consumer non-durables.

non-executive director A company director who is not a full-time executive employee of the firm. Non-executive directors are usually chosen either for their expertise in areas relevant to a company's activities, or because they have titles or hold other positions which lend respectability to bodies they join. They may well be executives of other companies.

non-inflationary growth Growth of economic activity without any tendency to inflation of prices. This is sometimes taken as the ideal target for macroeconomic management. It can be criticized as a target from various viewpoints. Some economists sceptical of the ability of the authorities to prevent minor fluctuations in the rate of inflation urge the danger from the *liquidity trap if prices fall as indicating that a small positive average rate of inflation is a more sensible target than a mean inflation rate of zero. Others have suggested that a modest inflation rate may actually be good for growth, though believers in *rational expectations doubt this. Even those who accept non-inflationary growth as a long-run target fear that a very large cost in terms of real output may attach to attempting to reach such a target too rapidly.

non-intersecting curves Curves which have no point in common. For example, in a set of indifference curves each curve corresponds to a different level of welfare for the individual they refer to, so that they do not intersect.

non-linear function A function which cannot be expressed in the linear form, $y = ax + b$. It may be non-linear in the sense of being continuously curved, with $d^2y/dx^2 \neq 0$. Alternatively, it may be non-linear in the sense that, while it consists of linear sections, these differ in slope: the function is piecewise linear, but has sharp kinks at the points where the linear segments join up.

non-marketable debt Debt where there is no secondary market. The holders of such debt may have to wait until it falls due for redemption, or may be able to get it redeemed by the borrower at any time, but possibly on terms involving some penalty. This is the position, for example, with National Savings certificates in the UK. Holders cannot sell their rights to anybody else, though they may be used as collateral for loans from other financial institutions.

non-marketed economic activities Economic activities producing goods and services not distributed through markets. These may be conducted by individuals, organizations, or the state. Individuals perform for themselves or their families activities which can be and often are paid for: these include child-care, looking after the sick and the elderly, housework, driving, gardening and do-it-yourself home improvements. Many voluntary organizations such as charities and churches produce services which are given free rather than sold. A great many government services, including health, education and personal social services are provided free, to some recipients at least. Between them these various forms of non-marketed activity constitute a significant share of a modern economy.

non-monetary job characteristics Job characteristics other than financial. These include hours and working conditions, holidays, training provision, opportunities for promotion, location of the workplace in a pleasant area, and a congenial boss and fellow-workers. These are contrasted with purely financial conditions, including pay and bonuses, pension rights, free or subsidized medical insurance, and assistance with house purchase. Some job characteristics have a financial value which is difficult to measure explicitly, such as job security, provision of child-care facilities, or training which improves a worker's other job opportunities.

non-negative A real number which is either positive or zero, written $x \geq 0$.

non-parametric statistics Statistical techniques which do not assume particular functional forms for the relations between variables. Correlation of the rank order of two variables is an example of this. Use of such techniques is only appropriate when there is reason to expect the relation to be monotonic, and it is hard to apply them to relations between several variables.

non-performing debt Debt on which the interest and redemption payments due are not in fact being made. Non-performing debt is an embarassment to lending institutions: they suffer not merely direct financial loss, but also damage to their reputation for sound judgement in picking borrowers. There is thus a temptation to camouflage non-performing debt by making fresh loans to finance repayment of earlier ones.

non-positive A real number which is either negative or zero, written $x \leq 0$.

non-price competition Competition for markets using methods other than price cuts. These include quality of product, quality of advertising, information and instructions, reliability of promised delivery dates, reliability in use, and after-sales service. Non-price competition is particularly important when there are legal or cartel restrictions on price-cutting, and where consumers use price as a signal of quality and assume that cheaper goods must be nastier. Even when firms do compete on price, they frequently use non-price methods of competition as well.

non-satiation The assumption that consumers can always benefit from having additional spending power. Their demand for particular goods may have a finite limit as their total spending increases, but there is always some good or service they would benefit from having more of.

non-systematic risk *See* idiosyncratic risk.

non-tariff barriers All forms of man-made obstructions to international trade other than tariffs. Non-tariff barriers have proliferated in recent decades, and they now involve a wide variety of devices, including: prohibitions and quotas; oppressive and dilatory procedures for the routing and documentation of imports; regulations allegedly for health and safety purposes; requirements for prior deposit of the cost of imports in blocked bank accounts; the requirement of licences or specific foreign currency allocations; and *voluntary export restraint agreements (VERs) with foreign exporters. In all cases where licences, allocations or approvals are required, in some countries it may be necessary to add to any fees, and the real costs of delay and documentation, the cost of bribing officials enforcing the rules.

non-tradables Goods and services which cannot be traded internationally. There is no direct motive for making the prices of non-tradables in different countries equal. Given that both have tradable substitutes, however, there is an indirect connection between their prices. Even goods which are very expensive or impossible to transport can still be consumed by tourists and by people visiting a country for medical treatment or education, so it is hard to say that any good is completely non-tradable; whether goods are tradables or non-tradables is a matter of degree.

non-voting share A share which gives the holder the same right to dividends as a voting ordinary share, but no vote at company meetings. Non-voting shares are issued to enable a company to raise equity finance without diluting control. They normally have a lower price than voting shares.

normal distribution The bell-shaped frequency distribution which results when variations are caused by a large number of independent and additive random factors. The frequency distribution of a normally distributed variable x with mean μ and variance σ^2 is given by

$$f(x) = [1/\sqrt{(2\pi\sigma^2)}]\exp[-\tfrac{1}{2}(x-\mu)^2/\sigma^2].$$

A normal distribution is symmetrical about its mean, since $f(\mu + z) = f(\mu - z)$ for all z. The fact that x is normally distributed with mean μ and variance σ^2 is denoted by $x \sim N(\mu, \sigma^2)$. If x is normally distributed, about 68 per cent of cases lie between $-\sigma$ and $+\sigma$ of μ, about 95 per cent between -2σ and $+2\sigma$ of μ, and about 99.7 per cent between -3σ and $+3\sigma$ of the mean.

Frequency

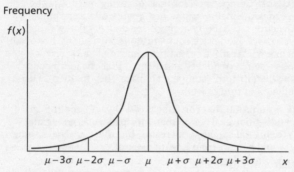

FIGURE 23: *Normal Distribution*

The horizontal axis shows the value of some variable, x. The vertical axis shows its frequency. The total area under the curve is thus always 1. x is normally distributed with mean μ and standard deviation σ. This is written $x \sim N(\mu, \sigma^2)$. Its formula is given by $f(x) = k\exp[-\tfrac{1}{2}(x-\mu)^2/\sigma^2]$, where k is a constant chosen to make the distribution sum to 1. The distribution is symmetric about μ.

normal good A good whose consumption increases with income. Thus any good is normal which is not inferior; this applies to most goods. Normal goods are divided between necessities, with *income elasticities of demand of less than one, and luxuries, with income elasticities of demand of over one.

normal profits The level of profits which is regarded as usual in any economy. Levels of profitability higher than this tend to stimulate entry to an industry, and levels of profits lower than normal tend to cause exit. The actual level regarded as normal depends on attitudes to risk-taking in a society, and on the distribution of wealth, which affects the ability to go into business on one's own account.

normative economics The aspects of economics concerning how the economy ought to be run. The main considerations concerned are *efficiency and *equity. On the efficiency side, it asks whether any given objective could be achieved using fewer real resources. If this could be done, it would leave more resources available to achieve other desirable ends. On the equity side, it asks whether the distribution of costs and benefits is desirable, given objectives such as equality, fair rewards for effort, and not disappointing people's reasonable expectations. These aims are not always mutually consistent, and normative economics has to consider the trade-offs between them and between the equity and the efficiency effects of any arrangements.

North American Free Trade Agreement (NAFTA) An agreement reached in 1993 between Canada, Mexico and the United States making the three countries into a *free-trade area.

North Sea Oil The rise of oil production in the North Sea. A combination of advances in oil technology and the rise in oil prices in the 1970s led to a dramatic rise in UK-based oil production. Output rose from approximately nil in 1973 to a level equal to 9 per cent of productive sector output by 1979. This dramatically improved the UK's balance of payments: in 1974 net imports of fuel were equal to 3½ per cent of GDP, while in 1983 net exports of fuel were equal to 4 per cent of GDP.

no-strike agreement An agreement between a firm and the union(s) representing its employees that in the event of disagreements which cannot be resolved by negotiation, both sides will accept the results of arbitration rather than resorting to strike action.

NTBs *See* non-tariff barriers.

null hypothesis The hypothesis that a variable has no effect. For example, in investigating the relation between income and saving, the null hypothesis could be that the income level of an individual does not affect the proportion of income that is saved. Observations of a sample of individuals' income and saving are then used to see whether any observed deviations from the null hypothesis could have arisen purely through sampling error. If richer individuals are found to have significantly higher savings ratios than poorer ones, the null hypothesis that the savings ratio is independent of income is not accepted.

number *See* complex number, imaginary number, rational number, and real number.

numeraire A good used as the standard of value for other goods. The price of the numeraire is defined to be 1. Any good can in principle be used as numeraire provided that it always has a strictly positive price.

NYSE *See* New York Stock Exchange.

O

Objective 1 region A region with under 75% of the average EU per capita incomes, which is eligible for financial assistance from the EU budget to improve its social overhead capital and employment prospects.

obsolescence Loss of value of equipment due to changes in techniques or tastes. Equipment may become obsolete because consumers no longer want the goods it produces, or because *technical progress in other industries means that intermediate goods it produces are no longer needed. It may become obsolete because new techniques in its own industry allow production with less labour, fuel or materials, or because it does not comply with improved health and safety regulations. Obsolescence is contrasted with loss of value through wear and tear or the passage of time.

occupational pension A pension provided by an employer for former employees. In contributory pension schemes employees are required to contribute part of their pay to help meet the cost of the scheme; in non-contributory schemes the entire cost is borne by the employer. Fully funded schemes build up sufficient funds to meet the actuarially expected cost of pensions. In unfunded schemes the pensions are paid for out of current revenue by the employer. In partially funded schemes there is a fund, but not one sufficient to meet the full forecasted cost of pensions due. Defined contributions schemes fix the contributions by employers and employees to the pension fund: pensions depend on the financial peformance of the fund. Defined benefit schemes fix what the pensioners receive, the employer making up any deficiency in the fund's financial performance. Defined-benefit schemes may fix benefits in cash terms, or index-link them, either to prices or current earnings.

odds, fair *See* fair odds.

OECD *See* Organization for Economic Cooperation and Development.

off-balance-sheet finance The use of leased rather than owned buildings and equipment. This reduces the capital required to run a business, and reduces the risk of loss due to technical *obsolescence of the equipment. Because the owner of leased equipment bears this risk, the rental on off-balance-sheet items may exceed the interest and amortization costs of owning them, so that use of off-balance sheet finance lowers current profits.

offer curve A diagram showing the willingness of the rest of the world to engage in trade. The offer curve shows the amount of trade any one country can do at various relative prices. For a small country, the offer curve facing it is a straight line, whose slope is proportional to world relative prices of exports and imports. For a country with monopoly or monopsony power, the offer curve facing it is concave, and by using tariffs to restrict its own willingness to trade a large country can improve its terms of trade. The offer curve is a purely theoretical concept: in a multi-country and multi-commodity world actual offer curves are impossible to discover.

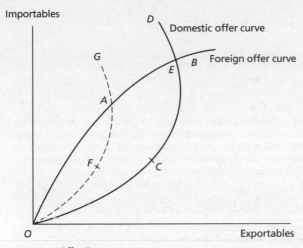

FIGURE 24: *Offer Curves*

The horizontal axis shows amounts of good X, assumed to be the exportable of the country concerned; the vertical axis shows amounts of good Y, assumed to be the importable. *OAEB* shows the trade the rest of the world is willing to do at any given relative prices. For a very small country *OAEB* is a ray through the origin: the terms of trade available are simply given. For a larger country, *OAEB* is concave: to do more trade the country has to accept worse terms of trade, as more units of exports have to be paid per unit of imports. *OCED* shows the amounts of trade the country's residents are willing to do at each relative price. They buy more imports as the terms of trade improve; the offer curve may turn back at some level of exports, as drawn, but need not do so. *E* represents free trade equilibrium, where the domestic and foreign offer curves intersect. A tariff raises the internal relative price of importables for any given external relative price. This makes residents less willing to trade, and shifts the domestic offer curve inwards to a position such as *OFAG*. Equilibrium shifts to *A*, and the terms of trade improve, except in the small country case when the foreign offer curve is linear and the terms of trade are unchanged.

Office for National Statistics (ONS) The UK government agency responsible for the collection and publication of UK economic statistics. The ONS was formed in 1996 by merging the Central Statistical Office and the Office of Population Censuses and Surveys.

Office of Fair Trading (OFT) The government body responsible for administering UK competition policy. It is responsible for maintaining the register of restrictive agreements, monitoring restrictive and anti-competitive practices, and regulating consumer credit. It can refer proposed mergers to the *Monopolies and Mergers Commission (MMC), now the Competition Commission (CC).

Office of Management and Budget (OMB) An office of the US President responsible for preparing the annual Federal budget for presentation to Congress. Once the budget is passed, the OMB controls its administration and provides data on the actual performance of Federal finances.

Office of Telecommunications (Oftel) The official body set up to regulate the UK telephone industry after the privatization of British Telecom.

official financing The official element in the *balance of payments. If a country's current and capital account balances do not sum to zero, the difference has to be found by the authorities. If the sum is a deficit, the central bank may meet this by running down its *foreign exchange reserves, or by borrowing from other central banks or from international institutions, particularly the *International Monetary Fund (IMF). If the sum of the current and capital accounts is a surplus, the central bank can repay past borrowing, or increase its foreign exchange reserves.

offshore fund A fund operating in a country which is not the residence of the holder. Use of offshore funds may assist in tax avoidance or evasion.

OFT *See* Office of Fair Trading.

Oftel *See* Office of Telecommunications.

Ohlin *See* Heckscher–Ohlin model.

oil Mineral oil, as contrasted with vegetable or animal-based oils. Oil is used mainly for fuel, but also in the manufacture of lubricants and chemicals. It is the most important single fuel source in the world at present. While stocks are finite, so that it is a depletable resource, the world's oil reserves are far from fully explored, and exhaustion of the stock is not imminent.

oil crisis A situation in which there is a sudden fall in the availability and/or a large increase in the price of oil. For the many economies which rely mainly on oil for their energy requirements, a fall in the quantity available would produce a major slump in real output. For countries importing their oil a large price rise produces an immediate and severe balance-of-payments problem. The oil crisis of 1973–4 occurred when the members of the *Organization of Petroleum Exporting Countries (OPEC) raised the price of oil by a factor of four and some Middle Eastern oil producers threatened a boycott of supplies to countries regarded as sympathetic to Israel in the 1973 Arab–Israeli war.

oil embargo A refusal to supply oil to countries whose policies are disliked. As bulk oil is mainly carried in pipelines and large and easily recognized tankers, an embargo on bulk oil supplies is relatively easy to enforce. Oil is so widely used as a fuel that this can create severe economic problems for the victim of an embargo. Refined petroleum products, which can be carried in smaller vehicles, barrels, or cans, can much more easily be smuggled, so that an effective embargo is difficult to police.

oil price The price of bulk oil, usually quoted in US dollars per barrel. The real oil price drifted downwards in the post-war period, until in 1973–4 the *Organization of Oil Exporting Countries (OPEC) increased it by a factor of four. This set off a severe bout of world-wide inflation, and the real price of oil since the 1970s has fluctuated severely, illustrating the tendency of price-fixing cartels to be unstable.

Okun's law The proposition that in cyclical fluctuations, the ratio of actual to potential real output generally rises by a greater percentage than the fall in unemployment. On the basis of data on the US economy from 1960 to 1980 Okun put the ratio of proportional changes in output to those of unemployment at around 3. This effect is believed to be due partly to short-run increasing returns to employment, and partly to a tendency for some workers to drop out from the labour force when laid off, rather than appearing as unemployed.

oligopoly A market situation with only a few sellers, each anticipating the others' reactions. Each firm has a sufficiently large share of the market to need to consider the individual reactions of the others to changes in its price or output. Equilibrium thus depends on how each oligopolist forecasts the others' reactions. This is contrasted with *monopolistic competition, in which each firm regards its own demand curve as downward-sloping, but no firm feels the need to take account of the individual reactions of the others.

oligopsony The situation where there are only a few buyers in a market, who take account of each other's reactions in deciding how much to buy. This is the equivalent on the demand side of *oligopoly on the supply side of a market.

OLS *See* ordinary least squares.

OMB *See* Office of Management and Budget.

ombudsman An official responsible for investigating complaints against the administration of institutions. In the UK the use of the ombudsman system started with government bodies, through the Parliamentary Commissioner for Administration; it has since spread to other areas, including banking, finance and insurance. An ombudsman's conclusions are not usually legally binding, but have considerable moral force, and disregarding them in particular cases can lead to political pressure for changes in the law.

on-the-job training Training by working under supervision by an experienced worker. This is contrasted with training by formal courses of instruction, provided by the employer or an outside body. Many employers make use of both training methods.

opaque policy measures Policy measures where it is difficult to discover what they are, who decides on them, and what they cost. These are contrasted with *transparent policy measures, where these points are relatively clear. Opaque policy measures are widely used. For example, suppose that the government wishes to encourage public transport on loss-making routes. This can be done by the transparent policy of offering a subsidy to any firm that will provide the services, or by the opaque policy of giving some firm monopoly rights over profitable routes, on condition that it uses part of the profits on these to cross-subsidize loss-making services.

OPEC *See* Organization of Petroleum Exporting Countries.

open economy An economy which has transactions with the rest of the world. These may include trade in goods and services, movements of capital, transfers of information and technical know-how, and migration of labour.

Most economies are at least partially open for some of these forms of contact; very few if any are completely open for all of them.

opening prices The bid and offer prices quoted when stock or commodity markets open on any working day.

open market operations The purchase or sale of securities by the central bank as a means of changing interest rates and the money supply. This is one of the major instruments of *monetary policy. If the central bank buys securities their prices rise, interest rates fall, and the money supply increases. If the central bank sells securities their prices fall, interest rates rise, and the money supply decreases.

open outcry The system of trading in commodities, securities or currencies by traders meeting together and calling out the trades they are offering. Open outcry is a system for trying to ensure that full information is available on an equal basis to all participants in the market. A similar function is performed in many modern markets by having offers and trades continually reported on screen in a computer network.

open position A situation when a trader in securities, commodities or currencies is at risk if market prices rise or fall. This may involve selling for future delivery items not either held or hedged by contracts to buy, in which case the trader will make a loss if market prices rise, or contracting to buy without hedging by contracts to sell, in which case the trader will make a loss if market prices fall. An open position is contrasted with covered arbitrage, where contracts are balanced and the trader is not exposed to risk of loss through price changes.

operational research The application of mathematical and statistical methods to the practical problems facing businesses. This techniques used include linear programming, critical path analysis, and queuing and inventory models. These have been applied to problems including finance, purchasing, production, marketing, delivery systems, and inventory control.

opportunism The tendency for one party to a bargain to try to change the terms in their favour once the other party has committed itself. For example, if a firm has incurred sunk costs in installing equipment to fulfil an order, the customer faces the temptation to try to negotiate a lower price, knowing that the supplier has bought specialized machinery with no alternative use. Equally, the supplier may be tempted to demand a higher price, knowing that the customer has left it too late to find an alternative source. Opportunism can be countered either by stringent and enforceable *contracts, or by continuing dealings with the same trading partners, where a reputation for fair dealing is valuable, so that fear of losing it acts as a restraint.

opportunity cost The amount of other goods and services which could have been obtained instead of any good. If it had not been produced, the resources used in making it could have been used to produce other goods and services instead. If it had not been bought, the money spent on it could have been used to buy the other goods.

optimal growth theory *See* optimum savings.

optimality, Pareto- *See* Pareto-optimality.

optimization The choice from all possible uses of resources of that which gives the best results. This is often represented by maximizing an objective function. Critics of optimization argue that there are unlimited numbers of different ways of using given resources. People actually choose between a very limited number of the possibilities, using often crude 'rules of thumb' both to select the possibilities considered and to choose between them.

optimum currency area The best area to use a single currency. To see what determines this, assume there are two separate currency areas, and consider the gains and losses from uniting them. The gain is the reduction in transactions costs in respect of trade and financial transactions between them, and the reduction in currency risk affecting such transactions. This is greater, the larger such transactions are relative to national incomes. The loss is that if the areas are affected by asymmetric *shocks, or have different preferences about any trade-off between stable prices and stable real output, having a single currency removes changes in the exchange rate between them as a possible equilibrating mechanism. How important this is depends on one's view as to whether exchange rate changes are effective in inducing shifts in real behaviour, or whether they simply promote inflation in the area whose currency is devalued. For any given level of transactions costs, the net advantage of a single currency increases the more similar the areas are in their preferences and the shocks they are expected to sustain, and decreases the more their preferences and expected shocks differ. The desirability of a single currency also depends on the effectiveness of the other available means of adjustment. The more prices are flexible and factors of production are mobile, the less the need for exchange rate adjustments, so the greater the net benefits of a single currency. If incomes in the two areas are liable to different patterns of fluctuation, a common fiscal system assists in coping with the resulting shifts in relative incomes, so some economists believe that a common currency requires a common fiscal system. The question of whether a single currency for the *European Union (EU) is desirable is extremely controversial.

optimum savings The theory of answers to the question, what proportion of income should be saved and invested? There is a trade-off between present consumption and future growth: more consumption now means a lower marginal utility of consumption now, but less investment means slower growth of output, which limits the rate at which consumption can grow in the future. Optimum savings theory suggests that in a competitive economy the time-path of aggregate consumption should be chosen so that the marginal utility of consumption decreases over time at a rate equal to the marginal product of capital.

optimum tariff A tariff which maximizes a country's welfare, trading off improvement in the *terms of trade against restriction of trade quantities. For a small economy which cannot affect world prices in the markets in which it trades, the optimum tariff is zero. For a country with monopoly power in its export markets or monopsony power in import markets, the optimum tariff is positive, but not so large as to eliminate trade entirely. Calculation of an optimum tariff structure in a multi-good economy would require information on cross-elasticities of supply and demand in world markets which no country possesses. The optimum tariff model also assumes no retaliation by trading partners. The main lesson of the model is to point to the advantages of multinational agreement to refrain from attempting to use tariffs to improve the terms of trade.

option A contract giving the holder the right but not the obligation to trade in a commodity, a share or a currency on some future date at a pre-agreed price. A 'put' option gives the holder the right to sell at a pre-agreed price. This can be used to reduce risk by somebody who has to hold the actual asset and is worried that its price may fall; it can equally be used to speculate on a price fall. A 'call' option gives the holder the right to buy at a pre-agreed price. This can be used to reduce risk by people who expect to need the asset in the future and are worried that its price may rise before they buy; it can equally be used to speculate on a price rise. An options market is a market in which options are traded; these exist for many widely traded goods, shares and currencies. Share options give a right to buy company shares at a future date at a pre-agreed price; they are used by companies as incentives for their executives. An option is contrasted with a futures contract, which carries the obligation as well as the right to trade. *See also* call option, put option, share option, and stock option.

option value The value of being able to put off decisions. If one invests in a project now one's capital is sunk in it. Market conditions may then change to make the project more or less profitable. If the decision is deferred, one can invest next year if the market improves, or abandon the project if the market worsens. Option value is the expected benefit from delaying a decision. The option value of ability to delay investments helps to explain the existence of liquidity preference, since holding cash does not commit one to any particular form of future expenditure. If a market is expected to improve rapidly, or there is a danger that competitors may enter it first, option value may be negative, in which case it pays to invest now.

order book The value of orders received but not yet carried out by firms in certain sectors, mainly construction and engineering, where output is mainly produced to order, and not sold off the shelf. The size of an industry's order book may be expressed in cash terms, or as months' output. Changes in order books are a leading economic indicator. Order books are liable to catastrophic declines in slumps, when purchasers may cancel orders, or go out of business.

order-driven market An asset market where the role of intermediaries is matching buy and sell orders. In such a market orders to buy at given prices or below, and to sell at given prices or above, are accumulated until a set time, for example noon daily. A *market-clearing price is then worked out, and orders consistent with this price are executed. This is contrasted with a quote-driven market, where the role of intermediaries is to act as *market-makers, offering to buy and sell at stated prices, up to some quantity limit, and transactions can take place at any time when the market is open.

order of integration The minimum number of times it is necessary to difference a time-series to produce a *stationary series. A series which has to be differenced n times is integrated of order n, written $I(n)$.

orders, new *See* new orders.

ordinal utility The view that in comparing welfare levels, the direction of differences can be observed but the magnitude of differences cannot be measured. This is contrasted with *cardinal utility, which assumes that welfare levels and therefore welfare differences can be measured. In considering decisions under certainty, ordinal utility is adequate except for dealing with income distribution. In considering decisions under uncertainty, however, economists have found it convenient to assume cardinal utility.

ordinary least squares (OLS) The simplest linear regression technique. OLS involves fitting a linear equation with the coefficients chosen to minimize the sum of squares of residual errors. In estimating systems of simultaneous equations, where the left-hand variable of each equation appears as a right-hand variable in others, OLS produces biased results, and is replaced by *two-stage least squares, or more sophisticated methods of estimation.

ordinary share The UK term for a share in the equity of a company. The US equivalent term is common stock. The holder of an ordinary share is entitled to share in any distribution of dividends in proportion to the number of shares held. Ordinary shares usually but not invariably entitle their holder to vote at company meetings. They are contrasted with *debentures and preference shares. Debenture holders normally have a fixed entitlement to interest, but no vote provided the interest is paid and any other conditions are complied with. Preference shareholders have no votes but must be paid their dividends before any distribution to ordinary shareholders is allowed. In the event of winding up a company, ordinary shareholders rank last in any claim to company assets, but get an unlimited part of any residual there is after paying off the others.

organizational slack *See* slack.

Organization for Economic Cooperation and Development (OECD) An international organization set up to assist member states to develop economic and social policies to promote sustained economic growth with financial stability. OECD members have been mainly free-market industrialized countries: in Europe this includes Austria, Belgium, Denmark, Finland, France, Germany, Greece, Iceland, Ireland, Italy, Luxembourg, the Netherlands, Norway, Portugal, Spain, Sweden, Switzerland and the UK. Outside Europe the OECD includes Australia, Canada, Japan, New Zealand, Turkey and the United States. Mexico became the first newly industrialized country (NIC) to join, in 1993, and the Czech Republic the first former planned economy to join, in 1995.

Organization of Petroleum Exporting Countries (OPEC) An organization of oil producing countries, set up to coordinate their policies in negotiating with the oil companies. Since 1973 OPEC has attempted to operate a world oil-exporting cartel, setting an agreed price and allocating export quotas. The members of OPEC have included Algeria, Iran, Iraq, Kuwait, Libya, Nigeria, Saudi Arabia, the United Arab Emirates (UAE) and Venezuela. OPEC's members have had difficulties in agreeing and policing a joint monopoly policy, and the real price of oil has fluctuated considerably since the 1970s.

organized labour That part of the labour force that belongs to *trade unions. The use of trade unions to negotiate pay, hours of work, and working conditions is widespread, and is believed to obtain better terms from employers than workers could obtain by individual bargaining. Trade unions also represent and assist their members in disputes over discipline, sick leave, or redundancy. Organized labour may also engage in political activities, in particular those aimed at ensuring that the legal and social security systems are arranged for the benefit of workers rather than employers. Critics of organized labour argue that when it uses its bargaining power to drive up wages it damages the employment prospects of 'outsiders', and when it obstructs changes in working practices and manning levels it may even damage the long-term interests of 'insiders'. *See also* insiders and outsiders.

organized sector Those parts of the economy which operate through institutions which feed figures into official statistics. This includes firms organized as companies, payments made via the banking system, incomes reported to the tax authorities, sales reported to the VAT authorities, and employment reported to the National Insurance authorities. These constitute the vast majority of total economic activity in advanced economies. The organized sector is contrasted with the informal or *unofficial economy, in which individuals, voluntary bodies and criminal organizations engage in trade, mainly for cash, which is not reported to the tax authorities, and employment, also for cash, which is not reported to the tax or social security authorities. In national income accounts, data on the organized sector is largely based on written records of transactions, while data on the informal sector is based on guesswork.

origin The point on a graph indicating zero for each dimension. A diagram may contain more than one origin: in a two-good, two-factor *box diagram, for example, the total available amounts of the factors are shown on the two axes: the amounts employed in one industry use one corner of the box as origin, while the amounts employed in the other industry use the opposite corner as origin. *See also* certificate of origin.

oscillation *See* amplitude of oscillation, and period of oscillation.

oscillatory function A function $y = f(x)$ which has regular oscillations in y as x increases. The trigonometric functions $y = \cos(x)$ and $y = \sin(x)$ take this form, each fluctuating between an upper limit of $+1$ and a lower limit of -1 as x increases, with peaks and troughs at regular intervals of 2π. Any linear combination, such as

$$y = a\cos(bx) + c\sin(dx)$$

takes a similar oscillatory form, with different limits.

other things being equal *See* ceteris paribus.

outcry, open *See* open outcry.

outflow, capital *See* capital movements.

outlier An entry in a set of statistical data which lies a long way from any pattern apparent in the rest of the data-set. The presence of an outlier suggests two possibilities which warrant further investigation. One is that something really exceptional occurred to cause it; such an occurrence is a shock. The other possibility is that the outlier occurred because of a mistake in recording or processing the data. Some statistical programmes exclude outliers in calculating trends or regressions; others include them but draw the user's attention to them.

output The result of an economic process, available for sale or use elsewhere. Where a process produces goods, measurement of output is straightforward. Where a process produces services, measurement of output raises problems: an airport fire crew, for example, produces safety even in a year with no fires for them to put out. In the output approach to national income, the cost of inputs to non-marketed services has to be taken as a proxy for their output. *See also* demand-determined output, and potential output.

output–capital ratio *See* capital–output ratio.

output effect The effect of a rise in output on the use of any particular input, holding input prices constant. Where the most economical proportion in which to combine inputs varies with the level of output, a rise in output causes use of some inputs to increase proportionally more than others.

output–input *See* input–output.

output method The method of calculating domestic product using information on the net outputs of various sectors of the economy. This is contrasted with the expenditure method, which uses information on the expenditures of various sectors of the economy including consumers, investors, and the government, and the income method, which proceeds by adding up the incomes of the various factors of production.

output per hour worked A measure of output per unit of labour input. (This is often referred to as output per manhour, which is inappropriate now that a large proportion of the labour force is female.) Output may be measured in physical quantities, or in value terms. Output per hour worked is used in comparisons of productivity in different plants, firms or countries. Variations occur because of differences in the skill and experience of the labour force, the degree of effort, the amount and age of capital equipment, and the level of managerial competence and technical expertise.

output per manhour *See* output per hour worked

outside money Money which is an asset to those who hold it, but is not a liability for anybody else in the economy. This is the case for gold coinage, but not for bank balances. Outside money is contrasted with inside money, where the asset for the holder is balanced by a liability of the bank issuing the money. It is a matter of definition whether money which is a government liability is outside or inside money.

outsiders and insiders *See* insiders and outsiders.

outsourcing The practice of buying goods and services from outside suppliers, rather than producing them within a firm. This is widespread among both firms and government agencies. Outsourcing may be used because specialist outside suppliers can apply more specialized skills, and can benefit from economies of scale or scope not available within the firm. It may also be used because adjusting output to variations in demand and maintaining the quality of inputs may be easier via enforcing contracts with outside suppliers than in dealing with a strongly unionized internal workforce.

over-capacity working Production in a firm or an industry above what is normally regarded as its *capacity. This is possible because capacity itself is calculated on a conventional basis which may be inaccurate. It is also possible to boost output temporarily above normal capacity levels in an emergency, by working more than the normal number of shifts, deferring staff holidays and training and maintenance of equipment, or making use of obsolete equipment which is so expensive to operate that it is not normally counted as part of capacity.

overdraft A negative balance in a bank account, so that the customer owes the bank money. This is normally allowed only by prior arrangement, though a normally reliable customer may be allowed to overdraw without prior arangement. Overdrafts are normally allowed only up to a set limit, and incur interest and possibly extra service charges for the customer.

overfull employment Levels of employment so high relative to the available labour force that they give rise to excess demand for labour. Difficulty in filling job vacancies causes wages to rise, and labour scarcity results in shortages of goods and services, so prices rise. Overfull employment thus produces and accelerates demand inflation. *Inflation leads to policy reactions designed to slow it; and the effect of inflation on expectations reduces the power of excess demand to elicit higher levels of real activity. Overfull employment is thus not permanently sustainable. Because of frictional and structural unemployment, overfull employment does not imply zero unemployment. The level of demand at which overfull employment sets in is itself a function of the organization of the labour market and social security system, the degree of monopoly in an economy, and the attitudes of its price- and wage-setters.

overhead capital, social *See* social overhead capital.

overhead costs Fixed costs a business must incur for production to be possible. Overheads may be avoidable in the short run, if output is temporarily cut to zero; or they may be avoidable only in the long run, if the possibility of future production is given up. They may include sunk or irrecoverable costs, which cannot be saved even if the firm is permanently closed down.

overheating A level of activity leading to excess demand. High output levels relative to capacity, at least in some important sectors, lead to shortages of factor inputs, or unusually high levels of imports. Overheating produces inflationary pressure internally and a deterioration in the trade balance externally; if this causes devaluation of the currency this gives a further boost to inflation.

overlapping generations The assumption made in models that individual agents have finite lives, but that each lives for more than one period. In each period there will be a new generation of agents who were not there before, and an old generation for whom this is their final period. Overlapping generations models are widely used in analysing savings behaviour, pension schemes, and security markets.

overmanning The excessive use of labour in any business. This is difficult to identify, since most businesses normally employ more labour than would strictly be necessary to do the work required if everybody was fully trained and always present at work. Actual employment needs to take account of the fact that on any given occasion some varying proportion of the labour force will be undergoing training, on holiday, off sick or absent for other personal reasons. If the pattern of demand is subject to regular or random variation this will also lead to extra workers being employed to enable firms to cope with peak periods, especially if these are liable to occur without warning. Overmanning, however, is used to describe the employment of even more workers than would be justified by these considerations. It may be imposed by law, or may result from collective bargaining or from managerial choice. Management may choose overmanning through incompetence, or in the belief that demand is likely to expand in the future, and that it is cheaper to hoard labour for the time being than to lay off redundant workers now and have to recruit and train replacements in the future.

overseas bank The UK term for a foreign bank with a branch or subsidiary in the UK, usually in London.

overseas investment *See* foreign investment.

overshooting The possibility that after a shock to the economy, some variables will move further in the short run than it is necessary for them to adjust in the long run. This occurs because of differences in speeds of adjustment. Suppose, for example, that after some shock it is necessary in the long run for a country's exchange rate to be 5 per cent lower than before. Some trade flows adjust only slowly in response to exchange rate changes, so that it may be necessary in the short run for the exchange rate to fall by more than 5 per cent. This is partly to produce larger changes in those parts of trade which can adjust promptly. Once the sectors which adjust slowly do react, the exchange rate can rise again to its long-run equilibrium level. The prospect of gains on their loans when the exchange rate recovers may also help to induce foreign lenders to finance a temporary deficit.

over-stimulation The adoption of monetary and fiscal policies that increase the level of effective demand so far that inflation begins to speed up, or substantial balance-of-trade deficits occur.

over-subscription The situation when the number of shares applied for in a *new issue exceeds the number on offer. This means that some applications have to be refused, and makes it likely that when the market opens the shares will stand at a premium over the issue price.

over-the-counter market A market in securities not regulated by a stock exchange. The UK has no OTC market; the US has the National Association of Securities Dealers Automated Quotation System (NASDAQ).

overtime Work in excess of normal working hours per week. Overtime is used by firms when high demand or emergencies make a temporary increase in labour inputs necessary. Overtime is normally paid at premium hourly rates. This may well be cheaper, however, than incurring the recruitment costs of taking on more workers. In addition the normal labour force is presumably familiar with the work, and may well do it better than newly-recruited outsiders. Where overtime is routinely worked, it amounts to a locally negotiated extension of working hours and rise in pay.

overtime ban A refusal by employees to work for more than normal working hours. This is used in *industrial disputes to inconvenience employers, and to press them to increase the numbers employed, in particular to avoid redundancies. While an overtime ban reduces workers' pay, it causes a much less severe drop in their incomes than a strike.

overtrading Carrying on business on too large a scale for a firm's capital. This creates a high risk that the firm will be unable to meet its commitments if it encounters temporary problems, for example delay in obtaining payments due from a debtor. Also, it may have to pay high interest rates for credit, since the shortage of capital makes lending to it risky. For a private firm overtrading is harmful to itself, and is discouraged by its bankers and creditors. For banks and some other financial intermediaries overtrading is also a danger to the public, as failure of one institution might be infectious and start a general financial panic. Bank regulators therefore try to prevent overtrading by requiring minimum levels of *capital adequacy.

over-valued currency A currency whose exchange rate is too high for a sustainable equilibrium in the balance of payments. With no capital movements a currency is overvalued if its exchange rate is too high to produce a balanced current account. With autonomous capital movements a currency is overvalued if its exchange rate is too high to produce a current account deficit that can be financed by a sustainable flow of inward capital movements. A currency can be held for some time at an overvalued rate by using high interest rates to induce inward short-term capital flows, but this causes external debt to rise at a rate which is not permanently sustainable. High interest rates needed to prop up an overvalued currency are also unlikely to be consistent with internal balance in the economy.

owner-occupied housing The system by which a house or flat is owned by its occupants. This is in contrast to rented housing, where the owner and the occupant are different people. Owner-occupied housing is the largest single form of housing tenure in the UK and many other industrial countries. It is encouraged by the tax system where, as in the UK, the *imputed income received by owner-occupiers is not counted as part of taxable income. Owner-occupiers are responsible for maintenance and insurance of their homes. These may be owned outright, or be financed by a *mortgage, using the house as collateral for a loan. While owner-occupation is very popular, it is not suitable for the very poor, who cannot afford to buy, the incompetent, who cannot cope with the maintenance problems, or the very mobile, who find the transactions costs involved in frequent house purchase and sale excessive.

ownership The right to exclusive use of an asset. The owner of an asset normally has the right to decide what use shall be made of it, and cannot be deprived of it except by law. The state, however, claims the right to regulate the use of many assets, and to tax income derived from them. The use that can be made of land and buildings is subject to planning permission, and rent from them is subject to income tax. The state also has rights of compulsory purchase of land needed for public works. Other people have contractual rights over assets, such as tenancies; and the general public has some rights, for example public rights of way. The extent to which ownership confers exclusive control over the use of an asset is thus a matter of degree. *See also* public ownership.

ozone layer A layer of the stratosphere protecting the earth's surface from harmful radiation. Depletion of this layer is believed to be due to human activities, the use of chlorofluorocarbons (CFCs), halon and other chemicals releasing chlorine molecules which, with a delay of around a decade, affect the stratosphere. Control of emissions requires global agreement, since each user of CFCs benefits from its own activities while most of the resulting damage affects the world as a whole. An agreement to replace CFCs and halon was reached in 1987 in the *Montreal Protocol.

Paasche index *See* current-weighted index.

package of policies A number of *policy measures all introduced at the same time. Governments resort to policy packages for two reasons: minimization of side effects, and uncertainty about the effects of particular policy measures. Any economic policy, such as changing the interest rate, is bound to have side-effects which are not wanted as well the effects for whose sake the policy is adopted. The use of any single policy measure means using it very energetically, which produces a lot of side-effects, which are both unwanted and noticeable: for example, sudden large changes in interest rates may destabilize some financial intermediaries. If several measures are used, each at a moderate level, the side-effects are smaller and less detectable. Also, there is often uncertainty about the size and timing of the effects of particular policy measures. Use of a mixture raises the chance that some at least will produce effects fairly quickly. It does, however, make it difficult to sort out statistically the separate effect of each measure: this perpetuates the uncertainty which led to choice of a package in the first place.

paid-up capital The part of the authorized capital of a company that has actually been paid by shareholders. The difference may arise because not all shares authorized have been issued, or because issued shares are only partly paid-up.

panel data Data collected over a period by repeated surveys of individuals or firms. Surveys may proceed by taking a fresh random sample of the population in successive periods, or by selecting a randomly chosen panel of respondents and following them over a prolonged period. Use of panel data means that more accurate and consistent data can be collected, but prolonged surveys impose a considerable burden on the informants, which may bias the membership of panels.

paper *See* green paper, and white paper.

parabola The graph of a quadratic expression. If $y = ax^2 + bx + c$, where $a \neq 0$, then y always has an extreme value when $x = -b/2a$. This is a minimum if $a > 0$ and a maximum if $a < 0$.

paradox of thrift The argument that a rise in the *ex ante propensity to save, that is, the share of incomes that people want to save, may not increase the ex post level of savings and investment in the economy, which may even decrease. Advocates of this view argue that in a depressed economy attempts to save more from present incomes reduce consumption and thus income levels. If this were the whole story, ex post savings and investment would not change. They go on, however, to argue that the fall in incomes discourages investment, so that ex post savings and investment actually fall: this is the paradox of thrift. The opposing argument says that in a prosperous economy, at any given income level, having more savings available makes it either easier or cheaper to borrow to finance investment; the fall in consumption thus 'crowds in' investment, so that ex post incomes are unchanged and savings and investment rise. The arguments for and against the paradox of thrift each appear to be capable of being correct in some circumstances; which actually applies in any particular situation is a matter of fact.

paradox of voting The fact that there is no reason to expect committee decisions to show transitive preferences. This is best shown by an example: suppose there are three members, 1, 2, and 3, and three policies, A, B and C. Their preference patterns, in descending order of preference, are for 1, A, B, C; for 2, B, C, A; and for 3, C, A, B: this pattern is known as cyclical preferences. In a vote between A and B, A wins since 1 and 3 prefer A to B. In a vote between A and C, C wins since 2 and 3 prefer C to A. In a vote between B and C, B wins since 1 and 2 prefer B to C. Thus there is no stable committee equilibrium: any proposal can be defeated by some other. This is an application of Arrow's impossibility theorem.

parameter A quantity which is taken as given in any particular piece of analysis. In comparative statics parameters may change, but such changes are assumed to be *externally imposed, and not generated as part of the solution to a problem. The parameters of one piece of analysis may be treated as variables in other contexts. For example, in analysing the behaviour of buyers and sellers in a competitive market, each is assumed to treat price as a parameter which their own actions cannot affect. In analysing the market as a whole, however, price is treated as a variable to be determined.

Pareto-optimality A situation in which no feasible change can raise anybody's welfare without lowering that of somebody else. This applies to reallocation of final goods between different users, reallocation of factors of production to different industries, and changes in the composition of final goods produced. Pareto-optimality is best understood through a series of negatives. If at the existing allocation two consumers have positive consumption of two goods and the consumers' *indifference curves between them differ in slope, an exchange between the two can make both better off, so the situation is not Pareto-optimal. If for two goods with positive output levels the indifference curve for any consumer and the transformation curve for any producer differ in slope, changing the composition of the goods produced can make somebody better off without harming anybody else, so the situation is not Pareto-optimal. With constant or decreasing returns to scale everywhere in an economy, Pareto-optimality is often defined in terms of marginal equalities. If there are increasing returns anywhere in an economy, however, Pareto-optimality cannot necessarily be ensured purely by pursuing marginal equalities: a local optimum may not be a global optimum, and an optimal situation may involve corner solutions.

Paris Club *See* Group of Ten.

parities, Smithsonian *See* Smithsonian parities.

parity, purchasing power *See* purchasing power parity.

partial adjustment A process of adjustment where decision-takers aim to remove in any one period only part of any discrepancy between the actual level and their target level of the variables they control. Partial adjustment is adopted for two reasons: costs of adjustment and uncertainty. If costs of adjustment rise more than proportionally with the speed of adjustment, it is cheaper to spread any required adjustment out over several periods. Some adjustment costs do take this form: for example, a gradual fall in the labour force can be achieved through natural wastage while a rapid fall requires redundancies, which are costly and unpopular; and a gradual rise in the labour force poses fewer problems of recruitment and training than a sudden large increase. The other motive for partial adjustment is uncertainty. The target for any variable has to be based on available information. Gradual adjustment allows time to gather further information to check whether an apparent change in circumstances is permanent or only temporary.

partial derivative The derivative of a function of two or more arguments with respect to any one argument, holding all the remaining arguments constant. Thus if $y = f(x, z)$, the partial derivative of y with respect to x is the derivative of y with respect to x, holding z constant. This is written $\partial y/\partial x$, or sometimes f_x or f_1, the derivative of $f(.)$ with respect to x, its first argument. Similarly the partial derivative of y with respect to z is the derivative of y with respect to z, holding x constant. This is written $\partial y/\partial z$, or sometimes f_z or f_2, the derivative of $f(.)$ with respect to z, its second argument.

partial equilibrium The method of analysis dealing with some part of the economy, deliberately ignoring possible implications of changes in this part for what happens in the rest of the economy. In studying the effects of changes in the supply and demand for a particular good on its equilibrium price and quantity a partial equilibrium analysis ignores changes in the rest of the economy, due for example to consequent changes in income distribution. This is contrasted with *general equilibrium analysis, in which the repercussions of changes in any one market throughout the rest of the economy are taken into account. General equilibrium models are necessarily either much more generalized or much more complex than partial equilibrium models. Partial equilibrium analysis is most useful when events in the sector studied have only small effects in the rest of the economy.

participation rate The percentage of the population in any given age group who are economically active, either as employees, self-employed, or unemployed, on the assumption that the unemployed would all work if jobs were available. Participation rates can be found for men, women, or both combined. Participation rates tend to vary with age, being lower among the young, many of whom are still in full-time education, and among the old, who are frequently retired; they are highest among those aged 20–50.

partnership A business which has more than one owner but is not incorporated, the individual partners remaining fully responsible for its debts. Partners need not all be equal: in professional partnerships it is common for senior partners to get a larger share of the rewards and do a smaller share of the routine work than junior partners. The senior partners' contribution is their capital, experience, and reputation. Partners may also be either active participants in the business, or 'sleeping partners', who provide capital, reputation, or guarantees while other partners do most of the work.

part-time work Working for less than the number of hours per week normal for full-time workers in the country and occupation concerned. This may suit the preferences of employers or employees. Employers may prefer part-time to full-time work because it fits the time pattern of their need for labour, or offers more flexibility. Employers may also prefer part-time workers if they enjoy less stringent legal protection than full-time workers, or tax and social security contributions for them are lower. Workers may prefer part-time work because this is convenient given other claims on their time: for example, parents with young children, part-time students, or voluntary workers. Older workers may prefer part-time to full-time work as it involves less physical and mental strain. In many cases, however, either the worker or the employer would prefer a full-time contract if they could get one.

par value The price at which a security is due to be redeemed. A safe security which is considered certain to be redeemed will stand below par if current interest rates are above its coupon yield, and above par if current interest rates are below the coupon yield.

patent A legal device to encourage and reward *invention by giving exclusive rights to inventors. In many countries the inventor of a new product or process can apply for a patent, giving the holder the exclusive right for a number of years to produce the good or use the process. This right can be used either through their own business, or by charging a licence fee to other users. This clearly provides an incentive to create inventions. It can be argued, however, that patents slow down the diffusion of new technical knowledge once it has been created. On the other hand, the right of a patentee to charge a fee reduces the incentive to keep new processes secret, which would hinder diffusion even if there were no patent protection.

paternalism The attitude favouring laws and policies which seek to control people's actions, overriding their preferences for their own good. This is inconsistent with the view usually taken in welfare economics, that people are the best judges of their own interests, at least in the case of sane and sober adults. Their actions should thus be constrained only when this is necessary to prevent them from harming other people or the environment. It can be argued that there is some degree of paternalism in many economic regulations, such as those concerning consumer protection and employment. It is possible to attempt to justify paternalism by the argument that the state can afford expert advice, which means that it knows better than individuals what is really good for them. Many people are not fully convinced by such arguments.

pay *See* performance-related pay, and profit-related pay.

pay as you earn (PAYE) The UK system of collection of *income tax on earned incomes at source. Employers are required by law to deduct personal income tax and National Insurance contributions from their employees' earnings at the time of payment, and forward the tax collected to the Inland Revenue. This improves the speed and reliability of the government's income tax revenue. As employers are required to apply tax codings taking account of allowances, which are different for each employee, the PAYE system imposes a considerable administrative burden on employers.

pay-as-you-go pensions Schemes where the pensions of the retired are paid for by their former employers, by contributions from those still in employment, or from general taxation. Pay-as-you-go pension schemes are contrasted with funded pension schemes, where current pensions are paid out of a fund built up from contributions during their working lives by members or their employers. A funded pension scheme might be preferable, as the pension fund could be invested, thereby increasing national capital and hence national income. If a country starts from a pay-as-you-go pension scheme, changing over to a funded scheme is difficult, since those whose working lives fall in the transition period will have to pay twice over, once to pay the pensions of the previous generation and again to build up a fund to pay their own pensions.

pay-back period The period during which a firm requires that it get back the cost of new equipment in profits, if it is to invest. Pay-back period is not an economically rational investment criterion: it passes a project which brings in 101 per cent of its cost in the first N years and nothing thereafter, even though the *present discounted value of the expected profits is well below 100 per cent, and fails a project which brings in only 99 per cent of its cost in the first N years, but is expected to do so well later that its present discounted value is 200 per cent of costs. It is, however, used as a rough and ready first step in sorting out projects worthy of closer study.

pay control Control over wage rates, as part of a *prices and incomes policy. As there are thousands of wage rates, no control body could actually determine them all from first principles: pay control has usually been content with limiting increases, either to some percentage or some flat-rate increase. A pay freeze is a particularly drastic form of pay control where the target rate of increase is set at zero.

PAYE *See* pay as you earn.

pay freeze A total standstill on wage rates imposed as part of a *prices and incomes policy. This can only be temporary, as the structure of wage rates at the moment a freeze is imposed is likely to contain anomalies due to the exact timing of the wage–price spiral in the period leading up to the freeze. The structure of wages also needs continual adjustment in the face of changes in techniques and tastes in the economy.

payments, balance of *See* balance of payments.

payment, side- *See* side-payment.

payments in kind Payment of employees in goods or services rather than money. Standard arguments of welfare economics suggest that in the absence of tax-related motives, it is more efficient to pay workers in money and allow them to choose what to buy. If they choose the same goods as they would have received in kind, they are no worse off, and if they choose any other set of goods they are better off with cash payment. In the UK payment of wages in kind is illegal, but many fringe benefits are provided in kind. Tax rules may make this privately beneficial, if it attracts less tax than a cash payment of equal value.

payments union An arrangement by two or more countries to pool their *foreign exchange reserves. The advantage of this is that it reduces the total reserves they need to hold, and sets them free to trade with one another without worrying about the effects on their reserves. The disadvantage is that they need to entrust their monetary policy to a combined central bank, or to agree on co-ordinated monetary policies. Unless this is done, a payments union is liable to find its combined reserves run down by the most extravagent member.

pay-off matrix A matrix showing the pay-offs to each player in a two-sided game. The rows show the results of each choice of *strategy by one player, and the columns the results of each strategy choice by the other. There may be one matrix for the pay-offs to each player; alternatively, each box in a pay-off matrix may contain two figures, for the pay-offs to the two players. In a zero-sum game the pay-offs to the second player are equal and opposite to those for the first, so only one set needs to be shown explicitly.

payroll A list of those employed by a given firm, or the amount paid to them. A payroll tax is a tax on wage payments.

payroll tax A tax on wage payments. The UK's National Insurance contributions, for example, are a payroll tax. Many other countries have similar taxes, which make up a large part of the *tax wedge between the costs of employment and wages received. Payroll taxes tend to discourage employment, so their use seems a strange policy in countries where unemployment is a serious social and economic problem.

peace dividend The resources made available for other purposes if a reduction in international tension allows cuts in defence expenditure. In this context 'peace' refers to a reduction in aggressive intentions towards other countries and/or fears of aggressive conduct from them, rather than formal agreements with them.

peak The highest point of a fluctuation. Where an economic variable has a trend, it may be necessary to distinguish between a peak in the sense of an absolute local maximum, and in the sense of a maximum relative to trend. If a country's real GDP has a trend growth rate of 3 per cent, for example, one may wish to identify as a peak in the trade cycle a year following which GDP growth falls below 3 per cent, even though it is still rising in absolute terms.

peak-load pricing A price structure in which more is charged for units supplied at peak-load periods than for units supplied at other times. The argument for peak-load pricing is that the total *capacity needed for a power, transport, or telephone system is determined by the maximum output it has to provide. If demand fluctuates daily or seasonally, charging higher prices at times of peak-loading makes prices reflect the extra capacity costs imposed by peak-period users. It also gives an incentive for customers who can avoid the peak period at low cost to themselves to do so.

peg, adjustable See adjustable peg.

pendulum arbitration Arbitration in which two sides set out their proposals and the arbitrator is required to choose between them. The parties could be trade unions and employers, or firms involved in a commercial dispute. Frequently arbitrators work by splitting the difference between the parties' claims, so that it pays each party to make exaggerated demands. Pendulum arbitration is designed to avoid this problem by giving each party an incentive to make proposals which the arbitrator will regard as more fair and reasonable than the other side's suggestions.

penetration, import See import penetration.

pension A regular income paid by the state to people above pensionable age, or by former employers to people who have retired from work. State pensions may be conditional on having made contributions to an insurance fund during one's working life. Occupational pensions may be contributory or non-contributory. Pension schemes normally give members pensions for their own lives; they vary in their provision for surviving spouses and other dependents. The self-employed can purchase personal pensions via insurance companies. *See also* occupational pension, pay-as-you-go pensions, and portable pension.

pensionable age The age at which a pension becomes payable, from the state or an occupational pension scheme. This varies between occupations and countries, and in the UK between the sexes.

pension fund A fund from which pensions are paid. Pension funds receive contributions from employers, employees, or both. The funds are then invested to give an income and accrue capital gains until the pensions are paid. Pension schemes may be fully funded, when the fund is actuarially solvent; or partially funded, when the fund relies on the employers to make up the sums necessary to pay for the promised pensions. Pension funds are held by trustees, but these are usually nominated by the employers, and often invest part or all of the accumulated funds in the employer's business.

pension rights Rights to receive pensions, from the state or from former employers. The value of pension rights refers to the actuarial value of expected pension receipts, given the age and other individual characteristics of the pensioner; what is received in any individual case depends on how long they survive to draw the pension. Pension rights are one of the main forms of personal wealth in modern societies. They are, however, a rather illiquid form of wealth: it is not easy to use them as collateral for borrowing.

pension scheme *See* contributory pension scheme, non-contributory pension scheme, under-funded pension scheme, and unfunded pension scheme.

PEP *See* personal equity plan.

per capita income The national income of a country, or region, divided by its population. Per capita income can be calculated per person, counting everybody; per adult; or per 'adult equivalent', using weights to count children of various ages as equivalent to fractions of an adult. Countries or regions with a high proportion of children rank lower when per capita income is compared using a measure which gives more weight to children than using income per adult.

per capita real GDP A country's real GDP per member of the population. This may be calculated using the total population, adults only, or 'adult equivalents', giving children of various ages weights equal to a fraction of an adult. Per capita real GDP is lower than per capita income in a country with net external assets which yield an income, and greater than per capita income in a country with a lot of inward investment, so that net property income payments have to be made abroad.

percentage change The change in a variable, expressed as a percentage of its previous value. If the variable is x_t, the change is defined as $\Delta x_t = x_t - x_{t-1}$, and the percentage change as $100\Delta x_t/x_{t-1}$. For example, if x_t is 50 and x_{t-1} was 40, the percentage change is $100(10)/40 = 25$ per cent.

percentile The values separating hundredth parts of a distribution, arranged in order of size. The 99th percentile of the income distribution, for example, is the income level such that only one per cent of the population have larger incomes.

perfect capital mobility A situation when capital is perfectly free to move between countries. If this occurred, the risk-adjusted returns to capital, net of tax, would be equal in all countries. Perfect capital mobility is prevented partly by controls on capital movements, and partly by lack of information about foreign countries, which makes the risks of investment or lending abroad appear greater than those for home country activities.

perfect competition An ideal market situation in which buyers and sellers are so numerous and well informed that each can act as a price-taker, able to buy or sell any desired quantity without affecting the market price. Although very few real world markets are like this, perfect competition is often regarded by economists as a bench-mark with which to compare actual market situations. Perfect competition is contrasted with monopoly, where there is only one seller, and monopolistic competition, in which there are too few market participants for them to act as price-takers.

perfect equilibrium An equilibrium concept applicable to situations where decisions are made in two or more stages. At every stage all market participants choose whichever strategy is best for them, given the information they have to hand. At every stage but the last, decisions are taken on the assumptions, first, that market participants cannot now alter the decisions taken at earlier stages, even though new information may mean they now regret their previous decisions, and second, that all market participants will choose whatever is best for them at all subsequent stages. It is not consistent with perfect equilibrium to make threats which it would not pay one to carry out.

perfect market A market in which the conditions for perfect competition are satisfied. This implies a homogeneous commodity, and large numbers of buyers and sellers who are well-informed about trading opportunities, none of whom receives preferential treatment.

perfect substitute A good which is indistinguishable in use from another. If two goods are perfect substitutes, their prices must be the same if both are to be used: the elasticity of substitution between them is infinite, and any price difference will lead to all consumers choosing the cheaper. Any *indifference curve between them is a straight line. Goods may be perfect substitutes in some but not all uses, so that only a limited section of any indifference curve between them is linear.

performance-related pay Pay related to the output or profits of the employer. This normally takes the form of bonuses over some agreed rate if the firm does well. Pay may be related to the performance of the firm as a whole, that of a division or part of a firm, or to team or individual results if these can be measured. The argument for performance-related pay is that it provides motivation for effort and co-operation to maximize results for the firm, and that it is good for morale if staff get more when profits are good. An argument against it is that it transfers part of the risks of a firm to its workers, who if they are risk-averse might prefer incomes which were smaller on average, but safer.

peril point A point where any further reduction in US tariffs would, in the opinion of the US Tariff Commission, lower import prices to a level threatening the continued existence of the US domestic industry.

period, accounting *See* accounting period.

period of gestation The period between the start of an investment project and the time when production using it can start. Because this period is usually quite long, particularly for major investment projects, expectations about market conditions when the project is complete are necessarily very uncertain; long gestation periods make investment both more risky and more difficult to predict.

period of oscillation The length of time it takes an oscillatory function to return to any given point in its cycle. The functions $y = a\cos x$ or $z = b\sin x$ have a period of oscillation of 2π; if the cycle reaches a given point, such as its peak, at time t_0, it returns to the same point at times $t = t_0 + 2\pi$, $t = t_0 + 4\pi$, etc. If the oscillatory function takes the form $y = a\cos cx$ or $z = b\sin cx$, the period of oscillation will be $2\pi/c$, and the cycle returns to the same point as it was at t_0 whenever $2\pi/c$ or any integer multiple of it is added to t_0.

periphery An outlying region of an economy, with poor communications and sparse population, which hinder its prosperity. The periphery is contrasted with the core, central regions with good communications and high population density. Some regional economists argue that differences between the periphery and the core tend to increase, as poor facilities in the periphery provoke outward migration and deter investment. Small populations also give peripheral regions low voting power, which causes government policies to be less responsive to peripheral than to core needs.

permanent income The amount that an individual can spend consistently with being able to maintain the same level of spending in the future. This is a forward-looking concept, depending on expected levels of earned income, unearned income, and transfers from the state or other individuals due to be received over a whole lifetime of unknown length. Permanent income cannot be objectively measured, and is extremely difficult even to estimate. Some theories of consumption and liquidity preference suggest that consumption spending and desired money holdings depend on permanent rather than measured income.

permission, planning *See* planning permission.

permit to pollute A permit allowing the emission of a given quantity of pollution to the atmosphere, rivers or the sea. One possible method of restricting pollution is to issue a limited quantity of permits to pollute, and forbid pollution without a permit. If the permits are tradable this means that the limited amount of pollution allowed will be allocated to those firms for which the costs of avoiding it are greatest. If permits are not tradable, the limited amount of pollution will be less efficiently allocated, and the permits will act as restrictions on entry to the industries concerned. Permits to pollute are an alternative to a tax per unit of pollution. If pollution standards are tightened, allocating tradable permits to pollute to firms in proportion to their past emissions gives them some compensation for the tightened standards.

perpetual inventory method The method of estimating a country's total *capital stock, starting from the level of real investment in each past year.

Investment is classified by type of capital goods, such as buildings, plant and machinery, and vehicles. An appropriate rate of write-off each year, based on the estimated lives of the various goods, is applied to each type of capital. The present capital stock is taken to be equal to the sum of past investments, written down in this way. The perpetual inventory method is contrasted with attempts to measure directly the actual levels of different types of capital goods in the economy.

perpetuity A security which yields an income for ever.

perquisites Payments in kind attaching to jobs. These may be of various forms; company cars, company sports facilities, and company medical facilities or insurance are common, and there are some idiosyncratic ones, such as company boxes at the opera. These perquisites are provided openly and some are taxed now; others are subject to periodic attempts by the Inland Revenue to tax them. Other perquisites are less open: pay is subject to tax and national insurance, while minor pilferage connived at by employers is not.

personal disposable income Personal incomes after deduction of income tax and national insurance contributions. This is the sum available to be divided between personal savings and consumption.

personal equity plan (PEP) A UK system, established in 1986, by which individuals could invest a limited sum each tax year in shares and unit trusts, through a financial intermediary. PEP investments were then free from both income and capital gains tax, subject to a minimum holding period. The financial intermediaries charged for their services in managing PEPs. PEPs were introduced to encourage savings, and to promote individual involvement in the company sector. They were replaced by Individual Savings Accounts (ISAs) in 1999.

personal income distribution The distribution of income between different individuals. This can be measured before or after the deduction of direct taxes and receipt of income transfers. Personal income distribution is distinguished from *functional income distribution, which is concerned with the division of total incomes between the owners of different factors of production.

Personal Investment Authority (PIA) A UK Self-Regulating Organization (SRO) under the *Securities and Investment Board (SIB), responsible for regulating the branches of the investment business dealing mainly with private investors. The PIA was formed in 1994 by merging the Financial Intermediaries, Managers and Brokers Regulatory Association (FIMBRA) and the Life Assurance and Unit Trust Regulatory Organization (LAUTRO).

personal loan A loan, usually from a bank, to an individual, who is not necessarily required to produce any specific security for it. Personal loans are widely used to finance the purchase of expensive items such as cars and furniture. Repayment is usually at an agreed rate over a period of months or years. Personal loans are more risky for the lenders than secured loans such as mortgages, and normally bear higher interest rates. They are, however, usually a cheaper method of financing than *hire purchase.

personal preferences Individual tastes, as regards both consumption and work. No two individuals are precisely the same in their choices between the available goods and services to consume and work to perform. This means that it is not possible to find a *utility function which will predict what every individual will do in response to any given set of prices and wage rates. Industry demand curves for goods and supply curves of labour are based on the average behaviour of large numbers of individuals, not on precise observation of a uniform behaviour pattern. The existence of innumerable idiosyncratic differences between individuals is a strong argument for making use of the *price mechanism in distributing goods and tasks between them.

personal sector The part of the UK economy consisting of households, unincorporated businesses, life assurance and pension funds, and private non-profit-making bodies serving persons, such as charities. This is distinguished from the corporate sector, consisting of companies, financial institutions and public corporations, and the government sector.

PESC *See* Public Expenditure Survey Committee.

peso problem The tendency in countries with a past history of high inflation for interest rates to remain higher than abroad. This problem occurs where experience of inflation and currency depreciation in the past has led to expectations that the future will be similar. Even if such a country succeeds in stabilizing its price level and exchange rate, until market expectations adjust to this new stability, interest rates remain higher than in countries whose currencies are expected to remain stable. An interest premium is needed to compensate both domestic and foreign investors for the risk they feel exposed to when holding a currency whose stability they mistrust. The name 'peso problem' links it to Mexico, but many other countries, including the UK, have suffered from the same problem.

petro-currency The currency of a country heavily dependent on oil exports. The exchange rate of a petro-currency is strongly influenced by the world price of oil.

petro-dollars Balance-of-payments surpluses of oil-exporting countries which were invested abroad, often in US dollar securities.

Phillips curve A curve plotting the rate of increase of wages against unemployment. Lower unemployment is associated with greater increases in wages. The original Phillips curve was named after its inventor. The model has since been extended in two ways. First, the rate of inflation is often shown instead of wage increases, on the assumption that wage increases will lead to price increases, and that low unemployment is associated with excess demand, which leads directly to price increases. Second, the model has been extended to take account of inflationary expectations; the short-run *expectations-augmented Phillips curve plots actual inflation against unemployment, with given inflation expectations. In the long run it is assumed that *rational expectations leads the expected inflation rate to equal the actual rate, so that the long-run Phillips curve is very steep or even vertical at the *non-accelerating inflation rate of unemployment (NAIRU).

The horizontal axis shows the unemployment rate. The vertical axis shows the rate of wage increase. The Phillips curve *ABC* is drawn for a given level of expected price increase. *B* corresponds to the level of unemployment, *OD*, which gives rise to wage increases consistent with the expected rate of price inflation. Wage increases can exceed price increases to the extent that

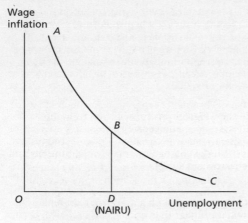

Wage inflation

FIGURE 25: *Phillips Curve*

productivity is rising. *OD* is thus the non-accelerating inflation rate of unemployment (NAIRU). If actual unemployment is less than *OD*, inflation increases and *ABC* shifts upwards; if actual unemployment is greater than *OD*, inflation falls and *ABC* shifts downwards. *ABC* is usually assumed, as drawn, to be concave upwards: low unemployment is more effective in increasing inflation than high unemployment is in reducing it. *See also* expectations-augmented Phillips curve.

physical capital Capital in the form of physical goods, either fixed capital or stocks and work in progress. Physical capital is contrasted with both financial and human capital. Financial capital includes both cash holdings of firms, and net trade credit extended to customers. *Human capital includes both technical know-how, whether or not embodied in patents, and the skills of the workforce. The ability of economies to recover rapidly after wars and natural disasters is thought to indicate that physical capital is less important than human capital as a long-run determinant of productivity.

phytosanitary measures Restrictions on trade designed to protect the health of humans, animals or plants. While some restrictions on trade are necessary to prevent the spread of diseases such as BSE or foot and mouth, there is a danger that restrictions purporting to be phytosanitary will be used to protect domestic producers of the goods concerned.

pi (Greek letter π) The ratio of the circumference of a circle to its diameter. π is a constant, equal to 3.141593 to six decimal places; π is a transcendental number whose value cannot be given precisely in any number of decimal places. Upper case Π is used to express the product of N numbers $x_1, x_2, \ldots, x_N$ in the form $P_x = \Pi_i x_i$. Lower case π and upper case Π are also widely used in economics to stand for variables ad hoc.

PIA *See* Personal Investment Authority.

picket, flying *See* flying picket.

picketing The procedure during *strikes of placing strikers outside workplaces to inform other workers that they are in dispute, and to attempt to persuade other employees, and those of suppliers and customers, not to enter the premises. Actual picketing varies between the normal procedure of entirely peaceful demonstrations by small numbers of strikers outside their own workplaces, and very occasional violent intimidation by large numbers at the premises of firms not involved in a strike.

picking winners The idea that governments can promote economic development by selecting particular projects for financial and technical support. This form of industrial strategy only promotes economic growth if the government is better than private investors at picking projects likely to succeed. The strategy runs two risks: the government may support projects which would have been adopted anyway, so that its support merely makes them more profitable; or it may pick too high a proportion of unsuccessful projects. The alternative is for governments to concentrate on providing general technical education to produce a skilled labour force, and promoting efficient financial markets to provide capital, and leave private businesses to select the most suitable particular projects for development.

piecewise linear function A function which consists of a number of linear sections, with different slopes. The function relating UK income tax payable to taxable income, for example, is piecewise linear: from 0 to some threshold level no tax is payable, then there is a band with a lower rate, then a band with basic rate payable, and then a point above which tax is payable at the higher rate.

piecework The system of pay by which a worker's wages are proportional to output produced. This system is suitable only when a worker's output can be reliably measured, and when variations do not arise from factors over which the worker has no control, for example late delivery of materials. It is contrasted with time rates, where pay simply depends on hours worked.

pie diagram A diagram used to display the relative size of variables. For example, the shares of a country's exports going to various regions of the world can be shown by the size of their slices of a circular pie. Pie diagrams can also be used to compare totals, for example a country's total exports at different dates. A circle with a radius λ times that of another has an area λ^2 times as great: pie diagrams with radii of 1 and $\sqrt{2}$ can be used to show, for example, that exports doubled between 1980 and 1990.

Panel 1: Shares in period 1 are shown by the relative sizes of slices A, B and C. These could be shares in anything, for example output in three sectors of the economy.

Panel 2: Shares in period 2 are shown in the same way. The size of the diagram is unchanged, so only changes in shares can be shown.

Panel 3: Shows both changes in shares, found by comparing the angle of each slice at the centre of the circle with Panel 1, and changes in total quantities, shown by the size of the pie. Multiplying the radius by λ multiplies the area by λ^2, so if the radius of the Panel 3 pie is twice that of Panels 1 or 2, it shows that the total quantities concerned were 4 times as large.

Pigou effect The argument that price and wage flexibility could prevent unemployment. If prices and wages fell sufficiently in a slump, full

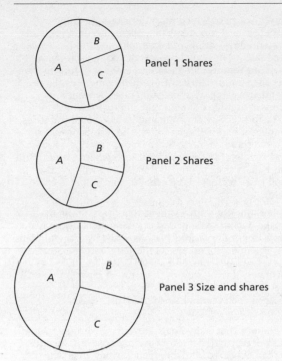

Panel 1 Shares

Panel 2 Shares

Panel 3 Size and shares

FIGURE 26: *Pie Diagrams*

employment would be restored because of the resulting increase in the real money supply. In practice nobody relies on such a mechanism. In an economy with money debts, large falls in prices would damage the solvency of many firms, and probably cause the collapse of some financial institutions. Perfectly flexible prices and wages might ensure real stability in the economy; if prices and wages fell gradually, however, the prospect of further falls to come would bring the liquidity trap into play, with adverse effects on real spending, so the short-term effects of greater price and wage flexibility might well make slumps worse. In practice nobody knows how far prices would have to fall before increased real balances started a recovery.

Pink Book The Office for National Statistics (ONS), formerly the Central Statistical Office (CSO) annual publication, *United Kingdom Balance of Payments*. This is a source of data on UK visible and invisible trade, capital movements, and overseas assets and liabilities.

placing Sale of shares by a UK company to selected individuals or institutions approached directly, rather than by an issue open to the general public. A placing may be preferred on grounds of lower costs, or because it gives the company a chance to choose its new shareholders.

planned economy An economy in which the government takes all major decisions about what should be produced and who should get it. This is contrasted with a market economy, in which most decisions are taken by independent individuals and firms. Proponents of a planned economy claim that planning enables wasteful duplication and unemployment to be avoided and goods to be distributed fairly. The actual process of taking decisions and seeing that they are carried out requires an enormous amount of information and officials to administer the system. Critics of planned economies claim that they have been bad at discovering what consumers really want and motivating firms to produce it, and have shown inflexibility in the face of a changing environment. The former Soviet Union and its associated countries provided large-scale examples of planned economies. The results proved so unsatisfactory that since 1990 these countries have shifted towards a more market-based system. Most real world economies fall somewhere between full central planning and a pure market economy. In the UK, for example, the government directs several large sectors of the economy, including defence, roads, education and health.

planned investment The amount of investment that firms, individuals, or public bodies intend to make during some period. Actual investment may not correspond to planned investment for various reasons. Fixed investment plans may be frustrated because the investment goods required cannot be obtained, as is likely in booms, or because the arrangements for financing the expenditure collapse, as is likely during slumps. Investment in stocks may fall short of planned levels because of unforeseen increases in demand, or may exceed planned levels because goods cannot be sold, so that stocks accumulate until production can be cut back.

planned savings The amount that individuals, firms, or governments plan to save. Savings plans may not be carried out for two main reasons. Income may be larger or smaller than expected, and emergencies may arise which require unanticipated spending or prevent spending plans from being carried out. Planned savings should be distinguished from contractual savings, such as mortgage repayments or life insurance premiums. Individuals are committed to such savings by contracts which may be impossible or expensive to break, but there are many other forms of savings, and it is perfectly possible to plan to fund contractual savings by incurring debts or running down other assets.

planning, central *See* central planning.

planning (land-use) Controls by central or local government over the use of land. These are widely used, because of the importance of *externalities resulting from land use. Land-use planning is used to keep activities causing harmful externalities, such as noise or visual intrusion, away from places where they are believed to be particularly harmful. Land-use controls usually operate more strictly on changes of use and new activities than on continuation of existing activities.

planning permission Permission granted by local or central government for the owners of land to use it for specific purposes. Normally permission has to be sought for changes in land use, for example from agriculture to residential use, or from residential to shops or offices. Planning permission for a transfer of land from a less to a more profitable use may add a great deal to land values.

player The term used in *game theory for any participant in a situation being modelled. A player is any individual, firm, or government that has to make a choice between different *strategies.

PLC *See* public limited company.

plough-back The system of financing investment in firms by retaining profits. This is contrasted with financing investment by borrowing or issuing new *equity capital. The advantage of plough-back is that it retains control, and reduces *gearing if the firm has borrowed in the past. The disadvantage is that complete reliance on internal finance limits a firm's possible growth rate, and it cannot be applied in new firms.

point, basis *See* basis point.

point elasticity The ratio of a proportional change in one variable to that of another, measured at a point. For example, if p is price and q is quantity, the elasticity of demand is defined as $-(p/q)(dq/dp)$. This is the limit of $-(\Delta q/q)/(\Delta p/p)$ as Δp and Δq tend to zero. In contrast to arc elasticity, which is defined for finite changes in p and q and can thus be based on direct measurement, point elasticity can only be found by statistical inference, fitting a continuous function $q = f(p)$ to the actual observations, and calculating the elasticity by differentiating this function.

point of inflection A point where a function changes its curvature. This means that its *second derivative changes sign. For example, consider the function $y = ax^3 + bx$, for which $dy/dx = 3ax^2 + b$ and $d^2y/dx^2 = 6ax$. The sign of d^2y/dx^2 thus changes when $x = 0$; if $a > 0$, $d^2y/dx^2 < 0$ for negative x and $d^2y/dx^2 > 0$ for positive x. y thus has a point of inflection at $x = 0$. This may not be a stationary value: in the case above y is stationary at $x = 0$ if and only if $b = 0$.

points (change in index) The change in an index in terms of the units in which it is measured. If a stock exchange index, for example, moves from 456 to 459, it rises by 3 points. This is contrasted with the percentage increase, which is $3/456 = 0.66$ per cent.

polarization The rule introduced by the UK Securities and Investment Board (SIB) that bodies such as banks and building societies must choose either to give independent advice on all brands of life insurance and unit trusts, or confine themselves to selling the products of only one company. The intention was to ensure either that advice was truly independent, or that customers were aware that it was not. The actual effect may have been to reduce the amount of information available to consumers of investment products.

policy(ies) *See* beggar-my-neighbour policy, commercial policy, competition policy, discretionary policy, fiscal policy, mix of policies, monopoly policy, prices and incomes policy, regional policy, reputational policy, rules-based policy, stabilization policy, and supply-side policy.

policy co-ordination The argument that national fiscal and monetary policies would produce better results if countries collaborated. The fiscal and monetary policies followed in each country have effects abroad as well as at home. Policy co-ordination points out that better results could be obtained if each country made less use of policies which harmed other countries than they would choose independently, and more use of policies that benefited the others. The benefits of policy co-ordination also apply to collaboration between the monetary and fiscal authorities within a country.

policy, credit *See* credit control.

policy instrument A policy measure under the control of the monetary or fiscal authorities. This could be a measure such as a change in the money supply or in tax rates, or the imposition of price or quantitative controls. Policy instruments are distinguished from policy targets and policy indicators. Policy targets are aims such as high employment and low inflation; the authorities cannot decide these, but can only try to influence them through policy instruments. Policy indicators are used in taking policy decisions; the indicators are not necessarily themselves targets, but may be used in deciding policy in preference to targets, because they can be measured more reliably or earlier than the targets.

policy measures *See* opaque policy measures, and transparent policy measures.

political business cycle The theory that some economic fluctuations are due to governments seeking political advantage by expanding the economy in advance of elections. Governments may also choose to make painful reforms immediately after elections, to give the electorate a chance to forget the pain and start reaping the benefits in time for the next election.

political economy The original name of what is now known as economics. The name is still used by some Economics departments. It can be argued that it is actually a better name for the subject, as it draws attention to the political motivation of economic policies: policy-makers and lobbyists are often more concerned with the income distribution than with the efficiency effects of policies.

poll tax A lump-sum tax levied on every citizen at the same rate regardless of income. A poll tax is necessarily regressive, taking a larger proportion of small incomes than of large ones. The UK *Community Charge of 1989–93, though it was labelled 'the poll tax' by its critics, was not a true poll tax, as it had exemptions for some citizens and lower rates for some taxpayers taking account of their lower incomes. Because of income inequalities, the total revenue it is possible to raise by a poll tax is very limited.

pollution Damage to the environment by the emission of noxious substances, which may be dirty, toxic, radioactive, or sources of infection. This may affect water, air, or land surfaces, in some cases over wide areas. Pollution resulting from economic activities is a major source of *external diseconomies. *See* also permit to pollute.

pollution control Methods of reducing pollution. These include taxing polluting activities, and the imposition of quantitative restrictions on pollution. Quantitative methods may take the form of prohibition of polluting activities, the imposition of pollution standards, which limit the permissible amount of pollution per unit of an activity, or the issue of a restriced number of permits to pollute, which may or may not be tradable. Prohibition of pollution may not be possible if there is no alternative production method available. Longer-term policies to reduce pollution include education of firms and the public about its effects, which can reduce pollution when cheap alternatives are available, and research into alternative less- or non-polluting technology. Restriction of the overall level of economic activity could reduce pollution, but is unlikely to be acceptable to any but the richest countries for the foreseeable future.

pollution standards The method of controlling *externalities by laying down standards for polluting activities. Firms may, for example, be required to clean waste products up to some minimum standard before discharging them into rivers or sewers, or there may be standards of maximum tolerated emissions from road vehicles. Standards are contrasted with the use of the price mechanism to control pollution, by taxing emissions of polluting substances. A disadvantage of emission standards is that in order to avoid crippling economic activity, some level of pollution must be allowed: having reached this, a standard gives firms no incentive to reduce pollution further. Also, the costs of avoiding pollution are higher for some firms than others: a tax will reduce emissions where they are most cheaply avoided, whereas under a standard the marginal cost of reducing pollution to the permitted level may vary widely between firms.

polynomial A function of the form $y = f(x)$, defined in terms of a sum of terms each of which is a coefficient times a power of x. A linear function is a first-order polynomial, such as

$$y = ax + b.$$

A quadratic is a second-order polynomial, such as

$$y = ax^2 + bx + c.$$

A cubic is a third-order polynomial, such as

$$y = ax^3 + bx^2 + cx + d.$$

In all cases it is assumed that $a \neq 0$, though any of the remaining coefficients may be zero. An Nth order polynomial takes the form

$$y = a_N x^N + a_{N-1} x^{N-1} + \ldots + a_0.$$

An Nth order polynomial can be shown to have N roots, that is N values of x for which $y = 0$. These roots may be real, imaginary or complex numbers. If the N roots are known, y can be factorized, that is, written as

$$y = a_N (x - r_1)(x - r_2) \ldots (x - r_N).$$

Linear and quadratic polynomial equations can be solved analytically by simple formulae. The cubic can in principle be solved analytically, but the procedure is so complicated that numerical methods are normally used instead. For quartics and above numerical methods have to be used to find the roots of polynomial equations.

population census *See* census.

population trap A situation where no increase in living standards is possible, because population is increasing so fast that all available savings are needed to maintain the existing capital–labour ratio. This is the position of some less developed countries (LDCs), especially in Sub-Saharan Africa. Escape from the trap requires an increase in savings, a cut in population growth, or both.

portable pension An occupational pension which allows a person to change employers without loss of *pension rights. A pension may be made portable when an employee leaves a firm in two ways. One method is for the employee's accrued pension contributions to be frozen in the former employer's pension fund until the employee reaches pensionable age, when the fund will pay part of their pension. The other method is for the former employer to transfer an agreed capital sum equal to the present discounted value of accrued pension rights either to the new employer's pension fund, or to a personal pension scheme, independent of any employer, operated by an insurance company.

portfolio A set of different assets in the possession of an individual or firm. A variety of assets may be preferred to holding a single type of asset for several reasons. Holding a variety of assets reduces risk, and allows a combination of some assets with higher income but poor *liquidity, and others with lower income but more liquidity. Large institutions may also hold a variety of assets because there is not enough of some attractive assets to absorb all their funds or, more likely, if they invested all they could in any one asset their holding would be too large relative to the market to be liquid. *See also* loan portfolio, and property portfolio.

portfolio selection The choice of the proportions of different assets which should be held in order to obtain the maximum expected benefit from any given stock of wealth. This depends on both the characteristics of various assets and the objectives of the person or institution holding them. Assets differ in their yield, either in the form of the mean expected income or capital appreciation, and in their riskiness. Riskiness depends both on the frequency distribution of their expected returns and on its correlation with the returns expected on other assets. The variance of expected returns, and covariance with other assets, are often used in portfolio selection, but these are not the only possible measures of risk. If variance is taken as the appropriate measure of risk, an efficient portfolio is one which gives the minimum variance available with any given expected mean returns, or the maximum returns available accepting any level of variance. As the returns on various securities are not perfectly correlated, the variance of returns on a portfolio can be reduced by holding more different securities. However, after a quite limited number the increased transactions costs of smaller holdings means that further diversification does not pay. The choice of which efficient portfolio to hold depends on the degree of *risk-aversion of the investor. An individual pensioner, or a pension fund, may have a strong preference for a safe income, without much concern about short-term fluctuations in capital value. A bank or other financial intermediary may have a much stronger preference for stable capital values, even at the cost of a variable income.

port, free *See* free port.

position *See* long position, open position, and short position.

positive Greater than zero. If this means strictly greater than zero it is written $x > 0$; if the inequality is of the weak form, including $x = 0$ as a borderline case, it is written $x \geq 0$.

positive economics The study of how economic processes work. As it is concerned with what actually happens, it needs a lot of institutional and statistical information. Positive economics is contrasted with *normative economics, which is concerned with how the economy ought to be run. Positive economics also analyses how economic processes would work given certain assumptions about institutional conditions, for example the existence of monopoly, or about motivation, for example profit maximization. To analyse what would happen given certain assumptions, positive economics uses models, which are stylized and simplified representations of the real world. Economic policy needs to be based on both positive and normative economics. Normative economics helps determine the aims of policy, but competence at positive economics is essential for policy-makers, since any policy, however laudable its objectives, is bound to fail if it is not capable of producing the results aimed at.

post, ex *See* ex post.

Post Office Savings *See* National Savings.

potential competition Competition from possible as well as actual rivals. If an industry has constant returns to scale and freedom of entry, potential competition is a powerful deterrent to monopolistic conduct by existing firms, even if the industry currently has a highly concentrated structure. *Limit pricing is setting of prices by incumbent firms low enough to deter entry by potential competitors.

potential output The output which could be produced with the available labour, capital, and technology. For an individual firm, potential output is the output that could be produced with present capital and technology, allowing for recruitment of necessary unskilled labour. In some cases old and inefficient capital equipment could only be used profitably at higher output prices. Potential output for the economy as a whole is not necessarily the sum of potential output for all firms, since while any one firm could obtain extra inputs of fuel and unskilled labour, it might not be feasible for them all to expand at once. In any case, many firms have spare capacity suitable only for producing goods of particular sorts: total potential output thus depends on the composition of extra demand.

pound (£) The UK currency unit; this is often referred to as the pound sterling. The name is also used for the currency units of several other countries, including Cyprus, Egypt, Lebanon, and Syria. If no type of pound is specified, the reference is normally to sterling, unless the context suggests that it is the local currency unit.

poverty Inability to afford an adequate standard of consumption. What this standard is once actual starvation is avoided is very much subject to variation between countries and over time. Economists have differed as to whether poverty should be considered in absolute terms, as falling below some fixed minimum consumption level, or whether it should be defined in relative terms, so that poverty means inability to afford what average people have. If an absolute standard is accepted it is at least conceivable that technical progress will eventually lift everybody above the poverty line. If poverty is relative, the poor will be always with us. The *poverty line is an income level supposed to be just enough to avoid inadequate consumption. The *poverty trap is a tax and social security system which makes it difficult for the poor to escape from poverty.

poverty line An income level supposed to be just enough to avoid inadequate consumption. Where this level lies depends on numerous factors: people vary in their number of dependents; in the extent to which they are addicted to expensive vices including alcohol and tobacco; in their need to pay interest on loans contracted because of previous over-spending of their incomes; and in their competence at spending such money as they have. Societies vary in the extent to which some needs, like medical attention, are provided for communally. Because of these variations, poverty is likely to cause considerable suffering unless the minimum income level is kept somewhat above what would suffice for an average family with average intelligence, no debts, no vices, and perfect health.

poverty trap A situation when *means-tested benefits mean that a person does not gain from moving from unemployment into a job, or from obtaining a better-paid job. They may be no better off, or even worse off financially than before, or too little better off to make the extra effort appear worth while. The poverty trap thus tends to perpetuate unemployment and low productivity work.

power 1. Strength in arranging the terms of one's dealing with other firms or people. *See* bargaining power, countervailing power, and monopoly power.
  2. An instruction to multiply a number of times. The nth power of x is 1 multiplied by x, n times; n is the exponent of x. Powers may be positive or negative; x^{-n} is one divided by x, n times. They may also be fractional; if $y = x^{1/m}$, y is the mth root of x.

PPP *See* purchasing power parity.

practices, restrictive *See* restrictive practices.

precautionary motive The motive to hold money to provide for the unexpected. This is distinguished from the transactions and speculative motives.Whereas the *transactions motive is to hold money for convenience in transactions which are anticipated, the precautionary motive is to hold money to deal with transactions necessary because of emergencies or problems whose precise nature cannot be anticipated.

pre-commitment *See* commitment.

predatory pricing Pricing low with the intention of driving rivals out of a market or preventing new firms from entering. This is good for consumers in the short run, but may be bad in the long run if a firm which has used predatory pricing to establish a *monopoly position then raises its prices.

predetermined endogenous variable A variable in a dynamic economic system which is determined within the system, but by past and not current variables. At any one time it is thus independent of other variables in the system. The capital stock, for example, is historically determined at any moment by past investment, but the past investment itself was determined within the economic system and not exogenously given.

preference(s) *See* consistent preferences, liquidity preference, personal preferences, revealed preference, single-peaked preferences, and time preference.

preference share A company share which carries no vote, but ranks before ordinary shares for dividends.

premium 1. The price paid for an insurance policy. This may be a monthly or annual payment, or it is possible to take out a single-premium policy by a lump-sum payment.

2. A share price higher than the issue price. A share traded at a price higher than its issue price stands at a premium.

3. An addition to interest rates required to compensate lenders for risk. *See* risk premium.

4. A suggestion of superior quality, as in premium petrol.

5. A premium bond is a UK government security offering monthly prizes instead of interest.

premium bond A UK government security where the interest goes into a fund which provides for lotteries held at regular intervals, in which all bond-holders are entered. In the UK premium bond scheme the prizes are tax-free.

prescriptive statement A statement about what ought to be, as opposed to a positive statement which is concerned only with facts. In many cases statements which are formally of one type carry strong implications of the other. 'Smoking can seriously damage your health', for example, is in form purely positive, but carries the prescriptive implication 'so don't smoke'.

present discounted value The present value of a payment due to be received in the future. If the payment is due t periods into the future and the proportional interest rate is r per period, the present discounted value of a sum A to be received t periods in the future is given by

$V = A/(1 + r)^t = A(1 + r)^{-t}.$

The present dicounted value of a stream of receipts spread over time is the sum of the present discounted values of the various parts of the stream.

present value, net *See* net present value.

pressure group An organization trying to bring about changes in laws or policies. These may be in the interests of its members, or of some wider cause such as the environment. Pressure groups may work via various forms of propaganda or public demonstration, or via lobbying of national and local governments.

pre-tax profits The profits of a company before deduction of corporation tax, or of an unincorporated business before deduction of income tax. In each case pre-tax profit is calculated after deduction of other taxes the business has to pay, including value-added tax (VAT), business rates, and employers' national insurance contributions (NICs).

price The amount of money paid per unit for a good or service. This is easy to observe for many goods and services: in any ordinary shop, customers will find displayed a price at which as many or few units as they wish can be purchased. For some goods and services, however, price is less easy to observe. Special terms may be available for large orders, for repeat orders, or for particular types of customer. In some markets buyers and sellers haggle over the price of each item. The price of similar goods varies over time and place, and goods with the same name vary in quality. A price index measures the prices of goods of some specified type: for example, consumer goods, raw materials, or exports. Wholesale prices are the prices charged by wholesalers; factory gate prices are the prices charged by manufacturers.

The **price mechanism** refers to the role of prices in organizing the production and distribution of goods and services in an economy: the prices people are willing to pay convey information about the valuation they put on different goods and services, and the prices charged by suppliers convey information on how they value the effort and inputs needed for production. Shadow prices are the prices that economic model-builders believe would need to be charged if consumers and producers were to be induced to take full account of external costs and benefits.

In national income accounting, market prices are the prices consumers pay. The prices facing producers, equal to market prices minus indirect taxes plus subsidies, are referred to as factor cost. Current prices are the prices prevailing at the time when transactions take place; constant prices are the prices of some chosen base period, used to revalue transactions to obtain a measure of real activity. *See also* administered price, ceiling price, closing prices, current prices, distorted prices, exercise price, exit price, factor prices, flexible prices, floor price, forward price, law of one price, market prices, mid-market price, opening prices, relative prices, shadow prices, spot price, shut-down price, sticky prices, and strike price.

price and quantity adjustment *See* adjustment, price and quantity.

price control The setting of maximum prices by law. This may affect particular markets, for example domestic rents are often subject to special controls, or apply in an economy generally. As it is administratively impossible to set millions of prices from first principles, price controls have generally worked by covering a limited number of essential goods, and imposing limits or a total ban on price increases. There is a danger that this will induce firms to divert resources towards goods whose prices are not controlled, and to change the specifications of goods to introduce new products to which the rules do not apply.

price discrimination Charging different prices to different customers for the same good or service. This is possible only if the supplier has some monopoly power, and can identify the customer, and if the customer cannot resell the good, or it is expensive to do so. Price discrimination is profitable for a monopolist if different customers have different *elasticities of demand, so that marginal revenue in different markets is equal only if price is not. First-degree price discrimination implies selling every unit at the maximum the consumer would pay, so that there is no consumer surplus and the producer takes all potential benefits from a good. Producers usually lack the information needed to discriminate this much, but first-degree price discrimination defines an upper limit to what producers can gain. Second-degree price discrimination occurs when producers cannot tell which group customers belong to, but offer alternative contracts which induce consumers to identify themselves. Third-degree price discrimination occurs when sellers can identify different groups of customers, and offer different prices to each group.

price–earnings ratio (P/E ratio) The ratio of the current market price of a company's ordinary shares to its most recently published earnings for equity per share. A relatively high price–earnings ratio may mean that earnings are expected to grow rapidly, or that they are regarded as relatively safe. A low price–earnings ratio indicates either that earnings are expected to grow slowly or fall, or that the company is regarded as relatively risky.

price elasticity The ratio of a proportional change in quantity supplied or demanded to a proportional change in price. The elasticity of supply is $(p/q)\,(dq/dp)$, where p is price and q is quantity. The elasticity of demand is usually defined as $-(p/q)(dq/dp)$, so that it is normally positive; not all authors adopt this usage, which needs to be checked.

price fixing Agreement between two or more firms about the prices they will charge. This is considered to be anti-competitive, and is forbidden by monopoly legislation in many countries.

price index An index number of the prices of goods of some given type. If only one good i is concerned, period 0 is the base period and period t the current period, where p_{it} is the price in period t, the price index is given by p_{it}/p_{i0}. This gives the index in ratio form: to obtain it in percentage form multiply by 100. If a class of goods $i = 1, 2, \ldots, N$ is concerned, the price index is a weighted average of the indices of their prices. The weights are the values of the goods purchased in some period. If q_{it} is the quantity of good i in period t, the base-weighted or Laspeyres price index is defined as $p_B = (\Sigma_i\, p_{it}\, q_{i0})/(\Sigma_i\, p_{i0}\, q_{i0})$ and the current-weighted or Paasche price index is defined as $p_C = (\Sigma_i\, p_{it}\, q_{it})/(\Sigma_i\, p_{i0}\, q_{it})$. Again these are in ratio form: to obtain them in percentage form multiply by 100. Price indices can also be found for securities or wage rates.

price index, commodity *See* commodity price index.

price leader A firm whose price changes tend to be followed by other sellers in its markets. This may be by agreement, which is illegal under monopoly legislation in many countries, or by collusion, which is considered anti-competitive but is difficult to prevent. A price leader may be a particularly large firm, or one with particularly aggressive management.

price level The general level of prices in an economy. This may refer to consumer goods prices, in which case it is measured by a *retail price index (RPI), or to all goods produced, including investment and government purchases as well as consumer goods, in which case it is measured by a *GDP deflator. *Inflation is a persistent increase in the price level.

price-maker A firm which sets the price of a good or security, by offering to buy and sell at announced prices. To act effectively as a market-maker it is necessary to hold a stock of the good, so as to be able to provide it when buying orders exceed selling, and a stock of money in order to be able to buy the good when selling orders exceed buying. The market-maker's selling, or offer, price will exceed its buying, or bid, price, to provide a margin to cover expenses and profits on capital employed. A price-maker is contrasted with a price-taker, which is a competitive firm or individual who has to treat the market price as given.

price mechanism An expression referring to the role of prices in a market economy in conveying information and providing incentives. The market mechanism is an alternative phrase making the same point. The prices people are willing to pay for goods and services convey information about how much they value them, and the prices producers ask convey information about how their inputs are valued. The price mechanism provides incentives to allocate resources where their value is highest, and to satisfy wants from the cheapest sources. Quantities also convey information under the price mechanism, however. In many markets price is set in the short run by a market-maker, who derives from the quantities bought and sold at these prices information about how prices should change.

price reform The shift from arbitrary controlled prices towards a system in which prices reflect opportunity costs. Such a shift is a principal element in the transition from a centrally planned to a *market economy. Systems of price control have typically fixed some prices too low relative to opportunity costs. This has led to excess demand, as there was too little incentive to provide such goods or to economize on their use. The two dangers of price reform are that decontrol of prices may lead to rapid *inflation, and that large changes in relative prices may have adverse effects on some people's real incomes. Actual price reform programmes may therefore stop short of a total and instant abolition of controls. The merit of price reform is that it helps to lead to more efficient production, and to an end to perpetual shortages and the wastes involved in eternal queuing.

prices and incomes policy Attempts by government to control prices and incomes directly, by persuasion or law. Such policies are distinguished from influencing prices and wages through monetary and fiscal policies, or setting prices by acting as a buyer or seller in particular markets. There are far too many prices in a modern economy for the task of setting them all from first principles to be administratively feasible. Prices and incomes policies therefore tend to work either by setting some important prices and leaving others to the market, or setting limits to price increases. Either alternative produces distortions in the structure of relative prices, and becomes increasingly difficult to enforce as time passes. Economists tend to agree that prices and incomes policies cannot in the long run be a substitute for effective monetary, fiscal, and supply-side policies. They disagree about how far prices and incomes policies may help in the short run to gain time for other measures to work, or speed up convergence to equilibrium.

price-sensitive information Information about a company which could affect its share price. This includes figures on profits, employment, turnover, innovations, mineral finds, changes in senior management, or takeover bids. Preferential access to price-sensitive information is what makes 'insider traders' insiders. *See also* insider dealing.

price support Government policies to keep the prices of commodities up to some minimum level. This applies mainly to agricultural products, to raise the incomes of producers. Price support works either by buying the product to prevent the market price from falling, or by paying the producer a subsidy to cover any shortfall of market price below the support price.

price-taker An individual or firm trading on a market where they do not believe that their own transactions will affect the market price. This may be because there are large numbers of traders on each side in a perfect market, or because the individual or firm is a small trader on a market where the price is fixed by a market-maker.

price volatility The extent to which a price fluctuates. Fluctuations may be measured on any time-scale, from year-by-year to minute-by-minute. Volatility over short time intervals tends to be lower when prices are administered than when they are set in a competitive market. Price volatility over any time interval tends to be higher when supply, demand, or both are liable to large random shocks, and when the elasticity of both supply and demand is low. Price volatility tends to be higher for commodities, shares, and exchange rates than for industrial products.

price–wage spiral *See* wage–price spiral.

price war Charging low prices to harm competitors' profits. In a price war one or more firms charge prices below those that would maximize their own profits, to inflict losses on rivals. A price war may aim to punish competitors for breaking a cartel agreement, to weaken their finances to force acceptance of a takeover bid, or to drive them out of business completely.

pricing *See* average cost pricing, cost-plus pricing, full cost pricing, limit pricing, marginal cost pricing, peak-load pricing, and transfer pricing.

primary sector The sector of the economy making direct use of natural resources. This includes agriculture, forestry and fishing, and extractive industries producing fuel, metals, and other minerals. This is contrasted with the secondary sector, producing manufactures and other processed goods, and the tertiary sector producing services. The primary sector is usually most important in less developed countries (LDCs); in industrial countries it is normally less important.

principal 1. A person or firm employing another to act as their agent. A person using an estate agent to sell a house, for example, is a principal; the estate agent is the agent. The principal–agent problem is concerned with how agents can be induced to act in the interests of their principals rather than their own.
  2. The amount lent at the start of a loan.

principal–agent problem The problem of how person A can motivate person B to act for A's benefit rather than following self-interest. The principal, A, may be an employer and the agent, B, an employee, or the principal may be a shareholder and the agent a director of a company. The problem is how to devise incentives which lead agents to report truthfully to the principal on the facts they face and the actions they take, and to act for the principal's benefit. Incentives include rewards such as bonuses or promotion for success, and penalties such as demotion or dismissal for failure to act in the principal's interests.

prior The initial value attached to a parameter in Bayesian statistics. The prior is regularly revised using a weighted average of the prior and the most recent obervations. The prior itself is not explained: it may derive from other people's observations, economic theory, rumour, or pure guesswork. The important point is that however beliefs originated, in Bayesian models they are revised in the light of experience.

prisoners' dilemma A game theory concept showing the disadvantages of not being able to reach binding agreements. The name originates from a situation of two prisoners who must each decide whether to confess without knowing what the other will say, where a lighter penalty follows if you confess when the other does not. An economics example would be two duopolists, who each have to set their price without knowing what price the other is setting. A pay-off matrix can be constructed as follows, where 1 and 2 are the players and A and B the strategies: in this case A is price high and B is price low. The matrix shows the pay-offs, that is, profits, to 1 of the four possible combinations of strategies. A similar matrix can be drawn up for 2.

		2's strategy	
		A	B
1's strategy	A	5	1
	B	7	3

1 knows that if 2 plays A, that is, prices high, 1 does better pricing low. Also if 2 plays B, that is, prices low, 1 does better pricing low. If no agreement can be reached, 1 will price low. For parallel reasons, so will 2. Thus they finish up each making profits of 3, when if they had both priced high they could each have made profits of 5. They may be unable to agree because anti-monopoly legislation forbids them to meet, or because they simply do not trust each other to keep to any agreement they reach. If they collude and each price high, their profits can be raised to 5 each.

private company A limited liability company in the UK restricted to between 2 and 50 shareholders, not counting present and past employees. Shareholders cannot transfer their shares without the consent of other members, and shares cannot be offered to the general public.

private cost The cost of providing goods or services as it appears to the person or firm supplying them. This includes the cost of any factor services or inputs bought by the supplier, the value of work done, and the use of land, buildings, and equipment owned by the supplier. Private cost excludes any external harm caused to other people or the environment, such as noise or pollution, unless the supplier is legally obliged to pay for it. Private cost is contrasted with social cost, which includes any external costs as well as the direct cost to the supplier.

private enterprise The system by which economic activity is undertaken by independent individuals or firms, rather than under central direction. Supporters of private enterprise claim that it is generally beneficial not so much because it is private, as because it is enterprising, which makes for greater efficiency and more technical improvements than centrally controlled firms would produce. Critics point out that because private enterprise is private it has no incentive to worry about *externalities, and that its enterprise is often directed to *rent-seeking, lobbying the government for subsidies and protection.

private good Any good or service which if used by one individual or firm is not available to others. Most ordinary consumer and capital goods are private goods. They are contrasted with *public goods, where one person's use does not decrease the amount available for others: services such as radio and television transmissions are pure public goods. Some goods, like the services of roads, are almost public goods at times of low usage, and almost private goods at peak periods when congestion means that one person's usage reduces the space available for others. Whether such goods are private or public is thus a matter of degree.

private property Things which the law recognises as belonging exclusively to particular individuals or organizations. This is contrasted with things which are owned by the government, such as public highways, and things which are held to be available for use by anybody, for example the works of Shakespeare and other authors whose copyright has expired. Things which are private property can only be legally transferred with the owner's consent, or by due legal process, for example compulsory purchase of land needed for public works. There are usually restrictions on the use which can be made of private property, to avoid danger or inconvenience to other people: for example, planning permission is required for building on private land.

private sector The parts of the economy not run by the government. This includes households, sole traders and partnerships, companies, and voluntary bodies such as charities and churches.

private sector balance The excess of savings over investment spending by the private sector. It is a national income accounting identity that the private sector balance, government sector balance, and current account deficit of the economy must sum to zero. Thus, for any given government balance, an increase in the private sector balance must reduce the current account deficit.

privatization The transfer to private ownership and control of assets or enterprises which were previously under public ownership. Privatized assets may have been under direct state ownership, or owned by local authorities, for example council houses in the UK, or by state-owned public corporations. Privatization may be adopted because of a belief that assets will be used more efficiently under private ownership, to reduce the power of central authorities, to raise revenue for the government, or to attempt to spread property ownership more widely in society.

probability The likelihood that a random event will occur. This must lie between 0 and 1: probability is 0 if the event is certain not to occur, 1 if it is certain to occur. Expectations concerning probability may be derived from past experience of how frequently events of this type have occured, or from theoretical models about how the economy works, which suggest how often such events should be expected.

probability distribution *See* frequency distribution.

process innovation Innovation where an existing product is made in a new and cheaper way. This is contrasted with product innovation, where a new or improved product is introduced. Many innovations involve both new processes and new products.

procurement Government purchase of goods and services. The large scale of government purchases makes corruption or inefficiency in procurement a serious drain on government finances. It is also common for government procurement to discriminate between domestic and foreign suppliers: unless this is necessary on grounds of national security, it is a form of protectionism which is an important source of inefficiency.

producer good A good intended for use as a capital good or intermediate product by producers, rather than for direct use by consumers. Some goods are both consumer and producer goods: cars, for example, are bought by both individuals and firms, and fuel oil is used both privately and commercially.

producer's surplus The excess of total sales revenue going to producers over the area under the *supply curve for a good. If the supply curve is perfectly elastic there is no producer's surplus, but if the supply curve is upward-sloping, those productive resources which would have stayed in the industry at a lower price earn quasi-rents.

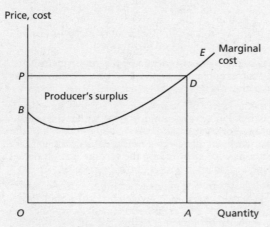

FIGURE 27: *Producer's Surplus*

The horizontal axis shows quantity produced; the vertical axis shows costs and price. *OA* is quantity produced; *BDE* is marginal cost curve (*MC*); and *OP* is price. *OBDA* is total variable cost, *OPDA* is total revenue (= price × quantity), and *BPD* is producer's surplus if there are no overhead costs. If there are overhead costs, producer's surplus is *BPD* minus overheads.

product 1. What is produced, by an individual firm, an industry, or the economy as a whole. See also gross domestic product, marginal product, national product, product differentiation, product innovation, product life cycle, and staple product.

2. The result of multiplication. The product of two numbers, algebraic expressions, vectors or matrices may be indicated by dots, multiplication signs, or simply writing them in sequence; thus $f(x).g(y)$, $f(x) \times g(y)$ and $f(x)g(y)$ are all equivalent. The product of N numbers $x_1, x_2, \ldots, x_N$ is the result of multiplying them all together, written $\Pi_1^N x_i$, or $\Pi_i x_i$ when the range is thought to be obvious.

product differentiation The marketing of generally similar products with minor variations which make them imperfect substitutes for consumers. This may involve real differences in material, design, workmanship, or other aspects of quality, or differences in advertising and the reputation of producers for quality and reliability. Often products differ in both respects. Product differentiation is associated with the use of trade-marks and *brand names.

product innovation Innovation where a new or improved product is introduced. This is contrasted with process innovation, where an existing product is made in a new and cheaper way. Many innovations involve both new products and new processes.

production The use of resources to make goods or services which have value. The expression 'means of production, distribution, and exchange' seeks to divide economic activity into changing the physical form of things, changing their location, and changing their ownership. It is not clear how such a classification can apply to services, nor that it is of any economic relevance as applied to goods. The notion that 'production' is particularly meritorious leads to paradoxes: for example, making sweets to rot children's teeth is productive, while dental treatment to preserve them is not. The economic problems of the former planned economies are believed to have been partly due to an irrational preference for 'productive' activities over distributive and other services. *See also* batch production, census of production, factor of production, government production, household production, joint production, and mass production.

production externality An external effect of production, which neither harms nor benefits the person or firm controlling the production. Adverse production externalities include noise and air pollution. Beneficial externalities include the public's pleasure from seeing lambs playing or barley growing. Activities producing adverse externalities are liable to be extended too far for maximum social welfare, since those controlling them have no incentive to take account of the externalities. For similar reasons, activities producing beneficial externalities are liable to be too restricted.

production function A function showing the maximum output possible with any given set of inputs, assuming these are used efficiently. The marginal product of any one input is normally positive, but decreasing. If the production function is written as $y = f(x, z)$, where y is output and x and z are inputs, the marginal product of x is $\partial y/\partial x$. A 'well-behaved' production function is one in which, for fixed positive x, the marginal product of z tends to infinity as z tends to 0, and tends to zero as z tends to infinity.

production possibility frontier A diagram showing the maximum output of one good or service possible with the available resources, given the output of other goods. In a two-dimensional diagram with its origin at the SW corner, the production possibility frontier (PPF) usually slopes downwards: its slope shows the opportunity cost of each good in terms of the other. Limited supplies of specific factors of production, and differences in factor proportions between industries, tend to make the PPF concave to the origin. Increasing returns in one or both industries tend to make it convex to the origin. A PPF can be drawn up for a firm, an industry, a country, or the world as a whole.

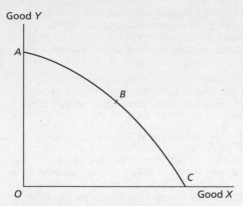

Good *Y*

A

B

C

O   Good *X*

FIGURE 28: *Production Possibility Frontier*

The horizontal axis shows output of good *X*; the vertical axis shows output of good *Y*. *ABC* shows the maximum amount of either good that can be produced consistent with any given output of the other, through efficient use of the available factors of production. This is the production possibility frontier. *ABC* is normally downward sloping at all points, including *A* and *C*. *ABC* may be concave or convex downwards at any point, according to the production functions for the two goods. *ABC* tends to be made concave by decreasing returns to scale in either industry, or by differences in the factor proportions used by the two industries. *ABC* tends to be made convex downwards by increasing returns to scale in either industry. *ABC* must be concave if there are constant or decreasing returns in both industries, and the factor proportions used are different.

production subsidy A payment by the government to producers of a good or service, at a fixed sum per unit produced. This is available only to domestic producers and not to importers. A production subsidy is contrasted with a consumption subsidy, which is an amount per unit paid to domestic consumers, or more usually distributors; it is thus available on imported goods, but is not given to exporters.

productive efficiency *See* efficiency.

productivity The amount of output per unit of input achieved by a firm, industry, or country. This may be per unit of a particular factor of production, for example labour employed, or per unit of land in agriculture, or 'total factor productivity' may be measured, which involves aggregating the different types of factor. Productivity per worker can be increased by longer hours, more effort, or improved skills on the part of the labour force, or by more capital equipment, improved technology, or better management. Productivity is also affected by the level of output, if *returns to scale are not constant.

product liability Liability for damage caused by a product of the original producer, as well as the immediate vendor. This implies that car crash victims injured by defective vehicles, for example, can sue the manufacturer as well as the firm which sold or hired a car.

product life cycle A model of how products go through a series of phases over time. In this model, new products start as small-scale specialities produced by innovators. Prices are initially high, both because of high costs due to small-scale production and because initially the innovators have cost advantages of know-how, equipment, and possibly patents, which give them a quasi-monopoly position. As knowledge of the new product spreads, costs fall through increased scale and greater experience, other producers enter the market, and prices come down. Once the product becomes mature, with large-scale production by techniques now regarded as standard, production tends to shift to areas with low labour costs, often in newly industrialized countries (NICs). Eventually the product is replaced by something new and drops out of the economy.

professional body An organization of people with particular professional qualifications. Such an organization may seek to set standards of professional competence, to control entry to ensure that its members are able to maintain professional standards, to monitor the conduct of members to ensure that they do, and to exclude them if they do not. Professional bodies may also lobby for legal restrictions on the right of non-members to provide professional services. This is designed to protect the public from possible damage by incompetent or dishonest practitioners; it is also possible to use entry requirements to keep down numbers so as to keep up the price of professional services, and to use codes of conduct to restrict competition between members of the profession. It is noteworthy that whereas accountants, doctors, and lawyers all have professional bodies in this sense, economists and statisticians do not.

profit An excess of the receipts over the spending of a business during any period. This includes credit transactions and asset revaluations as well as cash transactions and changes in holdings of real assets. Profit for a period is equal to dividends and profits taxes plus the excess of net assets at the end of the period over net assets at its start. So long as a business is a going concern, its profits are a matter of judgement rather than objective fact. Only when a business has been finally wound up and its assets converted to cash can profits be objectively measured. Until then, judgement is required as to the valuation of physical and financial assets, particularly if they are not traded on liquid markets, and as to the quality of debts due from credit customers. *See also* excess profits, gross profit, monopoly profit, net profit, normal profits, pre-tax profits, supernormal profits, and undistributed profits.

profit-and-loss account An account of an organization's receipts and spending over a period. Both sides of the account include credit transactions and asset revaluations as well as cash transactions and changes in holdings of real assets. An excess of receipts over spending is profit; an excess of spending over receipts is loss. The profit-and-loss account is contrasted with the other part of the accounts, the balance-sheet, which records the composition of assets and liabilities on a particular date.

profit maximization The aim of making as much profit as possible for a business. This is a slogan which raises many questions. Over what time horizon are profits to be maximized? There is liable to be a conflict between short-run profits and long-run growth. If the aim is maximizing the present discounted value of all future profits, what is the right discount rate to use? Profit maximization is a sensible objective only if the owners are risk-neutral: there is normally a trade-off to be made between risks and mean expected profits. Also, the directors or owners may have their own objectives: these range from desire for an easy life, a large empire, or jobs for their relatives, to a reputation as patrons of the arts, sport, or the environment. All these have to be traded off against profits. Other things being equal, however, businesses prefer higher profits to lower, as these allow directors more scope to pursue any aim. Finally, behaviourist critics argue that maximization itself is made impossible by lack of information and attention-span: actual businesses are run by *satisficing.

profit motive The desire for gain as a motive in economic activity. This motive is obviously both widespread and powerful. It is not the only motive in life for most people: they want a vast assortment of things, ranging from a quiet life, power, sex, friends, honours, the satisfaction of getting things to work, self-respect, and the respect of others that derives from a reputation for hard work and honesty. Other things being equal, more profits allow a relaxation of constraints on the attainment of any other objective. If the three great forces driving the social donkey are sticks, carrots, and ear-stroking, the profit motive corresponds to carrots. While profit-making can be pushed too far, it is probably less harmful than firing squads and brain-washing, the unacceptable faces of sticks and persuasion.

profit-related pay The system of making pay a function of the employer's profits. This normally takes the form of additional payments when profits are good, either as a rise in pay scales or as *bonuses. Bonuses are more usual, since the level of profits continually varies, and is not usually known until well after normal pay is received. Employers hope that relating pay to profits will make workers more co-operative in trying to achieve profits, decrease labour turnover, and improve morale generally. Employees who are *risk-averse may prefer smaller but safer incomes.

profit-sharing Giving employees a share in a firm's profits. This may be done either by profit-related pay, or by enabling employees to become shareholders, by giving them either shares or options to buy shares on preferential terms. Profit-sharing is intended to improve motivation by giving employees an interest in the firm's profitability. It is more frequently adopted for management than for other employees. This is probably because managers have more influence on profitability than other workers, and may be less *risk-averse, so that profit-sharing incentive schemes are relatively attractive to them.

profit-taking Selling an asset in order to realize an accrued *capital gain. The holder of any asset has to decide whether to hold on to it or sell it. A sale means that capital gains are realized, which may mean paying *capital gains tax (CGT). Holding on involves the risk that the price may fall, so that accrued capital gains are never realized at all. This applies to all assets, whether traded on a market, like shares, or subject to ad hoc negotiation, like houses and takeovers. Knowing when to take profits is part of the art of successful speculation.

program, entitlement *See* entitlement program.

program, mandatory spending *See* mandatory spending programme.

programming, linear *See* linear programming.

progression *See* arithmetic progression, and geometric progression.

progressive tax A tax where the revenue collected rises more than proportionally to income. *Income tax is made progressive by having exemptions for very small incomes, low rates for the first slice of taxable income, and higher rates for the largest incomes. Indirect taxes can be progressive if there are exemptions or low tax rates for goods heavily consumed by the poor, for example the UK's zero VAT on food, and higher rates on luxury items more heavily consumed by the rich.

progress, technical *See* technical progress.

prohibitive tariff A tariff set at so high a rate that no trade in the good concerned can take place. Prohibitive tariffs have the disadvantage that they raise no revenue, and make smuggling profitable.

proliferation of products *See* product differentiation.

promotion, export *See* export promotion.

proof by contradiction A proof which works by showing that assuming that a proposition is false leads to a contradiction. That is, assuming the original proposition is false allows one to prove both some statement and its opposite: thus the initial assumption that the proposition was false cannot have been correct. For example, consider the proposition that the square root of 2 is not a *rational number. Assume the contrary, that $\sqrt{2}$ is a rational number, x/y. If both x and y are even, divide both by 2, and continue until left with a rational x/y where at least one is odd. Now the square of any even number is even, and the square of any odd number is odd. $x^2 = 2y^2$ so x must be even. Set $x = 2z$. Then $4z^2 = 2y^2$, so $y^2 = 2z^2$, so y must be even. But at least one of x and y was by construction odd. This shows that the assumption that $\sqrt{2}$ is a rational number produces a contradiction, so $\sqrt{2}$ cannot be rational.

proof by induction The method of proving a sequence of statements by showing that if one particular case is true, the next must also be true; but it is true for the first, so it must be true for the rest. Consider for example the statement that the sum of the first N terms of a geometric progression a, ar, ar^2, etc. is given by

$$S_N = a(r^N - 1)/(r - 1).$$

This is clearly true for $N = 1$. Suppose it is true for N. The $N + 1$th term is ar^N. But

$$S_N + ar^N = a(r^N - 1 + r^{N+1} - r^N) / (r - 1)$$
$$= a(r^{N+1} - 1)/(r - 1).$$

This is S_N with $N + 1$ substituted for N, so if the formula for S_N is correct for N it is correct for $N + 1$. But we know it is true for $N = 1$, so it must be true for all $N \geq 1$.

propensity to consume The proportion of disposable income which individuals desire to spend on consumption. The average propensity to consume is total desired spending as a proportion of total disposable income;

the marginal propensity to consume is the proportion of additional income that an individual desires to consume. The marginal propensity to consume is normally less than 1. The size of both the average and marginal propensities may be affected by factors such as the consumer's total assets, liquidity, and expectations of inflation.

propensity to import *See* import propensity.

propensity to save The proportion of disposable income which individuals do not desire to spend on consumption. The average propensity to save gives total desired saving as a proportion of total disposable income; the marginal propensity to save is the proportion of additional income an individual desires to save. The sum of the propensity to save and the propensity to consume, average or marginal, is always 1. The size of the average and marginal savings propensities may be affected by factors such as a person's total assets, liquidity, and expectations of inflation.

property 1. Land and buildings; the UK legal term for these is real property. Property forms an important part of a country's capital stock. Property prices are the values of land and buildings, which are liable to large fluctuations. The amount of land normally cannot be changed at all, except where land can be reclaimed from the sea, as in the Netherlands. Buildings can be constructed or demolished, but planning and building large projects takes time, and once in place buildings wear out very slowly. If there is a surplus or a shortage of buildings, this can take a long time to set right, and in the mean time their prices may be abnormally low or high. Property investment is thus very risky.
2. Ownership of assets by private individuals or organizations. These assets may include property in sense **1**, but may also include securities and intellectual property such as patents. Property incomes are incomes derived from such assets. Expressions such as 'a man of property' or 'property-owning democracy' refer to property in both senses. *See also* intellectual property, and private property.

property company A company whose principal activity is owning and developing property. This may be industrial, commercial, or residential. Property companies may specialize on letting existing properties, or in new developments and conversion of properties with a view to selling them.

property developer An individual or firm which buys property with a view to changing its use, or constructs new property. Property development is inherently risky: this is partly because of the liability of the property market to large price changes, and partly because of uncertainty about obtaining planning approval for changes of use and new building. Large variations in property prices occur because the total stock of property can change only slowly; the planning process is a special cause of delay and uncertainty.

property income Income derived from the ownership of property of any sort. This includes rents, dividends, and interest. This is also sometimes known as unearned income; it is contrasted with income from employment. Income from self-employment is a mixture of earned and property income.

property income from abroad Incomes of residents of a country derived from rents, dividends, and interest received from abroad. Net property income from abroad is these receipts minus similar items of property income paid by residents to non-residents.

property lending Lending to finance purchases of property. Such lending normally uses the property concerned as collateral, via mortgages on it. Property lending can be very risky if the loans cover a high percentage of the property's valuation: if property prices fall the collateral may be worth less than the loan, leaving the borrower with *negative equity. Individual borrowers and small businesses usually continue to service such mortgages as they need their houses or workplaces, but corporate borrowers may well default, or be able to force renegotiation of the terms of their loans.

property market The system by which land and buildings are bought and sold. There is no central institution for this market, which works through an informal network of estate agents and other specialized intermediaries. The property market is extremely imperfect, as every property is different in location, and properties in close proximity differ in several characteristics. These include: the type of buildings on them and their condition; access to transport facilities; and amenity aspects, such as proximity to either sources of pollution such as rubbish dumps or sources of pleasure such as parks. Also, most individuals move fairly seldom, owing to high costs of movement, and firms move even more seldom. Thus most buyers and sellers have little recent experience of the market, and most properties are not available to be traded at any point in time. Property prices are thus subject to large fluctuations.

property portfolio A collection of properties held by a company. Such a portfolio may be held for income or with a view to development. Property companies hold portfolios rather than single properties partly to reduce risk, since any particular property may be refused planning permission for proposed developments, or may fail to find a tenant.

property rights The rights of an owner over property. These generally include rights to use property, and to exclude others from it. Property rights are not absolute: the use of assets may be subject to legal controls, such as the need for planning permission for changes in the use of land and buildings. The law also restricts the methods owners may use to exclude others from their property: for example, in the UK dwellings can only be reoccupied by their lawful owners through the courts and not by force. It is a hindrance to economic efficiency if it is not clear who owns property, and what their rights over it are; investment is made unnecessarily risky if the identity and rights of owners are not clearly defined.

proportional tax A tax where the revenue collected rises proportionally with income. A tax system could be made approximately proportional by having a uniform rate of income tax with very few exemptions, and indirect taxes levied at similar rates on as many goods and services as possible.

proprietor, sole *See* sole proprietor.

prospectus A document provided by a company wishing to sell newly issued shares or debentures to the public. A prospectus must provide information on the aims, past financial history, and capital structure of the venture, and may contain profit forecasts. Prospectuses in the UK have to be lodged with the Registrar of Companies, and there are penalties for making false claims in a prospectus.

protection 1. The use of trade policy to raise profits and employment in industries liable to competition from imports. Protection may be via tariffs, import quotas, or voluntary export restraints (VERs) and other non-tariff barriers to trade. Nominal protection is the proportional excess of domestic over foreign prices of imported goods. Effective protection for an industry is the proportional effect on value added in the industry of a tariff system which taxes both imports and imported inputs. *See* contingent protection, effective protection, and nominal protection.

2. Government policies aimed at safeguarding the interests of consumers, producers, or the environment. *See* agricultural protection, consumer protection.

protectionism The belief that restriction of international trade is a desirable policy. The aim may be preventing unemployment or capital losses in industries threatened by imports, the promotion of particular types of industrial development, affecting the internal distribution of incomes, or improving a country's terms of trade by exploiting its international monopoly power. Some politicians regard protectionist measures as desirable for their own sake; many who do not approve of protection still support it, as they cannot afford to lose the votes or financial support of those who demand it. *See also* new protectionism.

provision, bad debt *See* bad debt provision.

proxy vote A vote exercised by one person on behalf of another. At company meetings proxy votes are normally allowed. Usually shareholders can nominate some other person to cast their vote, either in some specified manner or at the proxy-holder's discretion. It is common for proxies to be entrusted to the Chairman of a company meeting. In many cases the majority of votes cast are proxies, rather than those of shareholders attending a meeting.

PSBR *See* Public Sector Borrowing Requirement.

public choice The choice of the kind, quantity, and quality of public goods to provide, and how to pay for them. Public goods are available to everybody, so if their provision is left to individuals or voluntary organizations, it is likely that too few will be produced, since most of those who benefit do not have to pay the cost. The state can levy taxes to cover the cost, but still has to decide what public goods to provide. If public choice is delegated to elected or appointed individuals or committees, they will be tempted to choose public goods in accordance with their own preferences rather than those of the rest of society. There are genuine problems in discovering what public goods the public really wants. There are far too many detailed decisions to be made for voting on anything except very general principles to be practicable. People asked to value public goods who believe they will be expected to contribute to the cost in proportion to the value they name have an incentive to understate their true valuations. If they believe they will not have to pay at all, they have an incentive to overstate their true valuations. Public choice thus poses more questions than answers.

public company *See* public limited company.

public corporation The UK form of organization for nationalized industries. Public corporations were supposed to operate in the public interest, using capital provided by the government, but with managerial autonomy in day-to-day business. In fact there was considerable government intervention in their management, particularly in relation to investment spending and pricing policy.

public expenditure *See* government expenditure.

Public Expenditure Survey Committee (PESC) A UK government interdepartmental committee that reviewed expenditure plans in the process leading to the annual Public Expenditure White Paper. The plans referred both to the coming financial year and to forward projections for the following four years. The PESC has now been abolished.

public finance The study of the financing of government. This includes taxation, spending by public bodies on real goods and services, provision of transfer incomes by the government, government property incomes, government borrowing and debt, and the financial relations between various levels of government.

public goods Goods or services which, if they are provided at all, are open to use by all members of society. Examples include defence, law and order, and public parks and monuments. As nobody can be excluded from using them, public goods cannot be provided for private profit. Public goods can be and frequently are provided privately, by individuals and voluntary organizations, from motives of altruism or ostentation. Really expensive public goods such as defence are necessarily provided by government bodies, which alone have the power to raise the taxes needed to pay for them.

public interest The good of the general public, as contrasted with the particular individuals or firms involved in a decision. The instructions for managers of publicly owned enterprises, or bodies appointed to regulate monopolies, often contain phrases such as 'operate in the public interest'. In the absence of any objective method of determining what the public interest is, those given such instructions must necessarily use their own judgement, or rely on precedents set by similar bodies.

public limited company (PLC) A UK company registered under the Companies Act. Its name must end in 'PLC'. The Act lays down minimum capital requirements, and sets the form for its memorandum. Such companies can offer shares and securities to the public with *limited liability. The rules governing public companies are stricter than those for private companies.

public ownership Ownership of enterprises by the government, or a government-controlled body. This may include direct operation by the central government, as for example with military establishments or the civil service; operation by local authorities, as with many public amenities, and in the UK local authority housing; and operation by government-appointed bodies, as with the UK National Health Service. It is also possible for the government to own part or all of the shares of companies.

public procurement The purchase of goods and services by the public sector, at all levels of government. Because of state activities in providing defence, law and order, health, education, and other public services, public procurement accounts for a considerable fraction of total national expenditure. In running an efficient economy it is important to ensure that the considerable sums involved are spent efficiently, and that the process of allocating government contracts is free from corruption. In international trade negotiations there is concern that government procurement should not be used as a vehicle for protection, though considerations of national security make governments reluctant to open defence procurement entirely to foreign competition.

public sector Those parts of the economy which are not controlled by individuals, voluntary organizations, or privately owned companies. The public sector thus includes government at all levels, national and local; government-owned firms; and *quasi-autonomous non-government organizations (quangos). Where government money is provided to bodies such as charities or housing associations, or privately owned public utilities are subject to close regulation by government-appointed bodies, the distinction between the public and private sectors is not clear-cut.

Public Sector Borrowing Requirement (PSBR) The amount the UK government has to borrow each year, when the government's expenditure exceeds its income. The PSBR must lead either to sales of securities to the public, which may raise interest rates and crowd out private investment, or borrowing from the banking system, leading to inflationary increases in the money supply. The PSBR has been regarded as an important indicator of the government's fiscal stance. It does not include the proceeds of selling off privatized industries, which are thus effectively treated as current government income.

public sector debt *See* government debt.

Public Sector Debt Repayment The amount of debt the UK government is able to repay in any period. This is the equivalent of a negative *Public Sector Borrowing Requirement (PSBR), and occurs if there is a budget surplus, that is, the government's total revenues exceed its expenditure.

public spending *See* government expenditure.

public utility The label given to the group of industries providing water, gas, and electricity to both domestic and business consumers. Such businesses are regarded as special partly because everybody needs their services, and partly because of economies of scale and the need to disturb both public and private property in operating their distribution networks. These industries are usually either in public ownership, or subject to some form of public regulation of their charges and conditions of supply.

public works Construction projects paid for by the government. These can include both new construction and improvements to roads, bridges, schools, hospitals, government offices, and publicly owned housing. There is normally a large programme of public works in progress. An increase in the programme is a possible means of stimulating the economy during slumps. Owing to the need for detailed planning, and delays in obtaining planning permission, preparing new projects mostly takes too long for them to be suitable as counter-cyclical measures, but it is ususally possible to bring forward the timing of projects which have already been approved.

pump priming The theory that it is possible for the government to bring about permanent recovery from a slump by a temporary injection of purchasing power into the economy. The argument is that if incomes are low because lack of confidence in the future prevents investment, a temporary rise in government spending, financed by borrowing rather than taxes, can raise incomes through its multiplier effects, which will allow investment to recover. Once a cumulative recovery process gets going, it will be possible to remove the extra government spending. The government may even eventually receive sufficient extra tax revenue to restore government debt to its original level. The name comes from a mechanical analogy with pumps that need an initial charge of water before they will work.

punishment strategy A strategy by which a player in a game who is injured by another player's actions responds by taking actions which punish the player causing the injury. The punishment may be temporary or permanent: the aim is to pitch the punishment at the right level of severity to ensure that the prospect of it will deter the victim from actions which incur it. Players have to consider the cost of punishment strategies to themselves, as it may be necessary actually to inflict punishment while building up their reputation, even if once deterrence is achieved the punishment will not need to be used.

purchase tax A UK tax on consumer goods, at rates varying between goods and over time. It was replaced by *value added tax (VAT) in 1973.

purchasing power The amount of real goods and services each unit of money will buy. Purchasing power is thus the reciprocal of a suitable *price index: if prices go up, the purchasing power of money goes down. Purchasing power is clearly dependent on consumer tastes: if relative prices change, for example meat prices rise and dairy prices fall so that the average consumer's purchasing power is unchanged, the purchasing power of vegetarians rises and that of meat-eaters with an allergy to dairy products falls.

purchasing power parity (PPP) The theory that *exchange rates between currencies are determined in the long run by the amount of goods and services that each can buy. In the absence of transport costs and tariffs, if the price of tradable goods were lower in one country than another, traders could gain by buying goods in the cheaper country and selling in the dearer: relative price levels thus determine the equilibrium exchange rate. Not all goods are tradable, and even for tradables transport costs and tariffs mean that prices need not be equal, but the same forces of arbitrage limit their differences, and thus limit the deviations of exchange rates from PPP. An alternative form of PPP says that changes in the equilibrium exchange rate are determined by changes in relative price levels.

pure floating exchange rate A *floating exchange rate which is set by the market without any intervention by central banks or governments. A pure or 'clean' float is contrasted with a managed or 'dirty' float in which there is some official *intervention in the foreign exchange market. Under pure floating the exchange rate is whatever private speculators believe it should be. There is thus a risk of extreme fluctuations in exchange rates, and for this reason very few countries allow a completely clean float for their currencies. Most countries attempt some degree of official intervention intended to stabilize the foreign exchange markets.

put option A contract giving the right but not the obligation to sell a good, security, or currency on some future date at a price fixed when the contract is first taken out. A put option will only be exercised when the date arrives if the spot market price is below the option price; if the market price is higher than the option price it will pay better to sell on the spot market. A put option can be used to reduce risk by somebody who has to hold the good, or as a speculation by somebody who expects a low spot market price.

pyramid scheme A financial scheme in which investors are offered a high rate of return provided they recruit at least n new members. Such schemes are inherently fraudulent; they can only pay the promised return as long as total membership rises fast enough, and once new entry slows down or falls they are bound to default on their promises.

Q

q, Tobin's *See* Tobin's q.

quadrant A section of a diagram, defined by its direction from the origin. Numbering of quadrants is somewhat arbitrary: a common labelling system is that quadrant I is North and East, that is above and right of the origin; quadrant 2 is North and West; quadrant III is South and West; and quadrant IV is South and East.

quadratic A function of the form $y = ax^2 + bx + c$, where $a \neq 0$, so that the highest power of x appearing is its square. The quadratic equation $ax^2 + bx + c = 0$ can always be solved by use of the formula

$$x = [-b \pm \sqrt{(b^2 - 4ac)}]/2a.$$

These roots are real and distinct if $b^2 > 4ac$, real and equal if $b^2 = 4ac$, and complex if $b^2 < 4ac$. The graph of a quadratic function is a parabola. A quadratic with $a > 0$ always has a minimum where $x = -b/2a$, and a quadratic with $a < 0$ always has a maximum where $x = -b/2a$.

qualification of accounts A report by *auditors that they are not, for some specified reasons, able to certify that its *accounts give a true and fair view of an organization's affairs. This may reflect either serious financial misconduct, or deficiencies in the organization's bookkeeping.

quality control The system for checking the quality of a product. This may be done before it is sold, and/or at earlier stages of production. Where the checking itself destroys or is liable to damage the product, quality control has to work via sampling batches of products chosen so that they are expected to have common properties, for example those processed on a given date by the same machine. The level of spending on quality control is affected both by commercial considerations of maintaining a reputation for quality, and by legal sanctions imposing penalties or awarding damages for defective products.

quality ladder The model of producer development by which firms steadily upgrade the quality of their products. Movement up the quality ladder includes making products more reliable and improving their specifications and design. In the process a product changes from being a cheap line aiming at the lower end of the market, to being a superior article aimed at more sophisticated and better-off consumers. This process is associated with the development of newly industrialized countries (NICs).

quality standards Minimum standards for goods, set by government bodies or trade associations. These standards are designed to protect consumers, by ensuring satisfactory levels of durability, electrical safety, fire-resistance, etc.

quango *See* quasi-autonomous non-government organization.

quantity and price adjustment *See* adjustment, price and quantity.

quantity demanded The quantity of a good demanded at any given price. If an arbitrary price is set, quantity demanded traces out the *demand curve as this price is changed. The *equilibrium price is that at which quantity demanded is equal to quantity supplied.

quantity discount A price reduction available only to purchasers of at least some minimum quantity. Such reductions may be publicly advertised, or available by negotiation. Quantity discounts may be due to lower costs made possible by economies of scale in supplying larger orders, or to the monopsonistic advantage possessed by large-scale buyers.

quantity equation An equation relating the price level and the quantity of money. The standard formulation of this is $MV = PT$, where M is the quantity of money, V is the velocity of circulation, P is the price level, and T is the volume of transactions. A standard form of the quantity theory of money urges that at any given time, T is determined by supply-side factors, and V is determined by the legal status and habitual working of monetary institutions, so that the price level P is proportional to the money supply, M.

quantity of money The amount of money in circulation in a country. There are several possible definitions of money: see the entries for M0 to M3-5 for details. The *quantity theory of money ascribes a major role in determining the price level to the quantity of money.

quantity supplied The quantity of a good supplied at any given price. If an arbitrary price is set, quantity supplied traces out the *supply curve as this price is changed. The *equilibrium price is that at which quantity supplied is equal to quantity demanded.

quantity theory of money The theory that the price level is proportional to the quantity of money. This is expressed by the quantity equation, $MV = PT$, where M is the quantity of money, V is the velocity of circulation, P is the price level, and T is the volume of transactions. It is argued by supporters of the quantity theory that T is determined by supply-side forces, which determine the level of real output, and institutional factors, which determine the ratio of total transactions to output; and V is determined by the legal status and operating habits of the financial system. Thus M and P must vary in proportion. These assumptions lead to Milton Friedman's statement that inflation is caused by increases in the money supply.

Critics of the quantity theory urge that it can only hold in the very long run, if at all. Desired holdings of *real balances are a function of the rate of inflation, so that if an initial increase in the money supply sets off an inflationary process, prices tend to outstrip the money supply as desired real balances fall. Even if the quantity theory worked for increases in the money supply, there is great doubt whether it would work symmetrically for decreases in M. Prices, and more particularly money wages, are resistant to decreases, and the initial effect of a reduction in M would be a rise in interest rates and a fall in T. Given the widespread use of contracts specified in money terms, if P fell significantly this would tend to impair the solvency of many borrowers and lead to bankruptcies, disrupting business activity and further reducing T. Maybe the quantity theory would work in the very long run, but it would be ages before this could be checked, and it gives almost no guidance on how V, T, or P would react in the first few years after any major change in M.

quarterly data Data for the four quarters of each year (that is, January–March, April–June, July–September and October–December). Quarterly data are produced for many components of the *national income accounts. They are often presented both before and after 'seasonal correction', that is statistical adjustment to allow for the estimated effects of seasonal factors.

quartile The values such that one-quarter of the observations in a distribution arranged in ascending or descending order lie above the upper quartile, and one-quarter lie below the lower quartile.

quasi-autonomous non-government organization (quango) A form of organization used when it is desired to provide government finance for an activity without making the day-to-day details of its operations subject to direct political control, and without making government ministers responsible for them. Governments appoint the governing bodies of quangos, and lay down their general objectives, but then entrust detailed decisions to their discretion. In the UK, for examples, quangos include the Arts Council and various research councils.

quasi-rent A payment for the services of a factor of production which in the medium term is like *rent. Whereas rent is paid for the services of land, which is provided by nature, quasi-rent is paid for the services of factors which owe their qualities to past sunk investment. It behaves like rent because in the short run the factors would not disappear if the payments were decreased. These payments are not true rents, since in the long run they have to be sufficient to induce new investment, for example renewing buildings or paying for professional training.

queue A number of customers for a good or service waiting for a turn. Queue discipline describes how turns are allocated: this may be first-come, first-served, in random order, last-in, first-out, or some system of priorities may be used. Where there is more than one server, there may be a separate queueing for each, or a common queueing for all servers. Use of a queueing system effectively allocates services by willingness to wait in place of price. The properties of queuing systems with simple patterns of arrivals and service times can be found analytically, the properties of more complex systems have to be found by simulation.

quits Termination of employment, for whatever reason. Quits may be initiated by the employee leaving voluntarily, for example to take a better job, or by the employer if an employee is unsatisfactory or redundant. Quits initiated by employees tend to be more common in booms than in slumps; quits initiated by employers tend to be higher in slumps than in booms.

quota A quantitative allocation. This may be set as a minimum or a maximum. A quota for jobs for disadvantaged groups, or for compulsory deliveries by former planned economy farmers to state marketing organizations, would be a minimum. A limit to imports of cars, or quantity of milk sold under the *Common Agricultural Policy (CAP), would be a maximum. In each case it can be argued that any objective achieved by a quota system could be achieved at lower cost by use of the price mechanism, through an appropriate tax or subsidy. The use of quotas tends to inhibit competition, directly if quotas are allocated to individual producers, and indirectly if they are fixed en bloc, as this encourages the formation of organizations to share out the market.

quota (IMF) The share of each member of the *International Monetary Fund (IMF) in its total funds. The quota allocated to each IMF member determines its voting power, the amount of gold or international currency and of its own currency that it initially subscribes, and its access to various borrowing facilities. A large quota is attractive to any IMF member in terms of prestige and borrowing power: the price of this is a large initial subscription and large liability to extend credit to countries that need to borrow. National quotas are periodically revised.

quota, import *See* import quota.

quota (OPEC) The maximum level of international oil sales allocated to each member of the *Organization of Petroleum Exporting Countries (OPEC) at its periodic meetings. There is an incentive for each OPEC member to exceed its quota, as the resulting increase in revenue accrues to the cheat, while any resulting decrease in world oil prices affects all producers.

quota sample A sample including representatives of different sections of the population being sampled in the same proportions as the overall population. This applies, for example, to choosing people from various sex and age groups. This is intended to improve the efficiency or decrease the cost of sampling.

quotation Acceptance of a company's shares to be traded on a *stock exchange. This is normally conditional on providing an acceptable level of information to investors. Market-makers are allowed but not compelled to quote prices at which they will buy or sell such shares, up to some quantitative limit.

quoted company A company whose shares have been accepted for trading on a *stock exchange. This makes it easier to raise capital, as shares once issued are made more marketable by being quoted on an organized exchange.

quote-driven market A securities market which operates by *market-makers quoting prices at which they will buy or sell, up to some quantitative limit. Prices are adjusted by the market-makers increasing their prices if they run short of stock, or cutting prices if they start accumulating excessive stocks. This is contrasted with an *order-driven market, where orders to buy at or below given prices,and to sell at or above given prices, are accumulated until at intervals, for example daily, a market-clearing price is found and buying and selling orders consistent with this price are executed.

racial discrimination A situation when the way an individual is treated depends upon his or her race. In economics this can apply, for example, to employment, insurance, access to housing, or access to credit. Such discrimination is widely recognized to be unjust, economically inefficient, and often illegal. It is nevertheless widespread, and has proved difficult to eradicate, for various reasons. Some individuals genuinely believe, however irrationally, that race is correlated with characteristics such as honesty and competence. Others do not believe this, but discriminate for fear of adverse reactions by their customers or other employees if they do not. Many people find it difficult to judge the characters of people from cultures other than their own: this makes dealing with them appear risky, and risk-aversion then leads to discrimination.

rain, acid *See* acid rain.

rain forest The zone of tropical forests, with high rainfall. The rain forest is of concern to environmentalists because of its role as a source of biodiversity, and as a sink for large volumes of carbon dioxide. There are fears that destruction of rain forests will lead to a rise in atmospheric carbon dioxide and thus to the greenhouse effect and *global warming. Destruction of rain forests is also liable to lead to severe erosion, and increased run-off of rain leading to flooding downstream on rivers draining rain forest areas.

R&D *See* research and development.

random sample A sample of a population, chosen by some method which ensures that every member of the population has an equal chance of being picked. A random sample is contrasted with a *quota sample, where the aim is to have the same proportion of different types, for example of people grouped by age and sex, as in the overall population.

random walk A situation when random changes in a variable at any time follow a pattern independent of previous changes. There is thus no tendency for a variable subject to a random walk to revert towards its own previous values. The longer this process goes on, the wider the dispersion of the frequency distribution of possible values.

range The difference between the largest and the smallest observed or possible values of a variable. The range can always be expressed in absolute terms: if the variable always has the same sign, it can also be expressed in relative terms, as the difference in the logarithms of the largest and smallest values. The range is not usually a good measure of dispersion, as it makes use of only two observations, which may each be *outliers, that is, the result of freak events or statistical mistakes.

rank correlation The method of checking the relation between two variables by correlating their rank orders. This is appropriate if the relation is believed to be monotonically increasing or decreasing, but its form is unknown. With N observations of each of two variables x and y, the rank correlation is found from

$$C = \Sigma_i (r_{xi} - \mu)(r_{yi} - \mu)/[\Sigma_i (r_{xi} - \mu)^2],$$

where r_{xi}, r_{yi}, are the rank orders of x_i, y_i, and μ is the mean rank $= (N + 1)/2$. C can take any value between $+1$ and -1; rank correlation between the variables is positive if $C > 0$, negative if $C < 0$, and they are independent in rank if $C = 0$.

RAROK *See* risk-adjusted return on capital.

ratchet effect A tendency for a variable to be influenced by its own largest previous value. For example, consumption from any given income may be higher, the higher the previous peak income; or the *real wages demanded by trade unions may be an increasing function of the highest real wage previously attained. The ratchet effect implies that variables are more sticky in one direction than the other. A ratchet effect may make inflation hard to stop, if varying speeds of adjustment have led to a situation where the sum of past peak real incomes of all sections of the community is considerably greater than the present total available.

ratable value The value placed on buildings in the UK for purposes of local taxation. Ratable values were originally supposed to be estimates of the rent which would be paid on a property, but over time have come to bear little relation to this. Ratable values are still used for the *business rate and as a basis for domestic water rates, but have been replaced and are not used as a basis for the *Council Tax.

rate, business *See* business rate.

rate, long *See* long-term interest rate.

rate of exchange *See* exchange rate.

rate of growth *See* growth rate.

rate of interest The cost of credit. Any borrower normally has to pay the lender more than the principal originally received: the excess is interest. The rate of interest is the interest which has to be paid for a 1-period loan, as a percentage of the principal. This is normally expressed as a rate per annum. If a loan is certain to be repaid, the pure rate of interest compensates the lender for loss of liquidity. If a loan is not certain to be repaid, the rate of interest is normally higher than the pure rate of interest, including a *default premium to compensate the lender for the average loss expected through default, and a *risk premium to compensate a risk-averse lender for uncertainty about how large such losses will be. The rates of interest on long- and short-term loans may differ; normally long-term interest rates are expected to be higher, as long-term securities are more liable to fluctuate in price if interest rates change.

rate of return The annual return on a loan as a percentage of its principal. Where interest is paid at intervals other than annual, the annual percentage rate (APR) is found by compounding the actual payments; for example, if 1.5 per cent a month is charged, the APR is $100 (1.015^{12} - 1) = 19.56$ per cent per annum. A rate of return may be given before or after deduction of income tax on the interest. *See also* internal rate of return and required rate of return.

rates A system of local taxation in the UK. The ratable value of properties is decided by District Valuers, and is still used as a basis of business rates and charges to domestic premises by water companies. Domestic rates, which were paid only by householders, were at levels per pound of ratable value, the rate in the pound being set by local authorities. Domestic rates were replaced in 1990 in England and Wales (1989 in Scotland) by the *Community Charge. A *Uniform Business Rate is now charged on business premises, at a level determined by the central government.

rate support grant A UK system of grants from central government to local authorities. As the name implies, these grants were to supplement the revenues of local authorities, which were not able to raise enough local taxation from rates to pay for their expenditure.

ratio The result of dividing one number by another. Ratios are widely used in economics to compare securities or institutions. A price-earnings (P/E) ratio, for example, is a share price divided by the earnings per share of a company; a reserve ratio is the amount of reserve assets held by a bank or other financial institution divided by its total liabilities. This allows meaningful comparisons of shares of different market values, or banks with different levels of total assets. *See also* capital-output ratio, financial ratios, liquidity ratio, price-earnings ratio, and reserve ratio.

rational expectations Expectations which are model-consistent, leading to behaviour consistent with the model of the economy used in forming them. Such expectations are not necessarily correct in particular cases, but on average they cannot be improved on by use of any available information. Enthusiasts for rational expectations urge that individuals, firms or governments will make losses in terms of utility, profits, or achievement of policy objectives if they do not use all available information, which is what makes 'rational expectations' rational. Critics urge that actually accessing and manipulating information is expensive, in terms of both money and effort. Methods of forming expectations using less information and less processing which produce tolerable results will be preferred to rational expectations. This is a parallel to the argument between believers in optimizing and in *satisficing.

rationality *See* bounded rationality, and consumer rationality.

rationalization Reorganization of production in the interests of efficiency or profits. It generally includes non-marginal changes: for example, production may be concentrated in fewer factories where it was previously scattered, or may be dispersed where it was previously concentrated. Rationalization is often used as an euphemism for sacking people. For any firm with elastic demand, however, improved efficiency is compatible with an increase in total employment, though not necessarily in the same jobs.

rational number A number which can be expressed exactly as the ratio of two integers, that is, of two whole numbers: for example, $1.5 = 3/2$. Many widely used numbers are not rational: for example, $\sqrt{2}$, π, and e, the base of natural logarithms. A non-rational or transcendental number cannot be evaluated exactly in any finite number of decimal places, or by recurring decimals.

rationing Allocation of scarce commodities by administrative decision rather than price. Many countries, for example, rationed food and clothing in wartime. The argument for allocating scarce essential goods by rationing rather than price was based on considerations of both equity and efficiency: governments wanted nobody to starve, and fit workers were needed for war production. Economists believe that rationing is normally inefficient, especially in dealing with goods where tastes differ widely. If quantity is rationed and the price is kept low, users who get little benefit from a scarce good have little incentive to economise on it, and producers have no incentive to increase the supply. If goods are needed irregularly, and rationing prevents enough being bought on those occasions when the need arises, every user has an incentive to take up their ration regularly to form an emergency stockpile. Thus, since more may be needed in dispersed small stocks than in one central reserve, rationing may actually encourage consumption and make shortages worse. The administration of rationing schemes itself also uses scarce resources. *See also* credit rationing.

Rawlsian social welfare function The social welfare function which uses as its measure of social welfare the utility of the worst-off member of society. This corresponds to the preferences of extremely risk-averse individuals who do not know in advance what position in society they will occupy.

raw materials The products of *primary sector industries, intended for use as inputs to production. The main groups of raw materials are plant crops such as cotton, animal products such as wool and leather, and assorted mineral products ranging from bauxite ore, used to make aluminium, to zinc. Raw materials form a decreasing proportion of international trade, but are still very important for many *less developed countries (LDCs).

reaction curve A curve showing the best price or quantity for one competitor, for each possible price or quantity of another. An equilibrium is where the reaction curves of two competitors intersect.

Reaganomics The policy combination of tight monetary policy to discourage inflation, and lax public finance to encourage real growth. This policy mix is so-called from its use in the United States during the presidency of Ronald Reagan. It led to large deficits in both the US government budget and the US balance of payments on current account.

real balance effect The effect on spending of changes in the ratio of money balances to income. During inflation, as prices rise, the real purchasing power of the money people already hold goes down. This is expected to make people more likely to save and less likely to spend their incomes. With a constant nominal money supply, this should eventually bring inflation to a halt. The Pigou effect considers a real balance effect during a depression: as prices fall, the real purchasing power of the stock of money rises, which should eventually lead to increased spending.

real balances The money supply divided by a suitable price index. This gives the amount of real goods and services which could be obtained by spending it. Changes in real balances are a function of changes in the money supply and changes in the price level: real balances rise if the money supply increases proportionally faster than the price level. The amount of real balances people wish to hold is an increasing function of their real incomes, and may be a decreasing function of interest rates and/or the rate of inflation.

real business cycle The theory that fluctuations in overall economic activity are due to real economic *shocks: for example, variations in the rate of technical progress. This is in contrast to more traditional theories of the trade cycle, which attribute overall fluctuations to a combination of real shocks, monetary shocks, and the inherent dynamics resulting from time lags in economic decision-making.

real costs The real resources used up in producing a good or service, or the *opportunity cost in terms of other possible outputs foregone. The real costs of a good differ from private costs if the inputs are taxed or subsidized, or if there are external costs which do not fall on the person or organization responsible for production.

real exchange rate The rate at which one country's real goods and services can be changed into those of another. If the home price level is p_h, the foreign price level is p_f, and the nominal exchange rate, measured as the home price of a unit of foreign currency, is e, the real exchange rate, r, is defined as $r = ep_f/p_h$. If each country produced only one type of good, so that home and export sales were at the same price, the real exchange rate would be the same as the terms of trade. As home sales typically include non-traded goods, and the composition of exports and home sales of exportables usually differs, the real exchange rate should not be confused with the *terms of trade.

real GDP Gross domestic product divided by a suitable price index, to express it in real terms. The price index used for this purpose is usually the *GDP deflator; as this covers the prices of investment goods and government purchases as well as consumer expenditure, it is more suitable than the *Retail Price Index.

real GNP Gross national product divided by a suitable price index, to express it in real terms. The price index used for this purpose is usually the *GDP deflator. Since this covers the prices of investment goods and government purchases as well as consumer expenditure, it is more suitable than the *Retail Price Index.

realignment of exchange rates A package of changes in exchange rates, negotiated by agreement between the countries concerned. Under the *European Monetary System (EMS) from 1979 onwards there were a series of realignments. These raised the relative par values of the currencies of countries with low inflation and balance-of-payments surpluses, and lowered the relative parities of countries with high inflation and balance-of-payments problems.

real income Income measured at constant prices. This is found by taking money income and deflating by a suitable price index. Because of continuous changes in the types and quality of goods and services available, measurements of changes in real income become steadily less reliable as comparisons over longer time periods are considered.

real interest rate The real return on loans. This is the money return, adjusted for *inflation. If the nominal interest rate is $100i$ per cent and the rate of inflation is $100p$ per cent, the real rate of interest of $100r$ per cent is given by

$(1 + r) = (1 + i)/(1 + p)$.

For low interest and inflation rates, the approximation $r \approx i - p$ is fairly accurate. At times when the rate of inflation is changing, the real interest rate can be measured on a forward- or a backward-looking basis. The backward-looking basis compares current interest rates with inflation over some recent period; the forward-looking rate compares interest rates with expected inflation over some future period. The forward-looking concept is more relevant to decision-taking, but depends on a model for estimating expectations, so the backward-looking measure, which can be based on published statistics, is more frequently used.

real money supply *See* real balances.

real national income The national income deflated by a suitable price index. This shows the level of real spending the country can afford. This is affected both by changes in its real productivity and by changes in the terms of trade. If a country's real production grows by 3 per cent, but it imports and exports amounts equal to a quarter of its national income and its terms of trade worsen by 10 per cent, the increase in real national income is only ½ per cent $(= [3 - (^{10}/_{4})]$ per cent).

real number What is normally thought of as a number. This is in contrast to imaginary or *complex numbers, which involve the use of the concept of $i = \sqrt{-1}$. Real numbers may be positive, zero, or negative, and may be rational or transcendental.

real terms Attempts to reduce changes in economic variables to changes in quantities. Real GDP, for example, is the value of gross national product, measured at current prices, deflated by a *'GDP deflator', or price index. Because of continual changes in the type and quality of goods and services available, measurement of changes in real terms becomes increasingly unreliable as longer time intervals are considered.

real variable A variable in economics which is measured in physical units of some sort: for example, the level of employment, or the volume of oil extracted in a year. Real variables are contrasted with the other two types of variable common in economics: monetary variables, such as the price level or the annual profits of a firm; and pure numbers or ratios, such as elasticities or the percentage of the labour force unemployed.

real wage resistance Difficulty in reducing real wages. This is partly due to opposition by trade unions to accepting wage settlements that do not at least compensate for price increases since the last agreement. Employers also know that workers dislike accepting reductions in their real incomes: wage offers involving real reductions are thought to be bad for morale, so employers are reluctant to make them. Real wage resistance is distinguished from nominal wage resistance, that is unwillingness to accept cuts in money wages. Real wage resistance is much worse than nominal wage resistance in obstructing adjustments in the structure of relative wages when these are necessary, and in making it difficult to bring an inflationary spiral to an end.

real wages Money wages deflated by a suitable price index. From an employee's point of view, the relevant price index is a consumer price index such as the *Retail Price Index (RPI); real wages show what workers can consume. From the employer's point of view, the relevant price is the price of the firm's output: a rise in wages relative to prices decreases profitability and discourages employment.

receivership The situation when a company has defaulted on its obligations, and a receiver is appointed to use the company's assets to pay off the creditors.

recession A situation when demand is sluggish, real output is not rising and unemployment is increasing. A recession is usually identified when real gross domestic product (GDP) falls for two successive quarters. It is not as severe as a depression.

reciprocal One divided by a number. Thus the reciprocal of 3 is $1/3$, the reciprocal of $1/4$ is 4, and the reciprocal of n is $1/n$.

reciprocity The principle of international economic relations by which country A treats the nationals of any foreign country in the same way as that country treats A's nationals. This is contrasted with multilateralism and the *most favoured nation (MFN) principle, by which all non-residents are treated equally. Supporters of reciprocity argue that it is both fair and likely to promote market access for one's own exporters; opponents argue that insisting on reciprocity is futile, because imports promote competition and lower prices, so that every country loses by its own trade restrictions. Reciprocity is difficult to interpret when countries are not symmetric: witness the prolonged disputes between the USA and Japan over their mutual trade.

recommended retail price A price that the producer of a good recommends should be charged to final customers. In the UK such recommendations are not normally legally enforceable. It is not clear why producers should wish to recommend retail prices rather than simply setting their own 'factory door' price and letting distributors decide their margins for themselves. One possibility is that the producers believe that price-cutting by low-cost outlets would eventually reduce total sales by driving low-turnover outlets out of business.

recovery The phase of a *trade cycle when output and employment are moving back from their slump troughs towards normal levels.

rectangular hyperbola *See* hyperbola.

recycling The reuse of goods which have served their original purpose: for example, empty bottles or worn-out motor vehicles. Recycling is advocated on both cost-saving and environmental grounds, as it reduces both the need for extractive industries and the dumping of waste products. Whether recycling actually saves real resources or protects the environment depends on how much fuel is required for the transport and processing of waste products.

redeemable security A security which the borrower is due to redeem at some date. This is contrasted with an irredeemable security, where the borrower has no obligation to repay the loan. As a redeemable security approaches maturity, its price comes to be dominated by its redemption value, that is the amount which is due to be repaid.

redemption date The date on which a security is due to be redeemed by the borrower. This may be a single date, or a range of dates within which the borrower has discretion to choose when repayment will take place.

redemption value The price at which a security is due to be redeemed when it reaches maturity.

redemption yield The interest rate at which receipts of interest and repayment on a security held till it matures need to be discounted to make their present value equal to its market price.

redeployment Shifting of factors of production from one use to another. When labour is redeployed, this can mean that workers no longer needed in one part of a firm are found jobs in another part. In many cases, however, new jobs are not available within the firm, and redeployment is a polite pseudonym for *redundancy, with no definite prospect of any alternative job.

rediscount To buy a bill of exchange from the holder before it reaches maturity. The original holder will have discounted it, that is, paid less for it than its face value. If the holder needs to obtain cash before the bill comes to maturity, it has to be sold on to another firm, again at a discount on its face value.

redistribution of income *See* income redistribution.

redistributive tax A tax designed to alter the distribution of incomes or property ownership, usually in the direction of greater equality. Any progressive tax is bound to have some effects of this type: the term is usually reserved for income taxes with high marginal rates on large incomes, and taxes on inheritance. The effect of deliberately redistributive taxes is largely to increase *tax avoidance and *tax evasion, and to enrich tax lawyers and accountants.

red-lining Refusal by banks to make loans or by insurance companies to issue policies to individuals or firms in particular areas. This is usually the result of bad experience with loans or policies in these areas. The practice is criticized as being a form of discrimination against ethnic groups concentrated in such areas.

reduced form A set of equations in which all current *endogenous variables are expressed in terms of either exogenous variables or pre-determined endogenous variables. This is contrasted with a set of structural equations, in which there may be simultaneity, with some current endogenous variables dependent on others.

reducing balance depreciation The method of depreciating fixed assets by writing off a constant percentage of their remaining value each period. The remaining fraction is then written off when they are finally scrapped. This is contrasted with straight line depreciation, where an equal sum is written off each period for a predetermined number of years.

redundancy Termination of employment without any fault on the part of the employees concerned, because of a fall in the employer's need for labour. Some UK workers have a legal right to compensation for redundancy. In many cases employers make redundancy payments in excess of legal requirements, to induce workers to accept offers of voluntary redundancy. This avoids the need for compulsory redundancies, which are objectionable to trade unions and bad for the morale of remaining employees.

reform *See* currency reform, and price reform.

reform, trade *See* trade liberalization.

refund, tax *See* tax refund.

refusal to supply Refusal by producers to sell their goods to all applicants. This is believed to inhibit competition between distributors. Firms may wish to restrict their outlets because they believe that some distributors would undermine the reputation of their products by selling them without proper storage facilities, advice to customers, and installation services, or in some cases simply by trading in sordid premises that would impair their prestige. Refusal to supply may also be because a producer prefers to sell through outlets which do not stock rival products. Refusal to grant trade credit on the usual terms may be due to doubts about a distributor's solvency.

regime, exchange rate *See* exchange rate regime.

regional aid Help by central government for regions with low per capita incomes or high unemployment. This may take the form of state funds for *infrastructure investment, subsidies or tax allowances to induce private firms to invest in depressed regions, or special assistance with projects such as technical education, designed to make the areas in need of aid more attractive to investors. The European Union (EU) also provides regional aid to depressed regions in member countries, through the European Regional Development Fund (ERDF) and the European Social Fund (ESF). In spite of large amounts of regional aid, regional differences in per capita incomes have been extremely persistent.

regional policy Policies concerning the distribution of income and employment between different geographical regions of a country, or in the case of the European Union (EU), a group of countries. Regional policies usually seek to bring regions with exceptionally low per capita incomes up towards the national average, and to lower the unemployment rates of regions with exceptionally high unemployment. They may also be concerned with relieving the social problems and congestion caused by over-concentration of activities on the most crowded regions. Regional policy works by seeking to direct both private and public sector investment into the more depressed regions. This may be done both by the direct use of government funds, and by tax concessions to encourage private investment in peripheral regions.

regional trade agreements (RTAs) Agreements between groups of countries to trade with each other more freely than with the world in general. There are a large number of RTAs, and most world trade is affected by one or more of them. RTAs differ greatly in their effectiveness. Some have major effects, notably the Common Market of the European Union (EU), and the North American Free Trade Agreement (NAFTA), including Canada, Mexico and the US. Many RTAs unite developing countries, for example MERCOSUR (Mercado del Sur), whose members are Argentina, Brazil, Paraguay, and Uruguay. It is thought that regional arrangements are preferred to full multilateral liberalization because of the extreme difficulty in reaching world-wide agreement; they are preferred to unilateral trade liberalization because of a desire to get improved access to foreign markets and worries about the effects of unilateral liberalization on the balance of payments. There is widespread disagreement as to whether RTAs are a step towards more general world free trade, or an obstacle to achieving it.

registered unemployed Unemployed persons in receipt of unemployment benefit or other forms of income support. This means that they are unemployed in the view of the official agencies responsible for administering benefits. This definition of unemployment is contrasted with that based on labour force surveys, which record the numbers who consider themselves to be unemployed. In the UK the registered unemployed figure is usually around 1 per cent of the labour force below that produced by labour force surveys.

register, share *See* share register.

Registrar of Companies A UK official responsible for registering companies, issuing certificates of registration, maintaining a register of companies, and receiving annual returns. One Registrar covers England and Wales; Scotland has a separate Registrar.

regression *See* linear regression, and multiple regression.

regressive tax A tax where the ratio of tax paid to income falls as income rises. The most regressive tax is a *poll tax, levied at a fixed rate per person regardless of income. A tax system can be made regressive by having a maximum direct tax charge irrespective of income, for example the UK employee's contribution to National Insurance; or by having indirect taxes levied at relatively high rates on goods heavily consumed by the poor, for example the former salt tax in India.

regulation A rule individuals or firms are obliged to follow; or the procedure for deciding and enforcing such rules. Modern societies abound in regulations. These may be designed to promote public health and safety: for example, rules on food hygiene and the coding of electrical wiring. They may be designed to promote competition and prevent unfair trading practices: for example, *monopolies and *mergers are controlled in most societies, and *insider dealing is forbidden in many countries. Regulations may be set and enforced by government bodies, or by *quasi-autonomous non-government organizations (quangos). In the last resort regulation relies on legal sanctions, but the largest proportion of effective regulation is done by the regulators setting standards which most respectable organizations then try to comply with as a matter of self-discipline. *See also* bank regulation, and self-regulation.

regulatory agency A body set up to decide on and enforce regulations. In some cases the government does this itself; in the UK, for example, town planning and weights and measures regulations are decided by the central government and enforced by local authorities. In many cases a *quasi-autonomous non-government organization (quango) is set up and the task of regulation deputed to it. This is largely because of the vast amount of detail involved, and also in an attempt to remove the influence of politicians from deciding on details, and to relieve them of responsibility for the results. In the UK, regulatory quangos include the Competition Commission (CC), formerly the *Monopolies and Mergers Commission (MMC) and the various bodies, such as the Office of Telecommunications (Oftel), set up to regulate the pricing and other policies of the privatized public utilities. Regulatory agencies may be set up from outside an industry, or use may be made of *self-regulation, by bodies representing firms in an industry. The advantage of self-regulatory organizations (SROs) is that practitioners in an industry can be expected to be aware of its problems; the danger is that they may tend to identify the public interest with protection of existing firms in an industry.

regulatory capture The tendency of regulators to identify with the interest of the industry they are supposed to regulate. This occurs when a public authority charged with regulating an industry in the public interest comes to identify the public interest with the interests of producers in the industry, rather than the interests of its customers, or the general public when externalities are involved.

reinsurance The system by which the issuers of *insurance policies pass on part of the risk to others, by themselves taking out further insurance policies. Reinsurance normally applies only to claims on a policy or group of policies in excess of some minimum amount. This limits the insurer's maximum possible losses if claims on the policies turn out to be higher than expected: it is thus a method of risk-spreading.

relationship banking Banking on the basis that there is a continuing relation between a bank and a customer. The bank is expected to take an interest in the customer's business, offering advice and support when in difficulties. This is contrasted with the view that a bank should simply operate a customer's account, and that the customer should take each type of transaction to whatever bank will handle it most cheaply.

relationship investor An investor who is an active participant in a business, as well as providing capital. Such participation may vary between appointing some members of the board of directors and informal consultation on a continuing basis. It involves a long-term connection between the investor and the company; a relationship investor is not in the business of selling out to make short-term speculative gains. Relationship investment is contrasted with the view that investors should merely hold shares, and let the existing management get on with the task of running a company.

relations, industrial *See* industrial relations.

relative income hypothesis The theory that *savings behaviour is affected by a person's relative position in the income distribution. Thus at a given level of real income, a person may be a relatively poor member of a rich community, or a relatively rich member of a poor community. The member of the richer community is expected to consume more and save less, as ideas of what constitutes a socially acceptable minimum level of consumption are influenced by what is habitual to their friends and neighbours. This analysis also applies to comparisons between different countries or regions, or the same country at different times.

relative prices The pattern of prices of different real goods and services. This is distinguished from actual money prices. Two sets of actual prices represent the same set of relative prices if it is possible to change one set to the other by multiplying by any constant λ. It has been argued that in any economy the level of absolute prices is mainly set by monetary factors, while the structure of relative prices is set by real factors. This cannot be true in the short run, as different prices are affected to differing extents by *contracts or government controls, so that during *inflation or deflation of the general price level actual prices do not correspond exactly to an equilibrium price structure. The relative prices of different financial assets are clearly not independent of monetary factors.

relief *See* debt relief, and mortgage interest relief.

remittances, migrants' *See* migrants' remittances.

reneging Going back on a promise or bargain. This may be motivated by sheer *opportunism: once the other party is committed to a bargain there is a temptation to renege on one's promises. In many cases a reneger will claim either that circumstances have changed, or that the consequences of the bargain are not what they had been led to expect. This is a highly suspect defence: in the nature of things circumstances are never exactly what anybody expected, and it is impossible to describe them exhaustively. It is thus in the essence of a promise or bargain that it should be binding except in the case of extremely radical changes in circumstances, or clear misrepresentation by the other party. General freedom to renege would make impossible many economically efficient bargains, for example those concerning loans and career choice.

renewable energy Energy produced by methods which do not involve using up irreplaceable natural resources. Burning fossil fuels—that is, coal, oil, and natural gas—is clearly not a renewable method. Using solar energy, either directly or by burning biomass grown by sustainable methods, or hydroelectric or tidal power, is renewable so far as the fuel is concerned, though building the necessary equipment may deplete other finite resources. Atomic energy is renewable so far as the fuel is concerned, but may in the long run lead to serious environmental problems, through accidents and the need to dispose of waste materials and decommissioned nuclear power-stations.

renewable resources Resources which are available for use on a continuing basis, for example tidal power. These are contrasted with depletable resources, which are used up when used at all, and must eventually run out. Unfortunately we do not always know whether resources are renewable, which may depend on the intensity of use. Underground water resources, for example, are renewable if pumping is restricted to what is replaced by rainfall, but can be destroyed by over-extraction, leading to drying up or replacement of fresh water by sea-water. Some resources which are in principle depletable, in fact exist in such large quantities that any possible exhaustion date seems very remote. It is almost certain, for example, that civilization as we know it will come to a bad end for some other reason before it runs out of deposits of iron ore.

rent A payment made for the use of land or buildings. If land is productive purely on account of its natural features or its location, rent is a pure surplus accruing to the owner, who put no inputs into creating it. The rent on buildings, or on land which has been improved, for example by drainage, is often termed *'quasi-rent', as it is partly rent and partly payment for the services of the capital invested in buildings or improvements. Payment for the hire of consumer durables or productive equipment is referred to as rental payments. Rent of ability describes payments for the work of people with exceptional and scarce talents, such as artists or lawyers, whose fees often exceed what they could earn in other occupations plus a normal rate of return on the cost of special training needed for their professions. *See also* economic rent.

rental payment A payment for the use of hired equipment. This may be productive equipment, such as cranes or scaffolding, or consumer durables. Such payments are in the nature of *quasi-rents: in the long run equipment will only be replaced when it is worn out if the rental payments are sufficient to cover interest and amortization.

rent control Government control of rents for houses and flats. This may involve setting the levels of rents, or restricting increases. It has been widely adopted, mainly for motives of income distribution, based on the assumption, often but not always correct, that landlords are richer than tenants, so that controlling rents produces a more equal distribution of real incomes. During inflationary periods lags in adjustment tend to make controlled rents fall below market-clearing levels: this produces excess demand, and necessitates protection of security of tenure for tenants. In the long run rent controls discourage investment in housing for rent, and also discourage maintenance work on rented housing, so that its quality deteriorates. A general situation of excess demand for housing impairs labour mobility, as sitting tenants are unable or unwilling to move.

rented housing Housing owned by somebody other than the occupant, who is a tenant and pays rent to occupy it. This is contrasted with *owner-occupied housing, where the owner and the occupant are the same. Rented housing may be owned by private individuals, by companies, by public bodies such as local authorities or HM services, or by *housing associations. It is the most suitable form of housing for two classes of people: those who lack the wealth to buy or the competence to manage owner-occupied housing, and those who choose not to take on the responsibilities of ownership in the interests of the mobility required by their work.

rentier A person whose main income comes from interest on assets, normally gilt-edged. This is contrasted with forms of property income connected with entrepreneurial activities.

rent-seeking Spending time and money not on the production of real goods and services, but rather on trying to get the government to change the rules so as to make one's business more profitable. This can take various forms, including seeking subsidies on the outputs or the inputs of a business, or persuading the government to change the rules so as to keep out competitors, tolerate or promote collusion between those already engaged in an activity, or make legally compulsory the use of professional services.

repeated game A game where participants expect that there will be future games of the same type. Participants in repeated games have an incentive to choose their *strategies taking into account how their actions in this game will affect their reputation, that is, how other participants will expect them to behave in future games. It may thus pay in a repeated game to adopt strategies which would not be chosen in a one-off game, where reputation does not matter.

replacement cost The system of accounting in which the assets of firms are valued and their depreciation allowances are calculated using the costs of replacing their buildings and equipment. Where buildings and equipment can be replaced exactly, this might seem an ideal accounting method. However, particularly in the case of equipment, owing to technical progress, exact replacements are frequently not available, and would not be worth installing even if they were. In such cases calculating the cost of appropriate replacements for equipment is very much a matter of judgement.

replacement ratio The income of an unemployed worker as a proportion of income when in work. If this ratio is too high it gives a disincentive to accept job offers: allowing for the cost of travel to work and other working expenses, and the value of leisure, a replacement ratio below 1 is needed to maintain incentives. Too high a replacement ratio may perpetuate unemployment, while too low a ratio inflicts severe suffering on the unemployed and their families. In practice replacement ratios vary widely, as income support is based on family size while wages are not.

representative firm The device of considering the behaviour of an *industry as if it were composed of a number of equal-sized firms. Where an industry actually consists of one large dominant firm or a small number of large firms, surrounded by a number of much smaller competitors, the 'representative firm' may not exist.

repressed inflation A situation in which price and wage increases are restrained by official controls. This is liable to lead to a burst of increases when the controls are relaxed, unless policies are adopted to remove excess demand pressure. A serious difficulty in ending repressed inflation smoothly is that in conditions of widespread *excess demand and controlled prices, nobody actually knows how much excess demand there really is, or how much any given price would rise if controls were removed.

repression, financial *See* financial repression.

reputational policy A policy which relies on other people believing the policy-maker's promises. For example, it is possible to attempt to control inflation by cutting the money supply immediately, or by promising to cut it steadily over some future period. The policy of promising a gradual cut in the money supply can only work if people believe the future cuts will actually be made: that is, the authorities' promises must be credible. If their past conduct has led people to regard official promises as worthless, a reputational policy is not available, and inflation can be controlled, if at all, only by immediate cuts in the money supply, possibly at a severe cost in unemployment. Reputational policies are only made possible by building up a reputation for keeping one's word, even in circumstances when immediate pain could be avoided by breaking it.

required rate of return The minimum rate of return on an investment needed to make it acceptable to a business. This may be higher than the rate at which the business can borrow: this is partly to take account of the risks involved in investment, and partly because of the fear in an imperfect capital market that extra borrowing now may increase the cost or difficulty of borrowing in the future.

requirement, margin *See* margin requirement.

resale price maintenance (RPM) The fixing by manufacturers of minimum prices at which their products may be resold by distributors. While RPM does not necessarily imply a price-fixing cartel of producers, it does make such a cartel easier to organize. RPM was stopped in the UK by the Retail Prices Act (1964) and the Restrictive Practices Act (1966), with some exceptions, including the Net Book Agreement, until it collapsed in 1995. Manufacturers can still set a 'recommended' retail price, but cannot legally enforce this.

rescheduling of debt A revision of a debt contract, by which interest and/or redemption payments are deferred to later dates than those originally agreed. This has been applied both to the private debts of companies in difficulties and the *sovereign debts of nations, especially *less developed countries (LDCs). Rescheduling is accepted by lenders because the alternative may be outright default on the debt, and the consequent requirement to write it off in their own accounts.

research and development (R&D) The use of resources to create new knowledge, and to develop new and improved products or more economic methods of production. Research is the part of this devoted to discovering new knowledge; development is the part devoted to bringing new ideas to the stage where production for the market can start. This includes devising methods of making the products, and testing that they work reliably and do not create hazards for health or safety. Development is generally far more expensive than research.

research, operational *See* operational research.

reserve asset ratio A required minimum proportion between banks' reserve assets and their deposits and other liabilities. This may be imposed or varied as part of a central bank's monetary policy, to enable it to control total bank lending by using *open market operations to control the amount of reserve assets, or as part of the regulations imposed to safeguard the solvency of the banking system. It is not very useful for this latter purpose, as banks with unsatisfactory non-reserve assets are liable to become insolvent, however strong their reserve position.

reserve currency A currency used as foreign exchange reserves by other countries. To be suitable for use as reserves, a currency needs to be *convertible, and to belong to a large country with a reputation for low inflation. The principal currency currently used as reserves is the US dollar. In the past the pound sterling was used as a reserve currency, mainly by *sterling area countries, and the French franc has been used, mainly by francophone countries. It seems probable that the Euro will be used as a reserve currency now that it has been adopted by many EU countries. Opinions differ as to whether countries gain by having their currencies used as reserves. Reserve currency countries receive cheap loans from the holders while the system lasts, but their currencies are exposed to severe speculative pressure if confidence in them declines, which inhibits independence in monetary policy.

reserve ratio The proportion of the total assets of a bank or other financial institution held as reserves, that is as money balances or some form of highly liquid asset. Minimum reserve ratios have been used both as instruments of monetary policy, and as regulatory methods of attempting to ensure solvency.

reserve requirements The minimum percentage of their total assets which banks or other financial institutions are required to hold in money balances, or in some form of highly *liquid assets. Minimum reserve requirements may be used as instruments of monetary policy, or as methods of trying to ensure the institutions' solvency. They are not satisfactory as guarantees of solvency, as they take no account either of the riskiness of the institutions' other assets, or of the adequacy of their capital. A financial institution whose assets depreciate so that they are worth less than its debts will be insolvent, regardless of the high liquidity of its remaining assets.

reserves *See* capital reserves, foreign exchange reserves, and loan-loss reserves.

reserve tranche (IMF) The first quarter of the quota of any member of the *International Monetary Fund (IMF), which is available to the member unconditionally if required. This corresponds to the part of each member's *quota originally deposited in gold or *convertible currency.

residual Anything which cannot be explained in an economic relation. For example, it is possible to try to explain the growth in real GDP by increases in the labour force and increases in the real capital stock. If these gave a complete explanation of the growth in GDP, it would be equal to the growth in the labour force times the marginal product of labour, assumed to be measured by wage rates, plus the growth in the capital stock times the marginal product of capital, assumed to be measured by profitability. Any excess of total growth over these is a residual, assumed by some authors to be a measure of technical progress.

residual error The difference between the value of any variable as predicted from a statistical model, and the actual level observed. For example, a fitted consumption function could be

$$c_i = \alpha + \beta y_i,$$

where c_i is the consumption and y_i is the disposable income of individual i. The values of α and β are found by minimizing the sum of squared residuals in the equation

$$c_i = \alpha + \beta y_i + \varepsilon_i,$$

where ε_i is an error term. The residual is thus

$$\varepsilon_i = c_i - \alpha - \beta y_i;$$

note that the convention adopted for the sign of the residual error makes it positive if the actual exceeds the predicted value of c_i.

residual, Solow *See* Solow residual.

resistance, wage *See* wage resistance.

Resolution Trust Corporation (RTC) A US federal agency set up in 1989 to wind up bankrupt *thrifts. The RTC is funded by the federal government, and supervised by the Federal Deposit Insurance Corporation (FDIC).

resource allocation *See* efficient resource allocation.

resources Anything which can contribute to economic activity. This includes natural resources, including both those located on land and those in or under the sea; human resources, including labour of various skills and qualifications; and capital goods, or man-made means of production. Economics can be defined as the study of how resources are, or should be, allocated. *See also* depletable resources, efficient allocation of resources, natural resources, and renewable resources.

Restart A UK scheme to assist the long-term unemployed to re-enter the labour market.

restraint of trade A term in a *contract that restricts a person's right to exercise a trade or carry on business. Such a term is common, for example, in the sale of a business, where the seller agrees not to set up in competition with the purchaser. Contracts of employment often include a term restraining employees from working for the firm's rivals for some period after they leave: this is to protect confidential commercial or technical information gained in the previous employment being passed to competitors. Agreements in restraint of trade are void in the UK unless the party relying on them can show that the restrictions are not unreasonable or contrary to public policy.

restraint *See* voluntary export restraint, and wage restraint.

restriction *See* credit control, exchange control, and import control.

restrictive practices 1. Practices which affect the ability of firms to compete freely in markets for their products and inputs. This includes discrimination between customers by suppliers, exclusive dealing arrangements, and agreement or collusion to share out markets, either geographically or by products. Agreements embodying restrictive trade practices may be made illegal, or may require registration, so that they can be referred to a regulatory body such as the UK *Restrictive Practices Court (RPC).
   2. Practices which affect the efficient use of labour. This may include demarcation of work between different employees, minimum manning levels on the workforce required for any given task, or refusal to co-operate with temporary or unqualified workers. Such practices are often justified as being necessary for the health and safety of workers, or of the general public: danger clearly can arise from having work done by staff who are insufficiently qualified, or too few to cope if anything goes wrong. However, they are criticized as being motivated by a desire to create more and safer jobs for 'insiders', and to restrict competition by 'outsiders'. The reduction or elimination of restrictive labour practices is frequently part of productivity agreements. *See also* insiders and outsiders.

Restrictive Practices Court (RPC) A UK court set up under the Restrictive Trade Practices Acts to judge whether restrictive trading agreements were in the public interest. The RPC was abolished in 1998, when its functions were transferred to the new Competition Commission (CC). The court was required under the Acts to rule against agreements unless they could be justified by reference to a list of factors, or 'gateways'. These are:

(1) that the restriction is necessary for public safety;
(2) that it confers substantial benefits on consumers;
(3) that it neutralizes monopolistic activities of others;
(4) that it is necessary to negotiate fair terms with strong buyers or sellers;
(5) that its removal would cause localized unemployment;
(6) that its removal would damage exports; and
(7) that it is necessary to support other restrictive practices adjudged to be in the public interest.

retail banking Banking involving transactions with the general public. Retail banks collect deposits from individuals and small businesses, and make loans to them. In both cases the sums concerned may be small. Retail banking is distinguished from wholesale banking, which concentrates on large-scale transactions with other financial institutions.

Retail Price Index (RPI) The official UK *cost of living index. The RPI is based on a monthly survey of the prices of UK consumer goods and services, and is used as the basis for payments on *index-linked government securities, and pensions and allowances. 'RPI' is in fact a misleading description, as it covers many forms of consumer expenditure such as rents, mortgage interest, and public utility charges which do not pass through retail outlets. The RPI measures prices inclusive of *value-added tax (VAT) and other indirect taxes, and so may change as the result of changes in indirect taxation. In many countries a similar index is referred to as a consumer price index (CPI).

retail price, recommended *See* recommended retail price.

retail sales The part of total consumption expenditure which passes through retail outlets, that is shops. This excludes many parts of consumer spending: for example, rent, mortgage interest, public utility charges, and insurance.

retained earnings The part of company profits which is not paid out in taxes or dividends, but is ploughed back into a business. Retained earnings may be used to finance fixed investment, to finance takeovers of other firms, to extend credit to customers, to pay off loans, or to increase liquid assets. Retention of earnings is an alternative method of financing to borrowing or raising equity capital through share issues.

retaliation A policy change made to punish another firm or country for its actions. In a *trade war, for example, country 1 retaliates to quotas on its exports to country 2 by imposing quotas on 2's goods. It is difficult in practice to distinguish between deliberate retaliation and policy changes which are simply a reaction to a worsening in country 1's position. If a fall in exports to country 2 worsens country 1's balance of payments, 1 may restrict imports for balance-of-payments reasons; while a fall in its exports injures country 2, this is a by-product rather than an objective of country 1's policy.

retirement, early *See* early retirement.

return on capital, risk-adjusted *See* risk-adjusted return on capital.

return *See* rate of return, tax return, and VAT return.

returns *See* constant returns, correlation of returns, decreasing returns to scale, and increasing returns to scale.

returns to scale The relation between a proportional change in inputs to a productive process and the resulting proportional change in output. If an *n* per cent rise in all inputs produces an *n* per cent increase in output, there are constant returns to scale. If output rises by a larger percentage than inputs, there are increasing returns to scale. If output rises by a smaller percentage than inputs, there are decreasing returns to scale.

revaluation 1. A change in the basis of valuing a company's assets in its accounts. This may be necessary because of general inflation, or because of changes in the real value of particular assets.
   2. A rise in the value of a country's currency: *see* appreciation, currency.

revealed preference A method of indirect proof that one set of goods is preferred to another. Consider three sets of goods, A, B, and C. An individual, who could have afforded something slightly better than B, chooses A: A is thus clearly preferred to B. If the consumer chooses A but could not afford C, it can in some cases still be shown that A is preferred to C. This is so if B is chosen when something slightly better than C could have been afforded: B is thus preferred to C. With consistent preferences, if A is preferred to B and B is preferred to C, A is revealed preferred to C, even if this could not be shown by direct comparison between A and C.

revenue 1. Receipts from sales. Total revenue is total receipts, that is, quantity sold times price; average revenue is revenue per unit sold; marginal revenue is the addition to total revenue from a small increase in quantity sold, per unit increase in the quantity.
   2. Government tax receipts. The Inland Revenue is the UK body responsible for collecting direct taxes, and a revenue tariff is a tariff imposed principally to raise income for the government.

revenue tariff A tariff imposed principally as a source of government revenue. This is contrasted with a protective tariff, imposed mainly as a means of assisting domestic producers to compete with imports. Many actual tariffs have effects in both ways, though a tariff on goods a country does not produce is clearly for revenue purposes only, while a prohibitive tariff can only be protective as it raises no revenue. Revenue tariffs are important for many less developed countries (LDCs), which find difficulty in collecting taxes from a largely informal internal economy.

reverse yield gap An excess of returns on *gilt-edged securities above those on *equities. This is likely to occur during periods of high inflation because equities are expected to provide capital gains to compensate for inflation while gilt-edged securities are not. During periods of stable prices the yield gap is usually positive: a greater yield on equities is needed to compensate investors for their relative riskiness.

revolution, green *See* green revolution.

revolving loan A loan which is formally for short periods, but which is habitually renewed. Such a loan would be made, for example, by a bank to a shopkeeper financing stocks on credit: sales allow the repayment of loans, but it is profitable for both parties to renew the loans to finance the purchase of further stocks. It is not easy to distinguish such loans from loans renewed because the borrowers cannot repay them.

Ricardian equivalence The argument that individuals' *savings behaviour will be affected in the same way by government spending, whether this is financed by taxes or borrowing. The argument is that whatever the government borrows now, it will have to repay in the future, so that future taxes will have to rise. The effect of government borrowing on the *permanent income of taxpayers is therefore the same as that of taxation. This argument is valid only if all taxpayers have *rational expectations, either believe they are immortal or value their heirs' welfare equally to their own, and are not liquidity-constrained. Few economists really believe in full Ricardian equivalence: the forces discussed may however make government spending less expansionary than naïve *Keynesian models suggest.

right-hand variable A variable included in an equation as an *explanatory variable, normally printed to the right of the equals sign. Thus if $y = \alpha + \beta x$, x is a right-hand variable.

rights issue An issue of new shares in a company which are first offered to existing shareholders in proportion to their present holdings: shareholders are entitled but not obliged to take up their rights. Where the issue price is below the market price of the shares, it may be possible to sell the rights. If rights are not taken up, the shares are sold in the market, and shareholders receive the excess if the shares fetch more than the issue price.The advantage of a rights issue as a means of raising capital is that the register of present shareholders provides a ready-made list of people who have already shown some interest in a company.

rights, property *See* property rights.

risk The fact that the results of any action are not certain, but may take more than one value. Risk is usually used to describe the form of uncertainty where, while the actual outcome of an action is not known, it is expected that it will be determined as the result of a random drawing from a set of possible outcomes whose distribution is known. Where this information is supposed to come from is usually not discussed.

The *variance of possible outcomes is frequently used as a measure of risk, but this should not be taken for granted. For some distributions of possible outcomes and some utility functions variance is exactly right as a measure of risk: this applies if the utility function is quadratic, or if the outcomes are normally distributed. For other utility functions and distributions, variance is only an approximate measure of risk, and indeed is not always defined.

Risk-neutrality means that utility is a linear function of the outcome: in this case only the mean matters and its distribution is irrelevant. Risk-aversion means that marginal utility is decreasing in outcomes, so that of any two projects with equal mean outcomes, that with the lower dispersion will be preferred. A risk-free asset is one with zero dispersion of outcomes; such assets are hard to find. With zero inflation, money is a risk-free asset, but with inflation at an uncertain rate, the real value of money can vary so that in real terms money is not risk-free. With inflation, an indexed bond without default risk can be regarded as risk-free. In a foreign currency loan, risk can be decomposed into two elements: default risk, because the borrower may not pay; and currency risk, because even if the borrower does pay, under flexible exchange rates the home currency value of a given foreign currency payment is uncertain. *See also* counter-party credit risk, currency risk, downside risk, exposure to risk, idiosyncratic risk, market risk, non-systematic risk, independent risks, settlement risk, and systematic risk.

risk-adjusted return on capital (RAROK) A method of comparing returns on different investment taking account of *risk. The actual return is adjusted by measuring how the assets held are exposed to risk, and adjusting downwards the returns on riskier assets. How useful RAROK is depends on how accurately the riskiness of different assets can be assessed, and on how well the penalties on riskier assets reflect the degree of risk-aversion of any given investor. For new types of asset, such as *derivatives, risk assessment is very uncertain, in advance of experience of how their prices will actually behave.

risk-averse Preferring safer returns, even if they are on average smaller. An individual with *decreasing marginal utility of total wealth will get less utility from a prospect with uncertain returns than from a safe project with the same mean expected returns. Such an individual will refuse actuarially fair gambles, and is risk-averse. Risk-aversion is sometimes characterized by saying that the individual values mean returns but dislikes variance: this is sometimes correct, but not for all utility functions implying risk-aversion. With a logarithmic utility function, for example, it is possible to find two projects with equal means where a risk-averse individual prefers the one with higher variance.

risk bearing Having or sharing responsibility for accepting the losses if projects go wrong. Most economic activities are capable of resulting in losses under some circumstances, however good the expected results may be. Somebody has to bear the risk of meeting any losses. The first risk bearer for any project is the *entrepreneur in a private firm, or the equity shareholders in a company. If the losses are sufficiently bad, other people connected with a firm are also at risk, including creditors, the tax authorities, customers who have paid deposits on goods, and workers left unpaid when a business collapses.

risk capital Capital which the owners are willing to invest in equity in new and untried projects, where there is a recognized chance that they will lose it. Venture capitalists are willing to take these risks if they expect that their successes will make sufficiently large profits to keep their average return positive, in spite of some losses. Venture capital may be provided by individuals who are almost or entirely *risk-neutral, or by investment banks and other organizations which are large enough to be able to spread their investments sufficiently to reduce risk to acceptable levels by *risk pooling.

risk-free security A security which is free of the various possible sources of risk. One is the risk that the debtor may default; this is thought to be absent in the case of UK and many other countries' government debt. A second risk is that the market price may be low at the time when a security has to be sold; this risk is high for securities with a long time to go to *maturity, and shrinks steadily as the maturity date gets closer. In money terms, a government obligation is risk-free if the holder has the option to have it redeemed at any time. In *real terms, so long as there is uncertainty about inflation no security is risk-free, unless it is suitably indexed. From any individual's point of view, the suitable index would have weights corresponding to his or her own tastes, and be kept fully up-to-date. Actual UK government indexed securities use the *Retail Price Index (RPI) with a lag of several months, so are not entirely risk-free in real terms.

risk-loving Preferring a project with dispersed possible outcomes to a certain project with the same mean return. Such preferences could arise from a *utility function with increasing marginal utility of total wealth: an individual with such preferences would always accept gambles at actuarially *fair odds, and would accept some gambles with less than actuarially fair odds. It is necessary to distinguish between risk-loving in this sense and *gambling for the sake of its entertainment value. Gambling for fun is extremely common in the real world; systematic risk-loving is not. Many people who bet on horses or lotteries still insure their houses: they are willing to accept gambles with a limited loss and a small chance of a large gain, but reject the gamble of an uninsured house where a limited gain from not paying premiums is balanced against a large loss if the house burns down.

risk-neutral Indifferent to the dispersion of expected outcomes. An individual with constant marginal utility of total wealth is interested only in the mean expected outcome of a project, and not in its distribution. Such an individual is risk-neutral, and is indifferent between accepting and rejecting any gamble at actuarially fair odds.

risk pooling Combining two or more risky projects, with returns which are uncertain but not perfectly correlated. The expected sum of the returns to such projects is less dispersed than the expected returns on the separate projects. Insurance companies work by pooling the risks on a number of separate projects, for example the chance that any one of N houses will catch fire. Risk pooling also applies to the portfolios of investment and unit trusts, which hold a number of different shares whose behaviour is at least partly independent. Risk pooling is one source of advantage for larger organizations relative to smaller ones.

risk premium The extra return required to induce a *risk-averse individual to undertake a project with uncertain returns. If the mean expected return on a project is x, and the individual is indifferent between this and another project with certain return y, $(x - y)/y$ measures the risk premium, or proportional extra return required to induce the individual to engage in the risky project. For a risk-neutral individual the risk premium is zero.

risk sharing Contracts which shift risk from one party to another. Suppose a firm wishes to finance a risky project. If it uses its own money, it bears all the risk itself. If it issues *equity capital to finance x per cent of the project, x per cent of the risk is borne by whoever buys the shares. If it sets up a new limited liability company, and buys its *debentures which bear fixed interest, while other people buy the equity shares, all the risk is transferred to the new equity-holders, unless the project does so badly that the new company defaults on its debenture interest. Any desired proportion of risk can be shared by a suitable combination of equity capital and fixed-interest debt.

risk taking Engaging in any risky activity when a safer alternative was available. This applies to many situations, for example trading on one's own account rather than working for an employer, making unsecured loans rather than secured ones, betting, or failing to insure one's home. Even *risk-averse individuals are prepared to take many risks: they would prefer a safer alternative if the mean expected return were the same, but believe that the risky alternative offers a higher return than the safe one.

river pollution The effects on rivers of dumping of industrial and agricultural waste products. These are liable to kill plants and fish, and to make the water unfit for bathing. Industrial use of water for cooling may also raise river temperatures, which interacts with the effects of chemicals. Where major rivers, such as the Rhine or Danube, run through different countries, cleaning them up requires international collaboration.

robustness of policies The property of economic policies that their merits are relatively insensitive to the exact specification of the underlying model of the economy. The effects of any policy measure can be predicted only by using some model of the economy, based on econometrics, theory, or more ususally some mixture of the two. If we are not sure that this model of the economy is correct, we cannot be sure of the effects any policy measure will produce. A policy whose predicted effects change markedly in response to small changes in the details of the model is not robust. A robust policy is one which will produce desirable effects for as wide as possible a range of specifications of the underlying model.

roll-over of loans Allowing borrowers to renew loans when they fall due for repayment, rather than actually paying them off. This is common in two cases. In many cases the loans have been used to finance profitable transactions, such as buying goods for resale: the borrower could repay the loan, but has good prospects of profit from similar further transactions if the loan is renewed. In other cases the borrower cannot repay the loan, and the lender has the choice of rolling over the loan or writing it off as a bad debt, with adverse effects on their own accounts. In such cases there is a strong temptation to roll over the loan, especially if there is some prospect that the borrower will eventually be able to repay it.

Rome, Treaty of The treaty setting up the *European Economic Community (EEC) in 1958. This was signed by the original six members: Belgium, France, (West) Germany, Italy, Luxembourg, and the Netherlands. The Treaty set up the various institutions of the EEC, including the European Parliament, the European Commission, and the European Court of Justice, and its terms have been accepted by members joining subsequently, including the UK.

root (of an equation) A value of the argument of an *equation which causes the equation to be satisfied. For example, if $2x - 4 = 0$, $x = 2$ is a root (in this case the only root) of the equation. The equation $y^2 - 7y + 10 = 0$ has two real roots, $y = 2$ and $y = 5$. A given equation may or may not have any real roots, and it may have one or many. In a few cases, the form of an equation tells us how many real roots there will be and allows us to locate them quite easily. In the linear equation $ax + b = 0$, where $a \neq 0$, there is always one real root, $x = -b/a$. If $ay^2 + by + c = 0$, where $a \neq 0$, there may be two real roots, possibly equal, or none. The roots are given by

$$y = [-b \pm \sqrt{(b^2 - 4ac)}]/2a.$$

If $b^2 > 4ac$ there are two distinct real roots; if $b^2 = 4ac$ there are two equal real roots, and if $b^2 < 4ac$ there are no real roots. For most types of equation there are no comparably simple rules; the existence and location of roots have to be checked by numerical methods. *See also* unit root.

root (of a number) The number, x, whose rth power equals y. If $y = x^r$, x is the rth root of y. For example, if $y = x^2$, x is the square root of y, written $x = \sqrt{y} = y^{\frac{1}{2}}$; if $z = x^3$, x is the cube root of z, written $x = \sqrt[3]{z} = z^{1/3}$. The number and sign of real roots depends on whether r is even or odd. If r is even, that is divisible by 2, if $y > 0$ it has at least two real roots; if $x^r = y$ then $(-x)^r = y$ also, because

$$(-x)^r = (-1)^r (x)^r = x^r = y.$$

If $y < 0$ and r is even, y has no real rth roots; all rth roots of y are imaginary numbers involving $i = \sqrt{-1}$. If r is odd, y always has only one real rth root, which must have the same sign as y, because all odd powers of -1 equal -1.

rounding error The error introduced when figures are rounded, that is, are shown to fewer decimal places than those to which they were originally measured or calculated. When two or more rounded figures are added, the rounded total may not agree with the sum of the components: for example, $1.3 + 1.4 = 2.7$; but if the figures are printed showing only whole numbers, they appear as 1, 1, and 3, which does not equal $1 + 1$. In more complex calculations, and in particular sequences of calculations, rounding errors may cumulate and make a large difference to the results. In consequence it is prudent to perform most calculations to more decimal places than one intends to use in presenting the final results, and the more elaborate the calculation, the more spare decimal places it is worth while carrying.

round, wage *See* wage round.

row A number of items listed side by side. These may be numbers, or algebraic expressions. A row may form part of a table, or a vector, shown by listing the variables in brackets and separated by commas, for example $(1, 2, 3, \ldots, N)$. Each row in a table should be labelled to show what it describes, for example the country or industry of origin of flows of goods or services. A row is contrasted with a column, which shows a number of items listed vertically.

royalties Payments to the owners of natural resources such as minerals or oil, made by mine operators. Royalties are so called because the owner is frequently a sovereign, or a state. Royalties are governed by agreements, which may specify them in amounts per unit extracted, or as a percentage of revenue. The term is also used for payments by publishers to authors, and by recording companies to composers.

RPC *See* Restrictive Practices Court.

RPI *See* Retail Price Index.

RPIX A retail price index excluding mortgage interest payments. This is contrasted with the UK's retail price index (RPI) which includes mortgage interest. In many other countries the commonly used retail price index is calculated excluding mortgage interest, so is already an RPIX. The main argument for using an RPIX is that under the UK system, if rising prices provoke a rise in interest rates to suppress demand, the impact effect is an increase in the measured rate of inflation. The main argument for including mortgage interest in the RPI is that people with mortgages do in fact have to pay it, and it absorbs a substantial proportion of personal incomes.

RPM *See* resale price maintenance.

RTC *See* Resolution Trust Corporation.

rules-based policy A policy which operates according to published or recognized rules. This may extend to rules about how the policy will change if circumstances alter. This is contrasted with *discretionary policy, where the authorities are expected to use their discretion about what changes should be made in policy instruments. The argument for rules-based policy is that it makes it easier for other economic agents to predict how the policy-makers are going to behave. If there are no known rules, then other agents have to guess what the policy-makers are going to do, and if they guess wrong the effect may be to destabilize the economy. The argument against rules-based policy is that changes may occur in the technical, political, or financial environment which were not imagined when the rules were devised. Such changes may make it undesirable to apply the existing rules unchanged, and may sometimes make it impossible.

rules of origin Rules applied in *free-trade areas to determine whether goods qualify for duty-free admission. Normally such rules specify a minimum percentage of inputs which have to come from member countries.

rules of the game The rules under which the *gold standard was supposed to operate. Under the 'rules of the game', countries losing gold were supposed to raise their interest rates and cut their money supply; countries gaining gold were supposed to cut interest rates and increase their money supply. Supporters of the gold standard argued that this would restore equilibrium in the balance of payments fairly quickly. Critics of the system argue that the incentive to obey these rules was much greater for the countries losing gold, who were in danger of running out of *foreign exchange reserves, than for the countries gaining gold. The countries gaining gold could afford to insulate their domestic economies from its inflationary effects by sterilizing the increase in their exchange reserves, and often did so; the countries losing reserves could not afford to sterilize the effects for long. This imparted a deflationary bias to the gold standard system as a whole. *See also* sterilization.

running yield The interest on a stock as a percentage of its current market price. For example, if a stock yields £8 per annum interest and its price is currently £70, the running yield is $8/70 = 11.43$ per cent.

rustbelt The area of the USA stretching from Pittsburgh to St Louis, containing a large concentration of traditional heavy industries. The rustbelt suffers from high obsolescence and relatively strong unionization of the labour force, which have both encouraged a tendency for economic activity to shift to the South and West.

Rybczynski theorem A proposition concerning the results of increasing only one factor of production. The proposition, named after its originator, concerns a two-good, two-factor economy with constant returns to scale, and economic growth due to an increase in one factor of production, holding other factors and techniques constant. This leads at constant relative prices to an increase in the output of the good intensive in the factor which has increased, but a decrease in the output of the industry using the factor which has not. This result at first sight seems surprising: the argument behind it is that with constant prices the techniques used in each industry must stay the same. To employ the extra supply of the growing factor, output rises in the industry using it intensively; but this also uses some of the other factor, so that less is left for the second industry, whose output therefore declines. *See also* factor-intensity.

S

sacking Dismissal of labour by an employer. This may be 'for cause', where some form of misconduct by the employee is given as the reason; in some cases UK employees may have rights to compensation for *unfair dismissal if this cannot be substantiated. Dismissal may also be due to *redundancy, when the work an employee was hired to perform is no longer required, and the employer has no other suitable job available. In such cases no misconduct on the worker's part is alleged, and such redundant workers may be entitled to compensation. Sacking is distinguished from voluntary quitting of employment, where it is the employee who takes the initiative.

sacrifice ratio The ratio between the amount of unemployment needed to reduce inflation and the reduction achieved. According to demand inflation models, a 1 per cent increase in demand when activity is high has more effect in increasing inflation than a 1 per cent fall in demand has in decreasing inflation when activity is low. It is therefore believed that the sacrifice ratio for any economy will be lower if disinflationary pressure is applied steadily than if the economy varies between spells of expansionary policy and occasional bursts of severe cuts in effective demand. It is also believed that the sacrifice ratio will be lower if the authorities' commitment to reducing inflation is regarded as credible.

saddle point A point at which a function of two variables takes a *maximum for movement in some directions and a *minimum for movement in other directions. The term is borrowed from geography, where a saddle is a low point in a range of hills. For example, if $y = x^2 - z^2$, $\partial y/\partial x = 2x$ and $\partial^2 y/\partial x^2 = 2$; thus if x is varied holding z constant, y has a minimum at $x = 0$. But $\partial y/\partial z = -2z$ and $\partial^2 y/\partial z^2 = -2$; thus if z is varied holding x constant, y takes a maximum at $z = 0$. The origin is therefore a saddle point for this function. The directions in which movement is considered need not correspond to the axes. Consider for example $y = x^2 + z^2 + 3xz$. Movement along the axes gives minima at the origin, as does movement in the direction where $dz = dx$; but movement in the direction where $dz = -dx$ gives $dy/dx = -2x$ and $d^2 y/dx^2 = -2$; thus if x and z are varied along one diagonal, y has a minimum, but for movement along the other diagonal y has a maximum at the origin.

safety at work *See* Health and Safety at Work Act.

safety net, social *See* social safety net.

salary A relatively dignified form of *wages. Traditionally, salaried workers were paid monthly, often into a bank account, and were not eligible for overtime pay; 'white-collar' workers were generally paid in this way. This was contrasted with wages, which were paid weekly, in cash, to 'blue-collar' workers, who received overtime if they worked more than normal hours. In modern economies the spread of bank accounts, less frequent pay days, and bonuses has blurred the distinction between wages and salaries, which have essentially the same economic function.

sales, retail *See* retail sales.

sales tax A tax on the sales of a business. A sales tax is normally a fixed percentage of total sales of some classes of goods and services. Sales taxes are used to raise revenue, for example, by some states of the US. While in principle a *value-added tax (VAT) is better for economic efficiency, a sales tax is much simpler to administer when a lot of the business being taxed is done by firms whose business spreads over several states.

sample A random selection of examples of a class of objects, whose characteristics are used to infer those of the whole class. Sampling is used where it would be impossible, too slow, or too costly to examine all the class. A sample may simply be picked at random from a list of possible cases: for example, electoral polls use samples drawn from electoral registers. A *quota sample tries to improve the efficiency or decrease the cost of sampling by using a sample selected to represent different sections of the population being sampled, for example including people in various sex and age groups, in the same proportions as the overall population. The reliability of inferences from samples to the whole population increases with the size of the sample, but normally considerably less than in proportion to sample size. *See also* quota sample, and random sample.

Samuelson *See* Stolper–Samuelson theorem.

sanctions, trade *See* trade sanctions.

satisficing A practical alternative to attempting to optimize as a rule of conduct. Critics of *optimization argue that information is expensive, incomplete and unreliable, and human rationality is limited. Thus optimizing, in the sense of considering all possible alternatives and choosing the best, is simply impossible. Any person or organization who has found a rule of conduct whose results they regard as satisfactory, for example 'always tell the truth', or 'always price your product at average cost plus *n* per cent', will not change it so long as nothing goes seriously wrong. This form of conduct is called satisficing. Satisficers change their rules of conduct only if circumstances change so that the current rules no longer produce satisfactory results. Even then, they do not try to optimize, but search for better rules by trial and error. Once they find an acceptable rule, they settle down to satisfice again.

saving(s) The excess of *income over *consumption. This is a way of acquiring *assets; for the economy as a whole it is the only way, since while individuals may gain or lose assets through inheritance or gambling, these cancel out on aggregation. The average propensity to save is the ratio of savings to income; the marginal propensity to save is the proportion of any addition to income that is saved. The interest-elasticity of saving measures the proportional response of saving to changes in interest rates.

Saving and savings are words which have caused great confusion in economics, as they are used to cover a number of different, though related, concepts, concerned with acquiring assets and ways of holding them. Saving is a flow; savings refers to stocks of assets and ways of holding them. 'Life savings' are a stock of assets built up by past saving. 'Saving up' for things means acquiring assets temporarily, with the intention of spending them at some time in the future. 'Small savings' are the assets of people who are assumed not to have many. *'National Savings' are UK government securities with their income and capital value guaranteed by the state; the amount any individual can hold is rationed. 'Savings banks', for example the Trustee Savings Bank (UK), are banks specializing, at least initially, in handling small savings. While saving and savings are related, they do not precisely correspond. 'Contractual saving' means payments such as mortgage repayments or pension contributions which are fixed for some period ahead by contract. A person's contractual saving may constitute net saving, but not if it is financed by running down other assets or by borrowing. Conversely, while savings must be held in some form of asset, people can and do save without committing themselves to hold assets of any particular type.

Savings is contrasted with *investment, the creation of real assets. Savings and investment for the economy as a whole must ex post be equal (on consistent definitions). They are not, however, necessarily equal either ex post or ex ante for any particular individual, firm, or government. The *IS curve in macroeconomics shows the combinations of income levels and interest rates at which aggregate ex ante savings and investment are equal. *See also* contractual savings, optimum savings, and planned savings.

savings and loan association (S&L) A US institution borrowing from the general public to provide housing finance. S&Ls are the nearest US equivalent to the UK's *building societies. During recent years S&Ls have encountered major financial problems through financing fixed-interest mortgages with short-term deposits, whose cost responds rapidly to changes in market interest rates.

savings function A function relating savings to its determinants. For an individual these include income, both actual and permanent, age, family status, assets and possibly *liquidity. At the aggregate level the savings function includes the effects of income, the age distribution of the population, and total assets.

Say's law The proposition that 'supply creates its own demand'. The argument is that in an economy with fully *flexible prices and wages, factors of production could always find employment and goods could always be sold. An *equilibrium with involuntarily unemployed labour and involuntarily held stocks could not occur. There seems no logical flaw in this, if full price and wage flexibility could be achieved. The problem is that lack of perfect information makes prices and wages somewhat sticky, which means that *involuntary unemployment can exist. If stickiness in prices and wages cannot be removed completely, reducing it may actually make matters worse. This is because downward movements in prices and wages lead to the *liquidity trap, in which real spending falls because hoarding money looks the most profitable activity available.

scale *See* diseconomies of scale, economies of scale, logarithmic scale, minimum efficient scale, and returns to scale.

scale (in graphs) The label on each axis of a diagram describing how distances in the diagram represent prices, quantities or other variables. The scale used should always be indicated. Any number of scales are possible; those most frequently used in economics are a proportional scale, where equal distances represent equal amounts of a variable x; an inversely proportional scale, where equal distances represent equal changes in $1/x$; and a logarithmic scale, where equal distances represent equal proportional changes.

scarce currency clause A provision in the original rules of the *International Monetary Fund (IMF), to deal with the problem that its stocks of any one particular currency might run out. The clause provided that if the IMF ran out of stocks of a country's currency, this could be declared a 'scarce currency', upon which members would be entitled and expected to discriminate against the country's goods in their trade policies. It was widely expected during the late 1940s that the US dollar would become scarce, though due to Marshall Aid and other US bilateral aid programs this did not in fact occur. *See also* discrimination.

scarcity The property of being in excess demand at a zero price. This means that in equilibrium the price of a scarce good or factor must be positive. At first sight one might expect that a good or factor that was never scarce would not be counted as an economic good at all. Some factors of production are counted as economic goods, however, because it is not known in advance whether they are going to be scarce. In a *linear programming model, for example, constraints are included, which may turn out to be effective constraints, with positive prices, or not, according to the objective function assumed and the amounts of other factors available.

scatter diagram A diagram depicting the relation between two characteristics of a number of subjects, which may be individuals, firms, or countries. Each point marked on the diagram shows an observation of the two characteristics, for example age and the income of individuals, measured on the two axes. This is often helpful in suggesting whether it is likely to be possible to find any significant statistical relation between the two characteristics, and what type of function it is worth trying to fit. It also draws attention to any outlying observations which may merit special investigation.

scenario A history of the future of an economy as it would be on given assumptions about how it operates. The assumptions, for example about government tax and spending policies, can be varied to produce alternative scenarios. The construction of alternative scenarios is common when considering the effects of policy changes, in models too complicated to be capable of analytical solutions.

Schedule A tax A former section of the UK income tax, levied on the imputed rent of owner-occupied land and houses. This tax was used before the Second World War; during the war the tax assessments were not revised, which reduced its real yield, and it was subsequently abolished.

scope, economies of *See* economies of scope.

screening Action taken by uninformed parties to induce other people with private information to act so as to reveal it. This can be done by second-degree price discrimination, where people are offered a choice of contracts, and information about their characteristics can be inferred from which contract they choose. Screening is contrasted with signalling, where people with private information take actions which they hope will convey this information to parties who would otherwise not possess it, or induce them to believe statements they would otherwise have no means of checking. In many cases, such as the job market, both screening and signalling occur.

scrip issue *See* bonus issue.

SDR *See* Special Drawing Rights.

SEAQ *See* Stock Exchange Automated Quotation System.

search unemployment Unemployment which occurs while an unemployed worker searches the job market for an acceptable job offer. In some occupations workers may leave one job voluntarily because search for another is more efficiently conducted while not working. In many professional occupations this does not happen, because being unemployed is itself a handicap in attracting offers: workers who want better jobs can search more efficiently while employed. If they lose their jobs involuntarily, however, search unemployment occurs if they do not simply apply for any job and accept any offer. Unemployed workers seeking jobs have reservation wages, that is, minimum acceptable pay offers, and cut-offs for the type of work they are willing to perform. If they do not receive acceptable job offers, their reservation wage and minimum job specifications change, probably falling as lack of income reduces their liquidity and failure to find acceptable jobs depresses their expectations about the distribution of potential offers.

seasonal adjustment Adjustment to correct for seasonal variations in economic variables. Seasonally adjusted figures for GDP or its components are believed to give a better impression of cyclical movements in the economy than unadjusted figures. Seasonal adjustment is liable to produce incorrect figures if anything happens to change the pattern of seasonal variation in the economy. National income data in the UK are provided both on a seasonally adjusted and an unadjusted basis.

seasonal unemployment Unemployment due to seasonal variations in the demand for labour. Some occupations have large seasonal variations, for example hop-pickers or Father Christmases. How far this leads to seasonal variations in overall unemployment depends on how far such variations are mutually offsetting.

SEC *See* Securities and Exchange Commission.

secondary market The market for resale of shares. This is distinct from the market for new issues: the vast majority of dealings in shares is in secondary markets. The existence of a liquid secondary market for shares is an important factor in making them saleable as new issues. If people intending to buy newly issued shares knew they could not sell them readily, but had to retain them permanently, they would be much more reluctant to risk buying them in the first place.

second-best The consideration in welfare economics of when it is a good thing to satisfy 'optimum conditions'. Economists can draw up sets of *necessary and sufficient conditions for the efficient operation of an economy. If all but one of these conditions were already satisfied, it would always be beneficial to satisfy the remaining condition: this would give rise to a *first-best situation. If, however, some of the necessary and sufficient conditions cannot be satisfied for any reason, then it may or may not be beneficial to satisfy any particular condition: this requires investigation case by case. A second-best optimum is one where the best decisions are made about whether or not to satisfy some optimum conditions when others cannot be satisfied.

second-degree price discrimination Price discrimination where customers are offered a choice of possible contracts, so that they reveal information about themselves through their choice of contract. Airlines, for example, offer lower fares to passengers who are willing to book in advance and travel at particular times. It is assumed that business travellers are willing to pay more to fly than tourists: airlines cannot tell which customers are travelling on business, but expect that business travellers will value their own time sufficiently highly to pay more for flexible travel arrangements. Second-degree price discrimination is contrasted with first-degree price discrimination, where producers charge the maximum their customers are willing to pay for each unit of a good, and obtain all the gains from the good's existence, and with third-degree price discrimination, where sellers have sufficient information about customers to be able to offer different contracts to different classes of customer.

second derivative The *first derivative of the first derivative of a function. The first derivative measures a function's slope; the second derivative measures how the slope changes as the argument increases: that is, it measures the function's curvature. The second derivative of $y = f(x)$ is written d^2y/dx^2; alternatively, the first derivative can be written $f'(x)$ and the second derivative can be written $f''(x)$. If $d^2y/dx^2 > 0$ the function is convex; if $d^2y/dx^2 < 0$ the function is concave. At stationary values, where $dy/dx = 0$, if $d^2y/dx^2 < 0$, y has a maximum, and if $d^2y/dx^2 > 0$, y has a minimum. (NB while these are sufficient, they are not necessary conditions for a maximum or minimum of y.)

second-hand Goods which have already had an owner other than the manufacturer or a professional distributor, and which may have been used. Second-hand goods are frequently cheaper than apparently similar new goods; the difference in price reflects doubts about how they may have been treated, and may also reflect doubts about whether any redress can be obtained if they subsequently turn out to be unsatisfactory. They may also possibly turn out to be stolen property which may be reclaimed by the rightful owner. On the other hand some goods, such as antique furniture, can only be obtained second-hand.

second-order conditions The sufficient conditions for a stationary value of a function to be a maximum or a minimum. If $y = f(x)$, the first-order condition for a stationary value is $dy/dx = f_x = 0$. If this is satisfied, $d^2y/dx^2 < 0$ is a sufficient condition for a maximum, and $d^2y/dx^2 > 0$ is a sufficient condition for a minimum. In the case of a function of two variables, for example $y = f(x, z)$, the first-order conditions for a stationary value are

$$\partial y/\partial x = f_x = 0 \text{ and } \partial y/\partial z = f_z = 0.$$

If these are satisfied, sufficient conditions for a maximum are that

$$\partial^2 y/\partial x^2 = f_{xx} < 0, \qquad\qquad \partial^2 y/\partial z^2 = f_{zz} < 0,$$

and

$$(\partial^2 y/\partial x^2)\,(\partial^2 y/\partial z^2) = f_{xx} f_{zz} > (\partial^2 y/\partial x\,\partial z)^2 = f_{xz}^2.$$

The point of the third condition is that it is needed to exclude the possibility that the stationary value is a *saddle point. Sufficient conditions for a minimum are that

$$\partial^2 y/\partial x^2 = f_{xx} > 0,$$

$$\partial^2 y/\partial z^2 = f_{zz} > 0,$$

and

$$(\partial^2 y/\partial x^2)(\partial^2 y/\partial z^2) = f_{xx} f_{zz} > (\partial^2 y/\partial x \partial z)^2 = f_{xz}^2.$$

Similar but more complicated conditions apply to maxima and minima of functions of more than two variables.

second order of magnitude Effects which are so small that they can be neglected for practical purposes. Economic models frequently approximate actual functions by local *linear approximations. If $y = f(x)$, and $y(u)$ is known, then if b is small, $y(a + b)$ can be approximated by

$$y(a + b) \approx y(a) + b\,dy(a)/da.$$

This approximation rests on the assumption that any further terms in the exact expression for $y(a + b)$ are of second order of magnitude.

sector A part of the economy. Sectors can be delimited in a number of different ways. One way is by the bodies organizing expenditures: thus the economy is divided between the public sector, that is the government at various levels and government-controlled bodies; the corporate sector, which is companies; and the private sector, which is individuals plus unincorporated businesses. For national income accounting purposes the rest of the world is sometimes regarded as a sector. Sectors may also be distinguished by the type of product; thus we have a primary sector, that is agriculture and mining; a secondary or manufacturing sector; and a tertiary or services sector. *See also* corporate sector, industrial sector, organized sector, primary sector, private sector, public sector and sensitive sectors.

secular stagnation *See* stagnation.

secular trend *See* trend.

secured loan A loan where the creditor has a claim on some particular part of the debtor's assets in the event of default. This is contrasted with an unsecured loan, where the lender has no right to take over any particular asset if payments are not made when due. In the event of the borrower going bankrupt or becoming insolvent, secured creditors rank before unsecured creditors for any available assets. Secured loans, such as mortgages, are thus safer than unsecured loans, and command lower rates of interest.

Securities and Exchange Commission (SEC) The main government agency responsible for supervising trading in securities and takeovers in the US.

Securities and Investment Board (SIB) A regulatory body set up to oversee UK financial markets. Its aim is to prevent fraud and insider trading. The SIB works via the system of each financial sector, for example, the stock exchange, having a Self-Regulating Organization (SRO) which reports to the SIB. The SIB is empowered to recognize investment institutions, and to finance itself by fees charged for recognition. SIB members are appointed by the Governor of the Bank of England and the Secretary of State for Trade and Industry. They are drawn from leading City institutions: this has the advantage that they are likely to be able to understand the activities they have to regulate, but the disadvantage that they may feel more concern about the welfare of the financial sector than that of the general public. The SIB does not have control over mergers, which are dealt with by the Takeover Panel. *See also* self-regulation.

securities market *See* stock exchange.

securitization The packaging of numbers of non-marketable assets, such as mortgage loans, into bundles which are marketable. Individual mortgages are not normally marketable because there is too much idiosyncratic risk in dealing with any one of them. A package of several similar mortgages reduces the riskiness, which allows the package to be marketed. The fact that mortgages are made marketable may enable them to be financed at lower interest rates.

security A paper asset. Securities include government debt, both long- and short-term, company shares, and company debt. Securities may be registered, where legal ownership depends on the entry in a register, normally run by a bank, and the paper is merely evidence of ownership, or in bearer form, where ownership is conferred by possession of the document. *See also* bearer bond, blue chip, collateral, fixed-interest security, gilt-edged security, irredeemable security, long-dated security, marketable security, redeemable security, risk-free security, short-dated security, and undated security.

security of tenure The right of some tenants renting or leasing houses, flats or business premises to continue as tenants, so long as they pay the agreed rent and abide by any conditions of tenancy. Security of tenure is clearly beneficial to existing tenants, as it protects them against the trouble and expense of moving if they do not want to, and the danger that they might not be able to find anywhere else to rent. Security of tenure may, however, discourage investment in property, and make the owners of existing property reluctant to let it: this harms those who are not currently tenants but would like to rent housing or business premises.

segmented market A market where there is restricted contact between different customers, or different suppliers. If different customers either do not know what prices others are paying, or are unable to resell goods and services to them, it is possible to discriminate in the prices charged or level of service offered to different parts of the market. Similarly if different suppliers are isolated from each other, it is possible to buy at discriminatory prices. The same applies in labour markets: if minority groups are segregated by social or language differences, for example, employers can pay separate groups different wages for similar work.

seigniorage The profits made by a ruler from issuing money. Originally this referred to the profits from the issue of coinage with a face value greater than its cost of production. Nowadays seigniorage refers to the ability of governments to obtain goods and services in return for newly created money. A growing economy needs some extra money, but if governments issue too much this produces inflation, which reduces the real purchasing power of the money they have already issued.

Select Committee on Estimates A committee of the UK House of Commons which considers items of projected government spending to enquire whether public money is being spent efficiently.

selection *See* adverse selection, and portfolio selection.

self-assessment, tax The system of tax assessment where the taxpayer reports all items of income and all allowances due, and works out how much tax is payable. The tax authorities then check this calculation. The alternative is the system where the taxpayer reports income and claims allowances, but the calculations leading to the tax assessment are made by the authorities. The disadvantage of self-assessment is that it demands both knowledge of the tax system and arithmetic competence: this is realistic for companies whose tax returns are prepared by professional accountants, but less so for small businesses and individuals, who are amateurs where the tax authorities are professionals.

self-correcting system A system where deviations from any initial position lead to reactions which tend to return the system to equilibrium. Such a system is self-stabilizing, and will return to equilibrium without any assistance from the monetary or fiscal authorities. It may still be possible for the authorities to speed up the return to equilibrium by policy measures.

self-employment Work carried out as a business, rather than an employee. The self-employed are responsible for their own tax, national insurance, and insurance, whereas those employed by others can leave these matters to their employer. The self-employed are also responsible for their own health and safety. Income from self-employment is a mixture of rewards for work, returns on private capital employed, and rewards for entrepreneurship.

self-financing Financing a business without recourse to borrowing or share issues. A business can only be started on a self-financing basis by those with some initial capital. The business can then expand only by ploughing back retained profits. The advantage of self-financing is that it combines safety with control: a self-financed business can be run without any regard for the opinions of creditors or shareholders. The main disadvantage is that an entrepreneur's initial capital and profits may not be large enough to allow full advantage to be taken of possible *economies of scale. In fact few businesses are completely self-financing.

self-fulfilling expectations *Expectations which induce people to take actions which bring about the situation that is expected. This is the case, for example, with expectations about the future prices of assets and durable goods. If prices are expected to rise, this gives an incentive to bring forward purchases and to postpone sales, which tends to produce excess demand and leads to price increases. If prices are expected to fall, this gives an incentive to bring forward sales and postpone purchases, which leads to excess supply and price cuts. Thus in the short run prices in speculative markets are dominated by expectations. If a shortage of a good is anticipated, this gives an incentive to lay in stocks while they are available, so that rumours of a shortage tend to produce one. Self-fulfilling expectations are contrasted with self-frustrating expectations: for example, producers who expect high price increase output, which tends to drive prices down, and producers who expect low prices cut output, which tends to drive prices up.

self-regulation A system where the approach of government to regulating a sector of the economy is to lay down general objectives, but entrust the task of devising and enforcing detailed rules to a body representing those engaged in the sector. The merit claimed for this is that people within the sector are better able than outsiders to diagnose problems and devise realistic methods of control. The danger with self-regulation is that it will operate too much for the protection of established firms in the sector, and too little in the interests of consumer protection or opportunities for innovators and new entrants to an industry.

sell 1. To part with any good, service, or asset for money. Where the asset concerned is a foreign currency, selling pounds for dollars is the same as buying dollars with pounds.
  2. To persuade somebody else to buy. Selling costs are expenditures on advertising or other methods of persuasion; a hard sell is a determined effort at persuasion.

seller's market A market in which conditions are much better for sellers than for buyers. If sellers are scarce and are in no hurry to dispose of their assets, while buyers are numerous and are under strong pressure to satisfy their requirements quickly, it is likely that prices will be high and that conditions of sale will be favourable for sellers.

selling costs Costs incurred in the process of selling products. This covers items such as the cost of advertisements on hoardings or the media, exhibiting at trade fairs, or employment of representatives or door-to-door salesmen. It does not normally cover the costs of design and quality control, though these may be more important than selling costs in making products marketable.

sensitive sectors Sectors of an economy which are particularly concerned about loss of markets and jobs through competition from imports. This applies particularly to sectors where developing countries have a comparative advantage. Agriculture, textiles and clothing, iron and steel, and basic chemicals fall in this category. Sensitive sectors in advanced economies have lobbied, usually successfully, for exemption from general trade liberalization measures.

separable utility function A utility function where the size of one *argument does not affect the result of changing another. For example, suppose that utility, U, is a function of consumption of two goods, x and y. In a separable utility function this can be split into two separate parts:

$$U(x, y) = f(x) + g(y).$$

Thus the marginal utility of x is independent of y, and the marginal utility of y is independent of x: this can be written as $U_{xy} = 0$. The same applies if utility is an increasing function of consumption, c, and a decreasing function of z, work done. If such a function is separable it can be written

$$U(c, z) = f(c) - g(z),$$

so that $U_{cz} = 0$. Separable utility functions are very convenient in constructing mathematical models, but very implausible as models of human behaviour.

separation of ownership and control *See* control (of a company).

sequestration 1. A UK procedure by which assets can be temporarily frozen by court order.
2. The US term for mandatory spending cuts in the budget proposed under the Gramm–Rudman–Hollings law on the deficit.

serial correlation The situation when the value of a stochastic time-series variable is not independent of its value in previous periods. If $x(t)$ is a time-series variable, observed at times $1, 2 \ldots t$, and $y(t)$ is its *trend value at time t, define

$$z(t) = x(t) - y(t).$$

There is zero serial correlation if the expected value

$$E[z(t) . z(t - 1)] = 0.$$

If

$$E[z(t) . z(t - 1)] > 0$$

there is positive serial correlation; if

$$E[z(t) . z(t - 1)] < 0$$

there is negative serial correlation. Many economic variables such as the rate of inflation or the unemployment rate show strong positive serial correlation.

series A sequence of numbers defined by an initial term and a rule for getting from each term to the next. For example, in the arithmetic progression $a, a + b, a + 2b$, etc., the first term is a, and the rule for getting to the next term is to add a constant b to the previous one. Such a series can be continued indefinitely. A *convergent series is one where the sum of the first N terms tends to a finite limit as N tends to infinity; a divergent series is one where the sum of the first N terms does not tend to a finite limit (an arithmetic progression, for example, does not converge). *See also* convergent series, and divergent series.

SERPS *See* State Earnings-Related Pension Scheme.

service *See* after-sales service, and debt service.

service contract A *contract for the provision of services. These may be routine services, such as inspection, regular maintenance, or cleaning, or emergency services such as repair after breakdowns, or provision of temporary staff to cover absence of permanent employees. Service contracts are useful where firms require services involving specialized labour, management skills, or equipment, but do not need them regularly enough to make it economic to provide them in-house.

service flows The services rendered by durable consumer goods. These count as consumption when they are bought, but items such as furniture, refrigerators, cars, or boats give services over years and often decades. Only in the case of housing do national income accounts follow the procedure of treating their purchase as investment when it occurs and the flow of services as *imputed income in later years. This means that when individual or national consumption expenditure falls during depressions or in wartime, the figures exaggerate the immediate fall in utility, which builds up gradually as stocks of *consumer durables wear out. Similarly, the real standard of living does not rise as fast as consumption spending during a recovery.

service industry The parts of the economy providing services. These may be to individual consumers, for example medical treatment or entertainment, or to businesses, for example architectural, cleaning, computing, engineering, or legal work. In some cases, such as restaurants, a combination of goods and services is provided. Service industries are collectively referred to as the tertiary sector, and are an increasing part of total activity in advanced economies.

services Economic goods which do not take a tangible and storable form. In some cases these require the physical presence of the customer, as for example with hairdressing, medical treatment or live entertainment. In other cases services can be performed at a distance: for example, legal representation or insurance.

services, social *See* social services.

set-aside Removal of land from agricultural production. Farmers may be either compelled or paid to set aside part of their land. Set-aside is part of agricultural policy, in particular the *Common Agricultural Policy (CAP) of the European Union (EU). Set-aside land may be allowed to lie fallow, or may be diverted to forestry, or, subject to planning permission, to amenity or residential use. The method of cutting agricultural production by set-aside rather than reducing the average intensity of cultivation on all agricultural land, for example by cutting use of fertilizers and pesticides, is both inefficient and environmentally unsound.

set, feasible *See* feasible set.

settlement The actual performance of a *contract to pay for or deliver goods, securities, or currency. Because of the documentation involved, and postal and clerical delays, many bargains are not carried out immediately, but some time is allowed. This may take the form of having a set date for completion of all contracts made during a given period, or of 'rolling settlement', where each bargain is allowed n days for settlement. Settlement risk is the risk that other parties may fail to fulfil their side of bargains. Prompt and reliable settlement is a major attraction of goods and securities markets. Failure to settle by a major financial institution could trigger a chain reaction of failures among other firms; fear of this is a major reason for financial regulation.

settlement risk The risk that other parties may fail to fulfil their side of bargains. Delay in settlement may merely cause inconvenience, but complete failure to settle could cause severe losses. To reduce counter-party risk many commodity and stock exchanges insert themselves as counter-parties for the actual traders, making payments to sellers and collecting payment from buyers. Failure to settle by a major financial institution could trigger a chain reaction of failures among other firms; fear of this is a major motive for financial regulation.

sex discrimination Treating individuals differently on account of their sex. This may apply to employment, membership of professional bodies, insurance, pensions, or access to credit. The attitude to sex discrimination of both the law and social practice in modern societies is a jumble: some forms of sex discrimination are illegal, while others are compulsory. Where a person's sex is really irrelevant, economic theory suggests that discrimination is inefficient. Problems arise in cases where a person's sex is statistically significant: in pensions and annuities, for example, actuaries are aware that on average women live longer than men, and this affects the policies insurance companies offer them. Whether this actuarial difference should affect the qualifying age for and/or the level of state pensions is a matter of some controversy. While many types of formal sex discrimination have been removed in modern societies, it is still generally the case that women on average are paid less than men, and are more likely to work part-time and in relatively junior positions.

shadow prices Relative prices of goods, services and resources which are proportional to their true *opportunity costs for the economy, taking account of any *external economies and diseconomies. If individuals and firms all made choices so as to optimize their situations subject to a set of prices proportional to the shadow prices for the economy, the results would be Pareto-optimal, that is, perfectly efficient. In a perfectly competitive economy with no price controls and no external economies or diseconomies, actual and shadow prices would be equivalent. In any real world economy, subject to monopoly, long-term contracts, legal price regulation and externalities, actual and shadow prices do not correspond. The *Lagrange multipliers appearing in *constrained maximum and minimum problems can be interpreted as shadow prices. *See also* Pareto-otimality.

shake-out The process of removing resources from some sector of the economy. This may occur within firms, or in industries by a reduction on the number of firms. Shake-out is liable to be set off by bad times: cuts in demand induce firms to reduce both their capacity and their labour force, and cuts in profits induce firms to make more effort to remove organizational slack and may compel them to leave an industry.

share A part of the ownership of a *company. Shares may be held by individuals or other companies. Company law requires companies to treat all shareholders of any given type alike as regards dividends, or division of the assets on liquidation. *Ordinary shares normally carry voting rights, though it is possible to have some non-voting shares. In some countries there may be limits on the total votes cast by any one shareholder. Preference shares rank before ordinary shares for dividends, but have no vote, and *debentures rank before preference and ordinary shares for dividends. Debentures carry fixed interest, but the holders have the right to take over control of a company if these are not paid. A share register is an official list of the names and addresses of shareholders; a share certificate is a document proving ownership. In some countries, but not the UK, companies can have bearer shares, where there is no central share register, and the holder of share certificates is deemed to own the shares. *See also* A-share, deferred share, non-voting share, ordinary share, preference share, and voting share.

share buybacks The practice of companies with good current profits but poor investment opportunities returning capital to their shareholders by buying in some of their own shares. Buybacks benefit shareholders by reducing their income tax bills. Share buybacks tend to raise the price of the remaining shares whereas distribution of the same amount in dividends tends to reduce it. This may benefit directors and other employees holding share options as part of their emoluments.

sharecropper A tenant who pays rent fixed as a share of crops produced rather than an agreed amount of money. This system is relatively common in backward regions and less developed countries (LDCs). Sharecropping has the effect of sharing risk between landlord and tenant, but discourages tenants from investing in fertilizers, irrigation, and other permanent improvements.

shareholder A person or company holding shares in a company. The ultimate say over control of a company lies with its equity shareholders, who can change the management either by using their votes at company meetings, or by accepting *takeover bids. A majority shareholder is one who holds a majority of voting shares; a minority shareholder holds fewer than half the shares. *See also* institutional shareholder, majority shareholder, and minority shareholder.

share index *See* share price index.

share indexes, Financial Times Actuaries *See* Financial Times Actuaries share indexes.

share, market *See* market share.

share option An option to buy shares at a pre-arranged price, granted as an incentive to company directors or employees. Share options will only be exercised if the option price is below the market price at the time. They are offered as incentives: the better a company performs the higher its share price will be, and the more holders of share options gain from exercising them.

share price The price at which a share can be traded. This is not any single amount: even for widely traded shares the offer price at which market-makers are willing to sell shares is higher than the bid price at which they are willing to buy. The mean of these, the mid-market price, is frequently quoted in the financial press. In the case of shares which are little traded, the reported price may simply be the last one at which any transactions were reported, and may give little guidance on the terms on which they can now be traded.

share price index An index of the prices of shares of some specific type. Share price indexes are published in all countries with stock exchanges. They vary in the range of industries they cover, and the number of companies whose shares are included. For US shares see the Dow Jones index; for the UK see the Financial Times Stock Exchange indexes; for Japan see the Nikkei index; for Hong Kong, the Hang Seng index, and so on.

share register The register kept by a limited company recording the names and addresses of shareholders, and the type and number of shares held. Entry in the register is proof of ownership: shareholders whose share certificates are lost or destroyed can obtain replacements on production of proof of identity.

shark repellent Contracts entered into to make a company unattractive to potential takeover bidders. Contracts may be made with directors, for example, entitling them to large payments on loss of office, or giving them options to buy critical parts of company assets, or the company's shares, at low prices.

shell company A company which does not trade, but has a legal existence, and possibly some non-trading assets. These may include a credit rating, and the right to carry forward losses for tax purposes. For anybody who needs a company to trade through, acquiring a shell company may be cheaper and quicker than registering a new company.

sheltered monopoly A monopoly protected from competition in some way. This could include legal restrictions on entry by competitors, or tariffs and non-tariff barriers (NTBs) restricting foreign competition.

shelter, tax *See* tax shelter.

Sherman Act The original US federal antitrust legislation. In 1890 this act prohibited 'all contracts, combinations and conspiracies in restraint of trade', and monopoly in interstate and foreign trade. The Sherman Act required subsequent amendment, including the *Clayton Act of 1914.

shift work Work scheduled so that the same equipment can be used by more than one set of workers in a day. Two- or three-shift working involves some shifts working at 'unsocial hours': this is likely to involve paying workers extra to compensate them for this, and may reduce their efficiency. It is worth incurring these costs in capital-intensive industries where equipment is too expensive to be kept idle for much of the time. Shift working is also necessary in some industries using continuous processes and in organizations such as the police, fire and ambulance services, providing round-the-clock cover.

shock An event which is different to an important extent from what people expected, or from what they could reasonably have expected given the information available to them. Actual economic events, such as goods prices, share prices, or income levels, are hardly ever exactly what people expected. A shock is an event which causes an actual outcome very different from what on average was expected. Examples include major geographical discoveries, major technical developments, and major political upsets such as wars and revolutions. There is no agreed system for identifying shocks in economic data. *See also* adverse supply shock.

shoe-leather costs of inflation The suggestion that one of the real costs of *expected inflation is that it increases transactions costs by inducing people to economize on their money holdings. The shoe-leather concerned was worn out making more frequent trips to the bank to avoid carrying large stocks of cash. A similar effect applies to other transactions costs.

shop steward A worker elected at shop-floor level to represent fellow-workers in discussions with management. Shop stewards are not trade-union officials, though they are normally union members. They can catch *industrial relations problems early and help to prevent them from escalating into industrial disputes.

shortage A situation when the demand for a good or service exceeds the available supply. This can only occur if price is not adjusted to clear the market. If there is a sudden rise in the demand or fall in the supply of a good, law or social convention may prevent the price from rising far enough to clear the market, thus creating a shortage. When this occurs, available supplies of the good must be allocated by some non-price method, such as formal or informal *rationing, or queueing.

short-dated security A security with under 5 years to maturity when first issued.

short position A contract to sell, for future delivery, goods or securities in excess of the amount a firm or individual actually holds. The holder of a short position relies on being able to produce or buy sufficient goods or securities to be able to fulfil the contract. When the time for delivery arrives, if spot market prices are lower than the contract price, the holder of the short position will be able to buy the goods at this lower price, and will make a profit. If the spot market price is higher than the price agreed in the contract, however, the result can be a loss, with no finite limit to its size. A short position is thus extremely risky.

short run A period in which some things cannot be changed, which could be changed given more time. In the short run, for example, a firm can buy more materials or fuel, and can hire more unskilled workers, but does not have time to build new plant or to recruit and train more skilled workers or managers. The short run is contrasted with the medium run, in which more things, but not everything, can be changed, and with the long run, in which everything can be changed that can ever be changed at all. Short-run supply and demand curves are typically less *elastic than the corresponding long-run curves.

short-run capital movements Movements of capital between countries which can be quickly reversed. This normally means holding *liquid assets, such as bank deposits or short-dated financial assets such as bills. It is possible to move funds short-term and buy shares or longer-dated bonds, but this adds to the risks. Short-run capital movements may be caused by differences in interest rates, where investors shift funds to countries with higher interest rates; or by expectations of exchange rate changes, where speculators shift funds out of currencies they expect to depreciate into currencies they expect to appreciate. Short-run capital movements may also be provoked by fears of persecution or breakdown of public order, or be part of the processes of money-laundering. It is believed that large-scale short-run capital movements have contributed to the instability of exchange rates during the flexible rates period.

short-run cost curve *See* cost curve.

short-run marginal cost *See* marginal cost.

short-run Phillips curve *See* Phillips curve.

short-termism The conduct of a business with too much regard to short-run relative to longer-run results. For industry, this means spending too little on *research and development (R&D), staff training, and investment in projects with a long lag in bringing in profits; for financial institutions, it means putting too much weight on short-term capital gains. Short-termism thus means *discounting the future too heavily. The concept is necessarily subjective, as there is no objective way of deciding the correct rate at which future costs and benefits should be discounted.

short-time working Cutting a firm's use of labour by reducing hours of work below a normal working week rather than laying some workers off. The merit of this is that it keeps the firm in contact with all its workers, so that more labour can be obtained very easily when it is needed. It is likely to be more acceptable to the workers than *redundancies if alternative jobs are difficult to obtain. Short-time working also keeps workers in practice, so that their skills are maintained. It is normally only used when the demand for labour is expected to recover.

shut-down price A price so low that at this or any lower price a firm prefers to shut its plant down rather than continue production. At prices just above the shut-down price the firm will usually be making a loss, but provided that the market is expected to recover, so that the firm is not planning to leave the industry permanently, this is preferred to the loss of contact with both workers and customers involved in a complete shut-down. The shut-down price is thus normally below marginal cost.

SIB *See* Securities and Investment Board.

SIC *See* Standard Industrial Classification.

sickness benefit Benefits paid to workers temporarily unable to work because of illness.

side-effects Unintended results of policies. These are frequently undesirable; for example, governments attempting to make essentials available cheaply to the poor by imposing maximum prices below the cost of production have found that the goods cease to be available at all. Side-effects can sometimes be beneficial; for example local councils which cut down on spraying roadsides with weedkiller to save money have incidentally encouraged the return of wild flowers.

side-payment A payment made by one or more parties in an agreement to other parties, to induce them to join the agreement. Suppose, for example, that in a group of firms, each has a profitable plant. They calculate that if one plant were closed and its output shifted to the remaining plants, total costs for the group would be lower and thus total profits would rise. If each firm gets its profits solely by selling the output from its own plant, no agreement can be reached, since the firm whose plant closes loses all its profits. The firms can thus only be induced to agree to a plan which includes side-payments, by which the firms whose plants remain open use part of their increased profits to compensate the firm whose plant closes down.

sigma A Greek letter, written as Σ in upper case, or σ in lower case. This is used in economics in various ways. Upper case Σ is used to denote the sum of the items following it; thus

$$\Sigma_1^N x_i = (x_1 + x_2 + \ldots + x_N).$$

Here the subscript 1 and superscript N after Σ denote the limits of the values i should take. In cases where the limits of the summation are obvious, Σ_i may be used. Lower case σ is used to denote the standard deviation, a widely used measure of dispersion, defined as the square root of the mean sum of squares of the distances between each x_i and their mean μ_x. Thus

$$\sigma = \sqrt{[\Sigma_i (x_i - \mu_x)^2/N]}$$

(this is true if μ_x is already known; if μ_x is itself being calculated from the same data set,

$$\sigma = \sqrt{[\Sigma_i (x_i - \mu_x)^2/(N-1)]}$$

gives an unbiased estimate). The symbols Σ and σ are also both frequently used in economics in other senses defined ad hoc.

signalling Actions taken not for the sake of their direct results, but to inform prospective customers or employers. For example, students may seek qualifications through formal examinations even though they have no interest in a subject, and it is well known that it will be of no use to them in actually doing a job. This is rational conduct if they believe that prospective employers will regard taking examinations as signalling energy, and doing well in them as signalling ability, so that success in examinations helps in getting a good job.

significance, tests of *See* tests of significance.

silicon valley The area of southern California containing a major concentration of computer and information technology businesses. This is a frequently cited example of the tendency to geographical specialization, caused by external economies resulting from the proximity of similar businesses.

simple interest The system by which repayment of a loan after n periods requires payment of a sum equal to the principal plus n times the interest payable for a single period. If the principal is P and the interest rate per period is r, at the end of n periods payment of $P(1 + nr)$ is required. As n increases, the proportional rate of return to the lender goes down, as the proportional return for the $n + 1$th period is $rP/[(1 + nr)P]$, which is a decreasing function of n. Simple interest is very rarely used, except for loans of very short duration where arithmetic simplicity may be felt to outweigh this defect.

simulation The use of quantitative models, normally mounted on a computer, to mimic the working of an economy. Given the assumptions about how an economy works, simulation is used to see how models respond to changes in these assumptions, changes in the distribution of stochastic shocks, or changes in economic policy. Simulation models normally use numerical methods, as their structure is too complicated for analytical conclusions about their behaviour to be obtainable.

simultaneous equations A system of two or more equations relating two or more variables. A solution to such a system is a set of values of the variables for which each equation is satisfied. In general as many variables as independent equations are needed for a system of simultaneous equations to be solvable, but this does not guarantee that any solution exists. For some particular systems, for example simultaneous linear equations, necessary and sufficient conditions for the existence of solutions can be stated, but such rules are specific to particular systems. For more complex systems, it may be difficult to establish whether solutions exist. If they do, there may well be multiple solutions. It is, however, always possible to check whether any proposed solution is correct: this is done by substituting it into the original equations and checking that each is in fact satisfied.

sine The ratio in a right-angled triangle between the side opposite to an angle and the hypotenuse. The sine of angle x is written sin x. If a circle of unit radius is drawn, measuring angles anti-clockwise starting from due East, sin x is the vertical coordinate of the point on the circle at angle x from the centre. Sin x fluctuates between a minimum of -1, reached when $x = 3\pi/2$ or $x = 3\pi/2 \pm n(2\pi)$, where n is any integer, and a maximum of $+1$, reached when $x = \pi/2$ or $x = \pi/2 \pm n(2\pi)$. [This is true measuring x in radians; if x is measured in degrees, sin x has a minimum when $x = 270°$ or $x = 270° \pm n(360°)$], and a maximum when $x = 90°$ or $x = 90° \pm n(360°)$. The sine function thus has regular oscillations as x increases. *See also* the figure for trigonometric functions.

single currency A currency used by two or more countries. It is necessary to decide how the amount to be issued is determined. This may be by agreement between two or more national central banks, or by commissioning a single supra-national institution to issue the currency. If a single currency is issued independently by more than one national authority, without any agreement between them, it is likely that too much of it will be issued. This is because the initial gains from additional currency accrue to the nation that issues it, while the losses resulting from inflation following excessive issue of a currency are spread between all countries using it.

Single European Act, 1986 An amendment to the Treaty of Rome, governing the conduct of the *European Community (EC). This made a large number of changes arising from the Cockfield Report (1985), *Completing the Internal Market*. These included permitting decisions by majority voting, an increase in the powers of the European Parliament, and recognition of the *European Monetary System (EMS).

single market The unified European market created in 1992 by the Single European Act. This was supposed to be achieved through the removal of all barriers to movements of goods, labour, and capital between member countries of the *European Community (EC). It was expected to have a substantial effect in raising European GDP by increasing efficiency, removing frontier controls, and opening up public contracts to EU-wide competition. These objectives have not (in 2002) yet been fully achieved.

single-peaked preferences An assumption about the pattern of individual preferences. This is that where any characteristic of a good or situation can be described by a numerical index, any individual has a unique most-preferred level of the index, and the valuation put on the good declines monotonically as the index departs from the preferred value in either direction. This means that any individual asked to choose or vote will always prefer the most-valued level to any other, and of any two alternatives on the same side of the most preferred value, will vote for that nearer the preferred value.

SITC *See* Standard Industrial Trade Classification.

size distribution of firms The number of firms of various sizes. Size can be measured in various ways: employment, turnover, and stock exchange capitalization are commonly used measures of size. On any measure the distribution tends to be skewed, with a lot of small firms and relatively few large ones in any industry or area, or a country as a whole.

skewness A measure of distributions, showing whether large deviations from the mean are more likely one side than the other. In a symmetrical distribution, deviations either side of the mean are equally likely. Positive skewness means that large upward deviations are more likely than large downward ones; the sum of cubes of deviations from the mean is positive. Negative skewness means that large downward deviations are more likely than large upward ones; the sum of cubes of deviations from the mean is negative. In many economic variables the distribution of deviations from the mean is skewed; for example, the distributions of individual incomes and the sizes of firms are both strongly positively skewed.

skilled work Work that can only be satisfactorily performed by somebody with appropriate technical qualifications, experience, or often both. Skilled workers are usually paid more than unskilled, and their jobs are typically more secure, because they would be difficult to replace, so that employers do not lay them off in the face of temporary falls in demand.

skills The ability to perform various tasks satisfactorily. Skills may involve physical dexterity, mental ability, or both. They can be learned either through formal instruction or through the apprenticeship system, working under the supervision of somebody who already has them. Individuals appear to differ in their ability to acquire skills. Workers with scarce skills can generally obtain better paid and more secure jobs than those without them.

slack Unused or under-used resources. Organizational slack occurs when firms or government bodies have more employees, equipment or buildings than they really need. Most organizations contain some slack: when demand varies, it is difficult to distinguish slack from necessary reserve capacity. In *linear programming a slack variable is the unused part of any resource: slack variables are non-negative by assumption, and are zero only if the constraint concerned is effective.

slavery The ownership of human beings by other people or organizations. While it has a long history, it is nowadays not generally practised, both on humanitarian grounds and because it is believed to be inefficient at providing incentives for work, and in particular for the acquisition of skills. It was widespread up to the nineteenth century, and labour practices in some countries even now are criticized as being akin to slavery.

slump A prolonged period of abnormally low economic activity and abnormally high unemployment. This is often accompanied by a tendency for prices to fall, or at least to rise more slowly than usual, and by a fall in the relative prices of primary products as compared with those of industrial products.

Slutsky equation The equation showing how the effect on demand for a good of a change in its price can be decomposed into the *substitution effect, which shows the effect of a change in relative prices at an unchanged level of real income, and the *income effect, which shows the effect of a change in real income holding prices constant.

Smithsonian Agreement An agreement reached in 1971 to try to restore a *Bretton Woods-style system of pegged exchange rates. The agreement was so named from the location of the conference at which it was reached, in the Smithsonian Institute in Washington, DC. The new Smithsonian parities lasted only a few months.

Smithsonian parities New parities for the world's major currencies agreed at the Smithsonian conference in 1971. These were intended to replace the *Bretton Woods system, which had broken down. The new parities agreed were rapidly found to be unsustainable.

smog Photochemical atmospheric pollution caused by emissions of hydrocarbons and nitrous oxides (NO_x). Named for its similarity to a cross between smoke and fog, smog is damaging to health. It results mainly from vehicle exhausts, particularly in heavily urbanized areas subject to temperature inversion which traps emission products near the surface. Smog is an obvious and conspicuous example of external diseconomies.

Smoot–Hawley Tariff Act A US act of 1930 establishing a protectionist tariff regime. It is widely believed that this act and similar measures in other major trading countries including Germany and the UK helped to produce the Great Depression of the 1930s.

snake in the tunnel An expression for an agreement by a group of countries in a flexible exchange rate system to intervene in the foreign exchange market to hold their currencies closer to each other than the generally permitted maximum deviation. The general limit is the tunnel, the closer limit is the snake. This system was operated by some European countries before the adoption of the *European Monetary System (EMS) in 1979.

social benefit The total benefit from any activity. This includes not only benefits accruing directly to the person or firm conducting the activity, but also external benefits accruing to other people who cannot be charged for them.

Social Chapter A chapter of the *Maastricht Treaty of 1993, dealing largely with social questions, including employment protection and works councils. The UK government chose originally to opt out of this section of the Treaty, but has since accepted it.

social charges Taxes on employment, whether levied on employers or employees. Social charges are levied in many countries, to pay for various social benefits such as unemployment insurance and pensions. In the UK social charges take the form of National Insurance contributions. Social charges make the cost of labour to employers higher than the earnings of their employees. High social charges are thought to contribute to high levels of unemployment in some EU countries.

social cost The total cost of any activity. This includes not only private costs which fall directly on the person or firm conducting the activity, but also external costs, which fall on other people, who are not able to exact any compensation for them.

socialism The idea that the economy's resources should be used in the interests of all its citizens, rather than allowing private owners of land and capital to use them as they see fit. Socialists have included believers in voluntary co-operation, believers in central planning, and believers in the use of the market mechanism in running a socialist economy. Socialists have tended to be egalitarian in principle, though not necessarily in practice. The use of planning rather than prices in running the economy makes the actual measurement of inequality difficult, and individuals can be as corrupt in a socialist as in a capitalist economy.

social opportunity cost The amount of other goods which has to be forgone because resources are used to make some particular good. When any goods or services are produced, the resources used to make them are not available for other purposes. Social opportunity cost takes account of any *external economies and diseconomies, as well as direct costs to the producers. It is contrasted with private oppportunity cost, which takes account only of direct opportunity costs to the producers, disregarding any external diseconomies.

social overhead capital Capital goods of types which are available to anybody, hence social; and are not tightly linked to any particular part of production, hence overhead. Because of their broad availability they often have to be provided by the government. Examples of social overhead capital include roads, schools, hospitals, and public parks.

social safety net A system of available payments in cash or in kind which will keep people's incomes from falling below some socially accepted minimum level. This needs to cover old age, sickness and disability, and unemployment. It may include *benefits in kind for people with special requirements: for example, health care, and publicly provided housing for those without the means or competence to house themselves privately.

social security benefits State payments designed to assure all residents of a country of minimum living standards. These benefits are typically provided to those over retirement age, and those unable to support themselves through disability, illness, or inability to find work. The benefits cover the recipient and any dependents, especially children. Social security benefits may be paid for by contributions from workers or their employers, or by general taxation. National insurance schemes, such as that in the UK, are usually not actuarially solvent, and have to be subsidized from general taxation. Social security benefits may or may not be means tested, where the recipients have any private income or occupational pensions. *See also* means-tested benefits.

social security contributions Charges levied on individuals or their employers to pay for the costs of social security benefits. The argument for having specific charges for this purpose rather than simply paying for social security through the tax system is the hope that such charges will be less resented than taxes, and that calling the benefits system an insurance scheme will remove any stigma from accepting benefits. There seems little evidence that taxpayers distinguish between the tax and national insurance elements of their overall tax bill, and the rationale of imposing high taxes on the use of labour in the presence of large-scale unemployment is not clear. Social security systems are normally not true insurance schemes: in the UK, for example, national insurance contributions are not sufficient to make the National Insurance system actuarially solvent.

social services The parts of social security requiring individual contact rather than cash payments. People's minimum consumption needs can be met by cash payments to those without sufficient incomes, through pensions and other benefits. Some citizens, however, need personal assistance with managing their lives as well as cash handouts. Personal social services cover matters such as home help for the disabled, advice and supervision for those on probation, advice and assistance in dealing with children and adults with behavioural problems, and supervision of parents thought to be in danger of harming their children.

social welfare function The idea that a measure of the total welfare of the members of a society could be constructed. This would be a function of the welfare of individuals, and the relation between them. Construction of such a function runs into extreme difficulties. A follower of Pareto or a utilitarian would argue, for example, that any change which made one individual better off and nobody worse off must be beneficial; but a believer in the importance of relative income might argue that £1 given to one of the richest individuals would actually decrease total welfare, as the poor would suffer more from envy than the rich would gain from extra spending. *See also* Rawlsian social welfare function.

society, co-operative *See* co-operative society.

soft budget constraint A limit to spending by some public body where those supposed to be subject to it believe that the consequences of breaching it will not be serious. For example, the managers of state-owned firms may believe that if they run at a loss, or make smaller profits than they have been instructed to, the state will meet the firm's losses, and not sack them. This is contrasted with a hard budget constraint, where the results of failure to break even, or to achieve required levels of profits, are expected to be catastrophic: for example, closure of the enterprise or dismissal of the management.

soft currency A currency which is not convertible into other currencies, or whose value in terms of other currencies is expected to fall. This is contrasted with a hard currency, which is freely convertible into other currencies, and which people want to hold because it is expected to maintain or improve its value in terms of other currencies.

soft landing A successful stabilization programme which restores price stability after a period of excess demand and inflation without provoking a recession in the process. The problem with achieving this is that if restrictive monetary and fiscal policy are not tight enough, the economy will not land at all, and inflation will continue; while if restrictive policies are too energetic there will be a slump in demand before stability is restored. A soft landing is contrasted with a hard landing, when restrictive policies are used too vigorously, so that excess demand is replaced by excess supply, and there is a recession before stability is restored.

soft loan A loan on terms less onerous than normal market rates. This may take various forms. A loan may carry a low rate of interest, the start of interest payments may be deferred, repayment may be spread over an unusually long period, it may be easy to arrange deferment of interest or redemption payments, or the debtor may be allowed to make interest or redemption payments in soft currency. A soft loan is contrasted with a hard loan, where interest is at market rates, and interest and redemption payments have to be made promptly in hard currency.

soil erosion Destruction of soil by wind or rain after vegetation cover is removed. Soil erosion is a particular problem in less developed countries (LDCs), where population pressure leads to deforestation and over-grazing. It also occurred in the American dustbowl. Water erosion can be controlled by contour terracing and the construction of small storage dams, and both forms of erosion can be prevented by planting ground-cover vegetation.

sole proprietor A person running a business, without partners or incorporation. The advantage of sole proprietorship is unity of control, as the owner and management are the same. The drawback of sole proprietorship is that in many industries *economies of scale are such that the minimum efficient scale of a business is well beyond the capacity of individuals to provide sufficient capital.

sole trader *See* sole proprietor.

Solow growth model A model in which the growth of total GDP is explained by population increase, technical progress, and investment. In this model there is full employment, with an aggregate production function showing *constant returns to scale. In the long run the rate of growth of GDP is determined by population growth and the rate of technical progress. Higher investment can speed up growth temporarily, but as the *capital–output ratio rises, an increasing proportion of GDP needs to be invested to equip the increasing labour force, and the capital–output ratio converges towards a finite limit, however high a proportion of GDP is invested. Similarly, low investment slows down growth, but the capital–output ratio falls towards a lower limit which is always positive for positive investment. This type of model is contrasted both with *Harrod–Domar growth models, which discuss the difficulties in maintaining full employment growth, and with *endogenous growth models, in which a higher or lower share of investment in GDP has a permanent effect on the growth rate.

Solow residual The part of the growth of national income which cannot be explained by the growth of labour and capital. This assumes that wages measure the marginal product of labour and profits measure the marginal product of capital. The residual is ascribed to technical progress.

solution A value of its argument such that an *equation is satisfied (or a set of values of their arguments such that all the equations in a system are satisfied). For an equation with only one argument, written as $f(x) = 0$, a solution is any value of x for which $f(x) = 0$. If the equation is a function of several arguments, written as

$$f(x_1, x_2, \ldots, x_N) = 0,$$

a solution is a set of values $x_1, x_2, \ldots, x_N$ for which

$$f(x_1, x_2, \ldots, x_N) = 0.$$

There is no general method for locating the solutions to equations, or even for establishing whether or not they exist, except for a few special cases such as sets of linear equations. It is always possible, however, to check whether any proposed solution is correct: substitute the values of the variables $x_1, x_2, \ldots, x_N$ into the equations, and check that they are all satisfied. The fact that a solution has been found does not in general indicate that there is no other solution, again with some exceptions for special cases. *See also* corner solution.

solvency Possession of assets in excess of a person or a firm's liabilities. Where the assets are either cash or marketable securities it may be obvious that a person or firm is solvent. It is an offence to trade knowing oneself to be insolvent, but if the assets are non-marketable solvency is largely a matter of judgement. Individuals can and do obtain unsecured credit, which they rely on future earnings to repay. Companies frequently trade successfully and pay off all their debts, when they would have been insolvent if forced into premature liquidation. In such cases the assets consist of patents, know-how, or contacts which could not be sold but were able to yield an income if kept together as a going concern.

sound money Money which preserves stable real purchasing power. This will only happen if the authorities issuing the money give priority in their policies to maintaining its value, and have an established reputation for such policy priorities, which in turn leads to market expectations of price stability. A sound money policy is in conflict with the Keynesian view that the primary responsibility of the monetary authorities should be maintaining a stable level of *effective demand. While a policy of priority for demand management does not directly lead the authorities to promote inflation, it does mean that the authorities tend to tolerate any inflation that does occur by *accommodatory monetary policy, which in turn leads to market expectations that inflation is likely.

sources of capital The sources from which businesses, whether private, corporate, or state-owned, obtain their capital. One major source is the savings of the owners of private businesses, and the undistributed profits of companies. A second major source is borrowing, either by selling bonds or borrowing from banks and other financial intermediaries. A further source of capital is selling equity shares. A large amount of fixed investment is financed from the depreciation allowances on existing equipment. Stocks of material are often financed by trade credit from suppliers. The government is also a major source of finance. Some businesses are publicly owned, and their capital is provided by the government. Governments make some capital transfers to finance investment, for example by housing associations.

They also frequently tax businesses under rules which decrease business taxes if investment is undertaken: companies which invest pay less tax, or are allowed to pay later, than companies with equal profits but less investment.

sovereign debt Debt of the governments of independent countries. With the debt of an individual or corporation, it is usually possible to use legal procedures to compel them to pay the interest and redemption payments due, or to hand their assets over to the creditor if they do not pay. Such legal sanctions are not available against governments, unless they choose to submit voluntarily to legal procedures. There is thus a risk that sovereign debt may be subject to repudiation, interest reductions, or compulsory rescheduling. The only protection for the creditors of sovereign debtors is the borrowers' concern about loss of reputation: default makes it difficult or expensive for them to borrow in the future.

sovereignty, consumer *See* consumer sovereignty.

spare capacity Capital equipment which is not currently needed for production. Firms like to have some spare capacity available, to meet sudden increases in demand for their products, and to be able to maintain production if equipment breaks down. Spare capacity is costly to purchase and maintain, however, so there is a limit to the amount that is wanted. Where firms have equipment which is too unlikely to be needed to be worth maintaining, this is *excess capacity.

special deposits Additional deposits that other banks are required to make with the central bank. These may carry low or no interest, and do not count towards any normal minimum reserve requirements. Special deposits reduce bank profits, and their ability to extend credit.

Special Drawing Rights A form of international money, created by the *International Monetary Fund (IMF) and defined as a weighted average of various convertible currencies. The IMF's official accounts are kept in terms of SDRs as units of account. Members have holdings of SDRs which can be used to settle balance-of-payments deficits between them, subject to rules governing the average amount to be held over any five-year period.

specialization Concentration on providing particular types of goods and services, and relying on others to provide what one does not produce. This occurs at all levels: individuals acquire particular skills or professional qualifications; firms concentrate on particular industries; districts, regions, or whole countries specialize in particular activities. Specialization may be total or partial. With total specialization, most activities are not carried on at all, and the goods and services concerned are entirely provided by others. This is very common at the individual and the firm level. With partial specialization, some but not all of particular goods and services are acquired from others. This is common at the regional and national level: many countries, for example, provide some but not all of their own food or fuel. Specialization has been a feature of all known human societies. At all levels, the *division of labour allows society to benefit from differences between individuals in abilities and between areas in natural resources. It also allows the development of specific skills, through both formal training and learning by experience. Specialization carries with it the danger that an economy based on very specific skills is liable to disruption by technical progress, changes in tastes, or man-made disturbances.

specific tax A tax levied at a fixed rate per physical unit of the good taxed, regardless of its price. This is in contrast to an *ad valorem tax, where the tax is proportional to the price of the good. Specific taxes have administrative advantages where measuring quantities is simple, for example in licensing cars or television sets, while the measurement of second-hand values would be very cumbersome. The disadvantage of specific taxes is that they are regressive, falling proportionally lightly on richer consumers who can afford better quality and more expensive goods, and proportionally heavily on poorer consumers who can only afford lower quality and cheaper varieties. The real yield of specific taxes is also rapidly eroded by inflation.

speculation Economic activity aimed at profiting from expected changes in the prices of goods, assets, or currencies. In a world of uncertainty, most transactions are capable of being interpreted as speculative, but the term speculation is reserved for transactions where expected *capital gains provide a major motive. Speculators may buy goods or assets they do not want but whose prices they expect to rise, or buy call options on such assets. They can contract to buy assets they do not have the funds to pay for. Speculators may sell goods, assets, or currencies they do not really want to part with, but whose prices they expect to fall, so that they will be able to buy them back more cheaply; or they may buy put options on such assets. It is also possible to contract to sell assets one does not actually possess. In Keynesian monetary theory, the *speculative motive for holding money implies that more than the usual proportion of assets is held in money when bond prices are expected to fall, and less than the usual proportion of assets is held in money when bond prices are expected to rise. If speculators hold stable expectations about the medium-term levels of prices, the reaction of speculation to short-term fluctuations in prices will be stabilizing. If the speculators themselves have unstable expectations, speculation is liable to amplify fluctuations in asset prices due to other causes. Whether speculation tends to stabilize or destabilize markets is controversial.

speculative bubble *See* bubble.

speculative motive The effects of expectations of changes in interest rates on the *demand for money. In Keynesian monetary theory such expectations are important. If it is believed that interest rates are likely to rise, and thus that bond prices are likely to fall, this makes bonds less and money more attractive to hold. This gives an incentive to sell bonds and hold money, or to defer buying bonds and hold on to money which would otherwise have been put into bonds to earn interest. Similarly, if interest rates are expected to fall, and bond prices to rise, this makes bonds more and money less attractive. This gives an incentive to reduce money holdings and buy bonds. The speculative motive for holding money is contrasted with the *transactions and *precautionary motives.

speculator An individual or firm taking *risks for the sake of expected profits. Speculators may be willing to do this because they believe they have better information and ability to forecast future prices than other market participants, or because they are risk-neutral, or less risk-averse than other market participants, who are willing to pay to transfer risks to somebody else. Speculators are often attacked as causing economic instability. Their defenders argue that speculators provide *liquidity for other people's assets, that on average their activities smooth price fluctuations rather than increasing them, and that without speculators many innovations could not have been financed.

spending, discretionary *See* discretionary spending.

spending programme, mandatory *See* mandatory spending programme.

spill-over A connection between different parts of the economy. Spill-overs may be pecuniary or non-pecuniary. A pecuniary spill-over occurs, for example, when changes in one industry affect factor supplies to another: if a new factory bids up the wages of unskilled labour so that local people find cleaners or gardeners more expensive, this is a pecuniary spill-over. Pecuniary spill-overs produce their effects through markets. A non-pecuniary spill-over occurs when one industry inflicts *external diseconomies on another: there is usually no market through which they can be paid not to do so. Non-pecuniary spill-overs provide a prima facie case for government intervention, by regulation or taxation, whereas pecuniary spill-overs do not, except on grounds of income distribution.

spiral *See* inflationary spiral, and wage-price spiral.

spot market A market for goods, securities, or currencies for immediate delivery (in some cases a short time is allowed for delivery). Spot markets are distinguished from *forward and *futures markets, in which delivery of the items traded is due at an agreed future date.

spot price The price of goods for immediate delivery. This is contrasted with forward or futures prices, which are for goods to be delivered at named future dates. Spot transactions are normally settled by actual delivery, whereas most forward and futures deals are paper transactions only.

spouses, independent taxation of *See* independent taxation of spouses.

spread The difference between the bid and offer prices quoted by a market-maker. The prices of securities at which market-makers are willing to sell are higher than those at which they are willing to buy. The spread has to cover the market-makers' operating costs and provide profits, and includes a premium against the risk that any particular customer has insider knowledge about the security being traded. Spreads tend to be smaller on more widely traded securities.

spurious relationship An apparent relation between two variables, which disappears when the effects of a third variable are taken into account. Suppose that variable y is regressed on variable x: estimating the relation

$$y_i = \alpha + \beta x_i + \varepsilon_i$$

gives an estimate of β which is significantly different from 0. However, if variable z is added, fitting

$$y_i = \alpha + \beta x_i + \gamma z_i + \varepsilon_i$$

yields an estimate of γ which is significantly different from 0, but an estimate of β which is not. The apparent relation between y and x is thus shown to be spurious.

squeeze, credit *See* credit squeeze.

stability conditions The conditions for a system to tend to revert to its original condition after a disturbance. The process of convergence may involve fluctuations, and the *equilibrium state to which a system reverts may itself be a stationary state, a steady-state growth path, or some form of limit cycle. Where a system can be described by a set of linear equations, the stability conditions for a linear *difference equation system are that all roots be less than 1 in absolute value; in a linear *differential equation system the stability conditions are that all roots be negative in their real part. In the linear difference equation system $y_t = a + by_{t-1}$, for example, the system is stable and will converge on the equilibrium level $y = a/(1 - b)$ if and only if $-1 < b < 1$. Stability conditions can be found for any linear system; for most non-linear systems stability can only be tested by numerical simulation.

stabilization Altering the behaviour of a system to induce it to return to equilibrium following disturbances, or to speed up the rate at which it does so. Where a system is affected by stochastic shocks, which cannot be forecast or offset without a time-lag, complete stabilization is impossible: it may be possible to reduce fluctuations, but not to eliminate them entirely.

stabilization policy The use of economic policies to reduce fluctuations. This may be applied at the macroeconomic level, to reduce fluctuations in real incomes, unemployment, inflation, or exchange rates, or at the microeconomic level, to reduce fluctuations in the prices of particular goods. Where a system is subject to stochastic shocks, to the extent that these can be predicted, stabilization policy can work by either preventing or offsetting them. If the shocks cannot be forecast or offset without time lags, some fluctuations are inevitable, and stabilization policy can seek only to reduce them. Stabilization may be pursued by creating automatic or *built-in stabilizers: higher marginal tax rates, for example, both reduce the *multiplier and speed up the rate at which the multiplier process converges. The alternative is to use *discretionary policy measures, such as changes in tax rates: this has the advantage that the authorities can react to new types of disturbance, but the disadvantage that unless the authorities stick to pre-announced or widely understood policies, it is necessary for other economic agents to guess what the authorities will do. If the other agents guess wrong this may simply act as a further source of stochastic disturbances, and destabilize rather than stabilize the economy. In particular, if the authorities attempt *fine tuning of the economy by vigorous and frequent changes of policy, they may make economic fluctuations worse rather than curing them.

stabilizers, automatic *See* built-in stabilizers.

Stackelberg duopoly A duopoly in which one firm is the leader and the other is the follower. The leader is assumed to act strategically, choosing a strategy taking account of the follower's expected reactions. The follower is assumed to act non-strategically, reacting to the leader's strategy but not anticipating the leader's reactions.

stag To subscribe to new issues of shares in the hope of selling immediately at a profit. A stag is an investor who acts in this way.

stages of economic growth The theory that countries develop through a series of modes of economic organization, each leading to the next. Various such sequences have been proposed: for example, Feudalism–Capitalism–Socialism; or Hunting-gathering–Herding animals–Agriculture–Industry–Service-based economy. In each case several economies can be observed to have followed such a sequence; whether all economies must do so, or whether the order can be changed or some stages omitted, is a matter of controversy.

stagflation The situation where a country persistently suffers from both high *inflation and high *unemployment. Economists at one time believed that inflation stimulated economic activity, and that high unemployment reduced inflation. If these beliefs were correct, no economy could long suffer from both at once, so stagflation would be impossible. Unfortunately, recent experience suggests that high unemployment and inflation are incompatible only in the extremely long run, if at all.

stagnation A situation in which there is little or no change in techniques or income levels. This is contrasted with development, when techniques are changing and income levels increasing.

stakeholder Anybody with some form of interest in a business. As well as *shareholders, this includes directors, managers, other employees, customers, subcontractors, and even the general public in cases where the firm's activities impact on the environment. A stakeholder is thus anybody who stands to lose if a business is run badly. While formally directors are supposed to run companies in the interests of the shareholders, in many cases they are expected by others, and often claim themselves, to consider the interests of the other stakeholders as well.

stamp duty A tax on transactions, levied by requiring that documents bear an official stamp to be legally valid. In the UK at one time there was a small stamp duty on cheques; it is now levied on some sales of property and on share transfers.

stamps, food *See* food stamps.

standard *See* dollar standard, gold standard, and technical standard.

Standard and Poor (S&P) One of the main US credit-rating agencies. It produces the S&P 500 stock price index, based on the prices of 500 principal shares traded on the New York Stock Exchange (NYSE). This covers about 80 per cent of the total value of stocks traded. The S&P 100 index covers many of the larger corporations' stocks, representing about 60 per cent of the New York Stock Exchange (NYSE) market.

standard deviation A commonly used measure of dispersion, defined as the square root of the mean of squared deviations of a variable from its mean. Thus if x takes N different values, x_i, for $i = 1, 2, \ldots, N$, and the mean is μ, the standard deviation is given by

$$\sigma = \sqrt{[\Sigma_i (x_i - \mu)^2 / N]}.$$

If μ itself has to be estimated from the N observations, the best estimator for the standard deviation is

$$\sigma = \sqrt{[\Sigma_i (x_i - \mu)^2 / (N - 1)]}.$$

standard error A measure of the reliability of an estimated parameter. The standard error is the standard deviation of the estimates that would be arrived at by taking repeated *random samples of a given size from the same population. The standard error is a decreasing function of sample size; the lower the standard error, the more reliable is the estimate.

Standard Industrial Classification (SIC) The method of classifying types of economic activity used in UK official statistics. This is consistent with the International Standard Industrial Classification (ISIC) issued by the United Nations (UN), and the Nomenclature des Activités établies dans les Communautés Européennes (NACE) used by the European Union (EU). The advantage of a similar classification of industries is that it facilitates international comparisons of the composition and the efficiency of industries.

Standard International Trade Classification (SITC) The system used to classify international visible trade. The main sections are denoted by single digits; for example, 0 is food and live animals, 1 is beverages and tobacco, etc. More detailed classifications are denoted by further digits, down to the five-digit level.

standardized commodity A commodity produced to uniform specifications, so that different units are interchangable. Standardized goods make possible lower costs of production through *economies of scale, but place some restriction on consumer choice. Only standardized commodities are suitable for being traded on forward and futures markets.

standard of living The economic component of people's welfare. This is often measured by consumption per head, or by consumption per equivalent adult, counting children as fractions of adults. This is not in fact a perfect welfare measure: it disregards some important factors contributing to overall welfare. First, it does not count services such as health care and education, which are sometimes provided free or at subsidized prices by governments, and sometimes have to be provided by consumers for themselves. Second, it takes no account of environmental externalities such as pollution, traffic delays or crime. Third, it can be argued that income saved contributes to welfare as well as income consumed, since the assets accumulated make their owners safer. Indeed, at the margin a rational consumer should equate the benefits of £1 consumed and £1 saved.

standard rate A now obsolete name for the rate of UK income tax applied to most incomes. This is now called *basic rate. There are usually lower rates for the first slice of taxable income, below some lower limit, and higher rates for income in excess of some upper limit. In the UK the basic or standard rate applies to the bulk of taxable incomes.

standby arrangement An arrangement by central banks to lend one another reserves if necessary to resist speculative pressure on their exchange rates. The existence of standby arrangements between a group of central banks decreases the total of *foreign exchange reserves that they need to hold between them, if speculative capital movements are likely to occur between their currencies.

staple product The most important product of an area or country. Domination of an economy by a single product is unusual except for some major oil producing countries, such as Kuwait, and a number of less developed countries (LDCs). Most modern economies have no single staple product, though some local areas are heavily dependent on particular industries.

State Earnings-Related Pension Scheme (SERPS) A UK government scheme to provide earnings-related pensions in addition to the basic flat-rate pension. Workers were required to belong to this unless they opted for a recognized occupational pension scheme or personal pension scheme. The SERPS scheme has been discontinued, but pensions from it are still being paid.

state enterprise A firm founded on the initiative of the state and run by it. The argument for state enterprises is that there are some activities which would be socially beneficial, but are not attractive to private entrepreneurs, and others which would be profitable but involve *natural monopolies and are therefore not to be trusted to private owners. An example of the first category would be factories to employ the disabled; of the second, provision of essential public services such as sewers. The argument against state enterprise is that as an owner the state provides a too soft budget constraint, and that the running of state enterprises is liable to capture by their management and workers, who run the business for their own benefit rather than that of the public. It is thus argued that it is better for the state to privatize such firms, subsidize them where necessary, and appoint regulatory bodies to supervise them, rather than running them itself.

state-owned company A company whose shares are owned by the state. This may be during the prelude to *privatization. If a company is privatized in stages, it is possible to have part of its shares state-owned, while the remainder are held privately.

state, welfare *See* welfare state.

statics, comparative *See* comparative statics.

stationary time series A time series in which the effects of shocks tend to zero as time passes. The process of convergence may include oscillations. Stationary time series are contrasted with series possessing *unit roots, where the effects of shocks persist indefinitely.

statistical discrepancy An item entered in tables by statisticians to show that data appear to be different when estimated by different methods, where if both methods were being applied without error the results ought to be the same. The alternative is to correct the results of one method to agree with those of the other. If the statisticians do not know which, if either, method produces a more accurate figure, it is more informative to include a statistical discrepancy to make this clear.

statistics 1. The collection of data and the mathematical methods used to draw inferences about the relations between different variables. This involves the use of techniques such as *linear regression and rank correlation. *See also* Bayesian statistics.
2. The numbers which are used to describe the functions fitted to data in summary form. Sufficient statistics are a set of parameters which contain or imply all available information about the functions they describe. If the fitted

function is a *normal distribution, for example, its mean and variance serve to describe it completely and uniquely.

statutory monopoly A monopoly protected by law from entry by rivals. Such monopolies are sometimes set up as a quid pro quo for an obligation to provide a universal service; the UK Post Office is an example of this.

steady state A state of the economy where all aggregates are constant. This includes zero population growth, zero net investment, no technical progress and a constant level of GDP. The composition of the labour force and capital stock change over time, but new entrants simply replace those who retire, and gross investment equals capital consumption.

steady-state growth A situation where all parts of the economy are growing at the same rate. This applies to the GDP, the capital stock, and the effective labour supply, which grows at a rate equal to the rate of population increase plus the rate of technical progress.

step function A function $x = f(y)$ where the value of the dependent variable, x, remains constant over ranges of the independent variable, y, then changes by discrete amounts at particular values of y. Step functions are extremely common in economic life, largely for administrative simplicity; consider for example the rules relating the cost of posting letters and parcels to their weight.

sterilization The method by which a central bank prevents *balance-of-payments surpluses or deficits from affecting the domestic *money supply. If there is a surplus in the balance of payments on current and capital account combined, this leads to a rise in the *foreign exchange reserves, and an increase in the money supply. If the central bank does not want the money supply to increase, it can prevent this by selling securities so as to sterilize the cash inflow. Similarly, if there is a deficit in the balance of payments on current and capital accounts combined, this leads to a loss of foreign exchange reserves and a shrinkage in the money supply. If the central bank does not want the money supply to fall, it can sterilize the cash outflow by buying securities. The central bank can choose to sterilize some proportion rather than the whole of the monetary effects of changes in foreign exchange reserves.

sterilized intervention *See* intervention in foreign exchange markets.

sterling The UK currency. The name originated from the pound Easterling, formerly used in trade with the Baltic. The sterling area was an arrangement under which a number of Commonwealth countries pegged their exchange rates to sterling and held their foreign exchange reserves in London: this system declined after 1950. Sterling M3 was a measure of the UK money supply excluding balances held in London but in other currencies.

sterling area A group of countries, mainly in the Commonwealth, which linked their currencies to sterling and held their foreign exchange reserves in London. This group was very important in the inter-war years and immediate post-war period, but declined in importance in the 1950s, mainly because of the UK's decreasing share in world trade and finance.

sterling M3 A former measure of broad money, including the following components:

(1) M0, that is, currency + banks' till money + banks' balances at the Bank of England;

(2) UK private sector sight bank deposits; and

(3) UK private sector time deposits + public sector sterling deposits.

This measure is now known simply as M3.

sticky prices Prices which do not vary in the face of small changes in costs or demand conditions.These are common in many manufacturing and service industries. This is because changing prices is administratively costly, and because of uncertainty about which way costs or demand conditions will move next. Firms may also believe that raising prices risks losing customers if competitors do not follow suit, while cutting prices runs the risk of starting a price war. If there are large changes in costs or demand conditions, prices usually do change.

sticky wages Wage rates that are not readily changed in the face of changes in market conditions. This frequently takes the form of either nominal wage resistance—an unwillingness to accept lower money wages—or real wage resistance—an unwillingness to accept real wage cuts, that is, wage increases less than the rate of inflation. Employers are also unwilling to increase wages in the face of temporary labour shortages, because of anticipated difficulty in lowering them again; and trade unions have been known to oppose their members accepting wage increases not negotiated through them.

stochastic Random, or affected by chance. A stochastic process is one where what happens is not exactly predictable, as it is affected by apparently random factors. It is often not known whether the apparent randomness is really so, or whether it is the result of the action of forces which are determinate, but so numerous that it is impracticable to model their effects.

stock 1. A variable which refers to the state of affairs at a point in time. This is contrasted to a *flow, which refers to the rate at which something happens over a period of time. For example the money supply, the price level, the assets of a firm, or the level of employment are stock concepts; whereas the national income, the profits of a firm, or the level of industrial production are flow concepts.

2. A synonym for stocks, a collection of goods held by an enterprise. *Stock appreciation is an increase in the value of stocks held due to price changes. A stockpile is a large holding of commodities, held for example by a government as a strategic reserve. *See also* buffer stock, and investment in stocks and work in progress.

3. A synonym for share. Common stock is the US term for ordinary share. Government stock is government debt instruments. A *stock exchange is an institution through which shares are traded. A stock option is a right to buy shares at a fixed price. *See also* alpha stocks, beta stocks, common stock, gamma stocks, and over-the-counter market,

stock appreciation The part of the change in the value of the stocks held by a business over any period which is due to price changes. Rising commodity prices cause this to be positive; falling commodity prices cause it to be negative. During inflationary periods stock appreciation causes real profits to be overestimated: firms may be allowed to subtract it in calculating their taxable profits, since without this adjustment they could be paying tax on nominal profits while real profits were in fact negative.

stockbroker A dealer in securities who acts only as an agent for others. A stockbroker sells stocks and shares for ultimate vendors at the highest available price, and buys for ultimate purchasers at the lowest available price. Stockbrokers may advise clients, or operate on the basis of simply executing orders, without giving advice. Brokers are contrasted with jobbers or *market-makers, who buy and sell securities on their own account.

stock dividend The situation when shareholders take their dividends in the form of new shares in a company rather than cash. This is a cheaper way of selling new shares than organizing an issue on the stock exchange, if only a small amount of new capital is required.

stock exchange An institution through which company shares and government stock are traded. Originally the exchange would be a building, where traders would gather and trade proceeded either by individual negotiation or by *'open outcry', where prices bid and offered were announced out loud so as to inform all traders within earshot. Modern stock exchanges are institutions with traders linked by computer networks and telephones. *Market-makers work either on a quote-driven system, announcing bid and offer prices at which they will trade with all comers, or on an order-driven system, where buy and sell orders are brought together and matched as far as possible at regular intervals, for example daily. In either case large deals usually get special treatment. Stock exchanges have rules about the information companies have to provide for their shares to be listed, the individuals or firms allowed to trade, the notification of trades carried out, and the procedure for settlement, that is actual delivery of shares and money payments. There are stock exchanges in all major world commercial centres, for example Frankfurt, London, New York, Paris, and Tokyo.

Stock Exchange Automated Quotation System (SEAQ) A screen-based dealing system allowing all *market-makers' buying and selling prices for a given security to be displayed to all traders simultaneously. This system was introduced in London after deregulation in 1986.

stock exchange listing The right of a company to have its shares traded on a stock exchange. Listing is usually conditional on the company providing a satisfactory level of information on its activities, and may be conditional on its size, or on making a sufficient proportion of shares open to the general public.

stock jobber An individual or firm who deals in shares, buying and selling as a principal. Jobbers are distinguished from stockbrokers, who act as an agents for buyers and sellers of shares, but do not trade on their own account. The role of stock jobbers has been taken over by *market-makers.

stock market *See* stock exchange.

stock market crash A sudden and drastic general fall in security prices on a stock exchange. For example, on 'Black Monday', 19 October 1987, the Dow Jones index in New York fell 23 per cent in a single day, and major falls occurred in London and other stock exchanges worldwide. A stock market crash is always possible, since the present price of shares is heavily dependent on opinions about future changes. A crash is most likely when a prolonged *bull market has pushed shares to high *price–earnings ratios.

stock option A right to buy shares in a company on some future date at a pre-arranged price. Stock options are often granted by companies to their directors and top executives as incentives. The greater the rise in the company's shares by the time the option can be exercised, the more the holder will gain, provided the market price is above the exercise price, so that the option is valuable. This gives a strong incentive to effort to improve the company's performance.

stockpile A large stock of a commodity. Stockpiles of goods such as wheat or tin may be held as strategic reserves, for use in emergencies such as wars or natural disasters. They may also be held to try to stabilize commodity prices, or more usually as the result of trying to hold commodity prices above a market-clearing level.

stocks and work in progress, increase in the book value *See* increase in the book value of stocks and work in progress.

stock split *See* bonus issue.

Stolper–Samuelson theorem A theory concerning the income distribution effects of *inter-industry trade. It shows the effects of trade in a two-good, two-factor model with constant returns to scale and incomplete specialization. The theorem shows that trade raises the real income of a country's plentiful factor, which is used relatively heavily by the exportables industry, but lowers the real income of the country's scarce factor, which is used relatively heavily in the importables industry. This is held to explain opposition to free trade. The model ignores the possible effects of complete specialization, of *intra-industry trade, and of fiscal action to compensate any losers from trade.

stop–go cycle A sequence of alternations of official policy between trying to expand and contract *effective demand. If the economy, when left alone, tended to produce alternating spells of depressed and excessive demand, stop–go policies could be defended as stabilizing. The suggestion of critics of 'stop–go' policies in the UK in the 1950s and 1960s was that the monetary and fiscal authorities applied the brakes and the accelerator alternately, in each case vigorously but too late. This set up tendencies to overshoot in each direction, destabilizing the economy. Stop–go policies were thus blamed for irregular growth.

store of value One of the functions of money. If asset prices are stable, money is unattractive as a store of value, as it brings in no income, but if asset prices are unstable, it is attractive to hold some part of total assets in money, as a safeguard against *risk. Money is particularly attractive as a store of value if there is believed to be any chance that prices generally will fall, and is less so the more inflation is thought likely.

straight-line depreciation The system of accounting for depreciation on an asset by taking an assumed life, say n years, and charging depreciation at the rate of $(1/n)$ of its cost each year until it is fully written down. The system is so named because if the remaining value is plotted against time on a graph the result is a downward-sloping straight line.

strategic entry deterrence Actions undertaken by a firm to deter competitors from entering their markets. Such actions could include making large investments of sunk capital, which make it unlikely that rivals could drive it out, or offering long-term low-price contracts to customers. For any given entry decisions by rivals, these policies do not maximize profits, but they may pay because they serve to discourage entry.

strategic game A game in which some players take account in choosing their own strategies of the way in which they expect this to affect the strategies chosen by other players. This is contrasted with a *Nash equilibrium, where each player takes the other players' strategies as given.

strategic trade policy A trade policy intended to influence the trade policies of other countries. A policy is said to be 'strategic' if it believed that while it would not be beneficial to adopt it if the policies of all other countries were taken as given, adopting it would in fact be beneficial because it would cause other countries to change their trade policies. For example, an export subsidy on good x might involve making losses if all other exporting countries continued to supply the world market, but might be beneficial if announcing the subsidy induced some or all foreign competitors to withdraw from the market.

strategic trade retaliation Retaliation to foreign trade restrictions which is imposed mainly to deter further restrictions. If country A raises its tariffs or cuts its quotas on B's goods, B has to decide whether to retaliate. If B could assume that A would take no further action, the best reaction might be to do nothing, on the argument that while A's action was harmful, retaliation would just make matters worse. However, B may fear that this would be interpreted by A as a signal that further restrictions would not be resisted, so B may take some form of retaliatory action simply to signal to A that they should go no further.

strategy A plan for dealing with uncertain future circumstances. This is a set of rules by which the actions to be taken depend on the circumstances, including natural events and the actions of other people. A *dominant strategy exists if one type of action by A is always best whatever is done by B, C, etc. A *mixed strategy uses a randomizing device, such as tossing coins, to choose between two or more sets of rules: this has the advantage of making it impossible for other people to predict your actions, as you do not know yourself how you will react until the randomizing device has been used. An open loop strategy is one where the rules to be followed are laid down at the start and do not change; a closed loop strategy includes 'feedback', that is, rules about changing the rules in the light of experience. *See also* dominant strategy, mixed strategy, and punishment strategy.

strengthening of a currency A rise in the price of one currency in terms of others. This is caused by an increase in the demand to hold it, which may be due either to an improvement of the country's current account, or to shifts into it from other currencies on capital account.

strike Withdrawal of labour by a group of employees, normally members of a *trade union. An official strike is one called or recognized by a union; an unofficial strike is one started without union authorization.

A no-strike agreement commits workers to accept arbitration of disputes, and not to resort to strike action.

strike ballot A vote of the members of a *trade union as to whether or not to resort to strike action. This may be required before a strike either by a union's own rules or by the law.

strike price The pre-arranged price at which an *option to buy or sell can be exercised.

Structural Funds Funds operated by the European Union (EU) to improve economic conditions in the poorest regions of member countries. Objective 1 funding, for example, is directed to regions whose per capita GDP is under 3/4 of the EU average. The intention of the Funds is to maintain political support for the EU by convincing people that it is beneficial for all its members, and not only for the more prosperous 'core' regions.

structural transformation A process of major change in a country's economy. This can involve a large-scale transfer of resources from primary to industrial sector activity, as in many *newly industrialized countries (NICs). It can also involve a shift in methods of economic organization, from a mainly planned to a largely market-based economy, as in many previously planned economies of the former USSR and Central and Eastern Europe.

structural unemployment Unemployment due to a lack of capital equipment which unemployed workers could use, or lack among unemployed workers of the skills necessary to produce anything for which there is a market. This can occur because investment has failed to keep pace with growth in the labour force: this is common in less developed countries (LDCs). It can also occur because of changes in demand, leading to the decline of industries which previously provided jobs. Structural unemployment cannot be cured by increasing effective demand, which would remedy *Keynesian unemployment, or by cutting wages, which would cure *classical unemployment; its cure requires major investment in new industries, or large-scale migration from depressed areas.

structure, market *See* market structure.

study, work *See* work study.

stylized facts Assumptions about the real world, claiming to be at least approximately true. An example is the assertion that a constant proportion of the national income goes to labour. While all aggregate statistics are over-simplifications, and many are inaccurate, they are at least based on an attempt to measure reality; 'stylized facts', by contrast, substitute dogma for measurement.

subcontracting The practice of the principal suppliers of goods and services buying in some of their inputs from independent firms, rather than using employees to produce them in-house. Subcontracting may be used because the work concerned needs specialized skilled labour or equipment which the principal producer does not need full-time. It also allows more flexibility in employment, if the principal's own employees are protected by employment laws or a strong trade union.

subsidiarity The principle that decisions on policy should be taken at the most decentralized level consistent with making them effective. Decisions affecting the global atmosphere, for example restrictions on the use of CFCs, need to be taken at an international level. Decisions on safety standards for vehicles need to be taken at at a national or possibly supranational level. There is a tendency in modern economies for an increasing proportion of policy decisions to be centralized, from local authorities to national governments, and from national governments to supra-national bodies such as the *European Union (EU). The main arguments for subsidiarity are first, that there are so many decisions to be taken that the centre should not be swamped in detail; and second, that there are national and local variations in income levels, traditions, and social attitudes, so that common rules which were hardly noticed in one area, where they merely formalise established habits, would be regarded as so outrageous as to be unenforceable in others.

subsidiary A firm which is owned or controlled by another. There are wide variations in the extent to which subsidiary companies are allowed to make decentralized decisions about matters such as investment projects, and choices between trading with other firms in the same group or with outsiders.

subsidization, cross- *See* cross-subsidization.

subsidized credit Credit provided on terms below normal market rates. Subsidized credit may be granted to encourage particular forms of activity, including for example exports, provision of affordable rented housing by *housing associations, or the growth of entrepreneurship among minority groups. It may also be granted as a corrupt favour to people or firms with political influence. Credit may be subsidized by governments, or lending institutions may cross-subsidize some borrowers out of the profits on other loans. Subsidized credit is particularly bad for economic efficiency in economies where the interest rate for favoured borrowers is below the rate of inflation, so that they borrow at negative real interest rates and are able to profit simply by holding unproductive assets

subsidy A payment by the government to consumers or producers which makes the factor cost received by producers greater than the market price charged by producers. Subsidies may be given on grounds of income distribution, to improve the incomes of producers or consumers. They are not usually efficient for either purpose: even goods consumed heavily by the poor, such as rice in India, are also consumed by the better-off, so that a lot of the benefit of a subsidy goes to those who do not need it. Similarly, farm subsidies benefit large rich farmers more than small poor ones. Export subsidies may be paid to increase exports in order to improve the balance of payments. *See also* export subsidy, farm subsidies, and food subsidies.

subsistence level The minimum level of consumption on which people can survive. This is an ambiguous concept: does it refer to the level of consumption needed for an individual to survive for some limited period, such as a year, or the level needed for the expectation of life normal in a given society? In any case subsistence level is well below what is regarded as a poverty line in modern societies.

subsistence wages The lowest level of wages consistent with the survival of the labour force. This is an ambiguous concept: does it mean wages sufficient for individual labourers to survive for some limited period, such as a year, or does it mean a wage level sufficient for the workers and their families to have the expectation of life normal in their societies? In modern societies 'subsistence wages' is a term of abuse rather than a definite quantity.

substitute A good or service which can be used instead of another. Every good is thus a substitute for other goods in general. A pair of goods are said to be substitutes if, holding the utility level constant, a rise in the price of one of them increases demand for the other. This relation between a pair of goods is contrasted with that of complements where, holding the utility level constant, a rise in the price of one good decreases demand for the other. *See also* perfect substitute.

substitution The possibility of switching consumption from one good or service to another in response to changes in their relative prices. Holding total utility constant, the *elasticity of substitution between two goods or services is the ratio of the proportional change in relative quantities consumed to the the proportional change in relative prices. If the price of one good changes, the prices of all other goods being held constant, the change in demand can be divided into a *substitution effect and an *income effect. The substitution effect is the change in consumption holding the utility level constant: it shows how consumption would have changed if consumers had been compensated for the change in prices. This is contrasted with the income effect, which is the change in consumption due to the effect of the price change on real income. *See also* elasticity of substitution, import substitution, and marginal rate of substitution.

substitution effect The part of the effect of a price change on demand due to the change in relative prices, assuming that the consumer is compensated sufficiently to remain at the same level of utility. The substitution effect is contrasted with the *income effect, which is the effect on demand of the change in real income caused by the price change, holding relative prices constant. The substitution effect of a fall in price is always non-negative, and is positive whenever any substitution is possible, whereas while the income effect of a fall in price is normally positive, it can be negative for an *inferior good. *See also* the figure for income effect.

sufficient conditions *See* necessary and sufficient conditions.

summation Adding up a number of items. The sum of all x_i, $i = 1, 2, \ldots, N$ is written using the Greek letter sigma, upper case, as $S = \sum_1^N x_i$, or, where the range of i is thought to be obvious, $S = \sum_i x_i$.

sunk costs Those parts of the costs of an enterprise which cannot be recovered if it ceases operations, even in the long run. These include items such as the construction costs of mines or tunnels, or the development costs of industrial processes. The existence of sunk costs tends to produce *hysteresis in the economy, and helps to explain the rarity of *contestable markets.

superannuation Payments to retired employees. Superannuation contributions are deductions from the pay of employees still working, to help to finance payments to those retired.

supernormal profits Profits above the level usual in an economy. Supernormal profits in an industry are likely to attract entry by new firms, and entry to the industry by firms already operating in other markets. How large profits can get before they are regarded as supernormal depends on how keen people in any economy are to become entrepreneurs rather than seeking safety as employees or rentiers.

Supplementary Benefit An additional UK social security benefit available on a means-tested basis to pensioners or others whose total income would otherwise be below some target level. The distinction between this and the basic retirement pension or unemployment benefit is that Supplementary Benefit is conditional on a *means test.

supply The amount of a good or service offered for sale. The supply function relates supply to the factors which determine its level. These include the price of the good, the prices of factor services and intermediate products employed in producing it, the number of firms engaged in producing it and their levels of capital equipment. The *supply curve relates the supply of a good to its price, holding the prices of inputs constant. If the producers are perfect competitors and act as price-takers, the supply curve is the horizontal sum for each price level of the marginal cost curves of the firms that take part in the industry at this price. Supply is more elastic, the more price rises attract firms to enter the industry and price falls cause them to leave it. If the producers are not perfect competitors the supply curve is not defined. *Excess supply is the excess of supply over the demand for a good or service at the existing price. *Supply-side economics is the view that output is more strongly influenced by factors affecting supply than by effective demand. *See also* adverse supply shock, aggregate supply, elasticity of supply, excess supply, inelastic supply, joint supply, labour supply, money supply, and refusal to supply.

supply curve A curve showing the amount that firms in an industry are willing to supply at each possible price. A supply curve is defined only if the firms are price-takers, who do not consider the effects of their own output on the price they can charge. With price on the vertical axis, the supply curve at any price is the horizontal sum of the marginal cost curves of the firms in an industry. The industry supply curve is at least as elastic as the supply of individual firms, and is more elastic if a rise in price induces more firms to enter the industry, or if a fall in price induces some existing firms to leave. *See also* backward-bending supply curve, and the figure for market equilibrium.

supply-side economics The view that real growth in the economy depends to a considerable extent even in the short run, and almost completely in the long run, on factors affecting supply rather than on *effective demand. Supply-side proposals to increase economic growth could include measures such as the reform of tax systems to encourage investment and innovation, the reform of restrictive practices, improvements in the infrastructure of transport and communications, better training and more assistance with mobility for unemployed workers, and reforming social security systems to encourage labour supply. This is contrasted with the *Keynesian view that the main factor affecting economic growth is the level of effective demand.

supply-side policy A policy intended to increase the aggregate supply available in an economy. Supply-side policies could include reform of the social security system to encourage the supply of effort; improvement of education and training to improve the productivity of the labour force; reform of restrictive practices and restrictions on market entry to improve efficiency; or reform of the tax system to encourage the devotion of more effort to production and less to tax avoidance and evasion. Such policies are contrasted with *demand management policies, which seek to increase and stabilize GDP by controlling effective demand. An ideal policy mix would combine supply-side and demand management policies.

support *See* income support, and price support.

surcharge *See* import surcharge, and investment income surcharge.

surplus *See* budget surplus, consumer surplus, current account surplus, export surplus, and producer's surplus.

surplus value The excess of what workers can produce over what they need to consume. As pointed out by Karl Marx, surplus value is essential if economies are to be able to afford either investment or 'unproductive' workers, producing goods or services which are not part of essential consumption. Political economists, including Marx, were concerned with the division of surplus value between various members of society. Marx believed that it would be appropriated by capitalists. In modern economies surplus value is divided between many sections of society, including consumption by workers of considerably more than their minimum needs.

surtax An additional income tax levied on large incomes. In the UK this has been replaced by having higher income tax rates on large incomes.

Survey, Current Population *See* Current Population Survey.

survey data Data collected by surveys of individuals or firms. Surveys may be total in their coverage, as with *censuses, or may be based on samples of the relevant population. They may be conducted by government bodies, either specifically set up for the purpose, for example the Office for National Statistics (ONS) in the UK, or in the course of their normal work. Data on UK incomes, for example, are collected by the Inland Revenue, and data on trade by the Department of Trade and Industry (DTI). Surveys are also conducted by private commercial bodies such as market research firms, by private bodies such as the Confederation of British Industry (CBI), and by academic institutions. Survey data are subject to difficulties from low response rates to surveys where replies are not compulsory, and poor incentives to give either complete or accurate replies to questions even when response is compulsory. This is particularly serious where the information requested is either confidential, or not available without special trouble and expense for the individual or firm concerned.

sustained yield A level of output which can be continued indefinitely, without impairing the future productivity of any *natural resources used. This is contrasted with over-cropping or resource mining, which reduces or destroys the productive capacity of the resources involved. Examples are found in agriculture, where good practice can improve the soil whereas over-cropping or over-grazing damage it; in forestry where a regular cycle of felling and replanting can be sustainable; or in fisheries, where a limited harvest can continue indefinitely whereas over-fishing destroys breeding stocks.

swaps, interest rate *See* interest rate swaps.

sweated labour Workers employed for low pay and often for long hours under poor working conditions. In many poor countries this is true of almost everybody who is employed at all. In more advanced countries, where such treatment is exceptional, workers treated in this way are often separated from the main labour markets by factors such as poor education, language differences, and sometimes by their status as illegal immigrants.

switching, expenditure *See* expenditure switching.

symmetrical distribution A *frequency distribution in which the value of a variable is equally likely to be a given distance above or below the mean. If $f(x)$ is the distribution, with mean value μ, the distribution is symmetrical if $f(\mu + z) = f(\mu - z)$ for all z.

syndicate (at Lloyd's) A group of *Lloyd's names who combine to provide insurance. Each member of a syndicate provides a stated amount of capital; if the syndicate makes a profit on the policies it has issued, all members of the syndicate gain in proportion to their share of the capital employed. If a syndicate makes a loss, each member is liable in proportion to his or her share in the capital, with unlimited liability as to the extent of the loss. Every member of a syndicate is also responsible to an unlimited extent for the losses if other members default on their share of the liabilities.

syndicated loan A loan provided by a syndicate of banks or other lending institutions. Such loans, often to less developed countries (LDCs), are normally arranged by one or a small group of leading banks negotiating the terms, and persuading a large number of other lenders to take up small parts of the loan. Participating in a number of syndicated loans gives lenders a less risky portfolio than negotiating loans for themselves with particular borrowers: borrowers can negotiate terms with a single body which they can trust to be able to raise the money by recruiting other lenders to join a syndicate.

synergy Benefits from combining different businesses. For example, if company A has a large stock of good ideas ripe for development but few production facilities or funds, and company B has a large fund of accumulated reserves and factories whose products face declining markets, the two can both benefit by combining. Benefits from synergy are normally claimed by the promoters of mergers, sometimes with little justification.

systematic risk Risk arising from disturbances which affect all projects in a class. This type of risk cannot be reduced by diversification. This is contrasted with non-systematic or idiosyncratic risk, where the disturbances affecting different projects are independent, so that the overall risk of a portfolio of assets can be reduced by dividing it between a number of projects. In the stock market, for example, risk is partly systematic: the trade cycle, or interest rate changes, affect most share prices in the same direction. It is also partly idiosyncratic: every industry, and every company is affected by different random disturbances. Some authors use the alternative term systemic.

Taft–Hartley Act The US Labor-Management Relations Act of 1947. This act restricted the rights of US trade unions in various ways, including banning the closed shop and authorizing states to enact 'right-to-work' laws.

take-off A stage of economic development at which an economy becomes capable of sustained growth in per capita income. An economy which has not reached take-off has savings and investment inadequate to do more than keep pace with population increase, at low and stagnant levels of per capita income. Take-off requires sufficient savings for investment in infrastructure and productive equipment, and institutions capable of providing education and public order.

takeover The acquisition of a company by new owners. The shares of the company are acquired by new owners, normally another company. They may be paid for in cash, or in the purchaser's shares.

takeover bid An offer to purchase all the shares of a company, thereby acquiring *control of it. Payment may be offered in cash, in the shares of the purchaser, or a mixture. A takeover bid becomes effective only if the holders of a majority of existing shares accept it. As ownership of a controlling interest by a single party leaves *minority shareholders at a disadvantage, stock exchange rules normally require that all shares be purchased on the same terms, and that no party or group can buy more than a certain proportion of the shares (30 per cent in the UK) without making a takeover bid for the remainder.

take-up rate The proportion of those entitled to a benefit who actually claim it. This may be restricted by lack of information, a cumbersome claims procedure which defeats the poorly educated, or embarrassment if the benefit is felt to carry some stigma. In spite of educational campaigns by welfare authorities and voluntary bodies, the take-up rate for most benefits is well below 100 per cent.

talk down The attempt to bring down any economic variable through persuasion by the authorities. The variable concerned could be inflation or the exchange rate. Talking down works via policy announcements by influential people such as Central Bank Governors or Finance Ministers. As a substitute for substantive policy measures such persuasion is likely to be unsuccesful, especially if the authorities have a reputation for ineffectiveness. As a complement to the use of practical policy instruments, talking down may help to bring about adjustment faster and at lower cost in terms of real activity than just using monetary or fiscal policy without explaining what results this is intended to achieve.

talks, trade *See* trade talks.

tangency A situation where two smooth curves touch but do not cross. For two curves $y = f(x)$ and $z = g(x)$ to be tangential at $x = x^*$, it is a necessary condition that $f(x^*) = g(x^*)$ and $dy/dx = dz/dx$ when both functions are evaluated at $x = x^*$, and it is a sufficient condition that $d^2y/dx^2 \neq d^2z/dx^2$. Thus the two curves both pass through one point at $x = x^*$: they have the same slope but different curvature.

tangency equilibrium An equilibrium which can be represented as a position of tangency between two curves. Consumer equilibrium, for example, is represented as the point where a *budget line, which is normally a straight line, is tangential to an *indifference curve, which normally has a positive second derivative. A tangency equilibrium is contrasted with a corner solution, where the budget line and the indifference curve need not have the same slope. At any point where consumption of both goods is positive, if the budget line and the indifference curve differ in slope, a change in consumption can always make the consumer better off. At a corner solution, with zero consumption of one good, the requirement for equilibrium is that the relative slopes of the budget line and indifference curve mean that increased consumption of the zero-consumption good does not pay: consumption cannot be decreased if it is zero already.

tangible assets Assets that can be touched. This should literally include only physical objects like plant and equipment, but it is usually also used to include leases and company shares, as these are mainly titles to tangible assets. It is contrasted with intangible assets, such as goodwill, trade-marks and patents.

tap issue An issue of UK *Treasury bills to other government departments. This is done at a fixed price, and does not go through the market; it is a piece of internal government book-keeping. It is contrasted with a *tender issue, by which Treasury bills are sold to non-government purchasers at a competitively determined price.

target An aim of policy. Economic policy targets include objectives such as high levels of employment and growth, low and stable levels of inflation, or maintenance of particular exchange rates. Policy targets are distinguished from both instruments and indicators: *policy instruments are variables the government or central bank can control, or at least influence, such as tax rates or the money supply. Policy instruments can themselves be targets, but often are not, and targets such as the rate of inflation are clearly not instruments. Policy *indicators are variables used in deciding on the use of policy instruments; indicators which are not themselves targets may be preferred to targets for this task because they are available sooner or can be measured more reliably than targets.

targeting Making benefits available to particular groups rather than to the public at large. This is intended to keep down the total cost of attaining a policy objective. Targeting can be done in two ways: providing *benefits in kind which appeal only to particular groups, or administrative restriction of the availability of benefits in cash or in kind. Some forms of targeting are simple: for example, nobody wants to use a wheelchair unless they need one. Other objectives are difficult to achieve: for example, providing a minimum retirement income. Universal pensions are very expensive, and much of the benefit goes to people with occupational pensions or other private income. Targeting implies means-testing state pensions; but *means tests are expensive to administer, and create *disincentives to saving before retirement and to work after retirement age.

target zone (exchange rates) A range within which a country seeks to keep its *exchange rate. The range may be broad or narrow, and may be specified in terms of some single foreign currency or some suitable basket of foreign currencies. A target zone can be interpreted in a strict or relaxed manner. With a strict target zone the country's central bank is committed to intervening to prevent the market rate moving outside the target zone, while retaining discretion over intervention while the market rate is within the zone. With a relaxed target zone, the central bank promises to adopt policies calculated to bring the market rate back within the target zone if it strays outside, but not necessarily to intervene in the market to achieve this result immediately.

tariff A scale of charges, for example in a restaurant. In economics a tariff was originally a schedule of taxes on imports; it now refers to the actual import duties. An ad valorem tariff is set as a percentage of the price of the goods imported. A specific tariff is set in money terms per physical unit of the good imported, and does not depend on its price. A non-discriminatory tariff taxes imports from all countries equally; tariff preferences mean that similar imports from different countries are taxed at different rates. *Non-tariff barriers are man-made obstacles to trade, such as quotas or *voluntary export restraint (VER) agreements. The tariff equivalent of a non-tariff barrier is the level of ad valorem tariff which would restrict imports by the same percentage. The *General Agreement on Tariffs and Trade (GATT) was an international organization devoted to codifying trade barriers, preventing increases in tariffs, and promoting multilateral negotiations to lower tariffs. Since 1995 these tasks have been entrusted to the *World Trade Organization (WTO). *See also* optimum tariff, prohibitive tariff, revenue tariff, and two-part tariff.

Tariff Act, Smoot–Hawley *See* Smoot–Hawley Tariff Act.

Tariffs and Trade, General Agreement on *See* General Agreement on Tariffs and Trade.

tastes Otherwise unexplained differences in consumer preferences. Even when faced with the same sets of goods at the same relative prices, consumers choose different bundles of goods. Some differences can be explained by differences in age, family status or physical condition: for example, only people with babies buy cots and baby food. Other differences can be explained by differences in income. This leaves many differences in preferences: some people are vegetarians or teetotallers, while others are not, and tastes in music, books or films are extremely varied. The existence of such taste differences is a factor leading economists to prefer distributing consumer goods through a market rather than a planned economy.

tax A payment compulsorily collected from individuals or firms by central or local government. A *direct tax is levied on the income or capital of an individual or company: the word direct implies the view that the real burden of such a tax falls on the person or firm paying it and cannot be passed on to anybody else. An *indirect tax is levied on sales of a good or service: the word 'indirect' implies the view that the real burden of such a tax does not fall on the person or firm paying it, but can be passed on to a customer or a supplier. These views on the real *incidence of taxes are not necessarily correct. *Income tax is levied on income; *value-added tax (VAT) is levied on the value-added of a business; and an *expenditure tax would be levied on income less net savings. A *wealth tax is levied on wealth; a *capital gains tax is levied on the increase in the value of assets. *Purchase tax was a UK tax levied on the purchase of certain goods. A *poll tax is levied on people, regardless of their circumstances. A *lump-sum tax is levied on a particular activity, regardless of its extent or the income of the taxpayer: for example the UK television licenses. A *specific tax is levied on goods at a rate fixed in money terms per unit of quantity, regardless of their price. An *ad valorem tax on goods is levied as a set proportion of their value. A *proportional tax increases in proportion to the taxpayer's income. With a *progressive tax the proportion of income taken in tax rises with the level of income; with a *regressive tax the proportion of income taken in tax falls with income.

Pre-tax income is income before direct taxes have been deducted; post-tax income is what is left after direct taxes have been deducted. Tax accounting is the activity of preparing and checking accounts in forms acceptable to the tax authorities, and advising on how to conduct one's affairs so as to minimize liability to tax. The incidence of taxation considers who ultimately bears the real burden of paying taxes. *Tax allowances are deductions in respect of particular activities, such as pension contributions, that individuals or firms are allowed to claim in calculating their taxable incomes. *Tax evasion is failing to pay taxes which are lawfully due; *tax avoidance is conducting one's affairs so as to avoid becoming legally liable for taxes. *Tax expenditure is the loss of government revenue due to granting tax allowances to encourage particular activities. The *inflation tax is the name given to the loss of real purchasing power when prices rise during inflation which is sustained by the holders of money and of government securities whose interest and redemption payments are fixed in terms of money. *See also* ad valorem tax, capital tax, capital gains tax, carbon tax, Corporation Tax, Council Tax, direct tax, emission tax, energy tax, expenditure tax, gift tax, income tax, indirect tax, inflation tax, inheritance tax, Inspector of Taxes, interest equalization tax, lump-sum tax, neutral taxes, payroll tax, poll tax, progressive tax, proportional tax, purchase tax, regressive tax, sales tax, specific tax, turnover tax, value-added tax, wealth tax, and withholding tax.

taxable income That part of income which is liable to direct taxes. Taxable income differs from total cash receipts in several ways. Some receipts are regarded as being of a capital nature: these may be liable to *capital gains taxes, but are not liable to income tax. Taxable income may include *imputed income, such as the rental value of owner-occupied houses (not in the UK). Total income may be reduced for tax purposes by various allowances, either personal allowances for all taxpayers, or allowances for particular categories, for example in respect of dependents, charitable donations, or pension contributions.

tax allowance A deduction from gross income allowed under the tax laws to reduce the taxable income of an individual or firm. This may be on grounds of *equity, because having to pay the deductible item, for example mortgage interest, lowers ability to pay relative to a taxpayer with the same gross income but no comparable liability. Tax allowances may be given to encourage certain forms of activity: for example, firms are given tax

allowances to encourage investment, and both individuals and firms get
tax allowances in respect of some charitable donations. Every tax concession
reduces the *tax base, which raises the tax rates needed to obtain any given
total tax revenue. This in turn stimulates people with other claims on their
income to seek further concessions.

tax assessment The determination of the amount of tax any individual or
company is liable to pay. This may be done in one of two ways. One is that the
taxpayers make tax returns, listing their income from various sources and any
facts affecting their entitlement to tax allowances. The tax authorities then
make the actual assessment. The alternative method is *self-assessment:
besides supplying information on their income and entitlement to
allowances, taxpayers produce their own assessments, applying the tax rules
to their own figures; these self-assessments are then checked by the tax
authorities. In the UK the assessment is made by an Inspector of Taxes if a tax
return is made within a time limit; after this taxpayers have to produce a self-
assessment.

taxation *See* tax, company taxation, double taxation, incidence of taxation,
independent taxation of spouses, and unitary taxation.

tax avoidance Arranging one's affairs so that tax is not legally payable. Tax
avoidance is thus entirely legal, as contrasted with *tax evasion, which means
finding ways of not paying tax that is in fact legally due, for example by
making false tax returns. While in theory tax avoidance and tax evasion are
entirely distinct, in many practical cases it requires expensive professional
advice from a tax accountant to determine which description applies to any
specific set of transactions.

tax base The set of incomes on which direct taxes, and transactions on
which indirect taxes, are levied. The tax base is lowered by all allowances and
exemptions: for example, the tax base in the UK is lowered by not including
the imputed income from owner-occupied houses in the tax base for income
tax, and by not including food and children's clothing in the tax base for VAT.
The more such exemptions there are, the higher the tax rates required on the
remaining tax base to raise any given total of tax revenue.

tax-based incomes policy A policy of using the tax system to reduce
*inflation through its incentive effects. This is distinguished from the
macroeconomic effect of higher taxes in cutting effective demand. The hope
of such policies is that if sudden increases in incomes attract punitively large
tax rates, firms will choose smaller wage and price increases. The dangers are
that firms with monopoly power will choose even larger price increases to
enable them to pay the taxes, and that such tax policies will encourage
*creative accounting, and drive economic activity into informal and untaxed
channels.

tax burden The total cost to the economy of having to pay taxes. This
includes not only the actual amount collected in taxes, but also compliance
and deadweight costs. *Compliance costs include the costs of additional
record-keeping required because of liability to tax, and the extra accounting
costs of devising methods of tax avoidance. Deadweight costs arise through
the loss of consumers' and producers' surplus. *Consumers' surplus is lost in
cases where consumers value goods above their production costs but below

their tax-inclusive price; *producers' surplus is lost in cases where people value leisure foregone less than the rewards of work before tax, but more than the rewards after tax. It is possible, however, that taxes on polluting activities may lower the total real tax burden, if they dissuade firms from activities which cause large *external diseconomies.

tax credit A procedure used in the UK when income tax on distributed profits is deducted at source. The shareholder receives dividends net of tax, and a tax credit equal to the amount of income tax deducted. The gross dividend including the tax deducted has to be reported, and is used in calculating the taxpayer's gross income and total tax payable. The tax credit is then treated as tax already paid. As tax at source is deducted at basic rate, only taxpayers with higher personal marginal tax rates have to make further payments; taxpayers with marginal tax rates below basic rate receive refunds of the excess tax collected.

tax evasion Failure to pay taxes legally due, for example by making a false tax return or failing to make a return at all. Tax evasion is thus illegal; it is contrasted with *tax avoidance, which means arranging one's affairs so that tax is not legally payable. While in theory tax evasion and tax avoidance are entirely distinct, in many practical cases it requires expensive professional advice from a tax accountant to discover which description properly applies to any given set of transactions.

tax exempt special savings account (TESSA) A UK system, intended to encourage small savers, by which individuals could invest a limited amount each year with a building society, the interest being tax-free. This system has now been closed to new investors, being replaced by Individual Savings Accounts (ISAs), but the capital part of maturing Tessas can be reinvested in an ISA which does not count against an individual's permitted annual total.

tax expenditure A means by which the government can encourage particular activities without appearing to spend money. If the government wants taxpayers, for example, to take out private medical insurance, it can either make specific grants for the purpose, which will appear as government expenditure, or it can pay implicitly by giving a *tax allowance which reduces net tax paid by an equal amount. The real economic effects of the two systems are exactly the same, except for those too poor to pay any income tax. Under the tax expenditure system, however, total government revenue and expenditure are both lower than under the grant system. Tax expenditures thus appeal to those who want the government to influence the economy while minimizing the apparent size of the state sector.

tax haven A country which provides foreign residents with opportunities to reduce their tax payments by doing business there. Tax havens can be used for *tax avoidance, when tax liabilities can legally be reduced by using foreign financial intermediaries. They can also be used for *tax evasion, for example by the use of confidential bank accounts to facilitate concealment of income and money laundering. Tax havens are not entirely evil in their effects, however: they have provided facilities to allow the victims of political and religious persecution to keep part of their assets out of the clutches of tyrannical governments.

tax holiday A limited period of tax-free operation, or of specially reduced taxation. This may be used to induce foreign firms to invest in a country, or domestic firms to invest in an industry or area which the government especially wishes to encourage. A tax holiday scheme may be very expensive in terms of lost revenue if firms which take advantage of it would have invested in any case even without it.

Tax Reform Act 1986 A US federal statute reforming and simplifying the federal tax system. Both individual and corporate income taxes were simplified, with fewer rates and lower tax allowances.

tax refund A repayment by the tax authorities of excess tax previously collected. This may occur because of mistakes in the original *tax assessment which are corrected on appeal. It may also occur when tax is deducted at source and the taxpayer is subsequently found to be liable for less tax than has been withheld. With a *pay-as-you-earn (PAYE) income tax scheme, as in the UK, a taxpayer who becomes unemployed part-way through a tax year may qualify for a tax refund.

tax return A report by a taxpayer to the tax authorities of his or her income, and of any facts affecting their entitlement to tax allowances. Tax returns may be demanded by the tax authorities, with legal penalties for failing to make returns. Alternatively, where a *withholding tax system is in force, it may be left to taxpayers to make tax returns as a condition for reclaiming any tax refunds to which they are entitled.

tax shelter An arrangement by which part of a person's income is protected from taxes. In the UK, for example, TESSAs, PEPs, and ISAs have enabled savers to enjoy some tax-free income.

tax wedge The difference, caused by taxes on employment and social security contributions, between the money benefit to an employee from addditional work, and its cost to the employer.

technical efficiency Those aspects of *efficiency concerned with getting the largest possible outputs for given inputs, or the smallest possible inputs for given outputs. This is efficiency in production. It is distinguished from efficiency in exchange, which is concerned with the distribution of outputs between different users, and the efficient choice of the set of outputs to produce. Thus while technical efficiency is a necessary condition for the overall efficiency of the economy, it is not sufficient: an economy could be better off producing the right mix of goods by technically inefficient methods, than producing an unsuitable set of goods with complete technical efficiency.

technical progress Improvement in knowledge of possible techniques. Such changes may allow more output to be obtained from unchanged inputs, the same output to be obtained from fewer inputs, or new forms of output to be produced which were not previously possible. Technical progress may be embodied or disembodied. If it is disembodied, improvements in productivity are purely due to new knowledge or improved skills, without the need for any new equipment. If it is embodied, exploitation of the new techniques requires investment in new capital equipment or new intermediate products. Actual technical progress is frequently partially embodied, some new equipment being needed while some of the existing equipment remains useful.

See also disembodied technical progress, embodied technical progress, Harrod-neutral technical progress, and Hicks-neutral technical progress.

technical standard A specification of the design of particular goods or components. Examples range from the gauges of screw on nuts and bolts to the voltages of electronic equipment. Technical standards are useful because they ensure that pieces of equipment fit together. Without them, for example, every compact disc player would take only particular makes of CD, instead of all CDs being interchangable. The use of technical standards is an example of *network externalities, where everybody gains from their equipment being compatible with everybody else's. In the early days of a new product, there is a considerable competitive advantage to a firm that can get its own design accepted as the technical standard.

technical substitution *See* elasticity of technical substitution, and marginal rate of technical substitution.

techniques, choice of *See* choice of techniques.

technological unemployment Unemployment due to technical progress. This applies to particular types of worker whose skill is made redundant because of changes in methods of production, usually by substituting machines for their services. Technical progress does not necessarily lead to a rise in overall unemployment. New methods of production are economic to adopt only if they lower costs, which allows a larger output to be sold at a lower price. If the elasticity of demand is high enough, overall employment in the industry concerned may rise, as will employment in the industry producing the machines. It is still possible, however, for technological unemployment to afflict workers with old skills, if the new jobs created are either lower-grade operative jobs, or require skills they do not possess.

technology The body of know-how about materials, techniques of production, and operation of equipment, based on the application of scientific knowledge. Technology requires the services of people who are literate, numerate, and nowadays normally skilled in the use of computers: to acquire these skills usually requires a high level of formal education. This is distinguished from craftsmanship, which is largely learned by experience, working under the supervision of people who already possess the skills. It is of course possible for the same individual to possess both technological and craft skills.

technology gap The difference between two countries in the techniques available for production. Technology gaps are based on differences in the education, training, and motivation of the labour force, the availability and quality of infrastructure, such as reliable power supplies and telecommunications, and market size.

technology transfer The transfer of techniques from countries where they are more advanced to other countries where they are less advanced. Technology transfer may involve foreign direct investment, transfers of skilled personnel from more advanced countries, training of workers from less advanced countries, or licensing of patents. Technology transfer is of great importance to less developed countries, who have most to learn, but it is useful to all countries, since no one country is the leader in every branch of technology.

tendering, competitive *See* competitive tendering.

tender issue An issue of *Treasury bills by inviting bids or tenders for a stated quantity, and accepting the bids from those offering the highest price. The actual sales are at the market-clearing price, bids at or above which are sufficient to take up the supply of bills on offer. This is contrasted with a *tap issue, where bills are made available at a stated price in whatever quantities are needed to absorb the spare cash of government bodies.

tend to infinity To increase beyond any finite size, however large. As a variable x tends to infinity, written $x \to \infty$, it becomes indefinitely large. Similarly, as $x \to -\infty$, it becomes less than any negative number, however great its absolute value.

Tennessee Valley Authority (TVA) A US public corporation set up in 1933 as part of the *New Deal. Its functions include power supply, flood control, development of natural resources and tourism, and training. Its power supply activities are self-financing; its remaining functions are funded by the federal government.

tenure, security of *See* security of tenure.

term loan A loan due to be repaid on a definite date. This is a US usage.

terms of trade The ratio of an index of a country's export prices to an index of its import prices. The terms of trade are said to improve if this ratio increases, so that each unit of exports pays for more imports, and to deteriorate if the ratio falls, so that each unit of exports buys fewer imports. This terminology can be misleading: if a country's terms of trade improve because of increased foreign demand for its exports, this is an improvement in its economic position. If the terms of trade improve because domestic inflation exceeds that abroad, however, the result may be problems with the *balance of trade, which cannot sensibly be regarded as an improvement in the economy. The commodity or 'barter' terms of trade are contrasted with the 'factoral' terms of trade, which is the amount of imports that can be obtained via trade per unit of factor services. A country's factoral terms of trade may improve either because of improvements in the barter terms of trade, or because of increased productivity. 'Terms of trade' with no adjective normally refers to the barter terms of trade.

term structure of interest rates The relation between the *redemption dates of various securities and the rates of return on them. The market prices of securities fluctuate with the rate of interest, and these fluctuations become larger as maturity dates increase. It is thus expected that if investors are *risk-averse, and on average interest rates are expected to stay the same, longer-dated securities will have higher rates of return than shorter-dated ones. If the term structure is displayed graphically as a *yield curve, this will slope upwards as maturity dates rise. This slope may be reversed if on average interest rates are expected to fall, while expectations of rising interest rates will tend to make it steeper.

TESSA *See* tax exempt special savings account.

testing, hypothesis *See* hypothesis testing.

test, means *See* means test.

theory of X *See* under X.

test discount rate The real rate of return required to justify investment projects undertaken for commercial reasons in UK nationalized industries.

tests of significance Statistical tests based on calculating the probability that a given result could have been obtained as the result of sampling errors. An estimate, for example, is statistically significantly different from zero at the 5 per cent level if, given the variance of the population, there is a less than 5 per cent chance that an estimate as far from zero as this could have been produced by a random sample of the size used.

Thatcherism A shorthand for the economic principles underlying the policies of the Thatcher government in the UK from 1979 to 1990. These included strengthening economic incentives by promoting competition, reduction of the role of government by deregulation and privatization, reliance on monetary policy to eliminate inflation, increasing individual choice, for example through the sale of council houses to their tenants, and a reduction in the powers of trade unions. These objectives fell well short of complete laissez-faire, and were only partially achieved.

third-degree price discrimination Price discrimination where sellers can identify different types of customer, and offer different contracts to different classes of customer. Special prices may be offered, for example, to students or pensioners. This type of discrimination is possible only when resale of goods or services is costly or impossible; if resale were costless, every customer would buy through the groups offered the lowest price. Third-degree price discrimination is contrasted with first-degree price discrimination, where the seller charges the customer the maximum he or she is willing to pay for every unit of a good, so that the producer gets all the benefits from the good's existence, and second-degree price discrimination, where the seller cannot identify a customer's type, but can induce customers to reveal information about themselves by offering a choice of contracts.

third-party insurance Insurance against the cost of compensating third parties, that is individuals or companies other than the insurance company and the policy-holder, for death, injury or damage to property. UK drivers are legally obliged to hold third-party insurance, whereas they are left to decide for themselves whether to insure against fire, theft and accident.

third world Poor or less developed countries. The term originated to cover countries which were neither part of the *Organization for Economic Cooperation and Development (OECD), the advanced capitalist bloc, nor of the former Soviet bloc. It is also used as a term of condemnation for the more sordid aspects of advanced countries, such as homlessness.

threat, credible *See* credible threat.

threshold The point at which an *indexation provision becomes operative. A wage bargain, for example, might provide that wage rates should be revised in proportion to the *Retail Price Index (RPI), but only if this rose by more than *n* per cent during the coming year. *n* per cent is then the threshold.

thrift Willingness to save and economy in spending. *See also* paradox of thrift.

thrifts United States non-banking financial institutions which collect savings from the public and finance mortgages. They are the nearest US equivalent to a UK building society. Many thrifts ran into severe financial problems in the 1980s, and had to be rescued with US government money.

tied aid Assistance to other countries, normally *less developed countries (LDCs), which has to be spent on goods and services from the donor. This is contrasted with untied aid, which can be spent in any way. Tied aid may be of less value than untied aid of an equal amount, as tying restricts the choices open to the recipient, though where the recipient imports a lot from the donor in any case tying may not be effective. As tied aid reduces the danger that giving aid may cause balance-of-payments problems for the donor, more aid may be available if it is given on a tied basis.

tied loan A foreign loan, normally to a less developed country (LDC), which has to be spent on goods and services from the lender. This is contrasted with an untied loan, which can be spent in any way. A tied loan may be of less value than an untied loan of equal size, as the tying restricts the choices open to the borrower, though where the borrower imports a lot from the lender in any case, tying may not be effective. As tied loans reduce the danger that making them may cause balance-of-payments problems for the lender, more loans may be available if they are made on a tied basis.

tigers, East Asian *See* East Asian tigers.

tight fiscal policy Fiscal policy which tends to restrict effective demand. This may include high taxes or low public spending. In both cases 'high' and 'low' are relative terms, comparing the current levels with whatever has come to be regarded as normal for the current level of real activity.

tight monetary policy A restrictive monetary policy. This is intended to restrict the level of effective demand by making loans expensive and difficult to obtain.

time *See* continuous time, and discrete time.

time-consistency The property of policies carried out over a period of time, that the policy choices made at later dates are independent of any commitments made at earlier dates. Where the policy authorities have no *credibility, a time-consistent policy is the only one available to them; there is no point in making promises that nobody expects you to keep. Where the authorities do have credibility, they may be able to get better results by the use of time-inconsistent policies: for example, inflation this year can be reduced by promises to cut government spending or growth of the money supply next year. When next year comes, the authorities would prefer to substitute cuts in the following year to keeping their promises; the incentive to keep promises is desire to retain the reputation which makes time-inconsistent policies posssible. *See also* reputational policy.

time deposit A deposit in a US bank or other financial institution where the depositor is required to give notice of withdrawal, or is subject to an interest penalty in lieu of notice. The UK equivalent is deposit account.

time discounting Placing a lower value on receipts or payments due in the future than on equal payments occurring immediately. This may be on account of pure time preference, uncertainty as to whether one will survive to benefit from receipts or make payments, or an expectation that higher incomes will make the marginal utility of money lower in the future than it is at present.

time horizon The most remote future period taken into account in making economic decisions such as investment. While in principle expectations about conditions in all future periods could affect present decisions, there are practical reasons for adopting a limited time horizon. One is that uncertainty increases rapidly as decision-makers look into the future. The other is that the calculations in formal models become more complicated the longer the horizon adopted.

time-inconsistency The property of policies carried out over a period of time, that the policy choices which would be made at later dates if the authorities were starting afresh are inconsistent with commitments made at earlier dates. Where the authorities have *credibility, they may choose time-inconsistent policies: for example, inflation this year can be reduced by promises to cut government spending or growth of the money supply next year. When next year comes, the authorities would prefer to substitute cuts in the following year to keeping their promises; the incentive to keep promises is desire to retain the reputation which makes time-inconsistent policies possible. Where the policy authorities have no credibility, a time-consistent policy is the only one available to them; there is no point in making promises that nobody expects you to keep. *See also* reputational policy.

time lags The delay, both in the real world economy and in economic models, of actions after the events which are believed to have caused them. Time lags arise in several ways. First, there are lags in the collection, collation, and dissemination of economic data. Second, even when the data are available, economic decision-makers often defer action while they wait for more data, to try to assess whether changes are temporary or permanent, or because of disagreement about what the response should be. Third, even when decisions have been taken, it takes time to put them into effect: in some cases, for example opening a new factory in response to a rise in demand, this delay may be considerable. Time lags are thus extremely common.

time preference The tendency to prefer goods and services now to the same goods and services at a future date. This may be due to three causes: uncertainty, decreasing marginal utility, and impatience. Goods now may be preferred to goods in 2020 because of uncertainty as to whether one will be alive to enjoy them; because one expects one's total income to be higher than at present so that the expected addition to utility from an equal addition to consumption is less; or through pure time preference or impatience. These are in practice almost impossible to distinguish.

times covered The ratio of a company's earnings for equity to its dividends to ordinary shareholders. A company with high *dividend cover may be retaining most of its profits to invest in expansion, leading to future growth in dividends, or it may be building up financial reserves or paying off debt to safeguard its ability to keep up dividends if business conditions become less profitable. A company with low or negative dividend cover may be a poor growth prospect, or a poor risk in a recession.

time-series data Data for the same variable at different times. The intervals may be of any length, varying from decades or whole trade cycles for economic historians to years or quarters for national income data, monthly for prices, and weekly, daily or even minute-by-minute for stock exchange prices. Data may refer to particular dates, or to the averages over periods such as a year, quarter, or month. Time-series data are contrasted with *cross-section data, which refer to different countries, firms, or individuals at the same time.

time-series, stationary *See* stationary time-series.

Tobin's q A ratio used to explain investment. q is the ratio of the valuation shareholders put on a firm to the market value of its assets; at the margin the shareholders' valuation is shown by the share price. The theory is that if $q > 1$ a firm should invest; if $q < 1$ the firm should run down or sell off its capital equipment.

token money Money where the face value of notes or coin is unrelated to the value of the material of which they are composed. Most money is now token money if it has any physical existence at all, and does not consist of book or computer entries.

Tokyo Round The round of international trade talks under the *General Agreement on Tariffs and Trade held in 1973–9. The round was named from its opening conference in Japan. It reached agreement on tariff cuts on most world trade in manufactures by about a third, implemented over the following five years. It failed to reach any agreement on agricultural protection or non-tariff barriers to trade.

total cost *See* cost.

total domestic expenditure The total of consumer expenditure, general government final consumption, and gross domestic capital formation. This is calculated without deducting either imports or *capital consumption.

total final expenditure The total of consumer expenditure, general government final consumption, gross domestic capital formation, and exports. Thus total final expenditure equals total domestic expenditure plus exports. This is measured before deducting anything for imports or capital consumption.

total revenue *See* revenue.

total utility A measure of the total welfare of an individual. This is only meaningful on the assumption that utility is cardinal, that is, measurable. Total utility is assumed to be a function of the quantities of goods and services consumed and the quantities of various forms of work done. A practical difficulty in applying the concept is that consumption is an activity of households rather than individuals.

tradables Goods and services of types which can be traded internationally. This applies whether or not the particular goods concerned actually are traded. Given the ability of tourists, students, and foreign customers for health care to buy goods and services in foreign countries, most goods are to some extent tradable; whether goods are tradables or non-tradables is thus a matter of degree.

trade **1.** A type of skill, such as that of a carpenter or a plumber; a fitter is referred to as a skilled tradesman. A *trade union was originally a combination of workers with similar skills.

2. The process of distribution, for example the motor trade. Restrictive trade practices are arrangements inhibiting competition in trade. The *trade cycle refers to major variations in the overall level of economic activity, which covers trade in both the productive and distributive senses. Buying and selling, or being in trade, was at one time regarded as socially inferior; the ghost of this archaic view still haunts the tradesmen's entrance.

3. Foreign trade, that is buying and selling abroad. A country's balance of trade is the excess of the value of its exports of goods over its imports. *Trade barriers are obstructions to international trade, such as tariffs and quotas. Trade preferences are differences in the rules applied to trade with different foreign countries. *Free trade means the absence of barriers to international trade. A *free-trade area is a group of countries with no barriers to trade between them, at least for most goods, though there may be exceptions, for example defence equipment or farm products. *Fair trade refers to attempts to devise ideal rules for the conduct of international trade by economists who do not acknowledge free trade as the ideal. *Trade talks are negotiations between governments on changes to the rules governing international trade. The *General Agreement on Tariffs and Trade (GATT) was the organization set up to codify and co-ordinate the rules on international trade, and to try to reach international agreement on the reduction of trade barriers. *See also* balance of trade, bilateral trade, fair trade, free trade, gains from trade, trade deficit, inter-industry trade, intra-industry trade, invisibles, managed trade, multilateral trade, restraint of trade, terms of trade, and visible trade.

trade association A voluntary body representing the firms engaged in a particular type of business. Trade associations promote the collection and exchange of information and discussion of technical standards; they also lobby government concerning legislation affecting the industry, and possible subsidies to it.

trade barriers Laws, institutions, or practices which make trade between countries more difficult or expensive than trade within countries. Some are deliberately designed to discourage trade: *tariffs, that is special taxes on imports, come under this heading. In many countries tariffs have been greatly reduced under the *General Agreement on Tariffs and Trade (GATT), and various groups of countries including the *European Union (EU) and the *North American Free Trade Agreement (NAFTA) between Canada, Mexico, and the United States have reduced or removed tariffs on trade between member countries. Other, *non-tariff barriers, such as quota restrictions and *voluntary export restraint agreements (VERs), however, have become increasingly common in recent years. Barriers to trade are also imposed by national differences in matters such as health and safety standards, labelling requirements, and weights and measures regulations. While these are not necessarily intended to act as barriers to trade, the need to modify products to conform to local requirements, and the documentation required to certify that this has been done, tend to impose costs and delays on international trade in excess of those experienced in domestic trade. Effective trade barriers are also imposed by public *procurement policies, which often give preferential treatment to domestic over foreign suppliers, as the result of legal requirements, through acts of policy, or simply through better information about domestic sources. The EU attempts to prevent this domestic bias in public procurement, so far as member countries are concerned, but with limited success.

trade bill *See* bill of exchange.

trade creation The effect of a *customs union in creating or increasing trade between member countries. This new trade results from the reduction in tariffs between the members and is generally welfare-increasing. Trade creation is distinguished from *trade diversion, which is the replacement of trade with non-members by trade between members. This occurs because the tariff-free prices of goods from members are lower than tariff-inclusive prices of the non-members who formerly supplied them. Trade diversion is generally welfare-decreasing. A customs union is beneficial to its members in the short run if their gains from trade creation exceed their losses from trade diversion.

trade credit The provision of credit by suppliers to their customers. It is common for customers to be required to pay for goods delivered not immediately, but within some normal grace period, varying from weeks for consumer goods to years for some capital goods. The need to provide trade credit accounts for a significant part of the capital needed in many industries.

trade cycle A tendency for alternating periods of upward and downward movements in the aggregate level of output and employment, relative to their long-term trends. These are also known as business cycles. In economic models trade cycles tend to be repetitive in duration and size. In the real

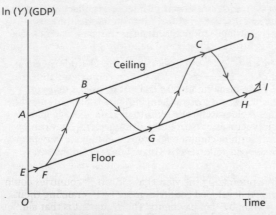

FIGURE 29: *Trade Cycles*

world economy, trade cycles have been observed for as far back as statistical records go, but these have been of very varied duration and severity.

The horizontal axis shows time; the vertical axis the level of GDP, on a logarithmic scale. *ABCD* is the ceiling, given by population increase, net investment, and technical progress. *EFGHI* is the floor, given by population increase, government policy on income support, and autonomous investment minus the maximum feasible rate of induced disinvestment. As shown by *FBGCH*, the economy fluctuates between the floor and the ceiling. Hitting the ceiling results in a slowdown in actual growth, which leads via the accelerator to a downturn. Hitting the floor leads to a resumption of growth; when the wearing out of capital has gone far enough, induced investment is switched on again and growth speeds up. It is also possible for a downturn to come before the celing is actually reached, or for a recovery to start before the economy hits the floor.

trade deficit The excess of imports over exports. This is also referred to as a trade gap.

trade diversion The effect of a *customs union in replacing trade with non-members by trade between members. This occurs because the tariff-free prices of goods from members are lower than the tariff-inclusive prices of non-members who formerly supplied them. Trade diversion involves shifting sourcing of imports from lower to higher cost suppliers, and is generally welfare-decreasing. It is distinguished from *trade creation, where new or increased trade between member countries resulting from the elimination of tariffs is generally welfare-increasing. A customs union is beneficial to its members in the short run if their losses from trade diversion are less than their gains from trade creation.

trade gap *See* trade deficit.

trade liberalization The process of reducing or removing restrictions on international trade. This may include the reduction or removal of *tariffs, abolition or enlargement of import *quotas, abolition of *multiple exchange rates, and removal of requirements for administrative permits for imports or allocations of foreign exchange, or at least simplifying the process of applying for them. The main argument for trade liberalization is that exposing a country's economy to international competition makes for greater efficiency. Elaborate administrative control of trade is also believed to promote corruption in the government, and preoccupation with *rent-seeking rather than productive efficiency in the private sector.

trade-mark A symbol, logo, or name used to enable the public to identify the supplier of goods. In the UK and many other countries trade-marks can be registered, which gives the holder exclusive right to use them. Trade-marks may be registered by manufacturers, distributors, or importers. They can be sold, and are an important form of commercial property. They are very poorly enforced in some less developed countries (LDCs), which is a serious source of international friction.

trade not aid A slogan epitomizing the view that industrial countries could help the development of less developed countries more by liberalizing their treatment of LDC exports than by *aid payments. The argument is that aid may be spent foolishly, on armaments or uneconomic prestige projects, whereas better access to OECD markets for LDC products such as textiles would promote sustainable development consistent with countries' *comparative advantage.

trade-off The process of deciding whether to give up some of one good or one objective to obtain more of another. The need to trade off goods or objectives against one another is a sign of economic *efficiency; if it is possible to get more of one good without accepting less of another, or to achieve one objective more fully without sacrificing another, the economy is not organized Pareto-optimally.

trade policy *See* liberal trade policy, and strategic trade policy.

Trade-Related Investment Measures (TRIMS) An agreement reached in the Uruguay Round to attempt to control national policies such as investment subsidies which have significant effects on international trade.

Trade-Related Intellectual Property Rights (TRIPS) An agreement reached in 1995 as part of the Uruguay Round, concerning countries' respect for other countries' copyright, patents, and trademarks. The OECD countries, which own most of these, were very keen on TRIPS; many LDCs were very suspicious of it, but some of the NICs, which are developing their own patents, supported it.

trader, sole *See* sole proprietor.

trade sanctions A restriction or prohibition by one country of trade contacts with another country of whose actions or policies it disapproves. Sanctions may be general, or applied to particular goods, especially armaments and oil. While it is difficult to enforce sanctions completely, as trade can be conducted by smuggling or the use of indirect routes, sanctions increase the costs involved in trade and so can bring some pressure to bear on the victims.

Trades Union Congress (TUC) The UK national organization representing *trade unions. Its main functions are to lobby the government on issues concerning workers, particularly legislation affecting employment and social security, and to settle disputes between member unions. The TUC has a fair amount of moral influence but no legal authority over its member unions.

trade talks Discussions on the arrangements for international trade. These may be conducted bilaterally between countries, by limited groups of countries, or on a world scale. Bilateral talks are common, in efforts to resolve minor disputes. Groups of countries hold talks to discuss the setting up and running of trade blocs such as the *European Union (EU) or the *North American Free Trade Agreement (NAFTA). World trade talks have been held under the *General Agreement on Tariffs and Trade (GATT). The last series, the *Uruguay Round, ended in 1994 with the setting up of the *World Trade Organization (WTO), which is now holding the *Millenium Round. The participants in trade talks are usually governments, but proposals for *voluntary export restraint agreements (VERs) may involve private trade associations as well.

trade union 1. An organization of employees, formed for the purpose of *collective bargaining with employers over wages, hours, conditions of service, job security, and manning levels. They collect subscriptions from which to fund services for members such as legal advice about unfair dismissal, and strike pay during stoppages. Trade unions have in the past provided *friendly society facilities for their members, including sick and unemployment pay, and may also negotiate price concessions for their members. They may engage in political activity to promote their members' interests, particularly over issues such as legislation affecting security of employment and the social security system. A union's membership may be confined to a narrowly defined groups of skills, or may be spread widely over the workforce in general unions. In the UK most unions belong to the *Trades Union Congress (TUC), an organization representing unions at the national level. Many US unions belong to the *American Federation of Labor and Congress of Industrial Organizations (AFL–CIO). The rights and duties of both UK and US trade unions are governed by extensive legislation.

    2. *Employers' associations; this sense is little used.

trade war A situation when countries try to damage each other's trade. Methods of trade war include tariffs, quota restrictions, or outright prohibitions on imports from the other country; and subsidies or subsidized credit for exports to the other country, or for exports to third countries where the opponent is a rival. During a trade war such methods may be intensified in a series of tit-for-tat reprisals for measures taken by the opponent. Economists believe that both parties usually lose from trade wars.

trade-weighted index number An index number where the weights are proportional to various other countries' shares in a country's trade. Such an index number is used to calculate a country's *effective exchange rate, when the other countries have variable exchange rates with one another. The weights may be based on imports, exports, or the sum of the two.

trading *See* computerized trading, and electronic trading.

trading, computerized *See* computerized trading.

trading currency A currency used to invoice international trade transactions. While the currency of either the buyer or seller is frequently used, in some cases transactions are invoiced in the currency of a third country; this is common where neither party's own currency is widely used. The US dollar and the Euro are often used as trading, or vehicle, currencies.

trading, insider *See* insider dealing.

trading profit, gross *See* gross trading profit.

tragedy of the commons *See* commons.

training The process of improving workforce skills. This may be done by formal instructional courses, provided by employers or by educational institutions, either before or during employment. Such courses may be full or part-time. Training can also be provided on-the-job by working under the supervision of more experienced workers. Most firms which provide any training at all make some use of both methods. Training may lead to some type of formal qualification, but need not do so. *See also* on-the-job training.

transaction cost economics An approach to the economic explanation of institutions. This considers the relative merits of conducting transactions within firms and between different firms using markets. It takes account of bounded rationality, information problems, the costs of negotiating contracts, and opportunism.

transactions motive The desire to hold *money balances in order to finance transactions. The transactions to be financed include both current and capital account payments. The amount of money required seems certain to be an increasing function of each type of transaction. There is no fixed ratio between transactions and money balances; use of *credit allows the timing of cash settlements to be deferred, and it is possible to economize on money holdings, at some cost in organizing cash budgeting and careful record-keeping. The desired ratio of cash to transactions may also be affected by interest rates and expectations of inflation. The transactions motive is contrasted with the *speculative motive, which considers the effects on desired cash balances of expectations of changes in security prices, and the *precautionary motive, which considers the effects on desired cash holdings of uncertainty about possible emergency cash requirements.

transfer earnings The amount any *factor of production could expect to earn in its best alternative use. To obtain factor inputs, an industry needs to pay factors at least their transfer earnings. If demand for factors is high, competition may force employers to pay factors more than their transfer earnings; the additional payments are an *economic rent.

transfer payments Payments of income which are not a return for the provision of current factor services. In many countries the state makes large-scale transfer payments, particularly to pensioners, the disabled, and the unemployed. Countries also make transfer payments abroad. Many transfer payments are also made by private charities. Transfer payments are not part of the *national product; as the name implies, they merely transfer spending power from one lot of people to another.

transfer pricing The prices of goods and services provided by one part of any organization to another. This applies particularly to transactions between firms and their branches, subsidiaries or affiliates in other countries. It is possible by using suitable transfer prices to shift overall profits between different parts of the same business. This may be advantageous when tax rates and rules differ in different countries, as they invariably do. It may also be politically advantageous if profits in one country are more likely to attract criticism, or the attention of regulators, than equal profits in another. Where there is a competitive market in similar products, blatant cheating through transfer pricing can be detected, but where there are no arms-length prices for comparable transactions the determination of fair transfer prices is a real problem.

transfers, capital *See* capital transfers.

transfers in kind *See* benefits in kind.

transformation *See* marginal rate of transformation, and structural transformation.

transformation curve *See* production possibility frontier.

transitional economy An economy in the process of major changes in its mode of economic organization. This may be from a centrally planned economy to a market-based economy, as in the former Soviet Union and many countries of Eastern Europe. It may also be from a highly dirigiste policy regime to a more liberalized one, as in many developing countries. Transitional economies face special microeconomic difficulties, as they may need to reform their institutions, for example by creating clear property laws and introducing bankruptcy procedures. They also face special macroeconomic problems, as they may need to reform their tax systems, and their monetary authorities may lack relevant experience on which to base their policies. Many transitional economies have experienced slumps in real output and bursts of inflation in the early stages of transition.

transitional unemployment Unemployment due to a major change in the way an economy is organized. This could apply to conversion from a wartime to a peacetime economy, industrialization of a less developed country (LDC), or a shift from central planning to a market economy. In any major change it is likely that managers and skilled workers will be needed to set up new systems and production facilities earlier than less skilled workers are needed to operate them. The less skilled are thus liable to suffer from structural unemployment during the transitional period.

transition, demographic *See* demographic transition.

transitive relation A relation, denoted by R, such that if $A\,R\,B$ and $B\,R\,C$, then $A\,R\,C$. The relations of equality, denoted =, and greater than, denoted >, are transitive, as is the relation of indifference or that of preference by any individual. The relation 'able to win a majority vote', however, is not transitive.

transmission mechanism The ways in which changes in incomes, prices, interest rates, etc. are spread between sectors, regions, or countries. This involves the working of both goods and capital markets, and the relation between them. A boom in industrial countries, for example, affects less developed countries through several channels: higher output increases the volume of LDC exports, and raises commodity prices so that their terms of trade improve, but higher interest rates worsen the balance of payments of indebted countries.

transparent policy measures Policy measures whose operation is open to public scrutiny. Transparency includes making it clear who is taking the decisions, what the measures are, who is gaining from them, and who is paying for them. This is contrasted with opaque policy measures, where it is hard to discover who takes the decisions, what they are, and who gains and who loses. Economists believe that policies are more likely to be rational if they are transparent than if they are opaque.

transplant A product made within a country which was previously imported. Transplants are normally made either by foreign firms, or by domestic firms in association with foreign suppliers. They are common, for example, in the motor industry, with US and European firms producing in Brazil and other less developed countries (LDCs), and Japanese firms producing in the US and Europe.

transport costs The costs of moving goods from place to place. These tend to be higher for goods which are bulky or heavy relative to their value, and for goods which are fragile and thus require careful handling, or which are perishable and thus require rapid transport. Where transport costs are high, it is economic to produce near to the market, and inter-regional and international trade are relatively unimportant. Where transport costs are low, production tends to be footloose. Transport costs have fallen considerably during the last century, which has contributed to an increasing ratio of trade to incomes. The development of cheap air freight has allowed rapid growth of international trade in perishable products such as fresh flowers and vegetables. On average transport costs between countries amount to well under 5 per cent of the total value of world trade.

trap *See* liquidity trap, and poverty trap.

Treasury The UK's ministry of finance. Her Majesty's (HM) Treasury is headed by the Chancellor of the Exchequer. It is responsible for collecting taxes, budgeting for and controlling government expenditure, and management of the *national debt. It used to be responsible for overall economic management of the economy; this responsibility is now shared with the Bank of England, which was made more independent in 1997.

Treasury bill A short-dated UK government security. Treasury bills bear no formal interest, but are promises to pay in 91 (occasionally 61) days time, issued at a discount on their redemption price. They are regarded as a highly liquid financial asset by banks and other financial institutions.

Treaty *See* Maastricht, Treaty of, and Rome, Treaty of.

trend A long-term growth path of an economic variable, around which there may be short-term fluctuations. Trends may be calculated by various methods. One of the simplest is to regress the variable on time using *ordinary least squares. If it is believed that there is a constant proportional long-run growth rate, the trend is found by regressing the logarithm of the variable on time. Alternatively, a curve can be fitted to the peaks or troughs of successive cycles. This is statistically less satisfactory, as there are fewer peaks and troughs than the observations for all available periods, and the apparent peaks and troughs themselves may result from freak events or

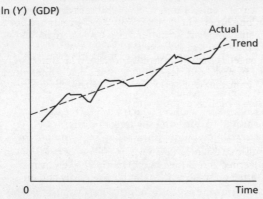

FIGURE 30: *Trend and Cycles*

errors in data collection. *Forecasting often works by projecting trends into the future: this is a risky procedure, as there is no natural law which prevents trends in economic variables such as income or prices from changing.

The horizontal axis shows time; the vertical axis shows Y = GDP, on a logarithmic scale. The trend is given by $\ln(Y_t) = \alpha + \beta t$, where α and β are found by regressing $\ln(Y_t)$ on t.

Treuhandanstalt A German institution set up after *German Economic and Monetary Union (GEMU) in 1990 to rationalize and privatize East German state-owned firms. This could be by handing them back to former owners or their heirs, or by sale of their assets to new or existing companies.

triangle of loss A measure of the loss attributable to setting an output level so that marginal cost and marginal benefit are not equal. In a market with an upward-sloping supply curve and a downward-sloping demand curve, if output is below the equilibrium level, the triangle of loss is the area between actual and equilibrium output above the supply curve and below the demand curve. If these units had been produced the marginal benefit to consumers would have been greater than the cost to producers. If output is above the equilibrium level, the triangle of loss is the area between equilibrium and actual output above the demand curve and below the supply curve. If these units are produced, the marginal benefit to consumers is less than the cost to producers.

trickle-down The proposition that economic development benefits the poorest members of a society mainly through the effects of increased national income on the demand for labour, rather than through explicit measures to assist them.

trigonometric function A function relating the properties of triangles to their angles. The sine of an angle x, written sin (x), is the ratio of the opposite side of an angle in a right-angled triangle to the hypotenuse (i.e. the longest side). x is the size of the angle measured in radians. The cosine, written cos (x), is the ratio of the adjacent side in the same triangle to the hypotenuse. The tangent, written tan (x), is the ratio of an angle's sine to its cosine. Trigonometric functions occur in the solutions to linear difference and differential equations of second order and above, whenever the roots are not all real. Sin (x) and cos (x) display regular oscillations as the angle increases; they can be expressed as infinite convergent series in x.

In Figure 31(on the next page) a circle of unit radius is drawn around the origin. Angles are measured from BC anti-clockwise. BE is at angle x, measured in radians (x = distance along the curve CE). ED = sin (x), BD = cos (x).

trillion A thousand billion = a million million = 10^{12}.

TRIMS *See* Trade-Related Investment Measures.

triple-A rating The highest grading available from *credit rating agencies. A triple-A rating (AAA) means that delay or default in payments of principal or interest on the security concerned is regarded as extremely unlikely. Any institution with a triple-A rating on its securities can borrow easily and on favourable terms.

TRIPS *See* Trade-Related Intellectual Property Rights.

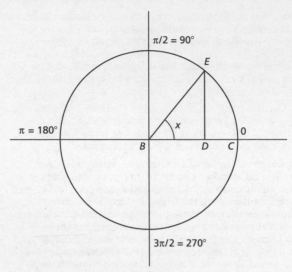

FIGURE 31: *Trigonometric Functions*

trough The lowest period for real incomes or activity in a *trade cycle. In a severe cycle the trough may be a minimum in absolute terms. In a mild cycle in an economy with a positive trend rate of growth of output, the trough may be a minimum relative to trend rather than in absolute terms.

true and fair view The property of *accounts which *auditors are supposed to check and certify. Accounts should not contain false statements; this is the true part. Neither, however, should they mislead by omission; this is the fair part. It requires more information to be sure that accounts are fair than that they are true.

trust 1. An arrangement through which one set of people, the trustees, are the legal owners of property which is administered in the interests of another set, the beneficiaries. Trusts may be set up to provide support for individuals or families, to provide pensions, to run charities, to liquidate the property of bankrupts for the benefit of their creditors, or for the safe keeping of the securities bought by *unit trusts with their investors' money. The assets which trusts may hold are regulated by law. These must be administered in the interests of the beneficiaries, and not for the profit of the trustees.
   2. A US term for a large or monopolistic business formed by amalgamation. This is why US anti-monopoly policy is called antitrust. *See also* investment trust, and unit trust.

trustee An individual or company who is the legal owner of property which he or she administers on behalf of a beneficiary. The beneficiary in turn may be an individual, a charity, the creditors of a bankrupt, or the investors in a *unit trust. Trustees may be paid for their services, but are bound to administer the trust in the interests of the beneficiaries and not for their own profit.

***t* test** A commonly used test of *significance of statistical estimates. The *t* ratio is the ratio of the *standard error of an estimate of a coefficient to its absolute value. This can be compared with tables of the ratios which for the sample size give any percentage chance that this estimate could have arisen by chance when the true value of the coefficient was zero. Estimates of fitted equations frequently print the *t* value for each coefficient immediately below it, in brackets. Thus the fitted version of the equation

$$y_t = a + bx_t + cz_t + \varepsilon_t$$

is printed out in the form

$$y_t = 102 + 0.375x_t + 1.23z_t$$

$$(3.45) \quad (4.27) \quad\quad (5.63)$$

TUC *See* Trades Union Congress.

turnkey project An investment project where a foreign firm contracts to build a factory, install equipment and train local labour, and hand it over as a going concern ready to start production. This system means that the supplier's experience of similar plants elsewhere is made available, and unexpected problems have to be sorted out before the host country takes over responsibility for the project. The name comes from the notion that the supplier simply hands over the keys when the project is completed.

turnover The value of total sales of goods and services by any organization during a given period, or the total value of transactions in a given market. *See also* labour turnover.

turnover tax A tax proportional to a firm's turnover. This gives an incentive to *vertical integration, as the tax may make it cheaper to produce an intermediate product within a firm than to buy a similar input produced more efficiently by an outside supplier. *Value-added taxes have been very widely adopted in preference to turnover taxes because they do not provide this artificial inducement to vertical integration.

two-gap model The proposition that development of less developed countries (LDCs) is constrained by two gaps: that between domestic savings and the investment required for take-off, and that between export revenues and the imports needed for development. National income accounting theory suggests that these gaps are not independent.

two-part tariff A pricing system by which customers pay more per unit for their purchases up to some given quantity, with a lower price per unit for further purchases. Such a system is only practicable when the customer can be identified, and resale is difficult. The argument for two-part tariffs is that the higher price for the first *n* units bought reflects the *overhead costs of supplying a particular customer: for example, gas, electricity, and water suppliers incur costs in connection to the mains, however much or little is then bought. Critics of two-part tariffs argue that the higher charge for the first *n* units is simply a form of monopolistic *price discrimination, to skim off some of the customer's *consumer surplus. They also point out that a two-part tariff results in higher average prices being charged to poorer customers, who usually buy less than richer ones.

two-stage least squares A method of estimating a set of simultaneous equations, where each variable appears as *dependent variable in one equation and a *right-hand variable in others. Each equation is run, then each right-hand variable is replaced by the value predicted from its own equation. The system is then re-run; the results give better estimates of each equation than those resulting from the first stage.

two-tier board A system of company organization in which there are two *boards of directors. Overall policy is decided by a supervisory board, on which employees as well as the shareholders are represented, and day-to-day management decisions are taken by a management board. The object of this division is to promote information and goodwill amongst employees by having their representatives on the supervisory body, while retaining the authority necessary for the managers to execute policies effectively through the management board. This system is relatively common in Germany.

type I and II errors The two types of mistake that can be made when deciding whether or not to accept a hypothesis. A type I error is rejecting a true hypothesis, that is, one there is really no good reason for rejecting. A type II error is accepting a false hypothesis: that is, accepting it as true when it should really have been rejected. When *hypothesis testing there is a trade-off between the two types of error. The best combination to choose depends on the losses arising from making the two types of error; in economic decisions these are frequently asymmetrical.

U

unbiased estimator A statistic which is on average neither too high nor too low. The method of estimation does not always produce estimates which correspond to reality, but errors in either direction are equally likely.

unbundling The sale of peripheral parts of a business to concentrate on its core activities. This may be because it is believed that the outlying parts of a business empire could operate more profitably if they became independent or joined different groupings, or to raise money to pay off debt.

uncertainty A consciousness of lack of knowledge about present facts or future possibilities. This is the normal condition of the human race, not only in economics. Some writers distinguish between *risk and uncertainty: risk covers cases where while individual events are not known, people believe that they know the frequency distribution from which they are drawn at random; uncertainty covers cases where such beliefs are absent. Events of the type covered by risk, such as individual deaths, fires, or motor accidents, are potentially insurable, while events of the types covered by uncertainty are not. Many authors, however, simply use risk and uncertainty interchangably.

uncompetitive Unable to sell at a profit. Goods or services may be uncompetitive because their prices are too high relative to alternative suppliers, or may be unsaleable because of defects in quality, where other suppliers offer better products. Inability to compete may apply to a firm, a region or a country. High costs may be due to dear or poor quality inputs of labour or materials, or to obsolete equipment and poor management. Products may be unsaleable at any price because of poor design, unreliability, failure to meet promised delivery dates, or failure to comply with health and safety regulations in possible markets.

UNCTAD *See* United Nations Conference on Trade and Development.

undated security A security with no set *redemption date. With such a security the borrower has only the obligation to pay interest as agreed, and need not redeem it. An undated security may be irredeemable, in which case the borrower has no right to redeem it, or it may be redeemable at the borrowers's discretion, as in the case of UK 'consols' (Consolidated Fund Annuities), where the government has the right but no obligation to redeem them at par at any time.

under-capitalized Having too little capital in relation to the business carried on or intended. If a business has insufficient capital, it is liable to become insolvent too easily in the face of the risks normal in its line of activity, such as delays in payment by customers. It is risky to lend or extent credit to an under-capitalized business, and being charged premium rates or refused credit is bad for its profits. For most businesses, under-capitalization is discouraged simply by being unprofitable, but in the case of banks and other financial institutions there is public regulation of *capital adequacy, because of fears that the insolvency of one institution could cause a general financial panic.

under-developed country *See* less developed country.

under-funded pension scheme A pension scheme with accumulated funds insufficient to meet the actuarially expected costs of pensions payable. The adequacy of funding is a matter of judgement, as it depends both on demographic forecasts of the expected lives of pensioners, and financial forecasts of the expected yield on the fund's assets.

underlying rate of inflation The rate of inflation as measured by a retail price index (RPI) excluding mortgage interest payments. This is contrasted with the 'headline' rate of inflation, which in the UK is the *Retail Price Index (RPI), which includes mortgage interest payments. The RPI in most other countries excludes mortgage interest, so this distinction is peculiar to the UK.

under-subscription Failure of applications for shares in a new issue to match the number on offer. This means that some shares will be unsold, or bought by underwriters, which makes it probable that when the market opens the newly issued shares will sell at a discount relative to the issue price. *See also* underwriting.

under-valued currency A currency whose exchange rates with other currencies are lower than is necessary for *external balance. This tends to improve the country's *balance of payments on current account, as relatively low prices make exports easy to sell and imports easy to compete with. It should also make it possible to borrow easily, if the market expects the exchange rate to rise. It is not easy to tell whether a currency is undervalued: for example, the current account may be in surplus during a recession even though the exchange rate is too high to be consistent with external balance once activity recovers.

underwriting The provision by merchant banks of a guaranteed market for a *new issue of shares. Firms making new issues cannot know in advance whether there will be sufficient demand for the shares they offer at the issue price, from the public or institutional investors. An underwriter removes the uncertainty as to whether shares will sell by promising to buy any the market does not take up. These shares then have to be sold, which may involve accepting a low price or a long wait. A commission is charged for this service.

undistributed profits Profits of a business which are neither paid out in taxes nor paid to the shareholders or owners. Undistributed profits are ploughed back into the business. While they may be kept as cash balances or marketable securities, they are usually invested in buying physical equipment, acquiring other companies, or extending trade credit to customers. They are a major source of finance for new investment in the economy.

UNDP *See* United Nations Development Programme.

unearned income Personal income derived from property ownership rather than work. It thus consists of rent, dividends and interest. At one time the UK income tax system collected tax at higher rates on unearned than earned incomes: this could be justified on the argument that unearned income was from permanent sources, while workers needed to provide for their retirement. The distinction has since been abolished.

unemployable People who are difficult or impossible to employ. Problems over employment may arise from physical, mental, cultural or behavioural characteristics. In all cases this is a matter of degree; physical and mental problems vary in severity, and relatively few people are completely unemployable. Physical disabilities restrict the range of jobs some people can fill: for example, the blind cannot be airline pilots. Mental problems also restrict the range of possible jobs: some work requires high intelligence, but there are many repetitive jobs which less intelligent people do well while clever ones become too bored to perform properly. Language problems limit the jobs open to some minority groups. The most severe difficulty arises with behavioural problems; it is very difficult to employ habitual thieves, violent drunks or those with severe drugs problems. How likely those with employability problems are to have a job depends on the overall state of the labour market. If ordinary workers are in excess supply, employers prefer to avoid the extra costs and trouble involved in employing problem cases. If labour is scarce, employers are willing to adapt jobs to suit the disabled, to provide special training for workers with language difficulties, and to put up with moderate degrees of misconduct, particularly by people who are good at their job.

unemployment Inability to obtain a job when one is willing and able to work. This can be measured in two ways: official registration with a state agency, which carries some form of income support, and self-assessment by a *random sample of the population. Self-assessment generally produces higher figures. The unemployment rate is the unemployed as a percentage of the total labour force, defined as employees plus unemployed. Official measures rarely correspond exactly to an economist's ideal definition of unemployment. They take no account of people who would prefer full-time work but can only find part-time jobs, or of people over pensionable age who would prefer to work. They do, however, include some people who are doubtfully employable, or simply do not want work.

Unemployment has been divided into various categories, corresponding to different causes; these probably do not operate independently, but interact. Demand-deficiency, or Keynesian, unemployment occurs when there is not enough demand for goods and services to provide jobs for all the workers available. This type of unemployment could be reduced by extra private or government spending. 'Classical' unemployment occurs if real wages are too high relative to productivity for it to be profitable to employ all the labour force. Unemployment of this type could be reduced by real wage cuts, or by improvements in productivity, through better training, or the reform of restrictive practices. Structural unemployment occurs through a mismatch between the skills and location of unemployed workers and unfilled vacancies. This could be reduced by measures to retrain or relocate unemployed workers, or to relocate firms and redefine jobs so as to use the skills of the unemployed. Frictional unemployment occurs if matchable unemployed workers and vacancies both exist, but the process of connecting them is slow or inadequate. Search unemployment occurs where workers are unemployed while looking for a suitable job. Frictional unemployment can be reduced by making the matching process more efficient, by creating or improving labour exchanges.

Some unemployment is due to the impaired employability of potential workers. Reduction of this requires an assortment of measures. Some potential workers could be made available for employment if there were better facilities for child-care, and assistance in caring for sick, handicapped, or elderly relatives. Others could be made employable by better facilities for the rehabilitation of alcoholics, drug abusers, or petty criminals. Some economists have distinguished between voluntary and involuntary unemployment, but others think this distinction too subjective to be useful. Some of the unemployed simply do not want work, at least of any form for which they are qualified. This again is due to a variety of causes. Some are simply idle, or have gainful occupations in the *unofficial economy. This form of unemployment might be reduced by *'workfare', where income support is made conditional on some form of work. Others are simply taking holidays between spells of hard and boring work; others again are engaged in educating themselves, or practising the arts. Unemployment is due to too many and complex causes for there to be any one simple cure for it. *See also* classical unemployment, cyclical unemployment, demographic unemployment, disguised unemployment, frictional unemployment, involuntary unemployment, Keynesian unemployment, long-term unemployment, natural rate of unemployment, non-accelerating inflation rate of unemployment, search unemployment, seasonal unemployment, structural unemployment, technological unemployment, transitional unemployment, and voluntary unemployment.

unemployment benefit Income support payments to the unemployed. Countries differ in the level of such payments, which may be at a fixed rate or an amount related to previous wages, and in the length of time for which they are available. Eligibility for unemployment benefit may be related to previous contributions to an unemployment insurance fund. Many of the unemployed and their dependents receive other forms of income support payment. In the UK, for example, fewer than half of the unemployed receive unemployment benefit, now rechristened jobseeker's allowance.

unemployment rate The number of unemployed as a percentage of the number of people either employed or unemployed. This rate takes no account of the number of the self-employed, nor of the number of people of working age not participating in the labour market. Unemployment rates can be calculated for a country as a whole, for men and women separately, or for different age, occupational, or ethnic groups, or different regions.

unexpected inflation *Inflation at a higher or lower rate than had been expected. If the expected rate of inflation has been taken into account in arriving at wage agreements and loan contracts, inflation higher than expected transfers real purchasing power from workers to employers or from lenders to borrowers; inflation lower than expected transfers real purchasing power from employers to workers or from borrowers to lenders. Unexpected inflation is believed to stimulate a temporary increase in real activity. It can be measured either via the use of a model of how expectations of inflation are formed, or by asking people what rate of inflation they expect and comparing this with the actual rate.

unfair competition Business practices complained of by firms whose rivals offer prices or use methods with which they are unable or unwilling to compete. For example, they may allege that foreign competitors receive help from their governments in the form of subsidies or cheap loans, which their own government does not provide; or that rivals are unhampered by laws on health and safety which they have to obey. A cynic might define unfair competition as competition viewed by the losers.

unfair dismissal Dismissal of an employee that the employer cannot show to be fair. Fair grounds for dismissal include the employees' conduct, lack of capacity or qualifications, or laws prohibiting their employment; or that while the employee is satisfactory, the need for their services no longer exists, so that they are redundant. Employees in the UK who believe they have been unfairly dismissed can apply to an industrial tribunal for reinstatement or compensation; not all groups of employees have this right.

unfunded pension scheme A pension scheme with no pension fund. The pensions of current beneficiaries are paid by a former employer out of current revenue or contributions by present employees, on a pay-as-you-go basis. Such pensions are safe only if the employer cannot become insolvent or cease to trade; this normally requires either state ownership or a state guarantee.

unified budget The system by which the UK Parliament is presented with a *budget covering both government spending and tax plans, to be considered together. In 1993 this replaced the previous system, under which the government's tax plans were presented to Parliament in the spring and its spending plans were considered in the autumn.

uniform business rate The UK system of property taxes on business premises in force since 1990. This replaced *rates set at varying levels by individual local authorities. *Business rates are now charged at a uniform percentage of valuation throughout England, so that local variations reflect differences in the valuation of property, rather than differences in local tax policies; Scotland and Wales have separate rates.

uniform distribution A *frequency distribution in which a variable is equally likely to take any value between known limits. If a variable x lies between a lower limit a and an upper limit b, with a uniform distribution, the frequency distribution is given by $f(x) = 1/(b - a)$ for $a \leq x \leq b$, and $f(x) = 0$ for $x < a$ and $x > b$.

union *See* customs union, payments union, and trade union.

unionized An occupation or workplace where the workers are organized in a *trade union, which is recognized as representing them in negotiations with employers over pay and working conditions. Workers may or may not all be union members.

union/non-union wage differential The excess of wages of workers in unionized firms over those of workers with similar skill levels in non-unionized firms. A positive differential is prima facie evidence that unions are beneficial for their members.

unitary taxation A system of taxing firms operating in several countries on the basis of a country's share in their total operations. If taxation of a *multinational firm operating in a country is based purely on its profits made in that country, tax can be avoided by accounting procedures. Measures to shift apparent profits out of the country include *transfer pricing, that is overvaluing purchases by branches of the firm from its branches in other countries, or undervaluing sales to them. Under unitary taxation a multinational firm is taxed on the basis of its world-wide profits times some measure of the proportion of its operations carried out in the country; such a measure could be employment or turnover. The adoption of unitary taxation would require changes in *double taxation agreements.

United Nations Conference on Trade and Development (UNCTAD) A United Nations (UN) organization established in 1964. It is intended to represent the *less developed countries (LDCs), and acts as a pressure group for increased aid and an international regime for trade and investment more favourable to LDCs. Proposals for a *New International Economic Order (NIEO) came from UNCTAD.

United Nations Development Programme (UNDP) A United Nations (UN) body formed to give technical assistance and make soft loans to *less developed counties (LDCs).

unit elasticity The case where a proportional change in one variable corresponds to an equal proportional change in another. In the case of a unit elasticity of demand, a proportional rise in price produces an equal proportional fall in quantity demanded: total revenue is thus constant, and marginal revenue is zero. In the case of the *income elasticity of demand, unit elasticity means that at any given price the proportion of income spent on a good remains constant as income changes.

unit-free measure A variable which is a pure number, independent of the units in which variables such as price or quantity are measured. Examples of unit-free measures are percentages, market shares, and *elasticities. Interest rates and growth rates are not unit-free measures, as while they are independent of the units in which prices and quantities are measured, they do depend on the units used to measure time.

unit of account The role of *money as the unit in which contracts are expressed and individual incomes or firms' profits are measured. High and fluctuating rates of inflation interfere with the performance of this function, which is believed to be bad for the efficient and equitable running of the economy.

unit root A tendency for changes in a system to persist indefinitely. A linear difference equation system of the Nth order has N roots. If the absolute value of any of these is more than 1, the system will explode, at least until it encounters some constraint which prevents it from continuing to be linear. If all roots are less than 1 in absolute value the system will eventually converge back to its original *equilibrium after any temporary disturbance. A root with an absolute value of exactly 1, or a unit root, will cause a permanent shift in the system, and a series of disturbances can cause unlimited divergence from the original position. Comparable results hold for linear differential equation systems, where roots may be positive, negative or zero in real part: the zero case corresponds to a unit root in difference equations. In recent years a number of statistical tests for the presence of unit roots have been developed.

unit trust A UK system by which small investors can benefit from diversified portfolios. Unit trusts sell units to investors, and use the funds to hold a portfolio of securities managed by the trust and held by a bank as trustee. Unit trust shareholdings may be widely spread, or concentrated on a particular sector or country. They may aim at varying combinations of income and capital growth. Investors get professional management and a diversified portfolio without high transactions costs. They can buy more units or sell their units back to the trust at published prices at any time. Unit trusts are distinguished from investment trusts, where investors buy shares in the trust company. *See also* portfolio of assets.

universal benefit A benefit available to all citizens of a country regardless of income. Universal benefits may be conditional on other criteria, such as age for pensions, or disability. The argument for making benefits universal rather than conditional on a *means test is that means testing is expensive and open to abuse, and an invasion of privacy. The objection to making benefits universal is that this is extremely expensive, and may involve most of the money going to people who are not in severe need. The alternative is to use means testing to target the available funds towards those in greatest need. In economies where the bulk of the labour force receives occupational pensions, state pensions could be larger if they were means tested. This however would create *disincentives both to saving before retirement age and to continuing work after it; pensions which are universal benefits have neither of these side-effects.

unlimited liability Liability for the debts an individual or business has incurred, without limit. This is contrasted with *limited liability, where shareholders in a limited liability company are not liable for its debts provided they hold fully paid-up shares. Unlimited liability for the debts of a business makes it difficult to raise capital for large and complex ventures, as without the protection of limited liability small investors are nervous of putting money into a business they do not fully understand and cannot control. The recent experience of some members of *Lloyd's illustrates the dangers of unlimited liability. Larger investors sometimes choose to operate with unlimited liability, as their reputation enables businesses run on this basis to get credit relatively easily and to borrow relatively cheaply.

Unlisted Securities Market (USM) A part of the London Stock Exchange dealing in the shares of smaller companies. The USM had less stringent requirements and traded shares in far fewer companies than the main market. It was abolished in 1995.

unofficial economy Economic activities which are not conducted through legally incorporated bodies and are not reported to the tax and social security authorities. This is also referred to as the informal or unorganized sector. Such activities range from part-time domestic cleaning, gardening and child-minding to large-scale organized crime and drug-trafficking. While many small-scale activities in the unofficial economy are harmless, the unofficial sector frequently involves ignoring health and safety regulations, restrictions on child labour and minimum wage legislation, absence of proper insurance for employees, evasion of income and value-added tax and social security contributions, and abuse of the social security system by drawing benefits when actually working. It is naturally extremely difficult to measure the level of unofficial economic activity, which lowers the reliability of official statistics on the economy.

unsecured loan A loan where the creditor has no claim on any particular asset of the debtor in the event of default. This is contrasted with a secured loan, where the lender has a right to take over some particular asset if repayments are not made at the due dates. In the event of the borrower going bankrupt or becoming insolvent, unsecured creditors normally rank below secured creditors for any available assets. Unsecured loans are thus riskier than secured loans, and require higher interest rates to compensate the lenders for this.

unskilled work Work not demanding formal qualifications or much experience. Such work is held in low social regard, and is generally poorly paid.

unsterilized intervention *See* intervention in foreign exchange markets.

untied aid Assistance to other countries, normally less developed countries (LDCs), which can be spent on goods and services from any country. This is contrasted with tied aid, which has to be spent on goods and services from the donor country. Untied aid may be of greater value than tied aid of an equal amount, as tying restricts the choices open to the recipient, though where the recipient imports a lot from the donor in any case tying may not be effective. As untied aid may cause balance-of-payments problems for the donor, less aid may be available if it is given on an untied basis.

unweighted average An average in which all the items have equal weights. Thus if there are N variables x_i, for $x = 1, 2, \ldots, N$, the unweighted average is given by

$$U = [\Sigma_1^N x_i]/N.$$

This is contrasted with a *weighted average, where the N variables are given weights w_i proportional to their importance, on some measure, and their sum is then divided by the sum of the weights, so that

$$W = [\Sigma_1^N w_i x_i]/[\Sigma_1^N w_i].$$

upstream *See* backward integration.

urban economics The study of the economics of urban areas. This includes the factors making for the growth first of towns and then of metropolitan areas, including *complementarity between industries and the attraction of proximity to markets. It also covers the special problems of conurbations, including congestion, pollution, and water supplies.

Uruguay Round The last round of trade talks under the *General Agreement on Tariffs and Trade (GATT); this round started in 1986 and finished in 1994. The Round managed for the first time to include some modest steps to restrict agricultural protection, and arrived at a new *General Agreement on Trade in Services (GATS). It also covered reform of the *Multi-Fibre Arrangement (MFA) on international trade in textiles, and the question of intellectual property rights.

U-shaped average cost curve The shape that average cost curves are believed to take. The argument is that any productive process has some overheads or fixed costs; these ensure that at low levels of output average cost is high. There are bound to be some inputs which cannot be increased indefinitely, at least in the short run. When output is high, shortages of these restrict the efficiency with which such inputs as can be varied contribute to more output. Thus at high levels of output marginal costs tend to be high, leading to increasing average costs. At some medium level or possibly range of output, average costs reach a minimum, hence the name. Whether long-run average cost curves must turn up or could remain flat for ever is a matter of some dispute.

USM *See* Unlisted Securities Market.

US Trade Representative An office set up to formulate US trade policy and conduct trade negotiations. The US Trade Representative forms part of the Executive Office of the President.

usury Charging excessive *interest on loans. The term was formerly applied to charging any interest, but now refers to interest rates the writer regards as unreasonable. Unfortunately there is no objective criterion of what constitutes a reasonable interest rate.

usury laws Laws restricting the level of *interest that could be charged or paid for loans. The intention of such laws was to restrain exploitation of those in need by money-lenders. If the highest permitted interest rate is too low to compensate for inflation and the risk of default or delay in payment, it creates excess demand for loans. This leads to their being rationed, either to borrowers with political pull or simply the safest risks; in either case the least fortunate cannot get loans when they need them.

util The unit in which *utility would be measured, if it could be measured at all.

utilitarianism The belief that rules and institutions should be judged by how good they are for people's *welfare. 'The greatest good of the greatest number' was a slogan of its inventor, Jeremy Bentham. A utilitarian attempts to tackle the question of how far the state should control and how far respect *private property by considering its usefulness and defects as a framework for economic activity, rather than asking how rules are related to either divine commandments or 'natural rights'.

utility A synonym for individual *welfare. A utility function gives an individual's welfare as an increasing function of the various goods they consume and a decreasing function of various types of work performed. Consumers are assumed to allocate their time and spend their available income so as to maximize their *utility functions. An indirect utility function gives utility as an increasing function of non-work income and wage rates for various forms of work, and a decreasing function of consumer goods prices, assuming that optimum choices of work and consumption are made subject to these prices. Economists have differed as to whether utility should be regarded as cardinal or ordinal: each view gives rise to problems. *Cardinal utility assumes that utility can be measured. While economists have found no practical way of doing this, without the assumption that it is possible there is no way of analysing decisions under uncertainty, or of answering questions about income distribution. *Ordinal utility assumes that consumers can only order the benefits they get from different combinations of work and goods, but cannot measure the differences between them. To a strict believer in ordinal utility the relative merits of different distributions of income are a matter of complete agnosticism, and changes can be recommended only subject to the Pareto-condition that somebody gains and nobody loses. This view makes most interesting questions about economic policy unanswerable. *See also* cardinal utility, expected utility, marginal utility, ordinal utility, public utility, and total utility.

utility function 1. An expression showing utility as a function of an individual's consumption of various goods and performance of various types of work. This is a direct utility function: utility is an increasing function of the quantity of each good consumed, and a decreasing function of each type of work performed.

2. An expression showing utility as a function of income, assuming that this is optimally divided between the various goods available. This is usually assumed to show decreasing marginal utility of income. Examples of such a utility function, where U is utility and C is the value of consumption, would be $U = \sqrt{C}$ or $U = A - (b/\sqrt{C})$, where A and b are positive constants.

3. An expression giving utility as a function of non-wage income, the price of each type of good, and the wage of each type of labour, assuming that the quantities of goods consumed and work performed are chosen optimally, so as to maximize utility. This is an indirect utility function, in which utility is an increasing function of non-wage income, a decreasing function of the price of each good consumed, and an increasing function of the wage rate for each type of work peformed. *See also* indirect utility function, and separable utility function.

utility maximization The device of explaining choice in consumption and labour markets by assuming that individuals have utility functions which they attempt to maximize. This is done by choosing the quantities of all goods consumed so that their marginal utilities are proportional to their prices and choosing the amounts of various forms of work done so that their marginal disutilities are proportional to their wage rates. Where choices have to be made under conditions of quantifiable uncertainty, or risk, the objective becomes that of maximizing expected utility. Where uncertainty is not quantifiable, applying the concept is difficult. It is far from clear, too, that people know their own utility functions; there may be no method—except experiment—of discovering how much one would enjoy a new product. As with the theory of the firm, some behavioural economists hold that *satisficing is a more relevant model than optimizing. Individuals spend partly out of habit and partly by random experiment.

They persist in any form of expenditure so long as it gives acceptable results, and react to unsatisfactory results or new opportunities by trial and error.

utilization, capacity *See* capacity utilization.

vacancy A post which an employer intends to fill if a suitable applicant appears. The number of *job vacancies is difficult to measure, as there is no one standard method of advertising or filling them. Job information is circulated by official and private employment agencies, public advertisement, and word of mouth among present and past employees. While some employers have very clear-cut ideas on how many vacancies they wish to fill, others follow an elastic policy, taking on promising candidates as they appear.

value 1. Value = price × quantity. For example, if between two years prices quadruple and quantities in the economy increase by 25 per cent, the money value of GDP rises to five times its former level.
2. A synonym for price. Valuables are goods which sell for high prices. A valuer is a professional who estimates what price goods would fetch if they were sold. The stock of a shop or firm is transferred from one proprietor to the next 'at valuation', that is for an amount set by a valuer. The labour theory of value attempted to explain the prices of goods by the amount of labour needed for their production. *Value added is the total value of a firm's output minus the value of inputs purchased from other firms. Value added is thus what is left to be divided between wages for its employees and profits for its owners.
3. A general term of praise. Value in this sense is a bit like price, but somehow more important, more permanent, and better. This usage is enshrined in the definition of a cynic as 'one who knows the price of everything and the value of nothing'. Advertisers claim that their goods represent 'value for money'; politicians claim the same for their policies.
4. The size of a variable or parameter. *See* modulus. *See also* book value, break-up value, expected value, labour theory of value, option value, par value, present discounted value, redemption value, store of value, and surplus value.

value added The total sales of a firm minus purchases of inputs from other firms. What is left is available for the wages of its employees and the profits of its owners. National income is the sum of value added in all enterprises in the economy. Trying to calculate national income by adding the outputs of all firms would involve massive *double counting.

value-added tax (VAT) An *indirect tax levied on goods or services as a percentage of their value added. The customer pays VAT on purchases in addition to the normal price; the seller then pays the government VAT collected on sales less the VAT they have paid on purchased inputs. VAT is levied in many countries: it was introduced in the UK in 1973. Goods may bear VAT at different rates. Some goods, for example food in the UK, are exempt, and VAT is not payable by businesses with turnover below some minimum level.

value index An index number of the total value of any economic aggregate at current prices: if p_t is the price and q_t the quantity concerned at time t, the value index is given by

$$V_t = (p_t\,q_t)/(p_0\,q_0),$$

where 0 is the base date. Where p_t and q_t are themselves index numbers, as is normally the case in dealing with aggregates, for example consumption, the value index V_t can be found as the product of a price and a quantity index; one of these must be base-weighted and the other current-weighted. Thus where there are i goods,

$$V_t = \Sigma_i p_{it} q_{it}/\Sigma_i p_{i0} q_{i0} = (\Sigma_i p_{it} q_{it}/\Sigma_i p_{i0} q_{it})\,(\Sigma_i p_{i0} q_{it}/\Sigma_i p_{i0} q_{i0}),$$

that is, the product of a *current-weighted or Paasche price index and a *base-weighted or Laspeyres quantity index; or alternatively

$$V_t = (\Sigma_i p_{it} q_{it}/\Sigma_i p_{it} q_{i0})/(\Sigma_i p_{it} q_{i0}/\Sigma_i p_{i0} q_{i0}),$$

that is, the product of a base-weighted price index and a current-weighted quantity index.

value judgement An opinion about the relative merits of two or more states of the economy, which cannot be empirically tested. For example, consider a proposed change which will affect A and B. Whether each gains or loses can be empirically tested, by asking whether they accept or reject the change, if the choice is left to them. Suppose the change benefits A but harms B. Whether or not it should be made then involves a value judgement, which cannot be empirically tested. The presence of value judgements is an essential component of *normative economics, and their absence a characteristic of *positive economics.

value of the physical increase in stocks and work in progress That part of the total increase in the value of stocks and work in progress which is due to changes in their quantities. This is distinguished from the part of the change in the total value of stocks and work in progress which is due to revaluations of the existing volume of stocks because of price changes. The value of the physical increase is part of the real *national product, whereas the increase due to revaluation of stocks is not.

value-subtracting industry An industry where the value of output is less than that of purchased inputs, so that *value added is negative. This situation can arise in two ways: the industry concerned may be heavily subsidized, either by the government or by *cross-subsidization from profitable parts of the same firms; alternatively, value subtraction may be apparent only if inputs and outputs are valued at prices other than those actually prevailing. In many former planned economies, for example, parts of state-owned industries were value-subtracting if inputs and outputs were valued at world prices.

variable A quantity which is liable to change. Variables may measure prices, interest rates, income levels, quantities of goods, etc. An exogenous variable is one where the changes originate from causes outside the scope of a given model; an endogenous variable is determined within the model. Variables which are exogenous in one model may be endogenous in another. *See also* dependent variable, discrete variable, dummy variable, nominal variable, predetermined endogenous variable, real variable, and right hand variable.

variable cost That part of cost which varies with the level of output. This is in contrast to fixed costs, which must be incurred for output to be possible at all, and do not depend on its level. It should be noted that this distinction is different from that of variability over time. The price of an input may be stable for years, but it is still a variable cost if the amount used depends on output. The price of another input may be volatile, but it is still a fixed cost if the amount used does not depend on the level of output.

variable factor proportions The ease with which one factor input can be substituted for another. Where factor proportions are variable, the *elasticity of technical substitution between inputs is high: a small change in relative factor prices causes a cost-minimizing firm to shift its use of factors strongly towards whichever has become relatively cheaper. If factor proportions are not easily variable, the elasticity of technical substitution is low, and firms change their relative use of factors very little as relative factor prices change.

variance A measure of dispersion. The variance of a set of N numbers is found by adding the squares of their deviations from their mean value, and dividing by N. Thus if the number are x_i, $i = 1, 2, \ldots, N$, and their mean is μ, their variance is given by

$$V = [\textstyle\sum_1^N (x_i - \mu)^2]/N.$$

See analysis of variance.

variation *See* coefficient of variation, compensating variation, and equivalent variation.

variety **1.** A particular good differentiated by specification or *brand name from other similar goods.
2. The existence of a large number of varieties in sense 1. Variety is good for consumers partly because their exact requirements differ, so that a wide choice gives more chance that they can obtain goods which are a good approximation to their ideal specification, and partly because individual consumers want the ability to vary their consumption over time. A large proportion of the real gains from economic growth and integration derives from increases in the variety of products available.

VAT *See* value-added tax.

VAT registration The procedure by which firms are added to the VAT register. This is the list of firms required to make VAT returns, and to pay VAT on their sales if these exceed the VAT exemption level.

VAT return A regular report of its sales of goods and services subject to VAT which is required of firms registered for VAT.

vector A compact notation used to refer to a list of variables, which may themselves be numbers or algebraic expressions. A vector may be written as a row, so that $\mathbf{x} = (x_1, x_2, \ldots x_N)$, or as a column, so that $\mathbf{x} = \begin{bmatrix} x_1 \\ x_2 \\ \cdot \\ \cdot \\ \cdot \\ x_N \end{bmatrix}$

A vector with N elements is said to be of dimension N. Vectors provide a convenient notation for referring to lists of the quantities or prices of goods.

vehicle currency *See* trading currency.

velocity of circulation The ratio of some aggregate of transactions, for example GDP, to some measure of the *money supply, for example M1. The ratio of money held to the value of total transactions can vary, but monetary economists have argued that such changes depend on changes in monetary institutions, and can thus be expected to take place only gradually. There are, however, reasons to doubt this. Even including only transactions on income account, there are normally several transactions per unit of GDP, as firms buy factors in one set of markets and sell their products in others, and there are many sales of fuel, materials, and components. The main scope for variations in the velocity of circulation, however, is the large amount of transactions on *capital account, trading in shares, bonds, and currencies. There is no reason why the volume of capital account transactions should bear any fixed relation to GDP, and many money balances are held primarily to finance capital market transactions.

venture capital Capital whose owners are willing to invest in new or small businesses, where the risk of losing it is high. Venture capital is necessary if people without sufficient capital of their own are to be able to start new businesses.

venture, joint *See* joint venture.

VER *See* voluntary export restraint.

vertical equity The place of *income distribution considerations in economic policies such as taxation. Consider for example the question of how far taxation should be progressive. While there is fairly general agreement that it is necessary to exempt the very poor from *income tax, so that some degree of progression is inevitable, the proper degree of progression is controversial. Some economists maintain that taxes should be as progressive as is consistent with preserving incentives for effort and saving, and the need to keep the rich within the official economy. Others prefer keeping taxes as nearly proportional as is consistent with exemptions for the very poor. Vertical equity is distinguished from *horizontal equity, which is concerned with considerations of fairness between people with roughly equal incomes. *See also* progressive tax.

vertical integration The combination in one firm of two or more stages of production normally operated by separate firms. Vertical integration may involve forward integration, for example an oil company running filling stations; or backward integration, for example an army running its own ordnance factories. Vertical integration may be beneficial for firms if it assists in co-ordination over the quality and reliability of intermediate goods which one independent firm would have sold to the other. On the other hand it may inhibit entry to and competition in an industry.

vertical merger A merger between two firms where one is a major supplier of the other. Examples would be a brewery and a chain of public houses, or a publisher and a bookshop. This is contrasted with a horizontal merger, which combines two firms operating at the same stage of production.

visible balance *See* balance of trade.

visible exports and imports *See* trade.

visible trade *See* trade.

voice The expression of preferences by attempting to change unsatisfactory situations: this may be by voting, lobbying, or use of complaints procedures or litigation. It is contrasted with 'exit', which means leaving an unsatisfactory situation: this may involve selling shares, changing jobs, or migration between areas or countries.

volatility Liability to fluctuate over time. Fluctuations may be measured in absolute terms, or relative to trend. Most economic variables are volatile, but some are much more so than others: for example share prices and primary commodity prices tend to be much more volatile than wage rates and the prices of manufactures. Volatility is often measured by the *coefficient of variation, which is the standard deviation divided by the mean for a series. This is not a satisfactory measure for series which can change sign, for example investment in stocks and work in progress. *See also* price volatility.

volume index An index of the real level of production or consumption, in the whole economy or some part of it. A volume index is a weighted average of the production or consumption of some suitably chosen bundle of goods. The weights are the prices of some period. Where 0 is the base period and t the current period, p_{it} the price and q_{it} the quantity of good i produced or consumed in period t, a *base-weighted, or Laspeyres, volume index is defined by

$$q_B = (\textstyle\sum_i p_{i0} q_{it})/(\textstyle\sum_i p_{i0} q_{i0}),$$

and a *current-weighted, or Paasche, volume index is defined by

$$q_C = (\textstyle\sum_i p_{it} q_{it})/(\textstyle\sum_i p_{it} q_{i0}).$$

voluntary exchange Exchange between two parties where each is free to refuse to trade. It is argued that under these circumstances both parties will gain, or at least not lose, from the exchange: support for a *market economy rests on this point. Critics of the market economy argue that if the parties to an exchange differ greatly in their access to information about alternatives, and their total wealth, the freedom of one party to refuse the terms offered may be illusory. Criticism on these lines has been applied both to relations between employers and unskilled workers, and to trade between advanced and less developed countries.

voluntary export restraint (VER) An agreement by a country's exporters or government to limit their exports to some other country. The limit set may be in terms of quantity, value, or market share. VERs may be 'voluntary' only in the sense of being accepted under duress, to avoid the threat of tariffs or other trade barriers. They may, however, be genuinely voluntary if exporting firms expect to make more profits from fewer export sales at higher prices. VERs were widespread in the 1970s and 1980s, but are being phased out following an international agreement in 1992.

voluntary unemployment Unemployment which is deliberately chosen by the person unemployed. 'Voluntary' refers to a state of mind which cannot be objectively observed, so the voluntary–involuntary distinction is unhelpful in analysing unemployment. An unemployed person may refrain from applying for jobs which they could have got had they applied, or may apply in such a way as to be refused the offer of a job. This could be because they do not want to work at all, at least at the present time, or because they do very much want work, but are searching for a better job opportunity.

vote, proxy *See* proxy vote.

voter, median *See* median voter.

voting, paradox of *See* paradox of voting.

voting share An *ordinary share in a company giving the owner the right to vote at the company's general meetings. This is distinguished from a non-voting share, which gives the holder equal rights to information about the company and to dividends, but no vote. In some countries companies can set a maximum on the number of votes which can be cast by any one shareholder, regardless of the number of shares held.

voucher A certificate usable in place of money, but only for a specific purpose. It has been proposed, for example, that parents or guardians should be issued with education vouchers to cover the cost of educating their children. It is claimed that such a system could combine the advantages of universal state funding of education with competition in its provision. The point of using vouchers rather than simply paying out money is to avoid the money being diverted to other purposes.

wage(s) Payment for work performed as an *employee. Wages and salaries were once distinguished: wages were paid weekly, or more frequently for casual work, in cash, while salaries were paid monthly into bank accounts. In recent years the growth of payments of wages by cheque has blurred the distinction, and wages and salaries are best regarded as a single total. Payments for work performed by the self-employed as independent contractors are not classed as wages. *See also* efficiency wage, flexible wages, minimum wage, money wages, real wages, sticky wages, and subsistence wages.

wage differential A difference in wage rates between two types of worker. Wage differentials may be on account of different levels of *skill, different formal qualifications, between unionized and non-unionized firms, or between workers of different age, sex, or ethnic groups. In the UK wage differentials based on age are legal, while those based on sex or ethnic group are not. The desire of groups to maintain traditional differentials within occupations makes some economists fear that *minimum wage laws would not just affect the unskilled, but would lead to general wage inflation. The desire to maintain differentials between occupations makes inflationary wage rises tend to spread around the economy. *See also* equalizing wage differential, and union/non-union wage differential.

wage drift The tendency for the average level of wages actually paid to rise faster than *wage rates. This may be due to increases in overtime, increases in special allowances, the operation of age-based salary scales, or up-grading of job descriptions. Wage drift is particularly likely during *booms when labour is relatively scarce, and during periods of attempted wage control, which firms try to evade.

wage flexibility *See* flexible wages.

wage freeze A prohibition on changes in *wages, imposed as part of a prices and incomes policy. As a temporary measure a wage freeze may help to cut inflation. It is very unlikely to be a practical long-term policy: the pattern of *wage rates in force at the time the policy starts is unlikely to equilibrate labour markets even at the time, and will become steadily less suitable. A wage freeze is difficult to enforce, as job descriptions can be changed, and operates unequally between workers on static wage rates and others on progressive salary scales.

wage–price spiral The tendency during inflation for wage increases to lead to price increases and for price increases to lead to wage increases, thus creating an *inflationary spiral. Wage increases tend to raise prices in their own industry by increasing costs, and in other industries by increasing demand. Price increases tend to lead to wage increases by increasing both the cost of living and the ability of employers to afford to pay higher wages. This makes *cost inflation hard to stop once it has begun.

wage rate The rate per hour paid for work of a given type. This applies where time rates are in force; some types of work are paid for at piece rates. The wage rate is taken as that applying to normal hours of working: special rates, usually higher, tend to apply to overtime, or work at night, weekends, bank holidays, or other unsocial times. Wage rates may be laid down by law, or decided by *collective bargaining or individual agreement. Wage rates are generally quoted exclusive of bonuses or allowances and before deduction of income tax, superannuation, or national insurance contributions.

wage resistance Difficulty in cutting wages. Real wage resistance applies to cuts in real wages, and nominal wage resistance to cuts in money wages. Both *trade unions and those bargaining individually with employers tend to regard wage rises lower than the increase in the cost of living as unacceptable, and nominal wage cuts as insulting. Indeed, most employers take the same view and are embarrassed even to suggest wage cuts unless their own economic survival seems to be at stake. Even unemployed 'outsiders', who want jobs, are reluctant to suggest accepting lower wages than the established rate in case this is regarded as *signalling that they regard themselves as inferior; and employers, who do take this view, are unwilling to take on workers who offer to undercut the market rate. Real wage resistance makes it very difficult to cure 'classical' unemployment. *See also* real wage resistance.

wage restraint Decisions by *trade unions not to demand wage increases, or to moderate their demands. Wage restraint is often urged on unions by governments trying to restrain inflation. From the point of view of workers as a whole, there is a sensible argument for wage restraint: if large demands are met, this is likely to lead to loss of jobs. If inflation continues, the authorities are likely to shift to restrictive monetary and fiscal policies, and even with given policies, higher money wages lead to higher prices, lower *real balances and thus lower effective demand. From the point of view of particular unions, each representing only a small percentage of the labour force, wage restraint is not a sensible policy unless it is needed to retain their own members' jobs. If the employers can afford wage increases without job losses, the gains accrue to their own members, while most of the macroeconomic effects of higher wages fall elsewhere in the economy.

wage rigidity The tendency of wage rates to be 'sticky', and not to adjust so as to clear the market in the short run. There are several reasons for this. Adjustment in the labour market involves the selection of suitable staff by employers and a search for suitable jobs by workers: this takes time, and at any moment nobody knows what the *market-clearing wage rate would be. Workers resist cuts in wages, and employers, who know that if wages are once increased there will be strong resistance to lowering them again, are reluctant to grant wage increases during a temporary labour shortage. Where wage rates are decided by *collective bargaining, neither side may be keen to disturb an agreement which cost much effort to reach. *See also* wage resistance.

wage round An annual sequence of pay negotiations. There is a tendency for later settlements to follow precedents set in earlier ones by major unions.

Wages Council A body set up by law to fix minimum wages for particular forms of work. In the UK Wages Councils operated from 1911 to 1994 in various industries, for example catering and agriculture. Wages Councils tended to be set up in industries where wages were low, and *collective bargaining was weak or non-existent, possibly because of dispersion of employment and low educational qualification of workers.

Wall Street The main financial area in Manhattan, New York. It is used as a symbol for high finance in the United States.

Walras's Law The proposition that in an economy with N markets, if supply equals demand in $N - 1$ of them, it must also do so in the Nth. This implies that in considering *general equilibrium, it is legitimate to ignore one market. In the *IS-LM model, for example, Walras's Law justifies ignoring the bond market, since if the supply and demand for both goods and money are equal, the supply and demand for bonds must also be equal.

war See price war, and trade war.

warming, global See global warming.

warrant A security giving the holder the right but not an obligation to buy shares in a company on some future date at a pre-arranged price. A warrant will be valuable if, when the date arrives, the market price is above the *exercise price. Warrants can be traded: a warrant is thus a traded option.

warranted growth rate The rate at which growth must occur in a *Harrod–Domar model if it is to be sustainable. If national income is Y, savings are S, and investment is I, savings are assumed to be a constant proportion of income so that $S = sY$. Investment is assumed to be given by an accelerator model, where investment is given by $I = v(dY/dt)$, where t is time. For *ex ante savings and investment to be equal requires that $sY = v(dY/dt)$. This implies that the growth rate of Y must be

$$w = (1/Y)(dY/dt) = s/v.$$

This is the only rate at which equilibrium growth is possible, so long as the savings ratio s and the capital–output ratio v are taken as fixed.

warranty A guarantee by the provider of goods or services as to their quality. A manufacturer's warranty is only of value to customers if it goes beyond the minimum properties of the good or service required by law. A warranty does not curtail the customer's statutory rights.

wastage, natural See natural wastage.

waste, hazardous See hazardous waste.

wasting asset An asset which diminishes over time. This wastage may be due to gradual destruction through use, for example the depletion of ore reserves by mining them. Alternatively, it may be due to the passage of time: for example, a *patent will expire on some future date, which draws closer as time passes. An individual or firm drawing income from a wasting asset needs to provide a fund which will replace the income when the asset is exhausted.

Ways and Means Advances Advances to the UK government made by the *Bank of England. These are made when necessary if government expenditure runs in advance of receipts from taxation plus borrowing from the public. They have the effect of increasing the money supply.

weakening of a currency A fall in the price of a currency in terms of other currencies. This is caused by a reduction in the demand to hold it, which may be due either to a worsening of the country's *current account, or to shifts into other currencies on *capital account.

wealth The total value of a person's *net assets. Wealth may be held in various forms: these include money, shares in companies, debt instruments, land, buildings, *intellectual property such as patents and copyrights, and valuables such as works of art. From this any debts owed are subtracted. The valuation put on these things is liable to uncertainty and fluctuations, as many of the assets are not marketed, and those that are may have volatile market prices. The wealth of individuals is believed to affect their choices about both consumption and money holdings. It is disputable whether wealth should include prospective accessions of assets: the actuarial value of pension rights can be calculated, but what pensioners will actually receive depends on how long they survive. Similarly prospective legacies have incentive effects comparable to actual wealth, but what will actually be received depends on how long testators survive, whether their assets change, and whether they change their minds about how to bequeath them. *See also* net wealth.

wealth effect The effect of the total wealth of an individual on his or her savings or *liquidity functions. It is generally expected that an individual with larger net assets will spend a larger proportion of current income, and save less, than somebody with the same income but smaller net assets. It is also expected that an individual with larger net assets will hold more money balances relative to income than somebody with smaller net assets. This implies that the level of total net assets in the economy will affect the *IS and *LM curves.

wealth, store of *See* store of value.

wealth tax A tax based on the personal wealth of individuals. Collection of such a tax involves regular valuation of the individual's assets. This raises problems where the assets are not traded in regular markets, or where their market prices are subject to rapid fluctuations. It is also difficult to measure assets which are easily concealed, such as jewellery, bearer securities, or bank deposits in foreign *tax havens. Actual wealth taxes tend to be levied at low rates on conservative valuations of restricted classes of assets.

wear and tear The cumulative damage done to equipment through normal use. Examples include the effect of driving in using up car tyres and oil. Normal wear and tear is not insurable, unlike accidental damage which can usually be insured against. Its effects are also excluded from cover by manufacturers' warranties. Wear and tear is one of the major causes of *capital consumption, the others being accidents and *obsolescence.

wedge, tax *See* tax wedge.

weighted average An average giving weights to different numbers in proportion to their importance. The weighted average of N numbers x_1, $x_2, \ldots, x_N$ is found by taking the sum of the numbers times their weights w_1, $w_2, \ldots, w_N$, divided by the sum of the weights, written

$$\mu_w = (\textstyle\sum_i w_i x_i)/(\textstyle\sum_i w_i).$$

Whether a weighted or an unweighted average should be used, and what the weights should be, depends on the purpose of the calculation. For example, if per capita income is $10,000 in country A and $20,000 in country B, the unweighted average is $15,000. However, if country A has 1 million inhabitants and country B has 3 million, the average per capita income of the region including both countries is given by the weighted average,

$$\$(10{,}000 \times 1 + 20{,}000 \times 3)/(1 + 3) = \$17{,}500.$$

weights in index numbers The relative importance attached to various components entering into any index number. The weights are thus chosen according to the purpose for which it is expected that an index number will be used. The weights in a consumer price index, for example, are chosen so that the bundle of goods and services whose prices are measured corresponds to what an average consumer would buy. These weights are based on surveys: for *base-weighted or Laspeyres indices the weights are derived from surveys conducted during the base period; in *current-weighted or Paasche index numbers the weights are based on surveys conducted as near the present as possible.

welfare Enjoyment of the necessary resources for a worth-while life. The welfare state is the attempt to organize society so that at least the minimum income and public services necessary for this are available to all a country's inhabitants. Welfare or *normative economics is the study of how economic activities ought to be organized, as distinguished from *positive economics, which studies how economies actually do work. Welfare criteria are rules for judging whether one state of the economy is better or worse than another. 'The welfare' is UK slang for the social security authorities responsible for income support, and 'Welfare' is US terminology for the income support itself.

welfare criterion A method of deciding whether a proposed change in the economy should be made. The Pareto criterion says that a change should be made if somebody gains and nobody loses. This is uncontroversial, but fails to answer the much more common question of whether or not to make changes with both gainers and losers. The Hicks–Kaldor criterion says that changes should be made if the gainers could afford to compensate the losers. If such compensation is actually paid, the criterion becomes similar to the Pareto criterion; but compensation for changes is usually not paid, especially when the losers are scattered and hard to identify. The Scitovsky criterion says that a change should be made if, after it has occurred, the losers could not afford to compensate the gainers for changing back. Differences between the Hicks–Kaldor and Scitovsky criteria arise if the change brings about alterations in relative prices. The Hicks criterion treats the pre-change distribution of real incomes as the status quo, the Scitovsky criterion is based on the post-change distribution. There is no general reason for preferring either distribution to the other. The absence of a generally acceptable welfare criterion forces economists to include value judgements about income distribution in any advice they give. *See also* Pareto-optimality.

welfare economics The part of economics concerned with the effects of economic activity on welfare. This includes the modelling of individual or household behaviour by utility functions; criteria for efficiency, including *Pareto-optimality and theories of the *second-best; criteria for judging whether changes in the economy are beneficial; consideration of how income distribution affects social welfare; and *cost–benefit analysis of activities involving *externalities. Welfare economics is largely synonymous with normative economics: it does not include study of the institutions, as distinct from the objectives, of the welfare state.

welfare state A state committed to ensuring for all its citizens at least some minimum standard of living, including housing, education, and medical services. Advocates argue that the welfare state is not merely equitable, but also efficient, since the absence of this provision leads to *externalities in the form of crime, poor public health, and failure to become employable. Critics point to its considerable cost, and the adverse effects on *incentives of both the taxes needed to pay for benefits and the *means tests used to limit them.

white knight A purchaser for a company, willing to rescue it from an unwanted *takeover bid by another buyer. A company threatened with takeover may welcome a competitive bid by a white knight as a means of improving the terms offered by the first bidder, whether or not the alternative bid is ultimately accepted.

white noise A time series whose observations are entirely independent, whatever the time lag considered. Economic modelling is much simpler when all random components take this form.

white paper A UK government publication, generally intended as a prelude to legislation. The eventual legislation may differ from the white paper's proposals in some respects. A white paper is contrasted with a 'green paper', a UK government publication intended to stimulate public discussion of an issue, without committing the government to legislating at all, or to the lines any legislation might take.

wholesale banking Banking by institutions which specialize on dealing with other financial institutions, large firms, and wealthy individuals. This is contrasted with retail or 'high street' banking, which also deals with numerous small firms and ordinary individuals. Wholesale banks do not need the dense network of branches which characterizes retail banks.

wholesale prices The prices of goods which are dealt with wholesale, mainly bulk goods, which are mostly inputs to production rather than finished commodities. A wholesale price index, for example, includes wheat and sheet steel, where a retail price index includes bread and cars. Because they involve goods that are dealt in before the production of final goods, and are held as stocks of inputs, wholesale price indexes tend to be leading indicators, moving earlier in trade cycles than the retail price index.

wholesaling The sale of goods to distributors, rather than the general public. Wholesale traders usually deal in larger quantities than retailers: they break bulk and sell in smaller quantities than their purchases from manufacturers. Wholesalers are able to compete with direct sales by manufacturers to retailers through *economies of scale and scope in stock-holding and transport.

widening, capital *See* capital widening.

wildcat strike A strike embarked on by groups of employees without being organized or supported by their trade union.

winding up Closing down a business, paying off its debts, and distributing any remaining assets to its *shareholders. Winding up or liquidation may be voluntary, when owners decide to retire or cut their losses, or may be imposed by the courts if the business has defaulted on its debts.

window, discount *See* discount window.

winner's curse The danger that the winner of a *contract will lose money on it. Where contracts are awarded by *competitive tendering, the winner is normally the firm offering the lowest price. Estimates of costs are subject to error, and there is a danger that the winner will be a firm which has made a large underestimate of the true cost, and will thus lose money on the contract.

winners, picking *See* picking winners.

Wirtschaftswunder German for the wonder economy, referring to the remarkable recovery of the West German economy after the Second World War. In 1945 West Germany was totally devastated by the war, and had to absorb millions of refugees from the East. By the 1960s West Germany had some of the world's most prosperous and productive industries, and an extremely strong currency.

withdrawal, equity *See* equity withdrawal.

withdrawals from the circular flow of incomes *See* leakages from the circular flow of incomes.

withholding tax A tax levied at a standard rate on all receipts of income from wages or dividends, regardless of the individual's tax liability. Taxpayers then make *tax returns so that their tax liability can be determined. Those liable to pay less than the withholding tax, for example because of low total incomes, then get tax refunds, while those liable to pay more get tax demands for the excess. This system helps the tax authorities as they get their money promptly, and taxpayers entitled to refunds have a strong incentive to file their tax returns promptly. It is disadvantageous for taxpayers, who get their refunds in arrears: it does however protect them from the danger that they may have spent too much of their income before the tax bill arrives. The US income tax system makes use of withholding taxes.

without-profits life insurance *See* with-profits life insurance.

with-profits life insurance *Life insurance where benefits to the policy-holders depend on the financial performance of the fund accumulated from their premiums. This is in contrast to without-profits life insurance, where a policy-holder gets a guaranteed level of benefits regardless of the financial performance of the fund. As with-profits policies involve far less risk for the insurance company than without-profits policies, premiums on with-profits policies are less than those on without-profits policies giving the same level of expected benefits at maturity. However, with equal premiums a without-profits policy offers more *cover during the early years of a policy. A with-profits policy offers much better protection against inflation over the life of the policy than a without-profits policy.

work Activities involving physical and/or mental effort. While a large part of this is in paid employment, or working for economic gain while self-employed, there are other forms of work. This is recognized in the terms voluntary work, where people perform for charities or political parties tasks other people are paid for, and housework, where people work for the welfare of their families. *See also* hours of work, part-time work, shift work, skilled work, and unskilled work.

worker-controlled firm A firm which is owned and managed by its workers, or a producers' co-operative. In an industry with low *capital-intensity, the workers may provide the firm's capital themselves; in more capital-intensive industries, it is possible for them to borrow capital, or to lease buildings and equipment. The advantage claimed for workers' control of firms is that it removes the conflict between owners and workers which besets ordinary firms. It does not, however, eliminate conflicts of interest between the more skilled and senior workers and the less skilled. There are relatively few successful worker-controlled firms. This may be because too few workers have the necessary willingness to take risks, or the necessary management skills. Many worker-controlled firms have failed after being tried as a last resort when other forms of organization had already been tried, and failed. *See also* skilled work.

worker, discouraged *See* discouraged worker.

worker participation Participation by workers in the process of decision-taking in a firm. This varies widely between firms. At the one extreme are producers' co-operatives, or worker-controlled firms, where the workers are the owners and elect the directors. At the other are firms with no worker participation except for any informal contacts between owners and workers, though in very small firms this may be quite effective. In between are firms with *works councils, where matters of general policy like manning levels and redundancies can be discussed, though management makes the final decisions. There are also firms with arrangements for workers to become ordinary shareholders, sometimes on concessional terms. It is possible for firms to co-opt directors nominated by workers, though this is uncommon. It is also possible, as in Germany, to have a *two-tier board: workers elect representatives to the upper tier, which decides general policy, but not to the lower tier, which takes operational decisions. Many firms consider that some degree of worker participation is in the interests of shareholders, as it is expected to reduce feelings of alienation, promote loyalty to the firm, and induce workers to take a more sympathetic view of its problems.

workers' compensation *See* employer's liability.

workfare A system making income support for the unemployed conditional on their performing some form of work for which they are suitable. Advocates of this policy argue that such work would benefit both society and the recipients, as it would improve their self-respect and future employment prospects. It would also reduce fraud on the social security system by those actually working in the *unofficial economy while claiming benefit. Critics argue that compulsory workfare would be very expensive: determining people's ability to work and supervising work by the unwilling would use scarce resources, which would be better spent on *training those who actually want work. Providing child-care for unskilled single parents could also cost more than the value of any work they might do.

workforce *See* labour force.

working capital The part of the capital of a business that is not tied up in land, buildings, or fixed equipment. Working capital is used to hold liquid balances, pay for wages and materials, and extend credit to customers.

working conditions The conditions under which employees have to work. This includes matters such as permitted breaks, the state of heating, lighting, and ventilation of workplaces, the safety and comfort of machinery, vehicles, and other equipment, normal manning levels, and disciplinary procedures. These conditions are affected by legislation, for example under the Health and Safety at Work Act, by *collective bargaining between employers and trade unions representing workers, and by voluntary improvements by employers who believe that better working conditions pay for themselves in terms of staff morale and loyalty.

working practices The ways in which the members of the labour force in an enterprise carry out their tasks. Working practices may be set by formal agreement between employers and workers' representatives, or by customs which have grown up and are followed without any formal agreement. They are concerned with who undertakes what functions, and how many people a given task is expected to occupy. For example, what level of repair and maintenance work is regarded as a normal part of somebody's job, and what tasks should be deputed to specialist fitters? Who is empowered to stop a production line if something goes wrong? Many working practices are based on long experience of what can go wrong: inexperienced workers or managers who take short cuts may not realize the trouble this could cause. Unnecessary working practices, however, can seriously impair efficiency.

working, short-time *See* short-time working.

work in progress *See* investment in stocks and work in progress.

works council A body where representatives of the management and workers of an establishment or a firm meet to discuss matters of mutual interest. These normally exclude wages, but include working conditions, health and safety, and individual or group grievances. Many managements find works councils useful in settling problems before they escalate into industrial disputes. They may also be used as a convenient occasion for briefing workers on the firm's prospects and profits. Works councils generally do not have the power to make executive decisions, but unless management takes considerable notice of their proceedings, discussion not followed by action is liable to make problems worse rather than better. In some countries, and under the *Social Chapter of the Maastricht Treaty, works councils are compulsory for larger firms.

works, public *See* public works.

work study The study of working procedures with a view to improving their efficiency, safety, or comfort. This includes looking at the order of operations to see whether rearranging them could save time or effort, and looking at the physical processes to see whether changes in equipment or in environmental features such as lighting could reduce fatigue or improve accuracy and reduce defects in the products. At what speed should production lines be run? If they run too slowly, workers waste time waiting for each task;

if they run too fast, workers are over-strained and make expensive mistakes. Work study also considers questions of specialization: should each worker's tasks be very narrowly specified, to reduce the skill level needed, or widened to make the work more interesting and improve flexibility?

World Bank *See* International Bank for Reconstruction and Development.

World Trade Organization (WTO) An international body to supervise and encourage international trade. An International Trade Organization was proposed following the Bretton Woods conference in 1944, but was never set up; the *General Agreement on Tariffs and Trade (GATT) was started instead. GATT organized the Uruguay Round trade talks, which concluded in 1994 by setting up the WTO to take over its functions in encouraging multilateral trade in goods and services.

worth, net *See* net worth.

write off To reduce the value put on an asset in a company's accounts. Depreciation is the process of writing off assets gradually over time. 'Write off' is also used of accidents severe enough to reduce an asset's value to zero.

wrongful dismissal Termination of employment by the employer contrary to the employee's contract of employment. Dismissal may be wrongful because the grounds given are not justified, or the procedure laid down by the contract of employment has not been followed.

WTO *See* World Trade Organization.

X-efficiency That part of overall *efficiency which consists of getting the maximum output technically possible from any given inputs, or producing a given output with the fewest possible inputs. X-efficiency thus implies the complete absence of *slack in production. Evidence for X-efficiency can take two forms. One is theoretical, showing that in principle better results are not obtainable. The other is empirical, showing that no other firm or organization is observed to do better.

X-inefficiency Failure of a firm or other organization to get the maximum possible output from the inputs it uses, or to produce its output with the minimum use of inputs. X-inefficiency implies that there is *slack in the organization. Its existence can be shown in two possible ways. One is the engineer's method, producing a plan of operations which is expected to do better. The other is the statistician's or bench-mark approach, showing that other firms or organizations manage to get more output from equal inputs, or the same output from fewer inputs.

Yaoundé Convention An international agreement by which many former French colonies became associates of the *European Community (EC).

year *See* budget year, financial year, and fiscal year.

yen (¥) The Japanese currency unit.

yield The income from a *fixed-interest security as a percentage of its price. The nominal yield is the interest per annum divided by the *par value. The running yield is the interest divided by the market price. The redemption yield is the interest equivalent to the actual interest payments plus capital gains (or minus capital losses) if the security is held to *maturity. A yield curve plots the yield on fixed-interest securities against their time to maturity. *See also* net yield, redemption yield, running yield, and sustained yield.

yield curve A graph plotting the yield on *fixed-interest securities against their years to maturity. As longer-dated securities are more subject to price fluctuations if interest rates change, and are thus less liquid than shorter-dated securities, it is normally expected that if interest rates are equally likely to rise or fall the yield curve slopes upwards; that is, longer-dated securities will have higher yields than shorter-dated ones. This slope may be temporarily reversed if interest rates are generally expected to fall, as the expectation of higher *capital gains on longer-dated securities makes them relatively attractive to hold. *See also* liquid assets.

yield gap The difference between the average dividend yield on *equities and the average yield on long-dated *gilt-edged securities. During periods of stable prices the yield on equities usually needs to be greater to compensate investors for their relative riskiness, so the yield gap is positive. During periods of high inflation the fact that equities are expected to provide *capital gains to compensate for inflation while gilt-edged are not can lead to a reverse yield gap, with returns on gilt-edged above those on equities. *See also* reverse yield gap.

Z

zero-base budgeting The proposal that the *budgets of government and other organizations should be designed starting from first principles, defining the aims of the organization and adopting the best method of achieving them. This is contrasted with normal budgetary procedure, which starts from the previous period's budget and makes marginal changes. As real world organizations are committed to contracts with their employees and suppliers, and are affected by the public's expectations about the prices they should charge and the services they should provide, zero-base budgeting is extremely difficult to achieve. Its critics argue that normal budgetary procedure exemplifies learning from experience, and is in any case preferable to a priori planning, which is what zero-base budgeting amounts to.

zero growth An economy without further expansion of activity. This term occurs in two contexts: in some poor and backward economies where it is a fact, it is called stagnation and is rightly regarded as a problem; in some very advanced and wealthy economies, however, worries about *pollution and the exhaustion of *natural resources lead to zero growth being propounded as an ideal. This raises two problems: first, if resources really are exhaustible then no positive rate of depletion is permanently sustainable, and advanced economies must evolve to survive; second, the vast majority of the world's inhabitants are far poorer than the advocates of zero growth. They would have to become far richer than they now are, consume vastly more resources and produce far more pollution, before they would be in the least likely to join in advocating zero growth as an ideal.

zero-rated (VAT) Goods or services included in the *value-added tax system, with a VAT rate of zero. Firms can reclaim VAT on inputs to zero-rated goods. These are distinguished from VAT-exempt goods and services which are outside the VAT system, so that VAT on inputs cannot be reclaimed.

zero-sum game A game in which the participants are determining the distribution of a fixed total of costs or benefits between them. *Market shares, for example, sum to 100 per cent by definition, so one firm's gain is another firm's loss. Zero-sum games are contrasted with positive-sum games, where gains for all participants are possible, for example international trade, and with negative-sum games, where the contest reduces the prize, for example war over the possession of resources.

zone *See* free trade zone, and target zone (exchange rates).

zoning The system of specifying that certain activities can only be carried on in particular areas. Some activities cause harmful *externalities, by emitting noise, smells, or dust, or by attracting heavy traffic. Zoning tries to minimize the harm done by such activities, by concentrating them where they do least damage, and separating them from residential, commercial, or amenity areas.

Appendix 1. **The Greek Alphabet**

LOWER CASE	UPPER CASE	LETTER
α	A	Alpha
β	B	Beta
γ	Γ	Gamma
δ	Δ	Delta
ε	E	Epsilon
ζ	Z	Zeta
η	H	Eta
θ	Θ	Theta
ι	I	Iota
κ	K	Kappa
λ	Λ	Lambda
μ	M	Mu
ν	N	Nu
ξ	Ξ	Xi
o	O	Omicron
π	Π	Pi
ρ	P	Rho
σ	Σ	Sigma
τ	T	Tau
υ	Y	Upsilon
φ	Φ	Phi
χ	X	Chi
ψ	Ψ	Psi
ω	Ω	Omega

Appendix 2. **Winners of the Nobel Prize for Economics**

A Nobel Prize for economic sciences was instituted in 1969, financed by the Swedish National Bank. The following have won the Prize since then:

1969	Jan Tinbergen
	Ragnar Frisch
1970	Paul Samuelson
1971	Simon Kuznets
1972	John Hicks
	Kenneth Arrow
1973	Wassily Leontief
1974	Gunnar Myrdal
	Friedrich Hayek
1975	Leonid Kantorovich
	Tjalling Koopmans
1976	Milton Friedman
1977	James Meade
	Bertil Ohlin
1978	Herbert Simon
1979	W. Arthur Lewis
	Theodore Schultz
1980	Lawrence Klein
1981	James Tobin
1982	George Stigler
1983	Gerard Debreu
1984	Richard Stone
1985	Franco Modigliani
1986	James Buchanan
1987	Robert Solow
1988	Maurice Allais
1989	Trygve Haavelmo

1990	Harry Markovitz
	William Sharpe
	Merton Miller
1991	Ronald Coase
1992	Gary Becker
1993	Robert Fogel
	Douglas North
1994	John Nash
	John Harsanyi
	Reinhard Selten
1995	Robert Lucas
1996	Jim Mirrlees
	William Vickrey
1997	Robert C. Merton
	Myron S. Scholes
1998	Amartya Sen
1999	Robert Mundell
2000	James Heckman
	Daniel McFadden
2001	George Akerlof
	Michael Spence
	Joseph Stiglitz
2002	Daniel Kahneman
	Vernon L. Smith
2003	Robert F. Engle
	Clive W.J. Granger
2004	Finn E. Kydland
	Edward C. Prescott

Great value ebooks from Oxford!

An ever-increasing number of Oxford subject reference dictionaries, English and bilingual dictionaries, and English language reference titles are available as ebooks.

All Oxford ebooks are available in the award-winning Mobipocket Reader format, compatible with most current handheld systems, including Palm, Pocket PC/Windows CE, Psion, Nokia, SymbianOS, Franklin eBookMan, and Windows. Some are also available in MS Reader and Palm Reader formats.

Priced on a par with the print editions, Oxford ebooks offer dictionary-specific search options making information retrieval quick and easy.

For further information and a full list of Oxford ebooks please visit: www.askoxford.com/shoponline/ebooks/

Oxford Paperback Reference

The Kings of Queens of Britain
John Cannon and Anne Hargreaves

A detailed, fully-illustrated history ranging from mythical and pre-conquest rulers to the present House of Windsor, featuring regional maps and genealogies.

A Dictionary of Dates
Cyril Leslie Beeching

Births and deaths of the famous, significant and unusual dates in history – this is an entertaining guide to each day of the year.

'a dipper's blissful paradise ... Every single day of the year, plus an index of birthdays and chronologies of scientific developments and world events.'

Observer

A Dictionary of British History
Edited by John Cannon

An invaluable source of information covering the history of Britain over the past two millennia. Over 3,600 entries written by more than 100 specialist contributors.

Review of the parent volume
'the range is impressive ... truly (almost) all of human life is here'

Kenneth Morgan, *Observer*

Oxford Paperback Reference

The Concise Oxford Dictionary of English Etymology
T. F. Hoad

A wealth of information about our language and its history, this
reference source provides over 17,000 entries on word origins.

'A model of its kind'

Daily Telegraph

A Dictionary of Euphemisms
R. W. Holder

This hugely entertaining collection draws together euphemisms from all
aspects of life: work, sexuality, age, money, and politics.

Review of the previous edition
'This ingenious collection is not only very funny but extremely
instructive too'

Iris Murdoch

The Oxford Dictionary of Slang
John Ayto

Containing over 10,000 words and phrases, this is the ideal reference for
those interested in the more quirky and unofficial words used in the
English language.

'hours of happy browsing for language lovers'

Observer

Oxford Paperback Reference

The Concise Oxford Companion to English Literature
Margaret Drabble and Jenny Stringer

Based on the best-selling *Oxford Companion to English Literature*, this is an indispensable guide to all aspects of English literature.

Review of the parent volume
'a magisterial and monumental achievement'

Literary Review

The Concise Oxford Companion to Irish Literature
Robert Welch

From the ogam alphabet developed in the 4th century to Roddy Doyle, this is a comprehensive guide to writers, works, topics, folklore, and historical and cultural events.

Review of the parent volume
'Heroic volume ... It surpasses previous exercises of similar nature in the richness of its detail and the ecumenism of its approach.'

Times Literary Supplement

A Dictionary of Shakespeare
Stanley Wells

Compiled by one of the best-known international authorities on the playwright's works, this dictionary offers up-to-date information on all aspects of Shakespeare, both in his own time and in later ages.

Oxford Paperback Reference

Concise Medical Dictionary

Over 10,000 clear entries covering all the major medical and surgical
specialities make this one of our best-selling dictionaries.

'"No home should be without one" certainly applies to this splendid
medical dictionary'

Journal of the Institute of Health Education

'An extraordinary bargain'

New Scientist

'Excellent layout and jargon-free style'

Nursing Times

A Dictionary of Nursing

Comprehensive coverage of the ever-expanding vocabulary of the
nursing professions. Features over 10,000 entries written by medical
and nursing specialists.

An A-Z of Medicinal Drugs

Over 4,000 entries cover the full range of over-the-counter and
prescription medicines available today. An ideal reference source for
both the patient and the medical professional.

Oxford Paperback Reference

The Concise Oxford Dictionary of Quotations
Edited by Elizabeth Knowles

Based on the highly acclaimed *Oxford Dictionary of Quotations*, this
paperback edition maintains its extensive coverage of literary and
historical quotations, and contains completely up-to-date material. A
fascinating read and an essential reference tool.

The Oxford Dictionary of Humorous Quotations
Edited by Ned Sherrin

From the sharply witty to the downright hilarious, this sparkling
collection will appeal to all senses of humour.

Quotations by Subject
Edited by Susan Ratcliffe

A collection of over 7,000 quotations, arranged thematically for easy
look-up. Covers an enormous range of nearly 600 themes from 'The
Internet' to 'Parliament'.

The Concise Oxford Dictionary of Phrase and Fable
Edited by Elizabeth Knowles

Provides a wealth of fascinating and informative detail for over 10,000
phrases and allusions used in English today. Find out about anything
from the 'Trojan horse' to 'ground zero'.

Oxford Paperback Reference

A Dictionary of Chemistry

Over 4,200 entries covering all aspects of chemistry, including physical chemistry and biochemistry.

'It should be in every classroom and library ... the reader is drawn inevitably from one entry to the next merely to satisfy curiosity.'

School Science Review

A Dictionary of Physics

Ranging from crystal defects to the solar system, 3,500 clear and concise entries cover all commonly encountered terms and concepts of physics.

A Dictionary of Biology

The perfect guide for those studying biology – with over 4,700 entries on key terms from biology, biochemistry, medicine, and palaeontology.

'lives up to its expectations; the entries are concise, but explanatory'

Biologist

'ideally suited to students of biology, at either secondary or university level, or as a general reference source for anyone with an interest in the life sciences'

Journal of Anatomy

More Art Reference from Oxford

The Grove Dictionary of Art

The 34 volumes of *The Grove Dictionary of Art* provide unrivalled coverage of the visual arts from Asia, Africa, the Americas, Europe, and the Pacific, from prehistory to the present day.

'succeeds in performing the most difficult of balancing acts, satisfying specialists while ... remaining accessible to the general reader'

The Times

The Grove Dictionary of Art - Online
www.groveart.com

This immense cultural resource is now available online. Updated regularly, it includes recent developments in the art world as well as the latest art scholarship.

'a mammoth one-stop site for art-related information'

Antiques Magazine

The Oxford History of Western Art
Edited by Martin Kemp

From Classical Greece to postmodernism, *The Oxford History of Western Art* is an authoritative and stimulating overview of the development of visual culture in the West over the last 2,700 years.

'here is a work that will permanently alter the face of art history ... a hugely ambitious project successfully achieved'

The Times

The Oxford Dictionary of Art
Edited by Ian Chilvers

The Oxford Dictionary of Art is an authoritative guide to the art of the western world, ranging across painting, sculpture, drawing, and the applied arts.

'the best and most inclusive single-volume available'

Marina Vaizey, *Sunday Times*

Oxford Paperback Reference

A Dictionary of Psychology
Andrew M. Colman

Over 10,500 authoritative entries make up the most wide-ranging
dictionary of psychology available.

'impressive ... certainly to be recommended'
Times Higher Educational Supplement

'Comprehensive, sound, readable, and up-to-date, this is probably the
best single-volume dictionary of its kind.'
Library Journal

A Dictionary of Economics
John Black

Fully up-to-date and jargon-free coverage of economics. Over 2,500
terms on all aspects of economic theory and practice.

A Dictionary of Law

An ideal source of legal terminology for systems based on English law.
Over 4,000 clear and concise entries.

'The entries are clearly drafted and succinctly written ... Precision for the
professional is combined with a layman's enlightenment.'
Times Literary Supplement

OXFORD

More Social Science titles from OUP

The Globalization of World Politics
John Baylis and Steve Smith

The essential introduction for all students of international relations.

'The best introduction to the subject by far. A classic of its kind.'
Dr David Baker, University of Warwick

Macroeconomics
A European Text
Michael Burda and Charles Wyplosz

'Burda and Wyplosz's best-selling text stands out for the breadth of its coverage, the clarity of its exposition, and the topicality of its examples. Students seeking a comprehensive guide to modern macroeconomics need look no further.'
Charles Bean, Chief Economist, Bank of England

Economics
Richard Lipsey and Alec Chrystal

The classic introduction to economics, revised every few years to include the latest topical issues and examples.

VISIT THE COMPANION WEB SITES FOR THESE CLASSIC TEXTBOOKS AT:

www.oup.com/uk/booksites